> "*I recommend this book as a companion book to* Partners in Prayer.
> *It contains what you need to experience God's power...regardless of your situation.*"
>
> JOHN C. MAXWELL

PIVOTAL
PRAYING

CONNECTING WITH GOD IN TIMES *of* GREAT NEED

JOHN HULL &
TIM ELMORE

WORDS OF PRAISE FOR *PIVOTAL PRAYING*

The last great unconquered frontier for the advancing cause of Christ may very well be the personal prayer life of His followers. My friends John Hull and Tim Elmore provide fresh and compelling insights. Read this book and get ready to tap the true power source—especially in times of need.

—DR. JOE STOWELL
President of Moody Bible Institute
and author of *Perilous Pursuits* and *Following Christ*

⧖

Pivotal Praying is a powerful, yet practical, manual for those compelled to see God's plan released in their lives—and the world!

—BECKY TIRABASSI
President, Becky Tirabassi Change Your Life, Inc.®

⧖

Who regards his prayer life as strong and adequate enough? John and Tim have given us a valuable resource to drive us closer to that elusive goal. *Pivotal Praying* will both instruct the minds and stir the hearts of all who want to pray well.

—RANDY POPE,
Pastor, Perimeter Church in Duluth, Georgia

⧖

Finally, a book that deals with prayer in the context of where we live! *Pivotal Praying* is a "dirt-under-your-fingernails" kind of book that, contrary to a lot of books on prayer, refuses to give you theory or theological surmise. It is a book you will read and use often, and it could change the way you look at prayer.

—STEVE BROWN,
Professor of Preaching at Reformed Theological Seminary

Tim Elmore and John Hull have effectively communicated how to pray when you least feel like it. *Pivotal Praying* reveals practical ways you can connect with God when you face your greatest challenges.

—ANDY STANLEY
Senior Pastor, North Point Community Church

⊠

With inspirational stories and insightful Bible study, John Hull and Tim Elmore teach us how to pray in the face of crises, unexpected turns in life's road, and at times of "crossroads" decision making. Someone has said that life is the accumulation of our choices. *Pivotal Praying* is a road map to making wise choices, because in those pivotal choice times, it directs our attention toward pursuing the heart of God.

—PAUL BORTHWICK
Author of *Six Dangerous Questions to Change Your World View* and *A Mind for Missions*

PIVOTAL
PRAYING

CONNECTING WITH GOD IN TIMES *of* GREAT NEED

JOHN HULL &
TIM ELMORE

THOMAS NELSON PUBLISHERS®
Nashville

A Division of Thomas Nelson, Inc.
www.ThomasNelson.com

Published in Nashville, Tennessee, by Thomas Nelson, Inc.

Library of Congress Cataloging-in-Publication Data

Hull, John D., 1958–
  Pivotal praying : connecting with god in times of great need / John Hull & Tim Elmore.
    p. cm.
  ISBN: 0-7852-6483-3
  1. Prayer—Christianity. I. Elmore, Tim. II. Title.
  BV210.3 .H85 2002
  248.3'2—dc21   2002007201

Printed in the United States of America

02 03 04 05 06 PHX 7 6 5 4 3 2 1

Dedicated to pastors and their prayer partners who daily experience the pivotal power of prayer.

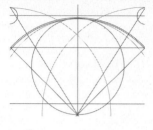

CONTENTS

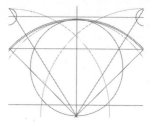

FOREWORD
BY JOHN C. MAXWELL

I believe you are going to enjoy this book.

In it are the stories of men and women who've learned to connect with the heart of God. Dozens of them. You'll feel as if you're sitting down over coffee and conversing with biblical personalities such as Solomon, Esther, and Job's friends. Each of them will shed some light on what he or she learned about pivotal praying. Some of them will share lessons they learned from their failure. Along with biblical characters, you'll also hear from contemporary people like you and me, and hear how they experienced God's supernatural invasion in their life—in response to their prayer. From President Bush dealing with the aftermath of September 11, 2001 to a set of parents who lost their daughter at the hands of a brutal murderer, you will experience the power of pivotal prayer and how it can change the course of our lives.

Along with each story, you will gain a principle you can use today. These chapters are loaded with handles on how to pray, not just 911 "panic" prayers, but handles on how to pray strategically and wisely in the midst of your worst days. You will learn how to pray when you face a new challenge, when you have failed, when you confront opposition, when your dreams don't come true, when you are in over your head, and when you just want to quit. I believe reading and practicing what you'll find in this book will make you a better parent, a better employee, a better daughter or son, a better supervisor, a better friend . . . a better person. Why? Because you will pray better.

Let's face it. While prayer is simply talking to God—and anyone can do that—some prayers connect with God's heart and others don't. Witness the story Jesus told of the Pharisee and the tax collector in Luke 18:9–14. Both went out to pray one afternoon, but only one connected with God. The Pharisee prayed a far more eloquent prayer, and demonstrated an accurate handle on Scripture. Unfortunately, that's not what God was looking for. The tax collector—full of humility and reckless trust in God—got the ear of his Father in heaven that day. The Pharisee went home empty.

As you set out to make a difference in your church and in your world, I can't think of a better place to start than by learning the power of pivotal praying. I recommend this book as a companion to *Partners in Prayer*. It contains what you need to experience God's power no matter what situation you find yourself in. This book will provide for you not only a great study on prayer, but a track to run on as you seek God in your life. The case studies are blueprints for your prayer life, and the principles are tools you can use to build it into something great.

The two men who wrote *Pivotal Praying* are my friends and colleagues. John Hull and Tim Elmore provide leadership to my EQUIP team in Atlanta. They play key roles as we attempt to equip one million Christian leaders around the world over the next six years. With a huge goal like that, they have to be men of prayer! Both have been on a journey over the years to learn to pray wisely and connect with God's heart each time they pray. I have seen the results of their prayers. I commend them to you as teachers. You'll find their style warm, easy to read, full of insight, and straight to the heart.

Take this journey with them. Decide now you are going to pray your way through this book, as they provide examples to follow from Scripture. I can only imagine what might happen if everyone who picks up this book would commit to pivotal praying from that day forward. I pray you take the challenge.

JOHN C. MAXWELL
Founder and Chairman of EQUIP
Author of the bestsellers *Partners in Prayer*
and *The 21 Irrefutable Laws of Leadership*

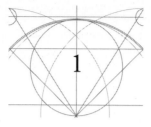

WHAT IS
PIVOTAL PRAYING?
(TIM ELMORE)

His life's dream was to be a missionary, and it looked as though it was finally coming true. As the nervous young man sat in the mission agency's office, he assured the interviewer that he and his new bride were committed to working hard, managing their resources as good stewards, and sharing Christ with as many people as possible. His future looked bright.

Then it all seemed to come crashing down. His dream began to fall apart. During their cross-cultural preparation, he and his wife realized she could never endure the rigors of life overseas. Her body was fragile and frail. If they went to Africa as planned, she would certainly die.

Confused and emotionally crushed, the young man returned home. His tragic tale continued as he failed to find a ministerial position. The first blow had left him devastated. This one left him depressed.

One night he awoke from sleep feeling the weight of his failed dream. His hands were clammy and his temperature ran high. He was angry. He was baffled. He began to wrestle with God over his calling. How could God call him to change the world, then close all doors to ministry? It was during this time in prayer that God reminded him of his original commitment—to work hard, to manage his resources, and to share Christ with as many people as possible.

Bingo! His entire attitude changed. It suddenly struck him that he could still remain true to his commitment, wherever he worked. So he prayed exactly for this.

He decided to work for his dad, a dentist who had a small business on the side that produced juice for church Communion services. As his father grew older, the young man took over the business and determined to use it to touch the world for Christ. He would keep his promise by financially supporting others who *could* go overseas as missionaries.

He built the company into a huge enterprise. In fact, you probably have purchased some of his juice. His name was Welch, and his grape juice is sold in supermarkets everywhere. Mr. Welch has not only given huge sums of money to world missions, he has impacted the world for Christ in a far greater way than if he had gone overseas himself.

It all began with a pivotal prayer. Just as with James.

James was a grocery clerk who started, with capital of $65, to peddle cheese from a one-horse wagon. To say he was a dismal failure would be kind. James continued to push himself but grew deeper in debt. He was young and inexperienced, so he sought the advice of a wise Christian friend.

"You haven't included God in your business," his friend observed. "You haven't let Him take over the work—you've only asked Him to be a part of it. That's not how God works."

This sent the young clerk into a tailspin. James was gripped with mixed emotions. He was offended that such a judgment be laid on him. At the same time he was struck by his friend's blunt honesty. It was a pivotal moment for him.

Days passed as the young clerk prayed and pondered. Finally he crossed a line in the sand. He wrote his friend, saying, "If God wants to run this cheese business, He can do it. I'll work for Him." And this is what he prayed.

From that moment on, God became the senior partner in his business, the chief Person consulted in every decision. A chair was left open in meetings, reminding key staff of His presence. Over the months the business grew and prospered. It eventually became the largest cheese company in the world. James L. Kraft's pivotal prayer made all the difference in the Kraft Cheese Company.

Unfortunately, it's easy to miss the opportunity to pray a pivotal prayer. You may remember hearing the name James Huberty back in the mid-1980s. He made the cover of magazines nationwide for one tragic reason: He was the mastermind behind the "McDonald's massacre." He walked into a McDonald's restaurant with an automatic weapon and gunned down more than twenty people in San Ysidro, California. A SWAT team showed up moments later and killed him, which was his goal—he didn't have the guts to commit suicide. When it was all over, bloodstains splattered the red-and-white tile of the restaurant. More than two dozen people had been murdered.

The store no longer serves hamburgers to local residents. It now stands as a memorial to the lives lost that day.

What makes this especially heartbreaking is that James Huberty mishandled a pivotal moment. After being released from his job, he became angry with his supervisor, his family, and himself. A colleague tried to encourage him. Sensing Huberty's anger, the friend pleaded with him to let his anger go. He urged him to surrender the issue to the Lord and trust Him to begin a whole new chapter in his life.

Sadly, Proverbs 18:19 proved true: "A brother offended is harder to be won than a strong city" (NASB). James Huberty never prayed the pivotal prayer that would have dissolved his bitterness. He suppressed his anger until he could hold it in no longer. The only way James

Huberty knew to deal with his losses was to take the lives of several persons, and hope that someone would end his own.

STOP, DROP, AND PRAY

Americans are probably more aware now of the need for prayer than we have been at any other time in our lives. For the first time I can remember, my kids' teachers actually told their classes to pray in class following the September 11, 2001 terrorist attack. People seemed to want to touch God as a nation. Yet that was only one of the many junctions we face.

Each of us encounters critical forks in the road on a regular basis: marriage, a new job opportunity, children, perhaps cancer or some other kind of sickness, or even a serendipitous meeting with someone who could change our lives. It is at these times that almost everyone prays.

But how do we pray at such junctions? Do we simply pray 911 prayers, or do we pray intelligently—strategically—and see results that take our lives to a whole new level? Do we pray about symptoms or root issues? Do we play offense or defense in our prayers? Are we able to look back at our prayers and say, "God did something then that I could never have done"?

This book is about *how* we pray and *what* we pray—especially at crucial times in our lives. It is about touching God when we most need to. It is about connecting with His heart and accepting what He wants to give us. It is about positioning ourselves to receive from Him, about praying well when we are tempted to panic or throw in the towel. It is about prayer that moves the heart of God.

Pivotal prayers come at pivotal moments. They produce pivotal decisions and result in pivotal consequences. Pivotal prayers embrace God and touch His heart, as David did after his sexual sin with Bathsheba (Ps. 51). Or as Jehoshaphat did before his nation faced an invading army much larger than his (2 Chron. 20). Or as Solomon did just before he took a job promotion and became king of Israel (1 Kings 2). Or even as Job did when he lost almost everything dear to him—his children, his livestock, his home, and his land (Job 1:20).

Job understood something many of us don't. The passage says that when all these things happened to Job, he fell on his face and he worshiped. Let me ask you a question: How could Job worship after all that tragedy? How would you respond after losing all your children and possessions? Somehow Job recognized that this was a junction. It was time for a pivotal prayer. He didn't want to merely react to the calamity. He knew that worship was the only response that would enable him to maintain proper perspective. God was God, and if there was ever a time he needed God's divine mastery and viewpoint, it was then.

Pivotal prayers increase as we mature spiritually. We learn to pray this way over time. This was vividly illustrated in November 2001, when *World Pulse* magazine reported the story of the three missionaries who had been kidnapped in 1993. All three worked with New Tribes Mission (NTM) and had turned up missing near the Colombian border. It wasn't until eight years later that New Tribes was willing to declare them dead.

Editor Deann Alford asked Dan Germann, NTM's vice chairman, how their prayers changed for the three men as the years went by. Dan responded, "When the guys were first captured, every one of us was praying, 'Lord, just bring them out safely. We know that You are able.' As time went on we started to pray, 'Lord, if they're alive, bring them home; but if they're dead, help us to know that as well.' Maybe six or eight months ago I heard us praying things like, 'God, if we never know, You'll still be God.' This was quite a difference from trusting Him to bring them out safely.

"In the end, God answered our prayers. We found a man in

prison who had cared for them. We received assurance from him that they were dead. This was a gift in the sense that we had come to the place where it was all right if God chose for us to never really know. Somebody looking on might think, 'How can you really accept that news?' All I can say is that God moved us down the road to where we could say, 'Lord, we want You to be glorified, even if we never know.'" [1]

Learning to pray this way isn't a cop-out. It doesn't mean we eventually stop trusting God to do miracles, and leave it to fate. It means we trust Him and His purposes regardless of our understanding. Do you remember Shadrach, Meshach, and Abednego? Daniel 3 tells the story of when these three Jewish men were about to be thrown into the fire by King Nebuchadnezzar. When he threatened to harm them unless they bowed down to worship his image, they responded with a pivotal decision: "O Nebuchadnezzar, we do not need to defend ourselves before you in this matter. If we are thrown into the blazing furnace, the God we serve is able to save us from it, and he will rescue us from your hand, O king. But even if he does not, we want you to know, O king, that we will not serve your gods or worship the image of gold you have set up" (3:16–18).

What those men said was no cop-out. They made a statement of faith: "God can and will deliver us." Then they made a statement of commitment: "But even if He doesn't, we will never bow down to any other god." That is a mature, pivotal decision. In their case, God was glorified by delivering them, causing the king and many others to repent.

Pivotal praying means we pray consistently from our hearts, not just from our heads. It is birthed out of relationship, not routine. Pivotal prayers move past clichés and perfunctory phrases to meaningful exchanges with God. This is the kind of prayer we all prefer but seldom practice.

Kevin was only five years old when his father carried him up the stairs to bed. As he crawled under the covers, the two of them folded their hands to say their prayers before falling asleep. Little Kevin was so tired, he shifted into automatic pilot and prayed these words: "Now I lay me down to sleep, I pray the Lord my soul to keep . . . If he hollers let him go—eeny, meeny, miny, moe."

We chuckle when we witness these kinds of episodes with kids, but are they not also a reflection of us as adults? How often do our prayer lives submit to the tyranny of meaningless, routine monologues? or to time constraints? or even to image-seeking as we pray in front of others?

If many Christians were to get honest, they'd admit their prayer lives border on superstition. We go through the motions, speaking a few worn-out phrases to make sure God is on our side before we head into our day.

The good news, though, is that pivotal praying isn't complex. In fact, it's often the simplest kind of prayer because it simply connects with the heart of God.

Jesus had something to say about pivotal praying. He told a story one day about two men who prayed—one of them connected with God, the other did not. The first was a tax collector and the other a Pharisee. The Pharisee was religious. He took pride in his sacrificial lifestyle, and his prayer was technically correct: "Lord, I thank you that I am not like other men—robbers, evildoers, adulterers—or even like this tax collector. I fast twice a week and give a tenth of all I get." The other man was a tax collector and could not even look to heaven, but instead beat his chest and said, "God, have mercy on me, a sinner" (Luke 18:10–14).

Interestingly, Jesus concluded that the tax collector's prayer—not the Pharisee's—was the pivotal one. It connected with God because of the posture of his heart. From this illustration we see that some prayers move the heart of God and cause Him to respond, and others, quite frankly, don't.

Years earlier, the prophet Jonah was sent to Nineveh to warn the Ninevites of pending destruction. The king of Nineveh repented, and God received it as a pivotal prayer. He responded by sparing the city. Ironically, Jonah got angry and failed to connect with God. He felt the Ninevites didn't deserve to be spared. Sometimes pivotal praying isn't the prayer that sounds pious or intelligent, but the one prayed from a heart that simply longs for God. In this case, the "bad guy" rather than the "good guy" prayed the pivotal prayer and the "good guy" didn't.

Be encouraged. The journey of learning pivotal prayer begins with a single step. The mere fact that you've picked up this book up demonstrates that you want to deepen your relationship with God and enlarge your prayer life. May this be the first step on your journey.

⊠

ENLISTING IN THE ARMY

I distinctly remember when God began to teach me about pivotal praying. It was 1981, and I was a junior in college. One morning I stumbled out of bed to spend some quiet time with God. As I mumbled through my usual prayer for myself, God interrupted me. In my mind I saw a startling picture. I saw our newly elected president, Ronald Reagan, being shot by a gunman. The vision was so shocking that my adrenaline began to flow. I remember thinking, *Wow! I sure hope that doesn't happen!*

As I continued to sit quietly, the picture lingered until I realized that God was communicating something to me. Immediately I began to pray for the president. I prayed for his safety and protection. Then I prayed that God would have His way and accomplish His purposes through Reagan's term of office. I must have prayed for thirty minutes. Afterward I sensed a burden lift from inside of me. I felt that everything was going to be OK. I took a shower and went on to class.

You can probably guess the rest of the story. Later that day I turned on my car radio and heard the news that President Reagan had been shot. As the details unfolded, I recognized them. They were precisely what I had seen in my mind earlier that morning. Later it was reported that the president was going to be fine and would fully recover, exactly as I had seen during my time in prayer.

I believe God was alerting many of His people to pray for the president that day. I believe He did so for the purpose of intercessory prayer. This is how God desires to accomplish His purposes on earth. When He can get His people to move beyond their selfish routines in prayer, He can use them greatly.

In Military Terms

Pivotal praying means we learn to pray at higher levels. Both the intimacy we share with God and the subject matter of our prayers deepen. Our prayers become more progressive, rather than merely accomplishing damage control. Our prayer becomes mission driven, not maintenance driven.

As television networks reported on America's war on terrorism, we began to hear the terms *logistical, tactical,* and *strategic initiatives.* These terms also describe three levels of prayer:

1. **Logistical prayer** focuses on my own personal needs. It is prayed from a temporal perspective. Imagine that you and I gather to pray before we lead the Sunday morning worship service. If we pray a logistical prayer, we might say: "Lord, help us to do well this morning. Help us to get through our program on time, help the microphones to work, and help us to be calm. Amen."

2. **Tactical prayer** focuses on helping others, but is still prayed

from a temporal perspective. If we were to pray this kind of prayer before our Sunday morning-worship service, we might say, "Lord, please bless all who participate in the service today, and bless those who attend. May it be inspiring to everyone. Amen." This prayer is better than the first one—but it still doesn't fully capture God's heart and purposes for the world.

3. **Strategic prayer** focuses on God's ultimate objectives for the world. It is prayed from an eternal perspective. It captures *His* heart and purpose, rather than mere human purposes. If we were to pray strategically before our Sunday-morning service, we might say: "Lord, raise up disciples from this service today. Regardless of what happens to the microphones, the musicians, or anyone else on the platform— use the service to glorify Yourself and bring Your kingdom more fully to this earth. Amen."

I am not suggesting that to pray for mundane things is selfish or evil. Nor am I saying that we are shallow anytime we pray for ourselves or for material things. I am saying that we should evaluate our prayer lives. How much of my prayer time surrounds "me" instead of others? How often do I ask God to bless *my* plans, rather than seek to fulfill *His* plans? Do I pray from my limited vantage point, or do I investigate His perspective on the issues?

The fact is, most Americans pray, but most of us pray selfishly. In 1993 I surveyed 2,000 church attendees, asking questions about their prayer habits. If their answers are any reflection of the general population, we have a lot of room to grow. The top three prayer subjects of those surveyed were meals, personal and family safety, and personal blessings. For many, their prayer time didn't go beyond praying over their Cheerios at breakfast! The average person spent less than seven minutes a day in prayer.

I am not implying this is evil—only that it is limited in potential. God yearns to accomplish so much more through our prayers, if we can only get on the same page He is on!

A Day in the Life of Jesus

Jesus demonstrated pivotal prayer. John 12 describes how He faced the final hours of His earthly life. The reality of a painful, brutal cross loomed in front of Him. He was in anguish. The Scriptures tell us His emotions were so intense that He sweated "great drops of blood."

So how did He pray? Recognizing the pivotal moment, He prayed, "Now my heart is troubled, and what shall I say? 'Father, save me from this hour'? No, it was for this very reason I came to this hour. Father, glorify your name!" (vv. 27–28).

Did you notice how Jesus contemplated what kind of prayer to pray? He could have prayed a logistical prayer: "Father, get me out of this mess!" That would have been natural. This might be what we would have prayed. Instead, Jesus prayed a strategic prayer—a pivotal prayer—at this crucial time. The result: the redemption of the world. *Key moment. Key prayer. Key decision. Key results.*

What's more, later in the Garden of Gethsemane Jesus was tempted once again to pray a logistical prayer. As He grieved over the execution He was about to endure, He prayed, "My Father, if it is possible, may this cup be taken from me." This is a normal reaction to His situation. However, He then added a strategic phrase: "Yet not as I will, but as You will" (Matt. 26:39). A pivotal moment. A strategic prayer.

As we leaf through the pages of Scripture, it is interesting to see how often God's people failed to pray strategically. Pivotal moments arose—but the people were caught up in themselves. In 2 Kings 3:5–18 we read of when the army of Israel faced the Moabites, who had a much larger military force. The king of Moab was in rebellion against King Joram, and was primed for attack. This was a pivotal moment.

Recognizing this, Israel's king rounded up two allies: the king of Judah and the king of Edom. The three men took their armies and livestock through the wilderness to face the Moabite army. But after a week they faced a crisis: They had run out of water.

They decided to go to the prophet Elisha to seek God's help. They begged for water. As the prophet sought the Lord, He responded through Elisha: *I will give you water—but this is a small thing for Me. I will also give the Moabites into your hands!*

In this pivotal moment, Israel had asked for the wrong thing. They saw only the small picture. They sought only the solution to their immediate needs. They prayed a logistical prayer. Graciously, God gave them what they *should* have asked for.

How many times do we miss God because we can't see beyond our own noses in a pivotal moment? Have you ever considered the fact that when we pray strategically, we'll receive every resource we need in the process? Had Israel asked for victory over the Moabites, they would have received water as well. God will take care of the logistics. "Seek first [God's] kingdom and his righteousness, and all these things will be given to you as well" (Matt. 6:33).

I imagine there have been hundreds of times in my life (maybe thousands!) when I have prayed shortsighted prayers, times when I couldn't see the pivotal moment. God may have wanted to do more, but I only asked for the small thing. He wanted to accomplish the ultimate, but I asked only for the immediate. It is the proverbial problem of missing the forest for the trees. Our focus and our vision are too small. We're like the woman and her son who got caught in a fierce tornado that swept through their tiny town in Texas. She grabbed hold of a tree for dear life, but in the process her son was taken up in the wind and blown into the air, and she lost sight of him. She cried out to God, "Lord, if You'll just bring my son back to me, I'll follow You. I'll obey You with all my heart. I will keep my eyes on You the rest of my life. I promise!"

Immediately the boy was dropped right in front of her. The wind stopped and set him down on the ground without a scratch. The woman looked at her son, then to heaven, and said, "Lord, he had a hat."

THE HISTORY AND MYSTERY OF PRAYER

In God's economy, prayer is vital currency. It provides us the opportunity to exchange our heart's cries for His gentle instruction. Throughout biblical history, prayer has been both a way and a means for believers to find help in time of need. When Jesus said, "Come unto Me," He knew a way to accomplish just that was prayer.

From the time of our creation, humankind has prayed—especially at pivotal moments (Gen. 4:26). Abraham petitioned God on behalf of the cities of Sodom and Gomorrah. Hannah, her womb barren and heart broken, called out to God in her misery. On the eve of inheriting a kingdom, Solomon petitioned God for wisdom and understanding.

How many times in your own experiences, perhaps jobless with little or no money in your bank account, or emotionally or physically impoverished, have you, too, called upon the name of the Lord?

Some people ask, "If God is sovereign and omniscient, why should I bother to pray?" This is a valid question. After all, God already knows what's going on before you call on His name, right?

Our friend Steve Brown is a professor of preaching at Reformed Theological Seminary. I love his answer to this very question: "He likes the sound of your voice." Isn't that great? Steve's answer paints the picture of a warm, loving companion. He continues: "God has created the relationship you have with Him so that He will often wait to act until you bring your concern to Him. Our daughter Robin is quite independent. When she was growing up, her attitude was often 'Please, Dad, I'd rather do it myself.' Sometimes I would know her needs and be perfectly willing to meet those needs. But I also knew that, for her sake, she needed to ask. I remember thinking, *I was just waiting for you to ask."*

God, our heavenly Father, is just waiting for us to ask. He loves us unconditionally. And in the context of that love He desires His children to come and share their heartaches, disappointments, and needs. So we go to Him with all our baggage and disillusionment— and there He is, at those pivotal moments. Moments when a husband walks away from twenty years of marriage; or a recession comes, bringing news of a job loss; or a brutal crime is committed against you or a member of your family.

When John Hull, my coauthor, was senior pastor at Peoples Church in Toronto, Canada, the first funeral he conducted was in early October 1993. Pamela, a young woman in her mid-twenties, had grown up in the church. After her university years she secured a job, resided with her grandfather, saved some money, dated a young Christian man, and was preparing for a bright future.

On a September evening, just minutes after sunset, Pam and her boyfriend were chatting in her grandfather's driveway. Suddenly a stranger with a weapon in hand appeared and forced the couple inside the house. The events that followed, too gruesome to describe, led to the execution-style murders of Pamela, her friend, and her grandfather.

John had known Pamela's parents, Carl and Barbara, for only a few weeks. They were stalwart church members, the kind every pastor loves to have in his congregation. They walked with God. And now, their daughter, Barbara's father, and a friend had become victims of a senseless crime. It was at this pivotal moment that Carl and Barbara asked God for grace and strength to help them through the darkest of days. Almost a decade later, Carl and Barbara continue in their walk with God. They prayed through this pivotal moment and passed the test.

LET'S TAKE A JOURNEY

These lessons from Carl and Barbara, Mr. Welch, Mr. Kraft, and Jesus beckon us to learn about pivotal praying. Such pivotal moments happen to us all. Fasten your seat belts; we're about to take a journey. In the pages of this book we will examine a variety of contexts every one of us faces during our lives. We will discuss how to pray pivotal prayers in every circumstance. We will learn from positive and negative examples in the Bible.

The chapters will focus on personalities from Scripture. We'll demonstrate the impact of that leader's prayer and action during pivotal seasons of his or her life. How each one prayed affected how he or she made decisions, and the ultimate results. We'll study the pivotal moment, the pivotal decision, and the pivotal outcome of that prayer.

Further, to illustrate the impact of pivotal praying, we will also include an example of someone who failed to pray a pivotal prayer in a similar junction. We'll provide a picture of a *type* and an *antitype* for pivotal prayer in each particular situation.

We want to study the kind of prayer that attracts God—prayer that moves His heart. We want you to learn how to pray so that God is responsive to you, as He wants to be. If this is the desire of your heart, let's get going.

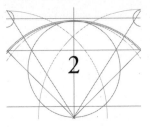

Pivotal Praying When You're Facing a Crisis

(John Hull)

When Jake called with the news, I was shocked. He came home one day to find that Sandra, his wife of four years, had moved her personal belongings out of the house, leaving only a note that she wanted a divorce. In subsequent conversations, Sandra made it clear to Jake that the marriage, from her point of view, was over. Final. Done. She wanted out without having to answer a lot of questions.

But Jake had questions. And as he asked Sandra those probing questions—starting with "Why?"—his frustrations grew because she wouldn't go there. Her responses were nebulous and inexplicable to him. This is where Jake was on the journey—confused and imperiled, facing the greatest personal crisis of his twenty-nine-year-old life—when he called and asked me to pray for him and for Sandra.

What in the world do you say to a friend at a crisis time like that? And how do you pray for him? More important, how does he pray for himself?

CRISIS AS A FULCRUM

"Crisis," writes Roy Zuck, "whether national or individual, reveals our human weaknesses and prompts us to turn to God. That's what the nation of Israel did in the wilderness. *'They cried out to the LORD in their trouble'"* (Ps. 107:6).[1]

Eugene Peterson draws this picture: "Prayer acts on the principle of the fulcrum." A fulcrum is a fixed position or defined point upon which a lever swings or turns. It is a necessary and strategic spot by where fluid motion can occur, and gradually great weight is transferred. Peterson passionately declares that prayer is "the small point (the fulcrum) where great leverage is exercised."[2]

Prayer is never more leveraged than at the fulcrum point of crisis—be it individual or national. Prayer is that specific point, in the context of a specific circumstance, at which our cries to God set in motion the leveraging of our crisis, moving its burdensome weight from our shoulders to His.

The very definition of the word *crisis* complements the image of a fulcrum. The word *crisis* means a pivotal, decisive, or crucial moment—a sudden time of testing, for better or for worse. It originates from the ancient Greek word *krisis,* which means a time of testing or judgment. The word *crisis* carries with it all the packaging within that pivotal moment when one may question his or her hopes, fears, and even faith, in rapid succession. It is in times like this that we pause in pain and utter bewilderment. Such times are the unexpected striking of a match that lights a fire that we can't control.

It's in these crisis moments that we come to a sort of emotional duality with what to do with this thing called prayer. Do we embrace it or neglect it? On the one hand, crisis often drives us to God because we know that there's no one else that can even begin to explain, much less make any sense of it.

On the other hand, if we've been negligent in our prayer lives, we may feel ashamed and awkward pursuing a new level of communication with God, now that crisis has come.

Crisis came to Jake's house. Maybe it has come to yours as well. Is this a fulcrum moment in your life? Are you at a point where you need some help?

CRYING OUT TO GOD

I think a lot these days about pastors of churches. Maybe it's because I was a pastor for almost twenty years prior to my present assignment at EQUIP, a ministry created to train pastors around the world in leadership. Maybe it's because I grew up in a minister's home. Whatever the reason, I have great compassion for pastors and preachers. I love them and I love to be around them.

You may not be aware of it, but pastors are like members of the emergency trauma center at your local hospital. These trained and talented men and women care for hurting souls on a regular basis, many of whom are experiencing genuine crisis in their lives. "Crisis care" is a normal part of the minister's daily work.

Mark Coppenger, a pastor in Evanston, Illinois, recently wrote about crisis and the church with some fresh frankness:

> The church is always in crisis mode. A new convert throws her live-in boyfriend out of the house, and now she has to make up the difference in rent. You get word that a junior high Sunday school teacher is telling her class that, without glossalia (speaking in tongues) they're second-rate Christians. A van load of youth are injured on the way to church camp. The local plant closes and three of your deacons are out of work. A staff member quits in a flurry of recrimination. A prominent church member shows up on the DUI list of the local paper. A business meeting ignites over item III. B in the budget. And that's just this week.[3]

I can remember times when I would sit, absolutely speechless, in my church study following a meeting with a parishioner and hearing the nature of his or her crisis. This person's crisis took my breath away.

You know what I would do? I would encourage this person to cry out to God. Many times in the center of my own crises I have cried, "Lord, what in the world am I going to do with this terrible situation I'm facing?"

It's so simple. Yet pride often prevents us from crying out to God and saying, "Lord, I didn't ask for this. I don't understand it. But now I've got to deal with it. God, please help me!"

When the people of Israel were wayward, even when it was of their own doing, prophet after prophet would cry out to God. Jeremiah cried out to God when he saw the people of Israel sliding toward doom and an inevitable national crisis. In fact, most of the Book of Jeremiah is his cry to God over Israel's disobedience. Deceit, adultery, and lying had become a part of the culture, and God was not going to ignore that. Judgment was coming. Crisis was near. And Jeremiah? He just kept crying out to God.

The writer of Psalm 107 mentions four groups of people going through crisis and how the Lord helps them. In verse 4 he speaks of some who "wandered"—those trying to make their way back to Israel from Babyonian captivity. "They were hungry and thirsty, and their lives ebbed away" (v. 5). These were people in a desperate situation. How did they make it through their crisis? Verse 6 says, "They cried out to the LORD in their trouble, and he delivered them from their distress."

The psalmist goes on to mention others in distress. He speaks of prisoners, the sick, and the storm-tossed. In each case these people "cried to the LORD in their trouble, and he saved them from their distress" (vv. 13, 19, and 28). Clearly, these segments of society experience crisis even today.

Abraham cried out to God when he learned that Sodom and Gomorrah, where his nephew and family lived, were going to be severely punished by God because of their decadence. He prayed that Sodom and Gomorrah be saved if only ten righteous persons could be found in the city. Abraham begged God not to "sweep away the righteous with the wicked" (Gen. 18:23). Like Jeremiah, Abraham saw a crisis looming and cried out to God for help. Sadly, ten righteous people could not be found in Sodom and Gomorrah, and the cities were destroyed. By God's grace, however, Lot and some of his family members were spared. I believe this was in answer to Abraham's prayer to save them. (Gen. 18–19)

If you are smack-dab in the middle of a crisis today, cry out to God. Tell Him exactly how you feel. He can handle it. Someone once told me that God is not embarrassed by the honesty of our prayers. Get gut-level honest with God and tell Him how badly you hurt, how angry you are, and that you need His help to get through this crisis. Don't worry about God—He can deal with this. When you cast (which means "to throw") your cares on Him, throw your best stuff at Him. He wants you to. It's a great first step toward praying appropriately in the face of a crisis.

Ask God for Wisdom
over the Next Few Days

James tells us that if we lack wisdom, we should ask God (1:5). When things are in crisis, life can get a bit crazy. Strange and hurtful things can be said and done. When crisis comes to your life, ask God to give you wisdom over the days that follow. Here are some suggestions for what to pray:

Ask God to Give You Wise Thoughts
Alan Bean, a former Apollo astronaut, shares the importance of wise thinking:

> Test pilots have a litmus test for evaluating problems. When something goes wrong they ask, "Is this thing still flying?" If the answer is yes, then there's no immediate danger, no need to overreact. When Apollo 12 took off, the spacecraft was hit by lightning. The

entire console began to glow with orange and red trouble lights. There was a temptation to "Do Something!" But the pilots asked themselves, "Is this thing still flying in the right direction?" The answer was yes—it was headed for the moon. They let the lights glow as they addressed the individual problems, and watched the orange and red lights turn off one by one. That's something to think about in any pressure situation. If your thing is still flying, think first, and then act.[4]

When we're in a crisis and the panic lights are blinking wildly, we're tempted to "do something!" But before you do anything, take time to think things through. Ask God for direction. Ask God for His timing. Ask God to clear your mind so that you can process what's going on.

Many people in crisis act before they think. A spouse, for instance, decides to make a major statement by moving out of the house. A business leader and others in the office resign their positions in anger, without considering the consequences of their actions.

During Jesus' ministry, Peter faced crises by acting impulsively or speaking out without first thinking it through. We've all done this. For some reason, in the midst of a crisis, we feel we need to do something right then and there. But this is not always the wisest move. Sometimes wisdom means being slow to act.

When you face a crisis, go to God and ask Him for wise thoughts.

Ask God for Wise Words to Say

One of the major emphases in James's letter is the role of the tongue—our words. Mark Twain once said that the difference between the right word and the nearly right word is the difference between lightning and a lightning bug. In other words, it's huge. What we say and don't say in the midst of a crisis matters.

James says, "With the tongue we praise our Lord and Father, and with it we curse men, who have been made in God's likeness" (3:9). Words have the power to heal and to hurt. They have the ability to win people over or wound them for years to come. It's very important that we choose our words wisely in a crisis period. God can help us with that if we ask Him. Just ask the Lord to give you wisdom in the selection of your words—especially to those who may be in the crisis with you.

This is especially true concerning family members. I've witnessed many fierce verbal exchanges between siblings while their mother is dying in the next room. I've heard cruel words thrown back and forth between a mother and father in the waiting room as their little son is holding on for dear life in the trauma center. Words really do matter. And in a time of crisis, the words spoken or not spoken can take on a life of their own long after the crisis is over.

Here is the kind of pivotal prayer a person in crisis offers when asking God for wise words to say: "God, I'm about to go see my family for the first time since this crisis has come into our lives. Help me not to say anything stupid!"

Ask God for Wise Counsel

At some point you'll probably want to talk to someone. Jake, in his marital crisis, called me. When I'm in crisis, I often want to talk to my wife or someone else close to me. Whom do you call for counsel?

After King Solomon died, his son Rehoboam became king. In 1 Kings 12, Rehoboam faced a crisis. His kingdom was divided, and national unity was at risk, A designated leader of the northern tribes of Israel, Jeroboam, met with King Rehoboam to negotiate a reduction in the tax and labor burden on the citizens in the north. Rehoboam said he wanted three days to think about it.

During this three-day period Rehoboam sought counsel from two groups within his kingdom. The first group was made up of older men who had served with his father, Solomon. They advised him to ease the work and tax load on the northern tribes. While not a perfect solution, it might buy some more time, continue the peace in the land, and give King Rehoboam time to establish his leadership.

The other source of advice came from a group of younger men, closer to Rehoboam's age. These younger leaders advised Rehoboam to play hardball—to take the approach, "If you think it's tough now, just wait and see how tough it's going to get."

Sadly, Rehoboam took the younger men's counsel. When he announced his decision three days later to Jeroboam and the leaders of the northern tribes, the response was highly negative, and as a result the country divided into northern and southern kingdoms.

In a crisis, Rehoboam sought counsel. But he followed the wrong advice and made the wrong decision. This led to a deeper and longer-lasting crisis: national division.

It's possible to make some very unwise decisions in a crisis. The consequences can be devastating. Seek counsel in a crisis situation. But before you do, ask God for wise counsel. And when you get counsel, ask God if what you've been advised to do is workable and consistent with His Word.

PRAY THAT GOD WILL NOT ALLOW THE SITUATION TO DETERIORATE

Many Old Testament prophets passionately went before the Lord, asking God in a crisis situation to stop the bleeding, and not let the nation continue to deteriorate. In the early days of his ministry at Brooklyn Tabernacle in New York, Jim Cymbala was frustrated that the ministry was having a tough time moving forward. In fact, things seemed to be going backward. It became a personal and professional crisis. Cymbala hungered for God to use him.

I despaired at the thought that my life might slip by without seeing God show himself mightily on our behalf. Carol [Jim's wife] and I didn't want to mark time. I longed and cried out to God to change everything—me, the church, our passion for people, our praying. One day, I told the Lord I would rather die than merely tread water throughout my career in ministry.[5]

Here was a transparent plea for God not to let the Brooklyn Tabernacle deteriorate any longer. Jim was asking God to stop the bleeding and to bring healing to the church. And God did. Today Brooklyn Tabernacle is one of America's most respected and influential churches!

There are times, however, when deterioration will continue and a crisis will escalate, regardless of our best efforts to stop it. If devastation is unavoidable and further deterioration seems certain, ask God to help you to do all within your power to manage the crisis. Consider former New York City mayor Rudy Giuliani: When New York was attacked on September 11, 2001, Giuliani helped the city cope in the aftermath. His crisis-management skills will long be lauded by the citizens of New York.

Crisis: When it comes, how do you pray?

- Cry out to God about your pain.
- Ask God for wisdom over the next few days.
- Ask God for the crisis situation not to deteriorate any further.

When I see Jake next, I'm going to sit down and share with him some points on this kind of pivotal praying. I'm going to reassure him that he will get through this terrible mess, one way or another. But however he does it, he will need to be transparent with God.

"Just call out to God; pour your heart out to Him," I'll say. Then I'll encourage Jake to seek God's wisdom over the next few critical days. He will need to be wise in his thoughts, in his words, and in the counsel that he seeks. Then I'll encourage him to pray that the critical situation he's facing won't deteriorate further.

And before I leave Jake, I might tell him this story about Thomas Edison: Edison's facilities in West Orange, New Jersey were heavily damaged by fire one night in late 1914. Edison lost about a million dollars' worth of equipment, along with a lot of paperwork containing the details of his inventions. Walking about the charred embers of his hopes and dreams the following morning, the sixty-seven-year-old inventor said, "There is value in disaster. All our mistakes are burned up. Now we can start anew."[6]

Take heart. Whatever the disaster, whatever the crisis, God gives us the capacity to start anew!

CLOSING PRAYER

A Pivotal Prayer When You're in Crisis

God, I cry out to You.
The news that's just hit me is so hard to bear.
I'm close to being in shock right now.
I don't know what to do.
I'm angry. I'm hurt. I'm confused.
So, Lord, I call out to You. Please hear my prayer.
Give me strength to get through this mess.
Help me to make wise choices
and not to say something that will
just make things worse.
Please, don't let this thing get any worse than it is.
And God, help me not to do anything stupid.
This is going to take a long time to get through;
and right now, I don't feel like I'll ever get on top of it.
So, here it is, Lord. A big mess.
Thank You that You're here to show me
how to clean it up.
Amen.

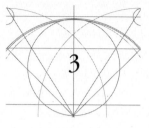

PIVOTAL PRAYING WHEN YOUR DREAMS DON'T COME TRUE

(TIM ELMORE)

Learning to pray well when your dreams don't come true has to be one of the toughest challenges in the world. Most of us have faced days when we've realized that some deep desire in our hearts isn't going to pan out. Few of us know how to pray in such pivotal moments. Many simply give up.

A friend of mine remembers his Little League coach giving a pep talk to the team before opening day of baseball season. He asked, "How many of you have a dream to one day play in the major leagues?" Almost every hand shot up. Almost every kid believed he could do it. You could see it in their eyes. The coach then told them, "If that is to happen—that dream begins now!" All the boys were so inspired by the challenge that they practiced hard and went undefeated for the next few years. All-star teams from other leagues would play them and lose!

Some twenty-five years later, my friend said he became a Little League coach himself. He brought all the kids together and gave the same pep talk he remembered his coach giving. "How many of you dream of playing in the major leagues one day?" Anticipating the response, he gazed at each of the kids. Not one hand was raised. Not one kid believed he could do it. You could see it in their eyes. My friend was shocked. The rest of his talk was meaningless, so all he could say was, "Really? Nobody? Well, get your gloves and warm up."

He thought about that day for a long time. What had happened in the twenty-five years since he was a kid? What had convinced those kids that they would never be more than what they were? What had come into their lives to steal their dreams?

It seems to me that this isn't a story confined to kids. As I talk to adults, most of them have had some dream they've given up on. They usually laugh about it and chalk it up to maturity or getting "real." Their ideals have given way to the realities of a mortgage payment, laundry to be done, meals to be planned, cars to be repaired, and monthly bills to be paid. They're not even praying about those dreams anymore. Douglas MacArthur once wrote, "People grow old by deserting their ideals. Years may wrinkle the skin, but to give up interest wrinkles the soul. Worry, self-doubt, self-distrust, fear and despair; these are the long, long years that bow the head and turn the growing spirit back to dust."[1]

When our dreams are selfish or born out of immaturity, it's probably wise to give up on them. In such instances we need a good dose of reality. Many times, however, our dreams are God–given. God gives them to us when we're still soft, when we've not been hardened by cynicism, and we still believe we can make a difference if we take a risk. "God dreamed us into existence," writes David Thomas, "and God, in turn, implants dreams within us. To pursue our hopes and dreams requires courage, which is the basic orientation of an act of hope . . . to fail to dream is to deny the God of faithful love, to deny ourselves our own birthright."[2]

So what do we do when our dreams don't come true? It's then that we come to discover the other side of this issue, which makes pivotal praying crucial. Nearly everyone who pursues a dream goes through a desperate season when it looks as though his or her dream will die.

This is sometimes called the "dark night of the soul." Bill Gothard has called this the "death of a vision." Yet this season is just as divine as the dream may be. And it is often necessary. Rarely does someone benefit from an easy dream and its speedy fulfillment. In fact, it is usually in the process of the dream's gestation period that God prepares us for its fulfillment.

Gordon MacDonald learned this lesson early. "I've come to see the dark moments of life as precious moments, times to ask, 'Is this a moment when God wants to speak to me?'" Such a pivotal moment came to him in the 1980s when a major Christian organization asked if he'd be willing to run for the office of their next president. Several wise people told him not to refuse—that maybe God was calling him to leadership at a world level. While other leaders were being considered for the job, his hopes were spiked when the headhunter called him, asking if he could come to Boston to visit.

The visit went extremely well—and soon Gordon and his wife, Gail, decided to get away to think and pray about their future. "Neither Gail nor I had ever asked God for omens or signs to determine our future direction, but during those weeks the dots seemed to line up. The books we read, the conversations we held, the prayers we prayed, the voice of God we heard in our souls—everything pointed to my taking this position. We believed that God was saying, "This is going to happen." It was a dream come true.

The final two candidates were asked to fly to the ministry headquarters for a final interview. Gordon was one of them. Gail told him, "They're going to ask you to be the next president." This surprised Gordon, as Gail was not prone to such pronouncements.

That Saturday, knowing the decision would be made Sunday afternoon, Gordon told his staff at Grace Chapel that he wanted to meet with them Sunday night after church. He was going to announce his resignation. He anticipated that by then the board chairman of the organization would have called.

As it turned out, Sunday afternoon came and went, but the phone did not ring. By the time the staff gathered that night at the MacDonald's home, he was in agony. Gordon didn't know what to do. He decided to be honest and tell the staff his story, and to admit that it didn't have an ending. For twenty-five minutes he shared how he and Gail had prayed and wrestled with this potential move—but that he felt it was a dream come true for them. Everyone was in a state of shock.

No sooner had Gordon finished than the phone rang. It was the chairman of the board. The other candidate had been chosen.

Gordon stumbled into the living room to tell the staff the news. He said stoically, "You've been with Gail and me on many occasions when God has said yes. Now you'll get to see how we handle things when God says no."

Ten days later the full force of what happened crushed him. "I submarined into the depths of disillusionment. At the subterranean level, I told God, 'You've made a perfect fool out of me. You drew me to the finish line and said, "I'm sorry."' I no longer understand your language. You speak a different language than I've been trained to understand."

Gordon reflected later, "I was questioning God—something I had never really done. I doubted whether it was possible to hear God speak." During this period, he resigned from Grace Chapel out of exhaustion, disillusionment, and bewilderment. By pursuing that position, he had lost trust with the leaders at Grace Chapel. By his own admission, his world had fallen apart.

Fortunately, during this period of time Gordon learned a new level of pivotal praying. Some fourteen years later he reflected,

I had to surrender to a much deeper and more mysterious God than I had known up to that moment. I had to surrender all of my prejudices and preconditions of knowing God. That takes time.

God wasn't in a hurry for Moses . . . and God certainly wasn't in a hurry for me.

In retrospect, I can say that if the board of that organization had picked me, I would have failed. I wasn't mature enough. The job required characteristics I don't have. Even so, there's a memory of those days that has stayed with me: Don't expect everything to be cozy with God, for He is a big God and His ways are beyond us.[3]

Pivotal praying, when our dreams don't come true, requires us to let God out of the box we've put Him in. Perhaps there is something He must do in us before the dream can be fulfilled. Perhaps He must tweak the dream before He can bring it to pass. Henri Nouwen gives us a model when he says, "Lord, let me at least remain open to your initiative; let me wait patiently and attentively for that hour when you will come and break through all the walls I have erected. Teach me, O Lord, to pray. Amen."[4]

GOING DEEPER

Let's face it: The easiest way to pray when our dreams don't come true is with anger or frustration. "Why didn't You allow it to happen, Lord?" "What is wrong with me?" "What are You doing, Lord? Are You breaking Your promise to answer my prayers?" "Why don't You fix this thing?"

In such pivotal moments it's easy to neglect the pivotal prayer. Each of these prayer requests misses the deeper truth God wants us to learn in the process. Oswald Chambers once said, "If God allows you to be stripped of the exterior portions of your life, He means for you to cultivate the interior." In other words, if your dream hasn't manifested itself on the outside, maybe there is more work to be done on the inside.

In an insightful article entitled "Beyond Prayer Requests," Wayne Jacobsen notes that in these situations we are far more likely to treat God like a genie in a bottle.[5] We let our human desires cloud the deeper work God wants to do. Take a look at the following prayer requests we make when things get rough:

The Trivial Prayer: "Help me get over this cold," or "Give us a sunny day for the church picnic." Our comfort and plans seem important to us, but perhaps God has something larger in mind. Perhaps the farmers around us desperately need the rain. Our prayer needs to reflect what we truly expect God to do, not our thoughtless hopes and whims. We must make sure the dreams we are praying about aren't shortsighted. We mustn't let our requests trivialize the awesome gift of prayer.

The Self-Motivated Prayer: "My brother's unit just got called up to go to Afghanistan. Let's pray he won't have to go." While I can understand the sentiment behind this request, it is still misplaced. If your brother is in the military, why shouldn't he go? God's purposes frequently include hardship and risk. Should we ask God to trump His purposes for our convenience?

The Controlling Prayer: "Please bless my plans. I've worked so hard, and I need this to work." Or, "Don't let my brother move into his girlfriend's house." This might be what you want for your brother, but if we ask God to force others to act according to our will, we are trying to control the situation. God never forces people to adhere to His will. Far too often we use prayer to try to control and don't even realize it. It is far better to pray, "Lord, reveal Yourself to my brother, and allow him to clearly see the choice he is making. Show me how to love him even if he makes a stupid mistake."

The Blaming Prayer: I heard about a church group who prayed for an infertile woman. They thought she wasn't getting pregnant because her husband wasn't godly enough, so they asked God to change him. She blamed him and tried to manipulate him to change. Everyone grew frustrated. Unfortunately they missed the point of prayer. Prayer isn't about blaming someone and pushing them to change. None of us qualifies for God's gifts. If God waited until everyone was ready to have a baby, no one would give birth.

The Manipulative Prayer: Not all prayer requests are directed to God. Sometimes people pray "at" others. Sometimes we even preach in our prayers. The messages may be subtle or not so subtle. In any case, when we do this we are manipulating on a horizontal level, among people. This is quite the opposite of what prayer is intended to do—to trust God for what only He can do.[6]

Consider this: When your dreams don't come true, you may be on the brink of learning to trust Jesus in a far deeper manner than you ever could have imagined. If all worked out well, you might put life on cruise control. What most enhances my relationship with Jesus is my ability to trust Him, no matter what the circumstance.

So what are we to do? During this time of pivotal praying, take time to make sure your dream is really God's agenda, not just yours. Use this time to grow deeper in your trust. You might even find it liberating to let go of your dream for one that is bigger—one from Him. "I am beginning to feel that we need a preliminary act of submission not only toward future affliction but toward future blessings," wrote C. S. Lewis. "I know it sounds fantastic; but think it over. It seems to me that we often, almost sulkily, reject the good that God offers us because, at the moment, we expected some other good."[7]

I remember a story about a man who was shipwrecked years ago on an uncharted island. He got caught in a storm, and the wind whipped his boat onto the shoreline, where it burst into pieces. He was exhausted but found strength to salvage a few valuables and crawl onto the beach. There he waited to be rescued. Surely people would notice he was missing.

For four days he watched and waited, but saw no ship or plane anywhere. He began to get hungry and depressed. He'd lost almost everything. Since he might be on the island a while, he decided he'd better build some kind of shelter for himself. So, he constructed a crude hut and put his valuables in it for safekeeping. At least he still had some possessions.

One day, however, he returned from a hunt for a meal to find the hut in flames. A fire had started somehow in the hot sun, and everything was burned up. The man was devastated. He dropped to his knees and wept. "God, how could You let this happen? This fire has consumed the only things I have left!"

Suddenly he stopped crying. Ironically, having lost everything, he felt as if he was liberated. He looked up to God and whispered, "It's OK, God. I surrender. I want Your plan for my life. I care nothing for my things, nor for my future anymore."

Within the hour a ship came into view to rescue him. He couldn't believe his eyes. As he climbed on board he asked the captain, "I've waited for days to be rescued. How did you know I was here?"

"It was simple," the captain replied. "We saw your smoke signal."

What We Learn from David and Absolom

Tucked away in the Old Testament are two leaders who pursued a goal and never reached it. David wanted to build a temple in Jerusalem. Absolom wanted to be the next king in Israel. Their stories are a picture of contrast: one prayed a pivotal prayer when his dream failed to unfold; the other forced the issue, coercing others to fulfill his dream. The pivotal prayer saved David. The manipulative spirit killed Absolom.

David's desire to build the temple is evident in 2 Samuel 7. David told the prophet Nathan he felt badly because he owned his own house, while God was confined to a portable tent, for several generations. David wanted to round up the finest materials in the area and construct a temple for God. From what we can tell, his motives seemed to be pure. The dream seemed to make sense. The idea appears to have been borne from a desire to glorify God and honor Him, as the Lord of hosts.

Nathan, however, heard from the Lord that same night. God told him David wasn't going to realize this dream. According to God's plan, David was excluded from the dream of building a holy place for God to dwell because he was a man of war. The temple would be built by David's successor, his son Solomon. God affirmed that it wasn't because David had done anything wrong or had fallen out of favor with Him. It just didn't fit into the divine plan.

The next day, Nathan shared these things with David. I'm sure the king grew quiet for a moment—this word flew in the face of everything he had planned. Consider this as well: David was the most powerful man in the Middle East at the time. He had the resources to force the issue and make his dream come true. He had the money, the manpower, and the favor of the people. He could have made fast work of it. But he didn't. In verses 18-29, David sat down and prayed a pivotal prayer. In it, he recognized God's sovereignty. He acknowledged his own humanity. He reminded himself of how well God had performed His will in the past, from the journey out of Egypt to the present day influence of the tiny nation of Israel. Finally, he affirmed his commitment to follow whatever God wanted, whenever He wanted it. Content that it was, indeed, God's dream, it didn't matter whether he got to do it, or someone else. He was only concerned for the name of God. David prayed well at the pivot.

In fact, his prayer led him to take another step. He went the second mile. On his own time and at his own expense, he began to round up the materials for the next king to use. Although Solomon had not yet been born, David prepared the way and simplified the task for him. He did all this even though he would not get to enjoy the temple himself.

I remember serving on the pastoral staff at Skyline Church with John Maxwell. John had had a dream for nearly fourteen years to relocate the church and build a new worship center on a mountain in Rancho San Diego. In 1995, after wading through a decade of red tape—from county planning committees, to environmental protection agencies, to the raising of millions of dollars—Dr. Maxwell decided to pursue his national ministry full time. He was going to leave the pastorate and his dream. He recognized he could not pursue both the local ministry and the national one.

What made this decision so hard was that this dream of relocation had consumed John for so long. Like David, he wasn't going to get to see the tangible building go up. What impressed me, though, was this: from the moment he announced his resignation in February until August when Jim Garlow assumed the role of senior pastor, John did everything he could to foster the fulfillment of that dream for a new generation. He met with teams of leaders, he continued to cast vision and raise money for the project, and he continued giving toward the building even after he moved to Atlanta.

John has said many times that it was hard leaving the pastorate, because people and buildings could be measured tangibly. Now that he is on the road, he can't always measure his success. One night, however, he had an encouraging pivotal prayer time that helped him make the move. He told me it was as though God said, "John, for the last twenty-five years, you kept score. For the next twenty-five years, I'll keep score."

My point is simply this: while it's on a much smaller scale than the building of Solomon's temple, John drew his strength, not from seeing the dream fulfilled himself, but in knowing he could prepare the way for a new leader and people to do so. Dreams belong to God, and must be held lightly. Both King David and John Maxwell learned that sometimes our role in the dream is submission. Both the temple and the worship center were built after they were gone.

THE DEATH OF THE DREAMER

Ironically, David's son Absolom never learned this lesson. He determined he was going to chase his dream, even if it cost him and everyone else their lives. David's death was an inward one—he had to die to the desire to force the dream to be fulfilled his way. Absolom's death was an outward one—it came as a result of his blind ambition and greed.

In 2 Samuel 15-16, we see that Absolom's story is a vivid illustration of a forced agenda. It's the story of a man who pushed to see his dream come true. He would stand at the city gate and use personal politics to get people to follow him rather than his father, King David. He became deceptive with his father about his agenda. He sent spies out to campaign for him and to announce that he would be the next king.

Absolom built such a following that David ended up fleeing Jerusalem. There is little doubt from the story that David and Absolom had some unresolved father/son issues. In defiance, Absolom entered Jerusalem with his own band of loyalists and set up shop. To demonstrate his power, he took his father's concubines and had sex with them on the rooftop, in the sight of Israel. This dream was a power trip.

Sadly, Absolom's journey ended in tragedy. As David's army met up with Absolom's men, they fought. In a rage to reach his goal, Absolom rode through the woods and was killed by Joab, David's captain. Absolom was blinded by his own ambition. He failed to see that the methods he used to fulfill his dream would sabotage his leadership afterward. He never understood that the end does not justify the means. He became so hardened and resolute to reach his goal, he failed to negotiate the path to get there. Here is the difference between Absolom and his father David: David was called, Absolom was driven. Moved by his calling, David cared less about who got the credit as long as God was honored. He could play a smaller role in the dream if it pleased God. Absolom was driven, not called. He felt he had to force the dream, and it killed him.

DREAMS AND RESILIENCE

When dreams fail, people have a choice. David made the decision to be flexible. Absolom had no flexibility. He demanded his dream happen as he wanted, when he wanted. This brittle spirit ruined his chances. Had he been adaptable, he might have been chosen to be the next king. He was certainly in line before Solomon.

One of the most helpful insights we gain from studies done on aging and longevity is the importance of resilience. Centenarians (those who live to be 100) and others who live to ripe-old ages are often those who are best able to accept personal loss and make new beginnings.[8] This isn't to say they don't feel the pain of major disappointments and even grieve them profoundly. Still, the point comes when they are able to put the past behind them and adapt to the loss. They are remarkably adept at making fresh starts.

Jeanne Calment was a stunning example of this resilience. This Frenchwoman, who died at 122, was the oldest person in the world whose birthday could be documented. She had suffered many misfortunes and failed dreams in her life. Her husband had died fifty years earlier from eating tainted cherries. Her only child died of pleurisy at age thirty-six. Her only grandchild died prematurely in a car accident. Through all this she kept dreaming and adapting, and maintained her sense of humor. When a reporter asked her on her 120th birthday what sort of future she envisioned, she replied, "A very brief one."

When dreams don't come true *we* need to adjust, instead of asking *God* to. We need to see the work He wants to do *in* us, before He does a work *through* us. A prerequisite for this is resilience. If we get stuck in a rut of how the dream is supposed to look, not only will we miss out on it, but we'll probably achieve one much smaller than what God planned. All around us are people who have lost a dream. Some overcame it. Others did not.

George O'Leary's dream was to become head football coach at the University of Notre Dame. While coaching at Georgia Tech during the 2001 season, he was finally asked to do it. It was unbelievable for him, almost surreal. He was realizing the dream of every Catholic kid who ever grew up in Long Island. After negotiations were complete, he traveled to South Bend, Indiana, for the announcement. On December 9, 2001, as the school's legendary fight song blared, thousands shouted his name as he was introduced as the head football coach at Notre Dame. It was emotional, even for an unemotional guy.

Then, it all came crashing down. Within days, a New Hampshire newspaper reported that O'Leary had never lettered in football at the University of New Hampshire, as his biography stated. When officials at Notre Dame called him to ask if this were true, he admitted that while he was on the team, a knee injury had kept him from playing and that an error must have been made by some sports writer that never got corrected. When the officials then asked if there were any other mistakes in the official biography, he admitted that he never received a master's degree in education. At that point, O'Leary offered to resign twice. Officials, however, rejected his offer. Later that night, O'Leary could not live with himself, and put his resignation in writing. He faxed it to the university from his hotel, and it was accepted. His career with Notre Dame was over after only five days.[9]

Today, George O'Leary is on the other side of a failed dream. Some might argue that it was his fault, but in any case the Notre Dame dream is over. He was forced to adapt to a new life. One minute he was on top of the world, the next he was unemployed.

Charles Dudish can understand this scenario. He was one of the most recruited athletes in America in the late 1960s. He was All-American in baseball and football. When he was a high schooler more than 200 colleges, as well as pro baseball teams, bid for his services

But Dudish never became the football star everyone expected. A high draft choice, he never made it in baseball either. Instead, he fell victim to drugs and alcohol, and his promising future came to ruin. The dream ended. "I went from having everything to being nothing," Dudish said. "It was a nightmare. By all rights, I should be dead."

But Dudish's story isn't a sad one. During this pivotal time he prayed. A friend led him to do so at a party. It was a prayer of surrender. He received Jesus Christ as his Savior and never took drugs again. His life was revolutionized—but with a new dream. A ministry began for him which allowed him to share Christ with teens. He is influencing students positively now in a way he could never have done before that prayer. Charles Dudish exemplifies what I'm attempting to say in this chapter. In fact, he summarized it better than I can: "You don't have to die just because your dreams do." [10]

May we all take that message to heart.

CLOSING PRAYER

Dear Lord,
I actually thank You today
that my dream was not realized in a quick and easy
fashion. I would have missed the growth You wanted to
bring about inside me. Deepen me as I wait and trust.
Alert me to keep my eyes open for opportunities to
pursue the dream. Help me to refuse to give up on my
God-given dreams.
In Jesus' name,
Amen.

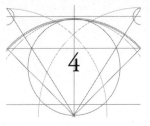

Pivotal Praying When You Want to Make a Difference

(John Hull)

Bob Hunter has been praying for Africa, especially Uganda, for over twenty-five years. During the 1970s, Uganda was known for its infamous and tyrannical dictator, Idi Amin. Amin made headlines around the world for his arrogant pomposity toward the developing world and his ruthless brutality toward his political enemies.

Bob and a few other fellow Christians began to pray specifically for Uganda, pleading with God to raise up at least one Christian leader in the nation's capital of Kampala. At a prayer retreat, Bob met a missionary nurse who just happened to work in a hospital in Kampala. Excitedly, Bob introduced the nurse to the leadership of his local church. That introduction sparked a relationship through which the church "adopted" the hospital as one of their major overseas mission projects. Bob's church alone has sent about three million dollars' worth of financial support, medical supplies, and other resources, while praying all the while for the nation's spiritual condition.

Bob first visited Uganda near the end of Amin's chaotic dictatorship. While there, Bob was able to build relationships with several rising government reformers. Over time, those strategic relationships, with leaders who would shape the future of Uganda, grew in mutual respect and trust. Suddenly Bob, just one "regular guy" in the United States who had simply prayed for a nation a few years earlier, was being invited by that nation to organize conferences in their country, focusing on themes of reconciliation between warring parties within the nation.

Over time, God opened doors for Bob to gain the attention of leaders in the United States Senate, the German Bundestag, and even former United Nations Ambassador Andrew Young. He became part of a process in Uganda that would heal past wounds and build a bridge of hope for the future.

Believing that his greatest ambassador was Jesus Christ, Bob shared the gospel with Uganda's leaders. And he continued to intercede for the nation, that it would encounter the positive realities of a relationship with the living God.

Bob struck up a friendship with an aide to Yoweri Museveni, who would eventually become Uganda's president. The aide was a follower of Jesus. Through his and Bob's relationship with Museveni, Museveni, too, became a Christian.

Remember Bob's and his friend's prayers years earlier? They had asked God to raise up at least one Christian leader in Uganda's capital city! God answered this prayer. President Museveni would later move his audience of listeners to tears at Washington's National Prayer Breakfast as he shared his love for Jesus Christ.

When South Africa released Nelson Mandela from prison in the early 1990s, President Museveni, who had just been appointed the chairman of the Organization of African Unity, called Bob to his office and proposed that Bob go to South Africa and tell the leaders there that the answer to their nation's woes was forgiveness and reconciliation. So, at the request of Uganda's president, Bob made his way to South Africa and met with Nelson Mandela, F. W. de Klerk, and other high-profile leaders. Later in that decade, as Mandela was elected president and South Africa began to reshape itself, the world press reported with great interest the country's efforts to work through their painful past through the government-appointed Commission on Truth and Reconciliation.

On New Year's Eve, 1999, President Museveni read a statement declaring Uganda as a nation embracing the lordship of Jesus Christ. In a formal covenant, the nation renounced its occult practices of the past and asked God to forgive Uganda for their sins against Him.

Years earlier Bob Hunter had prayed that a Christian leader would rise up in the capital city of Uganda. Today, five dozen government officials gather to pray every morning, five days a week, asking God to bless and guide their nation.

Bob Hunter's pivotal prayer to make a difference in Uganda has done just that.[1]

UNSELFISH PRAYING

Praying to make a difference is unselfish praying. In all likelihood, praying to make a difference is going to cost us something. It's probably going to make us uncomfortable and take us to places— spiritually and geographically—where we wouldn't dare go unless God had birthed it in our hearts.

Whether it's a relationship, a particular circumstance, or a cultural issue pressing for societal change, praying to make a difference in the lives of others is a refreshing engagement of God when compared to myopic mantras like "God bless me and mine," so often heard these days. The American Christian culture, nowadays so hypnotized by consumerism and self-interest, is plagued with egocentric prayer. We might as well say, "God, it's all about me!" because that's where we spend a lot of our prayer time.

But imagine for a moment the potency of pivotally interceding for others. To get beyond ourselves, our ailments, our discomforts, our problems, and to focus on those whose lives are far more desperate. It's not as if God doesn't care about our problems—of course He does. However, praying to make a difference in a nation and a world where so much difference is needed means connecting with God on behalf of others, even when our personal world is looking dim.

Jesus, with all the pressures of public ministry upon Him, facing growing opposition, knowing His destiny—the horror of His death and all the accompanying injustice—still pivotally prayed for others on a regular basis. The picture couldn't be clearer: Praying to make a difference in this world means we learn to get past ourselves and our problems and pursue a greater purpose. It's not that God doesn't want us to come to Him with our needs. He just doesn't want us to *stop* there. And let's be honest: We often do.

REJECTING THE STATUS QUO OF INJUSTICE

Britain's William Wilberforce, at the end of the eighteenth and the beginning of the nineteenth centuries, prayed pivotally to make a difference in the lives of slaves and slave owners. "May God enable me to have a single eye and simple heart, desiring to please God and to do good to my fellow creatures," he prayed. But outlawing slavery within Britain's Parliament and among England's financial power brokers would carry with it great sacrifice and personal discomfort.

Nevertheless, for twenty long years Wilberforce pivotally prayed and tenaciously worked with the nation's leaders to end what he called "a course of wickedness and cruelty as never before disgraced a Christian country."[2]

Wilberforce prayed and made a difference. His courage and Parliament's eventual vote to abolish slavery served as models for the growing abolitionist movement in the United States in the nineteenth century. It took an American civil war, but eventually slavery in America was also abolished.

When we pray to make a difference in the world, we are recognizing that something is already wrong. Somewhere there's injustice. Somewhere there's a person who needs help with an addiction or an abusive relationship. Somewhere there's oppression, a wrong that has to be made right.

Praying to make a difference also recognizes that change does not come easily. We can expect opposition, be it institutional or personal. Where there is wrong, there is usually some kind of power base—powered by either ignorance or self–interest—that will not go down easily.

Explorer/missionary David Livingstone met with tremendous criticism when he attempted prayerfully to reach inland Africa with the gospel. Some Christians thought him too secular (he wasn't exclusively a preacher and evangelist), and some humanitarians thought him too religious. But Livingstone made a difference and eventually became a catalyst in Zambia's aspirations to embrace Christ and eventually declare itself a Christian nation.[3]

Nehemiah's Prayer to Make a Difference

Imagine running into an old childhood friend at a local establishment. After the warm embrace, you ask how things are going in the town where you both grew up. Suddenly your friend's smile turns into a frown. She sadly reports that the town's water supply has been contaminated. Several of the townspeople are gravely ill. There's growing concern that many more will become sick. The town, she says, is defenseless, demoralized, and hopeless. Your friend asks you to pray. You leave feeling burdened and perplexed.

This is the kind of grave news Nehemiah received when he ran into some of his friends from his hometown, Jerusalem. Nehemiah had been a captive in Babylon for many years. However, he had managed to obtain a steady job serving as the king's cupbearer, or food taster. This was a position in which the king had to have great confidence. It was in some ways like being one of the king's security force.

Nehemiah's friends told him that Jerusalem was in ruins. The stone walls that had protected the city for generations were broken down, and the gates of the city were charred embers. The citizens were in trouble and were feeling greatly disgraced.

Nehemiah's heart broken, he immediately sat down and wept and prayed. He asked God to enable him to go back to Jerusalem and help his people. He wanted to make a difference. But he knew that the task was too large to do it by himself. He was going to need the king's support. So he asked the Lord for help: "O Lord, let your ear be attentive to the prayer of this your servant and to the prayer of your servants who delight in revering your name. Give your servant success today by granting him favor in the presence of this man [the king]" (Neh. 1:11). This was the first of Nehemiah's many prayers as he sought to make a difference in Jerusalem.

In the days that followed, Nehemiah and the king had a conversation. The king asked him why he looked so sad. He responded that his hometown of Jerusalem was in great peril. Then the king did a remarkable thing. He asked, "What do you want?" Nehemiah prayed again, then he answered, "If it pleases the king and if your servant has found favor in his sight, let him send me to the city in Judah where my fathers are buried so that I can rebuild it" (Neh. 2:5).

The king granted Nehemiah's request. Now Nehemiah was on his way to making a difference. Not too long after, he left for Jerusalem with the resources and support of the king. Once he arrived, it took less than two months to reconstruct the city walls.

Nehemiah's prayer was focused on something bigger than himself. Alone, he didn't have the resources or the influence to accomplish his goal. But he knew that the burden to rebuild Jerusalem was from God and that God would provide. His prayers expressed remarkably strong faith. In chapter 2, verse 20, he proclaims, "The God of heaven will give us success." Nehemiah's faith was so great that he believed God could touch the heart of an unbelieving king. His faith was so strong during the construction project that he believed the job could be completed.

Nehemiah also recognized that when someone prays to make a difference, that person may have to get off his knees and build relationships with others whom God can use to become agents of change for His glory. That's the king's role in this story. Nehemiah had a burden from God. He prayed that God would touch an agent for change—the king in this case—and suddenly all kinds of catalytic reactions began to take place.

PRAYER AND CATALYTIC RELATIONSHIPS

God uses prayer to make a difference. And God uses relationships to make a difference.

One Saturday night last fall, our son Andy had a friend sleep over at our house. After church the following morning, his mother came to pick him up. She goes to a different church than we do, so I asked, "How was the service this morning?"

She said, "It was great. But our pastor, Johnny Crist, is burdened. We desperately need to relocate due to growth, and we've found a great building that fits our needs. But our pastor has asked us to pray because we're having a difficult time finding a bank that will provide us financing at a reasonable interest rate, and this building we want is not going to be available too much longer." I told her that I just happened to be having lunch with her pastor in a few days and that I would talk to him about it. I wondered if God was up to something.

Immediately I thought of my friends at Peachtree Bank. That's where EQUIP banks. In fact, it's where I bank. The president, Monty Watson, is a wonderful believer, as are many of the board members. I remembered Monty telling me once that Peachtree Bank wanted to serve the nonprofit-ministry community, especially local churches in the Atlanta area.

When I met with Johnny later that week at a Mexican restaurant, he confirmed their need for financing. "Our people are really praying about this thing. This move is pivotal to the future of our church," he said. I told him about Monty Watson and Peachtree Bank, and he took down the information. On my way back to my office, I called Monty and left word that Johnny would be calling and what it was about. Johnny and Monty got together within days. Soon after, Peachtree Bank approved the loan. Johnny tells me that the dedication service in the new facility has been scheduled and the church is sky-high with anticipation.

Nehemiah prayed about making a difference and God opened doors by providing catalytic relationships. If you want to make a difference, be prepared for God to provide all kinds of catalytic relationships to accomplish His purposes. It may surprise you whom God will lead to join your team!

IS CHANGE NEEDED WHERE YOU LIVE?

Are there any changes that need to be made where you live? Are there wrongs that need to be made right? Praying pivotally can make a difference.

Is your local government making decisions that break God's heart and laws? Pray!

I read recently of a group of intercessors who began to go to city-council meetings, sit in the back of the room, listen carefully, and then silently intercede for the council members to make decisions that would be pleasing to God. They reported that the meetings took on a better atmosphere, members treated each other with greater respect, and the council's actions changed for the better.

Is your school in need of change? Pray! A Virginia pastor shared that a group of Christian mothers met to pray for their local high school—in a parked van near the high school. Right on the property, they stood in prayer against evil activity in the school, invoking God's grace, peace, and protection upon the students and the administration. As it became known that these moms were praying nearby, urgent prayer requests would be sent out to the van by students and teachers alike!

Does your church need a fresh touch from God? Has it lost sensitivity for the unchurched? In a San Diego neighborhood known for crime and upheaval, a local church was in steep decline. The church's leadership considered relocation. Instead they began to organize prayer teams to intercede for their neighbors. They started to cruise the neighborhood in their cars and ask God to bless the people who lived in the surrounding houses and apartments. The attitude of the church began to change. Instead of operating out of fear and isolation, they began to engage their surrounding neighbors with the love of Christ. Reports of crime decreased and church attendance increased!

Praying to make a difference in our community, nation, or world isn't an overnight experience. It wasn't for Bob Hunter and it won't be for us. In fact, praying to make a difference will require several things:

TIME

Any meaningful intercession takes time, especially intercession where revolutionary change is needed. William Wilberforce realized his antislavery sentiments were wildly opposed by the most prominent of British citizens. It took years to get his legislation before parliament, and another twenty years for it to become law.

In this day of microwave ovens and high-speed modems, we sometimes forget that things often take time in the spiritual realm of prayer. Praying to make a difference requires patience.

EFFORT

I have never met a person who has made a difference, regardless of his or her agenda, without putting forth a lot of effort. Politicians who want to make a difference work hard to get elected. Entrepreneurs like Bill Gates and Michael Dell work hard to show us that using computers can improve our lives. Entertainers work hard to move us emotionally.

If we are going to make a difference, our prayers must go hand in hand with effort. Prayer doesn't reduce our work. Prayer can make our work less stressful, more manageable, and more meaningful. And the hard effort accompanied by prayer makes the effort more expeditious and exciting.

EXPECTATION

Let's call this "faith expectation." When you pray for change that will bring God glory, expect Him to do something—and don't be surprised when He does. Humbled? Yes! Surprised? No.

A tale is told about a small town that had historically been "dry" until a local businessman decided to build a tavern. A group of Christians from a local church were concerned and planned an all-night prayer meeting to ask God to intervene. It just so happened that shortly thereafter lightning struck the bar and it burned to the ground. The owner of the bar sued the church, claiming that the prayers of the congregation were responsible, but the church hired a lawyer to argue in court that they were not responsible. The presiding judge, after his initial review of the case, stated that "no matter how this comes out, one thing is clear: The tavern owner believes in prayer and the Christians do not."

Henri Nouwen observed, "The paradox of prayer is that it asks for a serious effort while it can only be received as a gift. We cannot plan, organize or manipulate God; but without a careful discipline, we cannot receive Him either."[4] If we are going to make a difference, the disciplines of time, effort, and expectation will have to be continually cultivated. However, when they are working together it makes the journey through those pivotal moments much more exciting.

Where is God calling you right now? Is He leading you to make a difference? The vision God has given you may seem overwhelming, but remember Bob Hunter. This man, who now influences some of Africa's most important political leaders, just a few years ago prayed a simple but pivotal prayer: "Lord, raise up just one Christian leader in Uganda." And what a difference God has made!

CLOSING PRAYER

A Pivotal Prayer to Make a Difference

Lord, You have laid this concern on my heart.
It's very clear that what's going on is so contrary
to what Your Word teaches.
Would You help me to make a difference?
I really believe that's what You want me to do.
So I pray for wisdom to know how to begin,
the energy to do the job,
and the faith to believe that it will be done.
Help me to keep my eyes on what You've called me to
do, and help me to always remember that this
is all about making a difference so that
You might receive greater glory in the lives
of the people You touch.
Amen.

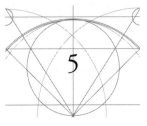

PIVOTAL PRAYING WHEN YOU HAVE FAILED

(TIM ELMORE)

Charles B. Darrow set a goal while still in his twenties. He determined he was going to become a millionaire. This isn't too unusual today, but Charles lived during the Roaring Twenties, a time when a million dollars was an enormous sum. He even married his wife, Esther, promising that they would be millionaires one day.

Then tragedy struck, 1929 rolled around: and the Great Depression began. Both Charles and Esther lost their jobs. In fact, they mortgaged their home, lost their car, and used up most of their life savings. Charles was crushed. He sat around the house depressed, until one day he told his wife she could leave him if she wanted to. After all, it was clear they were never going to reach their goal.

Esther wasn't about to leave. She told Charles they were still going to reach their goal, but that they would need to do something every day to keep the dream alive. "Keep it alive?" Charles responded. "It's dead! We've failed."

But Esther didn't believe this. Instead, she suggested that every night they take some time to discuss what they would do when they reached their goal. They began doing this each night after dinner. Soon Charles came up with the idea of creating play money—something quite appealing, since money was so scarce in those days. He would sit around with lots of time, and now lots of "easy money" to play with, as he and his wife pretended to buy things like houses, property, and other buildings.

Soon they turned it into a full-fledged game, with a board, dice, cards, little houses and hotels . . . and you guessed it: That was the beginning of a game you probably have in your closet right now. This is how the game Monopoly was born.

Charles's family and friends so enjoyed the game that in 1934 they persuaded him to approach the Massachusetts game firm, Parker Brothers. Executives there played the game and rejected it. They found it dull, the action slow, and the rules hopelessly complex. Charles persevered, however, again at his wife's encouragement. He approached Wanamaker's Toy Store and told an executive that if they'd stock the game, he'd take out a loan and create five thousand of them. The game took off, and suddenly Parker Brothers was interested. They replayed the game, and this time found it imaginative, fast paced, and surprisingly easy to master. The game was copyrighted in 1935, and Parker Brothers bought it from Charles Darrow. And do you know how much money they gave him for it? That's right. One million dollars.[2]

Most of us love stories like that. Rags to riches. Failure to fortune. It's something we all want to experience. The lesson of the story isn't new. Failure and tragedy are often doorways into marvelous breakthroughs. Charles Kettering broke his arm in a failed attempt to crank start his old jalopy. This failure led to his invention of the ignition system now used in automobiles. Jacob Schick grew angry when he cut himself shaving each morning. This fueled his invention of the electric razor.

Failure can be an insightful teacher. It can teach us how to prosper in adversity and make us resilient when we encounter defeat and trials. It can develop emotional muscles that would never grow if we only succeeded. It teaches lessons we'd never learn if we always had it easy. These are lessons we all should learn, as certainly every one of us has failed and will fail again.

I once heard of a college in the Midwest that offers a course entitled Failure 101. It's a business course that exposes students to the idea that failure is natural and that the sooner they learn to survive it—and even expect it—the better off they'll be. But I want to go deeper in this chapter. I want to wrestle with how we pray amid the worst kind of failure.

THE DEAL IS OFF

In this chapter, I want to talk about spiritual failure. What do you do when you fail God? What do you do when you crumble spiritually, and you don't even want to pray? How do you pray in such seasons?

I remember my first big failure spiritually. My family had moved to Southern California and I had just received Christ. I was almost seventeen. Within a few months I got the chance to visit my old friends back in Cincinnati, Ohio. This would be a chance to share my newfound faith with them. I was so excited, I packed shirts that had two pockets: one for my little New Testament and one for tracts. I was ready.

I called Rusty as soon as I arrived. When I told him I wanted to get together, he invited me to a party where many of my old friends would be hanging out. Hmmm. I wanted to build a bridge, not a wall in those relationships—so I accepted his invitation. I felt this would be a great chance to talk to a whole bunch of people at one time.

It was. I saw all of my buddies and got caught up on their lives. As we conversed, one of them offered me a beer. Hmmm. I didn't want to drink, but I wanted to build a bridge, not a wall with these guys, so I took one. And then another, and another. Within an hour, I was in no shape to share the gospel with anyone.

The next morning I woke up feeling awful. Most of my misery was spiritual. How could I have done this? I had intended to share my faith with these guys and failed miserably. I actually did the opposite of what I'd planned to do. Not only did I fail to be a good example— I was a *bad* example. I remember thinking, *God, is the deal off?*

I have friends who live on the East Coast. Bryan and Connie had been married for several years when she got cancer. She battled for a year through chemotherapy and radiation treatments. Bryan was a prince, fulfilling the role of both husband and father to their son and two daughters. After more than twelve months of struggle, Connie died. In the aftermath, Bryan changed. I'm not sure if it was his disappointment with God, or just that he was tired of fighting—but he walked away from God and the lifestyle he'd embraced as a Christian. He began to drink heavily and started dating a woman. Soon she was spending the night at their house. He started using language he'd never used as a dad and disciple of Jesus. It was as though Bryan was saying to God, "At least for now—the deal is off."

My wife and I have become acquainted with a married couple here in Atlanta. They have served in ministry for almost twenty years. Both of them are gifted—he in music and media, she in training and administration. God has used them greatly. One evening, however, he came home with an announcement. He told his wife he didn't love her anymore, and he walked out. It was over. She was stunned. There was no clear warning. Things had seemed fine and God had been moving in their lives. But something had happened that he couldn't live with anymore. Unfortunately for him, the deal was now off.

I met an atheist on an airplane just a few months ago. I like talking with atheists, so we struck up a conversation. As he shared his story, I soon discovered that he had not become an atheist through any extensive, objective research on theology. He had grown up in the church. He'd been involved in a faithful lifestyle. But somewhere along the way something happened and he became bitter and resentful. I don't know if he had failed God, if someone had failed him, or if he felt that God had failed—but I became sure of one thing during our conversation. As far as he was concerned, the deal was off.

I imagine you know people like this too. People who are casualties on the roadsides of their spiritual journey. They are bitter, apathetic, rebellious, depressed, arrogant, independent, or sometimes even suicidal. If they are honest, all of them can point back to an experience—I'm guessing a failure—and now "the deal is off."

FAILING GOD

This "I quit" mentality happens to all of us at some point in our lives. None of us enjoys the experience of failing at something. In fact, some of us hate it so badly we'll walk away from something we cherish if it represents ongoing failure to us. It is especially devastating when this involves failing God. Some people can never forgive themselves.

Failure doesn't have to ruin us. The "I failed" situation and the "I quit" mentality are two completely different things. I believe the "I quit" mentality stems from a wrong attitude toward both failure and God:

1. **I failed and that's final. The deal is off.**
   We cannot seem to let go of an experience and now it defines us. We walk away in an attempt to capture a new identity. Unfortunately, you can't face failure if you're walking in the other direction.

2. **God failed and that's fatal. The deal is off.**
   We somehow feel God has let us down. He failed to meet an expectation, and we feel deep disappointment, as though we can never trust Him again. We lump Him with all the other authorities who've failed us. We forget that He's all-wise and has an angle on what happened that we'll never

see if we walk away. We become lost in our narrow, short-sighted perspective.

There is a third category that many of us fit in. We have failed and we cannot let it go, but we've stayed in the church—lacking passion, wounded, walking with a limp ever since that experience. But no one knows why.

I believe the pivotal prayer when we've failed involves two steps: surrender and service. When we have failed God, two of the finest requests we can pray are "Lord, what would you have me surrender?" and "Lord, where would you have me serve?"

In the next section we will examine two disciples of Jesus, both of whom failed Him. You've heard of them both. One is Simon Peter. The other is Judas Iscariot. One failed Jesus accidentally. The other failed Jesus deliberately. Peter failed God out of weakness. Judas failed Jesus out of will. Believing that God had let him down, he turned against God and never returned.

As we study these two men, you will see why the issues of surrender and service are so crucial in the face of failure. As theologian Donald Bloesch puts it, "There is a time to argue and complain to God, and there is also a time to submit."[3]

I believe failure is a clear signal for surrender. In fact, surrender may be the one act that saves us. God asks us to take the first step of a lifetime in prayer, giving control of our lives to Him.

Mark Galli writes,

> For me, it's like going on a roller coaster. Whenever I sit in one, I realize I'm putting my life in the hands of a lot of other people: the designer of the roller coaster, the maintenance crew, the operators. For me, it's a pretty scary proposition.
>
> But it's also a heck of a lot of fun, with a number of jerks and drops along the way. Prayer is not much different a lot of the time.

It doesn't require a huge amount of humility to begin—just enough to buy a ticket and stand in line at first. But that's enough to get you started on this adventure.[4]

Then you simply continue submitting with each turn. Face it: You are not in control when you are on a roller coaster!

In his classic book, *Prayer,* Ole Hallesby sums it up this way, "Prayer and helplessness are inseparable. Only he who is helpless can truly pray. Your helplessness is your best prayer."[5]

WHAT WE LEARN FROM PETER AND JUDAS

The movie *Hoosiers* tells the Cinderella story of a small-town Indiana high school basketball team that won the state championship. One important character, an alcoholic named Shooter, played by Dennis Hopper, had failed at most things in life—but has a passion for the game of basketball.

The coach, played by Gene Hackman, works with Shooter to give him a second chance in life. He asks Shooter to be his assistant coach, and eventually Shooter agrees. The little-known Hickory High School team begins to win, and during a pivotal game the coach decides to get himself thrown out. He pulls the referee aside and says, "Take me out of the game." The ref doesn't know what the coach is up to, but he tosses him out.

Shooter is terrified. Now he is in charge. A few scenes earlier, after another drinking binge, Shooter had promised the coach he'd stay sober and remain the assistant coach on one condition: "Promise me you won't get kicked out of no games!"

The end of the game is near, and the score is tied. The Hickory players call a time-out. In the team huddle all eyes are on Shooter, including his son's, who never thought his dad should be in this situation in the first place. Shooter is paralyzed with fear. He can't speak.

Finally, his son says, "You reckon Number Four will put up the last shot, Dad?" That seems to jump-start Shooter, and he haltingly calls a play. The team goes back out on the floor and begins to execute it when Shooter calls time out.

Now he is completely engaged in the game, and his knowledge and passion for the game have overtaken his fear. He lays out a strategy: "All right, now listen to me. This is the last shot we got. All right? We're gonna run the picket fence at 'em. Merle, you're the swingman. Jimmy, you go solo right. All right, Merle should be open swinging around the end of that fence. Now boys, don't get caught watchin' that paint dry!"

The players are with him. They walk out onto the floor, run the play to perfection and sink the winning basket. Shooter and the players are deliriously happy. Amid the celebration, Shooter's son looks into his father's eyes and says, "You did real good, Pop. You did real good."

In this story, a weak, shame-filled alcoholic "did real good," because a coach decided it was worth it to take a risk on him. In many ways, that's exactly what Jesus did as he chose his twelve disciples, more than nineteen hundred years ago. It's what He continues to do today, with us. Like a gutsy, optimistic coach, He walks into our lives, despite what we've done—and wants to partner with us. He knows our failures better than we do. And yet, He still wants to give us an assignment.

A TALE OF TWO MEN

Two of Jesus' disciples deserve our attention as we consider pivotal praying when we've failed. On a single night, at the end of Jesus' earthly ministry, Simon Peter and Judas Iscariot both failed miserably. You might say, in the hour of Jesus' greatest need (humanly speaking), these guys not only failed to tarry with Him in prayer, but they outright turned on Him. On this night, they were utter failures.

It may surprise you to find that there are many similarities between Peter and Judas. In our Sunday school lessons, Peter is often the hero, and Judas is always the villain. However, both were very much like you and me in their humanity:

1. *Both were ambitious and influential.* Judas was a patriot from a wealthy background. He understood money as well as politics. He was selected to be the treasurer for the disciples and was put in charge of a large sum of money. The treasury must have been substantial, because Scripture says he used to steal from it, believing no one would notice. Judas was a man of zeal who had set tangible goals for his future. He was the only disciple not from Galilee—meaning he might have been the only "white collar" man on Jesus' team. He had a good circle of influence.

Peter was also an ambitious and influential man. His sphere of influence would have been more with fellow fishermen and blue-collar laborers. He was a fishing leader, the other disciples followed naturally. This is significant, in case we're tempted to naively assume that failure is just for the weak. Both Peter and Judas were going somewhere.

2. *Both chose to follow Jesus as disciples.* There was a moment when each of these men, individually, made a commitment to follow Christ. Even Judas. We can second-guess his motives, but I believe in the beginning he was devoted to this young rabbi, hoping to support his campaign and monarchy.

Peter also experienced a moment, like you and me, when he declared he belonged to Jesus and would follow Him wherever He led. Matthew 10 and Luke 5 record the selection and decision of each of these two men to follow the Master.

3. *Both questioned Jesus' leadership along the way.* Another interesting similarity between Judas and Peter is their flair for second-guessing

the Lord. For Judas it came the night Jesus allowed Mary to pour an alabaster vase of perfume on his feet (John 12). He began to grumble to the other disciples that the perfume could have been sold and the money given to the poor.

The minute we isolate Judas on this miscue, we must remember Peter did the same thing. One day, Jesus began to predict His death—and Peter scolded Him. Think about it for a moment. Both of these men questioned God—just like you and me do today.

4. Both failed Jesus and turned from their commitment to follow Him. You probably remember the Last Supper, when Jesus predicted Judas' betrayal:

Now when evening had come, He was reclining at the table with the twelve disciples. And as they were eating, He said, "Truly I say to you that one of you will betray Me." And being deeply grieved, they each one began to say to Him, "Surely not I, Lord?" . . . And Judas, who was betraying Him, answered and said, "Surely it is not I, Rabbi?" Jesus said to him, "You have said it yourself" (Matt. 26:20-22, 25).

Peter's failure looked slightly different but was just as real. Later we read:

Jesus said to them, "You will all fall away from Me this night, for it is written 'I will strike down the shepherd and the sheep will be scattered.'

But after I've been raised, I will go before you to Galilee." But Peter answered and said to Him, "Even though all may fall away because of you, I will never fall away." Jesus said to him, "Truly I say to you that this very night before the rooster crows, you shall deny me three times."

Peter said to him, "Even if I have to die with you, I will not deny you."

All the disciples said the same thing too (Matt. 26:31-35).

You might conclude that Judas' failure was a result of his hypocrisy, and Peter's was a result of his pride. There is little doubt that both stumbled over the way Jesus' ministry on earth was ending up. It just didn't meet their expectations.

5. Both experienced deep grief from their falling away. Finally, each of these men hurt deeply after his failure. The story of Peter's failure ends in Matthew 26:75. After cursing and swearing he never knew Jesus, the rooster crows. When he heard it, he went out and wept bitterly.

When Judas realized what he had done, he made his way back to the religious leaders confessing he'd betrayed an innocent man. They couldn't have cared less. To appease his guilt, he threw the money he had made onto the floor and left to commit suicide (Matt. 27:3-5). The evening ended in painful grief for both of these weak men.

SO, WHAT'S THE DIFFERENCE?

Here's the million-dollar question: What's the difference between these two men? Peter actually drew closer to the Lord after his dismal failure; Judas took a rope and hung himself. A huge difference. And I believe it all lies in two insights. First, they were different in how they approached failure. Second, they were different in how they approached the Lord, Himself. Let's take a look.

THEY WENT TO DIFFERENT SOURCES IN RESPONSE TO THEIR FAILURE

Consider this big difference. Three days after that fateful night, Jesus rose from the dead and called to the disciples who were out in a fishing boat. When Peter recognized the Lord, he couldn't wait to row back to the shore. He threw on his coat and jumped into the water. Once he reached the Lord, he embraced Him. On that shore, these two men reconciled the failure and their relationship. Wow. Instead of running *from* God in his failure, he ran *to* God. Obviously, the failure wasn't final. His relationship with Jesus was bigger than his failure.

Judas, however, never recovered. He never stuck around long enough to run to the Lord. Desiring to feel better, he returned the money to the chief priests. We never see him even pray about it. When the priests refuse to absolve his guilt, suicide seemed to be his only option. Why? I believe it's because Peter was a man content to live *under control;* Judas was a man who demanded to be *in control.* There is a world of difference. Peter could recover from his many mistakes because he lived under God's control. He wasn't in charge. Judas never relinquished control of his life. When we try to control people, our failures will always damage us. Too much of our identity will be wrapped up in them.

THEY APPROACHED JESUS DIFFERENTLY

This is the most crucial truth to grasp. These two men saw Jesus in fundamentally different ways. Peter was the first disciple to call Jesus, *Lord.* In Matthew 16:15-16, Jesus asked His men who they thought He was. Peter jumped in, declaring His Lordship. But that wasn't the moment he'd made that decision. When they first met, in Luke 5:1-11, Jesus told Peter to cast his fishing net out into the deep for a catch. Peter's response was: "Lord, we fished hard all night and caught nothing . . . " In other words, "Jesus, you are a carpenter, right? I am a professional fisherman. I know where they bite, I know when they bite . . . and they're not biting!" Jesus' instruction didn't make sense to Peter. However, the next phrase is key to his approach to Jesus: "Nevertheless, at your word, I will let down the net."

This phrase tips us off that Peter, from the very beginning, esteemed Jesus as Master of every issue. He's Lord. Even on subjects

Peter considered to be his strengths, he still considered Jesus as the final authority. His Lordship was established early on.

Judas, on the other hand, approached Jesus differently. Have you read his interactions with Jesus throughout the Gospels? Judas never once called Jesus, *Lord*. Even at the Last Supper, when each disciple said, "Surely not I, Lord?", Judas said, "Surely not I, Rabbi?" Later, when he betrayed Him in the garden, he kissed Jesus, and said, "Hail, Rabbi." Judas only went so far as to relate to Jesus as Rabbi. It means "good teacher." It's a term of respect. There's nothing wrong with it. However, there's a world of difference between "Lord" and "Rabbi." You don't surrender to a good teacher.

When Judas failed his world collapsed, because he was the center of it. Judas was lord of his own life—which means he would rise and fall with his own abilities. Unfortunately, when you live this way, failure can be devastating. While Peter felt horrible about his shortcomings, his world didn't collapse, because Jesus was still in control and at the center. Peter could run to Him and resolve things. Judas refused to surrender and stayed at the center and in control.

HOW ABOUT YOU?

I believe there are many of us today who follow Jesus in the same way. We like His principles. We want to raise our kids knowing the Bible. We truly believe He's a good teacher. But we never really settle the surrender issue. We want control. And it all comes out when we experience a major failure. Our world is rocked. Our prayers seem to do little good.

How can we tell if we've not approached Him as *Lord*? It's subtle, yet real. We say things like: "I've accepted Christ . . . I hope He can help me with my business." Or, "I'm trusting God will bless my life." Or, "You never know when you're going to need Him." These phrases are not evil, but they indicate *we* are still at the center of our spiritual journey. He is helping *us*. He is a "spare tire"—not a "steering wheel."

I have a friend who attended an annual church business meeting one Sunday night. During the meeting, the congregation began to argue over some insignificant issue, like the color of the carpet in the restrooms or the wallpaper in the Sunday school office. A division emerged among the people. Eventually, one lady stood and said, "I just wonder which side Jesus would be on!"

At that point, an elderly gentleman stood and spoke for the first time. He simply said: "Jesus didn't come to take sides. He came to take over."

This is the only hope we have of overcoming spiritual failure. We must stop trying to be "in control." Control is a myth anyway. No human being is in control. We must also recognize our lives cannot center around ourselves.

IT'S ABOUT SOMETHING FAR BIGGER

I enjoy college football. I also enjoy the great lessons that come from that world. Decades ago, Roy Reigels played in a game and received the unfortunate nickname: Roy "Wrong Way" Reigels. He got the name because just before half time the ball was fumbled, and Roy recovered it, hoping to score a touchdown. He got bumped and twisted in the process, however, and when he broke free—he began galloping the wrong direction, toward the other team's end zone!

It was exhilarating, because he could hear the hometown fans yelling, "Go, go!" Obviously, they were not yelling "Go, go!" they were yelling, "No, no!" Finally, Roy was tackled by his own teammate just before he would have scored for the opposition. When he looked up, he realized what he'd done. He was humiliated.

At half time, Roy slowly walked into the locker room, his head down. He didn't even want to look at anybody. His head coach gave a clear pep talk on what the team needed to do differently in the second half, making no reference to Roy's blunder. Then, he closed by saying: "I want the same team to start the second half, that started the first half." Everyone ran out onto the field, except for Roy. He remained on the bench in the locker room, dejected and embarrassed. The coach asked if he'd heard what he just said. Roy said he did, but told him he just couldn't go out there again after that failure.

At that point, the coach responded to Roy in a very insightful manner. He looked him in the eye and said, "Roy, this game isn't about you. It's about something far bigger. Now, get out there and play. I need you in there."

The coach said later that Roy played the best second half he'd ever seen anyone play. He was transformed.

And we can be, too. If you've failed God, I believe His word to you is simply this: "This is not about you. It's about something far bigger. Get in there and play. I need you."

But remember, He calls the shots.

CLOSING PRAYER

Dear Lord,
I want to begin with a confession.
I have failed. But I recognize that failure is an event,
not a person. I am not a failure.
I come to You in my humanity and surrender to Your
Lordship. I confess that life is not about me,
but You and Your kingdom.
Help me to see this failure through Your eyes
and not to fear new challenges in the future.
In Jesus' name,
Amen.

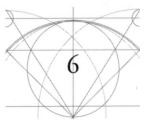

6

PIVOTAL PRAYING WHEN YOU NEED DIRECTION

(JOHN HULL)

Several years ago I heard this story shared in a sermon. Lloyd Olgilvie, chaplain of the United States Senate, was hiking through the deep woods of northern Ontario. As the sun was setting, Olgilvie, who had been exploring these woods for most of the day, realized that he was lost. Growing concerned as the minutes passed, he tried to make his way back to some kind of civilization. After a while he came upon what looked like an overgrown path. Thinking this might be the way, he followed it for several minutes. Then in the distance he saw an old, worn-out sign. On it was an arrow and these faded words: "This is the only way out!" Olgilvie took the sign's advice and soon found the main road.

If only life's decisions were that easy! If someone would just give us a sign and point in a direction, any direction, how good it would be. But life's woods and weeds aren't always as kind to us as they were to Lloyd Olgilvie. Sometimes it's very difficult to know what to do and what choices to make—especially when the sun is setting on a situation in our lives.

Many in our society spend a lot of time and resources just trying to get some direction about where to go and what to do in life.

Millions turn to their daily newspapers—not for sports scores or the status of the stock market, but for their horoscopes. Others turn to fortune-telling or magic. Still others dial up psychic hot lines! All of these fragile options—simply to get some kind of glimpse into the future.

The very first national "television preacher" in America was Bishop Fulton Sheen. The bishop was heard weekly, coast to coast, on the old Mutual Television Broadcasting network. Over time he became a sought-after speaker, especially among business and civic leaders.

Contemporary legend has it that Bishop Sheen was scheduled to speak in a city where he had never traveled before. Leaving the hotel and walking to his speaking engagement, he got distracted, a bit turned around, and then found himself completely lost. Seeing some boys playing on the sidewalk, he asked them how to get to his destination. The boys immediately knew where he was supposed to go and gave him directions. One of them said, "You just go down this street for two blocks, take a left, go down one more block, take a right, and the place is just across the street." The bishop thanked the boys and turned to walk away.

As he was leaving, one of the boys said, "What are you going to do there?"

The bishop said "I'm going to give a speech."

The boy said, "What are you going to speak about?"

The bishop said, "I'm going to tell people how to go to heaven. Would you like to come with me?"

The boy said, "No thanks. You don't even know how to get to City Hall!"

Sometimes we can't get our directions straight even to life's most obvious destinations. "Should I get married? And if I should, whom should I marry?" Or "What should I do with my life?" Or "Should I take that job and relocate to another city?" Or "Should I buy a car or lease it? And if I buy a car, should it be a new car or a used car?" On and on we go in life. Decisions and choices. Choices and decisions. We make thousands of them every day. Clearly, we are a people in great need of direction. Maybe we need a sign. Maybe we need someone to tell us what to do and where we should go.

And then there's prayer.

PURSUING GOD'S DIRECTION

Ministers are constantly asked by their parishioners, "Pastor, how can I know God's will for my life?" And ministers are constantly asking, "Lord, what is Your will for this church?" The search for God's direction in our lives never ends. The good news is that the resource of prayer is unending too.

A United Methodist pastor was starting a new project outside of Kansas City. The night before the new church was launched, he gathered together a small group of believers who would form the core families of the church. Here's what he prayed: "Lord, this church belongs to You. It's not ours. Our desire is to do what You want us to do and to be who You want us to be. You know the people You long to reach through this church. We place ourselves in Your hands and we long to be used by You."[1]

This is a good example of a pivotal prayer for direction. This simple prayer contains an intentional yieldedness: "Our desire is to do what You want us to do and to be who You want us to be." You can't go wrong praying this way. Such prayer acknowledges God's sovereign lordship in our lives. It expresses a heart that seeks to bring glory to God: "We place ourselves in Your hands and we long to be used by You." Think about it: There is no better place to be than in the caring hands of God.

As that fledgling church grows, the pastor has observed that frequent prayer is helping to shape the church's future. He says that frequency in prayer "keeps us aware of our subjection to God and our need for his direction."[2]

You may need God's direction for some major events or changes taking place in your life. Take a look in the Word of God and visit with a man who, early in his walk with Jesus, offered a pivotal prayer to discover God's direction for his life.

PAUL'S PIVOTAL PRAYER

Acts 21 tells the story of the apostle Paul's arrest in Jerusalem for teaching the gospel. This former persecutor of Christians was now in hot pursuit of God's will for his life. Paul would travel from synagogue to synagogue, challenging thousands of years of Jewish tradition and preaching that the Messiah had come in the person of Jesus. While making his point at a religious gathering in Jerusalem, Paul caused such an enormous stir among the traditional Jews that there was a near riot. Paul was arrested—which probably saved him from being beaten to death.

While behind bars, Paul shared his conversion experience with the government and prison authorities. He told them how, while traveling on the Damascus Road in pursuit of Christians—whom he had made a career of terrorizing—he had encountered the risen Lord. In dramatic fashion, Paul told them about the dialogue between Christ and himself that day. When Jesus identified himself, Paul had responded, "What shall I do, Lord?" Then Jesus instructed him to go into Damascus, saying, "There you will be told all that you have been assigned to do" (Acts 22:10).

The Lord has an "assignment" for all of us. Our challenge is to discover exactly what that assignment is. The very question, "What shall I do, Lord?" reveals a number of presuppositions that Paul had about God and his own future. Author Bill Thrasher offers the following suggestions as we seek to discern God's will for our lives:[3]

1. BELIEVE THAT GOD HAS A WILL FOR YOU

Paul believed that God had a will for his life. He simply asked the Lord, "What shall I do?" This is not complicated or hard to ask. But asking this question reveals that we indeed believe in God and in God's personal concern for our welfare and future. Thrasher says, "God will work with us where we are, and He can even weave the failures of a person with a repentant heart into something beautiful."[3]

Paul's previous life as the persecuting Saul of Tarsus didn't earn him the best of reputations. Maybe your reputation has been shaky too. Instead of living in fear that you have really blown it—that you have completely missed the will of God for your life—be encouraged that right now, no matter where you are on the journey, God has a will for you. He can take you right where you are and bring you back to His very best. Believe, just as Paul did, that God has a plan for you.

2. CONTINUALLY LISTEN TO GOD

A young professor beginning his first teaching assignment had joined a campus faculty. While settling into his office he was greeted by one of the tenured professors. As they talked, the younger professor asked the veteran scholar if he had any advice for him as he began his new life of teaching the next day. The older prof said, "In every class, you'll have at least one person who will always want to argue with you. Sometimes it will get annoying. But here's what I've learned: The person who's arguing is probably the only one listening!"

God speaks to us every day. But are we listening? For thousands of years God has been speaking *through the Bible.* The Scriptures clearly tell us that there are certain things that are right and certain things that are wrong. There's a right way and wrong way to treat people. There's a right way and wrong way to live in society. There's a way to God and there are ways that lead to destruction. The Bible is clear concerning God's view of such things, and we would be wise to listen.

God also speaks *through the Holy Spirit.* When an individual receives Christ into his or her life, that person receives the precious gift of the Holy Spirit, who comes and dwells within that person. Many times in the everyday relationships and responsibilities of life we do not have the Word of God handy. So God gives us the Holy Spirit to help us recall the Scriptures we do know and to guide our decision making. The Holy Spirit at times will prompt a Christian to give a particular gift or to share the gospel with another. Sometimes the Holy Spirit convicts us that we shouldn't be thinking or doing what we actually desire to think and do. At times, the Holy Spirit serves as a comforter, to be with us when difficulty—even devastating news—invades our lives. The Holy Spirit provides us power, if we utilize it, to make the right decisions. The Holy Spirit can become something of a godlike conscience living within our lives.

God also speaks *through people, events, and circumstances.* Sometimes when we're praying for direction, God will lead us to seek the counsel of someone who has been at that same pivotal point in his or her own life. Or God may send a person along to lovingly confront us concerning a particular sin and challenge us to deal with it before God.

God can also lead us to look back over events and circumstances that have become part of who we are. Being laid off unexpectedly may not have been what you thought was God's will for your life as the day began. But even in such circumstances God is able to work. He still loves you and He can use even an unexpected and upsetting circumstances to guide you into a new direction, with Him clearly at the helm.

During the aftermath of the September 11 tragedy, EQUIP, the nonprofit leadership-development ministry I lead, was hit hard by a downturn in donations. Many donor dollars were understandably directed to the relief efforts in New York City. Also, many of even our most faithful financial partners reported to us that their businesses were down 15 to 20 percent from the year before, and they just didn't have the resources at that time to continue giving to EQUIP. Consequently, as income diminished, our leadership at EQUIP had to make some hard decisions, including laying off personnel. I can't stand doing that kind of thing, but that goes with the job of being a leader.

One of the positions I had to eliminate was held by a man who has become a dear friend since we started working together. Stan Reiff is one of the world's great people. Everyone loves Stan. His professional and business skills are second to none. And because Stan worked so closely with me, he knew that with the upcoming changes his job might be in jeopardy. When I gave Stan the news that our reorganization would eliminate his position, he responded with class and character. He said, "You know, the Lord has always looked out for us, and we'll trust Him to continue. I just need to find out what He wants me to do next."

Stan and I, along with others on our team, began to pray about his future. Within thirty days Stan got a job with another ministry in the Atlanta area, with the same kind of responsibilities he had at EQUIP. But this time the ministry he's helping to lead is far more established and many times greater in size and budget than EQUIP.

Stan knew that God loves him and was able to use people, events, and circumstances to take him from one job to the next. He had placed God at the helm of his life. So even under the duress of losing his job, Stan listened to God from a fresh perspective, praying and asking others to pray for him to know what to do next.

When a person prays—as did Stan and the apostle Paul—"Lord, what shall I do?" and then reads the Word of God, listens for the promptings of the Holy Spirit, observes the experience of others, and pays attention to circumstances surrounding his or her life, that person is bound to experience not only God's direction, but also God's provision.

3. CONTINUALLY PURSUE THE PEACE OF GOD

This next topic is about passion. The same Paul who asked, "Lord, what shall I do?" later was to proclaim publicly, "I want to know Him [Jesus] and the power of his resurrection and the fellowship of sharing in his sufferings, becoming like him in his death, and so, somehow, to attain to the resurrection from the dead" (Phil. 3:10).

Paul was in passionate pursuit of God. He advised the Colossian Christians to let "the peace of Christ rule in your hearts" (Col. 3:15). The Greek word for "rule" here means "on top of everything else." It's the idea of something being the best. Think of the highest score on a test or winning the blue ribbon in a competition. That's what Paul means by "rule." In the first century this word was used to describe the kind of authority a judge had in a court of law or an umpire today has on an athletic field. Even in today's world, a judge or an umpire, in their respective arenas, has the final say.

Paul meant that the peace of God in our lives should act as a judge or an umpire when it comes to knowing God's will. When we have to make a decision, when we have inner turmoil, or when we're struggling about what to do, we should let the peace of God have the final say.

God would never tell us to do anything contrary to His Word, so we should study the Bible, seek the leading of the Holy Spirit, seek godly counsel, and review our circumstances in order to discern whether something is right or wrong. But often these aren't simple issues of right versus wrong, good against bad, or moral versus immoral. These are often choices between right and right, good and good, and moral and moral. Very often in my life the most difficult choices are not choices between right and wrong, but between right and right. Sometimes two choices, maybe three, that may dictate the future direction of my life are not choices between good and evil, but are choices of determining between what is good, what is better, and what is best.

SHOULD I HAVE THE SURGERY?

One time I was delivering the message "Let the Peace of God Rule" at a Bible conference. After the service a lady came up to me and said, "John, everything you said was exactly right!" (When a preacher hears those delightful words, he leans in a little closer!)

I smiled and said, "Tell me more, please."

She said that years earlier she had gone to the doctor for some tests and was diagnosed with a problem. The doctor recommended surgery, but he said, "I think you should get a second opinion." So she went to another doctor, who made the same diagnosis as the first doctor but concluded, "I don't think you should have the surgery. But I think you should get another opinion." She went to a third doctor, who came to same conclusion as the first two doctors and recommended, "Have the surgery. But before you do, get another opinion." Then she visited with a fourth doctor who made the same diagnosis as the first three doctors, but concluded—you guessed it—"Don't have the surgery!"

In utter frustration, she sought counsel from her pastor. She told him the situation and asked for his advice. He said, "Have the surgery."

Driving away from the pastor's office, she thought, *I wonder what my former pastor would tell me?* So she went to see her former pastor, told him her story, and he said, "I don't think you should have the surgery."

As the lady was telling me this story, she and I both laughed. But at the time she was experiencing this uncertainty, it was no laughing matter. I asked her, "What did you do?" She said, "John, I didn't know what to do. I had six well-meaning, informed persons giving me a variety of suggestions. It wasn't until one morning that my husband and I were having our devotions that I came across the very passage you just taught, Colossians 3:15: 'Let the peace of Christ rule.' And that was it for me. It was as if God was saying to me, 'You've prayed, gathered information, and sought counsel. Now do what you have peace about.' So my husband and I talked about it, and that morning we concluded that I had greatest peace about having the surgery." And just in case you're wondering, she had the surgery and is doing fine!

What Does Peace Look Like?

Tim Hansel describes peace this way:

> In my late twenties, a bunch of my friends and I decided to sail around the world. I have to admit though, at the time I was a bit worried. I hadn't sailed before. I was uneasy and anxious. So I spent a lot of time reading the Bible and praying about it, until it dawned on me that God was whispering, "Tim, I'll give you peace if you read some books on sailing. The reason you're anxious is not due to lack of prayer, but your lack of knowledge about sailing." I wasn't unprayerful; I was unskilled. So I took a step I needed to take to "let" God work his peace in my heart. I began reading about sailing.[4]

The Bible will not tell you whether or not to have surgery, or whether or not it's OK to sail around the world. It doesn't specifically tell you what job to take or where to educate your children. There's no verse specifically telling you whether to remain single or get married.

Nowhere in Scripture does it say that you should either buy or lease a car.

When you pray for direction and you aren't clear about what the Bible teaches on the matter, you can't seem to get insight into the Holy Spirit's leading, and advice and circumstances contradict each other, heed Paul's advice: "Let the peace of Christ rule." Let the peace of God the Son be the judge and the umpire. Let the peace of God make the call. Read the Bible, seek counsel, study the surrounding circumstances, gather information, and pray. And when you pray this way, pivotal events will begin to take shape in your life. The peace of God doesn't have to be a hunch or a guess. Hansel found the peace of God as he gathered information about a subject in which he was unskilled. As he studied the topic, he became more confident. God's peace began to rule in his heart. Peace for him came as an informed sense of rest.

Berit Kjos, in *A Wardrobe from the King,* writes about a man who sought the perfect picture of peace. Not finding one that satisfied, he announced a contest to produce this masterpiece. The challenge stirred the imagination of artists everywhere, and paintings began to arrive from far and wide. Finally the day of revelation arrived. The judges uncovered one scene after another, while the viewers clapped and cheered. But the tension grew as only two pictures remained veiled.

As the judge pulled the cover from one, a hush fell over the crowd. A mirror-smooth lake reflected lacy, green birches under the soft blush of the evening sky. Along the grassy shore, a flock of sheep grazed undisturbed. Surely this was the winner.

The man who had originally sought the perfect picture of peace uncovered the second painting himself, and the crowd gasped in surprise. A tumultuous waterfall cascaded down a rocky precipice; the crowd could almost feel its cold, penetrating spray. Stormy-gray clouds threatened to explode with lightning, wind, and rain. In the midst of the stormy scene a spindly tree clung to the rocks at the edge of the falls. One of its branches reached toward the torrential waters, as if foolishly seeking to experience its full power.

A little bird had built its nest in the elbow of that branch. Content and undisturbed in her stormy surroundings, she rested on her eggs. Her eyes closed and her wings covering her little ones, she manifested a peace that transcends all earthly turmoil.[5]

When we need direction in a world filled with noise and distraction, it's nice to know that there's a place—a quiet place—where God speaks and gives direction. This place is called *the peace of God,* and we should let it rule in our lives.

Like Lloyd Olgilvie, the sun may be setting on your need to make a decision. You may need direction. It's a pivotal moment.

Pray! Then go forward in the peace of God!

CLOSING PRAYER

Pivotal Prayer
When You Need Direction

Lord, I need to know what to do,
which direction to take.
Frankly, Lord, some of the options in front of me
are very inviting.
Like Paul years ago, I need to know soon,
"What shall I do, Lord?"
Help me especially to know
which way will give You the greatest glory.
Help me to discover Your peace.
And when I do make that great discovery,
give me humility to let Your peace
be the umpire and the judge.
Amen.

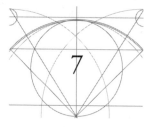

PIVOTAL PRAYING WHEN YOU DON'T SEE RESULTS

(TIM ELMORE)

Leroy strolled into the kitchen where his mother was making dinner. His sixth birthday was coming up, and he thought it was a good time to tell her what he wanted. "Mom, I want a bike for my birthday," he announced.

His mother smiled, thinking this would be a good time to talk about Leroy's behavior. He had the reputation for being a pest to his sister. And he had gotten into trouble at school that semester. She gently asked him if he thought he deserved to get a bike for his birthday. When he immediately responded that he did, she told him to go to his room and reflect on his conduct over the last year. Then she suggested he write a letter to God and tell him why he thought he deserved a bike for his birthday.

Little Leroy stomped up the steps to his room and sat down to write God a letter:

Dear God,

    I have been a very good boy this year and I would like a bike for my birthday. I want a red one.

                Your friend, Leroy

Leroy knew this wasn't true. He had not been a very good boy and knew God could see right past his words. So, he tore up the letter and started over:

> Dear God,
>   I have been an OK boy this year. I still would really like a red bike for my birthday.
>   Your friend, Leroy

Finally he convinced himself he had to be honest if he hoped to get any results with God. So he tore up letter number two and began the third letter:

> Dear God,
>   I know I haven't been a very good boy this year. I am very sorry. I will be a good boy if you just send me a red bike.
>   Thanks, Leroy

Leroy knew that even if this were true, it wasn't going to get him a red bike from God. By now, he was upset. He went downstairs and told his mom that he wanted to go to church. Leroy's mother thought her plan had worked, as Leroy looked very sad. "Just be home in time for dinner," she told him.

Leroy walked down the street to the church on the corner. He slowly opened the door and crept down to the altar. He looked around to make sure no one was watching, then picked up a small statue of the Virgin Mary. He slipped it under his shirt and ran out the door, down the street, into his house, and up to his room. He shut the door behind him, and sat down with a piece of paper and a pen. Leroy then wrote this letter to God:

Dear God,

I've got your mama. If you want to see her again, send the bike!

Signed, You Know Who

We may chuckle at little Leroy, but he's not much different from the rest of us. We Americans will do anything to get results. We are a results-driven, product-oriented society and have been since our country began. We are on a fast track to the bottom line. People get fired from their jobs if they don't produce results. Salespeople aggressively network with associates if they think it might help them close a sale or reach a goal. We even treat God this way.

Over the last twenty years I've had the privilege of leading dozens of chapel services for professional baseball and football teams. I can't tell you the number of athletes who will patronize a chapel service, treating God like some good-luck charm. They want Him on their sides so they'll play better that day. It's almost like a superstition. Anything that might help them get results.

According to a survey done by *Life* magazine, three of four Americans pray every day. Of those praying Americans, 95 percent say they have had their prayers answered. We tend to pray for the same reason we do anything else. We think it works.[1] So, what do we do when we pray, but we don't see results? This has got to be one of the toughest predicaments. A mother prays for her child to recover from leukemia, yet doesn't see any signs of improvement. A single, thirty-seven-year-old woman believes she is called to marry, longs to love a husband and children, but sees no prospect of marriage on the horizon. A man prays for thirteen years that his business colleague and friend will find Christ, but continues to witness that friend curse and drink and use God's name in vain. A midlevel manager works hard for years and prays for that job promotion, but his supervisor promotes his personal "buddies" instead.

Like Florence Chadwick, who gave up her swim from Catalina Island to the shoreline of California because the fog was so dense she couldn't see the coast in front of her, we find it hard to continue to pray when we cannot see any signs of an answer through the fog of our day-to-day experience. Any labor without some sign of progress becomes frustrating.

QUESTIONS TO ASK AS YOU WAIT FOR RESULTS

Let me say two things: First, if it's any encouragement to you, there isn't a praying person anywhere who hasn't felt the pain of waiting on answered prayer. It's part of the package of being a follower of Jesus. If all the answers came overnight, we would not be called a people of faith. Second, let me suggest a few questions that you may want to ask as you wait for answers to your prayer.

1. DOES GOD WANT TO DO SOMETHING DIFFERENT?

In other words, am I praying for the right result? It may never dawn on us that what we are praying for, while it sounds right to us, may not be what God has in mind. Acts 16:6–10 describes how Paul yearned for God to open doors in the East so he could take the gospel into pioneer territory that had never heard the message of Christ. It seemed biblically sound and logical. He discovered, however, that God had something else in mind. One night the Lord gave him a vision of a man in Macedonia crying out for Paul to come and share with them. Paul changed his plan. He went west into Europe instead of east into Asia.

2. DOES GOD WANT TO PURIFY MY MOTIVES?

In other words, am I praying for the right reasons? Have you ever noticed how consumed Jesus is with motives? In His Sermon on the

Mount He spoke specifically about this issue. When praying and fasting, He advised His hearers not to tell other people, but to do so silently before God. "And when you pray," He said, "do not be like the hypocrites, for they love to pray standing in the synagogues and on the street corners to be seen by men. I tell you the truth, they have received their reward in full. But when you pray, go into your room, close the door and pray to your Father" (Matt. 6:5–6).

Is Jesus against public prayer? Absolutely not. What He wants is for us to fight our way past pretension. How many times have you been in a prayer circle at church, where each person takes a turn to say something to God? Isn't it tempting to think, *Oh my gosh. Four more people, and it's my turn. What can I say that will sound profound?* Jesus said if that's what we seek, that's the only reward we'll get: the recognition of people. Sometimes even when we don't see results, God uses that time to purify our motives in prayer.

3. DOES GOD WANT TO CHANGE ME OR STRETCH MY FAITH?

This is a paramount question. C. S. Lewis noted that the best prayer is not for God to change our circumstances. It is for God to change *us*. While I believe God wants to change my circumstances from time to time, it is more important that I be changed in prayer than that prayer change my circumstances.

Consider this: The longer we wait for answers to prayer, the deeper the faith required. The book of Job illustrates this truth vividly. In chapter 1, Job is smitten by Satan with boils; with the loss of houses, barns, and property; with the death of livestock and even of his own children. Over the next forty chapters, his "friends" question Job's integrity and faith.

Job cries out for justice. But in the end he submits to the fact that God is just and knows his heart. He concludes, "Though he slay me, yet will I hope in him" (13:15). In chapter 42, God shows up and vindicates Job, talking about his great faith—faith that sustained him through the waiting process.

Let's face it: We don't like waiting on anything. (My vision of hell is one long line of people waiting). Yet God can use our waiting to stretch our faith. Ben Patterson, in his marvelous book *Waiting*, writes: "As important as the answer for which we wait, is the work God does in us, while we wait."[2]

I learned to ask these three key questions in 1980. While serving as a youth pastor, I wanted to introduce students to Christ. While driving through the small town where I served part-time at a church, I had an idea. I spotted an old theater that had been shut down years before. I thought to myself: *What a great place to fix up and show Christian movies!* We could lease the building, do some renovation, and show good, wholesome movies to teens who might never darken the door of a church. At the end of each movie I could take five minutes to share how to build a relationship with God—and see kids come to Christ!

The idea seemed perfect. I began to pray for God to open doors and bring this idea into reality. I leased the building, raised some money to begin covering the cost of renovation, and recruited workers from the church to start cleaning and painting. For the first few weeks we had momentum—everyone was excited.

But time took its toll. I was finishing my theology degree, and classes began demanding more of my attention. Volunteers had other obligations, and couldn't find time to get down to the theater to work. Our money soon dried up. I remember one night when it finally hit me that this idea was not going to happen.

I shared with the youth group and my adult sponsors how we just didn't have the time or money to finish. I wrote a letter to the donors, asking if they wanted their money back. It was difficult to face the fact that I had failed to reach my goal. I hated not seeing results.

One night, however, I was praying in my college dorm room. In that quiet hour, I recognized that I had not lost my heart for reaching students. The idea of the movie theater might be gone, but my vision remained. During this time in prayer, God taught me to ask the questions I've just posed to you. As they began to percolate in my mind, I saw the answers for the first time. Yes, God did want to do something different. (I was about to find out what!) Yes, God did want to purify my motives. (I was too caught up in the glamour of hosting the movie theater.) And, yes, God did want to change me and stretch my faith.

That evening a new idea came to me as I sat on my bed. Instead of asking kids to come to the movies, what if I took the movies to them? What if I were to assemble a multimedia presentation suitable to show in local high schools and colleges that would introduce students to truth? I could go into history classes and do a presentation on biblical prophecy, called "Where Is History Taking Us?" Hmmm. It just might work.

I began to check the prices of the equipment I would need and the production cost of each presentation. Ouch. It was more than the money I had raised for the movie theater. So I began to pray again.

As I begged God to provide the money for such a project, He impressed me with this thought: *Tim, I have already given you every resource you need for what I have called you to do.* As I sat quietly, this train of thought continued. God reminded me that I was in college on an art scholarship. It seemed He was prompting me to use my God-given gift in graphics and cartooning. I was to approach local newspaper editors in the area, show them my portfolio, and ask if I could draw editorial cartoons for their paper. They were buying nationally syndicated cartoons—mine would be on local issues. No one was doing that. I would charge ten dollars a cartoon, so the cost would be negligible.

The next Monday I put on a tie, swallowed hard, and took a step of faith. I spoke to an editor of a weekly paper, and within ten minutes I had the job. By week's end, four newspapers had agreed. By the next week I was overwhelmed with the number that had said yes. I began to draw the cartoons, copy them, and mail them out to the papers. I had my own little syndicate, and I was having a ball!

To make a long story short, by the end of the semester I had more than enough money to purchase the multimedia equipment for my presentations. Over the summer I put them together, and the next school year I trained my youth group in how to share Christ following the presentations in their schools. This time everyone got involved. Much to my surprise, the opportunities came quickly. Teachers turned entire days of classes over to me once they saw the presentation. By the end of the school year we had shared Christ with one out of every five students in the city.

My lesson is simple. Some of the greatest periods of growth in my life came when I didn't get results from the way I was praying. Call it a blessing in disguise, if you want. I just know that I'm in position to receive from God once I've answered honestly the three hard questions in this chapter.

What We Learn from Hannah and Michal

Over the twenty-eight years I have been a Christian, I've begun to see a pattern in the prayers that connect with the heart of God. At times I will pray an eloquent prayer and see no results. Other times I will pray a spontaneous prayer and God will surprise me with an answer beyond my wildest imagination.

Prayers come in all shapes and sizes, and the moment we turn prayer into some superstition—saying the same phrases over and over because we think they'll get some results—is the moment we'll be disappointed. The lessons have come slowly for me, but have stayed with me.

I guess you could say I've learned the same lessons we learn from two women mentioned in the Old Testament. Their names are Hannah and Michal. These women provide pictures of two different approaches to life when we don't see results. Hannah's response may be our ultimate test. Michal's response may be our ultimate temptation when we fail to get results. Let's compare and contrast their stories.

Hannah's story is found in 1 Samuel 1–2. She was a woman who prayed daily for a child. It was her heart's deepest longing. In fact, she was so consumed with it that Eli, the priest, thought she was drunk one day as she poured her heart out to God. She went for months—maybe years—without seeing results.

Michal's story is found in 1 Samuel 18:20–21 and 2 Samuel 6:20–23. She was one of David's wives. She possessed a different spirit from Hannah. Her father, King Saul, gave her to David to become a "snare" to him. She was controlling and stubborn. What she shared in common with Hannah was that she also was unable to have a child. Before we examine the differences between these two women, let's look at their similarities:

- Both were Hebrew women. They shared the same race and culture.

- Both longed to have a baby. In their Jewish culture, the greatest gift you could give your husband was a child.

- Both were barren.

That's where the similarities end. As these two women recognized they were not getting their desired result, they took two very different tracks to express their hunger and pain.

- Hannah trusted God, while Michal relied on human effort. Michal seemed predisposed to make it all happen. Hannah communicated to God that while she would do all she could, she would depend on Him for the results.

- Hannah was blameless, while Michal was a snare to David. Hannah kept her perspective. She knew the issue was out of her control. Michal seemed to become more frustrated as time went on. Her focus was on people, not on God.

- Hannah was consumed with honoring God, while Michal was consumed with her personal image. Hannah promised God that if He granted her a son, she would give him back to the Lord to serve Him. Michal's obsession with appearance is clear in 2 Samuel 6, when she scolds David for his worship and dancing before the Lord. It looked bad. He would ruin their reputations.

It is interesting to note how each story ends. Hannah was eventually granted a son. She named him Samuel, and he became the most influential priest in the history of Israel. Michal's obsession with image and reputation seems to have ruined her chances at receiving from God. Second Samuel 6 ends with the statement, "And Michal had no child to the day of her death."

If we were able to interview these two women, they would be a picture of contrasts. While Hannah wasn't perfect, her motive for having a son was to offer him back to the Lord. She didn't even get to enjoy raising him into adulthood. She wanted to honor God, and for her, bearing a child was the best way to do just that.

As far as we can tell, Michal couldn't get her eyes off herself. Her failure so engulfed her that she was blind to her need to trust God. We never read that she prayed. The motive behind her behavior seems to be how she looked in front of others, not how she could partner with God. It was appearance more than substance. It was image more than integrity that counted. Whenever our egos, or selfish ambitions, or obsessions with our images take precedence over the priorities of God, they will become roadblocks to getting results.

Michal couldn't get results from her prayer because she wasn't on the same page with God. This is why it's crucial to ask the questions: Does God want to do something different? Does God want to purify my motives? Does God want to change me and stretch my faith?

FROM ROADBLOCKS TO DOORS

So how do we dismantle roadblocks and open doors? This is what pivotal praying is about. We tear down roadblocks by listening to God's responses to the three questions we discussed earlier in this chapter. We open doors by learning the art of intercessory prayer.

In Matthew 7:7 Jesus says, "Ask and it will be given to you; seek and you will find; knock and the door will be opened to you." I think Jesus gave us three pictures of prayer in these statements. "Asking" prayer is what we do when we know the will of God and we pray the prayer of faith. We can pray for things like food, provision, and protection by simply asking in faith. We can lay hold of the answer by faith and stand on it because God has already communicated His will on the matter.

"Seeking" prayer is what we do when we don't know the will of God and so must seek His mind on the matter. We may not know how to pray about an opportunity to move across the country, or about taking a new job, or about a person we wish to marry. There is no chapter or verse in the Bible to tell us what God's will is for these. So we pray as Jesus did in the Garden of Gethsemane: "Lord, not my will but Yours be done."

"Knocking" prayer is where I'd like to focus for the remainder of this chapter. This is what we do when we know God's mind and will on an issue, but it involves the wills of others or factors that cannot be forced. It is a closed door on which we must knock.

For instance, we can pray for someone's salvation, knowing that it isn't God's will that any should perish but that all should come to repentance (2 Peter 3:9). However, we can't just "name it and claim it" because it involves someone else's will too. God doesn't negate the will of someone else. He will not force anyone into heaven. So we must "knock" to see the door open.

The word used in Matthew for *knock* is an interesting one. It describes a constant beating on a door, not a one-time tap. It connotes an incessant, almost annoying knocking until the desired result occurs. Jesus beckons us to persist as we partner with Him to accomplish His purpose. God's kingdom is set up in such a way as to require partnership between God and human "knockers." Our prayers are necessary in the fulfillment of God's plans. We can link our lives to His purposes for the world—and "knocking" prayer is often how we do this.

I love what David Cho has said about the "doors" prayer opens. Besides its common use as an entrance to a house or a building, the word *door* is used metaphorically as the entrance into any spiritual experience or opportunity. Jesus said, "I am the door" (John 10:7 NASB). Paul used the word as an entrance to an opportunity when he wrote, "I went to Troas to preach the gospel of Christ and found that the Lord had opened a door for me" (2 Cor. 2:12). Jesus, speaking through the apostle John, said, "See, I have placed before you an open door that no one can shut" (Rev. 3:8).

There are doors to nations and ethnic groups that can be opened as well. Once a door is open, those people are able to receive faith and believe.

Going through a door of opportunity means we may face spiritual opposition from the enemy. Paul wrote, "A great door for effective work has opened to me, and there are many who oppose me" (1 Cor. 16:9). We often think that if something is God's will, it will happen smoothly and effortlessly. This is often not the case at all.

Chapter 9 deals more in depth with the spiritual opposition we experience when engaged in God's work.

So how do we open the doors of faith and opportunity? As we have seen, Christ must open the door. However, as God has made us members of His body, He uses us to accomplish His purposes here on this earth. By lifting up prayers of intercession, we battle against the spiritual forces that strive to keep shut the door. Through our prayers, Christ can open the door and an entire city, nation, or race can be saved!

Paul wrote to the church at Colosse, "Pray for us, too, that God may open a door for our message, so that we may proclaim the mystery of Christ, for which I am in chains" (Col. 4:3–4). The bottom line is this: Only God can open a door; we have to knock! This gives new meaning to Jesus' invitation: "Knock and the door will be opened to you" (Luke 11:9).

Intercessory prayer is "knocking" prayer. While results may not come quickly, we align ourselves with God's purposes by continuing to pray. Sometimes intercessory prayer is praying for someone who cannot or will not pray for him- or herself. We may not see tangible results, but we cling to God's Word. This is the partnership God seeks with us. Let us not make the mistake we read about in Ezekiel, when God says, "I looked for a man among them who would . . . stand before me in the gap on behalf of the land so I would not have to destroy it, but I found none. So I will pour out my wrath on them and consume them." (Ezek. 22:30–31).

PRAYER THAT GETS RESULTS

Several years ago I was invited to speak at a Christian university. It was their spiritual-emphasis week. Months ahead of time, I began to pray for the many students on that campus who didn't know Christ, and for those who needed a more intimate relationship with Him.

Many of the leaders at this college informed me that they were praying as well.

Once there, I began to preach about the power of God. As we looked at the book of Acts, I shared that God's power was enough to change their lives, deliver them from the enemy's bondage, heal their bodies, and meet all of their needs.

At the conclusion of the Tuesday night service, a student named Darrell walked forward, a group of other students trailing behind him. He knelt at the altar to pray. When I asked him what he wanted to pray about, he informed me that he had a large cancerous growth in his leg and that he was to have it amputated the following Thursday. This tragedy was magnified by the fact that Darrell ran track and would have to give up his love for running. As I looked at all the students around him, I realized that now I had to pray as powerfully as I'd preached. I had just finished talking about the power of God—and now Darrell and his friends wanted to see it. (Part of me wanted to just slip out of the building and never come back!)

I prayed for Darrell that night. It was a simple prayer that God would reveal Himself to Darrell as His Healer and Savior. When we finished, I tried to encourage him by saying, "If it's any consolation, I have a chronic disease too. I have diabetes." Darrell looked at me forlornly and said, "I have that too." He was in sad shape. I encouraged him to continue to trust God, and that I would do the same.

On Thursday night I entered the chapel and had the surprise of my life. Darrell was standing in the lobby, both legs still intact. When I asked if he was supposed to get the cancerous leg amputated that day, he said yes, but that the doctors always do one last X-ray before the surgery. When they did, they were shocked: The cancer had shrunk down to almost nothing. Instead of spreading as they had feared it would, it was disappearing.

Needless to say, I was elated. "Didn't that make you feel wonderful?" I exclaimed.

Darrell responded, "Well, actually, I was feeling very weird at that moment. In fact, I asked the nurse if she could check my blood-sugar level, and when she did we discovered that with one swoop of God's hand, He had healed the cancer and the diabetes!"

That night we had one amazing service. Darrell stood up and shared what God had done. The Spirit of God moved on the students, and many of them came forward to accept Christ. The power of God saved, healed, and delivered many that night.

Our months or praying—of knocking at God's door—had paid off. God showed up. Dozens were saved. And Darrell was healed of cancer and diabetes.

Ironically, I am still a diabetic. I have wrestled with this disease for over twenty years. It's OK, though. I am still knocking.

CLOSING PRAYER

Dear Lord,
I'm tired of waiting for results.
Help me to see what You are up to.
Do You want to do something different
from what I'm asking?
Do You want to change me or stretch me in some way?
Help me to trust You with the results.
You lead.
I'll keep following.
Amen.

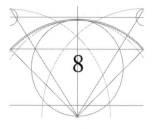

PIVOTAL PRAYING WHEN YOU NEED A MIRACLE

(JOHN HULL)

E d Dobson needs a miracle. This respected pastor of Calvary Church in Grand Rapids, Michigan, was diagnosed a few years ago with Amyotropic Lateral Sclerosis (ALS), better known as Lou Gehrig's disease. There is no known cure. If Ed is to live, he needs a miracle.

When he learned of the diagnosis, Ed realized that this suffering might lift his prayer life to levels he'd never known before.

> The truth was, I didn't feel like praying. I didn't feel like talking to God.
>
> When the doctor said, "You will lose your ability to walk, to sit up, to swallow, and to breathe, and all we can do is help you manage the pain," I went through several months where I felt like I was in Lazarus's tomb—cold, dark, trapped. You'd think my first instinct would be to pray for healing. I couldn't even bring myself to ask. I prayed for wisdom, because of all the medical options. But I didn't pray for healing for a long time.

As time has passed and the reality of his condition has worsened, Ed has come to pray in "pivotal prose":

I have three prayers for healing: a small-faith version, a medium-faith version, and a big-faith prayer. When my faith is small I pray, "Lord I give you my right hand. Just let the disease stop there." [Ed has muscle atrophy and nerve damage in his right hand and arm.] If I'm a little stronger in my faith, I'll pray, "Lord, stop it right where it is, no worse than it is today." If I'm feeling particularly bold I pray, "Maybe you could heal me, Lord. Maybe you could reverse this disease."[1]

POWERLESS, BUT LOST IN THE WONDER OF GOD

Recently a friend in the ministry visited Ed and anointed him with oil. His words of encouragement to Ed are for anyone praying for a miracle in his or her own life: "Ed, you need to get lost in the wonder of God. If you'll get lost in that wonder, who knows what He'll do for you."[2]

Lost in the wonder of God. What a refreshing perspective when we're looking for a miracle!

When we need a miracle, we usually get lost in the morass of the situation we're in or the overwhelming odds before us. But imagine being lost, completely lost, in the wonder of God. What a great place to be! When this happens, our prayers become focused on God, not on our problem, and we're truly able to pray, "God, whatever brings you greatest glory, do it!" Jesus prayed in the Garden of Gethsemane, "Abba, Father, . . . everything is possible for you. Take this cup from me. Yet not what I will, but what you will" (Mark 14:36).

When we pray for a miracle, we acknowledge that we are helpless on our own to bring about a God-honoring solution. The task is too great. The road is too hard. Our efforts, outside God's power, are futile.

DANIEL NEEDED A MIRACLE TOO

Daniel is one of the most captivating personalities in the Bible. A Jew deported by force to Babylon, he grew up in a completely alien culture. His life was tested early on when he was still in his teens. Immersed in a new culture, even given a new Babylonian name and introduced to food that contradicted Jewish dietary laws, Daniel vowed that he would not defile the faith he so dearly embraced and believed. "Daniel resolved not to defile himself with the royal food and wine" (Dan. 1:8). Although Israel was a long way off, God was near. As Daniel spent time with God every passing day, he got lost in the wonder of God.

This kind of profound commitment to God, along with a keen intellect and a strong work ethic, opened all kinds of doors for Daniel in Babylon. Over time his spiritual insights caught the attention of the kingdom's leaders. When King Belshazzar asked Daniel to interpret his dreams, Daniel did so with great accuracy, even to Belshazzar's doom. The Babylonians would be defeated, said Daniel, by the Medes and the Persians.

Word of Daniel's abilities reached Darius, ruler of the Medes and Persians. Soon Daniel became his political advisor and was given significant responsibility over the kingdom. But such upward mobility brought with it a price. A citizen of Judah excelling in the Median empire did not sit well with his colleagues. They became jealous of Daniel.

Daniel's enemies formed a conspiracy to undo him. But after a thorough investigation, they concluded that the only fault in his life was in his relationship with God. So the conspirators convinced Darius to outlaw prayer, knowing that Daniel would never stop praying. In fact, Daniel prayed three times a day.

When Darius banned prayer, Daniel's enemies saw this as his

death certificate. Daniel did indeed keep praying after the new law was enacted, so his enemies pressed Darius to enforce the law. Finally Darius arrested Daniel and sentenced him to die in a den of lions.

Daniel needed a miracle, but he never panicked. He just kept communing with God as he always had. He trusted that God was in control, no matter how bad the situation appeared. His prayer life enabled him to maintain a faithful perspective in the face of enormous pressures. "When Daniel learned that the decree had been published, he went home to his upstairs room where the windows opened toward Jerusalem. Three times a day he got down on his knees and prayed, giving thanks to his God, just as he had done before" (6:10).

I love the phrase, "just as he had done before." Once, while hoeing his garden, Francis of Assisi was asked what he would do if he were suddenly told he would die at sunset that very day. He replied, "I would finish my gardening."[3]

Daniel knew he was going to be arrested and would face execution. Still, lost in the wonder of God, he kept praying.

LOST IN THE WONDER OF ASA

Asa is not a famous name in biblical history, but he was a king of Judah. As leader of the Southern Kingdom, he had heard of God's faithfulness to His children through the years. Some of his predecessors had walked with God.

In the thirty-sixth year of his reign, Asa needed a military miracle, or—perhaps more accurate—*another* military miracle. On a previous occasion, God had delivered him from defeat because he had "relied on the LORD" (2 Chron. 16:8). Now Asa faced a greater threat, but this time he didn't turn to God for a miracle (16:2–3). Instead, he bribed a king in a neighboring region to break his alliance with Asa's greatest threat, King Baasha. The payoff would be substantial—silver and gold from Judah's treasuries. Things seemed to be going Asa's way. He had miraculously saved himself! . . . or had he?

The prophet Hanani confronted Asa with what he'd done: "Because you relied on the king of Aram and not on the LORD your God, the army of the king of Aram has escaped from your hand. . . . The eyes of the LORD range throughout the earth to strengthen those whose hearts are fully committed to him. You have done a foolish thing, and from now on you will be at war" (vv. 7, 9).

Hanani's sobering words remind us that no matter what we accomplish in life, it is God's power—not our soldiers or resources—that win the victory. What a reminder as to why we should pray. As a result of his independence from God, Asa would be at war for the rest of his life. Never would he know peace. Because he tried to be his own miracle worker, lost in his own wonder, Asa lived the rest of his life isolated from God.

Asa responded to the prophet Hanani by putting him in jail. Embarrassed yet increasingly proud, he then became more oppressive in his reign. Apparently Asa never repented of not relying on God. He spent the remaining five years of his life stewing in pride. Two years before his death he caught a rare foot disease. The Scriptures tell us that "even in his illness, he did not seek help from the LORD, but only from the physicians" (v. 1).

Unlike Ed Dobson, Asa never prayed a pivotal prayer for a miracle to occur in his life. He spent the rest of his life not lost in the wonder of God, but choosing to be lost in the fog of prideful disobedience.

THANKS IN THE MIDST OF PRESSURE AND PAIN

Ed Dobson is discovering that a prayer of thanks when you need a miracle is healing in and of itself. Daniel learned that too. While knowing his arrest was imminent, thankfulness was a key theme in his prayer. He gave thanks to God, "just as he had done before" (Dan. 6:10).

Dobson's perspective on thanks has changed considerably. "There's a world of thankfulness that we rarely explore . . . I used to never [pray] 'Thank you, Lord for getting me up in the morning.' I used to never thank God for that. After ALS, I do now. . . . The major change in my prayer life is that most of my prayers are now prayers of gratitude."[4]

Ed knows that unless God heals him, ALS will continue to torment his body. Yet he's giving thanks and experiencing a kind of healing within that he's never known before.

Daniel probably continued his prayers of gratitude while the lions growled just a few feet away. But he wasn't alone. In fact, the Bible says that the Lord sent an angel to the lions' den to be right there with him and to shut the mouths of the lions.

Daniel experienced his miracle. Asa did not. And whether or not God chooses to heal Ed Dobson from ALS, there's already a healing taking place in his life. Many in his congregation say his preaching has taken on new perspective. Ed's found himself calling on people with whom he had past disagreements or misunderstandings. He's been asking for and receiving forgiveness. "If I'm going to die, I want to die with a clear conscience and whole relationships."[5]

Ed Dobson—surrounded with torment, as was Daniel—just keeps giving thanks.

That's pivotal praying for a miracle.

CLOSING PRAYER

Pivotal Prayer
for a Miracle

Dear God,
I need a miracle—or at least I think I do.
This situation has me completely overwhelmed.
Instead of being lost in Your wonder,
I'm lost in the pain and the fear of an
uncertain future.
I need Your help.
Help me to call on You more often.
Please remind me that a life of bitter,
prideful ingratitude is empty.
Give me a taste of Your glory, Your wonder.
The lions are roaring, and I'm afraid.
Please help me!
Amen.

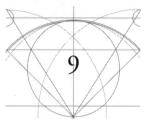

PIVOTAL PRAYING WHEN YOU FACE OPPOSITION

(TIM ELMORE)

I remember the first time in my adult life when someone really hated me. I was a twenty-five-year-old pastor on staff at a large church, responsible, among other things, for leading the college group. After returning home from a mission trip overseas, I was briefed on a conflict between two of my interns. The conflict was over a theological issue, and, quite frankly, I felt that the interns could and should work it out themselves. I was wrong. By the time I intervened, the division they had created was mammoth. The group had taken sides, and a faction had emerged.

I sat down with Sean, one of the interns, to talk it through. When I refused to take his side on the issue, he grew angry. His emotion far outweighed the issue at hand, and I wondered what the real problem was. I didn't find out until it was too late. Within a couple of weeks, Sean had resigned his position and, along with almost thirty other students, left the church.

I was crushed. I couldn't believe this was happening to me. I didn't talk to my wife about it for two weeks, knowing that she would absorb the pain on my behalf. I internalized the whole thing, allowing it to simmer inside me. I couldn't sleep at night. I became consumed with the conflict, and unfortunately, I faced it all alone.

After doing some homework, I discovered that Sean's dad had left his family when Sean had been very young. When I refused to support him in this conflict, I became simply one more male authority figure abandoning him.

I contacted Sean to seek forgiveness and resolve the conflict—but he had made up his mind. In his opinion, I had become demonic.

Since that experience almost twenty years ago, I have come to recognize some harsh realities about life as a Christian. First, being a believer doesn't eradicate my fleshly nature. Our fallen nature is in constant conflict with our faith. Second, although we are loved deeply by God—we are at war. Not with people, but with a very real enemy who often uses people for his purposes. Let me illustrate.

Have you ever seen a bullfight? Ken, a friend of mine, saw one during a trip to Mexico. He shared with me later the powerful spiritual analogy he caught as he watched the small, five-foot-four-inch-tall matador and the one-and-a-half-ton bull go at it.

Most of the action centered around the little red cape, handled by the matador. Two of the bulls chased the cape back and forth until they became frustrated and gave up. Another bull died that day at the hands of the matador. Suddenly it all became clear to Ken: If those bulls knew that the little red cape was not their real enemy, and began to pursue the real enemy, that little matador wouldn't have stood a chance!

This is also true for us. Satan often uses little red capes to frustrate us—capes such as long traffic signals, coworkers at the office, disruptive E-mails, bills, late deliveries, and even family members. These "capes" often come in the form of people. Once we recognize that these figures are not the real opposition, we can approach them far more wisely.

The apostle Paul wrote, "For our struggle is not against flesh and blood, but against the rulers, against the authorities, against the powers of this dark world and against the spiritual forces of evil in the heavenly realms" (Eph. 6:12). We must remember that we're all caught in the midst of heavy warfare—spiritual warfare—between the kingdom of light and the kingdom of darkness. Without over-spiritualizing the issue, let me be clear: Satan isn't really after you, he's after God—and you're tangled up between them, here on earth.

I heard about a high-school couple who broke up. The boyfriend wanted some space, so on their bike ride home from school he ended their relationship. The girl was so angry she couldn't even speak. She raced home, stormed into her room, and sulked on the bed for a while. Then she noticed a picture of her boyfriend—her ex-boyfriend—on her dresser. She grabbed it and threw it on the ground. She pulled the photograph out of its frame and ripped it into pieces. Finally she broke the frame. Afterward, she felt much better. Her adolescent emotions had been satisfied.

Consider this analogy for a moment. Did this girl hurt her former boyfriend as she ripped up his picture? Not at all. He was miles away—perhaps doing the same thing to her picture. What she hurt was the image of her boyfriend—his picture. And that's how Satan goes after you. You're made in the image of God. You are the closest thing to God he can strike at. Since he can't get directly at God, he strikes at you.

Praying in the Face of Opposition

A large part of my problem is that I forget we are at war. Perhaps many of us do. When we do this, the opposition surprises us. We feel violated, resentful—as though life isn't fair.

This is not the perspective of a soldier. When soldiers enlist, they *expect* opposition. It's part of the territory. May I remind you that when you signed up for the family of God, you also signed up for the *army* of God, to fight in His battles against the enemy. You've been enlisted.

We will continue to struggle in life if we attempt to remain civilians during this time of war. Civilians lose focus; soldiers do not. Recognizing that there is a real opposition forces us to focus.

We Americans prayed more effectively just after the September 11 terrorist attack than at any point that year. Why? Because we were made newly and acutely aware of the opposition. We were no longer preoccupied with petty issues. We were praying like soldiers. We had been attacked. John Piper writes, "The problem is that most Christians don't really believe that life is war and that our invisible enemy is awesome. How are you ever going to get them to pray? They'll say they believe these truths, but watch their lives. There is a peacetime casualness in the church about spiritual things . . . all is well in America, the Disneyland of the universe."[2]

God gave us the weapon of prayer to use in this battle against the opposition. Prayer is a vehicle not only to maintain relationship with our Father in heaven, but also to communicate and carry out His purpose of world conquest. Prayer is our vital lifeline in the midst of opposition. The primary reason prayer malfunctions in the hands of believers is their insistence on trying to take a wartime walkie-talkie and turn it into a domestic intercom![3]

Less than a month after the attacks on the World Trade Center and the Pentagon, America declared war on terrorism. Do you remember our strategy as we responded to the Taliban network in Afghanistan? It was the same strategy we used a decade earlier when we launched Operation Desert Storm. We determined to execute an effective air attack, then follow that with a ground attack. The air strike was to take out key enemy strongholds and disarm them from counterattack. Once this was done, our groundwork would be relatively easy. In Operation Desert Storm, this was called the 100-Hour

War. Why was it so quick? Because our air strike was thorough, the groundwork was simply cleanup.

I think you get the picture. As we face opposition, prayer is our "air attack." When we ask God to move in the hearts of others, to pave the way for His kingdom to enter a situation, the groundwork of interacting with the persons involved can be easier.

My church has established prayer teams to pray for specific persons in our city who do not know Christ. Then our outreach team will go out to share with them. We find that our work is accelerated due to the effective air attack! During the season we first set up our prayer teams, we saw a 32-percent increase in church attendance! The key to our outreach is prayer.

I don't know what opposition you are facing. It may not feel spiritual at all. What I do know is that opposition can make you pray better, if you let it. In fact, it can improve you in a variety of areas. Warren Wiersbe once said, "A realist is an idealist who has gone through the fire and been purified. A skeptic is an idealist who has gone through the fire and been burned."[4] Let the fire purify you.

This is exactly what the apostle Paul did two millenniums ago. Sitting in a Roman prison, chained to a Praetorian guard, and awaiting a trial that he thought might end his life, he wrote these words to the Philippian church:

> Now I want you to know, brothers, that what has happened to me has really served to advance the gospel. As a result, it has become clear throughout the whole palace guard and to everyone else that I am in chains for Christ. Because of my chains, most of the brothers in the Lord have been encouraged to speak the word of God more courageously and fearlessly. . . . But what does it matter? The important thing is that in every way, whether from false motives or true, Christ is preached. And because of this I rejoice. (Phil. 1:12–14, 18)

Here is a man who maintained perspective in the midst of opposition. These words don't sound as though they're coming from a man in prison. Paul continued to play offense, not defense in his ministry. How could he think this way? It's simple: He understood a secret very few of us understand. Paul knew he could either surrender to the circumstances around him, or he could surrender to a cause so great that the circumstances would never matter.

And so it is with us. We can either surrender to the opposition we face in our lives, or we can surrender to a cause, a mission, so great that the opposition doesn't matter—it only serves to help us focus. Paul let the opposition clarify his mission rather than cause him to fall into a self-centered life, consumed with his own struggles. He refused to live a maintenance-driven life, and insisted on living a mission-driven life.

In October of 1980 I faced a "prison" of my own. During my junior year of college I developed diabetes. I knew nothing about diabetes and almost slipped into a coma because I'd waited so long to get treatment. My blood sugar had skyrocketed. When the nurse came to my hospital room to explain diabetes, my life came crashing down. She told me I would have to take daily injections for the rest of my life, that there was no cure for diabetes, and that the average life span for persons with diabetes is about twenty years, once they contract the disease. Ouch. I could see my calling in life evaporate. I began to sink into a pool of self-pity. My prayer life became a session of whining and groaning.

Then God directed my attention to Paul's words to the Philippians. Watching how Paul responded to his prison, I suddenly realized that I had to refocus. I had to shift my sights from maintenance to mission. I walked out into the hallway and saw a candy striper pushing a cart of cottage cheese. I asked if I could take that cart for her and visit the rooms of the other diabetic patients on the floor. She let me take over, and that became my excuse to visit the other patients. I shared cottage cheese and Jesus with every one of them. Three of those patients came to Christ.

It was only after this experience that I understood Paul's words: "I want you to know, brothers, that what has happened to me has really served to advance the gospel. . . . But what does it matter? The important thing is that in every way . . . Christ is preached" (Phil. 1:12, 18).

The irony of kingdom living is that God will not only help us through the prisons of life, He will actually use those prisons to advance His purposes—if we can simply keep our perspective. Opposition can be reversed from foe to friend, if we see things from God's perspective. Our perception determines our prayer.

What We Learn from Samson and Jephthah

Some of the greatest lessons about praying in the midst of opposition come from unlikely people who lived centuries ago. Two such stories are tucked away in the Old Testament.

Some 3,500 years ago, during the time of the judges, Israel experienced a period of chaos. There was no king or standing army, so whenever a need arose, a leader—or "judge"—would step forth to solve the problem.

Samson and Jephthah were two such judges. Both men were self-starters. Both were warriors. Both faced enemies who represented fierce opposition to the Jews. For Samson it was the Philistines. For Jephthah it was the Ammonites. Had it not been for the initiative of these men, Israel would have been defeated.

There is a primary lesson about prayer to be learned from Samson and Jephthah. Both of them were terribly impetuous.

You likely know Samson's story better than Jephthah's. Samson was a picture of contrasts. He was physically the strongest man in Israel. He'd been known to slaughter hundreds of Philistines single-handedly. Unfortunately he was morally weak. You might say he had strong biceps but a weak backbone. On a whim, he would strike down a man, make a wager, sleep with a prostitute, or give away the secret of his strength to a woman named Delilah. Due to his impetuous spirit, the Israelites and the Philistines didn't trust him, and at the climax of his career his own people turned him over to the Philistines to save their necks.

Jephthah was also whimsical and impetuous. In fact, his worst nightmare occurred when, on the eve of his battle with the Ammonites, he made a vow to God. It was a stupid and impulsive vow:

> If you give the Ammonites into my hands, whatever comes out of the door of my house to meet me when I return in triumph from the Ammonites will be the LORD's, and I will sacrifice it as a burnt offering. (Judg. 11:30–31)

When he returned home after defeating the Ammonites, who should come out to greet him but his daughter, his only child. Jephthah was heartbroken. He began to tear his clothes in distress over his vow. And, like many of us, he began to blame someone else (his own daughter) for the trouble he had caused. Needless to say, she felt horrible and obliged to become a human sacrifice for the sake of her father's word.

What a needless tragedy for Jephthah. And what an important lesson for us. I believe our greatest temptation, when opposition arises, is to react impetuously. Think about it: Opposition heightens our survival instinct. Our emotions rise. Our adrenaline begins to pump. It usually boils down to fight, faint, or flee. Both Samson's and Jephthah's emotions clouded their perspective. Their pride and their survival instinct pushed them to act on an impulse. Sadly, we rarely maintain the big-picture perspective in times like these. Jephthah lost his daughter. Samson lost his freedom. I believe our greatest challenge, when opposition arises, is to maintain perspective.

SAMSON'S PIVOTAL PRAYER

Samson grew his hair back eventually. And although he became blind, enslaved, and grew older, he regained his strength while he labored in prison. The final four verses of Judges 16 describe how he avenged his impetuous acts. In a suicide mission, he placed his hands against the pillars of the Philistine assembly, prayed a pivotal prayer, and pushed. The pillars fell, and Samson—along with thousands of Philistines—died that day. He actually killed more Philistines in his death than he had all his life.

What enabled Samson to recover, pray, and win a victory? We can spot four factors in those final moments of pivotal praying.

1. Samson regained his first love and perspective. It took a while for Samson's hair to grow again. During this period, he was given a gift—the gift of time. It was in these days of solitude, when he couldn't react on an impulse, that he recaptured not only his love for God, but also his perspective. This is crucial if we're to pray pivotally in times of opposition. Judges 16:20 says that, at one point, Samson didn't even know the Lord had departed from him. By the end of the chapter, however, he was once again calling on the Lord for help. He was no longer Mr. Hot Shot, or Sir Self-Sufficient. He was needy and he knew it.

In his classic work *The Imitation of Christ,* Thomas à Kempis writes, "It is good that we at times endure opposition, and that we are evilly and unruly judged, when our actions and intentions are good. Often such experiences promote humility, and protect us from vainglory. For then we seek God's witness in the heart."[4] For the first time in a long time, Samson is thinking straight. He is depending fully on God for results—not on his own strength, not on his own wit.

May I encourage you, when you face opposition, to let it sharpen you. Allow it to provide you with perspective and focus. Permit the love of God to captivate you, weeding out all other petty distractions. This will make you different. You may seem odd to most people, but it will save you from acting on a human impulse.

On a balmy October afternoon in 1982, Badger Stadium in Madison, Wisconsin, was packed. More than sixty thousand die-hard University of Wisconsin supporters were watching their football team take on the Michigan State Spartans. MSU had the better team. What seemed odd, however, as the score became more lopsided, were the bursts of applause and shouts of joy from the Wisconsin fans. How could they cheer when their team was losing?

It turned out that, seventy miles away, the Milwaukee Brewers were beating the St. Louis Cardinals in Game Three of the 1982 World Series. Many of the fans in the stands were listening to portable radios, and responding to something other than their immediate circumstances.[5]

There's a vivid analogy here for us. Our perspective doesn't come from the ups and downs of the here and now. Scripture encourages us to fix our eyes, not on what is seen, but on what is unseen (2 Cor. 4:18). When we do this, we can maintain perspective and even rejoice in the face of opposition.

2. Samson sought strength from his God, not from his gift. In his pivotal prayer, Samson didn't waste words. He wasn't concerned about praying some fancy, poetic prayer. His goal was not to impress God or people. He simply prayed: "O God, please strengthen me just once more" (Judg. 16:28). To pray pivotally in times of opposition, we must look past our images and reputations. We cannot mince words. We shouldn't care about how we look as we pray. Our goal is not to preserve our reputation but to successfully defeat an enemy.

It is important to note that in adverse times our greatest temptation is to lean on our strengths—our gifts—to do the job. Our talent has gotten us through in the past; why not depend on it now? For those who are especially gifted, there is sometimes a "wing it" mentality. We think we really don't need to prepare for catastrophe. Our gift will see us through. This is how Samson had lived in his earlier day. In fact, we never once saw him pray about the opposition he faced during his life. He simply assumed his brute strength would carry him. In the end, this blind dependence on his gifts failed him. He needed God, and learned to pray as if he meant it.

This shift in dependence makes a huge difference. Let me illustrate. My friend Brett serves in the Navy and is stationed in Hawaii. He loves football. In fact, he has told me that he has a hard time waiting for the NFL Monday-night football telecast. In Hawaii, because of the time difference, the Monday-night game is played in midafternoon, but the local TV station delays the telecast until 6:30 P.M. When the Rams—Brett's favorite team—are playing he can't wait. He'll listen to the radio broadcast live. Then, because the Rams are his favorite team, he'll watch them later on TV too. If he knows the Rams have won, it influences how he watches the game on TV. If they fumble or throw an interception, it's not a problem. He'll think, *That's bad, but it's OK. In the end, we win.*

What a vivid illustration of how we as believers should live. We know the final outcome of all things. We win in the end. Jesus said, "In this world you will have trouble. But take heart! I have overcome the world" (John 16:33). When we lean on God, we can face opposition with absolute trust, knowing that all will turn out well.

3. Samson focused on a cause worth dying for. In Samson's final pivotal prayer, he is focused. But that's not strange. He was often focused in his life. This time, however, he was focused on the right issue. He wasn't focused on Delilah or on some game he was playing with the Philistines. He was focused on avenging his own and his peoples' losses. He was focused on restoring God's people to freedom. God's name had been blasphemed. He'd had enough.

I find it interesting to check my motives when I pray. What's my real mission? Samson was distracted many times in his life. I have been too. When I face opposition, though, things seem to change. Like Paul sitting in a Roman prison awaiting a trial, we'll fight, faint, flee . . . or focus. Paul was able to see how God could use even his imprisonment to help him accomplish his mission.

In 1990 I faced one of the scariest moments of my life. Serving with Youth for Christ in New Zealand, I was in a plane crash on the South Island. Four of us were in a single-engine Piper plane that crash-landed in a field. All of us were injured, but we all lived. As I lay on the grassy field waiting for medical attention, I knew I had to maintain God's perspective. I didn't blame Him for the crash, but I also knew He could accomplish something if I kept perspective. I prayed for God to accomplish His goal.

Because I was the least injured of the three, I stayed behind as my three companions were rushed to the emergency unit. I was taken to a bed nearby to rest and nurse my wounds. Within an hour I saw what God was up to. There was a knock at the door in the home where I was sleeping. When my host opened the door, there on the front porch was the news crew from the two national television networks. Evidently the plane crash was the number-one news story of the day!

They asked if anyone who had seen the plane crash was available to be interviewed. My host responded, "We have someone here who was actually in the plane crash!" Within moments they awakened me and escorted me out to the back lawn. They leaned me up against a tree and said, "Tell us what happened."

I don't know about you, but that sounds like an invitation to me! I proceeded to share about the divine protection we experienced, the saving grace of Jesus, and how to build a relationship with God! What's more, as we watched the interview on TV, the networks ran the whole story with very few edits. I got to share Christ with three million New Zealanders on both the evening and the late-night news broadcasts. What a divine reversal of a potential tragedy. My prison became a pulpit. I remembered Paul's words while he was in prison. We pray pivotally when we capture God's highest purposes and make them the focus of our prayer.

4. Samson no longer made survival his goal. In the end, Samson was willing to lose his life over the cause he prayed for. It was a "just this once" kind of request to God. I'm not suggesting that every prayer we pray must be a commitment to physically die. On the other hand, I am saying that surrender is a must.

The need to survive—"hold the fort," hang on, hold out, get by, stay alive, maintain—keeps more people from really living than anything else. If I cling to my desire to survive, the enemy (or opposition) has me right where he wants me. I'm playing defense. But when I can say, "I no longer have to survive," I free up all kinds of energy, resources, faith, and freedom to take risks. When I'm prepared to take risks, I'm in position to play offense and win. Maybe this is what Jesus meant when He said, "Whoever loses his life for my sake will find it" (Matt. 10:39).

Sooner or later all mature Christians must die to the self. This death to self is painful, but it settles all kinds of battles not worth fighting for. We no longer sweat the small stuff—or worry about it in our prayer times.

Harold Kohn wrote, "Brooks become crooked from taking the path of least resistance. So do people."[6] When we die to ourselves, we face reality for the first time. We remove what clouds our views of what God is really doing. We feel broken, almost wounded—because "self" is what we've leaned on for so long. But this broken-ness becomes our saving grace. "Where a man's wound is," writes Robert Bly, "is where his genius will be. Wherever the wound appears in our psyche, that is exactly where we will give our major gift to the community."[7]

This is because we are finally on God's track. God's point was never to help us turn over a new leaf—but to give us a new life. He wants nothing short of inward revolution. I love the way C. S. Lewis put it: "When I invited Jesus into my life, I thought he would put up some wallpaper and hang a few pictures. But he started knocking out walls and adding rooms. I said, 'I was expecting a nice cottage.' But He said, 'I'm making a palace in which to live.'"[8]

ONE LAST THOUGHT

Albert Einstein once said, "Great spirits have always encountered vio-lent opposition from mediocre minds."[9] In times of opposition, it may be your time to shine. Perhaps this is the time for you to take a stand, to hold fast to a conviction in the midst of a storm of adversity. Perhaps the difference you are making is the reason for the opposition you face. Don't give up. Seek God's strength.

Thomas Watson, chairman of the board at IBM, once said, "Strangely, the expounders of many of the great new ideas of history were frequently considered on the lunatic fringe for some or all their lives. If one stands up and is counted, from time to time one may get knocked down. But remember this: a man flattened by an opponent can get up again. A man flattened by conformity stays down for good."[10]

CLOSING PRAYER

Pivotal Prayer
When You're Facing Opposition

Dear Lord, I feel like I'm surrounded by enemies.
I feel drained by the adversity.
I want to throw in the towel one minute,
and fight back the next.
Help me gain Your big-picture perspective on the issues.
Help me to lean on You,
not on my own gifts and strengths.
Help me to focus on what really matters,
and to care more about Your name than mine.
I trust You to take care of me.
Amen.

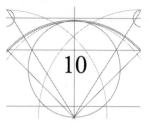

10

PIVOTAL PRAYING WHEN YOU NEED TO LET GO

(JOHN HULL)

Gordon Wilson and his daughter were buried in rubble after the bomb's blast. For many, it was just another explosion in Northern Ireland. But not for Gordon and his special girl. This time it happened in a public parade. Gordon held his daughter's hand as she died.

In a nationally televised interview in 1987, Gordon was asked his feelings toward the bombers. Did he hold any ill will? Gordon replied, "I shall forgive them tonight and every night. God forgave them, for they don't know what they do."[1]

There's an old story about a man walking through a section of woods unknown to him. To his surprise, he comes upon a steep drop and falls. In desperation, the man reaches out and grabs hold of a root sticking out of the side of the cliff and hangs there for dear life. An angel comes to him and says, "Do you believe I can help you?" The man says, "Yes!" Then the angel inquires, "Do you believe I will help you?" And again the man replies, "Yes!" The angel looks at him intently and says, "If you believe that I can and will help you, *let go!*"

Prayerfully letting go of wrongs or injustices caused by others is hard. But if we're to experience God's best for our lives, we have to

learn to let go. Letting go and allowing God to work toward healing our wounds will bring peace of mind and clarity of conscience.
Letting go means forgiving. Plain and simple. The Greek word for
forgive means "to let go." The act of forgiveness can be processed
and released through prayer—pivotal prayer.

It is a common human dilemma for even praying people to have
trouble forgiving others. Imagine how difficult it was for Corrie ten
Boom. As a younger woman, she helped Jews escape the Nazis during World War II. Ten Boom, a Dutch woman, along with her sister
Betsie, were caught and sent to a concentration camp. During that
horrific experience, Betsie died.

Corrie devoted the rest of her life to sharing with others the
power of Christ. One day her own theology was greatly tested when,
following a talk she had given, one of the camp soldiers who had been
so brutal to her and her sister approached her. After the war he had
personally experienced God's forgiveness and wanted to shake her
hand as an act of friendship and reconciliation. Suddenly, every
painful thing she had experienced years before in the camp flooded
her emotions. She thought of her sister's death, the inhumanity
toward those in the concentration camp, the injustice and the shame
of it all.

Silently she offered this pivotal prayer: "Jesus, I cannot forgive
him. Grant me Your power to forgive." Then she took his hand and
greeted him. Later she recounted, "From my shoulder, along my arm
and through my hand, a current seemed to pass from me to him,
while in my heart sprang a love for this stranger that almost overwhelmed me."[2]

While taking his hand, Corrie ten Boom actually "let go." That
level of forgiveness can indeed be overwhelming. Overwhelmed by
the love and forgiveness of the God who had forgiven her, she let go
of the hurt, the oppression, the loss, and the pain. It was Corrie who
famously observed, years later, that followers of Jesus "hold all things

loosely." This includes, she would say, all our grudges, our vindictiveness, and our thirst for revenge.

If we really desire God's best for our lives, we must embrace a greater understanding of what it means to pray pivotally for those who have hurt us, and work toward peace with them, letting go of what they have done to us.

As Christians we often find it hard to be at peace in a secularly minded culture where there is constant opposition, challenge, and even hostility to our core values and beliefs. The natural tendency within most of us is to stir things up—to fight, shout back, mobilize, and get in people's faces. But there are times when the best approach may be to calm down—bring peace.

PUTTING OUT FIRES

A handful of volunteer firefighters in a tiny town in Texas were accused of setting more than forty destructive fires in their community. When caught, they reported that they had simply been bored. "We had nothing else to do," they said. "We just wanted to see the red lights flashing and hear the bells clanging and the sirens roaring."

The job of firefighters is to put *out* fires, not to start them. The job of Christians is to help resolve conflict, not to start it. Jesus said "Blessed are the peacemakers" (Matt. 5:9). He did not say, "Blessed are those who are void of principles," but rather "Blessed are the peacemakers." This means we are called to pursue peace with others while taking a stand, fighting injustice, and hating sin.

The apostle Paul said that it's possible to be a Christian and live at peace with others. He wrote to Timothy that Christians have the capacity to "live peaceful and quiet lives in all godliness and holiness" (1 Tim. 2:2).

Where, what, or for whom do you need to pray, so that you, too, may live a peaceable existence? Is it personal revenge that you're seeking? Or is it a lawsuit? Maybe it's slander or rejection you've received and you're wanting to give it back. Are you angry and bitter toward someone? Then it's time to pray. It's time to let go.

Is there a war raging in your soul? Have you personally declared war on someone else? Have you started some fires, or are you building on fires that others have started? This is not God's best for your life.

God's best is for you to live at peace, even toward the person who has hurt you the most. God's best for your life is that you are able to pray for the person who's wounded you—to say "God bless this person, this person's family, and all this person does." This isn't easy, but it is possible for those who have experienced the authentic forgiveness of Jesus Christ. Sometimes we need to remember that Jesus didn't hang on the cross one minute longer for our enemies than He did for us.

You're probably thinking about who it is that's wounded you. Maybe you were used and abused as a child. Who out there is still denying responsibility for the havoc that he or she thrust upon your life? God wants you to have peace toward that person. This doesn't necessarily mean that you'll be reconciled with that individual; and it certainly doesn't mean that he or she will be exonerated for what was done to you. What it does mean is this: You forgive this person, you let go of the past, and you get on with the rest of your life. Speaker and author Beth Moore has said that to forgive doesn't mean that everything will be right in that relationship. It means that we will be right before God.

LAUNCHING FORGIVENESS

Prayer is the best place to launch forgiveness. Prayer molds us so that we can experience forgiveness. Does this mean that when you pray, all the pain of the past will go away? No. There may always be scars from the relationship. But through prayer and forgiveness that scar can become a brilliant reminder of the grace of God.

A precocious young boy took a hammer and drove a nail into a fine piece of his mother's antique furniture, creating an unsightly hole. When the youngster's father discovered what he had done, he scolded him firmly. Crying, the boy said, "But Daddy, I thought you loved me!" The father wisely responded, "I do love you. But the hole is still there."

There may be some holes in your life where there is incredible suffering for injustices done toward you. You've experienced God's grace and forgiveness through Christ, but the holes are still there. Prayerful forgiveness is the spackle that will begin to fill in those holes and start to recreate a different kind of person—not only on the outside, but on the inside too.

A single mom, with some holes in her life that needed filling, experienced such prayer and forgiveness one memorable evening. This woman was part of a "prayer walk" ministry at her church, in which the members would go in pairs into neighboring areas to pray specifically for the people living in those houses.

One evening she arrived late at the meeting, only to discover that the others had already left on their assignments. She and another latecomer teamed up, grabbed one of the remaining prayer maps, and headed out the door. They drove to the designated neighborhood where they were to pray, but as they turned down a certain street, she began to cry.

"I can't pray there!" she said.

"Why not?" asked her partner.

"That's the house where my husband lives . . . with his mistress!"

Later that evening, when the group regathered to talk about their experiences, this is what she shared:

We stayed in the car a long time, and I gave every reason I could why I should not have to pray there. My friend did not say much, except to cry with me and pray for me. When I'd given every reason I could, I realized God was speaking to me. "I've brought you here," He said. That was all. But that was enough—we both knew it. What else could we do? Tonight, I was going out to pray that people in bondage would be set free in Jesus. I learned that God also wanted to set me free. I forgave my husband and the woman, and I prayed for them. And tonight I was set free. I pray they will come to know this same wonderful freedom.[3]

This kind of pivotal praying empowers us to let go, to forgive, and to get on with the rest of our lives. Take a moment and consider some experiences or issues you have difficulty forgiving or letting go. It is essential that we forgive those who have deeply wounded us, and that we let go of past pain if we're to grow in the grace and knowledge of the Lord Jesus.

STEPHEN'S FORGIVENESS

Stephen, an early follower of Jesus, was the first martyr for the Christian faith. His death marks a memorable moment in the life of the early church.

Stephen was one of the first persons to be placed in a leadership position in the church. He had a sterling reputation as a man who exhibited great faith, wisdom, power, and grace. Even under great stress and criticism "his face was like the face of an angel" (Acts 6:15).

Stephen was arrested and tried for teaching that Jesus was the Christ and Savior of Israel. Before the Sanhedrin—the equivalent of the Supreme Court in America—Stephen boldly defended his beliefs about Christ and about the spiritual state of those who did not embrace the teachings of Jesus (Acts 7). He told the court, "You have betrayed and murdered him [Christ]" (7:52).

Stephen's accusers were enraged by what he said. They dragged him out of the courtroom and onto the street, where they stoned him to death.

As he was dying, Stephen prayed for his tormentors. Amazingly, he didn't ask for justice to be done toward them. Instead he prayed words similar to what Jesus said when He was on the cross: "Lord, do not hold this sin against them." Then Stephen died.

John MacArthur has observed, "How can anyone who has been so grievously wounded forgive so freely and so quickly? . . . Apart from Christ, it is well nigh impossible." Then he reminds us that because "we have the mind of Christ (1 Cor. 2:16), the Holy Spirit indwells and empowers us. Therefore, Christians are capable of superhuman acts of forgiveness." MacArthur continues, "My own brother-in-law went to jail to express his forgiveness and offer the forgiveness of God to the drug addict who murdered his son in a marketplace holdup."[4]

Sometimes we hear the expression, "Get over yourself!" And we should. But it's also important at times to "Get *outside* yourself!" There are times when we need to get beyond our nearsighted view of the world and see people the way Jesus does—from His perspective.

This is exactly what Stephen did. He was able to see his enemies through the eyes of Jesus, eyes of compassion. When he was arrested, tried, and falsely accused, Stephen got outside himself and looked at what caused people to pick up stones and hurl them with the intention to hurt, even to kill.

God's love did not end with Stephen. His love was extended to Stephen's most hostile enemies. It included the one who threw the stones the hardest and the one who was deadly accurate with his toss.

In that crowd of persecutors was a man named Saul (Acts 8:1). Later, that same man—the man who had organized this persecution of Stephen—encountered the forgiveness of Jesus Christ and became one of His most devout followers: the apostle Paul.

SEEING THROUGH JESUS' EYES

It is remarkable what happens when we begin to see people through the eyes of Jesus. Seeing things from Jesus' perspective enables us to forgive others in Christ.

Christ has forgiven us. Who are we, not to forgive others? Jesus made it clear that if we don't forgive those who have wronged us, our prayers will go unheard: "And when you stand praying, if you hold anything against anyone, forgive him, so that your Father in heaven may forgive you your sins" (Mark 11:25–26).

Think about it: Are you willing to allow future pivotal prayers to go unanswered because you insist on holding a grudge?

In Christ we are given the ability to forgive others. This is not a myth. This is not a television program that will eventually be canceled or a movie that fails at the box office. This is an eternal truth. We have in Christ the ability to forgive others. And our prayer can serve as a laboratory where we gain wisdom as to how to apply this forgiveness.

Christ's forgiveness is why Gordon Wilson could forgive the terrorists who took his daughter's life. It's why Corrie ten Boom could forgive her sister's oppressors. And it's why a deserted wife and mom could forgive her unfaithful husband and his mistress. These people were willing to let go.

Helmut Thielicke shares the following story:

I heard once of a child who was raising a frightful cry because he had shoved his hand into the opening of a very expensive Chinese vase and then couldn't pull it out again. Parents and neighbors tugged with might and main on the child's arm, with the poor creature howling out loud all the while. Finally, there was nothing left to do but break the beautiful, expensive vase. And then as the mournful heap of shards lay there, it became clear why the child had been so hopelessly stuck. His little fist grasped a paltry penny which he had spied in the bottom of the vase and which he, in childish ignorance, would not let go.[5]

Whatever your hurt, it's time to unclench your fist and release what's been plaguing you. It's time to let go.

When you pivotally pray to let go, asking God to help you release those who have hurt you or are hurting you now, you'll experience the first stages of a fresh walk with God. Your hands will be free to help others who are hurting, and your soul will be free to live in peace toward God and those around you.

CLOSING PRAYER

A Pivotal Prayer for Letting Go

Father, I am angry at _____.
Praying for _____ is very hard.
I am hurt by what this person has done,
but I don't want to live my life in bitterness.
So, I lift _____ before You and ask
that You will change my heart.
Help me to forgive.
Help me to let go.[6]
Amen.

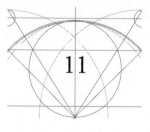

11

PIVOTAL PRAYING WHEN YOU'RE IN OVER YOUR HEAD

(TIM ELMORE)

During my freshman year of college, in the spring of 1979, my friend Dave walked into my dorm room with news that a local tennis club was sponsoring a professional match in town. When I failed to show much enthusiasm, he informed me that tennis star Jimmy Conners would be playing. I loved Jimmy Conners.

The two of us began to talk about how much fun it would be not only to see Conners play, but to talk to him and get his autograph. We decided it would be worth it to try to get tickets. When Dave left my room, I continued to ponder the thought of meeting Conners. The more I thought about it, the more I felt a burden not only to talk to him but to share Christ with him. After all, he needed the Lord just like we all do, and I had no idea how many Christian friends Jimmy Conners had. Before long, this became my personal mission. I began praying for an opportunity for Dave and me to share the gospel with Conners while he was in town.

The day of the match, Dave and I sneaked downstairs to the locker-room area. We waited for Jimmy to come out. We were prepared with a small Bible and with personal, handwritten tracts on building a relationship with Christ. To make a long story short, Jimmy walked through the door right where we were standing. Staring us in the eye was one of the greatest tennis players of his day. Dave and I both gulped, said hi, and told him we wanted to give him something.

He was courteous, but said we should leave it for him at the front desk or with his wife, since he was on his way to a match. We agreed, then attempted to encourage him to play well. Fortunately we were able to do what we'd promised. We left a copy of the tract at the front desk and later left the tracts with his wife. It was a spiritual adventure for two college students that day.

Little did I know that that episode was the beginning of a larger adventure for me. During my college years God began to open up doors of opportunity for me to share the gospel with a variety of celebrities. Each experience became a new lesson in trust and obedience. Over the years I have spoken with athletes such as Bill Walton, Steve Garvey, and Roberto Alomar, as well as musicians such as the members of KISS, Elton John, the Beach Boys, Ozzie Osbourne, Styx, Olivia Newton-John, John Ford Coley, John Denver, and others.

It was during those early days that God taught me about "pivotal praying when you're in over your head." I learned what it means to be burdened for a need. I learned to pray about that need until I identified with it. Ultimately I learned to take the appropriate risks to meet it.

In every case, I encountered some obstacle that reminded me I couldn't do this thing on my own—that I was in over my head. The night I spoke to the members of the heavy-metal band KISS, a bouncer the size of Goliath was my obstacle. He eventually helped me get to them, and I had a genuine conversation about Christ with all of them.

When I shared with Olivia Newton-John, the backstage guards told me I couldn't stay there unless I had a backstage pass or was willing to pay a little bribe. As I walked out, a friend working backstage opened the door for me.

The night I spoke to the Beach Boys, I wasn't sure I was at the right hotel. Just as I was about to walk away, in came their limousines. I got to talk to each of them.

My longest conversation was with Tommy Shaw and Dennis DeYoung of Styx, even though there were crowds of women around them in the hotel lobby. In each instance God opened up the door as I learned to lean on Him and pray a pivotal prayer. My lesson every time was seeing the difference between *giving up* and *surrendering*. I knew I couldn't give up—I felt I was sharing with these influential people as an act of obedience. However, I had to surrender my own agenda, my own presumptions about how it would work and how I could maneuver my way in and make it all happen.

You may or may not relate to my story. But I bet everyone reading this book has experienced an occasion when you just didn't have the wisdom, the strength, the influence, or the courage to face what was in front of you. You felt out of control. Perhaps you felt paralyzed. You were at the end of your own rope, without the tools to pull it off.

Maybe you can't get pregnant. Maybe you have a chronic disease. Maybe it's a strained relationship. In such situations, what do you do? Do you *react* or *respond?* Consider this: When a doctor prescribes medication to you, your body will either react or respond to it. If it reacts, your body has adjusted negatively. If it responds, your body has adjusted positively and cooperated with the medicine. When you're in over your head, reacting simply means you play defense. You reach down into your own arsenal and try to make something happen. You attempt to pull yourself up by your own bootstraps and do it yourself. Responding, on the other hand, means you play offense. You pause and consider God's role in this venture. Then you partner with Him in your action.

It is human to panic and react when we're in over our heads. As Americans, we've been taught to make it on our own. Be a pioneer. Welfare is for sissies. Stay in control. We must learn to *respond* in those pivotal moments. I even believe that's why God allows circumstances when we're in over our heads.

Reflect for a moment on some stories from the life of Jesus and His disciples. Do you remember when they were out in the boat in the middle of a storm? It was a violent storm and they were in over their heads. Jesus was asleep. The disciples were bailing water out as fast as they could. They were reacting. Finally they approached Jesus. They woke Him up and He quieted the storm.

Do you see what happened here? While the disciples were reacting, Jesus rested. But when they trusted Him to address the storm, He took control and they could rest.

We see this equation time and time again. Remember the story about how Jesus walked on the water to where His disciples were in a boat on the Sea of Galilee? Once again, they were in a terrifying storm. The Scripture goes on to say, "And seeing them straining at the oars, for the wind was against them, at about the fourth watch of the night, He came to them, walking on the sea; and He intended to pass by them" (Mark 6:48 NASB).

Did you notice that last sentence? Jesus intended to pass by them! Was it because He didn't care for them? Absolutely not. He saw that they were again in over their heads, and in walking by, He dared them to surrender to Him.

Luke tells a similar story. After Jesus' resurrection, the disciples still didn't understand what was happening. So in disguise Jesus approached two of them on the road to Emmaus. They didn't recognize Him. He explained the Scriptures to them, and "as they approached the village to which they were going, Jesus acted as if He were going farther" (Luke 24:28). I think we see a pattern here! Once again, Jesus was silently beckoning them to engage Him when they were in over their heads. When He does this, He doesn't come in as a mere helper, but as Master.

Ben Patterson, dean of the chapel at Hope College, writes that "sometimes God provokes you because you need the fight."[1] I agree. P. T. Forsyth writes in *The Soul of Prayer,* "Cast yourself into his arms not to be caressed but to wrestle with him. He loves that holy war. He may . . . lift you from your feet. But it will be to lift you from earth, and set you in the heavenly places which are theirs who fight the good fight and lay hold of God as their eternal life."[2]

I believe the purpose of the pivotal moment when we are in over our heads is to provoke a good fight. Really! Sometimes only a good fight will lead to genuine surrender. Like Jacob's wrestling the angel of the Lord all night, we must take God to the mat, not because of His reluctance, but because of our tendency toward self-sufficiency. Once Jacob fought all night, he was able to acknowledge who he was before God. Once the angel pinned him to the ground, and Jacob got honest about who he was and what he wanted, the angel said, "You . . . have overcome" (Gen. 32:28). It was Jacob who needed the fight that night, not the angel.

When Ben Patterson discovered that his son had Tourette's syndrome, he entered a battle with God and with himself that lasted for years. He struggled with thoughts of failure as a dad, and with not knowing how to deal with a disease that caused his little boy to twitch uncontrollably, obsessively repeat obscenities, and to experience random facial contortions. It scared both the boy and his parents.

Over the months, Ben made some wild discoveries about how God acts when we are in over our heads. He concluded that God is able to handle both his anger and his passionate and bewildering cries for answers. It is all part of the holy fight. Ben concluded that through such circumstances God nudges us, draws us, or jolts us into prayer. Suddenly we are faced with something that challenges our deepest securities, knocks away all our props, and violates everything we ever believed to be true about God and His ways.

President Franklin Roosevelt was weary of mindless small talk at

White House receptions. So he decided to try something, just to see if anyone was really listening to what he said. As he shook hands with folks, he would smile and say, "I murdered my grandmother this morning." With but one exception, the people would smile back and say something like, "You're doing a great job," or "How lovely." The exception was a foreign diplomat who said, "I'm sure she had it coming to her."

If from time to time we're shocked by something God says and does, we haven't been listening. How many of our prayers are like White House receptions? Does God feel about them as Roosevelt did?

"I read somewhere that the ability of a couple to express anger well can do wonders for their sex life," Ben Patterson observes. "It's true. It seems there can be no warm fuzzies without the opposite. Both anger and tenderness are forms of passion. So it is with prayer. God doesn't mind our anger. He even relishes it, if it drives us to Him instead of away from Him."[3] Better an outburst to God than a theologically correct—but spiritually dry—prayer. Routine, stale, tired prayers do little for our relationship with God.

No wonder we can get so bored with prayer. God is bored too. He wants to engage our hearts, not just our brains. We often engage Him best when we are in over our heads. C. S. Lewis once said, "God whispers to us in our pleasures, speaks to us in our labor, but screams at us in our pain: it is His megaphone to rouse a deaf world."[4] And why does He rouse us? I believe He wants us to wake up from our complacency and wrestle with Him over issues that matter most, to help us refocus.

The depth of God's person and plan is unsearchable. If our faith in God cannot be bewildered or perplexed, then we have domesticated Him. We simply have faith in some religious system—not in the limitless God. Consider this warning from Andrew Murray:

"Beware in your prayer, above everything, of limiting God, not only by unbelief, but by fancying that you know what He can do."[5]

TWENTY-SIX GUARDS

I believe we are in over our heads more often than we realize. A missionary on furlough told this true story while preaching to his home church in Michigan. While serving a small field hospital in central Africa, he traveled by bike to a nearby city every two weeks to get supplies. The trip took two days, with an overnight camping stop halfway there. On one of these journeys, he arrived in the city and observed two men fighting, one of whom was seriously injured. He treated him, then traveled two days back to his village, camping overnight without incident.

Two weeks later he returned to the city and met the man he had treated. This man told the missionary, "Some friends and I followed you into the jungle, knowing you would camp overnight. We planned to kill you, then take your money and drugs. But when we saw the twenty-six guards surrounding you, we left you alone." The missionary laughed and told the man he had been alone that night. The man insisted, "No, sir, I wasn't the only one who saw the guards around you that night. My five friends saw them too. We all counted them and decided not to attack."

At this point in the missionary's sermon, a man in the congregation jumped up and interrupted the missionary. He asked what day and time this had happened. The missionary told him, and the man smiled.

"On the night of your incident in Africa, it was morning here and I was preparing to go play golf. I had an urge to pray for you. In fact, the urging of the Lord was so strong that, instead of playing golf, I called men in this church to meet with me here in the sanctuary and pray for you. Would all those men who met with me on that day stand up?"

The men who had met together to pray that day stood up. The missionary wasn't so concerned with who they were—he was too busy counting how many he saw. There were twenty-six!

Thank God that when we're in over our heads, He isn't.

WHAT WE LEARN FROM PAUL AND THE SONS OF SCEVA

We almost got to meet her.

In the summer of 1997, our team from EQUIP ministries laid plans to go to India. We scheduled a meeting with Mother Teresa. In August, she passed away. I never got to greet her or thank her for all she had accomplished in Calcutta, and around the world.

Fortunately, we decided to visit her ministry anyway. The "Sisters of Charity" was gracious enough to let us visit and hear the story of how it all began. Teresa had been a teacher in a Catholic school for girls in Calcutta. As she looked out the window each day, she'd see the faces of impoverished, dying people who needed help. Eventually she asked the school leadership if she could leave her teaching post and serve the poor. When they insisted she stay, she explained to them that she saw Jesus in the faces of the poor. Finally she talked a priest into allowing her to go and minister to the poor. She left the school with no moral support or funding. She began her work by picking up limp bodies of those who were dying, so they could at least die with some dignity.

Quickly, Mother Teresa became overwhelmed by the volume of needs. There were thousands of desperate people. Trucks would drive through the streets in the morning to pick up the corpses of those who had died during the night. In addition, as a Catholic working in a Hindu culture she received little help or acceptance from others. Teresa felt so small and so alone. And she was.

But this drove her to her knees, and she wrestled in prayer. She wanted to make a difference in that huge city, but her belief was: If you can't *pray* a door open, don't *pry* it open. Perhaps she didn't know how pivotal her prayer for an open door was. She soon had the opportunity to serve in a most unusual way. A local monk became ill. According to Hindu belief, the outcome of his illness was to be left to fate; after all, they didn't want to mess with his future or his path of reincarnation. So he was left to die. When Mother Teresa saw him, she determined to help him out. Under her care he recovered, and later he became the doorway for many to accept her presence and ministry in Calcutta. Today, although she is gone, her legacy lives on. Her movement has mushroomed to become the largest order of its kind.

There are a number of great lessons to be learned when we are in over our head. Many of those lessons drive us to pray in that pivotal moment, just like in Mother Teresa's case. We see the value of being small. We actually pray better then. We're like the boy in G. K. Chesterton's parable who was granted a wish: he could be tiny or he could be a giant. The wish was granted. At first being a giant was great fun. The Pacific was a wading pool. The Rockies—a dirt-bike course. But after a while life was boring. Everything was beneath him. There wasn't much to do or anyone to do it with. It was lonely being a giant. Had he chosen to be tiny, his backyard would have been the Brazilian forest; his sand box, the Sahara. He could have spent a lifetime exploring the attic. What fun he could have had with a sled and a half gallon of ice cream! Life is more interesting for the small, the lowly.

This is what Scripture teaches us when it comes to pivotal praying. It is more interesting because there is room for God in it. When I think back to my early days of ministry, I shudder. I started as a pastor when I was nineteen years old. I knew very little about church work. I had an opportunity to go back and talk with those wonderful people who endured me in Sand Springs, Oklahoma. Even though I almost want to apologize to them for the things I did and said, I realize, now, that somehow God *did* use me, even though I was in over my head. Today, I have to remember that God is saying "What makes you think you're not in over your head now?"

PAUL'S THORN

The fact is, we are all small whether we know it or not. We must choose to see that we are small. This was the lesson Paul learned, more than nineteen hundred years ago. Part of his story is recorded in 2 Corinthians: "And because of the surpassing greatness of the revelations, for this reason, to keep me from exalting myself, there was given to me a thorn in the flesh, a messenger of Satan to buffet me—to keep me from exalting myself" (12:7 NASB).

It is clear Paul understood why the thorn was present. It wasn't from God—it was from the enemy. It was some messenger from Satan; Paul called it a thorn in his flesh. Yet God was able to use this awful thing for one primary purpose: to remind Paul he was small. He was in over his head. He couldn't pull off his life purpose on his own. You see, Paul had received more divine revelation than probably any apostle during his day. Certainly he wrote more Scripture than any other apostle. It would have been easy for him to think he could handle anything. He was smart. He was gifted. He was determined. He knew his mission, and he had a strategy for pulling it off. So, God used a thorn from the enemy to force him to wrestle: "Concerning this, I entreated the Lord three times that it might depart from me. And He has said to me, 'My grace is sufficient for you, for power is perfected in weakness'" (12:8-9a NASB).

Wow. Paul wrestled with God, and God responded with grace. I think it is easy for us to misread this story. God's answer wasn't, "No—I won't help you with this thorn." God actually did give him just the answer he needed: grace. Grace is what we need most when we are in over our head—and we are always in over our head! The grace that it took to save us and get us to heaven is the same grace we need daily to live the life we were intended to live. I remember when my kids were young. I would take them to swim in my parents' pool. They loved it. When I'd take them into the deep end, however, I would tease them about how deep the water was. I told them there was no way they could touch the bottom of the pool. Inevitably, they'd get scared and want to go back to the shallow end. What they failed to realize was that both ends were over their head! It mattered little where they were—they needed help. Paul had been given this reminder of grace because it was too easy to lean on his own great gifts rather than God's great grace. It kept Paul in a posture of humility. The one requirement to receive grace is humility: "God opposes the proud, but gives grace to the humble" (James 4:6).

Once again, God wanted Paul to engage in a fight. It wasn't an outward fight but an inward one. All of us need to wrestle like this. The wrestling will eventually break us of our self-life: self-sufficiency, self-promotion and self-righteousness. I love C. S. Lewis' account of his early days as a Christian. He was so full of pride he didn't want to associate with other Christians. He wrote:

> When I first became a Christian . . . I thought that I could do it on my own . . . and not go to churches . . . I disliked very much their hymns, which I considered to be fifth rate poems set to sixth rate music. But as I went on I saw the great merit of it. I came up against different people of quite different outlooks and different education, and then gradually my conceit just began peeling off. I realized the hymns (which were just sixth rate music) were, nevertheless, being sung with devotion and benefit by an old saint in elastic-side boots in the opposite pew, and then you realize that you aren't fit to clean those boots.[6]

The Apostle Paul may not have gotten the answer he anticipated, but he got the answer that could benefit him the most. He was in over his head—and he needed grace. He also recognized the only way he could get grace was to assume the posture of humility. His conclusion makes all kind of sense: "Most gladly, therefore, I will rather boast about my weaknesses, that the power of Christ may dwell in me. Therefore, I am well content with weaknesses . . . for when I am weak, then I am strong" (12:9b-10 NASB).

A PIVOTAL PROBLEM

Most of us agree with Paul's conclusion but have a difficult time living it out. To relish in our weaknesses—to be content with them— that's tough. But that's how we get the grace to face the times we're in over our head.

This is a lesson the seven sons of Sceva never learned. In Acts 19:13-17 we read their story. They were the sons of a Jewish chief priest. They saw Paul operating in this powerful grace and performing miracles—and they wanted a piece of the action. One day they met a man who was horribly demonized. He was at the mercy of an evil spirit. So they flippantly marched over to him and tried to exorcise the spirit. In fact, the Scripture quotes exactly what they said to the demon in an attempt to deliver the man: "I adjure you by Jesus, whom Paul preaches" (Acts 19:13 NASB).

They had plugged into the right formula. They used the powerful name of Jesus to cast this demon out. What they failed to recognize was the grace factor. In humility, Paul experienced healings, deliverances, and other miracles (Acts 19:11-12). All these boys wanted was to experience the same supernatural wonders, minus the humility. It didn't happen: "And the evil spirit answered and said to them, 'I recognize Jesus, and I know Paul, but who are you?' And the man, in whom was the evil Spirit, leaped upon them and subdued all of them and overpowered them, so that they fled out of that house naked and wounded" (Acts 19:15-16 NASB).

The problem wasn't in their methods. It lay completely in where they had put their trust. They couldn't see that they were in over their head. In fact, I see four distinct flaws in their failed attempt at a miracle. First, they assumed that their experience was enough to carry them during this encounter. Blinded to their spiritual poverty, they thought they had the tools it took to do the job. Wrong assumption.

Second, they failed to seek God on the issue. We never see them once praying. In fact, from what we can tell, they'd never even met the Lord. They used the name of Jesus "whom Paul preaches." Wrong approach.

Third, they tried to use God to accomplish a goal, using their own methods. They tried to use a formula. Chuck Swindoll once said the greatest sin in the church is our attempt to do God's will, our way. Wrong method.

Fourth, they gave up when their method failed. Instead of surrendering to God and receiving his grace for this "over their head experience," they ran. We don't read that they ever came back. When we find ourselves in over our head and our methods failing, this is designed to get us to drop to our knees in humility and receive grace. The sons of Sceva were humiliated but never got the grace they needed. They wrestled with a demon and gave up. God wanted them to wrestle with Him and surrender.

THE DIFFERENCE

The difference is clear. Paul began to love his weaknesses, because they reminded him he was always in over his head. He had nothing to prove, nothing to lose, nothing to hide. When he stared at huge challenges, he'd boast about God's strength: We've been surrounded and battered by troubles, but we're not demoralized; we're not sure what to do, but we know God knows what to do; we've been spiritually terrorized, but God hasn't left our side; we've been thrown down but we haven't broken" (2 Corinthians 4:8-9 The Message).

I have a niece named Sammi. She is one of my favorite people in the world. When she was barely five years old, she became aware that her mom and dad, Lisa and Craig, were trying to get pregnant. They were having trouble. Like so many couples, they were prepared to be good parents, but all their attempts to have a child were in vain. They had tried just about everything, and at one point just began to ask God what He was up to.

Sammi seemed to understand this concept of pivotal praying when we are in over our head. One night, she told her mom she wanted to pray with her. She folded her hands, and this five-year-old prayed this prayer:

"Dear Father, we just ask you now for a baby. We've tried everything else and don't know what else to do but ask you. My mom really wants a baby and you are the only one who can help. And if the devil gets in your way, just fight him and give us a baby. My mom really loves babies and we really need one. You are the only one who can help us—so thank you for giving us one. We don't want anyone to get killed. If someone does you should take them to the hospital—even if they're bad people—we don't want anyone hurt, we just want a baby, and you are the only one who can help. We love you so much Jesus. Thank you Jesus, Father for the baby because we really need one. We love you, Lord, thank you, in Jesus name we pray. Amen.

I'm no theologian, but I wonder if Lisa and Craig ought to get the baby room ready.

CLOSING PRAYER

A Pivotal Prayer
When You're in over Your Head

Dear Lord,
Thank You for the overwhelming predicament
I am in right now.
It might have been the only slap in the face I would pay
attention to that would get me to depend on You.
Jesus, help me to respond, not react.
Help me to seek You,
not lean on my own understanding here.
And Lord, help me to continue,
and not give up along the way.
You always finish what You start.
In Jesus' name,
Amen.

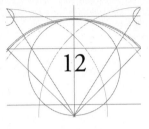

12

PIVOTAL PRAYING WHEN YOU WANT TO QUIT

(JOHN HULL)

A story circulates around the Deep South about a recruiter for Auburn University who annually visits a high-school football coach to check out his players for a possible collegiate gridiron future. As the coach sees the recruiter coming across the practice field, he says, "Well, what kind of player are you looking for this year?"

The Auburn man says, "Well, you know that guy on your team that, when he gets knocked down, he gets back up? And when he gets knocked down again, he gets back up? And when he gets knocked down again, he gets back up?"

The high-school coach says, "Yeah, I know who you're looking for. You want the guy that keeps getting back up."

The recruiter says, "No. I'm looking for the guy that keeps knocking him down."

Life is filled every day with events that can knock us down. We try to get back up, then here comes another blow and we get knocked down again. It's a sobering reminder that we live on a groaning, agonizing planet, stained with sin.

Be it health problems, finances, relationships, accidents, or tragedies, life seems to take some kind of sadistic, misguided delight in knocking us off our feet. Reality sobers us in the recogniation that while today may be "up," the next phone call or E-mail may have the kind of punch that will knock us down and take our breath away.

Such circumstances tempt us to simply throw in the towel and quit. We think, *Enough. I've had it!* We're tempted to curse and walk away. From that point on, we wonder if we should just drop out. After all, getting involved with people creates a lot of this heartache. And so, we ponder, should we quit praying? Maybe even quit God?

How do you bring yourself to go on when the roof is caving in on you at the same time as the floor is falling out from under you and the walls are crashing in? Is God even there?

Knocked-down emotions are not new to God. He doesn't find them strange or uncomfortable. In fact, He can handle them quite well. In biblical times, the psalmist said that sometimes when he prayed, the heavens were like brass. That's kind of an Old Testament way of saying that when he prayed, his words were just bouncing off the heavens just like sound bounces off brass.

THE CULTURE GROANS

What's even more sobering is to realize that there's no guarantee that when things are bad they're going to get better. Followers of Jesus are going to heaven, but we have no ticket that exempts us from the kind of pain that tempts us to quit. In all honesty, if our culture continues the present trend of moving away from moral absolutes, the challenge of being salt and light will become increasingly difficult. The planet groans in pain more and more every day, like a terminal patient. Yet people are seeking solutions from every source imaginable, outside the Great Physician. It's tough out there.

A sixth-grade boy had a paper route in his neighborhood. On his route was a ranch-style house with a carport on the side. Behind the carport and house was a chain-link fence. Inside the fence were two ferocious Dalmatian dogs. These were not the cute and cuddly Dalmatians in the Disney movie, but fierce dogs ready for confrontation.

Every day the boy would pedal his bike by the house and toss a newspaper onto the carport with some degree of hesitancy as the dogs barked. One day he missed his target, tossing the paper through the carport and over the fence, hitting one of the dogs squarely on the head. The dogs, now really upset, used their strong legs to jump over the fence and chase the boy on his bike. Seeing his life flash before his eyes, the boy began to pedal as fast as he could to his nearby house. Jumping off the bike and running into his house, he shouted, "Mommy! Mommy! Help me! Those *damnation* dogs are after me!"

When you read the paper or watch the news, do you sometimes feel as if the dogs of damnation have been set loose on our culture? At an alarming rate in the media and in our country, the graying of what is right from what is wrong and disrespectful rhetoric reflect a society groaning in disillusionment and selfishness. These damnation dogs sometimes just knock us down, and it's tough to get back up.

Some situations are so complicated and overwhelming that we're tempted to just walk away and quit. However, we need to explore what God's up to and what He's trying to teach us in the midst of tough times. At pivotal moments like these, we shouldn't push away from God, but run to Him in prayer.

MOSES DIDN'T QUIT

Moses faced some difficult and shocking circumstances that would test his leadership. Things had gotten so bad while he left his people to be alone with God that the fledgling nation's relationship with God was in jeopardy. Would he quit or stay at it?

Moses had just received the Law from God (Ex. 31:18). The Law, built on the Ten Commandments, would become bedrock truth and anchor Israel's future for generations to come. It was God's design for human conduct in a fallen, oftentimes inhuman world. At the core of the Law was the worship of the one true God.

However, when Moses returned from his intimate conversations with God, he discovered that the dogs of damnation had been set loose among the people. Descending from Mount Sinai, Moses witnessed the people in sordid idol worship and debauchery.

Some leaders might have quit—just thrown in the towel. But not Moses. While up on the mountain, he had heard God express His love for Israel. He had received a vision of what God wanted that nation to become. So in righteous anger he quickly acted by destroying their idols of worship and ordering that approximately three thousand unrepentant people be executed for their idolatry. He reorganized the leadership structure and brought back some sense of order to the culture.

Having taken these actions, Moses went before God concerning His long-term intentions for the Israelites.

> The LORD replied to Moses, "Whoever has sinned against me I will blot out of my book. Now go, lead the people to the place I spoke of, and my angel will go before you. However, when the time comes for me to punish, I will punish them for their sin. (EX. 32:33–34)

With dogged determination, Moses reminded God of His love for the Israelites and of the promises He had made to them. Moses pleaded with God to do justice toward their wrongdoing, but at the same time implored God not to leave their presence, as God was threatening to do.

Moses wouldn't quit. He begged God not to give up on the Israelites. And God didn't. Arguably, He wouldn't have anyway, but that's up to theologians to debate. What we do know is that Moses didn't quit, even though quitting would have been understandable.

Instead, in dependence and desperation, Moses called out to God and reminded Him of His promises. And God, in return, gave Moses the strength to carry on.

What was it that gave Moses the ability to press on in the midst of difficulty? What gave him the confidence to continue in prayer when his leadership and the young nation of Israel had been knocked down? How did he get back up?

Moses wasn't like the ten spies in Numbers 13 who wanted to call it quits because the circumstances seemed so overwhelming. Instead, Moses pressed on. What was it that motivated him?

MOSES KNEW GOD CARED ABOUT HIM

Moses had a foundational truth etched deep in his heart. He knew that, regardless of how bad things got, God cared about him. The apostle Peter knew this truth as well, and encouraged God's people to embrace it: "Cast all your anxiety on him because he cares for you" (1 Peter 5:7).

For years Moses had been in God's care. When he was a baby, at a time when other Hebrew babies were being killed, his mother saw to it that Moses would be looked after—an early sign of God's care in his life. When he struggled with whether or not he had the ability to lead the Hebrews out of slavery and captivity, God was there for him. When he had blown it as a leader and had become overly burdened with administrative responsibilities, God sent someone to offer advice and help him change some things for the better. God cared. To know someone cares, especially God, is vital to our spiritual health and serves as a tremendous motivator when we've been knocked down.

For four years, Frank Reed was held hostage in a Lebanese prison cell. During this period he was blindfolded for months at a time, living in complete darkness. He was chained to a wall and made to stay absolutely quiet. It was three weeks before he dared to peek out, and when he did he discovered that he was chained next to Terry Anderson and Tom Sutherland.

Although Reed was beaten, tortured, and tormented, what hurt him most was the lack of any caring. He said later, "Nothing I did mattered to anyone. I began to realize how withering it is to exist with not a single expression of caring around me. I learned one overriding fact: caring is a powerful force. If no one cares, you are truly alone."[1]

You may be saying to yourself, "God cares about me?" and be tempted to sneer. There may be times when, looking at everything that's happened to you, you're tempted to hold a grudge against God. We struggle with the unfairness of life and how it impacts us. As a result, it's very easy to become disillusioned with God. The last thing you want to do is pray.

Philip Yancey writes:

> If I stake my faith on a fault-proof earth, my faith will let me down. Even the greatest of miracles do not resolve the problems of this earth: all people who find physical healing will eventually die. We need more than a miracle. We need a new heaven and a new earth, and until we have those, unfairness will not disappear. . . . A friend of mine, struggling to believe in a loving God amid such pain and sorrow, blurted out this statement: "God's only excuse is Easter!" The language is non-theological and harsh, but within that phrase lies a haunting truth. The cross of Christ may have overcome evil, but it did not overcome unfairness. For that, Easter is required. [Because of the resurrection,] God will return all physical reality to its proper place under His reign. *Until then,* it's a good thing to remember that we live out our days on Easter Saturday (italics mine).[2]

Until then—until we see Jesus—this is a world where we're going to get knocked down. And how do we get back up? By remembering that God really does care *for us!* His incomparable care is expressed by

Paul in 2 Corinthians 5:21: "God made him who had no sin to be sin *for us,* so that in him we might become the righteousness of God" (italics mine).

Henri Nouwen shares a story about a family in Paraguay whose father, a medical doctor, spoke against the military regime in that country. The regime, known for its thuggery and human rights abuses, tried to silence the doctor by arresting and torturing his teenage son, whom they eventually killed. The community wanted the doctor to organize a march protesting this gross display of savage power. But the doctor refused. Instead, he went to the jail and brought his son's body back to the church for a funeral, displaying it as it had been when he found it behind bars. The boy's body was naked. His skin was scarred from electric charges and cigarette burns. The body did not lie in a coffin, but on the blood-soaked mattress from his cell. As the villagers viewed his body, their rage grew. Before them was a picture of gross injustice.

Nouwen goes on to say that this is exactly what Jesus did for us on the cross. All our sin was put on display as His body became a bloody picture of gross injustice. He took our sin, shame, and punishment.[3]

This past Easter season my son Andy participated in his high school passion play. Andy portrayed one of the thieves on the cross. And even though he wasn't playing the role of Jesus, this didn't diminish the fact that my son was up there, hanging on a cross.

I must tell you that I was enormously uncomfortable as a dad, watching Andy bloodied and in agony, graphically hanging on a cross with just a cloth covering the middle section of his body. It made no difference to me that this was just a dramatic presentation! I was gripped. My son was dying on a cross. And as I watched uncomfortably I asked myself, "Would I give up my son like that, for the loathsome characters at the foot of the cross and for a mass of others who didn't care?" Forgive me, but I'm not there yet and may never get there.

With God the stage was real, and His Son's death on the cross was no act. God gave His Son for us so that we might get back up after we've been knocked down by a sin-cursed world. He did it because He cares. God cared for Moses, and He cares for you and me.

Moses knew God cared about the big things and the little things in his life. Romans 8:28 is an important verse for folks who get knocked down a lot: "We know that God causes all things to work together for good to those who love God, to those who are called according to His purpose" (NASB). God cares about all things, including the big things in your life. Moses knew that God cared about the big items. Over the years God made it clear to Moses that He had big plans for the people of Israel. He had made an everlasting covenant with them. Parted water for them. Provided manna for them. Gave them a cloud by day and a fire by night. These were a people of promise. These were a people for whom God had a bright future.

And in all God's grand plans for Israel, there was also a great commitment for the little details. From Exodus 20 to 32, God gives Moses the intricate specifics of the Law and how it's to be carried out. God cared about the little things of their everyday lives, as well as the big things.

As humans we tend to focus on the immediate. Yet all the while, God is orchestrating the entirety of our lives, using specific details, specific people, specific circumstances, specific words. We tend to look at one piece of the puzzle, while God sees the whole picture as well as the detailed specifics within each piece. We see things in black and white, while God sees things in panoramic color.

If we don't recognize that God has a unique, detailed plan for our lives unfolding while we're on this earth, we'll be prone to quit. God sees both the big and the small pictures. Remembering this, when we've been knocked down, helps us to pray and ask God to get us back up.

Have you ever considered that sometimes you might get knocked down so that others might come to encounter God in their lives? Sometimes God allows us to experience injustice and unfairness so that others might be saved. God gave His Son to suffer unjustly so that others would be changed by the gospel. Why should we be exempt from such divine activity?

Donald Gray Barnhouse was a great preacher in his day. The following story is a powerful reminder of how God cares about both the big and the little things in our lives.

Dr. Barnhouse was conducting a week of services in a church. The pastor of the church and his wife were expecting their first child. During that week, Dr. Barnhouse teased the pastor about his being so uptight.

On the last night of services the pastor did not show up. Dr. Barnhouse assumed that he was at the hospital with his wife, so he went ahead with the service. Toward the end of the service he noticed the pastor slipping in quietly and taking a seat on the back pew.

When the service was completed, the pastor made his way to the front, dismissed everyone, and asked Dr. Barnhouse if he could see him in his office. As they shut the door behind them, the pastor wheeled around and blurted, "Dr. Barnhouse, our child has Down's syndrome. I haven't told my wife yet. I don't know what I'm going to tell her."

"Friend, this is of the Lord," Dr. Barnhouse responded. And then he read from the Old Testament: "And the LORD said to him [Moses], 'Who has made man's mouth? Or who makes him dumb or deaf, or seeing or blind? Is it not I, the LORD?'" (Ex. 4:11 NASB).

"Let me see that," the pastor said. As the pastor studied the passage, Dr. Barnhouse said, "My friend, you know the promise in Romans 8. 'All things work together for good'—including this special child—'for those who love the Lord'" (v. 28).

The pastor closed the Bible. Slowly he walked out of the office and went straight to the hospital room of his wife. When he arrived, she said, "They won't let me see my baby. What's wrong? I've asked to see my baby, and they won't let me." The young pastor took his wife by the hand and said, "'Who has made the dumb or deaf or seeing or blind? Is it not I, the Lord?' Darling, the Lord has blessed us with a child with Down's syndrome."

The pastor's wife cried long and hard. Then, as she began to settle down, she asked, "Where did you get that?"

"From God's own Word," he answered.

"Let me see," she said.

Meanwhile, news of the birth swept through the hospital. This information was of special interest to the switchboard operator in the hospital. She was not a Christian. In fact, she was a cruel woman who enjoyed seeing Christians crumble. She was convinced that, under pressure, there is really no difference between Christians and everybody else. When the pastor's wife called her mother to give her the news, the operator listened in, expecting the young mother to go to pieces.

"Mother, the Lord has blessed us with a child with Down's syndrome. We don't know the nature of the blessing, but we know it is a blessing."

There were no tears, no hysteria, no breakdown.

The operator was shocked. But when she absorbed what she heard, she began telling everyone. Soon the entire hospital was buzzing with the story of the pastor and his wife's response.

The following Sunday the pastor was back in his pulpit. In the congregation, unknown to him, were the telephone operator and seventy nurses and staff members from the hospital. At the conclusion of the service the pastor offered an invitation: "If you have never met Jesus Christ, I want to extend to you an invitation to do so."

That morning thirty nurses from the hospital came forward to receive Christ. All because of one special child and the faith of the young pastor and his wife.

Would God allow this child to be born with a handicapping condition for the sake of thirty nurses? Absolutely. Just as He allowed a man to be born blind, in order that His Son might heal him. And just as He allowed His own Son to be murdered, in order that many might receive eternal life. God allows suffering so that others might come to faith in His Son.[4]

God cares about the big things and the little things in our lives. No matter what.

Moses knew God cared about him enough to finish what He'd started. An artist begins to paint a beautiful picture. But the first strokes on the canvas make no sense at all. There's no form, no order, no clarity. He adds another stroke, then another here and another there. He spends hours at the canvas. After a while, the picture begins to take shape. Finally, he's finished.

As you look at the painting, you remember what it looked like when you first saw it. You couldn't understand it then—it didn't make sense. But now that it's finished, it's a thing of beauty. And in the corner is the signature of the artist, who cared enough to finish what he started.

When you want to quit, remember: "He who began a good work in you will carry it on to completion until the day of Christ Jesus" (Phil. 1:6).

Knowing that God cares about the big picture and the little strokes on that canvas gives us the ability to go to God, in pivotal moments, for comfort and strength when we get knocked down. So if you're tempted to quit, to throw in the towel, don't. Instead, at such a pivotal moment, pray!

CLOSING PRAYER

A Pivotal Prayer
When Tempted to Quit

Father, I'm tired and ready to throw in the towel.
This world just doesn't seem to get it.
Following You, doing what Your Word says,
is sometimes hard.
Sometimes I feel like no one's listening to me.
Sometimes my circumstances just knock me down.
But I know that You can pick me back up.
When I'm feeling sorry for myself,
help me to remember that You really do care about me
in all the big things and little things in my life.
Thank You that You care enough to finish in me
what You've started.
Amen.

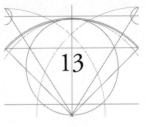

Pivotal Praying When You Confront a New Challenge

(Tim Elmore)

I chuckle when I read these words:

> Never be afraid to try something new. Remember: amateurs built the ark, and professionals built the *Titanic*.

They serve as a good reminder. When we are inexperienced, we tend to lean on God for results. We recognize how little we possess—and how much we need His help. When we are experienced, we tend to lean on our strengths and leave God out of the equation. We depend on our gifts rather than on our God. At least most of the time.

You may remember that five iceberg warnings were telegraphed to the ill-fated *Titanic*. When the sixth message, "Look out for icebergs," came in, the operator wired back, "Shut up! I'm busy." These were his last words over the wire before it all happened. Exactly thirty-five minutes later, the great vessel—about which the captain had said, "God Himself couldn't sink this ship"—was sinking. Hundreds of passengers and crew were drowned.

Reports of the tragedy say that when the captain gave the order to abandon ship, many passengers simply didn't believe the *Titanic* could possibly sink, and refused to board lifeboats. The crew was almost criminally complacent.

Why? They failed to recognize what a pivotal moment it was for everyone. The ship was new, the challenge was new, the voyage was new. It was the maiden voyage for the captain and his crew, including the man at the telegraph, but everyone believed that matters were under control. They were self-sufficient. They were invincible.

In the wee hours of that morning on Sunday, April 15, 1912, a woman was very weary but could not sleep. She was fearful for her husband, who was away. She gave in to the burden to pray and began to do so with passion. She forgot how tired she was, and prayed for hours, until 5:00 A.M. At that point, she felt a sense of peace, climbed into bed again, and slept. She had no idea what was happening to her husband, who was in the middle of the Atlantic Ocean aboard the *Titanic.*

It was during those hours that her husband, Colonel Gracie, was among the frantic hundreds trying to launch lifeboats from the great ship. He had given up all hope of being saved himself, and was doing his best to help the women and children. Wishing he could get a last message to his wife, he cried from his heart: "Good-bye, my darling." Then, as the ship plunged into its watery grave, he was sucked down in the giant whirlpool. Instinctively, he began to swim under the ice-cold water.

When he came to the surface he found himself near an over-turned lifeboat. Along with several others, he climbed aboard and was picked up by another lifeboat at about 5:00 A.M.—the very time that peace had come to his praying wife.

Pivotal moments. Pivotal decisions. Pivotal prayers. Pivotal results. Here, I believe, we see an illustration of both the sovereign prompting of God and the power of pivotal praying. Some recognized it. Some didn't.

Harry Emerson Fosdick wrote,

> Now if God has left some things contingent on man's thinking and
> working, why may he not have left some things contingent on
> man's praying? The testimony of great souls clearly affirms this:
> some things never without thinking; some things never without
> working; and some things never without praying! Prayer is one of
> the three forms of man's cooperation with God.[1]

God invites us to partner with Him to accomplish His purposes—but
He allows us to choose how we pray.

How do you pray when you face something new and different—
a new relationship? a new spouse? a new neighbor? a new baby? a new
colleague on the job? How do you handle a sickness or death in your
family? We've heard for years that "familiarity breeds contempt." I
believe that familiarity breeds self-sufficiency and complacency.
When we think we know the ropes, we're prone to think we control
those ropes ourselves. No one wants to feel out of control.

How do you pray when you face a new investment opportunity?
a pay raise? a glitch at work? a layoff? Or how about a new task added
to your job description, or even a new job opportunity? Learning to
pray pivotally means we understand how to pray strategically when
we face new challenges. We must gain the mind of God in those times
of uncertainty, and pray accordingly.

PIVOTAL PRAYER TODAY

Pivotal moments and pivotal praying have received the spotlight
since September 11, 2001. Everyone remembers where he or she was
that morning when the World Trade Center towers were hit by two
jets and the Pentagon in Washington D.C. was hit as well. It was terrorism at its worst. We witnessed a tragedy unlike any we had seen

before. In one blow, over three thousand people were murdered in an act of war. In my mind I can still see bodies falling from the towers. I can still see people running for safety as the towers crumbled. For weeks afterward, photos of missing persons were posted throughout the Manhattan area. Whether we knew what to call it or not—we all sensed it was a pivotal moment for America. Have you ever seen such display of patriotism in the last fifty years?

New York mayor Rudy Giuliani responded in an amazing way. He seemed to be everywhere. When he wasn't digging through the rubble, he was attending memorial services for people he never knew. He was a mayor and a chaplain simultaneously. Even more than Giuliani, however, President George W. Bush found his voice as a leader during the months that followed.

Both Democrats and Republicans agreed that George W. Bush was the right man for the moment. He responded tremendously to the grief-stricken families in New York and Washington, as well as to the sagging economy and the terrorist network in Afghanistan. What enabled this leader of the free world to respond so aptly to these crises? I believe it was a combination of factors, not the least of which was pivotal praying.

Soon after September 11, President Bush met with a group of church leaders from across the country. In that meeting Bush explicitly called those men to prayer. "Government will do some things, but you need to be praying." he stated flatly. "I think this is part of a spiritual awakening."

Bush suggested that there had never been a better time to lean on almighty God. Like Solomon, Bush could have prayed merely for survival—"God, help us make it through this tragedy." How easy it would have been to pray selfishly at this moment. He could have prayed merely for safety. Or cash flow. Or that he would look good in front of the American people. (Certainly that might have been on my mind if I were president!)

Instead he prayed a pivotal prayer, and found his voice in the midst of this new challenge. Gerald Kieschnick, president of the Lutheran Church, Missouri Synod, said to Bush: "Mr. President, I have just come down from the World Trade Center site in lower Manhattan. I stood where you stood. I saw what you saw. I smelled what you smelled. You not only have a civil calling, but a divine calling. . . . You are not just a civil servant; you are a servant of God, called for such a time like this."

"I accept the responsibility," Bush replied. Clearly, this crisis heightened his awareness of the divine calling of his office; and that pivotal moment led to pivotal prayer.[2]

PROBLEMS AT THE PIVOT

On the other hand, new challenges don't automatically cause people to respond well. Sometimes new challenges can derail once-flourishing careers. In the middle of a hard-fought battle in May 1862, for instance, Major General Gustavus Smith was suddenly handed the command of the Confederacy's largest army after his boss, Joseph Johnston, was wounded. There's a reason you don't see Gustavus Smith's name in any elementary-school textbook. The general simply froze. It has been said that new challenges cause you either to freeze or to focus. Smith froze, incapacitated by the hugeness of the responsibility. At one point he asked Confederate President Jefferson Davis what he thought of the ongoing battle. After less than a day on the job, Smith was relieved by one of Davis's aides, Robert E. Lee.[3]

During the Civil War, there were many pivotal moments—new challenges that stared leaders in the face for the first time in their lives. America had never been divided like this before. Praying in such times is not a cop-out. It is not a picture of a leader in denial who simply throws up his hands and says, "Well, Lord, whatever happens, I'll consider it Your will . . . *Que sera, sera.*" In fact, it is just the opposite. Pivotal praying happens when such a leader stands up, knowing that he or she must face this new challenge with confidence, but knowing that such confidence comes from God, not from some artificial smile displayed when the cameras are rolling. Such leaders recognize both their own inadequacy and God's sufficiency. Their confidence comes from knowing they are in step with Him. They are secure enough to admit their uncertainty, but they remain calm and poised because they are living in surrender to God. And that is how they pray.

What Are the Ingredients?

As I hear healthy leaders praying in the midst of new challenges, I notice a common thread. Their prayers express a handful of elements that make them pivotal. Let me tell you what I've observed:

First, they express submission. Although the person praying may not be a novice, he or she always sees the new challenge as a fresh opportunity to articulate dependence on God. Many even try to pray as if their slates of experience were clean and empty.

Second, they express the fact that they're seeking. They are on a search for God to do those things they cannot. In the next chapter, we will examine King Solomon, who at the beginning of his reign sought wisdom from God, since he didn't know how to lead such a large group of people. He wasn't afraid to "ask big." He specifically sought what he needed.

Third, they express surrender. At some point in their prayers they communicate that they put their trust in God, not in their own gifts. They will use the abilities God has given them, but they entrust the results to God. They are merely His servants.

The Unsinkable Ship

We began this chapter with a discussion of the *Titanic* and its tragic first venture on the Atlantic Ocean. What a miscarriage of equipment and what that ship was designed to accomplish. What a failed opportunity to see a pivotal moment and pray a pivotal prayer.

Just after the sinking, an American pastor was visiting in Belfast, Ireland. The *Titanic* had been built in Belfast, and there had been great local pride over the mighty ship. They'd been the first to herald it as "the unsinkable ship." Sixteen members of a church in Belfast, all skilled mechanics, had gone down with her.

The mayor said that Belfast had never experienced such grief or tragedy. When the news was finally verified that the gallant ship was certainly lost, so deep was the grief that strong men would meet in the streets, grasp each other's hands, burst into tears, and part without a word.

The visiting American preached the Sunday after the tragedy in the church that had lost the sixteen members in the *Titanic*. Not only was the building packed with people, but on the platform sat lords, bishops, and ministers of all denominations. In the audience, many newly-made widows sat, and orphans were sobbing on every side.

The pastor stood and announced his subject: "The Unsinkable Ship." But he did not apply this term to the *Titanic*. Instead, his message was about that other "unsinkable ship"—the frail, little boat on the Sea of Galilee, unsinkable because the Master of land and sea was asleep on a pillow in the back of the vessel. Because Jesus had said, "Let us go to the other side," the ship was destined to arrive successfully. He was in charge of that journey. The disciples, the waves, the wind, and the rain all assumed the posture of surrender.[4]

Not a bad place to start when we face a new challenge.

What We Learn from Solomon and Rehoboam

After moving to Atlanta in 1997, I became a fan of Chick-fil-A. This fast-food restaurant chain sells the best chicken anywhere, and have for over fifty years. Their slogan is, "We didn't invent the chicken, just the chicken sandwich."

As we entered a new millennium, Truett Cathy, the founder of Chick-fil-A, resigned as president and turned it over to his son Dan. It was a passing of the baton to someone Truett knew he could trust. After all, this was a huge responsibility. Chick-fil-A had become a billion-dollar business. By the year 2000 they had some 900 stores, not to mention headquarter staff in Atlanta. Dan would now oversee all of this and attempt to lead with the same values his father had embraced over the last five decades.

I once asked Dan, "What was the first thing you did, when you took over?"

He smiled and whispered, "I prayed."

Good answer! When facing a new challenge, prayer is the smartest first step for anyone to take. Think about it for a moment. New challenges do something to the human psyche. Something sparks. Adrenalin flows. Energy surges. Creativity surfaces, sometimes from out of nowhere. Sometimes it's scary, sometimes exciting. Depending on how you are wired, your tendency may be to say, "Bring it on," or "Let me hide." Some are predisposed to self-sufficiency, while others lean toward self-degradation. Neither are healthy responses.

Dan Cathy decided to take a route in between. When faced with the new challenge of leading Chick-fil-A, he recognized the pivotal moment and he prayed. He didn't shrink from it, but neither did he pretend to be self-reliant.

How would you have responded? Ask yourself: When is the last time I did something for the first time? How did I respond? How did I pray?

SOLOMON'S PIVOTAL PRAYER

Nearly three thousand years ago a young man was appointed to be king in Israel. His name was Solomon—known to have been the wisest monarch to ever sit on a throne. He is known for his wisdom and discernment, but he didn't begin that way. He began his reign young and inexperienced. He called himself a "little child" (1 Kings 3:7). Only twenty years old, he was apprehensive about the tasks before him. That's why he traveled to Gibeon to offer sacrifices to the Lord. He wanted God's favor so much, he offered a thousand burnt offerings on that altar. I'd say he was serious about getting God's attention!

And he did. The Lord appeared to Solomon at Gibeon in a dream one night and spoke to him: "Ask for whatever you want me to give you" (1 Kings 3:5).

Wow—talk about a pivotal moment! Almighty God appears—like some sort of genie from Aladdin's lamp—and invites him to pray for anything he wants! What an invitation. In the face of a new challenge, God said he could have anything he wanted! What would you have prayed for?

Solomon was ready to respond. His readiness for this new challenge was not a form of self-sufficiency or self-confidence. Quite the opposite. His readiness was in knowing how to pray at this pivotal moment in his life.

His dad, King David, had prepared him for it. David had spoken his last words to his son before he assumed the throne (1 Kings 2). He gave him a clear sense of the gravity of this new challenge. Then he told Solomon he was about to die, and that Solomon must be strong and show himself to be a man. David instilled in Solomon a sense of the magnitude of the job ahead.

David also gave him a clear sense of direction (v. 3). Solomon's character was paramount. David encouraged him to keep the charge of the Lord and to walk in His ways. David advised him specifically to follow the ordinances of Moses during his days as king.

Third, David gave him clear incentives to stay on course (v. 4). Solomon was to do all this in order that the Lord may carry out His promise to bless him, to cause him to succeed, and to keep the throne in His name forever.

Fourth, David warned Solomon about the obstacles before him (vv. 5–6). He mentioned the names of men who opposed his reign, and told him exactly what they had done. He counseled Solomon to deal with them firmly.

Finally, David gave Solomon clear insights from the past (vv. 7–9). David knew that the past is often filled with signposts that furnish direction for the future. There were other people and incidents that Solomon needed to know about.

All of this prepared Solomon to pray wisely. David had all but said, "This is a pivotal moment for you and the nation of Israel!" Solomon now confronted the daunting task of leading a nation that his father had built into a major military force, a nation now famous for its leadership, a nation prepared for the biggest building campaign it had ever seen—and the temple was Solomon's first big task.

In this pivotal moment, the young king made a pivotal decision. Instead of asking for survival or for wealth, fame, or long life—he prayed for wisdom and discernment:

> And now, O LORD my God, Thou hast made Thy servant king in place of my father David, yet I am but a little child; I do not know how to go out or come in. And Thy servant is in the midst of Thy people which Thou hast chosen, a great people who cannot be numbered or counted for multitude. So give Thy servant an understanding heart to judge Thy people to discern between good and evil. For who is able to judge this great people of Thine? (2 Kings 3:7–9)

Consider for a moment how easy it would have been to pray selfishly in that moment. Solomon could have asked that his name would be honored through the ages. He might have prayed for beautiful wives, unlimited income, or power over the surrounding nations. He could have just asked God to make him happy.

Instead, Solomon said, "I am depending on *You*, Lord, rather than on my own strength." That was pivotal prayer. Instead of flexing his muscles and his will, he voiced his own weakness. He became vulnerable and confessed how much he didn't know. Instead of strength, he expressed surrender. This is what made that prayer pivotal.

Jesus taught this truth a thousand years later on a hillside one day. Some scribes sent spies to Jesus, to trap Him in his own teaching. They asked him, "Lord, should we pay taxes to Caesar?" In asking Jesus this question they were setting Him up: If He said yes, He was submitting to Caesar instead of God. If He said no, He was evading the authority of Rome and could be arrested.

Jesus answered them with another question: "Whose image is on the coin?" This seemed a harmless question on His part. In fact, it was an easy one to answer. Caesar's image was on the coin. Then Jesus proceeded to silence them with one single sentence: "Then give to Caesar what is Caesar's, and to God what is God's" (Luke 20:25).

The next verse indicates how significant this statement was: "And astonished by his answer, they became silent" (v. 26). What was so astonishing about this answer? Jesus was teaching a principle about surrender. The principle is simple: When an object has a person's image stamped upon it, that object belongs to that person. The *coin* had Caesar's image on it—so they should surrender it to him. However, *they* had been made in God's image, so they should be surrendering themselves to Him!

Hidden within Jesus' statement was a paramount truth they missed as they squabbled over taxes. When they asked Him about money, He communicated an unforgettable message about surrender.

Because we have been made in the image of God, it is only appropriate for us to respond to Him in surrender. He isn't impressed with our gifts and talents. He gave them to us. He isn't moved by our strong will. He yearns for us to submit to His will. He is not amazed by our thoughts. His thoughts are far higher than ours (Isa. 55:9).

King Solomon prayed a pivotal prayer when he most needed to. Let's break it down. Facing his new challenge, Solomon's prayer included these elements:

1. He expressed his own inadequacy. Did you notice the first words out of his mouth were a confession of his own youth and inexperience? He was secure enough to admit his humanity. He didn't feel like "King David," his invincible father. He acknowledged that the new challenge might be bigger than he was. He was honest. He was human. He was humble.

2. He asked for the ingredient he didn't have. Next, Solomon specifically requested from God the item he needed most. He asked for wisdom and understanding in order to lead effectively. His request and his motive were right. "This is what I need, Lord, and this is why I need it." He wasn't afraid to say what he needed.

3. He surrendered to God. Finally, he communicated unconditional surrender to God. His submission is not covered; it is naked for all to see. This was most pleasing to the Lord.

God loved this king, who, despite having the most powerful position in the nation, didn't flaunt it. He surrendered to God, saying: "I need You. Give me Your understanding as I attempt to do this job. Give me Your wisdom as I make decisions. Give me Your discernment as I choose my staff, and insight as I judge between right and wrong."

God was so pleased with Solomon's prayer that He responded this way:

Because you have asked this thing and have not asked for yourself long life, nor have asked riches for yourself, nor have you asked for the life of your enemies, but have asked for yourself discernment to understand justice, behold, I have done according to your words. Behold, I have given you a wise and discerning heart, so that there has been no one like you before you, nor shall one like you arise after you. And I have also given you what you have not asked, both riches and honor, so that there will not be any among the kings like you in all your days. (1 Kings 3:11–13 NASB)

God gave Solomon everything he asked for, plus even things he didn't ask for but might have been expected to!

Some Just Don't Get It

Unfortunately, many never learn this. When King Solomon retired from his reign, he turned it over to Rehoboam, one of his sons. Did Rehoboam begin his monarchy as his father had? Nowhere close. He was arrogant, self-sufficient, and overconfident, even when he had to inquire of others what he should do. He was a pretender. Like many who face new challenges, he felt compelled to look strong, project an image, and appear to be in control. All the while, he had no idea what he was doing. He was spiritually bankrupt.

According to 2 Chronicles 10:1–19, Rehoboam blew it. He never became genuinely confident or strong because he refused to surrender. He missed his chance to pray pivotally. According to the passage, he never once prayed or sought God during this new challenge. He didn't even listen to the elders who had served his father Solomon. Instead, he began to seek the counsel of old friends. He listened for words that agreed with what he wanted personally. He never listened to the cries of the people he was leading.

Jeroboam even traveled miles from where he was staying in

Egypt to ask the king to lighten their workload. He promised that if Rehoboam helped them, they would serve him for life. The new king heard their words, but he never listened. He missed what God was saying to him in that pivotal moment. Consumed with himself, his image, and with success, he failed to see anything else. Rehoboam illustrates how personal preoccupation prevents pivotal praying!

What was the result? The kingdom of Israel split in two. Jeroboam returned home and led a revolt against Rehoboam. Some of the tribes went with Jeroboam, and Israel remained a divided, often captive nation until 1948. King Rehoboam failed to practice pivotal prayer and divided his country, losing both tribes and money. His life is summarized in 2 Chronicles 12:14, a testament of his failure in pivotal prayer: "And he did evil because he did not set his heart to seek the LORD" (NASB).

SOUND FAMILIAR?

Which of these men are you like when you face a new challenge— Solomon or Rehoboam? Do you rear back and pretend to know it all? Do you put on a facade of strength? Do you become preoccupied with yourself, with your own safety and survival? Or, like Solomon, do you surrender your own agenda and seek the mind of God? Do you think about the strategic opportunity for God to bring glory to Himself through this new challenge? Do you recognize the pivotal moment and pray accordingly? Do you seek out how to seize the moment, based on the need of the hour? Do you yearn for God to advance His rule through this new challenge?

When Dan Cathy took the reins at Chick-fil-A, his ultimate goal was to honor God in the position. This is what drives him. He has never once pretended he could do it without his Lord. The new challenge both motivates him and drives him to his knees.

My son Jonathan recently signed up for Little League baseball.

As a father, I was more excited about it than he was. However, after he saw who was on the team, he became scared. He was playing at a new level and felt a little over his head. As I tucked him in bed one night, he told me he didn't want to join the team after all. He was afraid.

I didn't want to force him to do something he didn't want to do. At the same time, I knew he could do it with a little coaching. I gave him Pep Talk Number 42, about how we could do it together if he would just give it a try. He finally smiled and replied, "OK, Dad. I'll do it—but only if you'll go with me and be my coach."

I imagine our heavenly Father loves to hear those same words.

CLOSING PRAYER

A Pivotal Prayer for Confronting Challenge

Dear Lord,
I have a challenge staring me in the face.
Keep me honest;
help me not to pretend I have all the answers.
On the other hand,
help me not to shrink from the challenge.
Instead, remind me that this is Your way to
foster fresh surrender to You.
I believe new challenges spark the need
for new submission.
You are the Master. I am Your servant.
Amen.

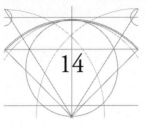

PIVOTAL PRAYING WHEN YOU NEED TO WAIT

(JOHN HULL)

S ince the day missionaries Martin and Gracia Burnham were kidnapped by political extremists in the Philippines on May 27,
2001, the folks back at their home church in Rose Hill, Kansas, had
been finding ways to cope—communicating with officials both in
the United States and Philippine governments, and keeping the press
aware of the Burnhams' plight. Gracia's mother, Betty Jo Jones, said,
"It's been up and down emotionally. So many times they tell us, 'It's
going to be soon.'"[1]

While some in the family and church worked the diplomatic and
media relationships, a group of men at Rose Hill Bible Church had
committed to pray daily—specifically for the Burnhams' release. Not
too many days after the shocking abduction, the men organized a
prayer vigil at the church on the couple's behalf. They met six mornings a week for one hour, to pray for the Burnhams' health, safety, and
their return.

Rose Hill's pastor, Robert Varner, didn't have any idea the
Burnhams' ordeal would last this long. Nor did the church
membership. "The initial thought was, 'This thing will be resolved in

thirty days or so,'" Varner says. But time slowly passed, and the church continued in its pivotal prayer.

When asked what the prayer group asked of God, Varner was quick to respond. "We prayed for their well-being and for their Christian testimony. We prayed that their ministry might be great, in spite of their situation."

Martin Burnham's parents, Paul and Oreta, were hopeful. Paul testified, "God will release them in time. God is working His will out in this. The Lord is sustaining us. He's using the prayers of His people to do that."

Earlier in 2002, Paul and Oreta had the opportunity to speak with Heather Mercer, one of the Christian workers held by the Taliban in Afghanistan in the early weeks of America's war on terror. Both were comforted by her words. She told them that she strongly believes she was released "because people were praying."[2]

For over a year, the people of Rose Hill Church watched the news, waited on God, and pivotally prayed for Martin and Gracia's release. At the time of this writing, press reports from the Phillippines communicated that Martin was killed during a rescue attempt on June 7, 2002. Gracia suffered a leg wound but survived and has since returned to the United States to be reunited with family members. Martin's body was recovered and returned to America for burial.

Just before boarding a flight for home, an exhausted and grieved Gracia acknowledged the sustaining power of pivotal praying during their fifty-three week captivity. She said, "We want to thank each and every one of you for every time you remembered us in prayer. We needed every single prayer you said during our ordeal in the jungle." An unidentified souce who was alongside Gracia the day after her rescue said she is "a strong woman of deep faith."[3]

Martin's brother, Doug, told reporters after his year of pivotally praying for their release, "Obviously, it hasn't turned out the way we hoped. But we are grateful Gracia is alive. Our faith in the Lord is the same. That hasn't changed."[4] The day the rescue was reported, I heard Matin's father, Paul, on the radio say that while he was saddened about his son's death, he looked forward to one day seeing him again in heaven. As I listened, I thought about the promises of Christ and hope of that reunion day. But I also thought that Paul will no doubt have times when he asks God at pivotal moments to give him and his family great patience to work through their pain and loss.

GIVE ME PATIENCE . . . AND I WANT IT NOW!

It has been said that the great American prayer is, "God give me patience and give it to me now!" Phillips Brooks was a New England preacher known for his quiet, methodical manner. At times, though, even he suffered moments of frustration and irritability. One day a friend saw him feverishly pacing the floor like a caged lion. "What's the trouble, Mr. Brooks?" he asked.

"The trouble is that I'm in a hurry and God isn't."[5]

Learning to wait, and learning how to pray while we wait, is challenging. It goes contrary to our culture, which craves immediate gratification and worships speed and results. Yet some of the greatest missionaries in the last few hundred years, people who have taken the gospel to places it had never been before, have waited long periods of time before ever seeing someone accept Christ.

William Carey worked for seven years before he led his first Hindu to the Lord in Burma. Adoniram Judson also served seven years before leading a soul to Christ cross-culturally. It took fourteen years of spreading the gospel in western Africa before the first reported conversion. In Tahiti it took sixteen years of evangelism, and in New Zealand it was nine years before the first persons said yes to Jesus Christ. David Livingstone went through his entire missionary career in Zambia leading only one soul to Christ, and there is some question among historians as to whether or not that person later recanted.

Why did their efforts, and our efforts in what we do, seem at times to take so long? Well, maybe in the eyes of the One who holds eternity in His hands, what seems a long time to us isn't that long at all. Gordon MacDonald wisely observes, "This Mysterious One . . . moves with agonizing slowness on some days and lightning speed on others. One lays no demands, no time lines, and no measurements before Him. One bows, speaks the language of the soul, and then waits. And often does not tell others what he is waiting for. Conversation from soul to heaven is enough."[6]

Patience is not a virtue in the eyes of our contemporary world. Yet reality and history remind us that when we make decisions too quickly, it often leads to regret. Robert Schuller has shared the following story:

> I remember one winter my dad needed firewood, and he found a dead tree and sawed it down. In the spring, to his dismay, new shoots sprouted around the trunk. He said, "I thought sure it was dead. The leaves had all dropped in the wintertime. It was so cold that twigs snapped as if there were no life in the old tree. But now I see that there was still life at the tap root." He looked at me and said, "Bob, don't forget this important lesson. Never cut a tree down in the wintertime. Never make a negative decision at a low time. Never make your most important decisions when you are in your worst mood. Be patient. The storm will pass. The spring will come."[7]

The Scriptures are full of lessons on the importance of waiting on God and the critical role of prayer in the process of waiting. Yet they are also full of stories about people who suffered because they were unwilling to wait.

Adam and Eve were impatient. They wanted what God said they shouldn't have and—well—we know the rest of that story. Moses refused to be patient, lost his temper, hit a rock when he should have spoken to it, and the results? He never entered the promised land. These were people who loved God, but they just couldn't wait for spring to come—when there would be greater clarity as to what they should do.

One of the saddest examples of impatience in the Old Testament is modeled by Sarah, the wife of Abraham. Sarah became impatient in wanting to have a son, and engaged the services of a surrogate mother (her servant Hagar) to bear her a child by Abraham. Her impatience and Abraham's caving in to her shortsighted desire for a child continues to have lasting implications in the Middle East. From Abraham's seed, through two women, would emerge two civilizations: Jews and Arabs.

When God makes a promise, He keeps it. That was true for Abraham and it's true for us. God had promised Abraham and his wife Sarah that they would become the parents of a nation, and that their descendants would be abundant: "Look up at the heavens and count the stars—if indeed you can count them. So shall your offspring be" (Gen. 15:5).

What a spectacular promise! But Sarah wanted a child right away. So she told Abraham to have a sexual relationship with her maid-servant, Hagar. Sarah seems to have been impatient with God when she said, "The LORD has kept me from having children" (Gen. 16:2).

So, with the intent of building a family through a surrogate mother, Abraham and Hagar became intimate and consequently she became pregnant. Sarah was immediately filled with jealousy toward Hagar once she learned the news. In fact, the entire episode became so fractious that one wonders how those associated in this love/hate triangle kept their sanity. There was deception, false accusation, jealousy, rejection, detachment, and frustration. Not the components of a happy home.

The Lord showed compassion on Hagar and told her that she, too, would give birth to a son (Ishmael) who would have many offspring. That offspring would eventually become known as the Ishmaelites. The Ishamaelites would form the early outlines of what would eventually become the Arab world.

Psalm 83:5–6 pictures a hostile relationship between the Ishamaelites and the Israelites (the descendants of Abraham and Isaac). These verses prophesied that the tents of the Ishmaelites, the Edomites, the Moabites, and the Hagrites would form an alliance against the sons of Abraham. And for thousands of years, up to contemporary history, the conflicts between the descendants of Ishmael and Isaac are legendary, and even today quite worrisome. Much of today's global tensions in that part of the world are rooted in Sarah's inability to wait on God. The result was a birth that has bred mistrust among these groups of people from ancient days to the present. Oh, the consequences of an impatient pivotal decision made apart from God's guidance!

TWO PATIENT PEOPLE

But not everyone in the Bible is known for impatience. There's a refreshing account in the New Testament of two people, a man and a woman, who, like the family and friends of Martin and Gracia Burnham, were willing to wait on God to fulfill His promise.

Simeon and Anna had seen many things in their lives. Simeon was a righteous man of good reputation. He had been promised by the Holy Spirit that before he died he would see the Messiah. Anna, too, was known as a spiritual person. In fact, she was a prophetess. As an elderly woman of eighty-four, she stayed in the temple area fasting and praying.

One can only imagine how many times Anna had prayed for the Messiah to come. If she had prayed only once a day in her adult life for this promise, she would have asked God about it over twenty-five thousand times. That's patience!

On the eighth day of Jesus' life on earth, Mary and Joseph brought Him to the temple for the customary circumcision. When they brought Jesus to Simeon, who was responsible for the ceremony, the old man who had long waited for the promised Messiah held Him in his wrinkled hands. Here is his prayer:

> Sovereign Lord, as you have promised,
> you now dismiss your servant in peace.
> For my eyes have seen your salvation,
> which you have prepared in the sight of all people,
> a light for revelation to the Gentiles
> and glory to your people Israel. (Luke 2:29–33)

Not too far away, Anna, who had also been waiting, approached Jesus and thanked God for this child who would bring redemption. She went up to Jesus and His parents and "gave thanks to God and spoke about the child to all who were looking forward to the redemption of Jerusalem" (2:38).

A good thing, a great thing, had come to these precious folks who had waited on Jesus. These two elderly adults had seen many things. But one thing they were still waiting to see was the coming of "the Lord's Christ," as He is referred to in connection with Simeon's expectation (v. 26).

My grandmother, now in her nineties, is in quite poor health. She was born in the early days of the last century. When I visited with her recently, I was reminded of all the changes that have taken place in her world since she was born. There I was with a small cell phone in one pocket and a wireless Palm Pilot in another. Just the day before, I had flown on a jet from a city several thousand miles away. I came to see her in a car that has a lot of bells and whistles.

None of those things were a part of her childhood or even most of her life. And yet she sat there, somewhat detached and at peace. Patiently, day by day, my mother and father care for her. Patiently my grandmother goes through her remaining days with dignity, thanks to my parents. Patiently, she waits to see Jesus. Not in the way Simeon and Anna waited until their senior years to see Him as a baby. But she waits, through uneventful days and brief visits with loved ones who come and go, for the day when—through the passage of death—she will see Jesus as He is. She's been patient for a long time, and God's going to reward her patience with a new home in heaven and a glorified body.

Patience for the Long Haul

Trinity Church in Cambridge, England, may sound like a nice place to pastor, but it wasn't for Charles Simeon. A bishop within the Church of England had assigned Simeon to lead the church in 1782. He arrived against the will of the congregation. The reason? He preached the gospel and proposed that men and women needed to experience the forgiveness of sin and the supernatural regeneration of Christ. This wasn't what the congregants at Trinity Church wanted to hear!

For over a decade the people wouldn't let him give the afternoon sermon. And they refused to attend the morning services. They even locked the traditional small doors that gave access to the pews, so that even visitors could not be seated. For twelve years Charles Simeon preached to those who came to a worship service as they stood in the aisles. This level of opposition went on for twelve long years.[8]

Simeon would stay as pastor of Trinity Church for fifty-four— that's right, fifty-four—years! In a day when most pastors in North

America stay at a church for an average of two years or less before moving to the next spot, we might wonder how he managed to endure. How did he have such patience? How could he wait like that? Here's what he wrote:

> In this state of things I saw no remedy but *faith* and *patience* [italics mine]. The passage of Scripture which subdued and controlled my mind was, "The servant of the Lord must not strive." It was painful indeed to see the church, with the exception of the aisles, almost forsaken; but I thought that if God would only give a double blessing to the congregation that did attend, there would be on the whole as much good done as if the congregation were doubled and the blessing limited to only half the amount. This comforted me many, many times when without such a reflection, I should have sunk under my burden.[9]

I don't know if there's any connection between the name "Simeon" and the word *patience,* but beyond the irony of these two men possessing the same name, both have served as models of patience. Simeon and Anna waited for the day when they would see with their tired eyes the One who had been promised to come. The One who would bring salvation to their people. God rewarded their patience by allowing them to be among the first to bear witness to Jesus Christ.

Charles Simeon waited twelve years just to win a hearing with the people of his own congregation! Before he died, he was noted as saying that the way he managed to live such a life of patience was to look to Jesus. "When I look to Him, I see nothing but faithfulness—and immutability—and truth; and I have the sweetest peace—I cannot have more peace."[10]

Because they kept their eyes on Jesus, Simeon, Anna, Charles Simeon, and even my failing grandmother have learned how to wait on God.

A key ingredient to learning how to wait, I'm convinced, is keeping our eyes focused on Jesus Christ; our faithful, true, and immutable Savior! There's something very clear and compelling in these words of the author of Hebrews: "Let us run with perseverance [patience] the race marked out for us. Let us fix our eyes on Jesus, the author and perfecter of our faith, who for the joy set before him endured the cross, scorning its shame, and sat down at the right hand of the throne of God" (Heb. 12:1b–2).

Because Simeon and Anna kept their eyes on the promise of Jesus' coming, blessing followed. Sarah, in contrast, took her eyes off the promise of God and, as a result, great burdens followed—burdens that rocked the ancient world then and the modern world now. A traditional Hebrew story illustrates this principle:

Abraham was sitting outside his tent one evening when he saw an old man, weary from age and journey, approach. Abraham rushed out, greeted him, and invited him into his tent. There he washed the old man's feet and gave him food and drink.

The old man began eating without offering a prayer or blessing. Abraham asked him, "Don't you worship God?"

The old traveler replied, "I worship fire only and reverence no other god."

When he heard this, Abraham became incensed, grabbed the old man by the shoulders, and threw him out of his tent into the cold night air.

When the old man departed, God called to his friend Abraham and asked where the stranger was. Abraham replied, "I forced him out because he did not worship You."

God answered, "I have suffered him these eighty years although he dishonors me. Could you not endure him one night?"

Oh, for the patience to endure life's afflictions for just one more night. Such endurance comes through prayer. Martin and Gracia discovered that in the jungle of the Philippines. Night after night, in horrid conditions, they waited on God. And now that that ordeal is over, Martin's dad and other grieving members of the Burnham family are discovering their need for patient endurance in the nights to come. Today and tomorrow they face the future without Martin in their lives. Pivotally they pray for the strength to endure. I join them in that prayer in their hour of need. And I join you in prayer in your great hour of need too.

Keep praying—and keep your eyes on Jesus!

CLOSING PRAYER

A Pivotal Prayer for Patience

Lord, I find it very hard to wait.
I want all the answers now,
and yet Your Word tells me that if I'm going to
grow in my walk with You,
I'm going to have to learn how to wait.
It's especially hard to wait for justice.
When I see all the wrongs in the world,
I want to see them all made right immediately.
I ask that You grant me grace to wait—
through the disappointments, through the surprises,
even through the victories.
Help me to wait, Lord,
and to trust You.
Amen.

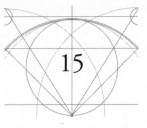

PIVOTAL PRAYING WHEN YOU ARE UNDER PRESSURE
(TIM ELMORE)

Heather Mercer and Dayna Curry were used to being roused from their cell beds by ranting soldiers toting AK-47s. These two young women spent three and a half months under Taliban captivity in Afghanistan. You may remember hearing their story in November of 2001. Their captors had kept the two American aides and six other Western hostages on the run almost every night when the U.S. began bombing Afghanistan the month before.

One night, however, things began to change. New jailers took charge and herded them into a van packed with rocket launchers and other military equipment. The new men seemed frighteningly on edge, much less hospitable than the previous ones. After a three-hour trip down dark roads lined with tanks, the van stopped and the soldiers forced the hostages into a cold, metal shipping container. Heather and Dayna curled up into a fetal position and waited out the night. "We knew the only way we'd get out of this was if God intervened," recalls Curry.

The next morning the prisoners were trucked to another makeshift jail as U.S. air strikes began. This time the bombs came terrifyingly close. From the window the hostages saw Taliban soldiers fleeing the town. Then there came an eerie silence. Thirty long minutes passed before suddenly there was a violent rattling at the door.

"We thought it was the Taliban coming back, and it was the end of the road," Heather said later. But then a soldier burst through the door screaming words too good to believe: "You're free! The city is free!"

The prisoners ran into the streets, where women cast off their burqas and began to sing, and men played music and fired Uzis into the air to celebrate.

When Dayna and Heather returned to the United States, we heard their story. They had gone to Afghanistan to help feed and clothe victims of the Muslim world's strictest state. Then they were accused of preaching Christ to children, a crime punishable by death. Both women testify that it was prayer that enabled them to go on.

At night, huddled under a blanket with a flashlight, Dayna and Heather would write letters to their church in Waco, Texas. "When I am afraid, I remember that Dad hears the cries of his children and answers them," Heather wrote, substituting the word *Dad* for *God* so her Taliban censors would pass the letters on to her lawyer, who would then give them to her parents, who would then e-mail them to the States.[1]

Praying in such a tough situation galvanized their faith and made them relentless in their determination not only to endure but to continue working in the country. Upon returning home, they immediately told their families they wanted to go back.

Heather and Dayna's experience may seem surreal—so far from the day-to-day pressures you and I endure. But let's face it: The word *pressure* may need to be redefined after September 11, 2001. Who would have ever thought we'd need to consider the possibility of a commercial jet flying into a building and leveling it to the ground? or that we would fear boarding an airplane? or dread receiving mail with a white powder on it? It's all like a Hollywood movie.

Yet, even prior to September 11, we lived in a world with more self-imposed pressure than any generation in history. Kids today are under pressure to make the team, make the grade, and then make the money. Parents feel pressure to be supermoms and -dads, as well as super employees at the job. I've talked to countless adults who say their careers demand their souls. Our lives are 45 percent more hectic now than when I was a kid in the 1960s and 70s. Although most of us say we want to simplify our lives, we continue to take on activities and commitments that push us harder.

I saw a cute cartoon showing two girls walking off a soccer field. One said to the other: "You've got ten minutes between soccer practice and piano lessons? What are you going to do with all that free time?"

MIRROR, MIRROR ON THE WALL

The truth of the matter is, pressure is neither good nor bad. In itself it is neutral. I like to think of it as a mirror. It reflects precisely who we are. It is the great revealer. Nothing will unveil your true colors more quickly than a day full of pressure.

Someone once said Christians are like tea. Our true colors come out when we're in hot water. Pressure can serve to disclose at least three things about us:

1. where we place our trust

2. what we are made of

3. whom we belong to

When the pressure is on, we see who we really are.

The story doesn't always have a fairy-tale ending. Even in Scripture we read about men who succumbed to pressure. A young man named John Mark quit Paul and Barnabas's mission team. He couldn't take the pressure.

Demas did the same thing. He preferred the pleasures of a life at ease over the fulfillment of obeying God in difficult situations. So he left Paul's team and settled into a life of compromise.

The rich young ruler approached Jesus one day and asked what he must do to inherit eternal life. Jesus was honest with him and spoke of surrender. The man walked away. Too much pressure. He had too many things to give up. We never hear of him again.

Early in 2002, America began to hear tragic stories of executives caught in the Enron scandal. The corporation had lost hundreds of millions of dollars belonging to their employees' 401Ks due to the poor management of Arthur Anderson. Before facing the embarrassment of legal proceedings, at least one of the executives committed suicide. Too much pressure. In their response to pressure, I believe we see where they placed their trust, what they were made of, and to whom they belonged. Pressure is the great revealer.

THE KEY QUESTION

I have always hoped I will respond well when faced with pressure. I've hoped I wouldn't compromise my faith and that I would stand for the principles I believe in. I got an early test when I was twenty years old.

When I developed diabetes in 1980, I remember sitting in the hospital bed, struggling with how I would respond. What should I pray? If I prayed for healing, should I refuse to take insulin, since that would demonstrate my lack of faith in God's healing power? I remembered a story in the Old Testament about God punishing a man because he put his faith in doctors rather than in God. I certainly didn't want to be guilty of that compromise.

On the other hand, if I didn't pray for healing, would I be

compromising God's power in my life? What if He wanted to perform a miracle? I didn't want to dilute the work of God because I was a spiritual wimp! Do I trust God or take insulin? This was heavy pressure for me, a young theology student in college.

I remember receiving some hope from God during my prayer time. It was as though He gave me a vision. It was a picture of a bicycle and a car. Then God posed a question: *Tim, if you were trusting me for a car to drive around town, would you be lacking faith if you rode a bike until you got the car?* I thought for a moment, then said, "No. That wouldn't be bad at all. It would simply be a temporary solution while I waited for the real solution. I would still continue to pray for the car."

Then it all became clear to me. In the same way that riding the bike would not demonstrate lack of faith, neither would taking insulin be a sign I wasn't trusting God. Insulin wasn't going to heal me anyway. It would simply keep me around as I waited for God to do whatever miracle He wants to do. I was still trusting Him.

The key question is always the same: Where am I placing my trust? If we place our faith in the doctor to heal us, or our jobs to pay us, or our supervisors to provide our sense of identity—our faith has been misplaced, and pressure will reveal this one day. Those instruments will fail to provide all we need. Our faith must be firmly placed in God, the great Provider. Anything else, and pressure will reveal our weakness.

WORK AND PRAY

This brings us to our point of application. When we are faced with pressure, are we to work at solving it, or to simply pray? Is praying sufficient? Are we to sit idly, and talk to God—expecting Him to resolve our pressure situations? Or are we to work to solve the problem? Doesn't working indicate we are trying to fix the situation ourselves, without trusting in God? How should we respond? How do we pray in this pivotal moment?

When faced with this dilemma, one king in the Old Testament escaped the tension by doing both. When threats of attack mounted from the Assyrian empire, King Hezekiah both used his skills and he prayed—all the while trusting God for the outcome. He demonstrated faith and total commitment by destroying the idolatrous shrines his father Ahaz had built (2 Chron. 28:22–25). King Ahaz knew little about trusting God under pressure. He'd given in to Assyrian pressure for years. In contrast, his son Hezekiah renewed Israel's covenant with the Lord (2 Chron. 29:10). He personally destroyed the people's favorite relic—the bronze serpent of Moses—because it distracted the people from trusting in Yahweh. He was determined to make things right with God.

However, Hezekiah's faith was as practical as it was devoted. He wisely took steps to protect the city's water supply by constructing a tunnel to the spring of Gihon (2 Chron. 32:30). When enemy troops besieged the city, they were unable to prevail. Hezekiah had preserved what they needed to survive.

Still, Jerusalem's survival was due to more than their king's foresight. When surrounded by well-trained troops who tried to dismay the Jews with propaganda, the king trusted God rather than turn to foreign allies, as Ahaz had done. The Lord honored Hezekiah's faith with the miraculous departure of the Assyrians (2 Chron. 19:35–36).

So what's our takeaway? Simple: The issue is not work versus prayer when we're under pressure. We are to do both. We must simply make sure that our work *deepens* our trust in God, rather than *distracts* us from trusting God.

I love the picture David provides for us in the Psalms. He describes his relationship with God as a "weaned child" (Ps. 131:2). Think about this metaphor. He was not a baby—he was weaned. This meant that he could do some things himself in cooperation with his

Father in heaven. (Babies just lie in their cribs and cry, eat, and soil their diapers.) On the other hand, he still called himself a "child," meaning he was dependent on his heavenly Father for provision. It reminds me of the little boy who boasted to his friends one day: "When I grow up, I'm going to be a lion tamer! I'm going to walk right up to the lions in the circus, with a whip and a chair, and I won't be afraid." Then he paused and added, "Of course, I'll have my dad with me."

This is how Hezekiah acted. This is how David acted. Under pressure, they acted with courage but also acknowledged, "Of course, I have my Father with me." When pressure comes to us, it isn't wrong to act. Many times we *should* take action. But we must let that pressure reveal to us where we really place our trust. Then, as we remember our identity in God, we can both pray and act, fully trusting the outcome to Him. Let the pivotal moment find you praying as well as using your skills—always trusting the One to whom you pray and for whom you work.

Pressure is the great revealer. It comes to us whether we're ready or not. As you recognize such pivotal moments in your life, let the pressure push you toward God, not away from Him.

What We Learn From Peter and Rhoda

Seldom do we face the kind of pressure the early Christians did in the book of Acts. They frequently found themselves facing threats because of their faith in Jesus. I got a little taste of this myself as I shared Christ on the streets.

I was with a friend named Eric when we approached a group of young men who were wearing leather, chains, and lots of metal. We asked if they had a minute to talk. One of them grunted an affirmative. The trouble began when we inquired if they had ever built a relationship with Christ or ever been to church. The ringleader walked up and got right in our face. When he got close enough, he pulled out a knife and held it up to our throats. He laughed as we grew very tense. After a moment or two, he said to us, "I don't think you really believe that religious b— s—, do you?"

Eric and I both looked at each other as if to say, "Go ahead and answer the man." He laughed some more and held the knife closer. He was now touching our necks as he moved it back and forth. With a smirk he asked the question again. This time, we both looked at him and found a way to say, "Yeah, we do believe what we're talking about." We paused. Then, I spoke again. "We wouldn't be out here if we didn't believe the Scripture. We're just hoping to help others find a relationship with Jesus, too." Then, Eric chimed in. "And if you were to kill us with that knife, tonight," he said, "it would just be graduation day for us."

There was a pregnant moment of silence. Then, the guy pulled his knife back, and put it in his pocket again. He said, "That's good." (Silently, both Eric and I were thinking, "Yes—that's really good!") Then, this young man went on. "I see you religious people out here all the time, pawning your message like some plastic televangelist. I just wanted to meet one of you who actually believed in what you were saying."

That comment launched an hour-long conversation, ending up in a prayer time that revolutionized that young man's life. He asked Christ to take over his life.

Sometime later, I was out sharing with people on the streets again and came upon another group of similar looking young men— leather, chains, ear and nose rings, haircuts you could get hurt on. When I spoke to them and asked if they had a minute to talk, one of them responded by saying, "What do you wanna talk about?"

When I told them I wanted to talk about their faith in God, the spokesman for the group, Damon, started cussing at me. He let me know explicitly they didn't want to talk about spiritual "stuff" that night. Wanting to oblige, I told them we could talk another time and started to walk away.

Just as I got to the perimeter of their little gang, I heard Damon start talking about his back. Evidently, he had injured it on a construction site a day or two earlier. He was swearing as he described the pain he was in. I could tell it was very real. In that moment, the Lord spoke to me in a still, small voice. He whispered that He wanted me to go back and pray for that young man. I was stunned. I whispered back to the Lord, reminding Him that the guy just told me he wasn't interested in talking about spiritual "stuff" (as if God needed my reminder). When the Lord wouldn't let me get away, I said to Him, "Alright. I'll go back and pray for the guy. But if he gets mad, it's Your fault!"

I stepped back within earshot and asked Damon if I had heard correctly about his back. When he started in with the cuss words again, I knew I had. I cleared my throat, and managed to say, "Well, I know you guys told me you didn't want to talk about spiritual stuff tonight, but I believe in the power of prayer." Everyone was quiet. I decided that was my cue to go on. "I don't know what you believe, but would you mind if I took a minute and prayed for your back?"

"You wanna what?" Damon inquired, without a cuss word this time.

I repeated my offer. He couldn't turn it down. All of a sudden, you'd have thought I was just introduced to sing the national anthem. They took off their hats, bowed their heads, put their hand on their hearts. I put my hand on Damon's back and prayed a straightforward, simple prayer. I prayed: "God, show these guys You are real, and that You care for them. Reveal Yourself to them as the Great Physician. Amen."

The minute I ended my prayer, Damon stood straight up and yelled, "What'd you do to me?"

I said, "Nothing. I promise." I didn't want to get in any more trouble that night.

"No. You did something. I felt all the pain leave my back when you said 'Amen.'"

At that point, I suddenly got it. Calmly, I began to explain the love of God and the power of God to those unchurched young men. I had their undivided attention. After my little explanation, some of the others formed a little "healing line," wanting prayer for their wrist, their eyes, their back, or their neck. We prayed several times that night. The next week, I was back out on the street, and noticed they were waiting for me, with a lawn chair for me to sit in! It was awesome. Two of them gave their heart to the Lord.

LESSONS FROM THE BOOK OF ACTS

I had always hoped I would respond well in a pressure situation. I don't always, but on those two occasions it was so rewarding to see God come through when I was in a tough spot. I love it when I get to experience miracles like those we read about in the book of Acts. In almost every chapter, we read about someone who found themselves in a pressure situation. I believe there are lessons to be learned from how they responded.

RHODA'S PRAYER GROUP

In Acts 12:5-17, we read about Rhoda's prayer meeting. It was held in Mary's home, John Mark's mother While they prayed, there was a knock at the door. To Rhoda's surprise, when she answered the knock, Peter was at her doorstep. It was a miracle. He had just been released from prison by an angel during the prayer meeting. In utter amazement, she slammed the door on him and ran back to tell the others their prayers had been answered! Instead of rejoicing with her, they burst her bubble. They refused to believe her. They had been toiling in prayer—but never really trusted God to answer. Sound familiar?

There are many insights we can learn from this little episode. This prayer group was praying at a pivotal moment. The religious leaders had turned up the heat on the early church. The pressure was on. And while God miraculously set Peter free, I believe it was in spite of this group of people. Let me suggest why I say this.

First, this prayer group failed in their experience. They were going through the motions, not acting on convictions. Had they prayed their convictions, they would not have been so surprised at Peter's release. They would have seen it as a direct answer to their specific prayer.

Second, their prayer group failed in their expectation. They failed to connect the power of prayer to this miracle. They may have said the right words, but they never expected them to be answered, and so they refused to believe Rhoda's report.

Third, their prayer group failed in their explanation. They had the audacity to suggest other alternatives as to why Rhoda thought she'd witnessed a miracle. They explained it away as a hallucination or a ghost. Instead of taking the time to go and see for themselves, they wasted time attempting a believable theory.

PETER'S PRAYER GROUP

Remember, praying under pressure reveals where we are placing our trust, what we are made of, and who we belong to. Rhoda's prayer group missed the mark.

Earlier, in Acts 4, Peter had participated in a little prayer group of his own. This group stands in stark contrast to the one in Acts 12. In order to comprehend the pivotal moment, let me share the context. Peter has just been reprimanded by the religious leaders for preaching Christ. When he is told to keep quiet, he says: "Whether it is right in the sight of God to give heed to you rather than to God, you be the judge; for we cannot stop speaking what we have seen and heard" (vv. 19-20 NASB).

At that point, Peter returns to his friends who hold a prayer meeting, not unlike Rhoda's. But they pray differently. Under the threat of torture, they begin by worshiping God, reviewing how faithful He'd been through history. Then they pray: "And now, Lord, take note of their threats, and grant that Thy bond-servants may speak Thy word with all confidence, while Thou dost extend Thy hand to heal, and signs and wonders take place through the name of Thy holy servant Jesus" (vv. 29-30 NASB).

What a prayer! Do you see how they stayed on the offensive and prayed from conviction? I'm sure they were tempted to cave in and panic. Their lives were threatened but they didn't even flinch. Remembering where they were placing their trust, and Who they belonged to, they spoke from deep conviction. They operated out of principles—truths they had chosen to live and die by. That's why their prayer was the same under pressure as it was any other time. Isn't that what we all want—consistency under pressure?

PUTTING GOD ON THE SPOT

Some have told me that this is idealistic—that conjuring up this kind of courage sets us up to put God on the spot. And, as a result, we pray things far beyond what we should. I disagree. I believe we fail to see God move more often because we're afraid to pray what He is really capable of doing. Think about it. If anyone can stand being on the spot, it is God. But He allows us to choose how we pray and act under pressure. If there is a journey of a thousand steps between us and God, He will take all but one. He will leave the final one to us. The choice is ours.

Dr. Helen Roseveare was a famous British missionary doctor in

Zaire. Her autobiography, *Give Me This Mountain,* is full of stories of such prayers under pressure. She spoke of one evening when a mother died giving birth to her baby. The mom left behind not only a premature newborn, but her two-year-old daughter to be cared for. They had no incubator or electricity and the nights were cool. An assistant fetched a hot water bottle, but soon returned in desperation because it had burst. They simply held the baby as close to the fire as they could through the night.

The following day, Helen held a prayer time with the children in her orphanage. She told them about the baby and the two-year-old girl, who now had no mother. Ruth, a ten-year-old girl prayed with the typical, brutal directness of African children: "Please God, send us a hot water bottle. Tomorrow will be too late, God, because the baby will be dead by then, so please send it this afternoon." Helen took a deep breath because of the prayer's directness, then heard little Ruth continue: "And while You're at it, would You please send a doll for the little girl, so that she knows that You really love her?"

To be honest, Helen could not believe God would do that. Oh, yes, God can do anything—she knew that theoretically. It is written in the Bible. But there are limits, aren't there? Helen hadn't received any parcels from home in four long years. Further, if anyone did send a parcel, why would they send a hot water bottle to tropical Africa?

Late that afternoon, she heard a car had come by the orphanage while she was away. Whoever it was had left a package on the veranda of her living room. She could feel the tears welling up inside. She took it into the room where the girls were playing, and looked inside. Apart from clothes and bandages, the parcel contained—she could hardly believe her eyes—a hot water bottle!

Helen just sat and cried. She'd seen no packages in four years, and today one came with precisely what they needed. She dared not ask God for it, but little Ruth had. When the water bottle was removed from the box, Ruth ran up to the front, shouting, "If God sent the hot water bottle, he must have sent the doll, too!"

She dug to the bottom of the parcel and pulled out a beautiful doll. Her eyes shone. She had not doubted God for a moment, even under pressure. "Can we go to the little girl and give her the doll so she knows God loves her?" she asked.

The parcel had been on its way for five months, sent by a Sunday school class. It had been mailed months before a ten-year-old girl named Ruth would pray, "God, we need it this afternoon." The words in the Bible are true: "Before they call, I will answer them" (Isaiah 65:24).

You see, even though we're under pressure most of the time, God never is.

CLOSING PRAYER

A Pivotal Prayer
When You are Under Pressure

Dear Lord,
I'm feeling stress right now.
I'm under pressure and I want to fix it.
Help me to relax and cast my cares on You.
Remind me through this day that I belong to You,
and that I can trust You.
You're never under pressure.
When I act, enable me to work in cooperation with You,
and not be distracted by what I do.
Thank You, Lord.
In Jesus' name,
Amen.

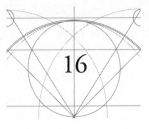

PIVOTAL PRAYING WHEN YOU
NEED TO TAKE A STAND
(JOHN HULL)

Stroll through a bookstore these days and visit the biographical section. You'll find there a growing number of books about the life and presidency of Ronald Wilson Reagan. From Lou Cannon, who followed Reagan's political career when he was first elected governor of California in 1966, to Peggy Noonan, who was one of his presidential speech writers, the literature on Ronald Reagan is growing.

Reagan was known as "The Great Communicator." From his earlier careers as a radio broadcaster and screen actor, Reagan had acquired the ability to use words and phrases that touched the hearts of Republicans, Democrats, and independents alike.

When Reagan spoke, his words had conviction. Compared to recent presidents before and after, Reagan arguably possessed that unique blend of style and substance rooted in character.

Granted, during his administration some of Reagan's opponents complained that he was simply the "Teflon president"—so smooth that nothing stuck to him. They argued that he was all style and no substance. But as time has passed, such perceptions of him have changed. What was it about this man, the oldest person to ever hold the office of president, that—two decades after he was first elected—increasingly endears him to the American people?

Peggy Noonan argues that it was his character. Reagan, she believes, had the courage to act on his convictions—convictions based in a value system that embraced a personal faith in God and a fundamental belief that the American people could accomplish goodness and greatness with God's help. Reagan loved freedom and hated tyranny. Noonan writes,

> He had courage. He always tried to do what he thought was right. And when doing what was right demanded from him great effort or patience or tenacity, or made him focus on unending attacks and criticism, he summoned from within the patience and the tenacity and the courage to face it all. To face it down. And when his great work was finished he left and went peacefully home.[1]

Reagan wasn't afraid to express his convictions, even when they were unpopular, or to act on his convictions when he felt he needed to draw a line in the sand with the enemies of freedom.

Call it raw conviction. Call it courage. Gordon MacDonald says:

> Character and conviction are closely associated concepts. We use the word "character" to describe the overall demeanor of a person. It provides a picture of how we see this individual living day in and day out through routine events. . . . Convictions are principles of life that grow out of the soil of our belief. They arise from the soul. A more modern word might be *values.*[2]

For eight years Ronald Reagan took a stand on most issues that crossed his desk, and most Americans respected him for it. He had core values that he wouldn't compromise, and the courage to stand upon those convictions regardless of the cost. He knew how to draw the line and communicate his convictions clearly. He also warned of the consequences of crossing that line. Just ask the air traffic controllers who went on an illegal strike early in Reagan's administration. He fired them all!

Sometimes life puts our convictions and courage to the test. In a university classroom where the very existence of God is questioned, it takes enormous courage to say with conviction, "I disagree!" In a business context, where ethics are sometimes clouded and morals are often compromised, to stand courageously for what you believe may cost you your livelihood. At moments like these our prayer takes on new depth and dimension. After all, these are the scenarios when the pressure is on and our convictions are tested.

DRAWING OUR OWN LINE

A few decades ago, baseball's Kansas City Royals went to the World Series. Their first baseman was Willie Mays Aikens. Named by his mother after the San Francisco Giant immortal, Willie Mays, Aikens became a center of attention and national conversation in the Series, not for what he did with his bat but for what he did before he even stepped up to the plate.

Aikens, a left-handed batter, had the deliberate habit of gradually moving his left foot out of the rear chalk line of the batter's box. He'd slowly begin to dig his spikes into the ground where the line was, kicking and mixing the white lime into the brown dirt. After a few at bats, the back line of the batter's box was just about gone. Aikens knew that the farther back he was in the batter's box, the better his advantage in getting around on a pitch and successfully getting a base hit.

As the World Series progressed, the announcers brought attention to Aikens's routine. The cameras began to focus on his left foot kicking the lime into the dirt. By the third or fourth game into the series, it had become something of a novelty to watch. Aikens would come to the plate, move his left leg and foot with that kicking-and-mixing motion, and gradually move his foot outside the batter's box.

Amusing? To the fans, yes. But to the umpires, no. While what Aikens did was captivating, it was also against the rules. In baseball, a batter has to have both feet inside the batter's box.

A few games into the series, Aikens walked up to bat. As he stepped into the box the home-plate umpire took the bat from Aikens's hands, tilted the thin end toward the ground, and with the bat drew a line to clearly mark where the back of the batter's box ends. Then he told Aikens that if he crossed that line he was out!

There are times in our lives when a clear line has to be drawn. When things become contorted in the culture and God's truth is being mocked, when people cease to abide by rules of right and wrong, these are times when God's people have to draw the line. And when Christians take a stand at such pivotal moments, there had better be some prayerful reinforcement.

Drawing a line in the sand takes courage. Telling someone he is out of bounds in his conduct is risky. The possibility is high that we'll be rejected and marginalized. But if we are to be the kind of people God calls us to be, we sometimes have to prayerfully draw the line.

Standing Up in Terrible Times

When the former Soviet Union was rapidly losing its Communist hold on the nation in the late 1980s, then president Mikhail Gorbachev, a charming and brilliant man who was admired by many in the West, sank in popularity with the Russian people. Gorbachav was seen by the many Russians as part of the old way of doing things. It was a terrible time in Russia, and the people wanted a new kind of leader.

In the midst of all the uncertainty, a lesser-known Russian politician rose to the occasion, literally by standing on top of a tank on a crowded street before thousands of people, cheering them toward democracy. Boris Yeltzin gained worldwide recognition and respect as a new leader and a fresh face. The people saw him as a real reformer, and later, in a constitutionally democratized Russia, elected him to become their president.

Courage is the ability to stay the course when it looks like the course is dangerous and unpopular. Aristotle said, "We become brave by doing brave acts." He continued, noting that people who take a stand "despise things that are terrible."

THESE WERE THE DAYS OF ELIJAH

In ancient Israel a prophet of God, Elijah, witnessed some terrible things taking place in Israel concerning their worship. He was forced to draw a figurative line in the sand, communicating that the people of Israel were way out of line when it came to the will of God. Under enormous pressure and hostile surroundings, Elijah showed amazing courage and a faith that was rooted in prayer.

Imagine Elijah as a David, and everyone around him as a collective Goliath. Never was praying more sensible, or more needed.

The scene was Mount Carmel in Northern Israel. Elijah was sent by God to confront the Northern Kingdom with their unfaithfulness to God. The Northern Kingdom had never had a godly king. Each kingly administration seemed to lead the people deeper and deeper into idolatry. The culture was in rapid spiritual and moral decline as they aggressively worshiped their false god, Baal.

Elijah courageously confronted the king of the north, Ahab, with an announcement: "There will be no rain in the next few years except at my word." One can only imagine the faces of the people who heard him make this statement. They must have wondered if he had lost his senses.

Elijah then departed the scene and did not come back to King

Ahab for several years. As he had predicted, there was no rain in the land since he had spoken those ill-fated words. Instead there was drought and despair.

Soon Elijah arranged a meeting with King Ahab and hundreds of false prophets. Over half of these false prophets had sworn their allegiance to Baal. Then Elijah took his stand. Before a relatively silent crowd, he asked a powerful question: "How long will you waiver between two opinions? If the LORD is God, follow him; but if Baal is God, follow him" (1 Kings 18:21).

The people were quiet. They weren't prepared to make a decision. It takes courage to make hard decisions. Elijah had made his: He would follow the Lord God.

During World War II, Winston Churchill was forced to make a painful choice. The British secret service had broken the Nazi code and informed Churchill that the Germans were going to bomb Coventry. He had two alternatives: (1) evacuate the citizens and save hundreds of lives at the expense of indicating to the Germans that the code was broken; or (2) take no action, which would result in the loss of hundreds of lives but would keep the information flowing, ultimately saving many more lives. Churchill followed the second course.[3]

The people on Mount Carmel also had two alternatives: follow God or follow Baal. When Elijah gave the challenge, the crowd was silent. Then, trusting in God, he did something unprecedented: He told the people,

> Get two bulls for us. Let them choose one for themselves, and let them cut it into pieces and put it on the wood but not set fire to it. I will prepare the other bull and put it on the wood but not set fire to it. Then you call on the name of your god, and I will call on the name of the LORD. The god who answers by fire—he is God. (1 Kings 18:24)

So the people did exactly that. And all day long, after careful preparations, they called on Baal. And called on Baal. And called on Baal. They shouted, cried, danced, you name it—still no fire. Elijah told them to shout louder. They did. Still no fire. Then they started cutting themselves open, moving more into a mindless frenzy. On and on they went, and still no fire.

Then Elijah said, "Come here," and began to teach them a new lesson about God. He rebuilt the broken altar of God, which had been ignored by Ahab's administration, and dug a trench around it. He stacked wood and the sacrificial remains of an animal upon it. Then, oddly, he instructed them to pour four large jars of water on the altar and the wood. He instructed them to do this not once but three times. After the third time, there was enough water to fill the trench.

Elijah then, with great courage, prayed this pivotal prayer as he prepared to take his stand for God: "O LORD, . . . let it be known today that you are God in Israel" (1 Kings 18:36).

As hundreds, perhaps thousands, looked on, Elijah stood alone and asked God to come through big time. He put it all on the line. Humanly speaking, he took a stand against all odds!

I sometimes think of Elijah's plight as the plight of those surrounded by Santa Anna's armies at the Alamo. The commandant, William Barret Travis, wrote of this occasion, "I am besieged by a thousand or more of the Mexicans under Santa Anna. I am determined to sustain myself as long as possible and die like a soldier who never forgets what is due to his own honor and that of this country."[4]

Elijah, besieged by hundreds of prophets who worshiped idols, sustained himself in the power of God and prayed. In an incredible moment, God answered Elijah's prayer, sending such fire from heaven that it consumed the altar, the wood, and even the water in the trenches.

Elijah had drawn the line: "Let God be God." You may find yourself surrounded by opportunities to compromise what matters most to you. And if you're not careful—if you don't make up your mind and decide for yourself—someone else may decide for you.

The Courage to Make up Your Mind

Ronald Reagan had an aunt who took him to a cobbler for a pair of new shoes. The cobbler asked the young Reagan, "Do you want square toes or round toes?" Unable to decide, Reagan didn't answer, so the cobbler gave him a few days.

Several days later the cobbler saw Reagan on the street and asked him again what kind of toes he wanted on his shoes. Reagan still couldn't decide, so the shoemaker said, "Well, come by in a couple of days and I'll have your shoes ready."

When the future president did so, he found one square-toed shoe and one round-toed shoe. "This will teach you to never let people make decisions for you," the cobbler said to the indecisive Reagan.

"I learned right then and there," Reagan later said, "that if you don't make your own decisions, someone else will."[5]

Is there something you need to make a decision about? Don't let others make it for you. Do you need to take a stand on a defining issue? Don't cave in to pressure. Don't just go with the flow. Don't look the other way. It's time for you to "let God be God" in your life.

Don't let the shadow of indecision constantly follow you. Sure, it's tough now. The enemy is attractive, powerful, and strangely sensible sometimes. But you have God and you have prayer! If God has called you to a life of courage, to take a stand, to do what is right regardless of the cost at this pivotal moment, call on Him to give you courage to do the right thing—to draw a line in the sand—to be a person of character and conviction for the glory of God.

CLOSING PRAYER

A Pivotal Prayer
When Taking a Stand

God, this is a situation in which, quite frankly,
it would be fine for me to be just another
face in the crowd.
Taking a stand means I'll probably stand out,
and that isn't something I feel comfortable doing.
I thought that was for others,
like my pastor or those preachers on TV.
Yet if I don't take a strong stand now,
I'm going to have a hard time living with myself.
Help me to be firm, but fair.
Help me rise to the occasion,
not with anger, but with a smile on my face.
Lord, this is going to be hard for me.
I'm going against the tide on this one.
Help me not to drown!
Amen.

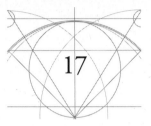

17

911
PRAYERS
(JOHN HULL)

He was sipping a Coke as he did every morning when he got to his desk at the Pentagon. Slipping off to the rest room on this September morning, Lt. Col. Brian Birdwell, a Gulf War veteran, contemplated the day before him, as well as the news he'd just received that a plane had just crashed into one of the Twin Towers in New York City.

Three to four steps out of the rest room, he was thrown to the ground by a tremendous impact. "Bomb!" Birdwell thought, as the blast tore through the building.

A jet flown by terrorists had flown directly into the Pentagon, only three windows from Birdwell's office. As he got up, Birdwell realized that his entire body was on fire.

"Jesus," he prayed, "I'm coming to see you."

At that pivotal moment, believing he was minutes from death, Birdwell sent this emergency prayer to heaven. By God's grace, Birdwell, a committed Christian, survived the explosion and is slowly recovering with the love and support of his wife, Mel.[1]

There are times when unexpected, emergency situations hit our lives. Out of utter desperation, we call directly on God for help. Nothing else will suffice.

When our daughter Mary Alice was born, Sharon and I were delighted. During the delivery process, though, Mary Alice had turned and twisted inside Sharon so much that the umbilical cord was wrapped tightly around her neck. When she was delivered, she was blue. Within seconds, the doctors and nurses grabbed Mary Alice and put her on a table in an adjoining room to resuscitate her.

Sharon, who just seconds earlier had gone through the pains of childbirth, looked at me in total fear.

"What happened?" she asked.

I told her something was wrong with Mary Alice, but that I didn't know what. All I could do was hold her hand and glance back and forth between her and the room where they were trying to save our newborn daughter. Sharon burst into tears, exhausted from the birthing experience, and simply prayed, "O Jesus! O Jesus!"

Mary Alice is now a thriving teenager. Still, as I relive that day some thirteen years ago, it brings tears to my eyes. In that emergency situation, all we could do was call out His name, "Jesus." But that was enough. He was listening and He knew the pain we were experiencing.

They say that 911 emergency systems are state of the art. All you need do is dial those numbers, and you will almost instantly be connected to a dispatcher. Displayed before the dispatcher will be a readout that lists your telephone number, your address, and the name by which that telephone number is listed at that address. Also listening in are the police, fire department, and paramedics.

A caller might not be able to say what the problem is. Or a woman whose husband has just suffered a heart attack may be so traumatized that all she can do is scream hysterically into the telephone. But the dispatcher doesn't need her to say anything. All of the vital information is there. Help is on the way.[2]

There are times in our lives when, in our desperation and pain, we say "911 prayers." Sometimes we don't know the words to speak.

Someone might say, "Jesus, I'm coming to see you." Someone else might say, "O Jesus! O Jesus!" But whatever the words, no matter how fearful they may be, God hears. He knows our names and our circumstances. Help is on the way.

CLOSING PRAYER

A Pivotal
911 Prayer

*Lord, I never expected something like this to happen.
I'm afraid, I'm hurting,
and I just don't know what to do.
So, God—I'm turning to You.
Only You know the answer to this awful situation.
Only You can give me the peace I so
desperately need right now.
Please, help me.
Amen.*

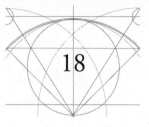

THE MOST IMPORTANT PIVOTAL PRAYER YOU'LL EVER PRAY

(JOHN HULL)

A widowed Scottish minister named John Harper and his six-year-old daughter were on board the *Titanic* the tragic night it sank. When the ship began to sink, Harper, traveling second class, handed his daughter to an officer on an upper deck, who put her into a lifeboat. He then began to help those on his deck. Others were doing this as well, but Harper's assistance was unique because of his instructions, heard over and over during the chaos: "Women and children and the unsaved into the lifeboats first. Women and children and the unsaved into the lifeboats first."

John Harper recognized the moment as the threshold of eternity. He was ready to face God, but knew that many on board were not.

As a minister, Harper's lips had often declared God's love for the lost. Now his life jacket declared it as an ultimate act. When he came upon a man without a life jacket, Harper took off his own and put it on the man.

Later, floating in the emptiness of the dark chilling waters, a survivor came within sight of a man struggling to stay afloat. It was John Harper. Rather than asking for help, Harper called out to the man, "Are you saved?"

"No," came the answer.

"Believe on the Lord Jesus, and thou shalt be saved," Harper said.

The man's reply was one of silence as they drifted out of sight of one another. A little later, the man spied Harper again, and again Harper called out to him.

"Are you saved now?"

Again the answer, "No, I can't honestly say that I am."

Again the refrain, weaker but still clear, "Believe on the Lord Jesus Christ and thou shalt be saved." Then silence, as John Harper slipped below the surface and into the arms of God.

Later, in a meeting in Ontario, Canada, the survivor stood up and told this story. He ended with these words: "Shortly after he went down, and there, alone in the night with two miles of water under me, I believed."[1]

Paul wrote to the church at Rome, "If you confess with your mouth, 'Jesus is Lord,' and believe in your heart that God raised him from the dead, you will be saved" (Rom. 10:9).

John Harper proclaimed these words to anyone who would listen as he treaded the icy waters of the Atlantic Ocean that fateful night. These were not the words of a lunatic fearing death, but of a man who understood that eternity for him and others was just around the corner. He was ready, and he wanted others to be ready as well.

John Harper knew that people don't just drift to heaven. They need to be told about Jesus and then must receive Him into their lives. He shared with those fearful passengers that Jesus loved them and that He would save them from their sins and for eternity. He wanted them to believe on the Lord Jesus Christ and receive Him into their lives. He wanted them to pray the most important pivotal prayer they could ever pray.

Have you confessed that Jesus is truly Lord and meant it with all your heart? Do you believe that Jesus died for your sins and that three days later He rose from the dead? If you haven't prayed this pivotal prayer, why not do so now?

Pray, won't you, the most important pivotal prayer you can ever pray, which you'll find on the next page.

CLOSING PRAYER

A Pivotal Prayer
for Salvation

Lord Jesus, I know I have sinned and cannot save myself.
Please forgive me.
I believe You died on the cross for my sins.
I thank You for that.
And I believe that You rose from the dead
and that You live forever.
I truly desire that You come into my life.
Right now I open the door of my life
and ask You to come and live in me.
I receive You now, Jesus,
as my Lord and Savior.
Thank You for answering my prayer.
Help me to live for You.
Make me the person You want me to be.
Amen.

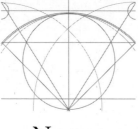

NOTES

CHAPTER 3

1. *World Pulse Magazine,* November 2001.

CHAPTER 2

1. Roy Zuck, *Praying in Times of Crisis* (Garland, Tex.: American Tract Society, 2001), 1.
2. Eugene Peterson, *Earth and Altar* (Downer's Grove, Ill.: InterVarsity Press, 1985), as quoted at www.ivcf.org/crisis/prayer.html
3. Mark Coppenger, *Leading in Troubled Times: Responding to Crisis,* as quoted at *www.lifeway.com/pastor,* October 2001.
4. Capt. Alan Bean, "Crises," *Reader's Digest,* as quoted at *www.christianglobe.com/illustrations*
5. Jim Cymbala, *Fresh Wind, Fresh Fire* (Grand Rapids, Mich.: Zondervan, 1997), 23.
6. Alan Loy McGinnis, *The Power of Optimism,* (New York: HarperCollins, 1990).

CHAPTER 3

1. Douglas MacArthur, as quoted in *Leadership* 3, no. 2 (spring 1985): 2.
2. David Thomas, as quoted in *Marriage Partnership* 7, no. 3 (fall 1990).
3. Gordon MacDonald, *Pastor's Progress,* as quoted in LeadershipJournal.net at *www.christianitytoday.com/le/713/713078.html*
4. Mark Galli and James Bell, *The Complete Idiot's Guide to Prayer* (Indianapolis, Ind.: Alpha Books, 1999), 16.
5. Wayne Jacobsen, "Beyond Prayer Requests," *Leadership* 23, no. 4 (fall 2001): 48–52.
6. Ibid.

7. C. S. Lewis, *Letters to Malcolm,* as quoted in *PreachingToday.com* 31, no. 13.

8. Blaine Smith, *Moving Ahead After the Letdown,*www.spiritualcrosswalk.com, article display, PTID74456.

9. Tony Barnhart, "O'Leary's Shining Hour Ended in Gloom," (The Atlanta Journal-Consitution, 16 December 2001).

10. Guy Curtright, "??????," (The Atlanta Journal-Constitution, 22 July 2001).

CHAPTER 4

1. Luis Palau and Jonathan Graf, "Moving Mountains," *Pray* (March/April 2002): 34–37.

2. John Piper, "Coronary Christians," *World* (23 February 2002): 37.

3. Ted Olson, "One Nation Under God," *Christianity Today* (4 February 2002): 36.

4. Randy Sprinkler, *Follow Me* (Birmingham, Ala.: New Hope, 2001), 85.

5. Henri J. M. Nouwen, *Reaching Out,* as quoted in *Christianity Today* 32, no. 6.

CHAPTER 5

1. Charles Panati, *Extraordinary Origins for Ordinary Things* (New York: Harper & Row, 1987).

2. Donald Bloesch as quoted in Galli and Bell, *The Complete Idiot's Guide to Prayer*, 28.

3. Ibid.

4. Ole Hallesby, *Prayer* trans. by Clarence J. Carlsen (Minneapolis, Minn.: Augsburg Fortress, 1994).

CHAPTER 6

1. Adam Hamilton, "Rehearsing the Covenant," *Leadership* (fall 2001): 40.

2. Ibid., 42.

3. Bill Thrasher, *Living the Life God Has Planned* (Chicago: Moody Press, 2001), 157–74.

4. Tim Hansel, *Holy Sweat* (Dallas: Word, 1987), 63.

5. Berit Kjos, *A Wardrobe from the King* (Colorado Springs, Colo.: Chariot Victor, 1988), 45–46.

CHAPTER 7

1. *Life* (March 1994).

2. Ben Patterson, *Waiting* (Downers Grove, Ill.: InterVarsity Press, 1989), 11.

CHAPTER 8

1. Eric Reed, Marshall Shelley, and Drew Zahn, "Leave Room for God: An Interview with Ed Dobson," *Leadership* (fall 2001): 28–34.

2. Ibid.

3. George Sweeting, *Too Soon to Quit* (Chicago: Moody Press, 1999), 9.
4. Reed, Shelley, and Zahn, "Leave Room for God," 28–34.
5. Ibid.

CHAPTER 9

1. John Piper, "Prayer: The Power That Wields the Weapon," *Mission Frontier* (June–July, 1989): 15.
2. Ibid., 16.
3. Warren Wiersbe, "The Patented Preacher," *Christianity Today* 38, no. 5, as quoted in *Leadership* (winter 1997).
4. Thomas à Kempis, *The Imitation of Christ* (Nashville: Thomas Nelson Publishers, 1979), 119.
5. Edward K. Rowell, *Fresh Illustrations for Preaching and Teaching* (Grand Rapids, Mich.: Baker Books, 1997), 172.
6. Harold Kohn as quoted in Alan Nelson, *Broken in the Right Place* (Nashville: Thomas Nelson Publishers, 1994), 64.
7. Ibid., 125.
8. Ibid., 19.
9. Marshall Shelley, as quoted in *Leadership* 4, no. 3: 3.
10. Thomas J. Watson, as quoted in *Leadership* 1, no. 1.

CHAPTER 10

1. Vera Sinton, *How Can I Forgive?* (Oxford: Lion Publishing, 1999), 8–9.
2. Ibid., 9–10.
3. Sprinkler, *Follow Me,* 56–57.
4. John MacArthur, *Forgiveness* (Wheaton, Ill.: Crossway Books, 1998), 114.
5. Helmut Thielicke, "How to Believe Again," *Leadership* 6, no. 2.
6. Steve Brown, *Approaching God* (Nashville: Moorings, 1996), 203.

CHAPTER 11

1. Ben Patterson, "Holy War," *www.ChristianityToday.com/le/9l2/9l2116.html,* 1.
2. Ibid., 1.
3. Ibid., 5.
4. C. S. Lewis, *The Problem of Pain* (New York: MacMillan Publishing Co., 1962), 71.
5. Franklin Roosevelt as quoted in Galli and Bell, *The Complete Idiot's Guide to Prayer,* 109.
6. C. S. Lewis as quoted in Galli and Bell, *The Complete Idiot's Guide to Prayer,* 68.

CHAPTER 12

1. Lynn H. Pryor, as quoted in *Leadership* 12, no.1.

2. Philip Yancey, *Disappointment with God* (Grand Rapids, Mich.: Zondervan, 1997), 187.

3. Ibid., 185–86.

4. Henri Nouwen as quoted in Charles Stanley, *How to Handle Adversity* (Nashville: Thomas Nelson Publishers, 1989), 37–39.

CHAPTER 13

1. Paul Lee Tan, *Encyclopedia of 7700 Illustrations*, (Rockville, Md.: Assurance Publishers, 1983), 287.

2. Harry Emerson Fosdick, *The Meaning of Prayer*, as quoted in *Leadership* 10, no. 4: 20.

3. Tony Carnes, "Bush's Defining Moment," *Christianity Today* 45, no. 14 (12 November 2001): 38–42.

4. Alynda Wheat, *Fortune Magazine*, 12 November 2001.

5. Joseph Grant, *The American Fundamentalist*, as quoted in *Encyclopedia of 7700 Illustrations*, (Rockville, Md.: Assurance Publishers, 1983), 288.

CHAPTER 14

1. Corrie Cutter, "Families of Hostage Couple Wait," *Christianity Today* (11 March 2002): 26.

2. Ibid.

3. "Special Report: Burnhams," New Tribes Missions, *www.ntm.org/connect/burnham/update.shtml*, 10 June 2002.

4. "Hostages Killed in Philippines," *cnn.com*, 7 June 2002.

5. "Patience," *Our Daily Bread*, as quoted at *www.christianglobe.com/illustrations*

6. Gordon MacDonald, *The Life God Blesses* (Nashville: Thomas Nelson Publishers, 1997), 203.

7. Robert Schuller, *Tough Times Don't Last but Tough People Do* (Nashville: Thomas Nelson Publishers, 1996), 49.

8. John Piper, *Future Grace* (Sisters, Ore.: Multnomah, 1995), 180.

9. H. C. G. Moule, *Charles Simeon* (London: InterVarsity Press, 1948), 204.

10. Ibid., 172.

CHAPTER 15

1. Ron Moreau, "Delivered from Evil," *Newsweek* (26 November 2001): 52–53.

CHAPTER 16

1. Peggy Noonan, *When Character Was King* (New York: Viking Press, 2001), 325.

2. MacDonald, *The Life God Blesses*, 172.

3. Klyne Snodgrass, *Between Two Truths: Living with Biblical Tensions* (Grand Rapids, Mich.: Zondervan, 1990), 179.

4. William J. Bennett, *The Book of Virtues* (New York: Simon & Schuster, 1993), 485.

5. Moody Bible Institute, *Today in the Word* (Chicago: Moody Bible Institute/Moody Press, 1991), 16.

CHAPTER 17

1. Angie Cannon, "Come Toward My Voice," *U.S. News and World Report* (10 December 2001): 29.

2. Craig Brian Larson, ed., *Illustrations for Preaching and Teaching* (Grand Rapids, Mich.: Baker, 1993), 187.

CHAPTER 18

1. Sprinkler, *Follow Me*, 12.

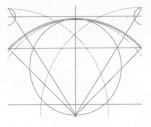

About
the Authors

Dr. Tim Elmore serves as vice president of EQUIP, a nonprofit organization founded by John Maxwell in 1997 to promote leadership development around the world, and is the author of *Nurturing the Leader Within Your Child* as well as other books on mentoring and leadership. He is a frequent speaker at colleges, companies, and organizations around the world, and heads Growing Leaders, an organization specifically committed to developing student leaders (www.GROWINGLEADERS.com). Tim and his wife, Pam, reside in Atlanta, Georgia, with their two children.

Dr. John Hull is President of EQUIP and former senior pastor at Peoples Church in Toronto, Canada. Hull is a frequent speaker at conferences and outreach events and has worked with organizations such as Ravi Zacharias International Ministries, Campus Crusade, Focus on the Family, Moody Pastors Conferences and the Billy Graham School of Evangelism. He and his wife, Sharon, reside in Atlanta with their two teenage children.

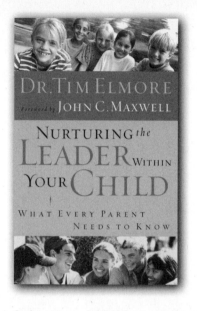

How do I bring out the best in my child? What can I do to help my children reach their full potential? Why is it important to encourage leadership in my child? John Maxwell protégé Dr. Tim Elmore answers these questions and others in *Nurturing the Leader Within Your Child*. Using a survey of over 3,000 students, he enters the minds of today's youth to understand their desire to affect their world, their way.

Beginning with a foreword by John C. Maxwell, the book contains four unique sections (What You Need to Know, What They Need to Know, When to Seize the Moment, How to Pass it On). Dr. Elmore gives practical tools for bridging the generation gap to foster character and growth in your children. Offering a list of fundamental qualities every leader must possess, Dr. Elmore helps parents and youth workers recognize teachable moments and equips them to structure an individual mentoring plan for each child. Finally, he offers evaluation methods for recognizing progress.

ISBN 0-7852-6614-3

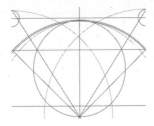

ACKNOWLEDGMENTS

When we first launched the idea of "Pivotal Praying" over a breakfast meeting, both of us took a deep breath. We knew that writing on prayer, a subject about which so many other books have been written, would be a formidable challenge. What could we say about prayer that hadn't been said before? Could we offer any fresh thoughts or new insights into this vital, supernatural link of communication between the believer and God? Thanks to the tenacious and disciplined guidance of our publisher, Victor Oliver, we pressed forward with what we believe to be an authentic attempt to encourage readers to connect with God in times of great need. Thank you, Victor!

John Maxwell's vision for one million Christian leaders to be developed around the world, as well as his faithful friendship continue to take us to higher ground. We are grateful for John's full support of "Pivotal Praying" from start to finish.

Sharon Hull, (John Hull's wife), provided much of the background research for this project. Sharon, once again, you found just what we needed to help make our points. Our assistants, Linda Kirk and Tracey Fries also made sure our schedules were protected for writing and our deadlines were met on time. We tremble when we think of office life without Linda and Tracey. Our thanks too to members of the EQUIP team, especially Pam Elmore (Tim's wife). They cheered us on with their hopeful words of encouragement.

A couple of dear ladies, Holly Moore of Atlanta and Mrs. Bertha Jackson of Toronto, Canada, faithfully prayed for us during the time of writing. They modeled the principles within this book by pivotally praying to God, asking for His wisdom, protection and guidance in our lives as we wrote and ministered. We continue to covet their pivotal prayers.

Finallly, we want to thank our parents, John and Agnes Hull of Atlanta, and Skip and Sally Elmore of San Diego for pivotally praying for us throughout our entire lives. We are both blessed to have grown up in homes where prayer was a familiar and cherished exercise of living faith.

—Dr. John d. Hull & Dr. Tim Elmore

GrowingLeaders.com—a website for developing your own leadership potential and the potential of those around you.

Leadership is not so much about positions or titles as it is about using your God-given influence for a worthy cause.

We believe everyone has some influence. So, whether you're a coach, a parent, a youth worker, a pastor, a teacher, or a student—Growing Leaders has something you can use to grow yourself, as well as the emerging leaders around you.

Growing Leaders provides you with the leadership conferences, books, tapes, mentoring guides, videos internships, and a leadership academy all designed to equip you as an emerging leader. It was founded by Dr. Tim Elmore, one of the author's of this book.

Our belief is that healthy leadership is servant leadership. It isn't about accumulating power, but about serving people. Good leaders lead by serving, and serve by leading. Influence grows as leaders develop their gift, and serve in the area of that gift. Along the way, they hone their skills in relationships, strategy, vision, communication, and so forth. Consequently, our resources are very practical and very relationship based.

We hope as you browse what we offer, you'll agree that if you will create the right environment, and provide the right resources, you can develop healthy, effective leaders.

For more information, see *www.growingleaders.com*

AIN'T NO MAKIN' IT

THIRD EDITION

Aspirations and Attainment in a Low-Income Neighborhood

JAY MACLEOD

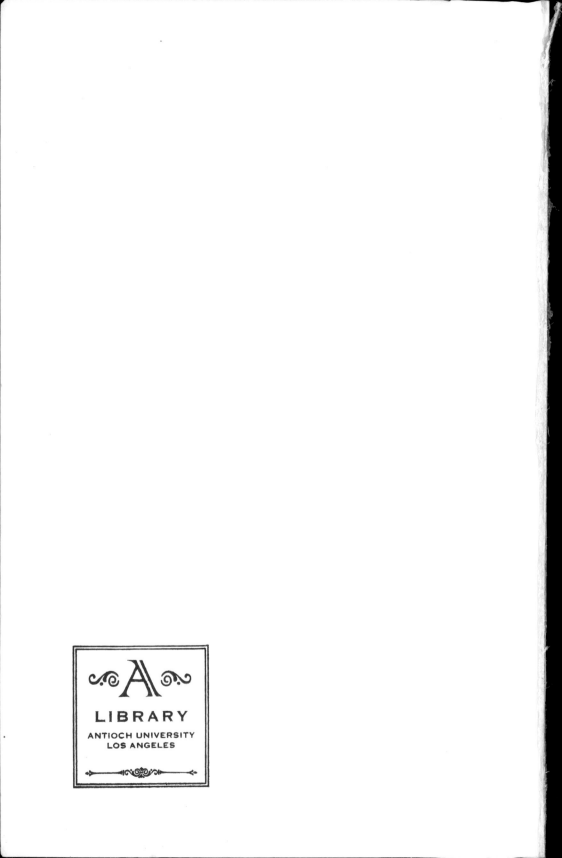

AIN'T NO MAKIN' IT

THIRD EDITION

AIN'T NO MAKIN' IT

Aspirations & Attainment in a Low-Income Neighborhood

JAY MACLEOD

Westview
PRESS

A Member of the Perseus Books Group

Designed by Trish Wilkinson
Set in 10.25-point Minion

Library of Congress Cataloging-in-Publication Data

MacLeod, Jay.
    Ain't no makin' it : aspirations and attainment in a low income
neighborhood / Jay MacLeod. — 3rd ed.
        p.   cm.
    Includes bibliographical references and index.
    ISBN 978-0-8133-4358-7
    1. Urban poor—United States—Case studies. 2. Youth with social
disabilities—United States—Case studies. 3. Social mobility—United States—
Case studies. 4. Equality—United States—Case studies. I. Title. II. Title: Ain't
no making it.
HV4045.M33 2009
305.5'690973—dc22   2008015528

10 9 8 7 6 5 4 3 2 1

CONTENTS

ACKNOWLEDGMENTS

The making of this book has spanned twenty-five years, and scores of people—too many to list—have helped along the way. Katherine McClelland and David Karen supported me from the start and made this edition possible. I am also grateful to John and Winnie Asher, Peter Bearman, Dean Birkenkamp, Jim Carroll, Stephen Cornell, John Dickie, David Finegold, Richard Harding, Greg Johnson, Rob Malley, Sue Vivian Mangold, Dan Porterfield, Michael Quirk, Ken Reeves, Jane Rosegrant, Debra Satz, John Stern, Andrew Sum, Douglas Taylor, Shelly Taylor, Hugh Thompson, Tina Tricarichi, Loïc Wacquant, David Webb, Paul Willis, and John Womack. Special thanks to John Clifford and Pat Glynn and to Barbara, Robert, Nancy, and John MacLeod. Steve Catalano of Westview Press has been helpful at every turn. I am also grateful to the Community of the Resurrection in Mirfield, the Monastery of Christ our Saviour in Turvey, and Bishop Woodford House in Ely for their warm hospitality when I holed up to work on this third edition. The Right Reverend Christopher Herbert, the Bishop of St. Albans, has been wonderfully supportive, as have colleagues John Tibbs, Neslyn Pearson, and Karamat Hussain, as well as the people of All Saints Parish Church. Sally Asher and our children, Asher, Kate, and Toby, have been forgiving of my domestic delinquency as I struggled to finish the book. Most of all, I would like to thank the Brothers and Hallway Hangers for so graciously letting me into their lives. To Boo-Boo (1966–1994) and to Sally Asher I dedicate this book.

—J. M.

We would like to thank Jay MacLeod for entrusting us with the important task of writing a conclusion to this new edition. It is a privilege to be included in this decades-in-the-making work of scholarship. We value Jay's friendship and we are once again beholden (we haven't forgotten Mississippi!) to him for giving us an inside look at processes of social inequality and social reproduction. We also wish to thank our friends who provided truly brilliant comments on this chapter: Janel Benson, Jerry Karabel, Annette Lareau, Krista Luker, John Noakes, and Judy Porter. They helped us sharpen our arguments, our prose, and our overall perspective. We are quite certain that each of them will see their suggestions in the final product, and we hope they won't be too disappointed by the errors that, no doubt, remain. We would like to thank Madeline Vellturo for helping us ensure confidentiality of the Brothers and Hallway Hangers by checking all the names and places across the three editions. Finally, thanks to Westview editor Steve Catalano for allowing us to play this critical role and for keeping us properly stoked with rare Springsteen tapes.

—*Katherine McClelland and David Karen*

PART ONE

THE HALLWAY HANGERS AND THE BROTHERS AS TEENAGERS

SOCIAL IMMOBILITY IN
THE LAND OF OPPORTUNITY

"**A**ny child can grow up to be president." So says the achievement ideology, the reigning social perspective that sees American society as open and fair and full of opportunity. In this view, success is based on merit, and economic inequality is due to differences in ambition and ability. Individuals do not inherit their social status; they attain it on their own. Since education ensures equality of opportunity, the ladder of social mobility is there for all to climb. A favorite Hollywood theme, the rags-to-riches story resonates in the psyche of the American people. We never tire of hearing about Andrew Carnegie, for his experience validates much that we hold dear about America, the land of opportunity. Horatio Alger's accounts of the spectacular mobility achieved by men of humble origins through their own unremitting efforts occupy a treasured place in our national folklore. The American Dream is held out as a genuine prospect for anyone with the drive to achieve it.

"I ain't goin' to college. Who wants to go to college? I'd just end up getting a shitty job anyway." So says Freddie Piniella,[1] an eleven-year-old boy from Clarendon Heights, a low-income housing development in a northeastern city. This statement, pronounced with certitude and feeling, completely contradicts our achievement ideology. Freddie is pessimistic about his prospects for social mobility and disputes schooling's capacity to "deliver the goods." Such a view offends our sensibilities and seems a rationalization. But Freddie has a point. What of Carnegie's grammar school classmates who labored in factories or pumped gas? For every Andrew Carnegie there are thousands of able and intelligent workers who were left behind to occupy positions in the class structure not much different from those held by their parents. What about the static, nearly permanent element in the working class, whose members consider the chances for mobility remote and thus despair of all hope? These people are shunned, hidden, forgotten—and for good reason—because just as the self-made individual is a testament to certain American ideals, so the very existence of an "underclass" in American society is a living contradiction to those ideals.

Hopelessness is the most striking aspect of Freddie's outlook. Erik H. Erikson writes that hope is the basic ingredient of all vitality;[2] stripped of hope, one has little left to lose. How is it that in contemporary America a boy of eleven can feel bereft of a future worth embracing? This is not what the United States is supposed to be. The United States is the nation of hopes and dreams and opportunity. As Ronald Reagan remarked in his 1985 State of the Union Address, citing the accomplishments of a young Vietnamese immigrant, "Anything is possible in America if we have the faith, the will, and the heart."[3] But to Freddie Piniella and many other Clarendon Heights young people who grow up in households where their parents and older siblings are undereducated, unemployed, or imprisoned, Reagan's words ring hollow. For them the American Dream, far from being a genuine prospect, is not even a dream. It is a hallucination.

I first met Freddie Piniella in the summer of 1981 when as a student at a nearby university I worked as a counselor in a youth enrichment program in Clarendon Heights. For ten weeks I lived a few blocks from the housing project and worked intensively with nine boys, ages eleven to thirteen. While engaging them in recreational and educational activities, I was surprised by the modesty of their aspirations. The world of middle-class work was entirely alien to them; they spoke about employment in construction, factories, the armed forces, or, predictably, professional athletics. In an ostensibly open society, they were a group of boys whose occupational aspirations did not even cut across class lines.

The depressed aspirations of Clarendon Heights youngsters are telling. There is a strong relationship between aspirations and occupational outcomes; if individuals do not even aspire to middle-class jobs, then they are unlikely to achieve them. In effect, such individuals disqualify themselves from attaining the American definition of success—a prestigious, well-paid job—before embarking on the quest. Do leveled aspirations represent a quitter's cop-out? Or does this disqualifying mechanism suggest that people of working-class origin encounter significant obstacles to social mobility?

Several decades of quantitative sociological research have demonstrated that the social class into which one is born has a massive influence on where one will end up. Although mobility between classes does take place, the overall structure of class relations from one generation to the next remains largely unchanged. Quantitative mobility studies can establish the extent of this pattern of social reproduction, but they have difficulty demonstrating how the pattern comes into being or is sustained. This is an issue of immense complexity and difficulty, and an enduring one in the field of sociology, but it seems to me that we can learn a great deal about this pattern from youngsters like Freddie. Leveled aspirations are a powerful mechanism by which class inequality is reproduced from one generation to the next.

In many ways, the world of these youths is defined by the physical boundaries of the housing development. Like most old "projects" (as low-income public housing developments are known to their residents), Clarendon Heights is architecturally a world unto itself. Although smaller and less dilapidated than those of many urban housing developments, its plain brick buildings testify that cost efficiency was the overriding consideration in its construction. Walking through Clarendon Heights for the first time in spring 1981, I was struck by the contrast between the project and the sprawling lawns and elegant buildings of the college quadrangle I had left only a half hour earlier. It is little more than a mile from the university to Clarendon Heights, but the transformation that occurs in the course of this mile is startling. Large oak trees, green yards, and impressive family homes give way to ramshackle tenement buildings and closely packed, triple-decker, wooden frame dwellings; the ice cream parlors and bookshops are replaced gradually by pawnshops and liquor stores; book-toting students and businesspeople with briefcases in hand are supplanted by tired, middle-age women lugging bags of laundry and by clusters of elderly immigrant men loitering on street corners. Even within this typical working-class neighborhood, however, Clarendon Heights is physically and socially set off by itself.

Bordered on two sides by residential neighborhoods and on the other two by a shoe factory, a junkyard, and a large plot of industrial wasteland, Clarendon Heights consists of six large, squat, three-story buildings and one high-rise. The architecture is imposing and severe; only the five chimneys atop each building break the harsh symmetry of the structures. Three mornings a week the incinerators in each of the twenty-two entryways burn, spewing thick smoke and ash out of the chimneys. The smoke envelops the stained brick buildings, ash falling on the black macadam that serves as communal front yard, backyard, and courtyard for the project's two hundred families. (A subsequent landscaping effort did result in the planting of grass and trees, the erection of little wire fences to protect the greenery, and the appearance of flower boxes lodged under windows.) Before its renovation, a condemned high-rise building, its doors and windows boarded up, invested the entire project with an ambiance of decay and neglect.

Even at its worst, however, Clarendon Heights is not a bad place to live compared to many inner-city housing projects. This relatively small development, set in a working-class neighborhood, should not be confused with the massive, scarred projects of the nation's largest cities. Nevertheless, the social fabric of Clarendon Heights is marked by problems generally associated with low-income housing developments. Approximately 65 percent of Clarendon Heights' residents are white, 25 percent are black,[4] and 10 percent are other minorities. Few adult males live in Clarendon Heights; approximately 85 percent of the families are headed by single women. Although no precise figures are available, the City Housing Authority acknowledges that significant numbers of tenants are second- and third-generation public housing residents. Social workers estimate that almost 70 percent of the families are on some additional form of public assistance. Overcrowding, unemployment, alcoholism, drug abuse, crime, and racism plague the community.

Clarendon Heights is well known to the city's inhabitants. The site of two riots in the early and mid-1970s and most recently of a gunfight in which two policemen and their assailant were shot, the project is considered a no-go area by most of the public. Even residents of the surrounding Italian and Portuguese neighborhoods tend to shun Clarendon Heights. Social workers consider it a notoriously difficult place in which to work; state and county prison officials are familiar with the project as the source of a disproportionately high number of inmates. Indeed, considering its relatively small size, Clarendon Heights has acquired quite a reputation.

This notoriety is not entirely deserved, but it is keenly felt by the project's tenants. Subject to the stigma associated with residence in public housing, they are particularly sensitive to the image Clarendon Heights conjures up in the minds of outsiders. When Clarendon Heights residents are asked for their address at a bank, store, or office, their reply often is met with a quick glance of curiosity, pity, superiority, suspicion, or fear. In the United States, residence in public housing is often an emblem of failure, shame, and humiliation.

To many outsiders, Freddie's depressed aspirations are either an indication of laziness or a realistic assessment of his natural assets and attributes (or both). A more sympathetic or penetrating observer would cite the insularity of the project and the limited horizons of its youth as reasons for Freddie's outlook. But to an insider, one who has come of age in Clarendon Heights or at least has access to the thoughts and feelings of those who have, the situation is not so simple. Part One of this book, very simply, attempts to understand the aspirations of older boys from Clarendon Heights. It introduces the reader not to modern-day Andrew Carnegies, but to Freddie Piniella's role models, teenage boys from the neighborhood whose stories are less often told, much less heard. These boys provide a poignant account of what the social structure looks like from the bottom. If we let them speak to us and strive to understand them on their own terms, the story we hear is deeply disturbing. We shall come to see Freddie's outlook not so much as incomprehensible self-defeatism but as a perceptive response to the plight in which he finds himself.

Although the general picture that emerges is dreary, its texture is richly varied. The male teenage world of Clarendon Heights is populated by two divergent peer groups. The first group, dubbed the Hallway Hangers because of the group's propensity for "hanging" in a particular hallway in the project, consists predominantly of white boys. Their characteristics and attitudes stand in marked contrast to the second group, which is composed almost exclusively of black youths who call themselves the Brothers. Surprisingly, the Brothers speak with relative optimism about their futures, while the Hallway Hangers are despondent about their prospects for social mobility. This dichotomy is illustrated graphically by the responses of Juan (a Brother) and Frankie (a Hallway Hanger) to my query about what their lives will be like in twenty years.

JUAN: I'll have a regular house, y'know, with a yard and everything. I'll have a steady job, a good job. I'll be living the good life, the easy life.

FRANKIE: I don't fucking know. Twenty years. I may be fucking dead. I live a day at a time. I'll probably be in the fucking pen.

Because aspirations mediate what an individual desires and what society can offer, the hopes of these boys are linked inextricably with their assessment of the opportunities available to them. The Hallway Hangers, for example, seem to view equality of opportunity in much the same light as did R. H. Tawney in 1938—that is, as "a heartless jest . . . the impertinent courtesy of an invitation offered to unwelcome guests, in the certainty that circumstances will prevent them from accepting it."[5]

SLICK: Out here, there's not the opportunity to make money. That's how you get into stealin' and all that shit. . . . All right, to get a job, first of all, this is a handicap, out here. If you say you're from the projects or anywhere in this area, that can hurt you. Right off the bat: reputation.

The Brothers, in contrast, consistently affirm the actuality of equality of opportunity.

DEREK: If you put your mind to it, if you want to make a future for yourself, there's no reason why you can't. It's a question of attitude.

The optimism of the Brothers and the pessimism of the Hallway Hangers stem, at least in part, from their different appraisals of the openness of American society. Slick's belief that "the younger kids have nothing to hope for" obviously influences his own aspirations. Conversely, some of the Brothers aspire to middle-class occupations partly because they do not see significant societal barriers to upward mobility.

To understand the occupational hopes of the Brothers and the Hallway Hangers—and the divergence between them—we must first gauge the forces against which lower-class individuals must struggle in their pursuit of economic and social advancement. Toward this end, the next chapter considers social reproduction theory, which is a tradition of sociological literature that strives to illuminate the specific mechanisms and processes that contribute to the intergenerational transmission of social inequality. Put simply, reproduction theory attempts to show how and why the United States can be depicted more accurately as the place where "the rich get richer and the poor stay poor" than as "the land of opportunity." Social reproduction theory identifies the barriers to social mobility, barriers that constrain without completely blocking lower- and working-class individuals' efforts to break into the upper reaches of the class structure.

Once we have familiarized ourselves with this academic viewpoint, we shall switch perspectives abruptly to the streets to consider how the Brothers and Hallway Hangers understand their social circumstances. How do they view their prospects for social upgrading, and how does this estimation affect their aspirations? What unseen social and economic forces daily influence these boys? How do they make sense of and act upon the complex and often contradictory messages emanating from their family, peer group, workplace, and school? In examining this terrain, we shall touch upon many theoretical issues: the role of education in the perpetuation of class inequality; the influence of ethnicity on the meanings individuals attach to their experiences; the causes and consequences of racism; the relationship between structural determinants (e.g., the local job market) and cultural practices (e.g., rejection of school); the degree of autonomy individuals exercise at the cultural level; the destabilizing roles of nonconformity and resistance in the process of social reproduction; the functions of ideology; and the subtlety of various modes of class domination. Our emphasis throughout, however, will be on the occupational aspirations of the Brothers and the Hallway Hangers, how these aspirations are formed, and their significance for the reproduction of social inequality.

Such an agenda can be addressed most thoroughly by a methodology of intensive participant observation. To do justice to the complexity and richness of the human side of the story requires a level of understanding and distinction that questionnaire surveys are incapable of providing. The field methods employed in this study are not unlike those of most sociological ethnographies in which the researcher attempts to understand a culture from the insider's point of view. But my methods are unique in some ways because of my previous involvement with the community. Having worked and lived in the neighborhood for three summers directing a youth program, I was already close friends with many Clarendon Heights residents prior to the beginning of my research. Without this entree into the community, as a college student from rural New Hampshire I would have faced massive problems gaining the trust and respect of my subjects. As it was, acceptance was slow, piecemeal, and fraught with complications. But with the hurdle of entree partially overcome, I was able to gather a large amount of sensitive data, most of it during a twelve-month period of participant observation in 1983 when I lived in the community.

This study concentrates not on Freddie Piniella and the other boys in my youth enrichment program, but on their high school–age role models whose aspirations are better developed. Only Mike, my oldest charge in the first summer of the youth program, later became a member of the Brothers and thus is included in the study. Nevertheless, my roles as community worker and researcher were never entirely distinct, and the dependence of the latter on the former is clearly illustrated by my first "interview," which was undertaken, strangely enough, not in Clarendon Heights but in my college dormitory.

One evening in late February 1983, Mike, with whom I had maintained a steady relationship since his graduation from the youth program a year and a half earlier, phoned my room. I had been down at the Heights that day and had stopped by his apartment, but Mike had not been home. His mother and grandmother had lamented to me about his poor performance in school, and I had offered to help in any way I could. On the telephone Mike gradually turned the conversation to school. He said he was doing fairly well, but he had failed English. I said I would help him prepare for tests, at which point he mentioned a report on Albert Einstein due in a few days. He had not had much luck researching the topic and hoped I could help. We arranged to meet the next day near the university. After reading an encyclopedia article on Einstein and photocopying it, we got something to eat in the college dining hall and went up to my room. While I did some reading, Mike worked on his paper at my desk.

Before I knew what was happening, my first unstructured interview was under way. Mike suddenly began talking about his future, about, in fact, his occupational and educational goals and expectations. The ensuing conversation lasted an hour and a half and touched on many subjects, but in that time Mike described the high school's curricula, spoke of his own experience in the Occupational Education Program, expressed his desire to work in the computer field, and graphically communicated the role of the achievement ideology in the school. His computer teacher, Mike mentioned, assured the class that a well-paid programming job could be secured easily upon graduation. When I asked Mike about all the unemployed teenagers in Clarendon Heights, his response manifested his own internalization of the achievement ideology: "Well, you can't just be fooling around all the time. Those guys, they was always fucking off in class. You gotta want it. But if you work hard, really put your mind to it, you can do it."

Thus began my formal research, which was to involve me deeply with the community during the next year. The data focus on the fifteen teenage boys who constitute the Brothers and the Hallway Hangers. Much time was spent with these peer groups during all four seasons and at all hours of the day and night. The simultaneous study of both groups was a difficult undertaking because of the animosity that exists between them and the consequent aspersions that often were cast upon me by members of one group when I associated with the other. In the end, however, the effort was well worth the trouble, as the comparative material that I managed to gather is of great importance to the study.

Field notes, a record of informal discussions, and transcripts of taped, semistructured interviews with each boy (individually and, on occasion, in groups) make up the main body of the data. In the few instances where interviews were not taped, the dialogue is not verbatim. Rather, it is my best rendering of what was said, which was recorded as soon after the discussion as possible. To round out the research, discussions with some of the boys' parents and interviews with teachers, guidance counselors, and career counselors also were undertaken.

This ethnographic account provides an intricate picture of how poverty circumscribes the horizons of young people and how, at the societal level, the class structure is reproduced. Before turning to the boys of Clarendon Heights and their families, friends, workplaces, and school, however, we must review the work of a number of social theorists who have tackled the problem of social reproduction. If we are to understand what we see on the streets, if we are to make sense of the forces that act upon these boys, and if we are to generalize from their experiences in any meaningful way, we must situate our work in a broader theoretical framework by letting theory inform our data and, ultimately, by allowing our data to inform theory.

NOTES

1. All names of neighborhoods and individuals have been changed to protect the anonymity of the study's subjects.

2. Erik H. Erikson, *Gandhi's Truth* (New York: Norton, 1969), p. 154.

3. Ronald Reagan, "State of the Union Address to Congress," *New York Times,* February 6, 1985, p. 17.

4. Part One, written in 1984, refers to African Americans as "blacks."

5. R. H. Tawney, *Equality* (London: Allen and Unwin, 1938), p. 110.

2

SOCIAL REPRODUCTION IN THEORETICAL PERSPECTIVE

Why is there a strong tendency for working-class children to end up in working-class jobs? It is this question, a perennial one in the field of sociology, that social reproduction theorists have addressed during the past thirty years. Drawing on the work of Max Weber, Emile Durkheim, and especially Karl Marx, reproduction theorists analyze how the class structure is reproduced from one generation to the next. They attempt to unravel how and why the poor are at a decided disadvantage in the scramble for good jobs. As reproduction theorists explore how the social relations of capitalist society are reproduced, they invariably are led to one site: the school. In the popular mind, school is the great equalizer: By providing a level playing field where the low and the mighty compete on an equal basis, schooling renders social inequality superfluous. Reproduction theorists, in contrast, show that schools actually reinforce social inequality while pretending to do the opposite. These theorists share a common interest in uncovering how status or class position is transmitted. But in doing so, they follow somewhat different approaches.

On one end of the spectrum are theorists who advocate deterministic models of reproduction; on the other end are those who put forth models that allow for the relative autonomy of individuals in their own cultural settings. Deterministic theories take as their starting point the structural requirements of the capitalist economic system and attempt to demonstrate how individuals are obliged to fulfill predefined roles that ensure the perpetuation of a class society. Culturally attuned models begin with the experiences of individuals, and only after understanding

11

people on their own terms do these models attempt to connect those experiences with the demands of capitalist social relations. In this review of reproduction theory, I shall begin with Samuel Bowles and Herbert Gintis, who represent the economic determinist end of the spectrum, progress through the works of Pierre Bourdieu, Basil Bernstein, and Shirley Brice Heath, and finally consider Paul Willis and Henry Giroux on the other end of the continuum.

SAMUEL BOWLES AND HERBERT GINTIS: SCHOOLED BY SOCIAL CLASS

As Marxists, Bowles and Gintis begin their analysis with the forces and relations of production. Marx writes in *Capital*, "The capitalist process of production . . . produces not only commodities, not only surplus-value, but it also produces and reproduces the capitalist relation itself; on the one hand the capitalist, on the other the wage-labourer."[1] Building on Marx's basic point, Bowles and Gintis show how the American educational system is subordinated to and reflective of the production process and structure of class relations in the United States. Thus, they suggest that "the major aspects of the structure of schooling can be understood in terms of the systemic needs for producing reserve armies of skilled labor, legitimating the technocratic-meritocratic perspective, reinforcing the fragmentation of groups of workers into stratified status groups, and accustoming youth to the social relationships of dominance and subordinancy in the economic system."[2] In short, argue Bowles and Gintis, schools train the wealthy to take up places at the top of the economy while conditioning the poor to accept their lowly status in the class structure.

Bowles and Gintis emphasize their "correspondence principle," which highlights the similarity between the social relations of production and personal interaction in the schools. "Specifically, the relationships of authority and control between administrators and teachers, teachers and students, students and students, and students and their work replicate the division of labor which dominates the work place."[3] Bowles and Gintis argue that strong structural similarities can be seen in (1) the organization of power and authority in the school and in the workplace; (2) the student's lack of control of curriculum and the worker's lack of control of the content of his or her job; (3) the role of grades and other rewards in the school and the role of wages in the workplace as extrinsic motivational systems; and (4) competition among students and the specialization of academic subjects and competition among workers and the fragmented nature of jobs.[4] In short, the social relations of the school reflect those of the capitalist mode of production; through its institutional relationships, the system of education in the United States "tailors the self-concepts, aspirations, and social class identifications of individuals to the requirements of the social division of labor."[5]

Insofar as these conditions apply to all students, however, their influence cannot explain the reproduction of class relations. An effective explanation must indicate the ways in which the educational system treats students differently depending on their social origins. In taking up this task, Bowles and Gintis elaborate the factors that contribute to class-based differences in socialization. They begin by demonstrating that there are major structural differences among schools. Schools serving working-class neighborhoods are more regimented and emphasize rules and behavioral control. In contrast, suburban schools offer more open classrooms that "favor greater student participation, less direct supervision, more student electives, and, in general, a value system stressing internalized standards of control."[6]

These variations reflect the different expectations of teachers, administrators, and parents for children of different class backgrounds. Working-class parents, for example, know from their own job experiences that submission to authority is an important value for success in the workplace; they will insist that the schools inculcate this value. Middle-class parents, reflecting their position in the social division of labor, will expect more open schools for their children.[7] Even within the same school, argue Bowles and Gintis, educational tracks, which cater to different classes of students, emphasize different values.

According to Bowles and Gintis, schooling functions at a material level to ensure the successful accumulation of capital by providing employers with trained workers. But the American educational system also functions at an ideological level to promote the attitudes and values required by a capitalist economy. Children of workers attend schools and are placed into educational tracks, both of which emphasize conformity and docility and prepare them for low-status jobs. By contrast, the sons and daughters of the elite are invited to study at their own pace under loose supervision, to make independent decisions, and to internalize social norms—all of which prepares them to boss rather than to be bossed. In short, Bowles and Gintis argue that schools socialize students to occupy roughly the same position in the class structure as that of their parents.

PIERRE BOURDIEU: CULTURAL CAPITAL AND HABITUS

Pierre Bourdieu, a prominent French sociologist, is more indebted to Weber and Durkheim than to Marx, yet Bourdieu also is influenced by the French structuralist movement, which seeks to delve beneath the surface of observed cultural forms to find the "deep" principles and logic according to which empirical reality functions. Drawing on these perspectives, Bourdieu forges an original theory in which class structure plays a more nuanced role, but one that does not preclude deterministic elements.

Bourdieu's most important contribution to reproduction theory is the concept of cultural capital, which he defines as the general cultural background, knowledge, disposition, and skills that are passed from one generation to the next. Cultural capital is the centerpiece of Bourdieu's theory of cultural reproduction. Children of upper-class origin, according to Bourdieu, inherit substantially different cultural capital than do working-class children. By embodying class interests and ideologies, schools reward the cultural capital of the dominant classes and systematically devalue that of the lower classes. Upper-class students, by virtue of a certain linguistic and cultural competence acquired through family upbringing, are provided with the means of appropriation for success in school. Children who read books, visit museums, attend concerts, and go to the theater and cinema (or simply grow up in families where these practices are prevalent) acquire a familiarity with the dominant culture that the educational system implicitly requires of its students for academic attainment. As Giroux contends, "Students whose families have a tenuous connection to forms of cultural capital highly valued by the dominant society are at a decided disadvantage."[8] Hence, schools serve as the trading post where socially valued cultural capital is parlayed into superior academic performance. Academic performance is then turned back into economic capital by the acquisition of superior jobs. Schools reproduce social inequality, but by dealing in the currency of academic credentials, the educational system legitimates the entire process.

Bourdieu's theory consists of four main points. First, distinctive cultural capital is transmitted by each social class. Second, the school systematically valorizes upper-class cultural capital and depreciates the cultural capital of the lower classes. Third, differential academic achievement is retranslated back into economic wealth—the job market remunerates the superior academic credentials earned mainly by the upper classes. Finally, the school legitimates this process "by making social hierarchies and the reproduction of those hierarchies appear to be based upon the hierarchy of 'gifts,' merits, or skills established and ratified by its sanctions, or, in a word, by converting social hierarchies into academic hierarchies."[9]

Bourdieu's model is not quite that simple, however. He recognizes, for instance, that the conversion of economic capital into cultural capital is not a precise one and thus that "the structure of distribution of cultural capital is not exactly the same as the structure of economic capital."[10] Moreover, in the upper reaches of the class structure, despite the decline of the family firm, economic capital is still passed on directly to the next generation, and the importance of educational attainment and cultural capital is correspondingly lower. Bourdieu also argues that "children's academic performance is more strongly related to parents' educational history than to parents' occupational status"[11] and contends that class-based differences in cultural capital tend to have a decreasing importance as one ascends the educational ladder. For Bourdieu, "social class background is mediated through a complex set of factors that interact in different ways at different levels of schooling."[12] Giroux captures the essence of Bourdieu's argument when he observes that "rather than being directly linked to the power of an economic elite, schools are seen as part of a larger social universe of symbolic institutions that, rather than impose docility and oppression, reproduce existing power relations subtly via the production and distribution of a dominant culture that tacitly confirms what it means to be educated."[13]

In addition to cultural capital, Bourdieu employs the concept of habitus, which he defines as "a system of lasting, transposable dispositions which, integrating past experiences, functions at every moment as a matrix of perceptions, appreciations, and actions."[14] The habitus "could be considered as a subjective but not individual system of internalized structures, schemes of perception, conception, and action common to all members of the same group or class."[15] Put simply, the habitus is composed of the attitudes, beliefs, and experiences of those inhabiting one's social world. This conglomeration of deeply internalized values defines an individual's attitudes toward, for example, schooling. The structure of schooling, with its high regard for the cultural capital of the upper classes, promotes a belief among working-class students that they are unlikely to achieve academic success. Thus, there is a correlation between objective probabilities and subjective aspirations, between institutional structures and cultural practices.[16]

Aspirations reflect an individual's view of his or her own chances for getting ahead and are an internalization of objective probabilities. But aspirations are not the product of a rational analysis; rather, they are acquired in the habitus of the individual. A lower-class child growing up in an environment where success is rare is much less likely to develop strong ambitions than is a middle-class boy or girl growing up in a social world peopled by those who have "made it" and where the connection between effort and reward is taken for granted. "The habitus is the universalizing mediation which causes an individual agent's practices, without either explicit reason or signifying intent, to be none the less 'sensible' and 'reasonable.'"[17]

The habitus engenders attitudes and conduct that enable objective social structures to succeed in reproducing themselves. The educational and job opportunity structures are such that individuals of lower-class origin have a very reduced chance of securing professional or managerial jobs. This fact filters down to the lower-class boy (for a girl the outlook is even bleaker) situated in his habitus from the experiences and attitudes of those close to him. Responding to the objective structures, the boy loses interest in school and resigns himself to a low-level job, thereby reinforcing the structure of class inequality. Essentially, Bourdieu posits a circular relationship between structures and practices, in which "objective structures tend to produce structured subjective dispositions that produce structured actions which, in turn, tend to reproduce objective structure."[18]

In Bourdieu's scheme, habitus functions as a regulator between individuals and their external world, between human agency and social structure. As Loïc Wacquant argues, habitus "effects, from within, the reactivation of the meanings and relations objectified 'without' as institutions."[19] It is the mediating link between individuals and their social world. As a conceptual bridge between subjective, inner consciousness and the objective, external constraints of the material world, habitus disposes individuals to think and act in certain ways.[20] Thus, Freddie Piniella announces in the streets of Clarendon Heights, "I ain't goin' to college," while an eleven-year-old counterpart across the city may enter his father's study to confirm a preference for Harvard over Yale.

Through the concepts of cultural capital and habitus, Bourdieu seeks to explain how social inequality is perpetuated and why this process of social reproduction is so readily accepted by exploiter and exploited alike. "Every established order," he notes, "tends to produce the naturalization of its own arbitrariness."[21] At the same time, the mechanisms of cultural and social reproduction remain hidden, because the social practices that safeguard the political and economic interests of the dominant classes go unrecognized as anything other than the only natural, rational, or possible ones. And schooling is crucial to the reproduction and legitimation of social inequality.

> Surely, among all the solutions put forth throughout history to the problem of the transmission of power and privileges, there does not exist one that is better concealed, and therefore better adapted to societies which tend to reuse the most patent forms of the hereditary transmission of power and privileges, than that solution which the educational system provides by contributing to the reproduction of the structure of class relations and by concealing, under an apparently neutral attitude, the fact that it fulfills this function.[22]

Thus success or failure in school is determined largely by social class. But cloaked in the language of meritocracy, academic performance is apprehended as the result of individual ability by both high and low achievers. Such is the magic of school-mediated exclusion: It implants in those it marginalizes a set of cognitive and evaluative categories that lead them to see themselves as the causal agents of a process that is actually institutionally determined. Bourdieu shows how schooling entrenches social inequality by reproducing class privilege and simultaneously sanctifying the resultant inequality.

BASIL BERNSTEIN AND SHIRLEY BRICE HEATH: LINGUISTIC CULTURAL CAPITAL

Whereas Bourdieu paints an elegant theory with broad brushstrokes, Basil Bernstein, an innovative British sociologist, zeroes in on one important link in the process of social reproduction—language patterns. Through his theory of language codification and its relationship to social class on the one hand and schooling on the other, Bernstein links micro- and macro-sociological issues. Influenced by Durkheim and the French structuralist movement, Bernstein, in some respects, goes well beyond Bourdieu in terms of methodological rigor by analyzing both structures and practices and actually demonstrating their relationship. Nevertheless, for all its distinctiveness, Bernstein's work is understood most easily in the context of Bourdieu's theory of cultural capital.

Bourdieu argues that schools require cultural resources with which only specific students are endowed; Bernstein looks specifically at the educational ramifications of divergent linguistic patterns among children of different social strata. Bernstein begins by tracing the implications of social class for language use. In a highly complex argument, he contends that class membership generates distinctive forms of speech patterns through family socialization. Working-class children are oriented to "restricted" linguistic codes, while middle-class children use "elaborated" codes. By *linguistic codes* Bernstein does not mean the surface manifestations of language such as vocabulary or dialect, but rather the underlying regulative principles that govern the selection and combination of different syntactic and lexical constructions.[23]

Linguistic codes, which ultimately are rooted in the social division of labor, derive from the social relations and roles within families. While rejecting an outright correlation between social class and linguistic code, Bernstein claims that working-class children generally grow up in homes where common circumstances, knowledge, and values give rise to speech patterns in which meanings remain implicit and dependent on their context (a restricted code). Middle-class families, in contrast, use elaborated codes to express the unique perspective and experience of the speaker; meanings are less tied to a local relationship and local social structure and consequently are made linguistically explicit.[24] In their introductory essay to *Power and Ideology in Education,* Karabel and Halsey explain how distinct class-specific forms of communication are engendered.

> Participation in working-class family and community life, in which social relations are based upon shared identifications, expectations, and assumptions, tends to generate a "restricted code," for the speaker who is sure that the listener can take his intentions for granted has little incentive to elaborate his meanings and make them explicit and specific. Middle-class culture, in contrast, tends to place the "I" over the "we," and the resultant uncertainty that meanings will be intelligible to the listener forces the speaker to select among syntactic alternatives and to differentiate his vocabulary. The result is the development of an "elaborated code" oriented to the communication of highly individuated meanings.[25]

Because "one of the effects of the class system is to limit access to elaborated codes"[26] and because schools operate in accordance with the symbolic order of elaborated codes, working-class children are at a significant disadvantage. "Our schools are not made for these children; why should the children respond? To ask the child to switch to an elaborated code which presupposes different role relationships and systems of meaning . . . may create for the child a bewildering and potentially damaging experience."[27] By conceptualizing the social structure as a system of class inequality, tracing this structure's implications for language, and demonstrating the ways in which schools value the elaborated codes and other linguistic devices characteristic of the upper classes, Bernstein puts forth a theory that focuses on a powerful mechanism of social reproduction.

Shirley Brice Heath's research into language patterns at home and in the classroom also highlights the importance of linguistic cultural capital. Whereas Bernstein elucidates the relationship among schooling, social class, and language in

Britain, Heath looks at race as well in her sensitive ethnography of schooling in America's Piedmont Carolinas. Heath examines the way language is used in Trackton (a working-class African American community) and nearby Roadville (a working-class white neighborhood). She uncovers important linguistic differences between the two neighborhoods, but the real contrast is between the language patterns of these two rural communities and the way the middle-class townspeople talk. The townspeople, including teachers, use discrete interrogative questions when they talk to their children at home. Through the everyday speech patterns prevalent in their households, these middle-class children are taught to label and name objects, to identify the features of the objects, and to talk about referents out of context: precisely the skills demanded of students in school. The children of Trackton learn different skills. They are less often questioned by their parents, who tend to use imperatives or statements. And in any case, questions that are asked at home usually require comparative or analogical answers rather than specific information. The result is that the black working-class children are not socialized to cope with the language patterns used in school and quickly fall into a pattern of academic failure. The white working-class children from Roadville fare better in that they develop many of the cognitive and linguistic patterns required in elementary school. But they fail to develop "the integrative types of skills necessary for sustained academic success."[28] Like their Trackton counterparts, only later, many Roadville students fall behind, drift through school in a fog of failure, or drop out altogether.

Heath's basic point is the same as Bernstein's: The mismatch between the language used at home and the language demanded by the school is a serious stumbling block for working-class and nonwhite pupils. Like many of the mechanisms of social reproduction, linguistic socialization is an invisible impediment that goes unacknowledged. Disadvantaged students blame themselves for failure, whereas wealthier pupils take their cultural capital for granted and accept full credit for their success. By stripping schools of their innocence, social reproduction theorists show that formal education actually functions "to certify lower status youngsters as socially inferior at an early age and to initiate the process that keeps many of them economically and socially inferior in adulthood."[29]

PAUL WILLIS: THE LADS AND THE EAR'OLES

Like Heath, Paul Willis, author of *Learning to Labor,* begins with the lived culture of his subjects. In this impressive ethnographic study of a group of disaffected, white, working-class males in a British secondary school, Willis undertook extensive participant observation in order to grasp this "counter-school culture's" distinctive pattern of cultural practices. Willis found that the complex and contradictory nature of the "sources of meaning" on which these boys draw and the determinants of their behavior "warns against a too reductive or crude materialist notion of the cultural level."[30]

This is not to say, however, that Willis denies the importance of structural influence. On the contrary, writing in the Marxist tradition, Willis believes that these boys' class background, geographical location, local opportunity structure (job market), and educational attainment influence their job choice. But he reminds deterministic Marxists that these structural forces act through and are mediated by the cultural milieu. If we are to understand social reproduction, we must understand

> how and why young people take the restricted and often meaningless available jobs in ways which seem sensible to them in their familiar world as it is actually lived. For a proper treatment of these questions we must go to the cultural milieu . . . and accept a certain autonomy of the processes at this level which defeats any simple notion of mechanistic causation and gives the social agents involved some meaningful scope for viewing, inhabiting, and constructing their own world in a way which is recognizably human and not theoretically reductive.[31]

By viewing social reproduction as it actually is lived out, we can understand the mechanisms of the process.

In his study of a working-class school, Willis finds a major division between the students. The great bulk of the students are the "ear'oles," who conform to the roles defined for students, aspire to middle-class occupations, and comply with the rules and norms of the school. The counterschool culture of the "lads," in contrast, rejects the school's achievement ideology; these nonconformist boys subvert teacher and administrator authority, disrupt classes, mock the ear'oles (to whom they feel superior), and generally exploit any opportunity to "have a laff," usually at the expense of school officials. In short, the lads use whatever means possible to display their open opposition to the school.

Willis directs almost all his attention to understanding the lads. Their rejection of school, according to Willis, is partly the result of some profound insights, or "penetrations," into the economic condition of their social class under capitalism. The lads believe that their chances for significant upward mobility are so remote that sacrificing "a laff" for good behavior in school is pointless. The lads repudiate schooling because they realize that most available work is essentially meaningless and that although individuals are capable of "making it," conformism for their group or class promises no rewards.[32] As Michael Apple puts it, "Their rejection of so much of the content and form of day to day educational life bears on the almost unconscious realization that, as a class, schooling will not enable them to go much further than they already are."[33] According to Willis, this type of insight into the nature of capitalism has the potential to catalyze class solidarity and collective action.

The promise of these cultural penetrations, however, is dimmed by certain "limitations" in the lads' cultural outlook. The lads equate manual labor with masculinity, a trait highly valued by their working-class culture; mental labor is associated with the social inferiority of femininity.[34] This reversal of the usual valuation of mental versus manual labor prevents the lads from seeing their placement in dead-end, low-paying jobs as a form of class domination. Instead, they positively choose to join their brothers and fathers on the shop floor, a choice made happily and apparently free from coercion. Val Burris, in a review of *Learning to Labor,* brings this point into sharp focus.

> What begins as a potential insight into the conditions of labor and the identity of the working class is transformed, under the influence of patriarchal ideology, into a surprising and uncritical affirmation of manual labor. It is this identification of manual labor with male privilege which, more than anything else, ensures the lads' acceptance of their subordinate economic fate and the successful reproduction of the class structure.[35]

The lads' nonconformist cultural innovations, which ultimately contribute to the reproduction of the class structure, are often complex and contradictory. An understanding of these mechanisms of social reproduction requires an ethnographic approach based on a theory that postulates the relative autonomy of the cultural sphere. Although a Marxist, Willis eschews theories based on economic determinism or a correspondence principle as explanations for the perpetuation of class inequality. Rather, he gives explanatory power to the cultural level and the social innovations of the individuals involved. In this way, we can see how structural forces are mediated by the cultural sphere through which they must pass.

Willis insists that the cultural attitudes and practices of working-class groups are not necessarily reflective of, or even traceable to, structural determinations or dominant ideologies. Although the mode of production wields a powerful influence on the attitudes and actions of individuals, people do not simply respond to the socioeconomic pressures bearing down on them with passivity and indifference. The cultural level is marked by contestation, resistance, and compromise. Culture itself implies "the active, collective use and explorations of received symbolic, ideological, and cultural resources to explain, make sense of and positively respond to 'inherited' structural and material conditions."[36] Subordinate groups can produce alternative cultural forms containing meanings endemic to the working class. Termed "cultural production" by Willis, this process is by nature active and transformative. Still, these behavioral and attitudinal innovations, as the lads illustrate, are often ultimately reproductive. As Liz Gordon remarks in her review of Willis's work, it may seem contradictory to refer to cultural production as both transformative and reproductive, but "Willis wishes to move away from an oversimplistic either/or model. He points out that there is no clear separation between agency and structure; these cannot be understood in isolation from one another."[37]

HENRY GIROUX: STUDENT RESISTANCE TO SCHOOL

Bridging the division between structure and agency maintained by theories of social reproduction has been one of the ongoing theoretical concerns of Henry

A. Giroux, who contends that separation of human agency and structural analysis either suppresses the significance of individual autonomy or ignores the structural determinants that lie outside the immediate experience of human actors.[38] Giroux insists on the need to admit "wider structural and ideological determinations while recognizing that human beings never represent simply a reflex of such constraints."[39] Structuralist theories, which stress that history is made "behind the backs" of the members of society, overlook the significance and relative autonomy of the cultural level and the human experiences of domination and resistance. "In the structuralist perspective human agents are registered simply as the effects of structural determinants that appear to work with the certainty of biological processes. In this grimly mechanistic approach, human subjects simply act as role-bearers."[40] Culturalist theories, on the other hand, pay too little attention to how structurally embedded material and economic forces weigh down and shape human experience. "Culturalism begins at the right place but does not go far enough theoretically—it does not dig into subjectivity in order to find its objective elements."[41]

Giroux argues for a rigorous treatment of ideology, consciousness, and culture in order to move reproduction theory past the theoretical impasse imposed by the structure-agency dualism. He proposes a dialectical treatment of subjectivity and structure in which structure and human agency are seen to affect each other and thinks it crucial "to understand more thoroughly the complex ways in which people mediate and respond to the interface between their own lived experiences and structures of domination and constraint."[42]

In exploring these issues, Giroux develops a theory of resistance. He takes as his starting point the ethnographic studies of Willis, Hebdige, and Corrigan, which analyze how socioeconomic structures work through culture to shape the lives of students.[43] Giroux follows their lead in examining student nonconformity and opposition for their sociopolitical significance. Giroux considers resistance a response to the educational system, a response rooted in "moral and political indignation,"[44] not psychological dysfunction. Student countercultures and their attendant social attitudes and practices, according to Giroux, need to be analyzed carefully for "radical significance"; not all forms of oppositional behavior stem from a critique, implicit or explicit, of school-constructed ideologies and relations of domination. The violation of a school rule is not in itself an act of resistance unless committed by a youth who, for example, sees through the schools' achievement ideology and is acting on that basis. The logic of resistance runs counter to the social relations of schooling and calls for struggle against, rather than submission to, domination.[45] By insisting that oppositional behavior be scrutinized and that resistance be mined for its broader significance, Giroux sets the program for future studies in social reproduction.

Student resistance represents a fertile area for academic study because it offers the possibility of transcending the structure-agency dualism. Resistance theory examines the ongoing, active experiences of individuals while simultaneously perceiving in oppositional attitudes and practices a response to structures of constraint and domination. Taking Willis's concept of cultural production seriously, Giroux suggests that working-class subordination is not a simple reaction to the logic of capitalist rationality. Rather, oppositional cultural patterns draw on elements of working-class culture in a creative and potentially transformative fashion. Thus, the mechanisms of class domination are neither static nor final.

As Giroux is well aware, a thorough understanding of student resistance is difficult to come by. Oppositional behavior is not self-explanatory. It must be linked with the subjects' own explanations of their behavior and contextualized within the nexus of peer, family, and work relations out of which resistance emerges.[46] Unfortunately, Giroux himself undertakes no such investigation, and most studies of social reproduction concentrate on the role of schooling in the perpetuation of class inequality, thus giving only token consideration to the other vehicles of socialization.

SOCIAL REPRODUCTION IN CLARENDON HEIGHTS

This book intends to delve beneath the surface of teenage behavior to recover the interests, concerns, and logic that render it comprehensible. In *Learning to Labor*, Willis gives us a complete and sophisticated analysis of how the lads experience the process of social reproduction. But what of the ear'oles? Both groups are working class. What causes the lads to respond to the school and to the occupational structure in a completely different way than do the ear'oles? Are the ear'oles, as Burris suggests, prepared for their economic fate by passive submission to structural and ideological forces? Or do the ear'oles actively respond to structural pressures bearing down on them and develop their own novel cultural practices and meanings? If economic determinants have the overriding importance that theorists such as Bowles and Gintis suggest, how can two groups from the same social location embody two distinctly different cultural orientations? Will the educational and occupational outcomes be much the same for the lads and ear'oles, or will they differ? In the process of social reproduction, what is the relationship between structural forces and cultural innovation? How much autonomy do individuals have at the cultural level?

Although the British and American contexts are obviously different, such questions are crucial to our understanding of how social inequality is reproduced in the United States. The chapters that follow examine in an intensive fashion two very different groups from the same social location and in the process illuminate some of the mechanisms, both structural and cultural, that contribute to social reproduction. In particular, occupational aspirations, as a mediating link between socioeconomic structures (what society offers) and individuals at the cultural level (what one wants), play a crucial role in the reproduction of class inequality. At the interface between structural determinants and human agency, aspirations offer the sociologist a conceptual bridge over the theoretical rift of the structure-agency dualism. Bourdieu and Willis both emphasize the importance of aspirations in their theoretical writings. For Bourdieu, the relationship between aspirations and opportunity is at the root of "the educational mortality of the working classes."[47] We have seen that a disparity in aspirations is the major difference between the lads and the ear'oles. Indeed, of all the factors contributing to social reproduction (e.g., tracking, social relations of schooling, class-based differences in linguistic codes), the regulation of aspirations is perhaps the most important.

Now that we have familiarized ourselves with some of the major aspects of social reproduction literature, we are in a position to examine in depth the male teenage world of Clarendon Heights. The experiences of the Brothers and the Hallway Hangers, if properly elucidated, bear on the issues of social reproduction more directly than any sociological theory ever could. Thus, it is to the boys of Clarendon Heights that we now turn.

NOTES

1. Karl Marx, *Capital* (Harmondsworth: Penguin, 1976), p. 724.

2. Samuel Bowles and Herbert Gintis, *Schooling in Capitalist America* (New York: Basic Books, 1976), p. 56.

3. Ibid., p. 12.

4. Ibid.

5. Ibid., p. 129.

6. Ibid., p. 132.

7. Ibid., pp. 132–133.

8. Henry A. Giroux, *Theory & Resistance in Education* (London: Heinemann Educational Books, 1983), p. 88.

9. Pierre Bourdieu, "Cultural Reproduction and Social Reproduction," in Jerome Karabel and A. H. Halsey, eds., *Power and Ideology in Education* (New York: Oxford University Press, 1977), p. 496.

10. Ibid., p. 507.

11. David Swartz, "Pierre Bourdieu: The Cultural Transmission of Social Inequality," *Harvard Educational Review* 47 (November 1977): 548.

12. Ibid.

13. Giroux, *Theory & Resistance,* p. 87.

14. Pierre Bourdieu, *Outline of a Theory of Practice* (Cambridge: Cambridge University Press, 1977), pp. 82–83.

15. Ibid., p. 86.

16. Pierre Bourdieu and Jean-Claude Passeron, *Reproduction in Education, Society and Culture* (London: Sage, 1977), p. 156.

17. Bourdieu, *Outline of a Theory of Practice,* p. 79.

18. Swartz, "Pierre Bourdieu," p. 548.

19. Loïc J. D. Wacquant, "Sociology as Socioanalysis: Tales of *Homo Academicus,*" *Sociological Forum* 5 (1990): 684.

20. Richard Jenkins, *Pierre Bourdieu* (London: Routledge, 1992), pp. 74–84.

21. Bourdieu, *Outline of a Theory of Practice,* p. 164.

22. Bourdieu and Passeron, *Reproduction in Education,* p. 178; translation adapted by Loïc Wacquant and cited in "On the Tracks of Symbolic Power," *Theory, Culture, and Society* 10 (August 1993): 2.

23. Paul Atkinson, *Language, Structure and Reproduction* (London: Methuen, 1985), pp. 66, 68, 74.

24. Basil Bernstein, "Social Class, Language, and Socialization," in Karabel and Halsey, *Power and Ideology,* p. 477.

25. Karabel and Halsey, *Power and Ideology,* p. 63.

26. Ibid., p. 478.

27. Ibid., p. 483.

28. Shirley Brice Heath, *Ways with Words* (Cambridge: Cambridge University Press, 1983), p. 343.

29. Carol Camp Yeakey and Clifford T. Bennett, "Race, Schooling, and Class in American Society," *Journal of Negro Education* 59 (Winter 1990): 5.

30. Paul E. Willis, *Learning to Labor* (Aldershot, U.K.: Gower, 1977), p. 171.

31. Ibid., p. 172.

32. Ibid., pp. 126–129.

33. Michael W. Apple, *Education and Power* (Boston: Routledge and Kegan Paul, 1982), p. 99.

34. Willis, *Learning to Labor,* p. 148.

35. Val Burris, rev. of *Learning to Labor,* by Paul Willis, *Harvard Educational Review* 50 (November 1980): 525.

36. Paul Willis, "Cultural Production and Theories of Reproduction," in Len Barton and Stephen Walker, eds., *Race, Class and Education* (London: Croom Helm, 1983), p. 112.

37. Liz Gordon, "Paul Willis—Education, Cultural Production and Social Reproduction," *British Journal of Sociology of Education* 5 (1984): 113.

38. Giroux, *Theory & Resistance,* p. 119.

39. Ibid., p. 38.

40. Ibid., p. 136.

41. Ibid., p. 135.

42. Ibid., p. 108.

43. Ibid., pp. 98–99.

44. Henry A. Giroux, "Theories of Reproduction and Resistance in the New Sociology of Education: A Critical Analysis," *Harvard Educational Review* 53 (August 1983): 289.

45. Ibid., p. 290.

46. Ibid., p. 291.

47. Bourdieu and Passeron, *Reproduction in Education,* p. 156.

3

TEENAGERS IN CLARENDON HEIGHTS
The Hallway Hangers and the Brothers

On any given day, except during the coldest winter months, the evening hours in Clarendon Heights are filled with activity. At one end of the housing development, elderly women sit on wooden benches and chat. In the center of the project, children play street hockey, kickball, stickball, or football, depending on the season. At the other end, teenage boys congregate in the stairwell and on the landing of one of the entries—doorway #13.

THE HALLWAY HANGERS: "YOU GOTTA BE BAD"

This doorway and the area immediately outside it are the focus of activity for the Hallway Hangers, one of the two main peer groups of high-school-age boys living in Clarendon Heights. Composed of a core of eight youths, but including up to ten additional people who are loosely attached to the group, the Hallway Hangers are tough, streetwise individuals who form a distinctive subculture. Except for Boo-Boo, who is black, and Chris, who is of mixed racial parentage, the Hallway Hangers are white boys of Italian or Irish descent. The eight members

25

considered here range in age from sixteen to nineteen. Five have dropped out of school, two graduated last year,[1] and one continues to attend high school. They all smoke cigarettes, drink regularly, and use drugs. All but two have been arrested. Stereotyped as "hoodlums," "punks," or "burnouts" by outsiders, the Hallway Hangers are actually a varied group, and much can be learned from considering each member.

Frankie, the acknowledged leader of the Hallway Hangers, is of only medium height and weight, but his fighting ability is unsurpassed among teenagers in Clarendon Heights. Missing two front teeth from one of his few unsuccessful encounters, Frankie maintains a cool, calculating demeanor that only occasionally gives way to his fiery temper. He commands the respect of the other boys because he is a natural leader and because he comes from a family that is held in high esteem by the city's underworld. His brothers have been involved in organized crime and have spent time in prison; four of them were incarcerated at the time I conducted my research. Although Frankie is the ringleader of the Hallway Hangers, he has never been arrested—no small feat considering the scope of the group's criminal activity.

Whereas Frankie combines physical toughness and mental acuity, Slick, although no weakling, clearly possesses an abundance of the latter attribute. Very articulate and perceptive, Slick scored high on standardized tests and fared well in school when he applied himself (he dropped out last year). Slick gets along well on the street, where his quick wit and sharp tongue are major assets. Although his status falls short of Frankie's, Slick is accorded much respect by the other boys of Clarendon Heights.

As Slick is known for the strength of his intellect, Shorty is known for his physical toughness. When a teacher at the local high school remarked, "What makes someone tough has nothing to do with size or even muscle—it's the fear factor. If someone's fearless, crazy, he'll do anything," he doubtless had Shorty in mind. As his nickname implies, Shorty is small but well built. His temper is explosive, and under the influence of alcohol or drugs, he has been known to accost strangers, beat up friends, or pull a knife on anyone who challenges him. On one occasion, he repeatedly stabbed himself in the head in a fit of masochistic machismo. Although Frankie and Slick also consider themselves alcoholics, Shorty's drinking problem is more severe. The county court ordered him to a detoxification center—an arrangement Shorty has slyly managed to avoid.

Like the other three boys, Chris is a self-professed alcoholic who also admits to being dependent on marijuana. Chris's father (who does not live at home) is black, and his mother is white, which gives Chris an ethnic heritage that makes his acceptance by the rest of the Hallway Hangers difficult. A tall, very slender youth, Chris is loud and talkative but without the self-confidence and poise of Slick or Frankie. He is often the object of the other boys' abuse, both verbal and physical, but nevertheless has some stature in the group largely because of his loyalty and sense of humor.

Boo-Boo, the other black member of the Hallway Hangers, is a tall, quiet, dark-skinned youth. His serious nature makes him a less frequent target of abuse, which begins as playful racial barbs but often degenerates into downright racial animosity. Like Chris, Boo-Boo is a follower. A sincere and earnest boy, his general demeanor is at odds with the violence and bluster that characterize the group as a whole. Nevertheless, Boo-Boo has been known to fight—and quite effectively—when seriously antagonized and generally is held in moderate esteem by the rest of the boys.

Like Boo-Boo, Stoney is a bit of a loner. The only Hallway Hanger to hold stable employment, Stoney works full-time in a pizza shop. His regular income, which he recently used to buy a car, earns him a measure of deference from the other boys, but Stoney lacks the cockiness and bravado necessary for high stature within the group. Skinny and averse to street fights, Stoney perpetually but ineffectively strives to rid himself of the label "pussy." Stoney does share with the other boys an enthusiasm for beer and drugs; he has been arrested for possession of mescaline and is psychologically dependent on marijuana. He has a steady girlfriend (another anomaly for the Hallway Hangers, who generally reject serious relationships in favor of more casual romantic encounters) with whom he spends much of his time, but Stoney still values the friendship of the Hallway Hangers and remains an integral member of the group.

Steve, Slick's younger brother, is the stereotypical project youth. Constantly on the lookout for a free ride, Steve is insolent and loud but lacks his brother's sophistication. He is courageous and full of energy, and fights well, but Steve is not particularly popular with the other boys, who tolerate him as Slick's brother and as a person who can be counted on for support and loyalty in the most trying situations. Steve is the only Hallway Hanger still in school; he expects to graduate in two years (1986).

In contrast to Steve, Jinx is a sensitive, shy boy who shares with Stoney and Chris a psychological dependence on marijuana. Although he is considered immature and is taunted as a "mama's boy" by some of the Hallway Hangers, Jinx seems to have inner reserves of confidence and self-esteem that protect his ego from such assaults. Lighthearted and understanding of others, Jinx is the only white member of the Hallway Hangers who is not overtly racist. Although he takes a good deal of abuse from the others, especially Frankie and Shorty, Jinx's acceptance as a bona fide member of the group is beyond question.

These boys come together in the late afternoon or early evening after dinner and "hang" in doorway #13 until late at night. They come to "see what's up," to "find out what's goin' down," to "shoot the shit," and, generally, to just pass the time. Smelling of urine, lined with graffiti, and littered with trash and broken glass, this hallway is the setting for much playful banter, some not-so-playful "capping" (exchange of insults), and an occasional fight. The odors of cigarette smoke, beer, and marijuana are nearly always present. During the weekend, there may be a case or two of beer, a nearly constant circulation of joints, and some cocaine, mescaline, or "angel dust" (PCP). Late at night, one occasionally stumbles upon a lone figure shooting up heroin.

In an inversion of the dominant culture's vocabulary and value scheme, the subculture of the Hallway Hangers is a world in which to be "bad" is literally to be good. A common characteristic of lower-class[2] teenage peer cultures, this emphasis on being bad is inextricably bound up with the premium put on masculinity, physical toughness, and street wisdom in lower-class culture. Slick, in articulating the prominence of this value for the Hallway Hangers, states in definite terms what being bad often involves.

(in an individual talk)

SLICK: You hafta make a name for yourself, to be bad, tough, whatever. You hafta be, y'know, be with the "in" crowd. Know what I mean? You hafta—it's just all part of growing up around here—you hafta do certain things. Some of the things you hafta do is, y'know, once in a while you hafta, if you haven't gotten into a fight, if you have a fight up the high school, you're considered bad. Y'know what I mean? If you beat someone up up there, especially if he's black, around this way . . . if you're to be bad, you hafta be arrested. You hafta at least know what bein' in a cell is like.

(in a group discussion)

JM: So how is it that to be what's good down here, to be respected . . .

SLICK: You gotta be bad.

FRANKIE: Yeah, if you're a straight-A student, you get razzed.

SLICK: Then you're a fucking weirdo, and you shouldn't be living here in the first place.

SHORTY: No, you got people down here who don't drink and don't smoke.

SLICK: Who? Name one.

SHORTY: Crane. Bruce Crane.

FRANKIE: Yeah, but like he's sayin', whadda we think of Bruce Crane?

SHORTY: Fucking shithead. [*all laugh*]

Thus, good grades in school can lead to ostracism, whereas time spent in prison earns respect. To be bad is the main criterion for status in this subculture; its primacy cannot be overemphasized, and its importance is implied continually by the boys.

Frankie carries the notion of being bad to the extreme, despite its offensiveness to conventional American values. In June 1983, John Grace, a bartender in a pub across the city, shot two police officers and was himself wounded in a gunfight in Clarendon Heights. All three survived, and at the time of this interview, Grace was awaiting trial in a county jail where two of Frankie's brothers were also serving time. "Fucking Grace, he's my man. He's taken care of. My brother says he'll have a fucking joint when he see him in his cell. He's in lockup, but they take care of him. He's a big fucking dude. He's respected up there, man. He's the baddest. He shot a fucking cop. He's golden, he's there. That's the best you can fucking do."

Although such a drastic view is seldom voiced or acted upon by the Hallway Hangers, success for members of the peer group does involve physical and emotional toughness. In addition, a quick wit is essential, for much time is spent capping on one another.

(in the hallway late one afternoon)

SHORTY: [*drunk*] Hey, Steve, what are you doing tonight?

STEVE: Nuttin'. Why?

SHORTY: You wanna suck my dick?

STEVE: You're the only gay motherfucker around here.

SHORTY: Yeah? Ask your girlfriend if I'm gay.

STEVE: Yeah, well, you ask your mother if I'm gay.

This type of sportive banter is common, a diversion to interrupt the boredom inherent in hanging in hallways for a good portion of the day.

JINX: Everyone gets ragged on out there. It's just when you're high, y'know, you're drunk—you start ragging on people. Helps the time go by.

Sometimes, of course, real venom lies behind the words. In that case, size and strength are the crucial elements for success in an altercation. For behind all the posturing lies the reality of the pecking order, which is determined primarily by physical toughness. Fighting ability is the deciding factor for status demarcation within the group; those lacking in physical stature must compensate for it with aggressiveness and tenacity or learn to live with a lot of abuse, both verbal and physical.

For the Hallway Hangers, being bad entails the consumption of alcohol and the use of drugs on a regular basis. The boys are intoxicated for a good portion of almost every weekend and drink heavily during the week. During the summer, the level of drinking reaches staggering proportions, often involving the consumption of two or more "beer balls" (the equivalent of two and half cases of beer pressurized into a plastic ball about two feet in diameter) a day for a group of eight to ten boys. Although none of the Hallway Hangers is drunk constantly, Frankie, Shorty, Slick, and Chris all consider themselves alcoholics.

FRANKIE: See, the way we are right now, technically we are alcoholics. Y'know, I can go days without drinking alcohol. It ain't like I need it, but right now I want it, y'know; it helps me get through. Y'know, get through problems, whatever; it helps me get through. Take away all the fucking problems down here, and there would be no problems with alcohol.

Shorty is honest about the debilitating effects of his dependence on alcohol.

(in a group discussion)

SHORTY: I think when you're an alcoholic like me, man, you ain't gonna be able to hold no fucking job. You say things you fucking forget.

FRANKIE: Yeah, yeah. I hear ya.

SHORTY: I mean, I don't remember trying to stab my own brother in the back; my other brother caught me. That's when I knew I was dead-up an alcoholic. Then I stabbed myself and three other people.

JM: How'd you get to be an alcoholic in the first place?

SHORTY: Being with these motherfuckers. [*all laugh*] These got me going. Frankie always used to drink before me. I only used to drink about a beer a night, and I used to get buzzed every night. It's like this now: six-pack—Monday through Friday. Friday, it's a case, and when summer comes, it's . . .

ALL: Beer balls!

Most of these boys began drinking beer regularly at the age of thirteen or fourteen; their preferences now include whiskey and peppermint schnapps.

The Hallway Hangers also began smoking marijuana when they were twelve or thirteen years old, a tendency that has led many to use an assortment of heavier drugs as well. Most of them describe stages in their adolescence during which they used PCP, mescaline, Valium, or THC (the chief intoxicant in marijuana). Only Chris admits to having used heroin; Frankie's experience is more typical of these boys.

(in a group interview)

FRANKIE: My drug was, my freshman and sophomore year, I was into THC, right? And you get a tolerance and shit, and you start doing three and four hits.

SLICK: Frankie was a junkie.

FRANKIE: Well, yeah, I didn't boot it [shoot it up], but I was addicted to it, definitely.

Having moderated what they now see as their youthful enthusiasm for different drugs, the Hallway Hangers generally limit themselves to marijuana and cocaine. All the Hallway Hangers smoke a great deal of marijuana; Chris, Jinx, and Stoney acknowledge their dependence on the drug. Marijuana joints circulate in doorway #13 almost as often as cans of beer, and all admit they get high before and during school.

(in an individual interview, before he dropped out of school)

JM: Chris, you get high a lot in school?

CHRIS: Oh, yeah. I'm high every time I go to school. I gotta be. Sometimes I even drink before I go—I'll have a few beers. It's too much if you don't. I'm a fucking alcoholic. I do a lot of cocaine. I'll do up cocaine whenever I can get it. Fucking expensive, though.

Despite their own widespread use of marijuana and occasional consumption of cocaine, the Hallway Hangers have no respect for junkies or "dustheads," those who are addicted to heroin or angel dust.

(in an interview with Shorty and Slick)

SHORTY: Little Tony and them, fuckin' ten, twelve years old, smoking pot, taking drugs. And that ain't good, at that age, cuz me and him don't do drugs, maybe coke, y'know? Coke and pot. But a lot of other dudes out here, they'll be taking; they'll be shooting up and everything. We don't even bother with them.

Obviously, underage drinking and drug use are illegal, and the Hallway Hangers have made their share of trips to the police station and the courthouse.

Stoney has three convictions, two for possession of narcotics and one for passing stolen property. Boo-Boo has been arrested for "hot boxes" (stolen cars). Chris has assault with a deadly weapon in addition to some less serious convictions on his record. Shorty has been to court for larceny, assault with a deadly weapon, and other less substantial crimes. One of the older teenagers on the fringes of the Hallway Hangers was convicted of rape and sentenced to eighteen months in the maximum-security state prison after his sophomore year in high school.

These, of course, represent only the crimes at which the Hallway Hangers have been caught. Their criminal activity is actually much more widespread. Those trusted by the Hallway Hangers are occasionally approached with offers for good deals on bicycles, stereo equipment, or musical instruments, all of which have been stolen. Chris makes serious money dealing drugs. Other Hallway Hangers make small amounts of cash selling drugs to friends and acquaintances.

JINX: We all know how to make a fast buck on the street. Buy the pot, roll up joints, sell 'em for two bucks a joint. Pay thirty for a bag; get twenty-five bones out of a bag—there's fifty bucks for thirty bucks.

Jimmy Sullivan, an experienced and perceptive teacher of the adjustment class in which Frankie, Shorty, and Steve are, or were at one time, enrolled, gives a good description of the Hallway Hangers' criminal careers.

JS: One thing about these kids: Crime pays, and they know it. . . . It's so easy to go over to the hallowed halls across the street there [a large university] and pick up a bike. I know three or four stores in the city that will pay thirty to forty dollars for a good bike, no questions asked. They'll turn it over for a hundred-fifty or two hundred bucks. What do these kids need money for? What do they care about? Beer, sneakers, joints. They're not going to work when they can make easy money through virtually riskless criminal enterprises. Only suckers are gonna work for that. As long as their expectations stay low and they only need a hundred bucks a week—as Steve said, "All I want is my beer money"—they're all set. Up to when they're seventeen years old there's no risk. But when they turn about eighteen, the peer group doesn't accept that anymore. If they could go on stealing bikes for the rest of their lives, I think they would. But when you're seventeen or eighteen and someone says, "Hey, man, where'd you get the cash?" it's unacceptable to say, "Oh, stealing bikes, man." You've got to be into cars, dealing drugs, or holding people up. That's when the risk and fear start coming into it. For many of them, the easiest route is to get a job. Of course, some of them don't, and they end up in jail.

Although this dynamic certainly plays a role in the Hallway Hangers' rationale, the legal system's distinction between a juvenile and an adult is more important in their determination of whether crime pays.

(in a group interview)

JM: Most of you are seventeen or over now?

SLICK: Only Chris is sixteen.

JM: Doesn't that make a big difference in terms of what you're doing to get money?

SHORTY: Hey, I'm doin' good. I don't deal no more, Jay. I got a good job coming at the weapons lab; most likely I'm gonna get my brother one there.

FRANKIE: Yeah, you slow down. Seventeen—you're an adult.

SLICK: Yeah, at seventeen you start slowing down.

SHORTY: You gotta start thinking.

(in a separate interview)

FRANKIE: Now that I think about it, I should've did more crime when I was a juvenile cuz when you're a juvenile you get arrested a good eight or nine times before they put you away. So I could've did a lot more crime, but I don't really mind. It was all right. But yeah, that's what most people do is once they go to seventeen, they smarten up and say that's big-time prison. And I've had many good examples of what not to do. I know jail ain't no place for nobody, even though some of my brothers make a living out of it.

Like many urban slums, the teenage underworld of Clarendon Heights is characterized by predatory theft, and some of the Hallway Hangers specialize in "cuffing" drugs, stolen merchandise, and money off those who themselves are involved in illegal activity. Shorty and Frankie have sold hundreds of fake joints, robbed other drug pushers, and forced younger or less tough boys to give them a share of their illegal income. The consensus among the Hallway Hangers is that this type of thievery is morally more defensible than conventional theft. More important, there is less risk of detection, for the authorities are unlikely to become involved.

(in a group discussion)

SLICK: You chump off thieves, and then you're, like, a hero. At least you got him back, y'know? You steal off a fucking thief who makes his life off stealing off other people, then its like you're fucking . . .

FRANKIE: You rip off illegal people, y'know? You rip off dealers.

SHORTY: That's why if you deal, you gotta be able to kill.

FRANKIE: Yeah, sometimes it could mean your life if you get caught. But you can't get put in jail.

For those raised with a strong sense of law and order, these attitudes are difficult to fathom. The Hallway Hangers, for their part, however, cannot understand the contempt and disdain the upper classes display for their lifestyle and launch a counterattack of their own.

(in a group interview)

SLICK: All right, you get people making fucking over fifty thousand dollars, and they fucking ask us why do we hang there? What the fuck, man?

CHRIS: What else are we gonna do?

JINX: They can go fuck themselves.

CHRIS: They want us to deal the drugs so they can buy them.

SLICK: See, they don't know what the deal is. See, they're just doing what we're doing, except they're doing it in a more respectable way. They're ripping off each other up there. That's all they're doing. They're all ripping each other off up there. But they're doing it in a fucking legal way.

FRANKIE: Yeah, check this out.

SHORTY: We ain't doin' it behind anybody's back.

FRANKIE: All them fucking businessmen, man. All them stockbrokers and shit in New York. All them motherfuckers are out to rip people off. There's more fucking scamming going on up there. They're, like, legally ripping everyone off.

SLICK: We're just doing it illegally.

This is an insightful, if incomplete, critique of the social order, but not one about which the Hallway Hangers get particularly upset. Rather, they accept it as a simple fact of life with an acquiescent attitude that is typical of their outlook.

An important characteristic of the subculture of the Hallway Hangers is group solidarity. Membership in the Hallway Hangers involves a serious commitment to the group: a willingness to put out for others and to look out for the rest of the group's wellbeing as well as one's own. This loyalty is the glue that holds the group together, and honoring it is essential. The requirements and limits of this commitment to the group are seldom expressed but are such that Slick would not leave Shorty "hanging with the cops," even though to stay with Shorty resulted in his own arrest.

SHORTY: See, that's how Slick was that day we were ripping off the sneakers [from a nearby factory]. He figured that if he left me that would be rude, y'know? If he just let me get busted by myself and he knew I had a lot of shit on my head, that's what I call a brother. He could've. I could've pushed him right through that fence, and he coulda been *gone*. But no, he waited for me, and we both got arrested. I was stuck. My belly—couldn't get through the fucking hole in the fence.

This cohesion between members of the Hallway Hangers is a striking characteristic of their subculture and one to which they constantly draw attention. Not only are they proud of their adoption of communitarian values, but they also see their "brotherhood" as inconsistent with conventional middle- and upper-class attitudes.

(in a group discussion)

SLICK: What it is, it's a brotherhood down here. We're all fucking brothers. There's a lot of backstabbing going on down here, down in the streets. But we're always there for each other. No shit. There's not a guy in here that wouldn't put out for one of the rest of us. If he needs something and I got it, I'll give it to him. Period. That's the way it works. It's a brotherhood. We're not like them up there—the rich little boys from the suburbs or wherever. There's a line there. On this side of the line we don't fuck with each other; we're tight.

FRANKIE: We'd chump them off [rob] on the other side, though.

SLICK: Fucking right. If he's got four hundred bucks in his pocket, there's more where that came from. Fuck him. But they also chump each other off; only they do it legally. How do you think they got rich—by fucking people over. We don't do that to each other. We're too fucking tight. We're a group. We don't think like them; we think for all of us.

FRANKIE: That's the fucking truth. If you don't have your fucking buddies, where are you? You're fucking no one. Nuttin'.

SLICK: If I had the choice, and this isn't just me but probably everyone in here, if I had the choice between being a good person and making it, I'd be a good person. That's just the way I am. If I had my bar exam tomorrow and these guys needed me, I'd go with them. That's just the way it is down here.

SHORTY: Yeah, you wanna be here with your family, with your friends; they're good people. You're comfortable with them. You don't feel right with these other people. I dunno. . . . You wanna be like them, y'know? You see they're rich; you wanna be rich. You can't be the poor one out of the crowd. You got all the crowd, and places like that—the suburbs—they're all rich. Y'know, a lot of places, they say quiet places; around here, you'll just be able to hang together, and nobody has that much money.

SLICK: But I'll tell you right now, you cannot find better friends because everybody's in the same boat. You'll find a few assholes, rats, whatever, but mostly when you have all of us, we all know everybody's poor. You're not better than me; I'm not better than him, y'know? Like, say if I have a hundred dollars or he has a hundred dollars, y'know, it's not just his or mine—it's *our* money. It goes between us, y'know what I mean? Like up there, it's not as tight. People aren't tight up there. I just came back from Fort Lauderdale, and I seen it up there. Real rich people, it's not like this at all.

These comments bear ample testimony to the solidarity that characterizes the subculture of the Hallway Hangers. This solidarity is not an ideal to which they only pay lip service; shared money, shared drugs, and shared risks in criminal activity are all facts of life in doorway #13.

At the same time that these boys affirm the lifestyle and values of people in their neighborhood, they assert with peculiar constancy their deeply felt desire to move with their families out of Clarendon Heights. Many of them want to make enough money to get their families out of the projects forever.

(all in separate discussions, unsolicited by me)

SLICK: Most of the kids down here, most of 'em wanna make money so they can help their families and help themselves to get out of this place. . . . My main concern is to get my family out of the projects.

CHRIS: I just wanna get my mother out of the projects, that's all.

SHORTY: All's I'm doing, I'm gonna get enough money, save enough money to get my mother the fuck out of here.

These statements are evidence of the stigma the Hallway Hangers, as public housing tenants, feel as a matter of course. Their pride in their lifestyle is pierced by the dominant culture's negative judgments. One implication of the culture's achievement ideology is that those of low socioeconomic stature are personally deficient. This negative evaluation and the inability of the Hallway Hangers to shield themselves completely from it combine to produce the deep ambivalence the boys feel toward themselves and their community.

Daily life for the Hallway Hangers is marked by unrelieved boredom and monotony. The boys are generally out of work, out of school, and out of money. In search of employment or a "fast buck on the street," high or drunk a good deal of the time, many are preoccupied with staying out of prison—a struggle some already have lost—and with surviving from one day to the next.

(in a discussion with Shorty and Slick)

SLICK: All through the teenage years around here, you hafta learn to survive, before you learn to do anything else.

SHORTY: Nobody learns anything from school around here. All it is is how to survive and have money in your pocket.

SLICK: You hafta learn how to survive first.

SHORTY: This is the little ghetto.

SLICK: Y'know, you hafta learn how to survive; if you can't survive, especially around here, that's why you see so many people who are just down and out. It's tough. That's what it is. It's tough.

Growing up in Clarendon Heights is indeed tough, and the frustrations of project life find release through the racist attitudes held by the boys. Racism among members of the Hallway Hangers runs very deep. Frankie and Shorty are violent in their prejudice against black people, while Slick, Steve, and Stoney are racist in a less strident manner. Only Jinx has a measure of empathy and respect for blacks.

According to the Hallway Hangers, their antipathy toward blacks stems from an incident in the early 1970s. At that time, a full-scale riot erupted in Clarendon Heights between the project's mostly white residents and black youths from the predominantly black Emerson Towers housing project a half mile away. The conflict lasted several days and involved the National Guard and riot police. Frankie describes how this event crystallized his own racist attitudes.

JM: So why is it, why is there, like, this tension between the whites and the blacks?

FRANKIE: Well, when I grew up here, when I was fucking second, third grade, there was racial riots right in front of my window every night. My brothers, I have seven brothers, were all out there, y'know, stabbin' niggers, beating niggers up. I was brought up thinking fucking niggers suck. Went over to Hoover School, no fuckin' black people there at all. Y'know, third grade, we had one black kid. His name was Sonny. Y'know, everyone fucked him up. So it was this through the racial riots. I was brought up to hate niggers.

Although the riots contributed to the racism of the Hallway Hangers, surprisingly enough, they also account for the acceptance of Boo-Boo and Chris into the group.

(in an interview with Jinx and Chris)

JM: Now, Chris, you're an interesting case cuz, except when Boo-Boo's around, you're the only black guy out there. How'd that come about?

CHRIS: It goes back to the days of the riots.

JINX: Back in the days of the riots, when the whites used to fight the blacks at the Heights . . .

CHRIS: Nobody fucked with my family.

JINX: Chris's family was always, like, neutral. They'd help out anybody. And besides, as he's grown older, I've related to him more because my brother married a black lady. And I got nieces and nephews that are like him: mulatto. I've just related to him more. I see things from his point of view more. Cuz I know how he feels when people start capping on him: "Hey, Breed."

JM: So that's how it came about with you?

CHRIS: Yeah. When the riots were going on, right, they'd be out there: the niggers against the whites; I'd be sleeping over his house and shit, y'know? His brothers would be fucking hating niggers, man; like his brother John, they'd be killing them.

Boo-Boo also gives a similar reason for his membership in the Hallway Hangers.

JM: What happened with your family during the riots?

BOO-BOO: My father knew both. He used to have all the kids in the house and shit.

JM: What happened with Chris's family?

BOO-BOO: People they knew wouldn't do nothing. If someone was hurting real bad and needed a towel or something, they'd get it. They knew both. Y'know, Chris's mother is real nice—she'd help both the whites and blacks.

Other factors have contributed to Chris's and Boo-Boo's affiliation with the Hallway Hangers. Boo-Boo's family was one of the first black households to be moved by the city's Housing Authority into the Heights. When he was growing up, he naturally made friends with white youngsters. His younger brother Derek went to a private grammar school; most other black youths who now live in Clarendon Heights had yet to move in. Boo-Boo's express reason for being a Hallway Hanger is simple: "I grew up with them, since I was real small."

The situation was much the same for Chris; in addition, his acceptance into the Hallway Hangers has been facilitated because he is half-white.

(in a group interview)

FRANKIE: It ain't like he's living with his black daddy; he's living with his white mommy.

SHORTY: His white brothers.

(in a separate discussion)

JINX: My brothers always liked his family, though . . .

CHRIS: Cuz my brothers were white, y'know.

JINX: His brothers were mulatto, but they looked like a white person. . . . It just looked like he had a nice tan all year round. And he was one of my brother's best friends. Y'know, it's just families hanging around.

Although both Chris and Boo-Boo are full members of the Hallway Hangers, their position often seems tenuous because of their race. Both take a lot of ribbing for their skin color. Chris routinely is referred to as nigs, nigger, breed, half-breed, or oreo; Boo-Boo gets less direct abuse but is the butt of racist jokes and occasional taunts. Both tend to deal with it in the same way: They "play it off," make a joke of it, or ignore it.

(in an individual discussion)

JM: So you naturally hung with Frankie and them. Are there any problems with you being black?

BOO-BOO: No. They say things but they're just fooling around. I take it as a joke. They're just fooling around. It doesn't bother me at all. If they hit me or something, that's a different story.

Chris occasionally will play along with the other Hallway Hangers by agreeing with their racist statements and denigrating other blacks.

One balmy night in late autumn, I walked into doorway #13 at about eleven o'clock to find Frankie, Chris, and two older guys on the fringes of the Hallway Hangers, Joe and Freddy, smoking a joint and drinking beer. I struck up a conversation with Frankie, but I was interrupted by Joe, a twenty-three-year-old man whose six-foot frame boasts a lot more brawn than mine. "Hey, Jay," he said in a mocking, belligerent tone, glancing sharply up at me from his two empty six-packs of Miller. "You're a fucking nigger. You're a nigger. You play basketball with the niggers. You talk like a nigger. You're a fucking nigger." This reference to a basketball game a few days earlier in which I played with the Brothers demanded a response that would not provoke a fight but would allow me to maintain some poise and dignity in front of the others. (I had learned long since that to confront the Hallway Hangers' racism was a fruitless exercise and not particularly conducive to entry into the group.) In the end, although I escaped with my pride and body intact, Chris was not so lucky. The exchange that followed highlights his deep ambivalence toward his ethnic identity.

JOE: Did you hear me? I said you're a nigger, a motherfucking nigger.

JM: What, you'd rather play four on six? It's not my fault we won; maybe it's yours.

JOE: You're a nigger, a fucking nigger. You act like a nigger.

JM: You must be really rat-assed drunk or that must be really good herb, cuz it isn't that fucking dark in here. My skin looks white to me.

FRANKIE: (*in an attempt to steer the conversation away from confrontation*) No, really, though, Jay, you don't have to have black skin to be a nigger.

CHRIS: Yeah, look at me. My skin is black, right? But I ain't a nigger. I ain't. It's not cool. The Brothers, I don't like them. I ain't like them. I ain't a nigger.

FRANKIE: Chris, you're a fucking nigger.

CHRIS: No, I ain't, Frankie. You know that.

Chris will go so far as to shout racial epithets at fellow blacks and to show enthusiasm for fighting with the Hallway Hangers against other black youths.

Much of this attitude, however, is expedient posturing that enables Chris to maintain his sometimes tenuous status in the group. His real feelings are quite different.

CHRIS: I've lived here for fourteen years. I've always hung with these guys. I dunno, maybe it's cuz I never knew many black people back then. These guys are all right, though. They fuck with me some, but not like with some kids. I mean, after fourteen fucking years you get used to them calling you nigger every ten minutes. It doesn't do no good to get upset. I just let it slide. Fuck it. I've gotten used to it. I'm glad you're not prejudiced, though. The only time they get real bad is when they've been drinking; then I gotta watch myself. I know how these guys think. That's something too—understanding how they think. I've been here fourteen fucking years, and I know how these motherfuckers think. Like, I can tell when they're gonna fuck with me. When they're trashed, they'll be looking at me a certain way and shit. Then another one will do it. I get the fuck out of there because I know they're gonna fuck with me. Yeah, when they're drunk, they'll get like that. Fucking assholes. But when they haven't been pounding the beers, they're the most dynamite people around. Really.

The rest of the Hallway Hangers are quick to deny any animosity toward Chris.

(in a group interview)

JM: Chris, it can't be easy coming from down here and being half-black and half-white.

SHORTY: The blacks bother him cuz he hangs with whites—us.

JM: Yeah, and you fuck with him cuz he's black.

FRANKIE: No, see, cuz we just razz him because he's black.

SHORTY: We done that all his life and he knows it.

CHRIS: It don't bother me.

Nevertheless, outright hostility toward Chris does come to the surface at times, especially when people are under the influence of alcohol or drugs. It seems that whenever Chris threatens the status of others in the group with his street hockey ability, his knack for making a fast buck selling drugs, or his success with girls, racial antagonism comes to the fore. One particular incident illustrates this dynamic. Frankie and I were talking in the doorway when we noticed two white girls giving Chris a few lines of cocaine on the landing above us. As they came down the stairs on their way out, Frankie demanded in a very abrasive tone, "What are you getting that fuckin' *nigger* high for? You don't fucking do that." As the door slammed behind them, Frankie muttered, "They want to suck his black cock, that's why. Fuckin' cunts."

Although the Hallway Hangers attribute their racist attitudes to the riots that occurred in Clarendon Heights during their childhoods, such an explanation cannot account for the racial antagonism that gave rise to the riots in the first place. Racism in Clarendon Heights is a complex phenomenon that does not lend itself to easy interpretation or explanation. Nevertheless, in the attitudes and comments of the Hallway Hangers, it is possible to discern evidence in support of the proposition that racism in lower-class communities stems from competition for scarce economic resources.[3] Shorty, for example, bitterly attributes his brother's unemployment to affirmative action policies: "He got laid off because they hired all Puerto Ricans, blacks, and Portegis [Portuguese]. It's cuz of the fuckin' spics and niggers." In a separate discussion of the harshness of unemployment, Smitty, an older youth on the fringes of the Hallway Hangers, put forth a similar view.

SMITTY: All the fuckin' niggers are getting the jobs. Two of them motherfuckers got hired yesterday [at a construction site]; I didn't get shit. They probably don't even know how to hold a fuckin' shovel either.

FRANKIE: Fuckin' right. That's why we're hanging here now with empty pockets.

The perceived economic threat blacks pose to the Hallway Hangers contributes to their racism. The racial prejudice of the Hallway Hangers, a subject of academic interest in its own right, also has important ramifications for social reproduction. In Chapter 11 we see how it not only harms blacks but is ultimately self-destructive as well.

Although the Hallway Hangers can be hostile to Boo-Boo and Chris, their real racial venom is directed against the Brothers, the black peer group at Clarendon Heights. Interestingly, when considering each member of the Brothers individually, the Hallway Hangers admit respect and esteem for a number of them. Considered as a group, however, there is little feeling aside from bitter racial enmity. As with Chris, the enmity is at its sharpest when the Brothers are perceived as threatening in some way. The following interview segment, quoted at length, captures the essence of the Hallway Hangers' attitude toward the Brothers.

JM: What do you think of Super and the rest of them?

SLICK: Fuck 'em, they're niggers.

FRANKIE: Fuck 'em, they're niggers, that's right.

SHORTY: They're niggers, man.

FRANKIE: Pretty soon, pretty soon, we're gonna be beefing [fighting] them motherfuckers, and they're not gonna like it.

SLICK: Once they're ready to take a beating, that's when . . .

FRANKIE: No, no. I'll tell you. They're ready; they're ready. Summertime. Summertime, we'll be fighting.

SLICK: Yeah, this summer we'll be fighting them.

FRANKIE: Definitely, we'll be fighting them.

SHORTY: Even though we did before, and they were the same age as us, but if we beat them up bad, they'd fucking, y'know . . .

SLICK: They'd call the cops and shit.

SHORTY: [*sarcastically*] Or their big tough fathers would come out. You see what we'll do to their fathers. We'll fight their fathers worse than we'll fight them.

JM: [*with my disgust undisguised*] So why are you so into that?

SHORTY: No, we ain't into it. We don't like their attitude.

FRANKIE: They don't like us, man. What're you, crazy? They're niggers.

SHORTY: They move in here. We don't bother them. Once they start with us . . .

FRANKIE: Hey, they're coming on our fucking land. Fuck them motherfuckers. They don't like us, man, and I sure as hell don't like them.

SHORTY: I've lived here all my fucking life, and no new nigger is gonna move in and fucking start [a fight] with me.

FRANKIE: And I'll tell ya, I'll stick any of them; I'll beat any of them. Fuck them fucking niggers.

SHORTY: Jay, listen to this. They move in here, right?

JM: But how do they move in here, huh?

SHORTY: They just move in here, y'know?

JM: But wait. Into the projects? It's not like you pick which one you wanna move into.

SHORTY: Bullshit!

JM: I think they said, "There's too many white people in here and people been complaining." So they started moving black people in here.

FRANKIE: [*still yelling*] Yeah, that's what happened last time. They moved too many fucking niggers in, and then in '71 and '72 we had the fucking riots.

SHORTY: The last time they did that was ten years ago. Watch!

JM: All's I'm sayin' is that it's not their fault that they moved in. It's the Housing Authority that sends 'em in.

SHORTY: Will you fucking listen, Jay?

JM: Yeah, but I mean, if you were black, would you wanna live here? I fucking wouldn't.

FRANKIE: [*very angrily*] They come in here with a fucking *attitude,* man. They ain't gettin' no [inaudible] attitude. Fucking niggers are getting *hurt* this summer. I'm telling you, man.

SHORTY: Jay, *listen.* When they first moved in here, they were really cool and everything. We didn't bother them. But once more and more black families moved in, they said, "Wow, we can overrun these people. We can overpower them." That's what their attitude was.

SLICK: Slowly but surely, man, they're trying to fucking fuck us over. It's gonna be '71 and '72 all over again.

SHORTY: They come in here walking with their buddies now with sticks and shit and look at us and laugh. Y'know what we could do to them so bad? It's just that a lot of us don't fucking wanna . . .

SLICK: No one can really afford to get arrested anymore, or we'll go away. No one wants to go away. No one wants to go to fucking jail.

FRANKIE: Yeah, but I'll tell you. Them niggers, man. It's just about time. This summer.

The resentment the Hallway Hangers feel toward blacks and the destructive consequences that flow from this hatred could not be more plainly exposed. By pointing to the economic and social factors that feed this racism, I do not mean to absolve the Hallway Hangers of responsibility for their racist attitudes and beliefs, much less for the violence to which these give rise. Racism is a sickness that rots American society, but those who see it simply as a matter of individual pathology overlook the social conditions that contribute to its outbreak and spread. We can blame the Hallway Hangers, but we also must blame the economic and social conditions of lower-class life under competitive capitalism.

THE BROTHERS: CONSPICUOUS BY THEIR CONVENTIONALITY

In contrast to the Hallway Hangers, the Brothers accommodate themselves to accepted standards of behavior and strive to fulfill socially approved roles. It is the white peer group from Clarendon Heights that is at odds with mainstream American culture. Nonconformity fascinates the sociologist, and if in this book undue attention is given to the distinctive cultural novelty of the Hallway Hangers, it should be borne in mind that the Brothers also pose an interesting and in many ways exceptional case. However, because my primary interest is the role that aspirations play in social reproduction, and because the Hallway Hangers undergo the process of social reproduction in a unique fashion, my emphasis in both the presentation of ethnographic material and in its analysis inevitably falls on the Hallway Hangers.

The most obvious difference between the two peer groups is in racial composition: The Brothers have only one white member. When one considers that this peer group emerges from the same social setting as do the Hallway Hangers, other striking differences become apparent. Composed of a nucleus of seven teenagers and expanding to twelve at times, this peer group is not a distinctive subculture with its own set of values defined in opposition to the dominant culture. The Brothers attend high school on a regular basis. None of them smokes cigarettes, drinks regularly, or uses drugs. None has been arrested.

Craig is a quiet, tall, dark-skinned youth with a reserved manner and easy smile, except on the basketball court. A graceful athlete, he is on the varsity basketball team at the high school. He moved to the projects six years ago and was one of a few black children to attend the neighborhood grammar school. His family is tightly knit; he lives with his parents, four brothers and sisters, and two stepsiblings. Self-assured and agreeable, Craig maintains a leadership role in the peer group, although such status demarcations are much less clearly defined among the Brothers than among the Hallway Hangers.

In contrast to Craig, Super is a fiery, loud, yet often introspective lad who, despite his medium size, never backs down from a fight. Hesitant in speech and uncomfortable with written material, Super struggles in the classroom. He is, however, a natural athlete. His speed, quickness, and agility lend themselves to football and basketball, but his carefree attitude toward sport and his flare for flashy moves do not sit well with high school coaches and have prevented success in these areas at the varsity level. Super's home life is turbulent; his temper, apparently, is matched by his father's, and the confrontations between father and son have prompted Super to leave home for safer environs for a week or two on at least three occasions.

Originally from the Dominican Republic, Juan is the only Brother to have finished school, but he currently is unemployed. He is slight of build, a sincere and sensitive youth. Juan speaks in somewhat broken English, was not particularly successful in school, and is not a good athlete. His loyalty, kind manner, and sense of fair play, however, are attributes that have earned him respect. Such remarks as these are typical of him: "Yup," he said, as he left one evening to meet his girlfriend, "there's the three things everyone needs—a job, a car, and a girl. And the girl's the most important. Because otherwise you'd be lonely. You need someone to talk to and somebody to love." In a neighborhood notorious for its toughness, such a comment is remarkable for its honesty and tenderness.

Mokey is a quick-tempered boy whose impatience with others often borders on insolence. Stocky and of medium height, Mokey commits himself with vigor and enthusiasm to whatever he is pursuing but has difficulty sustaining this drive for an extended period of time. One week he is enthused about his prospects on the school football team, but two weeks later he has quit the squad and exhibits a newfound zeal for track and field. Full of energy and constantly on the move, Mokey chafes against the tight rein his mother keeps on him but generally accedes to her wishes. When necessary, his father, who does not live with the family, is called in to straighten out any problems.

James, a junior at the high school, is very small for his age. He manages to compensate for his diminutive size, however, with a quick and caustic tongue. He is not as well integrated into the group as the other boys, perhaps because of a long, involved relationship with a girl that recently ended. A year ago, James was a fixture in one of the city's video arcades during school hours; now he attends school every day as well as on Thursday evenings to make up for failed subjects. This turnabout resulted from a serious talk with his father, whose presence in the household is sporadic. James's wit, sense of humor, and toughness have earned him the esteem of the Brothers.

Derek is Boo-Boo's half brother. The two boys have different friends, interests, and attitudes and are not particularly close, but they do maintain an amiable cordiality outside their home, which is a considerable achievement in view of the animosity between the Brothers and Hallway Hangers. (I take up the siblings' substantially divergent outlooks and membership in different peer groups in Chapter 8.) Their paths parted when, as a third-grader, Derek secured a government scholarship to a prestigious private school because of his scholastic achievements. Derek attended Barnes Academy through the eighth grade with great success; his grades were good, and he had many friends. Nevertheless, he decided to attend the city high school, where he has continued his academic achievement. Although lacking in athletic prowess, Derek is admired by the other boys for his academic success and personal motivation.

Mike is the sole white member of the Brothers. He lives with his mother and grandmother and rules the household. His large frame and strength have made him a valuable asset to the high school's football, wrestling, and track and field squads. His athletic ability and an aversion to drugs and alcohol inculcated by his mother as well as a strong and lasting friendship with Super all account for Mike's allegiance to the Brothers. He is subject to some abuse from his white peers on this account but seems to take their ribbing in stride.

The Brothers, in contrast to the Hallway Hangers, are not a distinctive subculture with its own set of shared values. The Brothers accept the dominant culture's definitions of success and judge themselves by these criteria. A night in the city jail would permanently tarnish a Brother's reputation rather than build it up. In the eyes of the Brothers, John Grace, the bartender who was involved in the shootout in Clarendon Heights, would be worthy only of disdain, and perhaps pity, rather than the respect Frankie accords him. While the Hallway Hangers have little concern for the judgments of the dominant culture, the Brothers become uncomfortable and embarrassed when recounting disciplinary problems they have had at home or in school. Such a "confession" for a member of the Hallway Hangers, on the other hand, might be accompanied by laughter and a sense of triumph.

Just as the Brothers accept the values of the dominant culture, their behavior generally conforms to societal expectations. Whereas the Hallway Hangers are conspicuous in their consumption of cigarettes and beer, the Brothers reject both. Although many of the Brothers drink beer in moderation every once in a while at a party or on a similar occasion, their consumption of alcohol is very limited. Likewise, although most of the Brothers have tried marijuana, they rarely smoke it, and they never use other drugs.

The Brothers are uncomfortable with simply "hanging"; they cannot tolerate such inactivity. They often can be found playing basketball in the park or the gym. If a pickup game of basketball cannot be mustered in the immediate neighborhood, they often will walk a half mile to the Salvation Army gym or another housing project. Energetic and spirited, the Brothers dislike the idleness of the Hallway Hangers.

DEREK: I would never hang with them. I'm not interested in drinking, getting high, or making trouble. That's about all they do. . . . I don't like to just sit around.

Although the Brothers do not adopt those practices that symbolize rejection of authority or basic societal values, their peer group does have its own distinctive attributes. The Brothers carry themselves in ways familiar to most urban black Americans, although somewhat scaled down. Their style of dress, mode of speech, and form of greeting clearly set them apart from other residents of Clarendon Heights. However, the caps, neck chains, and open shirts so prevalent among teenagers in the predominantly black sections of the city are lacking among the Brothers, whose residency in a white neighborhood has important implications for much more than their dress.

Athletics is one activity into which the Brothers channel their energies. Many excel in organized youth, church, and school basketball leagues as well as in regular pickup games. Mike, Super, and Mokey also play on the school football team. Only Juan and Derek are not good athletes, and even they maintain an interest in sports, often rounding out the teams for a pickup game of basketball.

Girls also claim much of the Brothers' time. A frequent topic of conversation, their interest in girls seems much more widespread than is the case for the Hallway Hangers. While the Hangers tend to go out with girls on a casual basis (typically for a weekend), the Brothers often have steady girlfriends, with whom they are constantly speaking on the phone, to whose house they are forever headed, and about whom they always are boasting. Whereas the Hallway Hangers focus on their beer and drugs, the Brothers have their basketball and girlfriends.

Since Juan bought an old worn-out Vega for two hundred dollars and fixed it up complete with paint job and functioning engine, cruising the streets also has become a favorite pastime for the Brothers. It gives them access to the "Port" and the "Coast," the black sections of the city. Considering the tense racial atmosphere of the Clarendon Heights community, it is no wonder that the Brothers do not spend as much time in the vicinity of the Heights as the Hallway Hangers do and instead prefer the black neighborhoods.

In addition to being the objects of many of the Hallway Hangers' racist slurs and insults, the Brothers suffer from even more substantive racial abuse. Super tells how the windows in his family's car have been broken year after year and how one morning last spring he awoke to find "KKK" drawn in spray paint on the side of the car. Juan recounts with anger accompanied by matter-of-fact acceptance how his mother was taunted by some members of the Hallway Hangers, which led his father into a confrontation with them. His father was lucky to escape unharmed from the ensuing argument. Juan has a measure of understanding for the Hallway Hangers: "When they call me a nigger, I usually don't let it bother me none. They drunk or high, y'know. They don't know what they're doing." In his freshman year of high school, however, Juan was beaten up by Shorty for no apparent reason; he still bears the scar on his lip from the fight, and the memory of it burns in his mind, fueling the resentment he feels toward the Hallway Hangers.

Although the Brothers are not submissive in the face of racial animosity from the Hallway Hangers, they are outnumbered and outmatched, and they usually find it expedient to walk away before a confrontation explodes into a street fight. They are accustomed to the violent racial prejudice of the Hallway Hangers. In fact, Craig, instead of being upset that a simple basketball game threatened to erupt into a racial brawl, merely commented, "That was good of Shorty to come over and tell us we better leave before his friends start all sorts of trouble." Although the Brothers are hesitant to answer openly the insults of the Hallway Hangers, they do vent their contempt for the Hallway Hangers in private discussions.

(all in separate interviews)

JUAN: I don't like their attitude, their gig, what they do. . . . They'll be there, hanging in front of the Heights, fighting and arguing and stuff like that. . . . It wasn't until I moved here that I heard the word *nigger*. I had heard about people in the projects; I knew they'd be a pain in the ass sometimes. . . . I swear, if I ever see one of them touching my mother or doing something to my car, I don't care, I'll kill them. Cuz I don't like none of them. I'm afraid I'm gonna hurt one of them real bad. Every time I hear them call me nigger, I just don't say anything, but I can't take the pressure of people getting on my case every time, y'know?

CRAIG: I don't know why they just hang out there being crazy and getting drunk and bothering people. Maybe cuz they need attention or something. They got nuttin' better to do so they might as well cause trouble so people will think they're bad and stuff. They're just lazy. They wanna take the easy way out—that is, hang around outside all day.

JAMES: They're not gonna get anywhere except for standing at that same corner going [*imitating someone who is very benumbed*], "Hey, man, got some pot, man? Hey, Frank, let's get high."

DEREK: We just have different attitudes. We like to stay away from the projects as much as possible, or they'll give us trouble. That's about all they do: make trouble.

SUPER: They smoke reefer; they drink. They ain't friendly like people, y'know what I'm sayin'? They go around the street laughing at people, ragging them out, y'know what I mean? They just disrespect people.

MIKE: They're just a bunch of fuckups.

Such perceptions are often voiced by the Brothers. The situation between the two peer groups, however, is not one of constant strife. Rather, there is a constant underlying tension that surfaces occasionally—often during basketball games or when the Hallway Hangers have been drinking excessively—but that threatens to erupt into considerable violence.

Aside from racial factors, the character of the two peer groups differs markedly in other ways. The Brothers have no pecking order based on fighting ability. Although Craig is generally respected most, there is no hierarchy in the group, hidden or otherwise; the Brothers do not playfully abuse each other, physically or verbally. Loose and shifting cliques develop among the members and sometimes encompass outsiders. Friendships wax and wane according to the season and the boys' extracurricular activities and responsibilities. During the winter, for example, Craig is so tied up with the basketball team that he effectively drops out of the group, and his best friend, Super, becomes closer to Derek and Mokey. During the school day, the Brothers often see little of each other and, once out, invariably break up into smaller friendship groups, coming all together only once in a while. In short, the Brothers are no more than a peer group, whereas the Hallway Hangers are a much more cohesive unit with its own subculture.

The Hallway Hangers, who reject the values of the dominant culture and subscribe to their own distinctive cultural norms, have a sense of solidarity that is noticeably absent from the Brothers' peer group. Internal cohesion and the adoption of communitarian values, in which the Hallway Hangers take pride, are missing among the Brothers. Although all the Brothers would support each other in a fight, the ties that bind them are not as strong and are not as strongly affirmed as those that bind the Hallway Hangers.

The Brothers do not compare themselves to members of the upper classes, nor do they feel as keenly the stigma or shame associated with life in public housing. (An explanation of these differences is undertaken in Chapter 7.)

Daily life for the Brothers is far less circumscribed than it is for the Hallway Hangers. Active, enthusiastic, and still in school, the Brothers are not preoccupied with mere survival on the street. Their world extends into the classroom and onto the basketball court, and it extends into the home a great deal more than does the world of the Hallway Hangers, as we shall see in the next chapter.

NOTES

1. All temporal citations in Part One have as their reference point February 1984, when the first draft of the book was written. Thus, "presently" and "currently" refer to the winter of 1984, and "last year" means June 1983. The present tense is used throughout the book, and no developments after February 1984 are included in Part One.

2. *Lower-class,* as the term applies to public housing residents, is not used in this book as an analytical construct but as a descriptive term that captures their position at the lower end of the socioeconomic spectrum. Similarly, the term *upper classes* is used to refer to all those whose position is higher on the socioeconomic scale; *middle class* refers more specifically to salaried white-collar workers, including professional and managerial personnel.

3. See, especially, David T. Wellman, *Portraits of White Racism* (Cambridge: Cambridge University Press, 1977); and Donald Neal, "A Theory of the Origin of Ethnic Stratification," *Social Problems* 16 (Fall 1968): 157–172.

THE INFLUENCE OF THE FAMILY

As the focal socializing agency, especially in the early years of a child's life, the family plays a crucial role in the process of social reproduction. In this chapter, we consider the particular circumstances of each boy's family and how the family influences his expectations for the future. In describing the families of these boys, we must be attentive to a number of factors, such as the presence of a father in the household, the occupational histories of parents and older siblings, and the length of the family's tenancy in public housing.

All families living in Clarendon Heights are lower class. For a family of four to qualify for federal housing projects, its annual income must not exceed $14,000; for state housing developments the limit is approximately $1,500 lower. These are, of course, the upper boundaries; the annual income of most families living in Clarendon Heights is well below the limit.

THE HALLWAY HANGERS' HOUSEHOLDS

Chris lives with his white mother and two younger sisters. Their father, who is black, moved out of the house a few years ago. "I kicked my father out," boasts Chris in a group interview. Chris also has two half brothers and one half sister who live on their own. His brothers work in unskilled, manual labor jobs; his sister is a part-time secretary. Chris seems to have free run of the household. His mother, a kind, friendly woman who has never married, has been pleading with Chris for two years to attend school regularly, but to no avail. Although she does not work regularly, for much of the year she babysits in her home for one and sometimes two young children from working-class families. In exchange for her labors (nine hours per day), she receives a small wage. Chris's family has lived in Clarendon Heights for sixteen years, prior to which his mother lived with her other children in private housing.

Boo-Boo also has lived in Clarendon Heights for his entire life. He and his older brother have a different father than his younger brother, Derek (a member of the Brothers), and his younger sister. Both fathers live out of state and very seldom venture to Clarendon Heights. Their mother, a high school dropout, has stable employment assembling computer and electronic parts in a nearby suburb. Boo-Boo's father, who graduated from high school, has been in the merchant marine "for a long, long time." Boo-Boo's older brother, Blade, has a drug dependency problem. He dropped out of high school a few years ago, recently has joined the army reserves and is struggling to acquire a General Equivalency Diploma (GED) so that he can join the army.

Stoney's mother's occupational history is a modest success story. She attended St. Mary's Catholic High School in the city but had to drop out during her freshman year to find work after her mother died. She subsequently earned a GED as well as a secretarial degree and has worked her way up to a supervisory position as secretary of a department in a state welfare office. Stoney's father's experience has been altogether different. Confined to the county house of correction a year and a half ago for passing a bad check, he broke out with only a month remaining on his sentence. With no place to go and unable to see his family, however, he subsequently turned himself in. After serving the remainder of his sentence plus some additional months for the escape, he has now found short-term work cleaning carpets. But like so many others from Clarendon Heights with a criminal record, Stoney's father probably will have a difficult time securing stable employment and is likely to end up back behind bars. Stoney's family moved to the Clarendon Heights neighborhood only three years ago; before that time they lived in Emerson Towers housing project, where Stoney's mother grew up. In contrast to the rest of the Hallway Hangers, Stoney's mother has a strong influence on him. A strict disciplinarian, she sets a nightly curfew for him, which he respects with diligence.

Frankie's family lived in the Heights for thirty years, and although his mother recently moved to another project in the city, Frankie spends nearly all of his time in the Clarendon Heights community. His mother and father both grew up in separate working-class neighborhoods in the city. Frankie's father attended City Tech for a few years before quitting school. He died when Frankie was seven years old. Frankie is the only Hallway Hanger whose mother graduated from high school; she currently works full-time at a camera factory. His sister also graduated from high school, but none of his seven brothers has earned a diploma. As mentioned earlier, all of Frankie's brothers have served time in prison; four of them presently are scattered around the state in various institutions. When out of prison, they find work in construction, landscaping, or painting. One of his brothers tends bar at the local pub, where recently he was shot trying to break up a fight. Most of Frankie's brothers work irregularly; at any given time, one or two may be unemployed.

Slick and Steve are the only members of the Hallway Hangers whose family has moved recently to public housing. Although their mother grew up only a few blocks from the Heights, the family lived in a neighboring city until they moved to Clarendon Heights about six years ago. Their father has never lived with the family, his background is hazy, and Steve's feelings about him are ambivalent. "I haven't seen that bastard for a long time. . . . I think he got put away when he was a kid." Neither parent graduated from high school. "My mom quit in the ninth or tenth grade. She quit cuz she had to put money in the house. And, y'know, she was on her own by the time she was eighteen," declares Slick. Currently out of work due to ill health, their mother, an aggressive and strong-willed woman, usually is employed as a nurse's aide. Slick and Steve have a brother and sister, both younger.

Jinx, like Frankie, is part of a large family that has lived in Clarendon Heights for close to thirty years. Both of his parents grew up in the city and are currently employed full-time. His father has worked for the city maintenance department for nearly thirty years, while his mother has been employed at a hotel as a chambermaid for six or seven years. Neither parent graduated from high school, nor did five of his six older siblings, including his only sister. The one high school graduate is in the navy; of the other three brothers, one paints houses, one works in a factory assembling clothes racks, and one is unemployed, having himself completed a stint in the navy. Jinx's fifth brother died of natural causes at the age of sixteen. His sister recently obtained her own apartment in Clarendon Heights; she has a small daughter to look after and consequently does not work. Given that the largest apartment in Clarendon Heights contains only three bedrooms, Jinx's family must have been very cramped before his sister and her daughter moved out. Even now, six people live in the unit.

Shorty's family is even larger. He has ten older brothers and sisters, three of whom have graduated from high school.

SHORTY: I got seven brothers. We lived here for thirteen years. . . . I mean, we been through the riots and everything. My brother Joe had to quit school when he was sixteen years old, just because my father was an alcoholic. He had to go out and get a job. My [other] brother, he was a bikey; he had to sell pot. But Joe was out gettin' a job at sixteen to support all the kids. . . . He [went back to school and was subsequently employed as] a cop for two months; he got laid off. He was working at the weapons lab as a security guard. You ask him. He's our father. That's what he really is—he's our father. My father got put away for nine months. He didn't live with us for six years. Every fucking penny that my brother got he threw right into the family, right into the house. Cuz my mother can't work. She almost died three times; she has a brain tumor.

Aside from this account, information on Shorty's family is very sketchy, as he will very seldom speak about his home life. In a separate interview, however, Shorty did mention that with the exception of Joe, all the boys in his family have at one time or another been in the military service, as was his father.

Despite the difficulty inherent in generalizing about such diverse family histories, it is clear that the Hallway Hangers share certain family characteristics that may affect their aspirations. Foremost among these are the duration of these families' tenancy in public housing. With the exception of Slick and Steve, all the Hallway Hangers and their families have lived in the projects for many years: Shorty for thirteen years, Chris for sixteen, Boo-Boo's family for at least eighteen, Jinx's family for twenty-seven years, and Frankie's and Stoney's families for thirty years. Like most of the project residents, the educational attainment of these boys' parents and older brothers and sisters is very low; of their parents, only Boo-Boo's father and Frankie's mother graduated from high school. The sporadic employment record of family members is another common characteristic. For those who are able to find employment at all, it is typically menial, low paying, and unstable. Other less widespread commonalities between the families of these boys include the fathers' absence from the household, the large size of the families, and the numerous encounters of family members with the law.

THE BROTHERS' FAMILIES

Super's family has lived in public housing for eighteen years. The family moved to Clarendon Heights only five years ago but prior to that lived in a large housing project in a nearby city. Super's mother and father came to the North from South Carolina and Tennessee respectively in the early 1960s. Neither graduated from high school. Super's mother does not work; his father is a general laborer in construction but currently is unemployed, a typical predicament for low-level employees in the seasonal construction business. Super has two younger sisters and an older sister who attends a Catholic high school. Super has left home repeatedly, citing his parents' strict and inflexible disciplinary code as the reason. Although many parents in Clarendon Heights use force when disciplining their children, Super is the only boy who admits to being abused physically by his father.

Details about Mokey's home life are scarce. Mokey is not sure whether his parents graduated from high school. Apparently a heavy drinker, Mokey's father is a custodian in an office building in the commercial and financial district of the city. Although his father moved out of the house at least four years ago, Mokey frequently meets him at work to help with the evening cleanup, especially during the summer. His mother works part-time at a nearby day care center. He has a brother who is two years younger than he is and a five-year-old sister who has just entered kindergarten. His family lived in a very small public housing development before moving into Clarendon Heights.

James has lived in the Clarendon Heights community for his entire life. His mother, who is originally from Georgia, quit school when she was in the eighth grade. She is unemployed temporarily because she injured her shoulder about six months ago, but she usually works as a nurse's aide for the elderly. James's father graduated from high school and currently works in a factory that manufactures zippers and buttons. When asked if his father lives in the household, James shakes his head no but adds, "He didn't really move out. He comes and he goes." James's two younger sisters are excellent students, but his thirteen-year-old brother has a much more lackadaisical attitude toward his education. As noted previously, James's approach to school recently has undergone a dramatic change from ambivalence to commitment.

Craig's family came to this country from Haiti about eleven years ago and has lived in the Clarendon Heights neighborhood for six years. Although the educational system is somewhat different in Haiti, both his parents attained the rough equivalent of a high school diploma. His mother works part-time as a "homemaker"; she prepares meals, cleans, and performs other domestic chores for an elderly couple. Craig's father works as a janitor for an engineering company. Craig took pains to explain to me that his father has worked his way up to a supervisory role in the maintenance department.

CRAIG: I think he's a supervisor.

JM: So what exactly does he do?

CRAIG: Before he used to do it himself—cleaning—but now he makes sure others do it.

Craig lives with his parents and six brothers and sisters. "Actually, I got four brothers and sisters, right? But since my father was messin' around, I got six brothers and sisters." The half siblings as well as his four full brothers and sisters all live in the household. His two older sisters have been very successful academically; there seems to be a supportive atmosphere for academic achievement in his home. His brother is in his second year at a technical college. One of the older sisters, who was a straight-A student in high school, is studying medicine at a local college.

Juan's family is also from the West Indies, in this case the Dominican Republic. His mother and father were divorced there, at which time Juan's mother came to the United States. Juan and his younger sister came to join her ten years ago; their three brothers preferred to remain in their home country. At some point, his mother remarried, and the family of four moved into Clarendon Heights in 1978. Juan's stepfather is presently unemployed.

JUAN: He can't find a job.

JM: What's his trade?

JUAN: He used to work in a hotel, like in management—a boss. He decided to quit, and then he went to another hotel. Then the same thing happened: He decided to quit. Don't know why.

Juan's mother does not work either. Both his stepfather and mother graduated from high school in the Dominican Republic. He sorely misses his older brothers and hopes to return to his homeland in the near future.

Mike lives with his unmarried mother and grandmother. His father, an Italian immigrant, was a very successful professional wrestler, but Mike knows of him only from television. Mike has lived in public housing since he was two years old, first in Emerson Towers and, since 1977, in Clarendon Heights. His grandmother retired from her work in a local factory a few years ago. His mother, a high school dropout, has held a series of jobs. Most recently, she worked at Woolworth's and subsequently on the night shift at a large hotel. She found that job physically draining and currently is employed as a homemaker who takes care of elderly people. Neither woman has much success disciplining Mike; periodically, however, his uncle is brought in to help with the task, which Mike loathes. A navy veteran, Mike's uncle is the stereotypical tough, no-nonsense blue-collar worker. His uncle recounts stories of painful encounters with his own father when his self-discipline slipped perceptibly and threatens Mike with the same type of punishment.

UNCLE: When my father said something, he meant it. When he said to be in at eleven o'clock, he meant eleven o'clock. I can remember being out with the boys one night and running all the way home—got in at 11:05. My old man was sitting there waiting for me. He looked at me, looked at the clock, and that was it. He knocked the shit out of me.

MIKE: [*grimacing*] That's crazy. Jay, tell him that's crazy.

UNCLE: It worked. And it'll work on you too. Damn right it will.

Indeed, the approach does have the desired effect, for now his mother exercises more control of Mike by threatening to summon his uncle.

In general terms, the Brothers' families are typical of lower-class households and are much like the families of the Hallway Hangers. Family structure is not of the conventional nuclear type; most are "broken homes." Educational achievement is low, and employment, for those who have a job, is typically in nondescript, uninteresting, unskilled work. There are, however, some differences between the families of the Brothers and of the Hallway Hangers in these areas. Whereas among the Hallway Hangers only Jinx's father lives regularly in the household, three of the Brothers have a male authority figure living with them. Nearly half the parents of the Brothers have graduated from high school; of the Hallway Hangers, only Boo-Boo and Frankie have a parent who has obtained a high school diploma. With the exception of Derek, all the Brothers are either the oldest male sibling or have older brothers and sisters whose educational achievement is significant; for the Hallway Hangers, on the other hand, it is more typical to find that an older sibling has been sent away to prison. In addition, all the Brothers' fathers work except Juan's, whereas among the Hallway Hangers, only Jinx's father works regularly. Moreover, the Hallway Hangers' families have lived in public housing for at least twenty years, and some are second-generation tenants (Stoney's, Jinx's, and Frankie's). The Brothers' families have lived in public housing for five to thirteen years (the exceptions are James, whose family has been in public housing for sixteen years, and Derek, who is Boo-Boo's brother). An even more pointed contrast arises when we consider how long the families of each peer group have lived in the Clarendon Heights neighborhood. Of the Hallway Hangers, only Steve's and Slick's family has moved to the area within the past twelve years. The opposite is true of the Brothers. Only James's family (and, of course, Derek's) has lived in Clarendon Heights for more than six years. In analyzing the feelings of hopelessness, immobility, and stagnation that plague the Hallway Hangers, this contrast will prove important.

The subjective side of these structural elements also shapes the boys' aspirations. Although rejection of parental authority is a common attribute of adolescent subcultures, the Hallway Hangers seem to respect the views of their parents, even though their parents do not play a large role in their lives. What we see in most cases is an unspoken but mutually accepted limitation of the parental role. At sixteen, seventeen, and eighteen years of age, these boys have gained a maturity from years of hard living on the street that is incommensurate with their chronological age. It appears that both they and their parents respect the notion that parental authority is incompatible with this maturity.

The boys' comments point to the limited role their parents play in their lives. In describing his mother's influence, Frankie says, "She wants me to do what I want to do." But, although she has little direct control of her son and does not exercise much authority, Frankie respects her wishes. He knew, for example, how badly she wanted one of her sons to graduate from high school. For reasons that will become clear in the next two chapters, Frankie wanted to leave school. "The only reason I got my diploma wasn't for me; it was for my mother. My mother wanted a diploma." The limited influence Slick's mother had concerning the same issue is apparent from the following exchange.

(in a discussion with Slick and Shorty)

JM: So did she [his mother] pressure you at all to stay in school when you decided to quit?

SLICK: No. She wanted me to stay in high school, but at the time, things were tough, y'know?

SHORTY: She knows his attitude is all right.

SLICK: She knows what I want, and she's not gonna stop me from getting it my way.

This type of interaction is typical of the relationship between parent and son among the Hallway Hangers.

The respect these parents have for the autonomy of their sons extends to the way in which they influence their sons' occupational aspirations. When asked about the effect their parents have on their ambitions, the Hallway Hangers are unanimous in their declaration that such a determination is left up to them alone. Indeed, even Stoney's mother, the most authoritarian of the parents, does not feel it is her place to sway Stoney's aspirations. She thinks it inappropriate to foster high aspirations in her children, fearing that unrealistically high goals only will result in disappointment, frustration, and feelings of failure and inadequacy. "It's not like he's growing up in the suburbs somewhere. Sure, he could probably make it if everything went right for him, but lemme tell you, the chances aren't great. He's got his goals, and they're probably good, realistic ones. I personally think he should've stayed in school. I think he fucked up by dropping out. But he didn't think it was worth it, and what the hell, maybe it isn't."

Other parents also are hesitant to encourage hefty ambitions in their children; as the Hallway Hangers tell it, there is little stimulus from home to raise their aspirations.

JM: What kind of work does your mother [do your parents] want you to do for a living?

(all in separate interviews)

BOO-BOO: Anything. She doesn't really care, as long as I'm working.

FRANKIE: She don't fucking care. I mean, I'm sure she cares, but she don't push nothing on me.

SLICK: She wants me to make a buck so I can move for myself.

STEVE: Anything, man. Somethin'. I dunno. Just a fuckin' job.

JINX: They don't talk about it. They hardly ever talk about it. Just as long as I'm not out of work. My mother hates when I'm unemployed.

If such an attitude is widespread among parents in Clarendon Heights, then the conventional sociological wisdom requires revision. The premise that lower-class parents project their frustrated ambitions onto their children in an attempt to reach their goals vicariously is a widely accepted notion among social psychologists and one to which Robert Merton alludes in his essay "Social Structure and Anomie." Citing work he and some colleagues undertook on the social organization of public housing developments, Merton reports that a substantial portion of both black and white parents on lower occupational levels want their children to have professional careers.[1] Before we challenge the sociological perspective on intergenerational mobility, however, we should consider the attitude of the Brothers' parents toward this issue.

In contrast to the Hallway Hangers, the Brothers' parents exercise a good deal of authority over them. All the Brothers have a relatively early curfew, which they conscientiously obey. They are expected to perform up to a certain standard at school, both in terms of academic achievement and discipline. Furthermore, they are expected to respect prohibitions against smoking cigarettes, drinking alcohol, and using drugs. Failure to meet expected standards of behavior invariably results in punishment. In these instances, the youth is confined to his family's apartment for specified times during the day. Sometimes one of the Brothers will be restricted to his room after school, occasionally for periods as lengthy as one month. By their obedience and consent to these restrictions the Brothers acknowledge the control their parents exercise. Comparable manifestations of parental authority are altogether absent among the Hallway Hangers. In fact, Craig explicitly made this point in comparing the differences in attitude and behavior between the Brothers and the Hallway Hangers. "I guess our parents are a lot tighter than their parents. Y'know, at least they tell us what to do and stuff. From the very beginning, ever since we were born, y'know, they'd always be telling us, 'Do this; do that.' Always disciplining us. As far as their parents go, I can't really say their parents are bad, but their parents aren't helping any."

Parental influence on the Brothers' aspirations accords with Merton's findings. James, for instance, feels that his parents project their own frustrated educational and occupational ambitions onto him.

JAMES: My father had to quit school when he had to go to work. But he went back to school. He was one of the top people in his class; he could've went to college. But he didn't have the money to go to college. He had to go to work. So now he wants us all to go to college.

(later in the same interview)

JM: What do your mother and father want you to do for a living?

JAMES: They wanted me to be a lawyer when I was a little kid. They wanted me to grow up and be a lawyer.

James also attributes his dramatic turnaround in school performance to his father's influence.

JM: So how'd you get back on track, then? Why've you started working hard now? This year.

JAMES: I decided I need to have good marks, so . . .

JM: Did anyone help you decide that or just . . .

JAMES: *Yeah.* My father.

JM: Yeah?

JAMES: He didn't hit me or anything; he just talked to me. Told me I wouldn't be able to go and do what I want to when school's over. Wouldn't be able to get no good job.

Other members of the Brothers indicate that similar processes are at work in their families.

SUPER: One thing I know they want me to do, they're always sayin' is finish school. They want me to go to college.

JM: They want you to finish high school and college?

SUPER: Uh-huh. . . . They want me to get a good job; I know that. And not no job with hard labor, y'know, standin' on my foot; they want me sittin' down, y'know, a good job, in an office.

Derek, Juan, and Craig also mention that their parents have high hopes for them. Craig's parents were the key figures in his decision to try becoming an architect. Juan's father wants him to get a job where "you can keep yourself clean." Derek's family nurtured hopes their son would enter a professional career. "They wanted me to be a lawyer. Ever since I went to Barnes Academy."

In addition to the Brothers' accounts, we have further evidence from the parents themselves. Mokey's mother, for instance, feels that her expectations heavily influence Mokey and undoubtedly will play a large part in whatever he decides to do. She insists that he pursue a career "which gives a successful future," such as management or ownership of a small business. She also believes that Mokey should "plan to be a success and reach the highest goal possible. The sky's the limit. That's what my mother told me, and that's what I tell my children. The sky is the limit."

Thus, the Brothers present a significant contrast to the Hallway Hangers with respect to their parents' influence in their lives. The Brothers' parents wield a substantial degree of authority, both in the present and in shaping their children's educational and occupational aspirations. These parents may be projecting their own unfulfilled occupational ambitions onto their children by nurturing in them high hopes for the future.

Some of the Brothers also have older siblings who serve as role models. Craig, Super, and James all have older brothers and sisters who have achieved at least moderate success in school. These three boys see that the path to academic achievement can be followed. Juan, Mokey, and Mike have no older siblings; they see a path that is as yet untried. In contrast, the Hallway Hangers, with the exception of Stoney and Slick, have older siblings who have failed in school; thus, the Hallway Hangers see a tortuous path that is difficult to negotiate. The Brothers all may not have older brothers and sisters who are high academic achievers, but, with the exception of Derek, at least they are not confronted exclusively with examples of academic failure, as most of the Hallway Hangers are. This difference between the two peer groups also has a significant impact on the boys' hopes for the future, which are the subject of the next chapter.

NOTES

1. Robert K. Merton, *Social Theory and Social Structure* (New York: Free Press, 1968), p. 213.

THE WORLD OF WORK
Aspirations of the Hangers and Brothers

Given that work determines one's social class, the perpetuation of class inequality requires that boys like the Hallway Hangers and the Brothers go on to jobs that are comparable in status to the occupations of their parents. Thus, the attitudes of these boys toward the world of work are critical to our understanding of social reproduction. In this chapter, their previous employment records, their general impressions of work, their aspirations and expectations, and their perceptions of the job opportunity structure are considered.

Before describing the boys' orientation toward work, I would like to make an analytical distinction between aspirations and expectations. Both involve assessments of one's desires and abilities, and the character of the opportunity structure. In articulating one's aspirations, an individual weighs his or her preferences more heavily; expectations are tempered by perceived capabilities and available opportunities. Aspirations are one's preferences relatively unsullied by anticipated constraints; expectations take these constraints squarely into account.[1]

THE HALLWAY HANGERS: KEEPING A LID ON HOPE

Conventional, middle-class orientations toward employment are inadequate to describe the Hallway Hangers' approach to work. The notion of a career, a set of jobs that are connected to one another in a logical progression, has little relevance to these boys. They are hesitant when asked about their aspirations and expectations. This hesitancy is not the result of indecision; rather it stems from the fact that these boys see little choice involved in getting a job. No matter how hard I pressed him, for instance, Jinx refused to articulate his aspirations: "I think you're kiddin' yourself to have any. We're just gonna take whatever we can get." Jinx is a perceptive boy, and his answer seems to be an accurate depiction of the situation. Beggars cannot be choosers, and these boys have nothing other than unskilled labor to offer on a credential-based job market.

It is difficult to gauge the aspirations of most of the Hallway Hangers. Perhaps at a younger age they had dreams for their futures. At ages sixteen, seventeen, and eighteen, however, their own job experiences as well as those of family members have contributed to a deeply entrenched cynicism about their futures. What is perceived as the cold, hard reality of the job market weighs very heavily on the Hallway Hangers; they believe their preferences will have almost no bearing on the work they actually will do. Their expectations are not merely tempered by perceptions of the opportunity structure; even their aspirations are crushed by their estimation of the job market. These generalizations may seem bold and rather extreme, but they do not lack ethnographic support.

The pessimism and uncertainty with which the Hallway Hangers view their futures emerge clearly when the boys are asked to speculate on what their lives will be like in twenty years.

(all in separate interviews)

STONEY: Hard to say. I could be dead tomorrow. Around here, you gotta take life day by day.

BOO-BOO: I dunno. I don't want to think about it. I'll think about it when it comes.

FRANKIE: I don't fucking know. Twenty years. I may be fucking dead. I live a day at a time. I'll probably be in the fucking pen.

SHORTY: Twenty years? I'm gonna be in jail.

These responses are striking not only for the insecurity and despondency they reveal, but also because they do not include any mention of work. It is not that work is unimportant—for people as strapped for money as the Hallway Hangers are, work is crucial. Rather, these boys are indifferent to the issue of future employment. Work is a given; they all hope to hold jobs of one kind or another in order to support themselves and their families. But the Hallway Hangers, like the lads in Willis's study, believe the character of work, at least all work in which they are likely to be involved, is essentially the same: boring, undifferentiated, and unrewarding. Thinking about their future jobs is a useless activity for the Hallway Hangers. What is there to think about?

For Steve and Jinx, although they do see themselves employed in twenty years, work is still of tangential importance.

JM: If you had to guess, what do you think you'll be doing twenty years from now?

(in separate interviews)

STEVE: I don't fucking know. Working probably. Have my own pad, my own house. Bitches, kids. Fucking fridge full of brewskies. Fine wife, likes to get laid. [*laughs*]

JINX: Twenty years from now? Probably kicked back in my own apartment doing the same shit I'm doing now—getting high. I'll have a job, if I'm not in the service, if war don't break out, if I'm not dead. I just take one day at a time.

As Jinx suggests, work is contingent on realities over which the Hallway Hangers have no control. Thus, far from being a priority in its own right, work makes possible more pleasurable activities. For the Hallway Hangers, as for many Americans, work is important not as an end in itself but as a means to an end—money.

In probing the occupational aspirations and expectations of the Hallway Hangers, I was able to elicit from them some specific hopes. Although Shorty never mentions his expectations, the rest of the Hallway Hangers have responded to my prodding with some definite answers. The range of answers as well as how they change over time are as significant as the particular hopes each boy expresses.

Boo-Boo's orientation toward work is typical of the Hallway Hangers. He has held a number of jobs in the past, most of them in the summer. During his freshman year in high school Boo-Boo worked as a security guard at school for $2.50 an hour in order to make restitution for a stolen car he damaged. Boo-Boo also has worked on small-scale construction projects through a summer youth employment program called Just-A-Start, at a pipe manufacturing site, and as a clerk in a gift shop. Boo-Boo wants to be an automobile mechanic. Upon graduating from high school, he studied auto mechanics at a technical school on a scholarship. The only black student in his class, Boo-Boo was expelled early in his first term after racial antagonism erupted into a fight. Boo-Boo was not altogether disappointed, for he already was unhappy with what he considered the program's overly theoretical orientation. (Howard London found this kind of impatience with academic study typical of working-class students in the community college he studied.[2]) Boo-Boo wanted hands-on training, but "all's they were doing was telling me about how it's made, stuff like that." Boo-Boo currently is unemployed, but he recently had a chance for a job as a cook's helper. Although he was not hired, the event is significant nevertheless because prior to the job interview Boo-Boo claimed that his ambition now was to work in a restaurant. Here we have an example of the primacy of the opportunity structure in determining the aspirations of the Hallway Hangers. One job opening in another field was so significant that the opening prompted Boo-Boo to redefine totally his aspirations.

In contrast to the rest of the Hallway Hangers who are already on the job market, Steve wants to stay in school for the two years required to get his diploma. Yet, he has a similar attitude toward his future work as do the other youths. He quit his summer job with the Just-A-Start program and has no concrete occupational aspirations. As for expectations, he believes he might enlist in the air force after graduation but adds, "I dunno. I might just go up and see my uncle, do some fuckin' construction or something."

Many of these boys expect to enter military service. Jinx and Frankie mention it as an option; Stoney has tried to enlist, but without success. Although Jinx refuses to think in terms of aspirations, he will say what he expects to do after he finishes school.

JM: What are you gonna do when you get out?

JINX: Go into the service, like everybody else. The navy.

JM: What about after that?

JINX: After that, just get a job, live around here.

JM: Do you have any idea what job you wanna get?

JINX: No. No particular job. Whatever I can get.

Jinx subsequently quit school. He had been working twenty hours a week making clothes racks in a factory with his brother. He left school with the understanding that he would be employed full-time, and he was mildly content with his situation: "I got a job. It ain't a good job, but other things will come along." Two weeks later, he was laid off. For the past three months he has been unemployed, hanging full-time in doorway #13.

Shorty has worked construction in the past and has held odd jobs such as shoveling snow. Shorty, an alcoholic, has trouble holding down a steady job, as he freely admits. He was enrolled in school until recently. Ordered by the court to a detoxification center, Shorty apparently managed to convince the judge that he had attended enough Alcoholics Anonymous meetings in the meantime to satisfy the court. He has not returned to school since, nor has he landed a job. Given that Shorty is often on the run from the police, he is too preoccupied with pressing everyday problems to give serious thought to his long-term future. It is not surprising that my ill-timed query about his occupational aspirations met with only an impatient glare.

Stoney is one of the few Hallway Hangers with a definite ambition. In fact, he aspires to a middle-class occupation—to own his own pizza shop. Although Stoney's goal is exceptionally high for a Hallway Hanger, ownership of one's own business, according to Ely Chinoy, is a common ambition for at least part of the blue-collar workforce.[3] Still, Stoney himself considers his aspiration unusually ambitious and is automatically defensive about his chances for success.

JM: What's your ambition?

STONEY: To *own* a store. One of these days I will. Watch. People might laugh at me now, but one of these days I will. It might be in fifty or sixty years. No, after a few years—if I'm about thirty years old, I can get a loan to get a store easy. Really. Get me some financial credit, buy me a little shop, work my way up.

Averse to both heavy manual work and "sitting behind a desk—I'd hate that," Stoney went straight to a local pizza establishment when he was put on a special work-study arrangement at school. He worked twenty-five hours per week, attending school in a special class from three to six in the afternoon. Stoney finally "got real sick and tired of school" and started working full-time, only to be fired soon thereafter. "I was working part-time anyway and I could work more if I wanted, so I told him [the boss] to put it up to thirty [hours per week] and I cut down my school more. Then I went up to forty. That's when I quit school. Then I got fired. [*laughs*]"

Stoney can afford to laugh. In contrast to Jinx, he has a marketable skill—making pizza—and immediately found another job in a small pizza shop in a different part of town. He soon left that "gig," returning to his original job. Shortly thereafter, he was fired once again for "being mouthy." The very next day, he was hired by a third pizza shop. Stoney has worked there for the past seven months, earning five dollars per hour under the table. He likes his boss, the small size of the operation, and the relatively good wage.

A year ago, however, when Stoney was employed by the larger establishment, was working for a boss he did not like, and was making only slightly more than minimum wage, he tried to join the navy. "I wanted to get into the navy and travel for a while. For two years, see the world, travel. I just found out real quick that they weren't gonna take me cuz of my drug record." Stoney was arrested last year for possession of mescaline. Although he could still have joined the army, he was not interested: "I don't want no bullshit army." According to Stoney, it is just as well that he was not accepted into the navy. "I like what I'm doing now, so I'll probably be here for a while."

Like most of the Hallway Hangers, Slick already has held quite a few jobs. Between the ages of nine and thirteen Slick worked under the table in a supermarket that his uncle managed. He also has worked construction and as a clerk in a shoe store as well as odd jobs such as snow shoveling and minor landscaping. Slick quit school his junior year and began bagging groceries in another supermarket. "I just decided I had to put any kind of money away; whatever was available I would do, right? When I went down there [*pointing to doorway #13*], a lot of people would say, 'Well, fuck it; it's just bagging, y'know? But you ain't gonna get no $20,000 a year job right off the streets anyway. You have to start somewhere, doin' somethin.'"

Just the same, Slick could not take bagging groceries for long. He quit that job last June and enlisted in the army the next day. Slick really wanted to join the marines, but without a high school diploma, one must score exceptionally high on the standardized tests the marines administer to potential recruits. Slick missed by one point.

Once he was reconciled to entering the army, Slick was disappointed to find that without a high school diploma, he did not qualify for many of the benefits. Not one to accept a setback so easily, Slick did something about it. "I started talkin' about the bonuses and shit [with the recruiter], cuz I seen them on the paper up there, and I asked him. He said, 'Well, you have to have your high school diploma.' So right across the street was the Adult Education Center." He enrolled in some classes at considerable cost and hoped to have a bona fide diploma by midwinter. Although originally scheduled to report for service in October, Slick postponed his entry until late December when he expected to have his diploma.

By December, however, Slick had what he considered a better job lined up as a security guard at a local defense contracting firm the Hallway Hangers call "the weapons lab." Although he would not be able to start that job until mid-January, Slick somehow managed to cancel his enlistment. Shortly thereafter, however, his contact at the weapons lab was fired, and with him went Slick's prospective job. He currently is unemployed and, like Jinx, spends much of his time hanging at the Heights.

Despite these setbacks, Slick dreams of becoming a lawyer. Apparently, I was the first person to whom he voiced this hope. In a subsequent group interview in which five of the Hallway Hangers were discussing their plans for the future, an embarrassed Slick mentioned his aspiration in front of the group. The manner of this disclosure, which amounted to a confession, and the response of the group are instructive.

SLICK: [*sheepishly*] I'm gonna be a lawyer.

(*This response elicits surprise and whistles from the group.*)

CHRIS: My boy ain't talkin' no petty cash.

SHORTY: My boy wants to be a lawyer. He ain't even graduated from high school. Got himself a shit-ass diploma. Signed up for the army.

FRANKIE: I know. My boy bought his diploma and shit.

Slick himself is the first person to admit that he is not likely to achieve this goal, although his pride prevents him from expressing his reservations to the group. Slick, like Jinx and the rest of the Hallway Hangers, realizes that there is usually little room for choice in occupational decisions. "Well, *if I had the choice*, if I couldn't be a lawyer, I'd like to either do landscaping or construction [*my emphasis*]." Although his expectations are far different from his aspirations, Slick is the only Hallway Hanger who aspires to a professional career.

Like those of so many of the Hallway Hangers, Frankie's aspirations and expectations are in a constant state of flux. What follows are Frankie's comments on his occupational expectations on four separate occasions spanning a one-year period.

(2/22/83)

FRANKIE: I'm getting out [of school] this spring.

JM: What are you gonna do then? I mean for work.

FRANKIE: I don't fucking know. Probably work construction. That'll be good. I'll make like seventy-five bucks a day. Under the table. Sixty or seventy-five bucks a day. I could do that for the rest of my life. I get paid cash, every day. My brother sets it up for me.

(4/15/83)

JM: Have any idea what you'll be doing for work when you graduate, Frankie?

FRANKIE: I don't fucking know. If I can't get anything else, I'll just join the fucking service.

On May 13, 1983, the day he graduated, Frankie was feeling very strongly the sense of uncertainty surrounding his prospects for future employment.

FRANKIE: [*unsolicited*] I gotta get a job, any fucking job.

JM: What about the construction?

FRANKIE: Yeah, I can work with my brother, but that's under the table. Besides, he's in Bradford [state prison] now.

During the summer, when he was unemployed, Frankie was on the verge of joining the army. Finally, he landed a temporary job as a garbage collector for the city. He was laid off in November and since that time has been out of work.

In an in-depth interview in December, Frankie articulated a new occupational aspiration, which he presently nurtures. "My kind of job is like, y'know, I did a lot of construction. That's the kind of job like I want. What I want to do is save up some money and go to tractor-trailer school and take heavy equipment. I don't wanna drive no eighteen-wheeler, but I want to do heavy equipment like payloading. Hopefully, some day I can do it. I got to get up the cash first."

An aspiration to blue-collar work, such as this, is not easy to achieve. Coming up with the cash, Frankie realizes, is no easy task. In addition, even if he were able to get his heavy equipment license, there would be no guarantee that he will land the job he envisions. Frankie is aware of the problems; the scenario he foresees contains many "ifs." "If I do get my license, and say if I get a job with a construction company, I'll tell 'em I got my license, but I'm starting off as a laborer anyway. Gettin' in fuckin' holes, y'know? Then if higher jobs come up in it, I'd have a better chance than anyone, instead of them sending someone to school. Y'know, 'This kid already got his license, give him a couple of days to get back in the swing of things.'" Considering these contingencies, it is no wonder Frankie has yet to act on these hopes.

Whereas Frankie is lucid about his aspiration and how to achieve it, Chris is in doubt about his future. He never has held a steady job for any significant period of time and presently makes his money dealing drugs (mostly marijuana and cocaine) in the Clarendon Heights neighborhood. He works quite hard, actively seeking out customers and making himself available through the afternoon and evening hours. Because he is currently the sole major outlet of drugs for the teenagers of Clarendon Heights, Chris makes a good deal of money (about $150 per week). Although dealing pays well, the risks are high. He admits that the police seem to be watching him closely, and if he is convicted of another offense, he may well be sent away. The threat of violence from other kids trying to make a fast buck is an additional and sometimes greater risk, one brought home to Chris when he mentioned his occupational aspirations in a group interview.

CHRIS: I wanna sell cocaine, no lie. I wanna deal cocaine, be rich.

SLICK: [*somewhat dubiously*] That's what he wants to do.

CHRIS: I'm just tellin' you the truth, man. That's what I'm s'posed to do, right, man?

SLICK: He's gonna get fuckin' blown away. [laughs]

FRANKIE: I'll cuff off him a thousand dollars.

Like Frankie, who also used to make his money illegally (and still does to a lesser degree), Chris may weigh the risks and alter his aspirations, or he may take his chances and try to make a future out of selling drugs.

One cannot help but be struck by the modesty of the Hallway Hangers' hopes for the future. Only Slick aspires to a professional career; Stoney is the only other individual who aspires to a middle-class job. Refusing the risk of hope, the remainder adjust their occupational goals to the only jobs that they perceive to be available—unskilled manual work. Many expect to enter military service, not because they find it particularly appealing but because of the paucity of other opportunities. The concept of an aspiration is essentially alien to the Hallway Hangers. Most simply expect to take whatever they can get.

The Hallway Hangers are quite honest about their occupational expectations and aspirations, but it is not comforting to look closely at one's future when bleakness is its main characteristic. When free of the psychological complications inherent in considering one's own future, the Hallway Hangers predict even more inauspicious outcomes for the peer group in general.

JM: What sorts of jobs do you think the rest of the guys will have?

(all in separate interviews)

STONEY: Shitty jobs. Picking up trash, cleaning the streets. They won't get no good jobs.

SLICK: Most of the kids around here, they're not gonna be more than janitors or, y'know, goin' by every day tryin' to get a buck. That's it. . . . I'd say the success rate of this place is, of these people . . . about 20 percent, maybe 15.

STEVE: I dunno. Probably hanging around here. I dunno. Shit jobs.

JINX: I think most of them, when and if a war comes, they're all gone. In the service. Everyone's going. But for jobs—odds and ends jobs. Here and there. No good high-class jobs. I think they'll all end up working for the city, roofers, shit like that.

In Frankie's answer to the same question, we get a real feel for the deep sense of pessimism that dominates the Hallway Hangers' outlook on their future. Listening to him talk, one can detect a poignant fear for his own destiny.

FRANKIE: Well, some of them are gonna do okay, but, I dunno, some of them are just gonna fuck up. They'll just be doing odd jobs for the rest of their lives, y'know. Still be drinking, y'know; they'll drink themselves to death, what's some of 'em'll do. That's what I hope I don't do. Yeah, some of them are gonna drink themselves to death, but some of them, y'know, they're gonna smarten up. Get married, have some kids, have a decent job. Enough to live off anyways, to support a wife and kids. But some of them, they're gonna fuck up; they'll be just a junkie, a tramp. They'll be sitting out on the lawn for the rest of their life with their fucking bottle. Going to work every morning, getting laid off. Fucking, y'know, they're just gonna fuck up. That's what I hope I don't do. I'm trying not to anyways.

The definitions of aspirations and expectations given at the beginning of this chapter suggest that an assessment of the opportunity structure and of one's capabilities impinge on one's preferences for the future. However, the portrait of the Hallway Hangers painted in these pages makes clear that "impinge" is not a strong enough word. But are the leveled aspirations and pessimistic expectations of the Hallway Hangers a result of strong negative assessments of their capabilities or of the opportunity structure?

This is not an easy question to answer. Doubtless, both factors come into play, but in the case of the Hallway Hangers, evaluation of the opportunity structure has the dominant role. Although in a discussion of why they do not succeed in school the Hallway Hangers point to personal inadequacy ("We're all just fucking burnouts"; "We never did good anyways"), they look to outside forces as well. In general, they are confident of their own abilities.

(in a group interview)

JM: If you've got five kids up the high school with all As, now are you gonna be able to say that any of them are smarter than any of you?

SLICK: [*immediately*] No.

JM: So how'd that happen?

SLICK: Because they're smarter in some areas just like we're smarter in some areas. You put them out here, right? And you put us up where they're living— they won't be able to survive out here.

SHORTY: But we'd be able to survive up there.

FRANKIE: See, what it is—they're smarter more academically because they're taught by teachers that teach academics.

JM: Not even streetwise, just academically, do you think you could be up where they are?

FRANKIE: Yeah.

CHRIS: Yeah.

SHORTY: Yeah.

JM: When it comes down to it, you're just as smart?

FRANKIE: Yeah.

SLICK: [*matter-of-factly*] We could be smarter.

FRANKIE: Definitely.

CHRIS: On the street, like.

FRANKIE: We're smart, we're smart, but we're just smart [inaudible]. It's fucking, y'know, we're just out to make money, man. I know if I ever went to fucking high school and college in a business course . . .

SLICK: And concentrated on studying . . .

FRANKIE: I know I could make it. I am a businessman.

JM: So all of you are sure that if you put out in school . . .

FRANKIE: Yeah! If I went into business, I would, yeah. If I had the fucking money to start out with like some of these fucking rich kids, I'd be a millionaire. Fucking right I would be.

Although these comments were influenced by the dynamics of the group interview, they jibe with the general sense of self-confidence the Hallway Hangers radiate and indicate that they do not have low perceptions of their own abilities.

If their assessments of their own abilities do not account for the low aspirations of the Hallway Hangers, we are left, by way of explanation, with their perceptions of the job opportunity structure. The dominant view in the United States is that American society is an open one that values and differentially rewards individuals on the basis of their merits. The Hallway Hangers question this view, for it runs against the grain of their neighbors' experiences, their families' experiences, and their own encounters with the labor market.

The Clarendon Heights community, as a public housing development, is by definition made up of individuals who do not hold even modestly remunerative jobs. A large majority are on additional forms of public assistance; many are unemployed. Like most old housing projects, Clarendon Heights tends to be a cloistered, insular neighborhood, isolated from the surrounding community.

Although younger residents certainly have external points of reference, their horizons are nevertheless very narrow. Their immediate world is composed almost entirely of people who have not "made it." To look around at a great variety of people—some lazy, some alcoholic, some foolish, but many energetic, dedicated, clever, and resourceful—and to realize all of them have been unsuccessful on the job market is powerful testimony against what is billed as an open society.

The second and much more intimate contact these boys have with the job market is through their families, whose occupational histories can be viewed only as sad and disillusioning by the Hallway Hangers. These are not people who are slothful or slow-witted; rather, they are generally industrious, intelligent, and very willing to work. With members of their families holding low-paying, unstable jobs or unable to find work at all, the Hallway Hangers are unlikely to view the job opportunity structure as an open one.

The third level of experience on which the Hallway Hangers draw is their own. These boys are not newcomers to the job market. As we have seen, all have held a variety of jobs. All except Steve are now on the job market year-round, but only Stoney has a steady job. With the exceptions of Chris, who presently is satisfied with his success peddling drugs, and Steve, who is still in school, the Hallway Hangers are actively in search of decent work. Although they always seem to be following up on some promising lead, they are all unemployed. Furthermore, some who were counting on prospective employment have had their hopes dashed when it fell through. The work they have been able to secure typically has been in menial, dead-end jobs paying minimum wage.

Thus, their personal experience on the job market and the experiences of their family members and their neighbors have taught the Hallway Hangers that the job market does not necessarily reward talent or effort. Neither they nor their parents, older siblings, and friends have shared in the "spoils" of economic success. In short, the Hallway Hangers are under no illusions about the openness of the job opportunity structure. They are conscious, albeit vaguely, of a number of class-based obstacles to economic and social advancement. Slick, the most perceptive and articulate of the Hallway Hangers, points out particular barriers they must face.

SLICK: Out here, there's not the opportunity to make money. That's how you get into stealin' and all that shit.

(in a separate interview)

SLICK: That's why I went into the army—cuz there's no jobs out here right now for people that, y'know, live out here. You have to know somebody, right?

In discussing the problems of getting a job, both Slick and Shorty are vocal.

SLICK: All right, to get a job, first of all, this is a handicap, out here. If you say you're from the projects or anywhere in this area, that can hurt you. Right off the bat: reputation.

SHORTY: Is this dude gonna rip me off, is he . . .

SLICK: Is he gonna stab me?

SHORTY: Will he rip me off? Is he gonna set up the place to do a score or some-thin'? I tried to get a couple of my buddies jobs at a place where I was work-ing construction, but the guy says, "I don't want 'em if they're from there. I know you; you ain't a thief or nothing."

Frankie also points out the reservations prospective employers have about hiring people who live in Clarendon Heights. "A rich kid would have a better chance of getting a job than me, yeah. Me, from where I live, y'know, a high crime area, I was prob'ly crime-breaking myself, which they think your nice honest rich kid from a very respected family would never do."

Frankie also feels that he is discriminated against because of the reputation that attaches to him because of his brothers' illegal exploits. "Especially me, like, I've had a few opportunities for a job, y'know? I didn't get it cuz of my name, because of my brothers, y'know. So I was deprived right there, bang. Y'know they said, 'No, no, no, we ain't havin' no O'Sullivan work for us.'" In a separate discussion, Frankie again makes this point. Arguing that he would have almost no chance to be hired as a fireman, despite ostensibly meritocratic hiring proce-dures, even if he scored very highly on the test, Frankie concludes, "Just cuz fuckin' where I'm from and what my name is."

The Hallway Hangers' belief that the opportunity structure is not open also emerges when we consider their responses to the question of whether they have the same chance as a middle- or upper-class boy to get a good job. The Hallway Hangers generally respond in the negative. When pushed to explain why, Jinx and Steve made these responses, which are typical.

(in separate interviews)

JINX: Their parents got pull and shit.

STEVE: Their fucking parents know people.

Considering the boys' employment experiences and those of their families, it is not surprising that the Hallway Hangers' view of the job market does not con-form to the dominant belief in the openness of the opportunity structure. They see a job market where rewards are based not on meritocratic criteria, but on "who you know." If "connections" are the keys to success, the Hallway Hangers sense that they are in trouble.

Aside from their assessment of the job opportunity structure, the Hallway Hangers are aware of other forces weighing on their futures. A general feeling of despondency pervades the group. As Slick puts it, "The younger kids have nothing to hope for." The Hallway Hangers often draw attention to specific incidents that support their general and vague feelings of hopelessness and of the futility of nurturing aspirations or high expectations. Tales of police brutality, of uncaring probation officers and callous judges, and of the "pull and hookups of the rich kids" all have a common theme, which Chris summarizes, "We don't get a fair shake and shit." Although they sometimes internalize the blame for their plight (Boo-Boo: "I just screwed up"; Chris: "I guess I just don't have what it takes"; Frankie: "We've just fucked up"), the Hallway Hangers also see, albeit in a vague and imprecise manner, a number of hurdles in their path to success with which others from higher social strata do not have to contend.

Insofar as contemporary conditions under capitalism can be conceptualized as a race by the many for relatively few positions of wealth and prestige, the low aspirations of the Hallway Hangers, more than anything else, seem to be a decision, conscious or unconscious, to withdraw from the running. The competition, they reason, is not a fair one when some people have an unobstructed lane. As Frankie maintains, the Hallway Hangers face numerous barriers: "It's a steeplechase, man. It's a motherfucking steeplechase." The Hallway Hangers respond in a way that suggests only a "sucker" would compete seriously under such conditions.

Chris's perspective seems a poignant, accurate description of the situation in which the Hallway Hangers find themselves.

CHRIS: I gotta get a job, any fucking job. Just a job. Make some decent money. If I could make a hundred bucks a week, I'd work. I just wanna get my mother out of the projects, that's all. But I'm fucking up in school. It ain't easy, Jay. I hang out there [in doorway #13] 'til about one o'clock every night. I never want to go to school. I'd much rather hang out and get high again. It's not that I'm dumb. You gimme thirty bucks today, and I'll give you one hundred tomorrow. I dunno. It's like I'm in a hole I can't get out of. I guess I could get out, but it's hard as hell. It's fucked-up.

THE BROTHERS: READY AT THE STARTING LINE

Just as the pessimism and uncertainty with which the Hallway Hangers view their futures emerge when we consider what they perceive their lives will be like in twenty years, so do the Brothers' long-term visions serve as a valuable backdrop to our discussion of their aspirations. The ethos of the Brothers' peer group is a positive one; they are not resigned to a bleak future but are hoping for a bright one. Nowhere does this optimism surface more clearly than in the Brothers' responses to the question of what they will be doing in twenty years. Note the centrality of work in their views of the future.

(all in separate interviews)

SUPER: I'll have a house, a nice car, no one bothering me. Won't have to take no hard time from no one. Yeah, I'll have a good job, too.

JUAN: I'll have a regular house, y'know, with a yard and everything. I'll have a steady job, a good job. I'll be living the good life, the easy life.

MIKE: I might have a wife, some kids. I might be holding down a regular business job like an old guy. I hope I'll be able to do a lot of skiing and stuff like that when I'm old.

CRAIG: I'll probably be having a good job on my hands, I think. Working in an office as an architect, y'know, with my own drawing board, doing my own stuff, or at least close to there.

James takes a comic look into his future without being prompted to do so. "The ones who work hard in school, eventually it's gonna pay off for them and everything, and they're gonna have a good job and a family and all that. Not me, though! I'm gonna have *myself*. I'm gonna have some money. And a different girl every day. And a different car. And be like this [*poses with one arm around an imaginary girl and the other on a steering wheel*]."

The Brothers do not hesitate to name their occupational goals. Although some of the Brothers are unsure of their occupational aspirations, none seems to feel that nurturing an aspiration is a futile exercise. The Brothers have not resigned themselves to taking whatever they can get. Rather, they articulate specific occupational aspirations (although these often are subject to change and revision).

Like all of the Brothers, Super has not had extensive experience on the job market; he only has worked at summer jobs. For the past three summers, he has worked for the city doing maintenance work in parks and school buildings through a government employment program. During the past year, Super's occupational aspirations have fluctuated widely. His initial desire to become a doctor was met with laughter from his friends. Deterred by their mocking and by a realization of the schooling required to be a doctor, Super immediately decided that he would rather go into business: "Maybe I can own my own shop and shit." This aspiration, however, also was ridiculed. "Yeah, right," commented Mokey. "Super'll be pimping the girls, that kinda business." In private, however,

Super still clings to the hope of becoming a doctor, although he cites work in the computer field as a more realistic hope. "Really, I don't know what I should do now. I'm kinda confused. First I said I wanna go into computers, right? Take up that or a doctor." The vagueness of Super's aspirations is important; once again, we get a glimpse of how little is known about the world of middle-class work, even for somebody who clearly aspires to it. Of one thing Super is certain: "I just know I wanna get a good job."

Although Super does not distinguish between what constitutes a good job and what does not, he does allude to criteria by which the quality of a job can be judged. First, a good job must not demand that one "work on your feet," a distinction, apparently, between white- and blue-collar work. Second, a good job implies at least some authority in one's workplace, a point Super makes clearly, if in a disjointed manner. "Bosses—if you don't come on time, they yell at you and stuff like that. They want you to do work and not sit down and relax and stuff like that, y'know? I want to try and be a boss, y'know, tell people what to do. See, I don't always want people telling me what to do, y'know—the low rank. I wanna try to be with people in the high rank." Although Super does not know what occupation he would like to enter, he is certain that he wants a job that is relatively high up in a vaguely defined occupational hierarchy.

Mokey has not given as much thought to his occupational aspirations as have most of the Brothers. His contact with the job market has been minimal. His only job has been part-time janitorial work with his father. Mokey plans to attend college and does not envision working full-time until after graduation, several years from now.

JM: So what do you think you wanna do when you get out of school?

MOKEY: I have no idea, really.

JM: Don't think about it that much?

MOKEY: Not really. Before, I wanted to be a motorcyclist, like motocross. That was it.

JM: Didn't you tell me mechanic?

MOKEY: And mechanic. That was when I wanted to be a motor mechanic. For motorcycles. I wanted to be a motocross, that's what I wanted to be.

JM: How'd you decide on that?

MOKEY: I seen a motorcycle race before and I've ridden a couple of minibikes before, and I just decided.

Usually, the aspirations of the Brothers reflect more thought than those Mokey articulates. Although his mother reports that he is interested in "general management, of his own or someone else's business," Mokey's aspirations are sketchy and contradictory.

In contrast to Mokey's, James's aspirations are defined clearly. Since his eighth-grade class visited the high school and James viewed the computer terminals, he has aspired to design video games. This is a goal to which James is strongly committed. His plans are well developed; he has even considered his prospective employers: Atari, Intelevision, or Colecovision. His enthusiasm for his foreseen occupation is unmatched by that of the other boys. "I like jobs that are fun and make money too. Like making computer games; it would be fun. . . . I want computers. I love computers. I fell in love with computers, so I know I want to do computers."

James is confident that he will achieve his occupational goal, despite the difficulty he has had finding any kind of summer employment. Last summer, after a two-month job search, James did maintenance work for the city recreation department. Paid and hired through the government job program, he spent the summer clearing parks and buildings.

The only boy whose plans are more definitively developed is Derek. He has never worked in his life; his summers have been spent traveling with a wealthy friend from Barnes Academy. Since he was a young boy, however, Derek has dreamed of joining the military. He wants to learn electronics and become a helicopter pilot, an aspiration Derek took a big step toward fulfilling by enlisting in the navy this past summer. He is on delayed entry until he receives his diploma this June; then he will report to basic training in July and will serve for six years.

Considering that the decision to enter the service is usually a last resort for most Heights teenagers, it is noteworthy that Derek aspires to a career in the navy, particularly given his success in high school and at Barnes Academy. Of all the Brothers and Hallway Hangers, he seems to have the best educational credentials and the best chance to move on to high-status employment. But Derek does explain his choice.

DEREK: At first, they [his parents] wanted me to be a lawyer. Ever since I went to Barnes. But there's no way I could do that. I need a job that has action. I need to be active. I couldn't sit behind a desk all week to make a living; that wouldn't be right.

JM: What do you mean, it wouldn't be right?

DEREK: I just couldn't do it. I like all the activities the navy has. And, y'know, sometimes I like to take orders. Carry them out. I don't want to just sit around.

This devaluation of white-collar work as inactive and boring, according to Paul Willis, is the main cultural innovation of the nonconformist lads that deters them from entering, or even trying to enter, white-collar work. This distaste for office work, which is bound up inextricably with the working-class culture's ideal of masculinity, serves to level the aspirations of the lads, thereby spurring them to work on the shop floor. A close examination of the Hallway Hangers and Brothers, however, reveals no such definitive cultural process at work, although we can detect traces of such an attitude among the Hallway Hangers (and with Derek). However, Super and his parents denigrate work that would require that he stand on his feet, a view shared by Juan.

Juan, whose previous employment record consists of a number of summertime jobs, aspires to be a cook. Like Super, he hopes to avoid manual work (a hope his father shares). "I like clean job, y'know, where you can keep yourself clean. That's what my father said. 'You should get a job where you can keep yourself clean.' I found out that the one that was better off for me was cooking. I like mechanic, but no, man, too rough for me."

Despite this aversion to auto mechanics, which Juan expressed last summer, he currently is seeking employment in precisely that area. The only Brother to have graduated from high school and thus currently on the job market, Juan has been unable to find work in food preparation. Although he retains his aspiration to be a cook because "it's fun; I like it," the unpleasant experience of unemployment for eight months has forced Juan to lower his expectations.

Craig, who like most of the Brothers has "never held a real job, just, y'know, summer jobs," hopes to be an architect. Craig has been a good artist since his earliest years and his father suggested that he consider architecture as a career. Craig has nurtured this aspiration since sixth grade and sees himself working for an architecture firm in the future. He adds, however, that if he is frustrated in his attempt to find employment in this field, he would like to be a computer operator or programmer.

This tendency to express contingency plans in case of failure is articulated fully by Mike. During the course of a year, Mike has revealed a hierarchy of aspirations and expectations. Mike's dream is to be a professional athlete: a wrestler, like his father, or a football player. He realizes this would come about only "if I get a big break." The occupational aspiration about which he talks the most is in the computer field, apparently a common aspiration for these boys because of the emphasis put upon the subject in high school. One step below that on his hierarchy of occupational preferences is more traditional blue-collar work, particularly as an electrician. Finally, he says, "If I don't make it in, like, anything, if I flunk out or something, I'll probably join the service or something."

Like most of the Brothers, Mike is very concerned about the quality of his future employment. "Mostly," he comments, "I just wanna get ahead in life, get a good job." Specifically, he wants to avoid the dull, monotonous type of work he experienced last summer as a stock boy in a large hardware warehouse. "It's for fucking morons," he exclaims. Mike also has held a summer job in which he learned some carpentry skills doing weatherization work for the City Action to Save Heat project, another CETA program. He hated taking orders from a strict supervisor who, Mike recalls, "just sat on his fat ass all day anyway. Then again," he adds upon reflection, "I wouldn't mind doing that."

Despite the Brothers' absorption with athletics and the status of professional sports in American culture, the Brothers have few illusions about the extent to which sports are a ticket to success. Although their younger siblings speak incessantly about "making it in the pros," the Brothers no longer aspire seriously to a career in professional athletics. Only Mike and Craig see sports as a means to get a college education.

Although not all the Brothers aspire to professional or managerial work, all do have hopes for the future. The notion of a career makes sense when applied to their visions of future employment. They are committed to acting on their hopes, and although they realize that there is no guarantee that their dreams will come to fruition, they are not resigned to failure. In short, the Brothers are optimistic about their future employment, while the Hallway Hangers are deeply pessimistic about their prospective occupational roles.

In contrasting the Brothers and the Hallway Hangers, however, we must resist the temptation to define the two groups only in relation to each other. Certainly in comparison to the Hallway Hangers, the Brothers have high aspirations. To assert that the Brothers aspire to middle-class jobs while the Hallway Hangers do not, however, would be overly simplistic. In a society in which the achievement of a prestigious occupation is considered a valid goal for everyone, it is significant that a few of the Brothers have only modest goals.

The Brothers display none of the cockiness about their own capabilities that the Hallway Hangers exhibit. Instead, they attribute lack of success on the job market exclusively to personal inadequacy. This is particularly true when the Brothers speculate about the future jobs the Hallway Hangers and their own friends will have. According to the Brothers, the Hallway Hangers (in Super's words) "ain't gonna get nowhere," not because of the harshness of the job market, but because they are personally lacking. The rest of the Brothers share this view.

JM: Some of those guys who hang with Frankie, they're actually pretty smart. They just don't channel that intelligence into school, it seems to me.

CRAIG: I call that stupid, man. That's what they are.

JM: I dunno.

CRAIG: Lazy.

(in a separate interview)

SUPER: They think they're so tough they don't have to do work. That don't make sense, really. You ain't gonna get nowhere; all's you gonna do is be back in the projects like your mother. Depend on your mother to give you money every week. You ain't gonna get a good job. As you get older, you'll think about that, y'know? It'll come to your mind. "Wow, I can't believe, I should've just went to school and got my education."

(in a separate interview)

MOKEY: They all got attitude problems. They just don't got their shit together. Like Steve. They have to improve themselves.

In the eyes of the Brothers, the Hallway Hangers have attitude problems, are incapable of considering their long-term future, and are lazy or stupid.

Because this evidence is tainted (no love is lost between the two peer groups), it is significant that the Brothers apply the same criteria in judging each other's chances to gain meaningful employment. James thinks Mokey is headed for a dead-end job because he is immature and undisciplined. He also blames Juan for currently being out of work. "Juan's outta school, and Juan does *not* have a job [*said with contempt*]. Now that's some kind of a senior. When I'm a senior, I'm gonna have a job already. I can see if you're gonna go to college right when you get out of school, but Juan's not doin' nothin'. He's just stayin' home." Juan, in turn, thinks that Mokey and Super will have difficulty finding valuable work because of their attitudes. He predicts that Derek and Craig will be successful for the same reason.

These viewpoints are consistent with the dominant ideology in America; barriers to success are seen as personal rather than social. By attributing failure to personal inadequacy, the Brothers exonerate the opportunity structure. Indeed, it is amazing how often they affirm the openness of American society.

(all in separate interviews)

DEREK: If you put your mind to it, if you want to make a future for yourself, there's no reason why you can't. It's a question of attitude.

SUPER: It's easy to do anything, as long as you set your mind to it, if you wanna do it. If you don't want to do it . . . you ain't gonna make it. I gotta get that through my mind: I wanna do it. I wanna be somethin'. I don't wanna be livin' in the projects the rest of my life.

MOKEY: It's not like if they're rich they get picked [for a job]; it's just mattered by the knowledge of their mind.

CRAIG: If you work hard, it'll pay off in the end.

MIKE: If you work hard, really put your mind to it, you can do it. You can make it.

This view of the opportunity structure as an essentially open one that rewards intelligence, effort, and ingenuity is shared by all the Brothers. Asked whether their chances of securing a remunerative job are as good as those of an upper-class boy from a wealthy district of the city, they all respond affirmatively. Not a single member of the Hallway Hangers, in contrast, affirms the openness of American society.

This affirmation of equality of opportunity is all the more astounding coming from a group of black, lower-class teenagers. Only Juan mentioned racial prejudice as a barrier to success, and this was a result of personal experience. Juan's mother was forced out of her job as a clerk in a neighborhood grocery store when some of the customers complained about the color of her skin. "Most of the time it depends on the boss, whether or not he has something against black. If they judge by the attitude, by the way they act, then that's it; there'll be an equal chance, but it's not usually that way."

Whereas the Hallway Hangers conclude that the opportunity structure is not open, the Brothers reach an entirely different, and contradictory, conclusion. Considering that both groups share neighbors and that the families of the boys have similar occupational histories, this discrepancy is all the more problematic. Indeed, we have uncovered quite a paradox. The peer group whose members must overcome racial as well as class barriers to success views the occupational opportunity structure as essentially open, whereas the white peer group views it as much more closed. The Brothers, whose objective life chances are probably lower than those of the Hallway Hangers, nevertheless hold positive attitudes toward the future, while the Hallway Hangers harbor feelings of hopelessness. To unravel this paradox is a challenge, one we shall face in Chapter 7.

If the Hallway Hangers view their predicament as a race in which they, as members of the lower class, must jump a number of hurdles, while the rest of the pack can simply sprint, the Brothers see it as an even dash. The Hallway Hangers believe a strong finish, given their handicap, is out of the question and drop out of the race before it begins. They cannot understand why the Brothers compete seriously. Apparently, explains Slick, the Brothers do not see the hurdles. "It's a question of you wanna see it, and you don't wanna see it. They might not wanna see all the obstacles. In the long run, it'll hurt them. You hafta hear what's going on, or it's gonna hurt you later on."

The Brothers, for their part, are lined up at the start, unsure of their ability, but ready to run what they see as a fair race. They do not understand why the Hallway Hangers fail to take the competition seriously. It is, after all, the only game in town.

DEREK: I don't know. I really don't. I guess they just don't realize what they have to do. It just doesn't get through to them. I dunno. I don't think anyone has really told them straight out what it takes to make it, to be a winner.

Before we analyze how the same race can be viewed in two fundamentally different ways, we must investigate how the two peer groups prepare themselves for the competition. School is the training ground, the place where this preparation takes place. As we might expect, the boys who plan to run the race competitively approach their training in a fundamentally different way than do those who already have conceded defeat.

NOTES

1. Archibald O. Haller undertook extensive conceptual and empirical work on aspirations and introduced this distinction between aspirations and expectations. The study that led to subsequent empirical work by Haller and others is Archibald O. Haller and Irwin Millers's *The Occupational Aspirations Scale* (Cambridge, Mass.: Schenkman, 1972). For a related study, see Kenneth I. Spenner and David L. Featherman, "Achievement Ambitions," *Annual Review of Sociology* 4 (1978): 376–378.

2. Howard B. London, *The Culture of a Community College* (New York: Praeger, 1978).

3. Ely Chinoy, *Automobile Workers and the American Dream* (Boston: Beacon Press, 1955).

6

SCHOOL
Preparing for the Competition

School is an institution in which the Hallway Hangers and the Brothers are forced into daily contact. Many of the attitudes we already have uncovered are played out in school and made manifest in the boys' conduct. Before we can consider this intriguing cultural and institutional mix, however, we must familiarize ourselves with the school itself.

Almost all the teenagers from Clarendon Heights who attend school go to Lincoln High School (LHS). LHS, a comprehensive school of more than 2,800 students and 300 faculty, is organized into four regular academic houses (A, B, C, D), four alternative programs (Enterprise Co-op, Pilot School, Achievement School, Fundamental School), and a separate Occupational Education Program that offers both academic and vocational courses. Two additional programs—the Building Trades and Services Program (BTS) and the Adjustment Class—also come under our purview.

Lincoln High School students from all four grades in the main academic program are sorted randomly into the four main houses of the school, as are staff members from all the academic areas. These 400 to 500 students and approximately 50 teachers are each assigned to one area of the building—their house. Freshmen and sophomores take most of their subjects within their house, while juniors and seniors often cross over to other houses as their elective program expands. The house system is designed to create a smaller setting that promotes better communication and accountability; it also is intended to build strong relationships between students' families and the administrators and counselors who work with the students all four years. In House D, in addition to the more than 300 students in the conventional curriculum, the Bilingual Program teaches the standard course work to about 200 students in their native languages: Portuguese, French-Haitian, Spanish, and Chinese.

According to the course catalog, the Occupational Education Program provides new options to secondary school students: a high school diploma as well as marketable skills in an occupation of one's choice. Karen Wallace, a career counselor at the school, describes the Oc. Ed. Program as "a spin-off from the old technical school. It's for kids who like to work with their hands." Students enrolled in Oc. Ed. carry an academic program that meets LHS graduation requirements, but they also carry a full vocational program that according to the course catalog "insures access to a career at a skilled level."

As freshmen, students in Occupational Education spend two periods each day in the exploratory program, in which they sample each of the twelve shops: auto body, auto mechanics, carpentry, computers, culinary arts, drafting, electrical, electronics, machine, metals, printing, and welding. According to Bruce Davis, guidance counselor for the program, at the end of the year each freshman lists three shops in which he or she prefers to major. In consultation with the shop teachers, the guidance counselors decide, on the basis of the interest, aptitude, and behavior each student has demonstrated, each student's shop major. Most of the students, claims Davis, end up with their first choice. During their sophomore year, students spend three periods per day in their shop. "During the third and fourth years," explains Davis, "they spend three periods in shop plus three periods per week in what we call a theory class, where they learn about the occupation itself." The Occupational Education Program enrolls approximately 300 students.

Enterprise Co-op is an alternative, career-oriented program that includes student-run businesses for dropouts and potential dropouts. The curricula of the standard English, math, and social studies courses also include academic work relating directly to the students' experiences in the businesses. A wood shop and extensive food services are operated in an atmosphere that simulates the real business world. Students receive shares in the co-op based on their productivity, and their dividend checks reflect the increase or decrease in profits for a particular pay period. "It is anticipated that, after one year of participation in Enterprise Co-op," states the course catalog, "a student will be prepared either to re-enter the mainstream high school program, or to secure entry-level employment in a career of his/her choosing."

The Pilot School, founded in 1969, is an alternative high school program that accommodates approximately 200 students. According to Wallace, the Pilot School came into being when a group of parents decided that the curriculum and atmosphere of the high school were too regimented. "The teachers act as counselors to the students; there are weekend trips and lots of outdoor activities. You have a much closer teacher/pupil relationship. The onus of responsibility is

on the student to take charge for his work." Candidates for admission are selected at random after steps have been taken to ensure that the student body approaches a representative cross section of the school population with respect to
geographical area, race and/or ethnic background, sex, academic interest, and
parental occupation. The course catalog bills the Pilot School as an attempt to
create a community of students, parents, and educators accountable to one another for the goals of the program and the successful operation of the school.

The Fundamental School, which originated when a group of parents decided
that the high school was not regimented enough, employs an educational philosophy at the other end of the spectrum. The school (with 400 to 500 students)
"emphasizes basic academic requirements with few frills." The catalog describes
this alternative program as one that "stresses academic excellence and student
accountability and enlists parental involvement and support in reinforcing the
discipline code." For Sammy, a ninth-grader who at his parents' insistence has
chosen to go into the Fundamental School, as did his brother Mokey, the Fundamental School is simply a lot stricter than the regular program: "I mean, you
can't cut class in Fundamentals. If you do, bang, you'll get caught."

"The Achievement School," according to Wallace, "is for kids who haven't
quite made it out of elementary school, but who are old enough to be in high
school." With a maximum student population of forty, the Achievement School
is designed to provide intensive compensatory education in the basic academic
subjects for students with special needs. Wallace explains that kids "do cross
over and are mainstreamed, but they have their own graduation."

Like Enterprise Co-op, the Building Trades and Services Program enrolls
"high-risk" students: dropouts and potential dropouts with truancy and disciplinary problems. Students from grades nine through twelve attend classes in
math, science, English, history, and social studies in a small, self-contained environment from 8:00 until 11:30 a.m. A lunch break follows; then from noon until 2:30 p.m. the students learn carpentry skills and occasionally travel to work
at small-scale construction sites around the city. Teachers seldom mention the
program, and when they do, it is typically in a negative vein: "There's Building
Trades with very easy academics. I don't know what the hell you learn to do
there, be a janitor or something."

Like all public high schools in the state, LHS has provisions for those students who are considered emotionally disturbed. These students are required to
meet regularly with an adjustment counselor. Depending on a psychiatrist's
perception of the severity of the problem, a student meets with his or her adjustment counselor weekly, daily, or for two periods each day. Adjustment counselors have more flexibility than do guidance counselors, which enables them to
spend a lot more time and energy on each of their assigned students. According
to Wallace, "[The adjustment counselor will] go to court with them, make sure
they see their probation officer, and that type of thing. The student is required
to spend a block of time with his adjustment counselor each week." Those with

severe problems are enrolled full-time in the Adjustment Class, the last step before residential schooling or institutionalization.

Whereas secondary school adjustment programs, according to state statutes, serve emotionally disturbed students, the teachers describe the youngsters assigned to the programs in a different manner. Wallace portrays them simply as "kids whose academics are very poor or who are in trouble" and "who are really into drugs, have bad home lives, or things like that." Lincoln students sense the ambiguity about whom the Adjustment Class serves. "That's more or less for the slow kids, but they say the crazy kids," relates Jinx. "Y'know, you gotta act stupid in school, go off, crazy, shit like that." The students in the Adjustment Class realize they are classified as emotionally disturbed, but if the seriousness with which they take their mandatory appointments with the school psychiatrist is any indication, they are none too concerned about the designation.

FRANKIE: I would toy with him more than he'd try to fuck with me. Y'know, like once I caught him with a tape recorder in his drawer. I would've been cool if he told me it was on. But he didn't tell me, and, like, I knew it was on, so I waited five minutes. He was asking me, "What bothers you?" I said, "You wanna know what bothers me? I'm pretty pissed that you fuckin' put that tape recorder on." I slammed open his drawer and shut the fucker off. I said, "That's what's pissing me off and I don't feel pissed off no more," and I sat back down. And, like, one time, y'know, I seen *Caine Mutiny,* and I went and I got some marbles. Y'know, Humphrey Bogart, he was a paranoiac, and he went in there always playing with marbles. So I went in there and played with marbles. The guy asked me why I was doing it. I says, "Cuz I know you're getting paid eighty-five bucks for this one hour, and I'm gonna make you work for it for once."

Jimmy Sullivan, the teacher of the Adjustment Class for fourteen years, describes his students variously as those "who've been in fights and are general pains in the ass," as "kids who have had emotional problems in the past and have shown an inability to be mainstreamed," as "those who couldn't hack the other programs," and as "kids who are tough, from very, very rough backgrounds." Sometimes he simply refers to those in his class as "crazy."

That the Adjustment Class is unique is beyond doubt. Walking into the room after school, one beholds a large, sand-filled punching bag suspended from the ceiling, weights and barbells sprinkled on the floor, magazines such as *High Times, Sports Illustrated,* and *Soldier of Fortune* left on the easy chairs and couches that line the room, and a small punching bag in one corner. Both Jimmy and his assistant have black belts in karate; the twelve kids in the class are encouraged to work out with the weights and to learn martial arts. Posters of Bruce Lee adorn the walls to provide further inspiration.

The program is very flexible. Students must arrive at school by nine-thirty in the morning and leave by twelve-thirty. Upon arrival, the boys (there are no girls in the class) pick up their folders, which contain their daily assignments in math, reading, vocabulary, history, and a lesson from a job opportunities book. Most of the reading is on a fifth-grade level; the daily math assignment includes basic addition, subtraction, multiplication, and division as well as work in decimals and fractions. In an interview, Jimmy expressed his teaching philosophy and gave an indication of the atmosphere that predominates in the class.

JS: The kids are judged on their ability to get the work done. They've got the folder; that's it. It doesn't matter if they have this problem or that problem; everybody's got a fucking problem. Regardless of the problems, you've got to get your work done. I'd say the work can usually be done in two hours. Y'know, they come in here, some take a nap on the couch, some get a cup of coffee over at the store. There's a lot of freedom, but they have to get the work done. If you come in three days but only did the work two days, that's a 40 percent. . . . They'll get twenty-five credits each semester for being in here; you need one hundred and eighty to graduate. They can get ten extra credits for my version of work-study. I didn't give any work-study credits this year. I mean, you have to hold a job for more than a fucking week.

With its unique approach, the Adjustment Class deserves a separate in-depth study of its own. Although we shall temporarily reserve judgment on the effectiveness of the class, considering the positive attitudes of the enrolled students toward the class and the respect they accord Jimmy, the class is, by the school's standards, unusually successful. In contrast to the other programs, the boys attend regularly and control themselves while in class.

LHS formally practices tracking (as do 80 percent of the country's public high schools); classes in almost all programs are organized so students of similar learning achievement or capability are put together. According to their performance in each subject area in grammar school, pupils are placed into tracks, which also are called ability groupings and streams. Almost all the subject areas are divided into general, intermediate, and advanced level courses. Of the basic academic subjects, only the Social Studies Department, reflecting a commitment to heterogeneous classroom populations, offers a significant number of nonleveled courses. Even outside the core academic areas, most courses in business education, home economics, art, photography, dramatic arts, music, and physical education are leveled according to ability or achievement. Classes in the Fundamental School as well as academic classes in the Occupational Education Program also are leveled. Only classes within the Pilot School are all heterogeneous and untracked. But at Lincoln High School there are actually two levels of tracking—among programs (with Oc. Ed., Enterprise Co-op, BTS, and the Adjustment Class at the bottom) and within them. The practice of tracking on both levels has widespread implications for students' academic achievement, self-esteem, and postsecondary school educational and occupational plans, implications that are considered later in this chapter.

Although racial tension at LHS never has been as severe as at schools in a city such as Boston, Massachusetts, an incident in 1980 nevertheless focused attention on the severity of the problem at Lincoln. In a fight between black and white students on school grounds, a white boy was stabbed fatally. The ensuing review of the schools' policies revealed a significant shortage of black teachers. When the school system moved to rectify the problem by bringing in more black staff, a backlash from a number of white students accompanied the changes. Wallace, who is black, reports that white students, especially those from the Clarendon Heights neighborhood, "resented the fact that the black students now had somewhere to go, someone to relate to. And they did come—in droves. The white kids thought they were getting special attention." Indeed, the Hallway Hangers continue to believe that black students are favored at the high school.

THE BROTHERS: CONFORMITY AND COMPLIANCE

Super, like all other pupils, had to decide in the middle of eighth grade what high school program he wanted to enroll in. As part of this process, the high school sends a guidance counselor down to each eighth-grade grammar school class to explain the various programs and curricula at the high school. Booklets detailing the programs and their constituent courses are distributed to students; tours of the high school by all eighth-grade classes are arranged; and parents are invited to the high school for an information night, during which high school counselors present each program and answer questions. Finally, a high school guidance counselor meets individually with every eighth-grader to discuss what the LHS course catalog calls his or her "high school choice, occupation or career plans, sports, interests and hobbies, and personal concerns." Considering the importance of the student's program choice and the implications it may have for his or her future, the provisions the high school makes to ensure an informed, carefully weighed decision are understandable. For thirteen- and fourteen-year-olds, however, the choice of programs is not always based exclusively on logic or long-term considerations. Super's expressed rationale for entering the Occupational Education Program is typical: "Really, I picked Oc. Ed. because my friends picked it. That's why, y'know?"

In contrast to the rest of the Brothers, Super changed his program after he entered LHS. Super was involved in several fights stemming from racial tension in the predominantly white Occupational Educational Program and was suspended from school (another anomaly among the Brothers) three months into his first term. Subsequently, he enrolled in House C, part of the regular academic program.

Super is now well integrated into the school. He respects his teachers and truly wishes to be successful academically. Super accepts the disciplinary code of the school. He occasionally cuts classes but openly chastises himself for this weakness in self-resolve. Similarly, although he later expresses regret, Super often ignores his homework for the pursuit of more pleasurable activities—playing basketball and flirting with girls. Super's scholastic performance is mediocre; his grade average (on the standard scale whereby 60 is the lowest passing mark) during the one-and-a-half-year period he has been enrolled in the high school hovers just below a 70.

A natural athlete, Super has been involved in sports at LHS, which is further evidence of his successful integration into the school. This past fall he played on the junior varsity football team; last year he made the freshman basketball team but quit when he found the daily practices too time consuming. Super's earnest involvement in both academic and athletic pursuits, with only fair success in each, typifies the Brothers' approach to school.

Mokey undergoes the rigors of schooling in a similar way. Enrolled in the Fundamental School at his mother's insistence, he is generally obedient and hardworking. Despite his positive attitude, Mokey's grades have not been good. He failed a course last year, thereby prompting him, again at his mother's urging, to apply to the Upward Bound Program, into which he was accepted. Upward Bound, a year-round, federally sponsored program for underachieving high school students, stresses development of academic skills and motivation for students who traditionally are not considered college bound. Mokey attended an overnight summer school at a nearby college campus and presently spends three hours every Thursday afternoon in the program. Although he now names four colleges he would like to attend, Mokey actually has fared less well in school since his participation in the program, having failed two classes in the fall semester of his junior year. Despite his unsatisfactory performance, Mokey's attitude toward school is positive. His conduct and effort seem to be at a high level, and, like Super, he enjoys playing on the junior varsity football team.

James's attitude toward school has fluctuated dramatically during the past three years. After a dismal sophomore year, during which he cut nearly all his academic classes and attended only his computer shop for three periods daily, James has made a real turnaround. He now attends every class assiduously and is making up last year's failed classes after school on Thursdays. Whereas last year James spent school hours playing video games in a local sub shop, this year he recently was elected president of the science club despite having failed his science course in the fall semester.

Of all the boys from Clarendon Heights, Derek has the most unusual educational history. After finishing third grade at the neighborhood grammar school, Derek was selected to attend Barnes Academy, a prestigious prep school located on the outskirts of the city. At Barnes, Derek enjoyed great success. He earned As and Bs and immediately gained the respect of students and staff. Nevertheless, instead of attending grades nine through twelve at Barnes, Derek chose to attend Lincoln High School. Tired of the heavy workload, sick of the pressure to achieve in order to requalify for his scholarships, and bored with his subjects, he transferred to House D in Lincoln.

DEREK: I like to work, but not too much. That's why I quit Barnes after eighth grade. I just lost interest. It got to be too much—all the bills and everything.

JM: You were on a scholarship, though. Didn't it pay for everything?

DEREK: Yeah, as long as I kept my grades up, then the government would pay for it.

Derek's scholastic achievement at the high school has been quite high; he has been on the honor roll several times and maintains a strong B average.

Although his grades are not as high as Derek's, Craig works very hard in school. Self-disciplined and conscientious, Craig spends a good deal of time each evening on his homework, often passing up pickup basketball games in favor of studying. Presently a senior, Craig picked the Fundamental School in eighth grade in part because it was at the time housed in a separate building located in the northern reaches of the city. By entering the Fundamental School, Craig hoped to avoid the racial tension in the main high school, a hope that went unrealized when the Fundamental School was moved into the Lincoln building just prior to his freshman year.

JM: You're in the Fundamental School, right?

CRAIG: Fundamental, yeah.

JM: Now, why'd you choose that one, way back in eighth grade?

CRAIG: Cuz I heard their reputation was something.

JM: What's their reputation?

CRAIG: Their reputation was that they have very good teachers and stuff. My sister and her friends said it was a very good school.

JM: Do they have technical drawing in Oc. Ed.?

CRAIG: In Oc. Ed.—oh, they have a lot of that stuff.

JM: How come you didn't decide to go into there?

CRAIG: I didn't know Oc. Ed. was like that. . . . I didn't want to go into it cuz I thought, I thought, really, I thought most of the kids in there are stupid.

JM: Do you think that now?

CRAIG: No, they're smarter than I am.

JM: In technical drawing?

CRAIG: Yeah, they went through a better program. See, if I was in Oc. Ed. I'd have, like, three periods each day.

JM: All this wasn't clear to you back in the eighth grade?

CRAIG: Well, to be truthful, the main reason I picked Fundamental was cuz the main high school was real tense. Y'know, there was fights up there—a white kid got stabbed to death, and when I was in the eighth grade it was still pretty bad. See, the Fundamental School used to be way up by, uh . . .

JM: Columbia Street?

CRAIG: Yeah. I thought by going up there I'd miss all the hassles. But then they moved the year I was graduating [from eighth grade]. They just moved into Lincoln.

Craig, during the course of his three and a half years at the school, has maintained a 75 average.

Juan, a 1983 graduate of the high school, studied culinary arts in the Occupational Education Program. Describing his performance in school as "pretty good," Juan never failed a subject and once received a 94 in a class for his efforts. In his honest, sincere, and straightforward manner, Juan describes his behavior in school. "I wasn't any angel in the class; most of the time I was okay. I was in between, because sometimes I came in a bad mood in some classes. But usually I wouldn't bother nobody, because I wasn't ready to go through no hassle. . . . Most teachers knew me as a nice kid. I don't know if I was a nice kid [*smiles widely*], but they know me as a nice kid." Although many of his black friends, like Super, eventually dropped out of the Occupational Education Program, Juan stuck with it.

Mike is generally obedient and disciplined, although he periodically cuts classes and occasionally sneaks down into the school basement with his girlfriend. Nevertheless, he respects the rules of the school; like many of the Brothers, he becomes embarrassed and almost apologetic when recounting episodes of misbehavior. Mike's academic performance is mediocre. Last year he failed English, which prompted his enrollment in a six-week summer school course. His grades have not improved much this year; his first semester's marks were a B, two Cs, and two Ds. Although his performance in the classroom has been dismal, Mike has excelled on the athletic fields. As a sophomore, he has made the varsity football, wrestling, and track teams.

In general, the Brothers are integrated fully into the school. Although many of them turn in only fair academic performances, they honor and respect the standards, conventions, and judgments of the school. They show no evidence of disrespect for teachers or other school officials, and their disciplinary records are for the most part clean. Their course of study is stable; once they choose a particular program, most of them stay with it until graduation. Their participation in extracurricular activities, especially athletics, gives them a chance to excel in an activity that is sometimes prized as highly as academics. In short, the Brothers are typical high school students.

THE HALLWAY HANGERS: TEACHER'S NIGHTMARE

For the most part, Frankie exemplifies the Hallway Hangers' attitudes toward school; he is unusual only in that he graduated. Placed in a special program limited to fifty students his freshman year (which has since been discontinued), Frankie was expelled from the high school for repeated fights, especially with black students, and for striking a teacher in the face. He was prevented from gaining entry into any alternative program and thus was barred from the school altogether. He then attended the King School, a certified, tuition-free, private alternative high school for low-income youths that employs a politically radical educational philosophy and curriculum. Dissatisfied with the teachers, whom Frankie variously terms "fuckin' liberals," "flakes," and "burnouts from the sixties," he left the King School after one year. When Frankie threatened to take Lincoln High School to court for refusing to readmit him, he gained entry into the Enterprise Co-op Program. Although he did well at first, he was struggling to stay in the program after the first month because of a drug problem that severely impaired his performance. Frankie was ingesting three and four "hits" of THC each day and was "gettin' real fuckin' high, veggin' out, not doin' my work." After a month, he was kicked out of Enterprise Co-op.

At that point, there was only one program in which Frankie could be enrolled—the Adjustment Class. A sympathetic guidance counselor who had gained Frankie's trust arranged for his admittance into Jimmy Sullivan's class. For the first time in his life, Frankie really admired and respected his teacher; he stayed in Jimmy's class for three years, graduating in 1983. The respect Jimmy elicits from his students is based on his toughness, his streetwise reputation, and the perception that his financial success (he has significant real estate holdings) is independent of his position as a teacher. In an interview before he graduated, Frankie comments on Jimmy's Adjustment Class.

FRANKIE: I didn't give a shit at the school. I used to tell teachers to their face to fuck themselves. That's why I like this class I'm in. Jimmy, he'll say, "You wanna fuck with me, then fight me." He's a fucking black belt in karate. . . .

Jimmy makes more fucking money than anyone else in that school. He's a real estate broker.

(in a separate interview)

FRANKIE: I went there, y'know. It was cool, cuz, like, you went in there, fuckin' you talk to Jimmy, and you know Jimmy's real cool. I never had a teacher that says, "Fuck this and fuck that" and "I'll kick your ass if you fuck up." The teachers in the King School, they were flakes; they swore and shit, but you just told them to shut the fuck up, and they shut up. They were scared. Jimmy, he ain't scared of no one.

Faced with the simple choice of doing his daily two hours of academic work and getting credit or of not doing it and failing, he attended school conscientiously.

FRANKIE: Jimmy, he says to me, "Look, come in and do your work if you want to; if you don't, screw! Get the fuck out of here." . . . I listened to him, y'know, sat there until was fuckin' got through my head. I fuckin' realized, hey, man, I gotta get my diploma, keep my moms happy. I started doing my work and, y'know, you fuck around and shit but Jimmy was cool. He let you fuck around—if you do your work you can do whatever you want to. I used to work out, used to do a lot of boxing and shit. . . . I was there for a while, three years. It was pretty cool.

Frankie was the first Hallway Hanger to enter Jimmy's class. In fact, when Frankie was first accepted into the class, he was the only student not to have been sent there by the court system. Most of the students had come directly from prison; some were shuttled daily from the county jail where they were incarcerated. Now, however, the average age of the students has fallen from nineteen to seventeen, and most are referred to the class after having problems in other high school programs.

Steve, for example, made a similar trek through the different programs, finally landing in the Adjustment Class. He picked Occupational Education in the eighth grade "cuz all my friends were there and I thought it'd be all right." Steve lasted only a month in that program before he was switched to regular academics, House C, because of discipline problems and excessive truancy. He lasted only two weeks in House C before he was assigned to Enterprise Co-op. "I didn't go. And I told them to go to hell, and I left. I didn't show up for school for a *long* time. Then they transferred me over to Co-op. And then so I went there. It was all right, but I really didn't like it either. Then I just said the hell with that and missed the whole rest of the year. Didn't get no credits either." When he returned to school the next year, Steve kicked in a window in a hallway, exclaiming that he wanted to be put in Jimmy's class. The Hallway Hangers acknowledge that Steve's antic amounted to a deliberate attempt to get into the Adjustment Class, and Steve himself admits, "Yeah, I wanted to cuz they had me on the list and shit, so I said fuck it, I'm in."

The effort paid off; Steve was admitted to Jimmy's class almost immediately, has attended for one year, and plans to stay in it until he graduates in two years. Like Frankie, he respects Jimmy and finds the class superior to the other programs.

STEVE: Jimmy's class has been real good for me, man.

JM: Yeah? What's it like in there?

STEVE: Oh, it's bad. It's way better than the other school. Come in at nine thirty, get out at eleven thirty. The guy is just like us; he swears and shit, tells all the other teachers to go fuck themselves; he don't care. Got weights, punching bag; we get out early.

Aside from the streetwise teacher and the unique atmosphere of the classroom, students in the Adjustment Class like the light academic workload. As Jimmy himself admits, "This is the easiest way to graduate." Whatever the reason, it is because of Jimmy's class that Frankie managed to graduate and Steve has stayed in school.

For Shorty, however, Jimmy's class was not enough. Shorty was admitted to the Adjustment Class because he was a chronic truant and had a habit of threatening teachers. Shorty accounts for his downward spiral into Jimmy's class this way.

SHORTY: You start school as a freshman and you start cutting one class, right, and when that teacher starts giving you a hard time—this is how it started with me: I wasn't good in history and spelling and shit—and he wouldn't ever have got me a tutor or nothing. So then I said, "Fuck it." He wasn't passing me, so then I stopped going to his class. Then he would spread the word around to the other teachers, and they would give me a hard time, and I'd stop going to their classes. Finally, I ended up in Jimmy's class.

Although he successfully completed one year of the Adjustment Class, Shorty, hearing that there was a warrant out for his arrest, became convinced that he would be sent to a detoxification center or prison and dropped out of school altogether this past November (1983). Although he managed to avoid incarceration, Shorty never went back to school, figuring he could not bring up his average enough to get credit for the fall semester.

Slick has a somewhat different educational history. He lived in a neighboring city until sixth grade and scored well enough on a test to gain admission to Latin Academy, a public school for gifted students. He attended Latin Academy for one year, enjoyed the challenging academic work, and was disappointed with the local grammar school when his family subsequently moved to Clarendon Heights.

SLICK: When I was at Latin, it was fucking real hard, right? Then I moved here cuz my grandfather died and my mother wanted to be closer to my grandmother so we could help her out. So we moved over here, and it would've cost three thousand dollars for me to go there [to Latin Academy, where nonresidents of the city in which it is located pay tuition], and we ain't got that kinda money, so I couldn't go. I went here [the local grammar school] during my seventh and eighth grade and then up the high school. It was a big letdown from Latin. It was much slower, and I knew everything they were teaching me. So I just didn't go to the school.

Given the apparently high level of his academic training at Latin Academy, it is curious that Slick chose to enter the Occupational Education Program upon entering the high school. In answer to my query, he revealed his logic. "Because I was already working with my brain. I wanted to try to learn something with my hands, know what I mean? If I just kept on doing fucking academics, it wasn't gonna fucking help me anyways. It was stuff I already knew." In a separate interview, Slick intimated that he thought at the time that he needed to learn a trade to maximize his chances of getting a job.

Once at the high school, however, Slick was dissatisfied with Oc. Ed. and switched to regular academics before his sophomore year. During his second year, bored with his classes, he started to cut more frequently. Like many of his friends, Slick voices dissatisfaction with what he perceives as favoritism toward black students at the high school. Indeed, this is the express reason that Slick quit school in the middle of his junior year.

SLICK: The regular academics I didn't like because there was certain favoritism. By my junior year, I quit school. Went to work.

JM: What do you mean? What was the favoritism?

SLICK: You see, because of what happened a few years ago, they have to lean towards the minorities more. Because of, you know, what happened, some kid got stabbed up there. So if there's like a fight between a white kid and a black kid, the white kid's always wrong. So I didn't like that; so I just quit school.

Jinx also began in the Occupational Education Program "because I wanted to learn a career for when I got out of school." As a field of specialization, he chose computers but left the program in favor of regular academics because he "couldn't deal with sitting at a desk all day typing. It was too fucking boring." Previously a strong B student (according to the other boys), Jinx started cutting most of his classes and spending his time at Pop's, a store about five blocks from the school. The Hallway Hangers and a number of other students frequent the back room of Pop's during school hours, playing cards, smoking marijuana, and drinking beer. This past fall, at the beginning of his senior year, Jinx dropped out of school. He already was working twenty hours per week and expected to be hired full-time. "I like working better than I like going to school. I just prefer working. Going to work, getting paid. I need the money. The holidays are coming; gotta buy them gifts. I got a part-time job now. When I quit school, it'll be a full-time job, my boss said." Shortly after Jinx quit school, he was laid off.

Aside from Frankie, Boo-Boo is the only other Hallway Hanger who has graduated from high school. He entered the Oc. Ed. Program "cuz everybody else was" and attended school diligently for two months before starting to cut most of his classes in favor of "smoking a few bones" at Pop's. Eventually, Boo-Boo stopped going to school at all for four months and did not receive so much as a phone call from the school authorities. Then Boo-Boo was arrested for auto theft in the middle of his freshman year (he was fifteen). After he was placed on probation as a result of his conviction in juvenile court, Boo-Boo's school performance was monitored by his probation officer. He was switched into the Building Trades and Services Program and began to attend school regularly. "I was only fifteen, and when you're on probation, you have to go to school. They kept giving me a hard time, and I didn't want to hear it, so I kept going." Boo-Boo stayed in BTS for four years and graduated in 1983.

Like many of the Hallway Hangers, Chris enrolled in Oc. Ed. his freshman year because he believed that knowing a trade would make it easier to get a job. During his freshman year, Chris was switched into BTS because "I was fucking up in Oc. Ed. I threw a chair at a teacher. I couldn't take the shit they were dishing out." Claiming that the academic work in BTS is far too simple ("We were just doing multiplication tables and shit—what a fucking joke"), Chris skipped all but his first two classes, hanging at Pop's the rest of the day. Unfamiliar even with the names of his afternoon teachers, Chris acknowledges that when he did attend school, he was impaired by drugs or alcohol. "Oh, yeah, I'm high every time I go to school. I gotta be. Sometimes I even drink before I go; I'll have a few beers. It's too much if you don't." This past fall, Chris quit school altogether. Although he still frequents Pop's to sell drugs and occasionally ventures onto school grounds for the same purpose, Chris is no longer subject to the school's authority, an arrangement he prefers.

Stoney chose to enter the regular academic program in the high school but attended classes for only two weeks before he started cutting regularly. "I never went. I'd go to a couple classes, and then I'd cut a class here, cut a class there, cut another class—before you know it, you got fifty cuts, detentions, and then I stopped going to school." According to Stoney, he was suspended a couple of times, and school administrators wanted to expel him, but because he was too young, they put him in a special after-school program. Working part-time and attending school from three to six in the afternoon, Stoney was satisfied with the situation until the middle of his junior year. Given the opportunity to work more hours and tired of the school routine from which he felt he was learning little ("We rarely did work in there. They thought I was stupid or something; they had us do stupid stuff"), he quit school completely and started working full-time.

As a group, the Hallway Hangers experience school in a way much different than the Brothers do. Whereas the Brothers are fully integrated into the school, the Hallway Hangers' attitudes toward the educational system can be summed up by Stoney's words: "Fuck school. I hate fucking school." Most of the Hallway Hangers have dropped out. While officially enrolled, most spent little time in school anyway, preferring the fun, companionship, and drugs at Pop's. When in class, they generally were disruptive and undisciplined. None of the Hallway Hangers participated in any extracurricular activities. By their own accounts, they were high or drunk much of the time they spent in school. No one picked a school program and stayed in it; they all switched or were switched into differ- ent classes, some spiraling down through the array of alternative programs at amazing speed, landing in the last stop on the line. Some stayed there; most have dropped out altogether.

What factors explain the wide discrepancy between the educational pattern of the Brothers and the Hallway Hangers? The school cites the personal prob- lems with which the Hallway Hangers are burdened. They are slow, unmoti- vated, undisciplined, or emotionally disturbed. More sympathetic teachers, like Jimmy Sullivan, attribute this type of fundamental difference between students to the ability of some to "talk about themselves in the long range, to project themselves into the future." However, a deeper level of analysis is necessary to explain the Hallway Hangers' and the Brothers' different experiences in school.

THE UNDERLYING LOGIC OF STUDENT BEHAVIOR

As with many urban high schools, Lincoln High School is preoccupied with maintaining discipline. The team of security guards policing the hallways is am- ple evidence of this fact. Aside from specific sanctions (suspensions, detentions, parent notifications), teachers attempt to secure discipline by reinforcing the achievement ideology: "Behave yourself, work hard, earn good grades, get a good job, and make a lot of money." This line of reasoning rests on two assumptions: what I shall term the efficacy of schooling—the notion that academic perfor- mance is the crucial link to economic success—and the existence of equality of opportunity. Although used primarily to ensure proper behavior by highlighting its eventual rewards, the ideology has more than a disciplinary function.

Before we move on to consider the implications of this line of reasoning, we must address the question of how commonly it is used in the school. This task is not difficult, for both students and teachers draw attention to its prominence. Karen Wallace, the career counselor, in an unsolicited remark, mentioned that this argument is constantly reinforced by teachers: "We tell them that if they try hard enough, work hard enough, and get good grades, then anything is possi- ble." On another occasion, Mike, excited about the prospects of securing a lu- crative computer job, recounted the computer teacher's remark about a friend who makes two thousand dollars a week working with computers. The teacher assured his students that comparable jobs are available in the computer indus-try "for those who don't fool around and really learn the trade." In another un-solicited remark, Chris drew attention to this tendency of teachers to forge a secure link between success in school and success on the job market: "They tell you they'll get you a job when you're done. They say that to you right at the be-ginning. They say it to you all the time." The difference between Mike and Chris, and more generally, as we shall see, between the Brothers and the Hallway Hangers, is that Mike believes this line of reasoning, whereas Chris reacts to it with: "That's *bullshit*. They don't fucking give you shit."

Swallowing the Achievement Ideology

In the previous chapter, I noted the Brothers' widespread belief in the reality of equality of opportunity. Like most Americans, they view this society as an open one. Crucial to this widely held notion is a belief in the efficacy of schooling. As the achievement ideology propagated in school implies, education is viewed as the remedy for the problem of social inequality; schooling makes the race for prestigious jobs and wealth an even one. The Brothers have a good deal of faith in the worth of schooling.

The Brothers' belief in the equality of opportunity and the efficacy of school-ing emerges very strongly from their responses to particular interview ques-tions. When asked whether they feel they have an equal chance to do as well in school as would a wealthy boy from an affluent part of the city, the nearly unan-imous response is "yes," as it is when they are asked if they have an equal chance to get as good a job as the same hypothetical wealthy boy would. With respect to their views on the efficacy of schooling, the Brothers' responses to the question of why they work hard in school are illustrative.

(all in separate interviews)

DEREK: I know I want a good job when I get out. I know that I have to work hard in school. I mean, I want a good future. I don't wanna be doing nothing for the rest of my life.

CRAIG: Because I know by working hard it'll all pay off in the end. I'll be getting a good job.

MIKE: Get ahead in life; get a good job.

When asked whether their academic achievement will influence the type of job they will be able to secure, the Brothers all agree that it will.

This viewpoint explains the Brothers' commitment to their schoolwork and the relatively high level of effort that characterizes their academic participation.

But whereas their acceptance of the achievement ideology accounts for the ease with which the Brothers are integrated into the school, their mediocre academic performance requires further explanation.

One cannot attribute the Brothers' lack of scholastic success to lack of effort; as we have seen, they try hard in school. Moreover, the Brothers generally are intelligent and able. Although their scores on IQ tests, which purport to measure intelligence, are not available, three years of acquaintance with the boys leaves me assured that, on average, they are not substantially less "gifted" or "clever" than my university classmates. What, then, accounts for the academic mediocrity of the Brothers?

In attempting to answer this question, we find ourselves in the company of many eminent sociologists who have tackled the problem of the "educability" of the lower classes. The consistent tendency of working-class children to perform less well in school than their middle-class counterparts is demonstrated by a wealth of empirical evidence,[1] but the actual processes and mechanisms by which this comes about remain almost completely obscured.

Many conventional sociologists look to the working-class family to explain differential academic performance by social class, an approach that has yielded little in the way of concrete results. As Olive Banks admits in *The Sociology of Education:*

> The consistent tendency of working-class or manual workers' children to perform less well in school, and to leave school sooner than the children of non-manual workers, calls for explanation, and it has seemed reasonable to look for that explanation in the working-class family.
>
> It would, however, be far from the truth to conclude that the attention paid by sociologists in recent years to this problem has taken us very far towards a solution. We have many studies into the relationship between social-class background and educational achievement, and many different aspects of that background have been suggested as causal factors in the link between home and school, but up to now we have very little knowledge of the precise way in which these different factors interrelate to depress intellectual performance.[2]

In addition to the inability of this approach to account for the problem of differential academic achievement, this emphasis on the family, in its extreme form, has produced some very dubious conclusions and destructive results. Propagated in the United States since the 1960s in an attempt to explain the low educational attainment of black and lower-class white children, the concept of cultural deprivation attributes their problems solely to the cultural deficiencies of their families. The view that the problem resides almost exclusively with the children and their families, and that some sort of cultural injection is needed to compensate for what they are missing, is not only intellectually bankrupt but also has contributed to the widespread popular notion that the plight of poor whites and minorities is entirely their own fault.

To understand the problems lower-class children face in the American educational system demands that attention be paid not just to their families but also to the school. Theories that give primacy to the family inhibit critical scrutiny of the nation's schools. The problem is not that lower-class children are inferior in some way; the problem is that *by the definitions and standards of the school,* they consistently are evaluated as deficient. The assumption of some mainstream sociologists that the problem must lie with the contestants, rather than with the judge, is simply unfounded.

Conventional sociologists as well as Marxist theorists have been singularly unable to put forth a convincing explanation of lower-class "educability." As Karabel and Halsey point out, the only explanation Bowles can muster is the vague assertion that the "rules of the game" favor the upper classes. Although this sentiment undoubtedly is true, he offers us no explanation of how the rules are biased and reproduced. Clearly, what is needed is a comprehensive analysis of how the educational system's curricula, pedagogy, and evaluative criteria[3] favor the interests of the upper classes.

Although such a formidable task has yet to be undertaken, the guiding theoretical concept for the endeavor has been provided by Bourdieu—the notion of cultural capital. To recapitulate: Bourdieu's theory maintains that the cultural capital of the lower classes—their manners, norms, dress, style of interaction, and linguistic facility—is devalued by the school, while the cultural capital of the upper classes is rewarded. As Halsey, Heath, and Ridge put it, "The ones who can receive what the school has to give are the ones who are already endowed with the requisite cultural attributes—with the appropriate cultural capital."[4] Although Bourdieu is primarily a theorist, Paul Dimaggio has substantiated Bourdieu's concept by analyzing data sets with measures for cultural attitudes, information, and activities for more than 2,900 eleventh-grade boys and girls. He found that the impact of cultural capital on high school grades is "very significant," which confirms "rather dramatically the utility of the perspective advanced here [by Bourdieu]."[5]

Although neither Bernstein nor Nell Keddie self-consciously situates his or her empirical work within Bourdieu's theoretical framework, both provide analyses of actual classroom processes that enforce class-linked differences in educational achievement. These analyses fit nicely into Bourdieu's theoretical perspective. As we saw in Chapter 2, Bernstein actually demonstrates how class-based differences in speech patterns affect academic achievement and place working-class students like Frankie and Craig at a disadvantage with respect to their middle-class counterparts. Keddie's study also demonstrates how observed classroom phenomena—the different expectations teachers hold for students of different social origins, the determination of what counts as knowledge, teacher-student interaction, the tracking of courses—serve to handicap the performance of the lower classes.[6] As Karabel and Halsey remind us, because dominant social groups determine what is valued in the educational system, it should not surprise us that subordinate social groups are judged deficient by the criteria set by the powerful.[7]

These complex mechanisms of social reproduction are embedded deeply in the American educational system; they are well hidden, and thus the Brothers are unaware of the processes that work to hinder their performance. The Brothers believe in equality of opportunity and reject the idea that they have less of a chance to succeed in school than do middle- or upper-class students. Instead, the Brothers attribute their mediocre academic performance to personal inadequacy—laziness, stupidity, or lack of self-discipline.

(all in separate interviews)

SUPER: I would try—if I had more study skills, I bet you I'd be trying my hardest. I bet I'd be getting good grades. . . . I dunno; I just can't seem to do it.

MOKEY: I try my best to do as good as anyone else. But there's some real smart people up there, plus I can't seem to get myself to work, especially during football. It's hard.

MIKE: I did horrible [my freshman year in high school]. I used to do good. I got all As in grammar school. Now I'm doing shitty. I guess I started out smart and got stupider.

If one accepts the equality-of-opportunity line of reasoning, those who are not "making it" have only themselves to blame.

Clearly, the self-esteem of the Brothers suffers as a result of their inferior academic performance. A careful review of the literature on the effects of academic achievement and particularly track placement on students' sense of self, undertaken by Maureen Scully in a 1982 unpublished essay, reveals that although we can expect academic self-esteem to vary according to scholastic performance, students' general self-esteem is often more resilient. Because some high school students do not value academic achievement very highly and instead emphasize nonacademic activities and values, their general sense of self-esteem is sheltered from the negative onslaughts of academic failure.[8] The Brothers, however, care a great deal about their academic performance, and thus their general self-esteem is sensitive to academic failure.

In summary, the Brothers believe that American society is open; equality of opportunity is perceived as a reality. Moreover, schooling is regarded by the Brothers as the means to economic success; consequently, they care about school, accept its norms and standards, and conform to its rules. As black lower-class students, however, the Brothers are lacking in the cultural capital rewarded by the school system—hence their poor academic achievement and placement into low tracks. The Brothers blame themselves for the mediocrity of their scholastic performance. The implications of this dynamic are important to an understanding of the overall process of social reproduction (which will be taken up in the next chapter).

Spurning the Achievement Ideology

The school experiences of the Hallway Hangers suggest that they are a group of disaffected, rebellious, undisciplined boys who have been labeled "emotionally disturbed," "learning impaired," and "slow." Beneath their uncooperative conduct and resistance, however, lies a logic that makes sense to these boys and informs their attitudes toward school.

The Hallway Hangers do not "buy" the achievement ideology because they foresee substantial barriers to their economic success, barriers this ideology fails to mention. It is important to note that the Hallway Hangers could reject the notion that equality of opportunity exists but accept the reasoning that school can still help them. Just because one does not have the same chance to succeed in school or on the job market as a middle- or upper-class student does not mean necessarily that achievement in school will be of no use in securing a job. Indeed, the connection between schooling and occupational achievement is so deeply ingrained in the minds of most Americans that it is difficult to imagine people completely rejecting it.

The Hallway Hangers, however, challenge the conventional wisdom that educational achievement translates into economic success. In their view of the opportunity structure, educational attainment is of little importance. Convinced that they are headed into jobs for which they do not need an education, the Hallway Hangers see little value in schooling. Jinx perfectly summarizes this view: "Even if you get a high school diploma, that don't mean shit. A lot of people say, 'Oh, you need it for that job.' You get a high school diploma, and they're still gonna give you a shitty job. So it's just a waste of time to get it."

Because this point of view runs counter to a deeply rooted, collective belief, it offends our sensibilities. In fact, however, it is a rational outlook based on experience. Jinx looks at his four older brothers, one of whom graduated from high school, and observes that the one with the diploma is no better off than the rest of them. The brother who struggled through the four years of high school is in the navy, as was another who did not graduate.

Stoney feels the same way. He insists that school performance has no effect on what kind of job one will get. He argues instead that "fucking experience, man, it comes in handy," particularly in the case of his current job in a pizza shop.

STONEY: So the very next day, I went looking for another job. Went into this place, told him my experience, made a few pies. That was it; he hired me on the spot. No application or nothing.

JM: No high school diploma.

STONEY: That's right. He didn't want one.

JM: For your goals, how would it help you to have a diploma?

STONEY: [*immediately*] It won't, cuz I don't need no diploma to open a store. Like I said, if you know how to do something, you do it. If you don't, you don't.

JM: Do you think it would help you at all if you got fired tomorrow, and you went up to another pizza shop somewhere? Do you think it would help you if you could show them a diploma?

STONEY: No, it wouldn't help me. They wanna see what you got, what you can do. If you can do the job. I used to always get hired on the spot. They'd look at me and be real surprised a young kid can make pizza this good.

Relevant job experience is much more important than educational attainment for landing a job in food preparation, at least in Stoney's experience. The same logic holds true for a prospective construction worker or auto mechanic.

Shorty draws on the experiences of his brothers, much like Jinx, to reach a similar conclusion regarding the efficacy of schooling. Two of Shorty's brothers have graduated from high school; one of these apparently graduated from college as well. Nevertheless, neither has been able to secure desired employment. The college graduate is working security at a local research firm. Despite relatively high educational achievement, "they don't seem to be getting anywhere," comments Shorty.

Frankie need only look at his own experience to assert that schooling is generally incapable of doing much for the Hallway Hangers. In interviews, he constantly reiterates this theme.

JM: Okay, so why is it that some kids, even coming from down here, will go to school, and they'll work real hard, go to all their classes, and do all the work? Why do some kids take that route?

FRANKIE: Well, none of my friends take that route. But I dunno. I never took that route. But I guess, I dunno, they're dopes. I dunno, I guess, y'know, they fuckin' think if they go through high school and go through college, they think they're gonna get a job that's gonna pay fifty grand a year. Y'know, a white-collar job. I don't think that's true.

JM: Do you think how you do in school is gonna affect what kinda job you get?

FRANKIE: I got my diploma, and you don't even need that. Y'know, my diploma ain't doing me no good. It's sitting in my bottom drawer. Y'know, it ain't gonna help me. I got my diploma, and you don't even need that. . . . All those Portegi [Portuguese] kids, they never went the fuck to school. Now they fuckin' got good jobs, cars—y'know, they fucking made it. They went out and fuckin' worked machinery and mechanics. So a high school diploma really isn't fucking shit.

(in a separate interview)

FRANKIE: They dropped out of school, and they got better fucking jobs than we do. I got my fuckin' diploma, and I ain't got jack shit. So it wasn't worth it for me to get my high school diploma. If I dropped out when I was sixteen—that was two years ago—I prob'ly would've already been through a job training program, and I'd already have a fucking job, saving me fucking money.

(following an assertion by me that schooling is of some use on the labor market)

FRANKIE: [*angrily*] But, but [*stuttering because he is upset*], still, I *did,* I did, I *did* the fucking, I did my school program, I went to school, I fuckin', I got my diploma, I went what you're s'posed to do. 'Cept you're s'posed to further your education—college and many more thousands of fucking dollars. Look how many fucking college graduates ain't got jobs. You know how fucking hard it is. They got educations. What the fuck they doin' with it? They ain't doin' shit. So fucking school ain't paying off for no one.

This last assertion—that school does not pay off for anybody—is not one to which all the Hallway Hangers would give their support. Even Frankie, in a less tense moment, would agree that some kids do "make it" and that success in school is a crucial ingredient for economic and social advancement. Nevertheless, although exaggerated in this case, Frankie's comment is indicative of the general attitude of the Hallway Hangers.

The Hallway Hangers do not maintain that schooling is incapable of doing anything for anyone because they all know Billy. He used to hang with the Hallway Hangers, getting high every day before, during, and after school, drinking excessively, and stealing cars. During his freshman year and the early part of his sophomore year, however, Billy underwent a number of personal crises out of which he emerged a much different person. Part of a large family, Billy had a father who was an alcoholic and has a mother who is mentally ill. In the span of a year and a half, Billy's mother was deemed unfit by the Department of Social Services to have custody of her children, so Billy moved in with his father, who died shortly thereafter. At about the same time, Billy's best friend was murdered brutally in an abandoned building a few blocks from Clarendon Heights. Billy, who currently lives in a three-bedroom apartment in Clarendon Heights with his aunt and uncle, three cousins, and a baby nephew, is a senior at Lincoln High School. Goalie of the varsity hockey team and recipient of a special college scholarship for "individuals of extraordinary ability and need," Billy has switched from Oc. Ed. to the Fundamental School in preparation for college.

The view among the Hallway Hangers is that Billy is "making it." He is living testimony to the fact that schooling can work, that it can pay off. So the Hallway Hangers are not of the view that success in school is irrelevant but rather that the odds of "making it" are simply too slim to bet on. In what can be likened to a cost-benefit analysis, the Hallway Hangers, much like Willis's lads, conclude that the possibility of upward social mobility is not worth the price of obedience, conformity, and investment of substantial amounts of time, energy, and work in school.

For the Hallway Hangers, perhaps the biggest cost of going to school every day is the deferred income from full-time work. As Giroux reminds us, the economic issue often plays the crucial role in a working-class student's decision whether to attend school full-time, part-time, or not at all.[9] The issue of potential work earnings entered into all the boys' decisions to drop out of school. Chris and Jinx comment on the tension between school and employment directly.

(in a joint interview)

CHRIS: Jay, lemme tell you how I feel about school. I wanna go to school; I'd like to go 'til like eleven thirty and then at about twelve o'clock work until about five. Y'know, so I could go to school plus make some money.

JINX: You won't like that, brother, cuz that's what I do. That's what I do. He'll start going to work, getting a little money in his pocket, and he'll always want more.

(later in the same interview)

CHRIS: So, Jay, people should fucking give us a break, y'know? [*laughing*] Pay us to go to school, y'know?

JM: How would that work?

CHRIS: Give us forty bucks a week to go to school 'til twelve o'clock. At twelve we go to work and make about fifty bucks.

JM: What would be in it for them?

CHRIS: They'd get a lot of people to go. [*laughing*] They'd get a helluva lot more than they got now, I'm tellin' ya.

CHRIS: On Friday, I'd say, "Oh, *yeah!* Got my job."

JINX: Got my ounce all paid for.

This last comment is revealing. The world the Hallway Hangers inhabit, with its preponderance of drugs and alcohol, demands financial resources. The pressure to come up with money is keenly felt by all these boys, a pressure to which Slick alludes often.

SLICK: [*motioning to doorway #13*] Hey, everyone out there has a goal. Their goal is one thing and that's money. You hafta have money, to make it. . . . That's what depresses them. That's what puts them into the pressure situation. They hafta make money; they know they hafta do it. The name of the game is money. You hafta get it. If you don't get it, there's no way you're gonna be able to do anything. You hafta make it.

Locked into the present by the pressing need for money, the Hallway Hangers, in contrast to middle-class teenagers, do not have the resources to bide their time while long-range educational or occupational plans come to fruition. Moreover, believing they have missed out on the indulgences of American consumerism, they are starved for immediate financial success.

(in a group interview)

SLICK: Y'know what it is, Jay? All of us down here, we just don't wanna make a buck; we wanna make a fast buck. We want it *now*. Right fucking now. And you know why? Not cuz we're stupid and can't wait for anything, but because we've never had it.

SHORTY: Fuckin' right. We're all poor as shit.

SLICK: No one in this room has thirty bucks in his pocket. Fuckin' right we want it. We've never had it.

The desire of these boys to go for the fast buck, to focus only on the present, becomes understandable in light of the uncertainty of the future and their bona fide belief that they may be in prison or dead.

In considering the experiences of the Brothers in school, we have seen that the effects of schooling on their self-esteem are significant. The Hallway Hangers also feel a measure of personal inadequacy with respect to their dismal educational attainment, but for them schooling is merely tangential to the overall experience of being a lower-class teenager in an urban setting. Hence, little of their self-esteem is tied up in school; academic performance has less effect on their sense of self. It is possible, however, that this apparent indifference toward school is itself in part a defense mechanism that protects the boys from assaults on their self-respect. Evidence for this type of failure-avoidance strategy has been documented in a number of quantitative studies of students' self-esteem.[10] For the Hallway Hangers, the prospects of failure in school and the accompanying feelings of inadequacy are further reasons not to invest themselves in education; the potential threat to self-esteem is another item on the cost side of the equation.

The cost of deferred work earnings, the price of obedience and conformity to rules and authority that run counter to the peer group's ethos, the risk of failure, and the investment of time and energy all make up the costs of school involvement for the Hallway Hangers. On the benefit side are improved prospects for social mobility resulting from educational achievement. For the Hallway Hangers, who see through the achievement ideology and have little faith in the efficacy of schooling, the improved prospects for social mobility are not worth the price that schooling exacts. Although their approach to school assuredly is not based on a rational cost-benefit analysis, these considerations do underlie their orientation toward education.

This logic dictates that the Hallway Hangers drop out of school or at least minimize their involvement with it. That most of the Hallway Hangers pursue this latter course is evident from their paths into the less demanding programs at Lincoln High School, such as BTS, the Adjustment Class, Enterprise Co-op, and the after-school program. With teachers for whom they have more respect, fewer rules, and lighter academic workloads, entry into these alternative programs sometimes minimizes the costs to the point where schooling becomes worthwhile. Both high school graduates (Boo-Boo and Frankie) and the one boy currently enrolled in school (Steve) are or were in such alternative programs. Even for the boys in these programs, however, schooling often is not worth the price that must be paid, and thus most have dropped out. For Frankie to stay in school, for instance, the added benefit of "keeping my moms happy" was necessary to swing the balance in favor of schooling.

Whereas at first glance the rebellious behavior, low academic achievement, and high dropout rate of the Hallway Hangers seem to stem from lack of self-discipline, dullness of wit, laziness, or an inability to project themselves into the future, the actual causes of their rejection of school are quite different. Their unwillingness to partake of the educational system stems from an assessment of the costs and benefits of playing the game. Their view is not that schooling is incapable of propelling them up the ladder of social mobility, but that the chances are too slim to warrant the attempt. The Hallway Hangers' alienation from school rests not so much on a perceived lack of the means to succeed in school as of the means to convert that success into success on the labor market. Convinced that they are headed into dead-end jobs regardless of their educational attainment, the Hallway Hangers dismiss school as irrelevant.

Given this logic, the oppositional behavior of the Hallway Hangers is a form of resistance to an institution that cannot deliver on its promise of upward social mobility for all students. Furthermore, Lincoln High School, like almost all American schools, is essentially a middle-class institution. Its curriculum, grading system, and disciplinary code all reward middle-class traits, values, and skills. In coping with the difficulties of growing up poor in America, the Hallway Hangers have developed a set of survival skills of which they are very proud. These skills, however, are accorded little or no recognition in the school setting; instead, students must relinquish their street identities and move beyond their neighborhood ties. The Hallway Hangers resent the fact that the school, because of its middle-class orientation, ignores the skills they have picked up on the street. Thus, they do anything they can to express themselves in an institution that denies and violates their cultural identities.

The maturity and independence the boys have gained from years of hard living in Clarendon Heights clash with the authoritarian structure of the school. Teachers, as the agents of repression, are especially difficult for the Hallway Hangers to tolerate.

(all in separate interviews)

CHRIS: I hate the fucking teachers. I don't like someone always telling me what the fuck to do. Especially the way they do it. They make you feel like shit. I couldn't take their shit.

SLICK: It's with the maturity here—you wanna do what you want to do, and you don't want anyone to tell you what to do.

JINX: You gotta get high to go to class. You gotta, to listen to the teachers talk their shit. Tell you, "Do this, do that, and do that," and a lot of people just say, "Fuck you. You do it yourself. I ain't doing shit for you."

Although teacher condescension and the institution's demand for unquestioning obedience to authority are sore points, the Hallway Hangers' resentment is not focused on teachers as a generic category as much as it is directed at middle-class teachers in particular. The Hallway Hangers constantly refer to the perceived social class disjuncture between themselves and the schools' teaching staff. Jimmy Sullivan, who comes from the same class as these students and still displays many characteristics of that class culture, is respected because "he doesn't take no shit from anybody," including students. The middle-class teachers at the King School, in contrast, are held in contempt by Frankie because "they swore and shit, but you just told them to shut the fuck up and they shut up." The Hallway Hangers are willing to accept the authority of Sullivan and Harry Jones, a former resident of public housing. The same authority in the hands of other teachers, however, draws nothing but scorn from the boys.

(in a group interview)

JM: What about the teachers? You all seem to like Sullivan and Jones. What's the difference between them and the rest of 'em?

CHRIS: The other ones are all pussies.

SHORTY: Cuz they don't know how to deal with us kids.

FRANKIE: And the reason Harry Jones is cool is cuz Harry was brought up in the city his whole life; he used to live in Emerson Towers and his brothers and shit—they ain't all fucking angels, y'know? That's why he's cool. . . . And, y'know, there's a couple of other teachers that are fuckin' from around here and know what the fuck is happening. Y'know, but other teachers, they live in the suburbs and shit. They're coming into a city to work. They don't know what the fuck city kids are.

(in a discussion with Shorty and Slick)

SLICK: Certain teachers you can talk to up there. But most of the teachers that are up there, a lot of them are too rich, y'know what I mean? They have money, and they don't give a fuck about nobody. They don't know how it's like to hafta come to school late. "Why'd you come to school late?" "I had to make sure my brother was in school. I had to make sure certain things—I had to make sure that there was breakfast."

SHORTY: Responsibilities. See, that's what I mean. Now, the teachers will not understand. He ain't got no father, right? The father ain't living there, just like me. He's the oldest kid now. And he has big responsibilities at home because his brothers are growing up and his sister—he's got to keep an eye on 'em. Now you gotta do all that, and you got teachers giving you a hard fucking time?

SLICK: It's tough.

SHORTY: You got teachers like Harry Jones. They know; they understand where you come from, that you're trying to support your family.

SLICK: Like Harry Jones, when I got into his class, he talked to me, y'know? He'd understand what I'm doing.

SHORTY: He grew up around here all his life.

(in a group interview)

FRANKIE: Y'know, I'll admit I fucked up, y'know? Hey, man, I got fucking problems, y'know? And the teacher just don't want to deal with it. Well, fuck them.

(in a discussion with Jinx and Chris)

JM: Do any of the teachers know the people?

JINX: A few. Like Harry Jones, Jimmy Sullivan. All the rest are all bitchy. They don't understand us; they don't try to understand us.

Similar effects of social class differences between teachers and students have been found in other studies. In his analysis of the culture of a community college, Howard London found that subtle class antagonism between students and teachers was at the root of problems in conduct, absenteeism, and negative attitudes on the part of both toward the school.[11] The expressed antipathy of the Hallway Hangers toward middle-class teachers should not surprise us, for they are the most obvious symbols of the middle-class orientation of the school.

The school demands respect for its staff. But for the Hallway Hangers to show respect or even deference for individuals who by their standards do not deserve it is a real struggle. Thus, in trying to understand the approach the Hallway Hangers take toward school, we also must be cognizant of the costs involved in meeting the school's requirement of respect for teachers (loss of self-respect, condemnation from peers, forfeiture of feelings of ascendancy over other students).

The Brothers do not have problems with respecting teachers, for in many ways the teachers symbolize what the boys hope to become. Many of the Brothers aspire to middle-class jobs and, in any case, harbor no ill will toward middle-class values and norms. Indeed, the Brothers, consciously or unconsciously, emulate the middle-class traits of the teachers and endeavor to embody middle-class values. This phenomenon, termed "anticipatory socialization" by Robert Merton,[12] is an important source of dissimilarity between the Brothers and the Hallway Hangers.

In marked contrast to the Hallway Hangers, the Brothers feel that they are headed up the ladder of social mobility and believe that schooling is going to get them there. That two peer groups of the same social class, indeed from the very same neighborhood, hold such radically different attitudes toward school presents a challenging puzzle to the sociologist. In the next chapter, I attempt to meet this challenge directly.

NOTES

1. See, for example, studies by the following: David Dillon, "Does the School Have a Right to Its Own Language?" *The English Journal* 69 (April 1980): 1460–1474; Warren G. Findley and Miriam M. Bryan, "Ability Grouping: A Review of the Literature," Part 3 (Washington, D.C.: Office of Education, 1970); Melvin L. Kohn, *Class and Conformity: A Study in Values* (Chicago: University of Chicago Press, 1977); Charles Miller, John A. McLaughlin, John Madden, and Norman M. Chansky, "Socioeconomic Class and Teacher Bias," *Psychological Reports* 23 (1968): 806–810; Ray C. Rist, "Student Social Class and Teacher Expectations: The Self-Fulfilling Prophecy in Ghetto Education," *Harvard Educational*

Review 40 (August 1970): 411–451; Morris Rosenberg and Roberta G. Simmons, *Black and White Self-Esteem: The Urban School Child* (Washington, D.C.: American Sociological Association, 1971); and Charles B. Schultz and Roger H. Sherman, "Social Class, Development, and Differences in Reinforcer Effectiveness," *Review of Educational Research* 46 (1976): 25–59.

2. Olive Banks, *The Sociology of Education* (London: B. T. Batsfield, 1976), pp. 68, 69.

3. These are the three major areas Bernstein has identified as crucial to our understanding of the socially determined value placed on various types of knowledge. See *Class, Codes and Control,* vol. 3 (London: Routledge and Kegan Paul, 1975), p. 85.

4. A. H. Halsey, A. F. Heath, and J. M. Ridge, *Origins and Destinations* (Oxford: Clarendon Press, 1980), p. 7.

5. Paul Dimaggio, "Cultural Capital and Social Success," *American Sociological Review* 47 (April 1982): 189–201.

6. Nell Keddie, "Classroom Knowledge," in Michael F. D. Young, ed., *Knowledge and Control* (London: Collier, 1972), pp. 133–160.

7. Jerome Karabel and A. H. Halsey, eds., *Power and Ideology in Education* (New York: Oxford University Press, 1977), p. 67.

8. Maureen Anne Scully, "Coping with Meritocracy" (Thesis, Harvard College, 1982), pp. 85–101.

9. Henry A. Giroux, *Theory and Resistance in Education* (London: Heinemann Educational Books, 1983), p. 95.

10. See the following: Viktor Gecas, "Contexts of Socialization," in Morris Rosenberg and Ralph H. Turner, eds., *Social Psychology: Sociological Perspectives* (New York: Basic Books, 1981); Rosenberg and Simmons, *Black and White Self-Esteem;* Morris Rosenberg, *Conceiving the Self* (New York: Basic Books, 1979); Morris Rosenberg, "The Self-Concept: Social Product and Social Force," in *Social Psychology: Sociological Perspectives;* Richard J. Shavelson, Judith J. Hubner, and George C. Stanton, "Self-Concept: Validation of Construct Interpretations," *Review of Educational Research* 46 (Summer 1976): 407–411; Arthur L. Stinchcombe, *Rebellion in a High School* (Chicago: Quadrangle Books, 1964).

11. Howard B. London, *The Culture of a Community College* (New York: Praeger, 1978).

12. Robert K. Merton and Alice S. Rossi, "Contributions to the Theory of Reference Group Behavior," in *Social Theory and Social Structure* (New York: Free Press, 1968), pp. 319–322.

7

LEVELED ASPIRATIONS
Social Reproduction Takes Its Toll

With the ethnographic description from the preceding chapters at our disposal, we now can attempt to analyze the forces that influence the aspirations of these two groups of boys from Clarendon Heights. That many boys in both groups do not even aspire to middle-class jobs is a powerful indication of how class inequality is reproduced in American society. These youths' prospects for socioeconomic advancement are doomed before they even get started; most of the boys do not even get a foothold on the ladder of social mobility. In this chapter, the task before us is to illuminate in as much detail and depth as possible the process of social reproduction as it is lived by the Hallway Hangers and the Brothers.

The regulation of aspirations is perhaps the most significant of all the mechanisms contributing to social reproduction; however, aspirations themselves are largely a function of structural mechanisms that should be considered when possible. Mention already has been made of the effects of tracking and the school's valuation of the cultural capital of the upper classes, both of which influence aspirations but also have independent effects on reproducing class structure. An additional and essential component of social reproduction is the process by which individuals in a stratified social order come to accept their own position and the inequalities of the social order as legitimate.

Whereas force and coercion often have ensured the cohesion of societies and the maintenance of oppressive relationships, ideology is more important in fulfilling this function in contemporary America. In particular, the achievement ideology is a powerful force in the legitimation of inequality and, ultimately, in

113

social reproduction. In short, this ideology maintains that individual merit and achievement are the fair and equitable sources of inequality in American society. If merit is the basis for the distribution of rewards, then members of the lower classes attribute their subordinate position in the social order to personal deficiencies. In this way, inequality is legitimated.[1]

In their theoretical formulations, both Weber and Marx touch on the role of ideology in the maintenance of social cohesion. In Weber's terms, ideology is the "myth" by which the powerful ensure belief in the validity of their domination. "Every highly privileged group develops the myth of its natural superiority. Under conditions of stable distribution of power . . . that myth is accepted by the negatively privileged strata."[2] Although Marx considered economics the major determinant in the perpetuation of class relations, he discusses the function of ideology in preserving exploitative relations in capitalist societies. Ideology, which is proffered to the subordinate classes as an accurate depiction of the social order, is actually a "false consciousness," an apparently true but essentially illusory set of views that disguises and distorts the true workings of the capitalist system. The ruling class, in order to justify its dominance, "is compelled . . . to represent its interest as the common interest of all the members of society. . . . It has to give its ideas the form of universality, and represent them as the only rational, universally valid ones."[3] Thus, by obscuring the truth of conflictual relations and exploitation, ideology serves to make capitalist societies appear legitimate.[4]

In contemporary America, the educational system, by sorting students according to ostensibly meritocratic criteria, plays a crucial role in the legitimation of inequality. Because the school deals in the currency of academic credentials, its role in the reproduction of inequality is obscured. Students believe that they succeed or fail in school on the basis of merit. By internalizing the blame for failure, students lose their self-esteem and then accept their eventual placement in low-status jobs as the natural outcome of their own shortcomings. If individuals are convinced that they are responsible for their low position in society, then criticism of the social order by the subordinate classes is deflected. The process of social reproduction goes on, unscrutinized and unchallenged.

If this legitimation function is working, then members of the lower classes will suffer from low self-esteem, which originally was developed in the school and then carried into later life to reconcile them to their position. In gauging the degree to which lower-class individuals accept the social order and their position in it as legitimate, we must determine whether they attribute their inferior social position to personal inadequacy or to external forces as well.

THE HALLWAY HANGERS:
INTERNALIZING PROBABILITIES, RESCUING SELF-ESTEEM

According to Bourdieu, the aspirations of the Hallway Hangers should reflect their objective probabilities for upward mobility. Immersed as they are in their social universe at the bottom of the class structure, their subjective hopes should be as modest as their objective chances are slim. Indeed, this is the case. The Hallway Hangers view their prospects for substantial upward mobility as very remote, which accounts for their low occupational aspirations. Drawing on the experiences of their families, and on their own encounters with the job market, the boys' appraisals of the possibility for social upgrading often preclude the formation of any aspirations at all. Moreover, the available evidence indicates that the boys' parents do not intercede significantly in their children's aspiration formation. In general, the parents of the Hallway Hangers have little influence in their sons' lives. Like most parents, they want the best for their children, but if Stoney's mother is any indication, they also are hesitant to encourage excessively high aspirations in their sons for fear of setting them up for disappointment.

Although the families of the Hallway Hangers have a pervasive influence on their aspirations, so have their own work experiences. All the Hallway Hangers have held summertime employment since they have been of working age. Apart from Steve, they are searching for full-time work. In their struggles to find meaningful, stable employment, all have been thwarted. Invariably, once they think they finally have found a decent job, the opportunity falls through. This type of firsthand experience on the job market further deflates any illusions they might have had about the openness of the opportunity structure. When a boy searches in vain for work that pays seventy-five cents more than minimum wage, his estimation of the prospects for significant upward mobility is bound to be low.

In addition to family and work, school has an important, if less direct, influence on aspirations. Because the school devalues the cultural capital of the Hallway Hangers, their chances for academic success are diminished substantially. Although the Hallway Hangers do not see the intricacies of this process taking place, half have remarked that students from "higher" social backgrounds have a better chance to do well in school. The Hallway Hangers have seen their older siblings fail in school; they see their friends fail as well. Even their Clarendon Heights peers who try to succeed in school meet with only modest success; for verification of this the Hallway Hangers need only look to the Brothers. Thus, the Hallway Hangers question their own capacity to perform well in school, a view that informs their assessment of the chances for social mobility.

Of more importance is the Hallway Hangers' belief that performance in school is of only tangential importance in securing a job. They challenge the widely held notion that success in school translates into success on the job market. But if they feel that schooling will not boost them up the ladder of social mobility, what will? In essence, the Hallway Hangers see a ladder with no rungs on it, or at least none they can reach. They believe that the educational system cannot deliver on its promise of upward social mobility for those who perform well in school. Thus, in part, their leveled aspirations reflect their feeling that schooling is incapable of doing much for them.

In concentrating on this point, however, it is easy to miss some of the intra-school processes that affect the aspirations of the Hallway Hangers. The school is distinctive not for what it does but for what it fails to do.

Lincoln School officials are aware of the process of social reproduction (although they would not conceptualize it in these terms). Bruce Davis, a young, enthusiastic, and dedicated guidance counselor in the Occupational Education Program, acknowledges social reproduction as a simple fact of life.

BD: These kids [those enrolled in the Oc. Ed. Program] go directly into hard jobs. They're generally from homes where people are laborers. I mean, kids who go to college are from families whose parents went to college. That's how it works, it seems to me. That's where these kids are coming from; they're geared to manual labor jobs, like their brothers, sisters, fathers, uncles, whatever—mothers, like the jobs they have.

Rather than attempting to use the resources of the school to mitigate this process, school officials seem content to let it unfold unhindered. The Oc. Ed. Program, for example, is designed to prepare its students for the rigors of manual work.

BD: We constantly stress to the kids that they have to be responsible, reliable, and dependable, that they can't be a screw-off. Really, we're just trying to make the kids accountable for themselves. Y'know, most of these kids won't go to college. When they leave here, they can't sleep 'til eleven and then get up and go to three classes. They've really got to be disciplined. They're going to be right out there working. In Oc. Ed., that's really what we're all about. We're trying to simulate a work experience, make class just like a job. It's not just their competency that matters; to be a good worker, your willingness to cooperate, your attitude, is so important.

Bowles and Gintis's argument that working-class students are socialized for working-class jobs and that the social relations of school mirror those of the workplace hardly could be better substantiated.

My point here is not that the school, consciously or unconsciously, levels the aspirations of some students but that it accepts and exacerbates already existing differences in aspirations. By requiring the Hallway Hangers, as eighth-graders, to choose their educational program, the school solidifies what is often a vaguely felt and ill-defined preference for manual work or a desire simply to be with one's friends into a definite commitment to a future in manual work. The decision is essentially their own, and it makes a good deal of sense considering that experience in a trade ostensibly will be of some advantage in a difficult job market. Slick's decision to enter the Oc. Ed. Program, despite his high level of achievement in grammar school, typifies the quandary of these boys. Very few middle-class students with decent grades would select a vocational program, but Slick felt the need to do so in order to improve his chances of getting work after graduation.

Although the boys chose their various programs, there are grounds for skepticism about the degree to which this was a completely uncoerced choice. James Rosenbaum, in his 1976 study of a working-class high school, found that guidance counselors and teachers applied subtle and not-so-subtle techniques to channel students into particular tracks and keep them there, sometimes against the students' wishes. But the school officials did this in such a manner that both the youngsters and their parents believed it was a free choice.[5]

Lincoln High School boasts a more liberal educational philosophy than that of Rosenbaum's school, so we hardly can extrapolate his findings to Lincoln High. Nevertheless, in response to a question concerning the process by which students choose their program, Wallace responded, "Oh, that's done for them in grammar school." Sensing that I had picked up on the "for them," she hastily went on to say that it is a process that initially involves a conference between the eighth-grade counselor and the student as well as parents. "According to however they performed in grammar school, the counselor will come up with a suggested schedule and send it home for approval. Of course, the parent can disagree and pick other courses."

Resolution of the extent to which this is a decision of self-selection requires detailed ethnographic data on the transition from grammar school to Lincoln High, without which we must stop short of Rosenbaum's conclusion that the school exacerbates and actually creates inequality by its discriminatory tracking procedures. There is no doubt, however, that the school, by requiring that such choices be made at a young age, reinforces existing differences in aspirations.

In trying to understand the impact of family, work, and schooling on the aspirations of the Hallway Hangers, Bourdieu's theory that the habitus engenders aspirations that reflect objective probabilities seems accurate. According to Bourdieu and Passeron:

> The structure of the objective chances of social upgrading according to class of origin and, more precisely, the structure of the chances of upgrading through education, conditions agents' dispositions towards education and towards upgrading through education—dispositions which in turn play a determining role in defining the likelihood of entering education, adhering to its norms and succeeding in it, hence the likelihood of social upgrading.[6]

But the concept of the internalization of objective probabilities, because it limits the scope for human agency and creativity, has little explanatory value when we consider the influence of the peer group on the Hallway Hangers. This is a serious deficiency because according to our ethnographic sketch the peer group, especially for the Hallway Hangers, is of primary importance in these boys' lives.

In a country in which success is largely measured by income and occupational status, the Hallway Hangers have a problem. Unemployed, living in public housing, at the very bottom of the socioeconomic spectrum, they are regarded as failures, both by others and, at least to some extent, by themselves, a phenomenon Sennett and Cobb document for working-class people in general in *The Hidden Injuries of Class*.[7] The Hallway Hangers have been enrolled in programs that are designed for "fuckups" (as Mike of the Brothers put it), have been placed in the lowest educational tracks, and have received failing grades; all these constitute part of the emotional attack the boys suffer in school. The Hallway Hangers may have little of their self-esteem tied up in school, but, as Scully argues, they cannot help but feel "a judgment of academic inferiority cast upon them, be it by teachers, classmates, or their seemingly objective computerized report card."[8] The subculture of the Hallway Hangers must be understood as an attempt by its members to insulate themselves from these negative judgments and to provide a context in which some semblance of self-respect and dignity can be maintained.

To characterize the subculture of the Hallway Hangers as a defense mechanism against these onslaughts to their self-esteem, however, would be incomplete. Scully argues that most student countercultures have both defensive and independent features;[9] studies by Sennett and Cobb, Stinchcombe, and Willis verify this duality. The Hallway Hangers, like Willis's lads, have their own distinct set of values. These values are indigenous to the working class; they do not arise simply in opposition to the school. The Hallway Hangers' valuation of physical toughness, emotional resiliency, quick-wittedness, masculinity, loyalty, and group solidarity points to a subculture with its own norms, which are passed on from the older to the younger boys. Frankie describes how the subculture of the Hallway Hangers is learned and passed on.

(in a group interview)

FRANKIE: We were all brought up, all we seen is our older brothers and that gettin' into trouble and goin' to jail and all that shit. Y'know, seeing people— brothers and friends and shit—dying right in front of your face. You seen all the drugs, Jay. Well, this place used to be a thousand times worse than it is now. We grew up, it was all our older brothers doing this. We seen many fucking drugs, all the drinking. They fucking go; that group's gone. The next group came. It's our brothers that are a little older, y'know, twenty-something years old. They started doing crime. And when you're young, you look up to people. You have a person, everybody has a person they look up to. And he's doing this, he's drinking, he's doing that, he's doing drugs, he's ripping off people. Y'know, he's making good fucking money, and it looks like he's doing good, y'know? So, bang. Now it's our turn. We're here. What we gonna do when all we seen is fuckin' drugs, alcohol, fighting, this and that, no one going to school?

By providing a realm in which to be bad and tough are the main criteria for respect, the peer group of the Hallway Hangers reverses conventional cultural norms. Like almost all subcultures, however, the Hallway Hangers cannot escape the dominant culture's definitions of success. No matter how strong and insular the group, contact with the dominant culture, especially through school and work, is inevitable. Listening to the Hallway Hangers describe their descent through the school's programs, one detects a sense of shame, despite all their bravado. For Frankie to report that he finally found work, but as a temporary employee with the city's sanitation department as a garbage collector, clearly involved quite a swallowing of pride.

This inability on the part of a subculture to shelter itself completely from the dominant culture's values and norms has been documented widely: Willis's lads are pained by teachers' insults; the children Sennett and Cobb describe as having developed their own "badges of dignity" still have much of their sense of self-worth tied up in academic performance and teacher approval; and the inside world of black street-corner men who congregate at Tally's Corner in Elliot Liebow's study "is no more impervious to the values, sentiments and beliefs of the larger society than it is to the blue welfare checks or to the agents of the larger society, such as the policeman, the police informer, the case worker, and the landlord."[10]

Despite the fact that the Hallway Hangers' subculture affords its members only partial protection from the negative judgments of the dominant culture, it does provide a setting wherein a person can salvage some self-respect. The Hallway Hangers, who have developed alternative criteria for success, understand their situation in a way that defends their status; they manage to see themselves differently from the way the rest of society sees them. This is not entirely a self-protective psychological inversion; their ways of understanding their situation also are real. The Hallway Hangers are not living a fantasy. The world of the street exists—it is the unfortunate underside of the American economic system, the inevitable shadow accompanying a society that is not as open as it advertises. Moreover, the Hallway Hangers *are* physically hard, emotionally durable, and boldly enterprising. Those of us who are supposed to be succeeding by conventional standards need only venture into their world for the briefest moment to feel as though our badges of success are about as substantive and "real" in that environment as the emperor's new clothes.

The subculture of the Hallway Hangers is at odds with the dominant culture. The path to conventional success leads in one direction; the path to a redefined success lies in another. A boy cannot tread both paths simultaneously; orthodox success demands achievement in school, a feat that can be accomplished only by respecting the authority of teachers, which is inconsistent with the Hallway Hangers' alternative value scheme. All the current members of the Hallway Hangers have chosen, more or less definitively, to tread the path to a redefined success. (It should be remembered, however, that this choice is not an altogether free one; the Hallway Hangers see the path to conventional success as blocked by numerous obstacles.) Nevertheless, some do choose the path to conventional achievement; Billy, who expects to attend college next year, is being studied carefully by the Hallway Hangers as a testament to what they may have passed up.

The decision to break away from the group and pursue conventional success is not just a matter of individual calculation, however. More complicated forces are at work, forces that strain the individualistic orientation of American society. The solidarity of the Hallway Hangers is very strong. We have seen, for example, that the sense of cohesion and bonds of loyalty are such that Slick would not leave Shorty at the scene of a crime, preferring to be arrested himself. These communitarian values act to restrain individual Hallway Hangers from breaking away from the group and trying to "make it" conventionally. Slick, for example, scores very well on standardized tests, attended Latin Academy for a year, and is very articulate. Despite class-based barriers to success, he had a relatively good chance of "making it." But Slick also demonstrates the strongest sense of loyalty to the group. In a group interview, for example, he commented, as the rest of the group nodded their heads in agreement, that "money is secondary to friendship; I think friendship is more important than money." Jinx realizes that this loyalty can constrain individuals from striving for upward social mobility.

(in an individual interview)

JM: Do you have anything else to add about kids' attitudes down here?

JINX: I'd say everyone more or less has the same attitudes towards school: fuck it. Except the bookworms—people who just don't hang around outside and drink, get high, who sit at home—they're the ones who get the education.

JM: And they just decided for themselves?

JINX: Yup.

JM: So why don't more people decide that way?

JINX: Y'know what it is, Jay? We all don't break away because we're too tight. Our friends are important to us. Fuck it. If we can't make it together, fuck it. Fuck it all.

One of the forces operating to keep the Hallway Hangers from striking out on their own is the realization that there is little chance of their making it as a group, and to leave the others behind is to violate the code of loyalty. Recall how Slick contrasts the Hallway Hangers and the "rich little boys from the suburbs." "How do you think they got rich? By fucking people over. We don't do that to each other. We're too fucking tight. We're a group. We don't think like them. We think for all of us." This group loyalty rests on some very strong communitarian values and vaguely parallels an affirmation of class solidarity over individual interests, a point to which I shall return.

With respect to the influence of the peer group on social reproduction, there are some complicated processes at work that Bourdieu's theory fails to capture. Conceptually "flat," the model Bourdieu develops with Passeron struggles to account for the resistance and nonconformity characteristic of the Hallway Hangers' subculture. To some extent, membership in the subculture of the Hallway Hangers tends to level one's aspirations. Although influenced by the definitions of the dominant culture, the value scheme of the peer group devalues conventional success; the norm among the Hallway Hangers is low aspirations. This ethos, passed down from older to younger boys, is a powerful force on the individual. In addition to the general climate of the peer group, there is a tendency among the Hallway Hangers to resist raised aspirations because to act on them would involve breaking one's ties and leaving the group, a transgression of the code of loyalty.

It is possible to examine the workings of the process of legitimation as it applies to the Hallway Hangers. We have seen that their self-esteem is relatively resilient to poor academic performance, for little of each boy's sense of self is invested in the school. In addition, the peer group subculture affords the Hallway Hangers additional protection for their self-esteem and alternative ways of generating self-esteem through the value system of the group. Although failure in school is psychologically debilitating for the Hallway Hangers in some ways, their self-esteem is partially buttressed from the assaults of the educational system.

If legitimation were functioning smoothly, the Hallway Hangers, in addition to low self-esteem, would internalize their failure and point only to personal inadequacy as the cause of their plight. But such is not the case; the Hallway Hangers realize that internal and external factors contribute to their low social position. Although they do blame themselves to some degree for their failure, they also recognize external barriers to success.

When the Hallway Hangers talk, one almost can feel the struggle being waged in their minds between the tenets of the achievement ideology and the lessons distilled from their own experiences. This tension produces a deep-seated ambivalence. At times the boys are prone to take full responsibility for their dismal social status, but on other occasions they blame external obstacles to their social advancement. Boo-Boo reproaches himself at the beginning of an interview ("I just screwed up") but later maintains that boys from a middle-class neighborhood have an advantage when it comes to achieving social and economic prosperity. Other boys hold a similarly dichotomous outlook.

CHRIS: I guess I just don't have what it takes.

(in a separate interview)

CHRIS: We don't get a fair shake and shit.

FRANKIE: We're all just fucking burnouts. . . . We never did good anyways. . . .
We've just fucked up.

(in the same interview)

FRANKIE: If I had the fucking money to start out with, like some of these fucking rich kids, I'd be a millionaire. Fucking right, I would be.

SHORTY: I'd go in there, and I'd try my hardest to do the work, right? I'd get a
lot of problems wrong cuz I never had the brains much, really, right? That's
what's keepin' me back.

(in a different interview)

SHORTY: Hey, you can't get no education around here unless if you're fucking
rich, y'know? You can't get no education. . . . And you can't get a job once
they find out where you come from. "You come from Clarendon Heights?
Oh, shit. It's them kids again."

The Hallway Hangers see through parts of the achievement ideology, but at
some level they accept the aspersions it casts on lower-class individuals, including themselves. However, although the Hallway Hangers do not escape emotional injury, neither does the social order emerge unscathed. In the eyes of the
Hallway Hangers the opportunity structure is not open, a view that prevents
them from accepting their position and the inequalities of the social order as
completely legitimate.

Although the legitimation of inequality could be working more efficiently
with respect to the Hallway Hangers, the whole process is not ready to collapse.
Like those of the lads in Willis's study, these boys' insights into the true workings of the system are only partial, and often vague and ill-defined at that.
Moreover, although they are cognizant of external barriers to success, the Hallway Hangers raise no fundamental challenge to the fairness or efficacy of the
system as a whole. For the most part, in the absence of any systematic critique of
capitalism, the Hallway Hangers simply are plagued by a sense of unfairness and
the uneasy conviction that the rules of the contest are biased against them.
Thus, there is a discrepancy between their strongly felt conviction that they are
getting "the short end of the stick" and their inability to understand fully how
this is so.

They conveniently fill this gap with racism. The Hallway Hangers seem to
believe that if they are stuck with the short end of the stick, it must be because
the "niggers" have the long end. Their feelings of impotence, frustration, and
anger are subsumed in their hatred of blacks and in their conviction that their
own plight somehow has been exacerbated, if not caused, by the alleged economic and social advancement of black Americans. Recall how Shorty attrib-

uted his brother's unemployment to the "spics and niggers." Frankie and Smitty account for their predicament with one reason.

SMITTY: All the fuckin' niggers are getting the jobs.

FRANKIE: Fuckin' right. That's why we're hanging here now with empty pockets.

Affirmative action affords the Hallway Hangers a handy explanation for their own demise. Slick, despite his perceptiveness, succumbs to the same misunderstanding. Although his decision to quit school was undoubtedly the result of many factors, Slick insists that he dropped out of school solely because of supposed favoritism toward black students at Lincoln High. In a different interview, Slick begins by accusing the school of class-based prejudice but muddles the issue by suddenly bringing blacks into the discussion: "They favor all them fucking rich kids at that school. All the rich people. They fucking baby 'em. They baby all the fucking niggers up there."

This confusion between class bias and alleged reverse racial discrimination is symptomatic of the Hallway Hangers' outlook. By directing their resentment at affirmative action and those who benefit from it, the Hallway Hangers can spare themselves blame, but then the social order also is spared any serious scrutiny. In Willis's terms, racism is a serious "limitation" on the cultural outlook of the Hallway Hangers. Just as the lads' reversal of the usual valuation of mental versus manual labor prevents them from seeing their placement into dead-end, low-paying jobs as a form of class domination, so does the Hallway Hangers' racism obscure reality.

Thus, the Hallway Hangers harbor contradictory and ambivalent beliefs about the legitimacy of their social position. Their identification of class-based barriers to success and their impression that the deck is unfairly stacked against them, insights that could catalyze the development of a radical political consciousness, are derailed by their racism. On the one hand, the Hallway Hangers puncture the individualistic orientation of American society by their adoption of communitarian values to the point where a realization that the entire group cannot "make it" prevents individuals from striving for conventional success—a point of view that runs in the same direction as a class logic. But on the other hand, the Hallway Hangers support some politically conservative values and leaders. The prevalence of this type of dual, contradictory consciousness, embodying both progressive, counterhegemonic insights and reactionary, distorting beliefs, is discussed at length by Antonio Gramsci.[11] More recently, Michael Mann has argued convincingly that ambivalence about social beliefs leads to "pragmatic acceptance" of the social order rather than complete acceptance of it as legitimate.[12]

It is instructive to compare in detail this analysis of the Hallway Hangers with Willis's depiction of how social reproduction takes place for the lads in his study. The Hallway Hangers, as residents of public housing, are from a lower social stratum than the lads, who are from stable working-class families. Moreover, the British working class, with its long history, organized trade unions, and progressive political party, has developed an identity, pride, and class consciousness that are lacking in the United States. Despite these differences, substantial similarities in the way each peer group experiences the process of social reproduction warrant a comparison.

Willis argues that the lads' rejection of the achievement ideology and of the values and norms of the educational system is based on some key insights into the situation of their class under capitalism. However, the crucial element in the process of social reproduction—placement into manual labor jobs—is experienced by the lads as an act of independence and self-election, not a form of oppression. Because of the value placed on machismo in the wider working-class culture, which the lads appropriate for their own, they choose to enter the bottom of the occupational structure. At the root of social reproduction for the lads is the cultural inversion by which manual labor, equated with the social superiority of masculinity, is valued over white-collar work, which is associated with the inferior status of femininity.

Whereas the lads reject school because it has no bearing on the manual labor jobs they intend to pursue, the Hallway Hangers reject school for different reasons. For the lads, the seeds of leveled aspirations, and hence social reproduction, lie in their cultural affirmation of manual labor. Like the lads, the Hallway Hangers place a heavy premium on masculinity; their emphasis on being cool, tough, streetwise—in a word, bad—indicates the prevalence of machismo in their cultural outlook. Nevertheless, this emphasis on masculinity seldom is linked with distaste for white-collar work. The subculture of the Hallway Hangers contains no systematic bias toward manual work; their depressed aspirations result from a look into the future that sees stagnation at the bottom of the occupational structure as almost inevitable. The Hallway Hangers' outlook is more pessimistic than that held by the lads; there is no room on the job market for independence, election, or even choice. Thus, the Hallway Hangers reconcile themselves to taking whatever job they can get. Given this resignation, their belief that education can do little for them, and their assessment of the costs of educational success, the Hallway Hangers reject the institution of school. Although they do not experience unemployment or entry into low-level jobs as acts of triumph but rather as depressing facts of lower-class life, neither do the Hallway Hangers incriminate the social order as entirely unjust. In both cases the structure of class relations is reproduced, largely through the regulation of aspirations, but the processes through which it happens for the lads and the Hallway Hangers vary. The lads' sexism keeps them from decrying class domination; the racism of the Hallway Hangers serves the same purpose.

It is difficult to conceptualize the process of social reproduction when it is depicted in general terms. To facilitate our understanding of how the aspirations of the Hallway Hangers are leveled, I now describe the mechanisms associated with social reproduction as they affect Jinx. By looking at his experiences, the processes we have been discussing can be rendered concrete.

According to one of his friends, Jinx was an A student in his freshman year. At first, he worked hard and conformed to the rules of the school, but during his sophomore year, he started to weigh the costs and benefits of attendance and hard work. Every morning, he would socialize with the rest of the boys at Pop's for about fifteen minutes, maybe smoke a joint, and then head to class. "Hey, man, what the fuck? Sit down and smoke another bone. Whaddya wanna go to school for? You like them teachers better than us?" After leaving the group to comments like this, in class his mind would wander back to his friends sitting in Pop's, getting high, relaxing. He would think about his brother who dropped out of school at the age of sixteen and had a union job at the shipyards. He would think about another brother who had graduated the year before and joined the navy, and about his oldest brother, who was dead. He would think about the older boys at the Heights, some graduates of high school, some dropouts—all unemployed or in lousy jobs. Gradually, Jinx's attitude toward school started to change.

JINX: I started hanging around, getting high, just not bother going to school . . . started hanging down Pop's. Cutting, getting high.

JM: What were the reasons behind that? Why'd you start going down to Pop's?

JINX: Friends, friends. . . . I'd go to my classes and meet them at lunch, but when I was with 'em, I'd say, "The hell with it. I ain't even going." Besides, I didn't really care to try in school. . . . You ain't got a chance of getting a good job, even with a high school diploma. You gotta go on to college, get your master's and shit like that to get a good-paying job that you can live comfortably on. So if you're not planning on going to college, I think it's a waste of time.

By his junior year, Jinx attended school only sporadically, and when he did go to class, he was often drunk or high, a necessity if he was to "listen to the teachers talk their shit."

Faced with the need for income to pay for, among other things, his weekly ounce of marijuana, Jinx began to deal drugs on a small scale, stopping only after a close call with the police. After four months of searching and waiting, Jinx landed a job and began working in the afternoons, attending school for a few hours each day. Convinced that school was doing him little good and faced with the opportunity to work full-time, Jinx quit school, only to be laid off shortly thereafter. Although his parents wanted him to finish school, Jinx downplays their influence on him: "They want me to graduate from high school, but I ain't gonna. They'll be mad at me for a week or two, but that's life."

Now that he is out of school, out of work, and out of money, Jinx does not have much to which he can look forward. Nevertheless, he is not as "down and out" as we might think. He has plenty of time for his friends and accepts his predicament placidly, with thorough disrespect neither for the system nor for himself. The situation is, after all, not much different than he had expected.

THE BROTHERS:
INTERNALIZING FAILURE, SHORN OF SELF-ESTEEM

If the mechanisms by which the Hallway Hangers and lads end up in dead-end jobs are somewhat different, the process of social reproduction as it operates with respect to the Brothers presents an even sharper contrast. Applied to the Brothers, Bourdieu's concept of the internalization of objective probabilities does not ring true. Undoubtedly, the Brothers do internalize their chances of "making it," and this calculation certainly moderates their aspirations. Yet, their view of the probabilities for social advancement is informed not only by the objective opportunity structure but also by their parents' hopes for their future and the achievement ideology of the school. In this sense, there is no such thing as the internalization of objective probabilities, for all perceptions of the opportunity structure necessarily are subjective and influenced by a host of intervening factors. The actual habitus of the Brothers is much more complex than Bourdieu and Passeron would have us believe. A theory stressing a correspondence between aspirations and opportunity cannot explain the excessive ambitions of the Brothers because it underestimates the achievement ideology's capacity to mystify structural constraints and encourage high aspirations. The Hallway Hangers reject the achievement ideology, but the situation for the Brothers is quite different.

Like the Hallway Hangers, the Brothers come from families in which their parents either hold jobs that are at the bottom of the occupational structure or are unable to find work at all. An important difference, however, is that, with the exception of Derek, all the Brothers are either the oldest male sibling in the family or have older brothers and sisters who attend college. Thus, the Brothers are not faced with a picture of nearly uniform failure in school. In addition, the parents of the Brothers actually encourage high aspirations in their children, as a tool to motivate them to achieve in school and perhaps as a projection of thwarted ambitions. Thus, from their families, the Brothers take away a contradictory outlook. On the one hand, they see that hard work on the part of their parents has not gotten them very far, an implicit indictment of the openness of the opportunity structure, but on the other hand, they are encouraged by these same people to have high hopes for the future.

For the Brothers, work is an exclusively summertime affair; only Juan is on the job market full-time. Thus, their experience on the labor market is very limited, and that experience has been sheltered from the rigors and uncertainties of finding work. Most of these boys have been enrolled almost exclusively in federal summer youth employment programs and only have had to fill out an application form to be placed in a summer job. Whereas the more extensive contact of the Hallway Hangers with the world of work tends to level their aspirations, a comparable process has not taken place for the Brothers—at least not yet.

The Brothers' peer group does not tend to level their hopes for the future. Because the Brothers do not comprise a distinctive subculture but rather accept the norms and values of the dominant culture and strive to embody them, their peer group does not provide them with a redefinition of success. The Brothers are achievement oriented, prize accomplishments in school and obedience to the law, and measure success as does the rest of society. The ethos of their group encourages high aspirations and reinforces behavior that contributes to the realization of their goals.

The Brothers unconditionally accept the school's achievement ideology, a step that requires a belief in equality of opportunity and the efficacy of schooling. But at the same time that their aspirations tend to rise because of their faith in these precepts, the Brothers are being prepared psychologically for jobs at the bottom of the occupational structure. In low educational tracks and the recipients of poor grades, the Brothers struggle in school. They blame themselves for their mediocre academic performances because they are unaware of the discriminatory influences of tracking, the school's partiality toward the cultural capital of the upper classes, the self-fulfilling consequences of teachers' expectations, and other forms of class-based educational selection. Conditioned by the achievement ideology to think that good jobs require high academic attainment, the Brothers may temper their high aspirations, believing not that the institution of school and the job market have failed them, but that they have failed themselves.

For most of the Brothers, this "cooling-out" process, documented by Burton Clark in his study of a community college,[13] will not be completed until they actually graduate from high school and are face-to-face with the job market. Armed with a high school diploma and a good disciplinary record, the Brothers will have a better chance to land suitable jobs than the Hallway Hangers do, but the Brothers' opportunities still will be quite limited. Juan, the only Brother to have graduated, already has begun to "cool out."

Juan, who left high school with a diploma and a skill (he spent 1,500 hours in school learning culinary arts), has lowered his aspirations significantly after six months of unemployment. Although he previously expressed distaste for a job in auto mechanics because of its association with dirty manual work, Juan now hopes to find work in precisely that area. We can expect many of the Brothers to undergo a similar reorientation after graduation.

From the description of the Brothers' experiences in school it seems clear that the legitimation of inequality is working smoothly for them. In general, the Brothers, without the protection of a peer group with a distinctive subculture, suffer from low self-esteem as a result of their academic performances. In addition, they do not acknowledge the existence of external barriers to their success in school and instead blame themselves for their mediocre performance. We can expect that the same will be true for what may turn out to be their low occupational status.

Whereas the Hallway Hangers are analogous to Willis's lads, the Brothers are closer to the ear'oles. Although our picture is complicated by the variable of ethnicity, the Brothers' experiences illuminate the process of social reproduction as it is undergone by conformist lower-class youth, a subject into which Willis does not delve. Reflecting their acceptance of the achievement ideology and the concomitant notion that all those who are capable can get ahead on their own merits, the Brothers have developed significant ambitions. Relative to the depressed aspirations of the Hallway Hangers, the middle-class aspirations of the Brothers attest to their belief that they are involved in a fair competition. If they fail to get ahead, they will probably attribute their social and economic fate to their own incapabilities, to their own lack of merit.

But we cannot be sure. Will the Brothers and the ear'oles become disillusioned with themselves when they are "cooled out," or will their disillusion encompass the social order as well? This issue demands a longitudinal study spanning a number of years, without which no definite pronouncements are possible. I suspect that although some cynicism about the openness of American society will result, the achievement ideology has been internalized so deeply by the Brothers that their subsequent "careers" will be interpreted in its light. Moreover, if one of the Brothers should be lucky enough to "make it," those who do not will be all the more likely to blame themselves. Far from contradicting the social reproduction perspective, the limited social mobility that does take place in liberal democracies plays a crucial role in the legitimation of inequality. ("If Billy can make it, why can't I? The problem must reside in me.") This "controlled mobility" encourages working-class self-reproach and goes a long way toward explaining why in the United States working-class students with Super's outlook far outnumber those with Jinx's perspective and why in Britain there are more ear'oles than lads.

When Super switched from the Occupational Education Program to House C in the regular academic program, he was placed in the lowest educational tracks for nearly all his subjects because of his low academic performance in grammar school and the fact that switching into the classes in the middle of the semester would have been difficult for him academically. Now in his sophomore year, Super still is enrolled in the "basic" tracks and maintains a high D average.

Super aspires to professional or middle-class work, which reflects his parents' insistence that Super aim for a white-collar job, the premium his peer group places on conventional success, his minimal contact with the job market, and the achievement ideology of the school. Within the course of a year he variously expressed hopes of becoming a doctor, a businessman, or a computer specialist. Reconciling these aspirations with his academic performance is a difficult exercise for Super. At the same time that he affirms the achievement ideology ("It's easy to do anything as long as you set your mind to it") and his own effort ("I swear, I'll be tryin' real hard in school"), Super admits that his performance is lacking ("I just can't seem to do it"). The only explanation left for him is that his own abilities are not up to par, a conclusion that Super accepts, despite its implications for his sense of self-worth. Every lower-class student who internalizes the achievement ideology but struggles in school finds himself or herself in this dilemma. Moreover, the way is clear for lower-class students again to attribute their failure to personal inadequacies when they find themselves in a low-status job. The feeling is a harsh one, but the American school system and the structure of class relations demand that it be borne by many. That Super and the other Brothers feel it strongly is evidence that the legitimation function of the school and the larger process of social reproduction are at work.

If schooling is the training ground at which students are prepared to participate in the race for the jobs of wealth and prestige, the Brothers are being cheated. Told over and over again that the race is a fair one and led to believe that they are given as much attention during the training as anyone, the Brothers step to the starting line for what they see as an equitable race. When the starter's gun goes off and they stumble over the first few hurdles while others streak ahead, they will in all likelihood blame only themselves and struggle to keep going.

The Hallway Hangers see that the race is unfair. They reject official declarations of equity and drop out of the training sessions, convinced that their results will be unsatisfactory no matter how hard they train. They expect to do poorly, and even those who might stand a chance stay back with their friends when the race starts. Instead of banding together, however, and demanding that a fair race be held, the Hallway Hangers never really question the race's rules and simply accept their plight.

This leaves us with an important question: How can the same race be viewed so differently? Why is it that the entrants who have racial as well as class-based hurdles to overcome are the ones who see no hurdles at all?

THE SOURCES OF VARIATION

Although the distinctive processes of social reproduction that have been detailed previously make internal sense, what accounts for the variance between them? What factors contribute to the fundamental incongruity between the two peer groups in the first place? Why is the influence of the family so different for the two peer groups? Why are their experiences in school so dissimilar?

To answer these questions, we must move to a deeper level of analysis that is centered on the role of the achievement ideology. The Hallway Hangers reject this ideology; the Brothers accept it. It is at this point that their paths diverge and the groups experience the process of social reproduction in different ways.

The achievement ideology runs counter to the grain of all these boys' experiences. Neither the residents of their neighborhood nor the members of their families have "made it." In a housing project plagued by unemployment and crime, we might expect both groups of boys to question the existence of equality of opportunity, yet only the Hallway Hangers do so. Of course, they have their own experiences on the job market to which they can point, but this explanation is only of limited value because in most instances they have dismissed the ideology even before experiencing the job market firsthand. The question remains: Why do the Hallway Hangers dismiss the achievement ideology while the Brothers accept it?

The Hallway Hangers reject the achievement ideology because most of them are white. Whereas poor blacks have racial discrimination to which they can point as a cause of their family's poverty, for the Hallway Hangers to accept the achievement ideology is to admit that their parents are lazy or stupid or both. Thus, the achievement ideology not only runs counter to the experiences of the Hallway Hangers, but is also a more serious assault on their self-esteem. Acceptance of the ideology on the part of the Brothers does not necessarily involve such harsh implications, for they can point to racial prejudice to explain their parents' defeats. The severe emotional toll that belief in the achievement ideology exacts on poor whites relative to poor blacks explains why the Hallway Hangers dismiss the ideology while the Brothers validate it.[14]

The Brothers believe the achievement ideology to be an accurate depiction of the opportunity structure as it exists in the United States today because they perceive the racial situation to be substantially different for them than it was for their parents. Whereas their parents were barred from lunch counters and disqualified from the competition before it began, the Brothers see themselves in entirely different circumstances. Mokey's mother, for example, in commenting on Mokey's chances of "making it," says, "I feel Mokey has a equal chance to [be successful], regardless of money or color. That's a chance I never had." We saw in Chapter 5 that of all the Brothers only Juan believes that young blacks face any racial barriers to success. Indeed, it is amazing how often the Brothers affirm the openness of the opportunity structure. Presumably encouraged by perceived gains made in the past two decades, the Brothers seem to believe that equality of opportunity exists today as it did not in their parents' time. This view allows them to accept the achievement ideology without simultaneously indicting their parents. Because the Brothers fully expect to "make it" themselves, embracing the achievement ideology involves little assault on their self-esteem.

This belief that the situation for blacks has improved in the United States also explains why the parents of the Brothers encourage high aspirations in their children while the Hallway Hangers' parents do not. Believing the situation that contributed to their own condition to have changed, the Brothers' parents are convinced that their children have a better chance of "making it" and see no danger in encouraging lofty aspirations. The Hallway Hangers' parents, in contrast, believe that the deck is stacked against their children as it was against them and are wary of supporting unrealistically high aspirations.

Quantitative studies on the generation of ambition have produced equivocal results about whether blacks have higher aspirations than whites from the same socioeconomic background. In general, more recent studies indicate higher aspiration levels for blacks, while those utilizing data from the 1960s and early 1970s find that whites maintain higher aspirations than blacks. The only issue on which there is a consensus among quantitative practitioners is that the aspiration levels of blacks seem to have risen during the past ten to fifteen years,[15] a finding consistent with the attitudes of the Brothers and their families.

A number of factors can account for the increased aspirations of blacks. Because black youths perceive a change in the opportunity structure their parents faced (a change that may or may not have occurred to the degree perceived), they may feel that affirmative action has reduced the occupational handicap of color and that discrimination in employment has abated. Or it may be that the incontrovertible gains of the civil rights movement (e.g., affirmation of basic political and civil rights for blacks, an end to legal Jim Crow segregation, the emergence of black leaders on the national stage) have imbued many blacks with a general sense of progress and improvement that has affected their occupational aspirations. Or political mobilization itself may have created feelings of efficacy and resistance to being "cooled out" that have led to the higher aspirations. To the extent that the civil rights movement was about aspirations and dreams and a refusal to be reduced to hopelessness, blacks may feel that diminutive aspirations are somehow a form of surrender and a betrayal of past gains.

The divergence between how the Brothers and Hallway Hangers react to the achievement ideology is not entirely racial. As I noted in Chapter 4, many of the Hallway Hangers and their families have lived in low-income housing projects for a long period of time, and some have been on public assistance for as many as three generations. This extended duration of tenancy in public housing cannot help but contribute to a feeling of hopelessness and stagnation on the part of the Hallway Hangers. With family histories dominated by failure, the Hallway Hangers' cynicism about the openness of the opportunity structure and their rejection of the achievement ideology are understandable.

The Brothers' situation is quite different. Their families have lived in public housing, on average, for less than half the time the Hallway Hangers' families have. The Brothers' families also have resided in the Clarendon Heights neighborhood for a substantially shorter period of time. Many of the families see their move to the neighborhood as a step up in social status; some families came from worse projects in the area, others from tenement flats in the black ghetto. Moreover, some of the Brothers' parents (Super's, James's, Mokey's) have moved up from the South, bringing with them a sense of optimism and hope about making a fresh start, feelings that have not yet turned into bitterness. For those families that have come to the United States from the West Indies in the past twelve years (Craig's, Juan's), this buoyancy is even stronger. Like the optimism felt by turn-of-the-century immigrants despite their wretched living conditions and the massive barriers to success that they faced, the Brothers' outlook encompasses a sense of improved life chances. Although at the bottom of the social ladder, the Brothers feel that they are part of a collective upward social trajectory, a belief that is conducive to acceptance of the achievement ideology.

Another factor that bears on the Hallway Hangers' rejection of the achievement ideology and the Brothers' acceptance of it is the way in which these peer groups define themselves in relation to one another. The character of the Brothers' peer group is in some measure a reaction to distinctive attributes of the Hallway Hangers. Thus, we can understand, in part, the Brothers' aversion to drugs and alcohol and their general orientation toward achievement as a response to the Hallway Hangers' excessive drinking, use of drugs, and general rejection of the standards and values of the dominant culture. As Super remarks pointing at a group of the Hallway Hangers loitering in doorway #13, "As long as I don't end up like *that*." Having moved into a predominantly white neighborhood that is generally unfriendly toward blacks and having been taunted and abused by a group of disaffected, mostly white boys, the Brothers react by disassociating themselves completely from the Hallway Hangers and by pursuing a distinctly different path—one that leads to success as it is conventionally defined.

For these and other reasons, the Brothers are not representative of poor black teenagers generally. One might discover black peer groups with a similar ethos in other lower-class, predominantly white communities, but if one ventures into any black ghetto, one finds an abundance of black youths hanging in doorways who are pessimistic about the future and cynical about the openness of American society. These youths have formed subcultures with values similar to those of the Hallway Hangers and present a marked contrast to the Brothers in outlook and behavior. The sources of these differences are explored in Chapter 8.

To view the general orientation of the Brothers' peer group as a mere reaction to that of the Hallway Hangers would be a vast oversimplification that fails to account for both the complexity of their reaction to the situation in which they find themselves and their powers of social discernment. We have seen that the Hallway Hangers see through the achievement ideology, not so much because of greater insight into the workings of the system but because of the assault this ideology makes on their self-esteem. The Brothers' acceptance of the ideology and their own individualistic orientations toward achievement are not entirely uncritical. The Brothers are not ideological dupes. They make their own partial "penetrations"[16] into their economic condition, and these insights inform their actions.

The Brothers' decision to "go for it," to work hard in school in pursuit of a decent job, makes a good deal of sense in view of the Hallway Hangers' decision to opt out of the competition. With the number of "good" jobs fixed, one's objective chances increase as individuals remove themselves from contention. Thus, the bipolarity between the Hallway Hangers and the Brothers should not surprise us. In deciding whether to purchase a raffle ticket, the wily individual takes note of how many others are buying them, conscious that the fewer sold, the more sense it makes to purchase one. Lower-class individuals generally do not have a good chance of "making it," but as one social group eschews the contest, others see it in their interest to vie seriously. Where we have a group like the Hallway Hangers, it is only natural that we have a group with the outlook of the Brothers. Willis notes a similar logic in *Learning to Labor:* "The ear'oles' conformism . . . takes on a more rational appearance when judged against the self-disqualification of the lads."[17]

The Brothers' orientation toward individual achievement is even more understandable when we consider affirmative action measures. Although a far cry from what is needed to ameliorate racial injustice in the United States, affirmative action for minorities does increase the Brothers' objective chances of securing stable employment. There is, of course, no analogous measure offered to the lower classes as a whole to mitigate class injustice in the United States, so the anger of the white working class about affirmative action should not surprise us. The perception among whites in Clarendon Heights is that blacks now have an advantage on the job market. There may even be a measure of support for this view among blacks. Chris, for example, believes that although the white boys will face unemployment, his fate could be different: "Watch when I go for a job for the city or something: I'll get it. They'll say, 'Minority—you got the job.'" The Brothers' decision to "buy into" the system also seems to be based on the understanding that, all other things being equal, affirmative action can give them an advantage over their white lower-class peers on the labor market. The sharpening of racial division in the lower classes about affirmative action policies, alluded to throughout this study, also has important political ramifications that are taken up in the final chapter.

There are, then, a number of factors that contribute to the dissimilarity between the Brothers and the Hallway Hangers. The Brothers, who have moved to the northeastern United States within the last generation and recently have moved into public housing, see themselves on a social upswing. This ambiance of ascension is intensified by their impression that racial injustice has been curtailed in the past two decades, thereby making the opportunity structure they face more pliant than the one their parents encountered. The Hallway Hangers have no such grounds for optimism, having been left behind when much of the white working class moved to the suburbs. Whereas Clarendon Heights seems a step up for the Brothers' families, the Hallway Hangers believe they cannot slide much lower. Hailing from families who have resided in the projects for many years, some in Clarendon Heights for three generations, the Hallway Hangers feel that little has changed and consequently are despondent about their own futures. We also might point to variances in the families of the two groups as a source of their divergent outlooks. The Brothers' family members, especially their older siblings, have achieved a slightly higher status in terms of educational and occupational achievement than have the Hallway Hangers' family members.

Although all these factors contribute to the optimism of the Brothers and the pessimism of the Hallway Hangers, they do not in themselves account for the wide disparity between the two groups, nor do they explain the distinctive subculture of the Hallway Hangers. This oppositional culture partially shelters the Hallway Hangers from the abnegations of the dominant society, the negative judgments they sustain as poor members of an ostensibly open society. The Brothers are pained by these appraisals, too, of course, but the achievement ideology represents a more potent assault on the Hallway Hangers because as white youths they can point to no extenuating circumstances to account for their poverty. The subculture of the Hallway Hangers is in part a response to the stigma they feel as poor, white Americans. Finally, the differences between the two groups seem to be amplified by their tendencies to define themselves in relation (i.e., in opposition) to one another.

Where are these two paths likely to lead? In all probability, the Brothers will be better off than the Hallway Hangers. With a high school diploma, a positive attitude, and a disciplined readiness for the rigors of the workplace, the Brothers should be capable of landing steady jobs. An individual or two may work his way into a professional or managerial occupation, and a few might slide into a state of chronic unemployment, but the odds are that most of the Brothers will end up members of the stable working class, generally employed in jobs that are toward the bottom of the occupational ladder but that afford some security.

The Hallway Hangers probably will end up quite differently. Dependent on alcohol or drugs or both, disaffected and rebellious, and without qualifications in a credential-based job market, the Hallway Hangers generally will end up as Slick predicts: "They're not gonna be more than janitors or, y'know, goin' by every day tryin' to get a buck." An alcoholic himself, who becomes more despondent every day that he remains unemployed, Slick may well meet the same fate, despite his exceptional intelligence and articulate nature.

Of course, the Hallway Hangers do not deny that upward social mobility is possible. Their rejection of school was based not on the premise that they could not succeed but on the premise that the prospects for limited social mobility did not warrant the attempt, given the costs involved in the try. This is a calculation they all now have come to question. Having experienced life on the streets without a job, the Hallway Hangers generally indicate that if they had it to do over again, they would apply themselves in school.

JM: Would you do anything different if you could do it over again?

(all in separate interviews)

BOO-BOO: Yeah, lots. Wouldn't screw up in school as bad as I did, wouldn't get high with my friends as much.

CHRIS: I dunno, man, wouldn't fuck up in school. I guess I shoulda learned to live with their shit. It's just the way I am. Like, if I decide, if I say I'm not going to do something, I don't give a fuck what they do to me. I'm not going to do it. That's just the way I am. I guess that's what's gonna fuck me over in the long run.

FRANKIE: Yeah, definitely. I wouldn't have fucked up as much. I coulda been a—I fucked it up for myself, maybe. Maybe I woulda tried going to school more. But still, I don't think I woulda come out much better. So, y'know, just fuckin' bein' less rude to people, truthfully.

STEVE: Yeah, I'd make sure I got more credits my freshman year. I only got five fucking credits, man. That's rough to fuckin' jump back on and shit. It's a bitch.

JINX: I'd probably get more interested in school, but it's too late now.

Almost any price would be worth paying to avoid the pain and misery of hopelessness at such a young age.

NOTES

1. Maureen Anne Scully, "Coping with Meritocracy" (Thesis, Harvard College, 1982), p. 6.

2. Max Weber, *Economy and Society* (Berkeley: University of California Press, 1970), p. 953.

3. Karl Marx and Friedrich Engels, *The German Ideology* (New York: International Publishers, 1947), pp. 65–66.

4. Scully, "Coping with Meritocracy," p. 3.

5. James Rosenbaum, *Making Inequality* (New York: Wylie and Sons, 1976).

6. Pierre Bourdieu and Jean-Claude Passeron, *Reproduction in Education, Society, and Culture* (London: Sage, 1977), p. 156.

7. Richard Sennett and Jonathan Cobb, *The Hidden Injuries of Class* (New York: Vintage Books, 1972).

8. Scully, "Coping with Meritocracy," p. 83.

9. Ibid., p. 85.

10. Elliot Liebow, *Talley's Corner* (Boston: Little, Brown, 1967), p. 209.

11. Antonio Gramsci, *Selections from Prison Notebooks* (London: Lawrence and Wishart, 1971).

12. Michael Mann, "The Social Cohesion of Liberal Democracy," *American Sociological Review* 35 (June 1970): 423–439.

13. Burton Clark, "The 'Cooling Out' Function in Higher Education," *American Journal of Sociology* 65 (1960): 576–596.

14. I am not arguing that blacks living in poverty are psychologically better off than their white counterparts. Given the internalized effects of racism on blacks, such is clearly not the case. It is only in considering the effect of the achievement

ideology alone that I am making a comparative statement about the emotional suffering of poor blacks and poor whites.

15. Kenneth I. Spenner and David L. Featherman, "Achievement Ambitions," *Annual Review of Sociology* 4 (1978): 388.

16. The term, of course, is borrowed from Willis, who first directed my attention to the penetrations of the Brothers after reading a draft of the book.

17. Paul Willis, *Learning to Labor* (Aldershot: Gower, 1977), p. 148.

8

REPRODUCTION THEORY RECONSIDERED

The theoretical literature composing reproduction theory was discussed in Chapter 2. Conceptualizing reproduction theory as a spectrum, with one end dominated by economically determinist theories and the other by theories asserting the autonomy of the cultural level, we reviewed the work of Bowles and Gintis on the determinist end of the spectrum and progressed through the theories of Bourdieu, Bernstein and Heath, and Willis and Giroux at the other end of the spectrum. Having examined in detail the specific mechanisms of the process of social reproduction as they occur in one low-income neighborhood, we are now in a position to assess the cogency of the theories outlined in the second chapter and to develop a revised theoretical perspective.

BUILDING ON BOURDIEU

This book's basic finding—that two substantially different paths are followed within the general framework of social reproduction—is a major challenge to economically determinist theories. Two groups of boys from the same social stratum who live in the same housing project and attend the same school nevertheless experience the process of social reproduction in fundamentally different ways. This simple fact alone calls into question many of the theoretical formulations of Bowles and Gintis. If social class is the overriding determinant in social reproduction, what accounts for the variance in the process between the Brothers and Hallway Hangers? Bowles and Gintis, in considering a single school, maintain that social reproduction takes place primarily through educational tracking. Differential socialization through educational tracking prepares working-class students for working-class jobs and middle-class students for middle-class jobs. But the Hallway Hangers and the Brothers, who are from the same social class background and exposed to the curricular structure of the school in the same manner, undergo the process of social reproduction in substantially different ways. The theory of Bowles and Gintis cannot explain this difference.

Bowles and Gintis do give an excellent account of the hidden structural and ideological determinants that constrain working-class students and socialize them for positions at the bottom of the heap. What the Brothers and Hallway Hangers demonstrate quite clearly, however, is the open-ended manner in which individuals and groups respond to structures of domination. Although there is no way to avoid class-based constraints, the outcomes are far from predefined. As posited by Bowles and Gintis, the fairly rigid structural correspondence between the educational and economic systems is simplistic and overdetermined. As Giroux points out, human subjects are viewed from this perspective as passive role bearers shaped by the demands of capital. Student nonconformity and oppositional behavior are not acknowledged. "What is disregarded in the notion of 'correspondence' is not only the issue of resistance, but also any attempt to delineate the complex ways in which working-class subjectivities are constituted. . . . We are presented with a homogenous image of working-class life fashioned solely by the logic of domination."[1] Bowles and Gintis pay scant attention to the active, creative role of individual and group praxes. Their work, like much social research, tends to treat categories such as the working class as undifferentiated monoliths. Although Bowles and Gintis break important ground by examining how the process of schooling reinforces relations of dominance and inequality among classes, their theory ultimately is too crudely deterministic to capture the complexity of social reproduction.

Paul Willis approaches the issue of social reproduction from the other end, so to speak: He begins with the lads themselves—with their concrete lived experiences and complex, often contradictory attitudes. To his credit, he goes to great lengths to understand the cultural dispositions and practices of the lads on their own terms before linking his ethnographic material with the structural requirements of capitalism. Willis resists the temptation to force the link between culture and structure in a false, facile manner. His ethnography does uncover the local and embedded manifestations of larger socially reproductive forces, but only after a long detour into the lived culture of the lads. For Willis, that is the only route that will work. And it does work stunningly in his story of how the lads simultaneously resist and collude in their class subjugation. But by considering only the nonconformist lads in his study, Willis is hard-pressed to illuminate the purely institutional mechanisms that constrain the social mobility of working-class individuals. And his insistence on the autonomy of culture means that his actual account of how the lads end up in manual labor occupations is remarkably free of attention to structurally embedded constraints.

The interface between the cultural and the structural is critical to our understanding of social reproduction. To capture this relationship, the agency-structure dualism must be bridged by an analysis of the interpenetration of human consciousness and structural determinants. Macro models that demonstrate the extent to which status is inherited and quantitative studies that measure how educational, occupational, and income structures mediate the effect of class origins are not enough. Such projects merely set the context for beginning to wrestle with the real issues of how social structures capture agents' minds and control their attitudes and how individuals resist and succumb to the inertial pressure of structural forces. Aspirations provide a conceptual link between structure and agency in that they are rooted firmly in individual proclivity (agency) but also are acutely sensitive to perceived societal constraints (structure).

According to his disciples, Bourdieu's concept of habitus dissolves the distinction between structure and agency and points the way forward.[2] The habitus, as understood by Giroux, comprises "the subjective dispositions which reflect a class-based social grammar of taste, knowledge, and behavior inscribed in ... each developing person."[3] In Bourdieu's scheme, habitus bridges the perennial poles in social thinking: micro and macro, agency and structure, volition and constraint, internal and external. (Interpreting Bourdieu, Wacquant states that habitus "effects, from within, the reactivation of the meanings and relations objectified 'without' as institutions."[4]) Basically, Bourdieu believes that people absorb from their social universe values and beliefs that guide their actions. Like the basketball player who instinctively cuts to the hoop to receive a pass, people do not stop and think about their actions, nor can they explain why they undertook them. They learn to act and react not from explicit teaching but from experience, from thousands of street games, from subtle cues on the court, from "clicking" with their teammates. As Richard Jenkins relates, "The power of the habitus derives from the thoughtlessness of habit and habituation, rather than consciously learned rules and principles. Socially competent performances are produced as a matter of routine, without explicit reference to a body of codified knowledge, and without the actors necessarily 'knowing what they are doing.'"[5]

Habitus is a clever concept, but it is also a slippery one. I have yet to discover from Bourdieu's own writings *how* the habitus mediates between structure and practice. Clearly, objective and external constraints from above shape the habitus, which then shapes the practices of agents below. Clearly, causality also runs in the other direction. But just how does this dialectical process work? Does the habitus merely dispose individuals to act in certain ways, or does the habitus virtually guarantee structurally prescribed and socially reproductive outcomes? Depending on how it is mined, Bourdieu's mass of empirical and theoretical work provides different (and confusing, if not confused) answers to these questions.

On the issue of aspirations, Bourdieu and Passeron's theoretical formulations in *Reproduction in Education, Society and Culture* imply a circular relationship whereby objective probabilities are internalized as subjective hopes that reinforce structures of constraint.[6] Working-class individuals develop depressed aspirations that mirror their actual chances for social advancement, and then these stunted aspirations effectively seal the social immobility and continued subjugation of the working class. But a closed loop between structure and agency is incompatible with the findings of the present study. The Brothers, whose objective life chances were originally lower than those of the Hallway Hangers because of racial barriers to success, nevertheless nurture higher aspirations than do the Hallway Hangers. By emphasizing structural determinants at the expense of mediating factors that influence subjective renderings of objective probabilities, Bourdieu and Passeron presume too mechanistic and simplistic a relationship between aspiration and opportunity. Their theory fails to fathom the numerous factors that lie between and mediate the influence of social class on individuals.

Fieldwork with the Algerian proletariat and the French bourgeoisie, on the other hand, prompts Bourdieu to acknowledge how complex and contingent the relationship between objective life chances and subjective aspirations can be. Although Bourdieu never gives an adequate sense of the internal structure of the habitus, his varied empirical work suggests that, although habitus is primarily a function of social class, other factors can be incorporated into it. For example, he differentiates people not only by class and gender but also by whether they come from Paris or not. On my readings, habitus is constituted at the level of the family, and factors such as ethnicity, educational history, peer associations, neighborhood social ecology, and demographic characteristics (e.g., geographical mobility, duration of tenancy in public housing, sibling order, and family size) are all constitutive of the habitus. Bourdieu himself alludes to the interplay of mediations within the habitus: "The habitus acquired in the family underlies the structuring of school experiences, and the habitus transformed by schooling, itself diversified, in turn underlies the structuring of all subsequent experiences (e.g., the reception and assimilation of the messages of the culture industry or work experiences), and so on, from restructuring to restructuring."[7] When understood along these lines, the concept of habitus becomes flexible enough to accommodate the interactions among ethnicity, family, schooling, work experiences, and peer associations that have been documented in this book. Indeed, Bourdieu's notion of habitus is quite helpful in understanding the Brothers and the Hallway Hangers. As Bourdieu predicts, the habitus discreetly integrates individuals into a social world geared to the interests of the ruling classes; habitus engenders attitudes and conduct that are compatible with the reproduction of class inequality.

FROM ETHNOGRAPHY TO THEORY

Once we descend into the world of actual human lives, we must take our theoretical bearings to make some sense of the social landscape, but in doing so we invariably find that the theories are incapable of accounting for much of what we see. The lives of the Hallway Hangers and the Brothers cannot be reduced to structural influences or causes; although structural forces weigh upon the individuals involved, it is necessary, in the words of Willis, "to give the social agents involved some meaningful scope for viewing, inhabiting, and constructing their own world in a way which is recognizably human and not theoretically reductive."[8] We must appreciate both the importance and the relative autonomy of the cultural level at which individuals, alone or in concert with others, wrest meaning out of the flux of their lives.

The possibilities open to these boys as lower-class teenagers are limited structurally from the outset. That they internalize the objective probabilities for social advancement to some degree is beyond question. The process by which this takes place, however, is influenced by a whole series of intermediate factors. Because gender is constant in the study discussed in these pages, race is the principal variable affecting the way in which these youths view their situation. Ethnicity introduces new structurally determined constraints on social mobility, but it also serves as a mediation through which the limitations of class are refracted and thus apprehended and understood differently by different racial groups. The Brothers comprehend and react to their situation in a manner entirely different from the response the Hallway Hangers make to a similar situation; ethnicity introduces a new dynamic that makes the Brothers more receptive to the achievement ideology. Their acceptance of this ideology affects their aspirations but also influences, in tandem with parental encouragement, their approach to school and the character of their peer group, factors that in turn bear upon their aspirations.

If we modify the habitus by changing the ethnicity variable and altering a few details of family occupational and educational histories and duration of tenancy in public housing, we would have the Hallway Hangers. As white lower-class youths, the Hallway Hangers view and interpret their situation in a different light, one that induces them to reject the achievement ideology and to develop aspirations and expectations quite apart from those the ideology attempts to generate. The resultant perspective, which is eventually reinforced by the Hallway Hangers' contact with the job market, informs the boys' approach to school and helps us understand the distinctive attributes of this peer group. Thus, although social class is of primary importance, there are intermediate factors at work that, as constitutive of the habitus, shape the subjective responses of the two groups of boys and produce quite different expectations and actions.

Having grown up in an environment where success is not common, the Hallway Hangers see that the connection between effort and reward is not as clear-cut as the achievement ideology would have them believe. Because it runs counter to the evidence in their lives and because it represents a forceful assault on their self-esteem, the Hallway Hangers repudiate the achievement ideology. Given that their parents are inclined to see the ideology in the same light, they do not counter their sons' rejection of the American Dream.

A number of important ramifications follow from the Hallway Hangers' denial of the dominant ideology: the establishment of a peer group that provides alternative means of generating self-esteem, the rejection of school and antagonism toward teachers, and, of course, the leveling of aspirations. In schematizing the role of the peer group, it is difficult not to appear tautological, for the group does wield a reciprocal influence on the boys: It attracts those who are apt to reject school and the achievement ideology and those with low aspirations and then deepens these individuals' initial proclivities and further shapes them to fit the group. But at the same time, the peer subculture itself, handed down from older to younger boys, is the product of the particular factors that structure the lives of white teenagers in Clarendon Heights.

In addition to the peer group, the curricular structure of the school solidifies the low aspirations of the Hallway Hangers by channeling them into programs that prepare students for manual labor jobs. Low aspirations, in turn, make the Hallway Hangers more likely to dismiss school as irrelevant. Once they are on the job market, the Hallway Hangers' inability to secure even mediocre jobs further dampens their occupational hopes. Thus, although each individual ultimately retains autonomy in the subjective interpretation of his situation, the leveled aspirations of the Hallway Hangers are to a large degree a response to the limitations of social class as they are manifest in the Hallway Hangers' social world.

The Brothers' social class origins are only marginally different from those of the Hallway Hangers. Being black, the Brothers also must cope with racially rooted barriers to success that, affirmative action measures notwithstanding, structurally inhibit the probabilities for social advancement, although to a lesser degree than do shared class limitations. What appears to be a comparable objective situation to that of the Hallway Hangers, however, is apprehended in a very different manner by the Brothers.

As black teenagers, the Brothers interpret their families' occupational and educational records in a much different light than do the Hallway Hangers. Judging by the Brothers' constant affirmation of equality of opportunity, the boys believe that racial injustice has been curbed in the United States in the past twenty years. Whereas in their parents' time the link between effort and reward was very tenuous for blacks, the Brothers, in keeping with the achievement ideology, see the connection today as very strong: "If you work hard, it'll pay off in the end" (Craig). Hence, the achievement ideology is more compatible with the Brothers' attitudes than with those of the Hallway Hangers, for whom it cannot succeed against overwhelming contrary evidence. The ideology is not as emotionally painful for the Brothers to accept because past racial discrimination can help account for their families' poverty, whereas the Hallway Hangers, if the ideology stands, are afforded no explanation outside of laziness and stupidity for their parents' failures. The optimism that acceptance of the achievement ideology brings for the Brothers is encouraged and reinforced by their parents. Thus, we see how in the modified habitus ethnicity affects the Brothers' interpretation of their social circumstances and leads to acceptance of the achievement ideology, with all the concomitant results.

Chief among these results is a positive attitude toward education that influences the Brothers' relations with teachers and reaction to the curricular structure of the school, thereby making it less likely for the boys to select a future in manual work via a vocational program. Their validation of the achievement ideology also affects the ethos of their peer group, which in turn influences each individual's orientation toward school as well as his aspirations. Because their contact with the job market has been minimal, the Brothers have yet to undergo experiences that might upset or alter their perspective. Once they graduate from high school, the Brothers probably will need to temper their aspirations as Juan has done. Whether they begin to question the achievement ideology and the openness of American society or whether they reproach themselves for frustrated ambition remains to be seen. From a political perspective this is an intriguing question, but from a sociological angle what is equally fascinating is the way ethnicity mediates the limitations of class, thereby creating a refractive effect that catalyzes the Brothers to construct meaning out of their existence in an entirely different manner from the Hallway Hangers.

A fundamental aspect of habitus (but hidden in this book because of its constancy) is gender. As boys, the Hallway Hangers can inhabit a subculture whose values receive a good deal of validation from the dominant culture. The cultural inversion employed to turn "bad" into good is based on a valuation of machismo taken to the extreme. Being tough, "cool," and defiant all derive from an overstated pride in masculinity, an ideal portrayed by a whole series of Hollywood actors. The Hallway Hangers exaggerate and manipulate this ideal, investing it with new dimensions until it is so distorted that John Grace can embody it. Lacking in nearly every category that defines success in America, the Hallway Hangers latch onto and inflate the one quality they still have: their masculinity.

Girls from Clarendon Heights experience and manipulate the structural forces of class, race, and gender in their own ways. Although we have no original empirical material to inform our analysis, a rich ethnographic study, undertaken by Jane K. Rosegrant in Clarendon Heights itself, offers us invaluable information on how lower-class girls understand their circumstances and what types of action proceed from these interpretations.

Rosegrant delves into the life histories of five women from Clarendon Heights in an attempt to determine the combined importance of the "distinct, yet intertwined threads of influence"[9] of class and gender on their lives. Although small, her sample cuts across racial lines, encompassing three whites, one black, and one Latina. These women and their daughters are subject to even more structural limitations than are the boys in this book because they have to contend with patriarchy as a mode of domination as well as class and race. Women in Clarendon Heights face a future that holds out little promise. Resolution of the structural forces acting on girls in Clarendon Heights, however, is radically different than for boys because, among other things, girls can realize a goal that seems to promise them freedom from the forces by which they, like the Hallway Hangers, feel trapped.

> It is at this juncture that the "mothering option" raises its head. As teenagers, the women of this study . . . underwent the same hardships and lived the same stigma that their brothers felt. Certainly they knew their families were poor, that they were living different lives than the ones they saw depicted on T.V., and that somehow it was their parents'—especially their father's—"fault" that they were in this position. They certainly felt bad when they did poorly in school and they did not look forward to the jobs they would hold in their lifetimes—work at least as dull as that for which the boys were headed. However, the girls could react to these pressures and find a respite from them, that the boys could not. Within the mainstream of our society, a clearly defined and lauded path existed which they could follow. Thanks to this "escape route," the girls were not forced to cope with an overwhelming image of themselves, either personal or societal, as failures. No matter how poorly they performed in school, or how dismal their employment outlook might have been, they had a route to respectability. The importance the aspiration to mother had in their lives can not be overestimated. In the midst of their often tumultuous childhoods, it gave them something concrete to cling to. Unlike their fathers, brothers and boyfriends, they were headed for a future they desired, one of which society supposedly approved. They could be mothers, and nothing and no one could keep them from realizing this goal.[10]

Rosegrant's finding is substantiated by the daughters of these women as well. When she asked these adolescent girls to what jobs they aspire, they were all indifferent about their future work roles but were unequivocal in their desire for children, despite their mothers' advice to the contrary. The response from eleven-year-old Sara is especially instructive: "Me? No, I want to get pregnant when I'm sixteen. Get an apartment, have a baby." One girl whose performance in school is exceptionally good nevertheless states, "I don't wanna go to college; I wanna have four kids."[11] While the Hallway Hangers attempt to escape the forces bearing upon them through the protection of their peer group with its celebration of masculinity, the girls look to parenthood and maternity.

As we might expect, however, the relief that mothering seems to hold out is largely illusory. Although none of the women in Rosegrant's study regretted having children, they all came quickly to the painful realization that being poor and a parent (usually a single one) is fraught with inestimable difficulties. As important as the practical burdens motherhood imposes is the denial these women felt when they failed to receive the respect that had been promised them. "If the Hallway Hangers of MacLeod's study felt betrayed by society as teens coping with school and work, these women come to feel this betrayal as young women coping with motherhood. They had done what they understood they were supposed to do—either willingly or by default—but society seemed to be reneging on its part of the deal."[12]

If motherhood, in spite of its promise, offers no relief from the structural forces impinging on lower-class girls, neither can girls expect consolation from a supportive peer group. Whereas the boys can construct a subculture offering alternative ways of maintaining some self-respect and dignity, the girls have no such avenue open to them. Consider the conclusion Anne Campbell draws from her extensive research on the lives of girls in New York street gangs.

> For these girls, there was no escape in the gang from the problems they faced: their female role could not be circumvented, their instability remained and was magnified, their isolation was covered by a rough veneer. The gang was no alternative life for them. It was a microcosm of the society beyond. Granted, it was one that had a public image of rebellion and excitement and offered a period of distraction (discussions of gang feuds and honor and death). But in the end, gang or no gang, the girls remained alone with their children, still trapped in poverty and in a cultural dictate of womanhood from which there was no escape.[13]

Denied the camaraderie and solidarity that "male bonding" affords the boys, girls in Clarendon Heights fulfill the roles that patriarchal society defines for them, particularly the role of "girlfriend," which effectively keeps them divided, dependent, and subordinate. Nonconformist girls may well drop out of the race but without the solace of a closely knit peer group that has modified definitions of success. In such a predicament, it is no wonder that the option of motherhood seems attractive.

Another case that demands our attention is the situation of blacks at the very bottom of the socioeconomic strata who react to their predicament in much the same way as do the Hallway Hangers. What aspects of their habitus produce an outcome so different from that of the Brothers? Across the city in the projects housing mostly black and Latino families, one finds an abundance of black youths "hanging" in doorways, pessimistic about the future and cynical about the American Dream. Because they share with the Brothers the three main structural variables of social class, race, and gender, we must look to other factors making up the habitus to understand the differences between the Brothers and their black peers across the city.

For a start, their family occupational and educational histories are slightly more desolate, and there is often a more extended stay in public housing (two or three generations). Living in a neighborhood where black failure (by conventional criteria) is ubiquitous, these boys are likely to view the economic gains of the civil rights movement as illusory. For them affirmative action is a token gesture that has little bearing on their lives—when the deck is stacked against you, being dealt one face card hardly guarantees a winning hand. Because they view the conditions that contributed to their parents' demise as largely intact, the ethnicity variable does not have the same refractive effect it has for the Brothers. Without the ambiance of improved life chances, the achievement ideology rubs harder against the grain of these boys' experiences, thereby spurring them to reject the dominant ideology, disassociate themselves from school, and organize themselves into peer groups with an ethos much different from that of the Brothers. Because these project youths see the path to conventional achievement as blocked and because they are susceptible to racially rooted negative judgments by the dominant culture, it should come as no surprise that they form protective peer subcultures whose evaluative criteria are much like those by which the Hallway Hangers measure success. To be bad is to be successful, at least in the limited sphere of one's peer group. Despite the class, race, and gender variables these boys share with the Brothers, the internal structure of their habitus is substantially different and gives rise to different expectations and actions.

This schematization of intermediate factors between the structural determinants of social class and individual social actors explains a great deal of the empirical material this ethnographic inquiry has uncovered. This depiction of the social landscape inhabited by lower-class teenagers accommodates both the Hallway Hangers and Brothers as well as other social groups about which we have limited empirical data. We also should be able to locate and make sense of the situation of individuals on this social map.

INDIVIDUALS IN THE SOCIAL LANDSCAPE

Boo-Boo and Derek pose an interesting challenge. Not only do they share the variables of class, race, and gender, but these two boys are also from the same family, yet have completely different outlooks on their futures. Because the boys have different fathers, their early home lives were somewhat varied. The crucial point of divergence, however, was Derek's acquisition of a federal scholarship to attend Barnes Academy after third grade. Enrollment at a prestigious private school not only objectively raised Derek's chances for success by providing him with a superior education and new opportunities—it also meant an entirely different form of socialization than that which Boo-Boo and other boys from the neighborhood were undergoing at the local grammar school. Derek was in white, upper-class educational environs for most of the day and spent most of his free time with his Barnes Academy friends. Thus, the two brothers had radically different peer associations. While Derek was spending his summers sightseeing around Texas, Mexico, and Martha's Vineyard with a rich friend and his family, Boo-Boo was hanging in the project with the Hallway Hangers. Both boys, although hesitant to speak about each other, draw attention to their different peers as an important source of variance between them.

JM: How'd you end up hanging with Frankie and them?

BOO-BOO: When I was in school, they was in school. My brother went to Barnes, started hanging with other kids. When he started hanging down here, Juan and Craig were around.

(in a separate interview)

JM: Why do you think your brother hangs with them [the Hallway Hangers]?

DEREK: I don't know. . . . I only started hanging with Super and Mokey and everybody a couple of years ago. Before that, I hung up by Mirror Lake with the guys from Barnes.

Thus, although the main variables of class, race, gender, and family are the same for Boo-Boo and Derek, the differences in other factors making up the habitus, especially schooling and peer associations, readily account for the existing disparity between the brothers.

Billy, the boy who has won a scholarship to attend college, also presents us with a challenge, for he used to be indistinguishable from the Hallway Hangers. He is still friendly with Jinx, Slick, and Frankie and speaks matter-of-factly about his early years in high school.

BILLY: I was getting high with them [the Hallway Hangers], having fun with them, cutting classes. . . . We all hung together. We all used to go out during lunch, about ten of us, get smashed. I'm serious. We'd come back hardly able to stand up and go to shop [Oc. Ed.]. . . . I used to smoke dope every single day. I swear to God, I don't think I went one day without smoking. Then I just went home, went to sleep, wake up, get high, go to sleep.

Billy's family background is similar to that of the other boys as well. Neither parent graduated from high school or worked regularly. But the death of his father and separation from his mother altered his family in a drastic way and thus instigated a reorientation of other intermediate factors that resulted in an outcome far different than that for most of the Hallway Hangers.

The upheavals in his family situation coupled with the brutal murder of his best friend somehow touched off a spark in Billy to buck the odds and "make something" of himself. "I want to become successful in life. I wanna be someone, y'know? I don't wanna live in a housing development or anything like that." In keeping with his suddenly high aspirations, Billy embraced the achievement ideology at the same time his peers were coming to reject it. "Do I have an equal chance to make it as some richer kid? Yeah, I have an equal chance as anyone does. You can be the smartest person if you want to be, unless you have some disabilities, cuz all it takes is hard work and study."

Having chosen Oc. Ed. in eighth grade because "it was the thing to do back then. All my friends, all people from where I live—that's where everyone was,"

Billy began to work hard in school. He gradually drifted away from the Hallway Hangers, stopped smoking marijuana, and earned a spot on the high school hockey team as the varsity goalie. This, in turn, led to a whole new set of friends with different values and a different lifestyle, a change about which Frankie comments.

FRANKIE: Yeah, Billy figured what the fuck, man. He said, "Hey, now I got a chance to fucking do something," and he did it. Good luck to him, y'know? I think he pulled a good move cuz he used to get high and shit all the time. . . . Now he started playing hockey, y'know, and met a lot of kids on the team, ended up hanging with them. That's good, y'know? Hang with them and these dudes are all the time trying to get good grades. Y'know, Billy said, "What the fuck, I'll check this out."

Jinx and Chris see Billy in the same way.

JM: Do you think any of your friends will go to college?

JINX: I think one might.

CHRIS: Billy?

JINX: Yeah, that's about it.

JM: Does he still hang with you guys at all?

CHRIS: No, and that's the only reason [that he might make it to college].

JINX: He used to hang with us.

CHRIS: He used to fuck up.

JINX: Like eighth grade, ninth grade. Then he just started going to school, doing all his work, started being by himself.

CHRIS: I think because his father died, mostly. He just said, "I wanna do something good with my life."

Billy won a scholarship and plans to attend a small liberal arts college next year. He may well "make it" and leave behind his old friends, the Hallway Hangers: "I think I'll come back five years from now and I'll see eight out of ten of them still hanging in doorway #13, bummin' money, doing nuttin."

Because his life illustrates the interplay among family, school, and peer group, Billy is a perfect example of the importance of mediating variables in the habitus and the complex relationships that exist among the various factors. If one variable is changed, it upsets the balance of the habitus, and the consequences can ripple through the other intermediate forces, changing all the interactions to mold a different outcome. Billy had some distinctive familial experiences that altered his aspirations. Changed aspirations led to new attitudes and behavior (in particular new interactions with peers and school), which led in turn to further alterations in expectation and action. Instead of hanging in doorway #13 next year, Billy expects to be settled on a college campus.

CULTURAL AUTONOMY WITHIN STRUCTURAL CONSTRAINTS

By taking as our starting point the peer cultures of Clarendon Heights and working upward from ethnography to analysis, we have discovered how a number of factors mediate the influence of social class on the individual actors at the cultural level. As long as Bourdieu's concept of habitus is fleshed out empirically and deepened theoretically to accommodate these factors, it is a valuable descriptive device for understanding the social world of Clarendon Heights. Individuals, with their distinctive assets and character traits, have a good deal of autonomy. But although we can in no way predict with confidence the precise effect a particular change in habitus will have on people, the factors that frame their existence and from which they derive meaning go a long way toward explaining their outlooks and behavior patterns.

Structural features of class, racial, and gender domination permeate American society, but this book has been concerned especially with class-based constraints embedded in the educational system. The school's valuation of the cultural capital of the upper classes and its depreciation of the cultural capital of the lower classes are the most important mechanisms of social reproduction within the educational system, but the discriminatory effects of tracking and of teachers' expectations also inhibit the academic performance of lower-class students. No matter how students from the lower classes respond, the dynamic of the race for the jobs of wealth and prestige remains unchanged. Although a restricted number of individuals of working-class origin may overcome the barriers to success, the rules of the race severely limit and constrain these individuals' mobility.

My analysis of the aspirations of the Brothers and Hallway Hangers shows clearly the autonomy individuals possess in their response to this received structure of domination. How poor youths react to an objective situation that is weighted heavily against them depends on a number of mediating factors and ultimately is contingent. The Hallway Hangers' leveled aspirations demonstrate the extent to which structural constraints can impinge directly on individual attitudes. Confronting what they regard as a closed opportunity structure, the Hallway Hangers attach very little significance to their own occupational preferences in formulating their aspirations. Thus, we see how structure can reach into human consciousness to encourage dispositions that ensure the reproduction of class inequality. With respect to the Hallway Hangers, Bourdieu's perspective is vindicated.

The higher occupational aspirations of the Brothers, on the other hand, indicate that the connection between objective structure and subjective attitudes is tenuous; ideology can cloud, distort, and conceal the mechanisms of social reproduction. Although structural determinants shape the aspirations of the Hallway Hangers, the Brothers attest to the power of ideology to mold perceptions. Cognizant of no external barriers to success, the Brothers consistently affirm the achievement ideology and the actuality of equality of opportunity. High aspirations may result from a capitalist society's contradictory need to present an ideology of openness and equal opportunity at the same time that the underlying structure of class relations is maintained. However, the Hallway Hangers prove that ideological hegemony is not a fait accompli; such hegemony often is contested and is realized only partially.

Although individuals can interpret and respond to constraint in different ways, they must still face the effects of class domination. As Giroux reminds us, "While school cultures may take complex and heterogeneous forms, the principle that remains constant is that they are situated within a network of power relations from which they cannot escape."[14] Cultural practices operate within the limits defined by class, gender, and racial barriers. In terms of the immediate perpetuation of class inequality, it matters little how lower-class teenagers respond to the vicissitudes of their situation. No matter how clearly they understand their lives, no matter what cultural innovations they produce, no matter how diligently they devote themselves to school, they cannot escape the constraints of social class. Conformists accept the ideology and act within the system but come up against the barriers of class; only a few break through. Nonconformists balk and do no better; in effect, they withdraw from the system, never test its limits, and generally find themselves in worse shape.

Structuralist theories are of value because they can show quite clearly why the end result turns out to be much the same, but in doing so they often obliterate human agency by ignoring "the complex ways in which people mediate and respond to the interface between their own lived experiences and structures of domination and constraint."[15] Culturalist theories give us a sense of the texture of individual lives but too often fail to contextualize attitudes and behavior as responses to objective structures. Giroux's insistence on a dialectical treatment of subjectivity and structure is correct: "Determination and human agency presuppose each other in situations that represent a setting-of-limits on the resources and opportunities of different classes. Men and women inherit these pre-defined circumstances, but engage them in a 'process of meaning-making which is always active' (Bennett 1981), and leaves their results open-ended."[16]

The results may be contingent, but neither of the outcomes documented in this study is positive. It is an open question whether the Hallway Hangers or the Brothers are worse off. The Brothers' mobility is defined by structural constraints that probably will result in the boys' entry into the stable working class. Because the institutional mechanisms of social reproduction hinder rather than block the Brothers' mobility, one or two of the Brothers may even break into the middle class. However, unaware of the constraints (but subject to their effects), the Brothers are prone to blame themselves for their plight. The Hallway Hangers, in contrast, see through the ideology, perceive the constraints, and realize the futility of high aspirations. They salvage some self-esteem but in the process forfeit any chance for individual social advancement. In a sense, cultural innovations like those of the lads or Hallway Hangers aid the process of social reproduction because nonconformists often relegate themselves to the bottom of the pile.

From a wider standpoint, however, the Hallway Hangers, who see with a certain crudity the true workings of the system, pose a threat to the stability of social reproduction. But as we have seen, the counterhegemonic elements of the Hallway Hangers' perspective are divested of their political potential; the Hallway Hangers' racism, among other factors, impedes the formation of any sort of critical consciousness.

Although the Hallway Hangers' capacity to see through the dominant ideology is not politically empowering, it does allow them to maintain some semblance of a positive identity. In puncturing the achievement ideology, the Hallway Hangers invert the dominant culture's definitions of achievement. Whereas the conventional American example of success might be J. Paul Getty, self-made millionaire, Frankie holds up as an example John Grace, bartender being tried for attempted murder. By turning the achievement ideology upside down, the Hallway Hangers reject the official, authorized interpretation of their social situation; in so doing, they become free to create their own cultural meanings. Because they see the spoils of economic success as beyond their reach, the Hallway Hangers invert the dominant ideology in a way that gives them access to "success," albeit in forms the dominant culture recognizes as failure.

My finding that the Hallway Hangers reject the official ideology and my speculation that the poorest members of the black community do the same makes a good deal of sense. We would expect those clinging to the very lowest rungs of the socioeconomic ladder to reject the achievement ideology, for although all other segments of society can use the dominant ideology as a means to feel superior to whomever is below them, poor whites and blacks have no one to look down on. Even those only marginally better off can and do use the achievement ideology as a means of self-validation. As public housing tenants, Clarendon Heights residents routinely are depicted as irresponsible, morally lacking, and indolent by the city's other inhabitants. Consider the light in which an auto mechanic living in a working-class neighborhood across the city sees Clarendon Heights residents: "These people are fucking animals. . . . I know what their habits are like; they won't stop at anything to rip you off. Fucking sponges, leeches, they are. They'll suck the blood out of anyone, anything. They suck it out of my paycheck every week. . . . At least I work for my money."

Willis writes that the working class does not have a structurally based vested interest in mystifying itself.[17] But, in the United States at least, the working class is so fragmented that only the very lowest strata have no use for the dominant achievement ideology. For the poorest segments of the population, both white and black, the only defense against the ideology is to turn it on its head and attempt to salvage as much dignity as possible via the redefined criteria for success. This is a struggle that will never be completely won, for the judgments of the dominant culture are capable of piercing the thickest individual or collective shells. Willis captures the issue in *Learning to Labor:* "One of the time-honoured principles of cultural and social organization in this country as it is enacted and understood at the subjective level is that of 'them' and 'us.' That the term 'them' survives in 'us' is usually overlooked. . . . Even the most 'us' group has a little of 'them' inside. . . . Ideology is the 'them' in 'us.'"[18]

The poorest black and white people in America, who are fodder for the rest of society's hunger for social superiority, ironically turn on each other to fulfill the same function. The Hallway Hangers continually strive to convince themselves of their superiority over "the niggers." We might expect that poor blacks vaunt themselves over the "white trash" living across the city. The more effective means of maintaining a measure of dignity and self-respect, however, seems to be the inversion of the dominant ideology, a cultural response to class domination by those at the bottom of American society.

The interaction between the cultural and the structural that I have posited— that class-based institutional mechanisms set limits on mobility, thereby ensuring social reproduction, while cultural innovations can be at once both functional and dysfunctional for social reproduction—fits the ethnographic data. By ignoring the cultural level of analysis, determinist theories cannot account for the distinctive cultural practices and attitudes of lower-class individuals; nor can these theories explain how such practices can contribute to and threaten social reproduction. Culturalist theories seldom manage to connect the micro processes they document to the macro forces that constrain working-class individuals.

By striving to understand the world of the Brothers and the Hallway Hangers on their terms, this book has managed to uncover some important mediating factors that influence individuals at the cultural level. It is to these factors that deterministic theories must pay more attention. In addition, theorists such as Bowles and Gintis and Bourdieu must recognize individuals' capacity for reflexive thought and action—in Willis's words, their potential "not only to think like theorists, but act like activists."[19] Individuals are not passive receivers of structural forces; rather they interpret and respond to those forces in creative ways. In asserting the autonomy of the individual at this cultural level, however, we must not lose sight of structural forms of class domination from which there is no escape. To paraphrase Marx, we must understand that teenage peer groups make their own history, but not under circumstances of their own choosing.[20]

NOTES

1. Henry A. Giroux, *Theory & Resistance in Education* (London: Heinemann, 1983), p. 85.

2. Loïc J. D. Wacquant, "Sociology as Socioanalysis: Tales of *Homo Academicus*," *Sociological Forum* 5 (1990): 684.

3. Giroux, *Theory & Resistance,* p. 89.

4. Wacquant, "Sociology as Socioanalysis," p. 684.

5. Richard Jenkins, *Pierre Bourdieu* (London: Routledge, 1992), p. 66.

6. Pierre Bourdieu and Jean-Claude Passeron, *Reproduction in Society, Education and Culture* (London: Sage, 1977).

7. Pierre Bourdieu, *Outline of a Theory of Practice* (Cambridge: Cambridge University Press, 1977), p. 87.

8. Paul E. Willis, *Learning to Labor* (Aldershot: Gower, 1977), p. 172.

9. Jane K. Rosegrant, "Choosing Children" (Thesis, Harvard College, 1985), p. 120.

10. Ibid., pp. 125–126.

11. Ibid., pp. 133–134.

12. Ibid., p. 127.

13. Anne Campbell, *The Girls in the Gang* (Oxford: Basil Blackwell, 1984), p. 266.

14. Giroux, *Theory & Resistance,* p. 63.

15. Ibid., p. 108.

16. Ibid., p. 164.

17. Willis, *Learning to Labor,* pp. 122–123.

18. Ibid., p. 169.

19. Paul E. Willis, "Cultural Production and Theories of Reproduction," in Len Barton and Stephen Walker, eds., *Race, Class, and Education* (London: Croom Helm, 1983), p. 114.

20. Karl Marx, *The Eighteenth Brumaire of Louis Bonaparte,* in *Selected Works* (New York: International Publishers, 1968), p. 97.

PART TWO

EIGHT YEARS LATER
Low Income, Low Outcome

THE HALLWAY HANGERS

Dealing in Despair

"**H**ey, Jay, what the fuck brings you back to the Ponderosa?" Greeted by Steve in July 1991, I surveyed a Clarendon Heights that had changed considerably since 1983. Steve jerked his thumb over his shoulder at a group of African American teenagers lounging in the area outside doorway #13, previously the preserve of the Hallway Hangers. "How do you like all the new niggers we got here? Motherfuckers've taken over, man." I asked Steve about Frankie, Slick, and the other Hallway Hangers. "I'm the only one holding down the fort," he answered. "Me and Jinx—he lives in the back. The rest of 'em pretty much cut loose, man."

Indeed, the Hallway Hangers' clique has broken up. Of those who have moved out of the neighborhood, only Slick and Shorty occasionally return to hang in the Heights. Although physically Clarendon Heights looks much the same, the surrounding neighborhood is slowly being transformed by gentrification. Students and young professionals have moved into the area, displacing Italian and Portuguese families. Ice cream parlors and posh restaurants that cater to the new clientele are replacing the pawnshops and family-owned five-and-dime stores. The vacant lot across from Clarendon Heights, once strewn with battered cars around a sagging basketball rim, is now the site of a smart office building. "Smile, you're on *Candid Camera*," Steve announced, pointing to small video cameras mounted on the office walls and trained on the area in front of doorway #13. "The cops've gone high-tech on us. But shit, it's too hot to deal out here now anyways, with all the spooks takin' over."

Later in this chapter I probe the siege mentality and racism of the Hallway Hangers, explore how their identities are formed around the axes of race, class, and gender, and recount their experiences of work. In their midtwenties, the seven Hallway Hangers should be in the labor force full-time. Most of them aren't: They are unemployed or imprisoned, or are working sporadically either for firms "under the table" or for themselves in the drug economy. Before considering these issues closely, I briefly sketch the fate of each young man since 1984.

Since 1984 Stoney has moved from pizzeria to pizzeria and from prison to prison. When I saw him in September 1987, Stoney was depressed. "I've been in and out of the can since you left, but it's been for stupid shit—not going to drug or alcohol classes, drinking in public, ignoring court summonses, possession— shit like that." Later that day he went to the courthouse and asked to serve a suspended six-month sentence for possession of cocaine. Hoping to cleanse his system of drugs, Stoney thought jail would do him good. When I visited him a month later in the county jail, he was miserable and could hardly believe his stupidity. Stoney is still dependent on Valium and, according to friends, has tried to take his own life several times. In 1988 he robbed a convenience store with a tire iron and spent two years in jail. He got out, found his girlfriend and two children living with another man, acquired another pizza job, fell in love, sold his belongings, and moved with his fiancée to the South where she had lined up a job. Stoney found work but her job fell through, and three months later they were back in town. Stoney was soon arrested another time for armed robbery, again after drinking and dropping Valium. He held up a pizza delivery-man, took forty dollars and a large pizza, and was sentenced to the maximum-security prison for up to five years. Due to overcrowding and good behavior, he had minimum-security status when I visited him in 1991. Remarkably healthy and upbeat, he looked better than I'd ever seen him. Stoney still hopes to own a pizza parlor. "Things haven't gone good," he said, "but it'll get better. I hope so anyway."

Steve has also been in and out of prison five times over the past seven years, mostly for violating restraining orders and beating his girlfriend. The father of two children, Steve admits that paternity "didn't faze me—I was a kid still." Apart from occasional babysitting, Steve offers little financial or moral support to their mothers. He cycles in and out of construction jobs and has dealt crack to supplement his income. Steve seems to have progressed from "the stereotypical project youth . . . constantly on the lookout for a free ride" to the stereotypical hood whose violent existence seems completely unanchored. Many people around Clarendon Heights consider Steve "crazy." Stoney, whose jaw was broken by Steve in a street fight, says, "Steve's a maniac. He's got a big heart, but he's a fuckin' maniac."

Shorty could easily wear the same label, having spent ten days in a state psychiatric hospital after attacking a police officer. In another fight in front of Clarendon Heights, he stabbed a boy named Rico in the stomach with a hunting knife. The boy went into a coma and Shorty was charged with attempted murder. Then Rico recovered, and upon discovering that Shorty was actually a distant cousin, he dropped the charge. Shorty ended up doing thirteen months, and when he refused to attend Alcoholics Anonymous (AA) classes after his release, he served another six. Shorty worked a few construction jobs before getting stabbed himself a few blocks from Clarendon Heights. He was in the hospital for fourteen days after his spleen was removed and his bladder repaired. True to form, Shorty refused to identify his assailant, even under intense police pressure. He still lives with his mother, works sporadically, and likes crack cocaine.

JM: What about women? Steady girlfriend or . . .

SHORTY: Yeah, got one girl. I stay with her. I don't go around fuckin' other broads. Maybe, maybe once in a while, once in a while I'll go out and grab another piece of ass, but I don't like to because I don't wanna catch no fuckin' AIDS. You gotta watch where you're poking your hose these days, you know. Fuck that.

Shorty's existence may seem unsettled but he finds it surprisingly composed. Asked if things had gone as he expected over the past seven years, Shorty replied, "No. I thought I'd be in jail for fucking life. Murder. I'll tell ya one thing, I didn't think I'd slow down like this."

Chris failed to slow down in pursuit of his teenage aspiration to be a big-time cocaine dealer. In 1984 he was moving up in the drug underworld of the city, expanding his clientele to other neighborhoods and to a nearby city. But as his market grew, so did his own appetite for drugs until, according to Jinx, "he became his own best customer." Having lost the trust of his suppliers, Chris increasingly turned to theft to support his heroin and cocaine habits. When I saw him in 1987 he had already been jailed several times and was awaiting trial on a breaking and entering charge. "I fucked up, Jay, that's all. Cocaine did it to me. What can I say? I'm at rock bottom and I'm fucking embarrassed for you to see me like this." But Chris was not at rock bottom in 1987 because he has sunk considerably since then. When I interviewed him in jail four years later, Chris described how he and his girlfriend, Samantha, had been homeless for the past several years, moving from one "base house" to another when kicked out by other addicts, sleeping in hallways and on the street. He recounted how he robbed friends and family and then resorted to increasingly risky theft: stealing radios and tape decks out of cars, breaking into dormitory rooms and houses, passing stolen checks, and finally sticking people up. Chris has been imprisoned six times, most recently for holding up three college students with a stick beneath his shirt in an effort that netted him ninety-seven dollars and probably seven years behind bars. Samantha cannot visit him because she jumped bail, and his family will not accept his collect calls. "Jay, I wanna have a normal life so bad. You don't know how bad I'm aching inside. I just want so bad to have a normal life."

Boo-Boo, the other black Hallway Hanger, is also in bad shape. In 1985 he began working at a car wash for $4.30 per hour. "It was a shit job for shit pay, but what else could I do?" After fourteen months and only a fifty-cent pay raise, Boo-Boo quit. He hung in Clarendon Heights and did a stint in jail after a drunken joy ride. After his release Boo-Boo was in high spirits. He was in love and had somehow been accepted into the army despite his record. On June 4, 1987, he was married and on June 8 he was inducted into the armed forces. But on July 15 he was given a medical discharge for bunions growing on his feet. Two weeks later, at his wife's insistence, their marriage was annulled. Shortly afterward, Boo-Boo met Ginger, a young Italian woman, and eventually moved in with her family in a housing project across the city. They moved out when Ginger gave birth, and another daughter was born a year later. In 1990 the Department of Social Services took custody of the girls because, according to Boo-Boo, their basement apartment was often flooded and perpetually damp, and because "the kids weren't being looked after right." Boo-Boo and Ginger moved to a nearby city and became enmeshed in the crack cocaine racket. They emerged unharmed, but since then Boo-Boo's family and personal life have completely crumbled.

Slick was also struggling in 1987 when I visited him in jail. He had joined the marines in 1984 but was discharged several months later. He worked "under the table" as a construction laborer, landed a permanent job with a roofing company, and was making over ten dollars per hour when he was arrested for disorderly conduct after a brawl. As part of his probation, Slick had to attend weekly AA meetings for several months. He missed the final two sessions and was sentenced to six months in the county house of correction for violation of probation. Once out of jail, Slick settled back into his roofing job and began to supplement his wages by dealing cocaine. He and his girlfriend, Denise, rented a condominium until Slick bailed out of the drug racket. Sitting in their current ramshackle apartment, Slick spoke of his determination to stay straight.

SLICK: What you do, you make money. You make the legal money and you make it and you make it and you make it. You just don't give in, man. Cuz I don't wanna go back to doing illegal things, know what I'm saying? . . . Lemme tell you what a good job is right now. Working five days a week, forty hours a week, working steady. That's what a good job is right now. Cuz there *ain't* no jobs out there right now. And a good guy, a good provider, is a guy that comes home with his paycheck every week and does the right thing. Doesn't go out drinkin' and druggin' and fuckin' going crazy and shit. That's a good person. That's what a lot of these people, myself included, are looking for. Just for something that you can say, "Hey, look, I work my forty hours a week, I work hard all week, I take care of my kids, I take care of my family, y'know, I'm doing it the right way. Know what I mean?

Slick currently earns over twelve dollars per hour, far more than the other Hallway Hangers. Still, the work is irregular: Slick gets laid off nearly every winter.

After "bouncing from job to job, just gettin' by, keepin' myself occupied, staying away from trouble," Jinx jumped into drug trafficking. Like Slick, he managed to climb out again, still intact, and currently has a steady job in a warehouse. Jinx lives in Clarendon Heights with his girlfriend and their six-year-old son. Apart from Steve, he seldom sees the Hallway Hangers.

JM: When you look back on the heyday, back in high school as teenagers, how do you look back on it?

JINX: It's, say, confusing. I can't say I'd want to change the way it was, but I can't say I'd want it to be the same way. You know, because we were all so close back then. But we all went our separate ways. And if we were as close as we thought we were, we wouldn't've parted our ways. No matter what happened to us, each havin' our own families, we would always still be the same people we were and be that close. Which we're not.

Now twenty-five, Jinx fears his successors hanging around doorway #13. "I don't feel safe not knowing this kinda kid standin' out front. I don't know one of them. I don't feel safe." This is more than caution bred by age. Jinx fears the new hallway hangers because they are black.

When Frankie moved out of state with his mother in 1984, he came back every weekend to hang with his friends. Now he lives within a mile of Clarendon Heights but hardly ever stops by. Frankie is a changed man. He touches neither drugs nor alcohol, attends weekly AA meetings, sees counselors regularly, receives motivational training, and prays "every morning and every night—and a few hundred times during the day." This metamorphosis occurred in 1989 when Frankie perceived that his substance abuse combined with his violent temper could prove fatal. Now Frankie lives quietly with his son, his girlfriend, and her family. Despite this internal revolution, Frankie is unemployed.

Taken individually, the Hallway Hangers are easily seen as simply losers, the relative success of Slick, Jinx, and Frankie notwithstanding. The Hallway Hangers are alcoholics and drug addicts. They fight, they steal, they deal crack. They treat women as objects and victimize people of color. They can't stay out of jail, much less hold down steady jobs. In short, the Hallway Hangers seem to have screwed themselves. But once we widen the camera frame beyond individual portraits, we begin to see the background factors that influence the Hallway Hangers' lives and push them toward self-destructive behavior. The social and economic structure, often obscured and ignored, determines the opportunities, influences the attitudes, and affects the actions of the Hallway Hangers. Their story is not just a narrative string of personal failures. Rather, their personal biographies are inextricably linked with the changing structure of the economy. Even when the Hallway Hangers straighten up, as Frankie has, they are hard-pressed to make progress. The racism, sexism, substance abuse, violence, and criminal exploits of the Hallway Hangers are all tied to their subordinate position in the class structure and their quest to fashion identities as poor white men. This is not to say that they are absolved of responsibility for their attitudes and actions, nor that crime ceases to be criminal if committed by someone clinging to the bottom rung. But to understand what has happened to the Hallway Hangers between 1984 and 1991, we must examine their collective experience on the legitimate labor market and in the underground economy, and then we must strive to fathom how they understand and project themselves as lower-class American men.

ON THE JOB

The Hallway Hangers have faced a job market completely different from the one their fathers entered as young men. With the restructuring of the U.S. economy—the shift from manufacturing to service employment—masses of traditional blue-collar jobs in industrial production have vanished. As markets and corporations have become internationalized, many American industries have reduced their labor and production costs by replacing workers with machines and by moving operations overseas. America's northern cities, hard hit by deindustrialization, now rely more on jobs devoted to the processing of information than on the production and distribution of goods. Clarendon Heights residents work in a city dominated by the economy of the service sector—administration, finance, and information exchange. In 1980 information-processing industries provided more jobs in the city than did manufacturing, construction, retail, and wholesale industries combined. In the mid-1950s, by contrast, jobs in the more traditional urban industries outnumbered data-processing employment by a margin of three to one.[1] By 1988 manufacturing jobs accounted for only 6 percent of all wage and salary jobs in the city.[2] Urban industrial transition is part of a larger national trend. Of the 23 million positions created between 1970 and 1984 across the country, 22 million were in the service sector, and today more than three-quarters of all employment is in the service industries.[3]

The rise in managerial, professional, technical, and administrative jobs, coupled with the precipitous drop in blue-collar employment, has landed high school dropouts in desperate straits. The number of jobs in the city held by those who did not complete high school declined by 59 percent between 1970 and 1980. Even those who finished high school have been stranded: Jobs held by high school graduates also dropped by 29 percent. Conversely, the quantity of jobs for college graduates grew by 71 percent.[4] In short, the new postindustrial economy has reduced opportunities for undereducated inner-city youths to a trickle.

The shift from a manufacturing to a service-based economy means that for the working class there are far fewer jobs with good wages, fringe benefits, and opportunities for advancement. Jobs in the service sector tend to be polarized between high-salaried, credentialed positions (such as those for attorneys and stockbrokers) and low-wage, menial positions that offer little security (such as those for janitors, security guards, and fast-food cooks). Many service jobs pay little more than five dollars per hour, whereas workers in unionized manufacturing industries have often made two, three, and even four times that amount. Between 1979 and 1987, 50 percent of all new jobs created in the United States were at or below the poverty level, only 38 percent were at the middle-income level, and a mere 12 percent were at the high-wage level.[5]

The occupational histories of the Hallway Hangers between 1984 and 1991 reflect the shift from a manufacturing- to a service-based economy. They have been employed as janitors, garbage collectors, cooks, caterers, couriers, cleaners, carpet layers, landscapers, inventory keepers, movers, packers, plumbers' assistants, groundsmen, soldiers, and store clerks. They have worked at car washes, junkyards, hotels, and restaurants. Although the Hallway Hangers have labored in the construction industry, most of these jobs were "off the books" and approximated service work rather than traditional blue-collar employment in terms of earnings, job security, and working conditions. And, as noted, the service sector tends to pay low wages, offer few opportunities for promotion, and encourage high turnover. The experiences of the Hallway Hangers bear this out.

Few of the Hallway Hangers have held stable jobs. Even Jinx, who has had his current job for over three years, has worked for nine different employers since February 1984. Frankie has held twelve jobs. Despite having been incarcerated for most of the period under consideration, Shorty and Stoney have had thirteen jobs between them. Boo-Boo has held six jobs in between periods of unemployment. In previous decades, most American youths, preoccupied with their peer group and prospective sexual partners, went through a period of labor market experimentation and adjustment before they settled down into a career job.[6] Many of the Hallway Hangers, however, have failed to hold a steady job even in their midtwenties. Although some of this turnover can be attributed to their behavior, much of it stems from the nature of the jobs the Hallway Hangers have held. Slick, Steve, and Shorty, for instance, have all been routinely laid off from their construction jobs during the winter months. Similarly, seasonal swings have forced Jinx to switch from one hotel job to another: "It would get slow around Christmastime. They were cutting my days from working five days to two days. . . . I skipped around, I jumped to three different hotels. Hey, you gotta pay for those Christmas presents." Shorty had two stints working for the city but was laid off just before qualifying as a permanent employee. Recent research suggests that the Hallway Hangers are not atypical. Paul Osterman's 1992 study shows that roughly a third of all high school graduates, and even more high school dropouts, fail to find stable employment by the time they are thirty.[7]

All of the Hallway Hangers have worked "under the table." Steve, Boo-Boo, Frankie, Shorty, and Jinx have worked in construction illegally. Most of Stoney's jobs at pizza places and Boo-Boo's two most recent jobs—at a scrap yard and a moving company—have been "off the books." Shorty's most recent employer, the owner of a liquor store, paid him cash.

SHORTY: The job in the liquor store, ha: five bucks an hour. But I needed the money. Anything goes, y'know? . . . I stayed there for five months. I asked him for a dollar raise, y'know, cuz I was doin' everything. I was doin' the inventory, the shipping, receiving, cash-registering, sayin', "I can't be doin' all this shit. Give me some more money." Y'know, he wouldn't give it to me, so I left.

JM: Do you like working under the table, or would you prefer to get a check?

SHORTY: At first I liked getting cash. No paperwork or taxes to worry about. Like he's doing me a favor, y'know? But really, I'm the one getting fucked. No fucking Social Security when I'm an old geezer, no unemployment when I get laid off. And no help if you get hurt, no what's it called—workmen's compensation. It's better to get a regular check. I was working carpentry for a real estate company. It was under the table. But then we went on the books because they had too many guys workin' for them.

JM: Did you have to take a pay cut when you went on the books?

SHORTY: No, I got a raise.

JM: Have you ever insisted on being paid by check?

SHORTY: What're you, fuckin' nuts, Jay? "Excuse me, mister, could I have a check, please?" I'd be on my ass at home the next day watching *General Hospital,* cuz there's a hundred and fifty fucking guys ready to work in my place.

Shorty suggests that "off the books" employment outside the framework of public regulation benefits employers while hurting workers and that a reserve army of unemployed people further undermines the position of employees. All of this is confirmed by Saskia Sassen, whose New York study indicates that the growth of the informal economy represents a structural feature of the post-industrial city.[8] Working "under the table," the Hallway Hangers, like so many other inner-city residents, sell their labor in a market unfettered by laws, job descriptions, or institutional constraints. Job security is nonexistent, as Shorty underlines by saying *when* rather than *if* he is laid off. Under such conditions, unprotected by the laws that the working class fought to institutionalize, a human being's labor is most nearly reduced to a mere commodity.

The hourly wages of the Hallway Hangers have ranged from $3.65 to $12.50, but most of their jobs paid between $5 and $7 an hour. Again, their experience is connected to larger economic trends. Over the past two decades, the real annual earnings of young adult men have deteriorated by 31 percent.[9] In contrast to most of the Hallway Hangers, who have been stuck in entry-level positions, Slick has more than doubled his earnings.

SLICK: When I started roofing I was making six dollars an hour, and now I make twelve-fifty. I went from a laborer to assistant foreman over about a six-year period of time with the same company.

JM: So although you usually get laid off in the winter, you're bringing in good money, now.

SLICK: Yeah, I bust my ass, but bills are still breaking my back.

JM: Tell me about them.

SLICK: I pay child support for my two kids, that's the first priority. Then five hundred dollars a month for rent. We gotta have a roof over our head. [Slick lives with his girlfriend, Denise, and Tyler, their infant son.] And this month I gotta pay three hundred dollars for Sean's christening. I gotta pay for the DJ and the hall—that's three hundred and fifty dollars. Then I got Denise's father's birthday this month—that's gonna cost us at least another hundred and a half. Then I got her cousin's christening this Sunday. That'll probably cost us half a yarder—fifty bucks. Plus all the photos of Sean. Not to mention the little stuff like eating, like food shopping and shit. It adds up like crazy. You work longer hours, know what I'm saying? But there's only so many hours in a week. And I didn't count the phone bill, the electric bill, the heating bill.

Most of the Hallway Hangers have earned roughly half of what Slick currently makes. Only Jinx, who makes $8.93 an hour after three years with one company, has also been able to set up a household with his girlfriend. The rest of the Hallway Hangers have lived with parents and friends, or have been incarcerated or homeless. All of them have worked for an hourly wage rather than a salary. None has owned a car.

Slick and Jinx are not the only Hallway Hangers to have received raises. Shorty's account of one of his "under the table" construction jobs has an interesting twist.

SHORTY: I started off at five dollars an hour. I was just a laborer, y'know, sweepin' up and shit after the carpenters. I stayed there about a year and I was making nine bucks an hour, carpenter's helper. They were paying me good. Then they just laid everybody off because we finished. What they were doing was makin' all them old buildings into condos, moving . . . all the poor people out. That's why all the kids, they started bringing all the fuckin' condos down and smashin' the windows every night. We go and put up nice siding and something like that, and they'd go buy fuckin' paint and throw it on there and everything, cuz they were moving all the poor people out and and movin' all the yuppies in and shit.

JM: So what did you think of that?

SHORTY: I thought it was wrong, y'know, but hey, I was getting paid for fuckin' work, y'know? Gotta make some money. Shit, the way I look at it now, those kids were helping me by trashing our work. Cuz I woulda got laid off sooner. But at the time I was pissed off. Come and see your work all fucked up each morning.

Frankie was also promoted in one of his early jobs when he was living out of state with his mother.

FRANKIE: I went in as like a dockperson, y'know, just unloading trucks, and I ended up doin' pretty well. It was a friend of a friend that helped me out. I ended up going from a dockworker to a shipper to a material control specialist. I was sittin' on a computer all fucking day.

JM: Tell me about how you were able to move up.

FRANKIE: Actually, it was because I knew this guy. A lot of it was luck. It was this guy who drank and couldn't make it in on Saturdays. I had to replace him, and they threw me on a computer, because they were so far behind. And they noticed I caught on real quick, and they sent me to school. I moved to shipper within six months and after that, I'd say within another six months, I became a material control specialist. What I was doin', I was keepin' a computerized inventory for them. They sent me to a few courses, y'know?

Frankie is the only Hallway Hanger to have received any formal training on the job.

The Hallway Hangers have generally worked at jobs for which few skills are required and few can be learned: dead-end jobs with little opportunity for advancement and little reward for seniority in the form of higher pay or a better position. Boo-Boo's experience, for example, contrasts with Frankie's.

BOO-BOO: I worked for this moving company. I worked for them a while, then I quit. I was gettin' ten dollars an hour, under the table. It was good. I was makin' like a hundred dollars a day. It was excellent. I was doing all right then.

JM: Why'd you quit?

BOO-BOO: Well, he started to get this attitude where, instead of promoting me, he was demoting me. First I was makin' ten dollars an hour, then he brought it down to seven-fifty, and I was takin' it for a while. But then, y'know, you move pianos, you move everything, anything, you name it, we're moving it. Big giant copy machines. All kinds of stuff. If anybody's working a job, working hard, doing a good job, and they're getting ten dollars an hour, you never get demoted. I've never heard of anyone getting demoted. Taking money away, cuz he said he was losing money. It was a self-made business, his own business. He made it himself. He has like three trucks. He owns his own house. Nice new Volvo. He was just getting real cheap about everything, so I just, like, broke loose. I said, "Sorry, dude, I can't work for you anymore." I just quit.

Most of the Hallway Hangers' jobs have been with small firms, which have a high chance of failure and are especially susceptible to downturns in the business cycle. Jinx did renovation work for a year and a half "'til the company went bankrupt on me and left out owing me twelve hundred dollars. How could I afford to fight it in court?"

Jobs in the service economy, especially with small firms, are seldom unionized. Of the Hallway Hangers, only Frankie has been in a labor union. He worked on a catering crew with clear lines of advancement and managed to move up.

FRANKIE: I ended up getting in a hotel/restaurant union. I started off as what they call a runner and within two days I went from becoming a runner to general service in the catering crew.

JM: What's a runner?

FRANKIE: A runner was just you run supplies from the kitchen to the entrees. And I ended up becoming general service for the catering within two days. From a runner to general service was like a buck-fifty raise within two days. And within the month I got another two-fifty raise because I became a steward on the crew. It was a union job with union rates and I was getting merit raises, too, y'know? I was makin' good money there. I was gettin' three squares [meals] a day. And the overtime was great. It was great. I was working hard, but it was also a learning process.

Frankie credits the union for helping to ensure a decent pay scale, opportunities for promotion, and a measure of job satisfaction. But he is most indebted to the union for the personal support it lent him. When in 1989 Frankie approached his shop steward about his addiction to drugs and alcohol, the union arranged for thirty days of residential treatment and then for placement in a halfway house. Back on the job, Frankie got into a fistfight when two colleagues ridiculed his temperance. He was fired and decided not to appeal against his termination.

FRANKIE: I just said, "Fuck it. There's so much booze around here anyway." And I left the job, y'know? I'm kickin' myself in the ass over that. But I just couldn't do it. So I left there. An' I tell you, I haven't been drinking in—it'll be two years next Thursday.

Jinx has worked at hotels as a cleaner and with banquet setups and convention services. He explained that none of his jobs were unionized, "but all the hotels around here, they keep competitive with the union wage, so they avoid everyone going into unions." Jinx made up to $6.95 an hour but kept having his workweek reduced during the off-season. Also, he hated his work hours.

JINX: I worked the graveyard shift, eleven p.m. to seven a.m., at one hotel, and then at the Marriott was swing shift. I would work one during the day, one at night. Same thing with the Hyatt Regency, was no set hours. It was whenever there was work to be done, I'd work.

Still, unlike most of the Hallway Hangers, Jinx received some employment benefits. "If anyone else out here [Clarendon Heights] gets sick, they're fucked, but I've gotten health insurance with most of my [hotel] jobs."

As with hotels, restaurants, and small businesses, the construction industry can be devastated by recession. In fact, in the years after the bottom fell out of the local economy in 1989, 45 percent of low-level construction jobs were lost.[10] Since then, with the exception of Slick, the Hallway Hangers could not even rely on casual work as day laborers. As Steve complains, "Nowadays, man, it's fuckin' tough [to get a job]." Slick concurs: "There *ain't* no jobs out there right now." By saying "nowadays" and "now," Steve and Slick emphasize their current difficulty finding work. The recession exacerbates the more permanent bias in the labor market against the unskilled. Between 1980 and 1990, the unemployment rate in the city for high school dropouts rose from 19 to 35 percent. For high school graduates the unemployment rate increased from 12 to 18 percent.[11] Unemployment, always a problem for the Hallway Hangers, has taken an especially severe toll since 1989. Shorty, Steve, and Boo-Boo have all had long bouts of unemployment, and none have qualified for unemployment benefits because their work has been "off the books."

Unemployment has been particularly difficult for Frankie to accept. Having quit drinking and doing drugs, he has been trying to turn his history of substance abuse into an asset on the job market. Frankie still attends Alcoholics Anonymous and Narcotics Anonymous meetings regularly and seldom visits Clarendon Heights, where he is now known as "preacher" for his sermons on the evils of alcohol and drug abuse. Unemployed, he is currently studying part-time and hopes to work as an apprentice in building maintenance, learning about heating, ventilation, and air conditioning. His tuition and part of his training wage will be paid by a government agency for the disabled. As a recovering alcoholic, Frankie is eligible for its programs. He has also learned job application and interviewing skills, and sees two personal counselors regularly. The irony is that Frankie held down a number of jobs while addicted. "It's fucked-up," he says. "Now I'm sober and I've got all this help, and I'm unemployed." Indeed, that so many of the Hallway Hangers could do their jobs while drunk or stoned says something about their attitudes toward work, but perhaps even more about the types of jobs they have held.

The Hallway Hangers have relied almost exclusively on one means of landing their jobs: connections. It was through his brothers that Jinx was offered a job laying carpet. And his mother, a long-term employee at the Hyatt, found him his first hotel job. Steve and Shorty secured construction jobs through friends, including Slick. After describing how scarce jobs are, Steve added, "I'm lucky I know a few people, that's about it." Shorty also found other jobs by exploiting personal contacts. "I got connections," says Shorty. "Look at my brothers; they're both cops. They know a lotta politicians." When he ran out of contacts, Shorty had no success on the labor market. "I went to a lot of places and filled out applications, but nobody called me. Fucking nobody." Boo-Boo also secured his position with the moving company through a Clarendon Heights friend. Frankie was offered nearly all of his twelve jobs through connections.

FRANKIE: The job on the catering crew was, like, the only job I actually went and applied for. Everything else was handed to me.

JM: How did that happen, those connections?

FRANKIE: I come from a big family, a pretty well-known family. Just from the local bars, y'know, that's the way it works. That's the bottom line. . . . Politicians, guys I knew who were already working for the city or for the state. Thing is, I've burned a lot of those bridges now.

What success the Hallway Hangers have had on the job market seems to have been achieved almost exclusively through informal networking.

The networks to which the Hallway Hangers have access, however, are inferior to those of the more affluent—a point that Jinx well understands.

JM: Have you found in your own working career that connections have been helpful?

JINX: Yes, the jobs I used my connections for, my mother, that was helpful. But even now, where I work now, I see my boss's son works for him, okay? He has this kid who graduated from college, he's a salesman. The kid shows up maybe one day a week, he does absolutely nothing. He's a complete moron, and he can do as he pleases because his father's the boss. Because he's got money it makes everything he does right, y'know, whether it be wrong or right. He can't do no wrong. I see it at my job and everywhere else, and it's just all over the world.

Jinx's mother helped him get entry-level jobs in hotels, and his brothers helped Jinx get a job laying carpet for a daily wage of thirty-five dollars. For that he is grateful. But Jinx is also aggrieved that middle-class youths, by virtue of their more privileged background, have access to superior social networks and hence better jobs.

Frankie has had a similar experience, not uncommon in small firms where managerial control in the workplace tends to be informal, unstructured, and concentrated in the hands of family members.

FRANKIE: I also became a material control specialist for a hearing-aid company. . . . I left there—it was a family-oriented business and they brang in their son, but he's a high school kid, y'know, and [*he says this incredulously*] he became my *boss*. And here he's only a junior in high school. I couldn't accept that. His mother was the personnel director, his father was the general manager, his two brothers were the other two managers, so they were weaning this kid in. So I went, y'know, my old method I woulda just left. But I went and had a discussion with his old man. I just told him, "I just can't find myself taking orders and shit from this kid." He said, y'know, he didn't blame me. But he also said, "You realize this is my son?" So I told him okay, I told him I'd hafta leave.

JM: Was it just the idea of having the kid as your boss, or was it how it worked out in practice, was the kid an asshole?

FRANKIE: He was an asshole. He didn't know the job, but he was trying to change standard operating procedures to his way. "I think it'd be better this way." And I'd say, "No, it's not, and this is why." Simple. He'd say, "Well, I don't care why." It was just a lot of that on a daily basis. What I felt was my old behavior, y'know, the old project self coming out of me, and I was gonna fucking whack the shit out of him, is what I was gonna do. But I know I was the only one gonna get hurt out of that. I finally learnt, I ain't gonna lower myself to this kid, so I gave two weeks' notice. I left but then I was unemployed for *a while*. . . . And it's been tough. Cuz, y'know, the economy fucking sucks.

For Frankie, the cost of maintaining his pride has been the trial of extended unemployment.

In fact, Frankie's job at the hearing-aid company had already been straining his sense of self.

FRANKIE: It was just a desk job, y'know, and that's not me. I'm not a desk-job guy. It was a good job if you could sit at a desk for eight hours a day.

JM: What was it about the desk job that . . . ?

FRANKIE: I just, it's just not me, man. You know me, I'm hyper. It was a lotta things. People's mothers, I remember these two ladies, they useta kill me. All they did was talk to me about how their sons hung out with little trouble-makers and punks and all that. And just the office atmosphere, I'm not big into gossip, never was and never will be. Just not able to leave these people, y'know? At least if you work in a warehouse or somethin', y'know, "I gotta go do something." You can only go to the bathroom so many times in an office. [*laughs*] I'm just too hyper, man. I just couldn't sit there. Y'know, they wanted me to wear a shirt and tie, and I'm a jeans and dungarees guy. That's just not me, y'know? Yeah, so I left there in August '90 when they brought their son in.

The humiliation of working under an incompetent youngster, combined with the passivity and social relations of white-collar work, spurred Frankie to quit the job.

The Hallway Hangers have been trapped in what economists call the secondary labor market—the subordinate segment of the job structure where the market is severely skewed against workers. Jobs in the primary labor markets provide wages that can support families and an internal career structure, but the rules of the game are different in the secondary labor market. Wages are lower, raises are infrequent, training is minimal, advancement is rare, and turnover is high. Neither seniority nor education provide much of a return for workers in the secondary labor market.[12]

Whereas many youths begin their working careers in the secondary labor market and then break into the primary sectors, the Hallway Hangers have been confined to the secondary sector. Slick, the highest paid among them, still struggles to support his family and will be laid off as soon as the snow flies. Jinx's warehouse job has provided more security than his hotel jobs but offers little scope for advancement and little job satisfaction. Frankie, the only one to receive formal training on the job, has been unemployed for several months, despite having undergone state-sponsored training to improve his job prospects. These have been the success stories. The remainder of the Hallway Hangers have eked out a subsistence wage on the margins of the American economy. When they have managed to find work, it has tended to be "off the books." Asked what his best job has been over the past seven years, Boo-Boo answered, "The one at the junkyard." He made five dollars per hour "under the table." Although their experiences on the job market have been varied, the Hallway Hangers have generally held menial, dead-end jobs in the secondary labor market.

WORKING THE STREET

When the legitimate job market fails them, the Hallway Hangers can turn to the underground economy. Since 1984 almost all of the Hallway Hangers have at least supplemented their income from earnings on the burgeoning, multibillion-dollar drug market. The street economy promises better money than does conventional employment. It also provides a work site that does not demean the Hallway Hangers or drain their dignity.[13] As workers in the underground economy, they won't have to take orders from a boss's arrogant son, nor will they have to gossip with office colleagues and strain to camouflage their street identities. They won't be asked, as Boo-Boo was, to take a 25 percent pay cut after several months on the job. Still, the informal economy is hardly a mecca of opportunity. The risks are serious and, in many cases, have been undertaken by the Hallway Hangers only when other options have been played out. After being cheap labor fodder for firms intent on avoiding unions and even the minimal obligations of a bona fide payroll, many of the Hallway Hangers have been unemployed but barred from the unemployment line. Ineligible for benefits and desperate for income, they have moved from outlaw "under the table" employment to illegal jobs dealing drugs. For most of them, the experience has proved as unsatisfactory as their work in the formal economy.

While there has been a shift in the U.S. economy from manufacturing to service jobs, a dramatic change has occurred in the Clarendon Heights drug economy with the arrival of crack cocaine. In early 1984 marijuana was still the most popular drug in Clarendon Heights. But with U.S. drug policy concentrating on interception at the borders, the price of marijuana has skyrocketed while the cost of cocaine has come down.

FRANKIE: Cocaine's getting cheaper. Now you can get a quarter [gram] for fifteen bucks. . . . Pot's outrageous nowadays. I mean, jeez, you're paying a hundred and eighty bucks for an ounce. When I first started smoking pot, it was forty bucks, you get a four-finger ounce. Pot's too high. It's too big to smuggle. C'mon, y'know? Seventy thousand dollars of cocaine you throw in your suitcase. You need a fucking truck for the pot.

(in a separate conversation)

SHORTY: Weed's too expensive. . . . You used to get a joint the size of your pinkie for a buck. Now you pay five dollars for a pinner. You get a couple of pieces of leaves, two twigs, and about ten seeds, and you're paying five bucks for it. . . . The cheapest thing is coke. Everybody and their mother's doing coke now.

As in the rest of the country, cocaine became much more prevalent in Clarendon Heights during the mid-1980s. In 1984 all of the Hallway Hangers enjoyed snorting powdered cocaine for its intense, euphoric high. Chris would occasionally dissolve the powdered cocaine into an injectable fluid and "shoot it up."

Then came the biggest change in the local drug economy: Cocaine began to be marketed in its unadulterated "base" form, known as "crack." Prepared and distributed in small crystalline quantities, crack sold for as little as five dollars, far less than the minimum price tag for powdered cocaine. And crack is easily smoked. Absorbed into the bloodstream through thousands of tiny capillaries in the lungs rather than through the nose's mucous membrane, crack cocaine provides a more intense high. And whereas powder can be "cut" and significantly adulterated, base or crack is purer and more addictive.

JINX: Crack, it's cheaper to buy [than powdered cocaine]. The high is better than just snorting coke, but it don't last as long. Everyone enjoys it more, but the only problem it's more addictive. You get addicted quicker to it. . . . It's a good high, but then after you're comin' down and you have no more money and you can't get no more, it's depression. It's even worse than comin' down from snorting it. You're like, "Wow, where did all my fuckin' money go?" And if you have anything in your pocket, you'll go give it to the dealer to get more crack.

(in a separate interview)

FRANKIE: Coke is faster-paced [than marijuana], it's more addicting and you need a lot more, and people realized that. That's why they developed crack, cuz it's even more addicting. . . . Everybody's out there to get their own, man, if you're hooked on the shit. I know personally, you take that first hit, and it feels fucking great. But after that, you're just chasing, man, feel like shit the rest of the time. And, y'know, you'll do whatever it takes to fuckin' get high.

The advent of crack capitalism in Clarendon Heights has changed the nature of dealing. Buyers no longer come into doorway #13, sample the merchandise, haggle over the price, and make their purchase. The transaction is now furtive and impersonal as money and prepackaged drugs change hands swiftly. The large volumes of cash and the desperation of addicts make the threat of predatory violence from customers and competitors as worrisome as police detection. "It's a fucking drugstore out here," relates Steve. "Twenty-four hours a day." Indeed, before the police cracked down, a convenient "drive-through" dimension had been added to the business. Customers placed their order at the curb, drove around the block, and picked up their drugs on the return pass.

The Hallway Hangers report that by dealing full-time they could make up to a thousand dollars a week. Some worked as street sellers; others worked out of their homes and out of bars. Chris, Slick, Jinx, and Frankie have all dealt intensively on a full-time basis, but none of them was able to stay in the drug business for more than a year. The other Hallway Hangers—Steve, Shorty, Boo-Boo, and Stoney—have peddled drugs sporadically over the past seven years to supplement their incomes.

If the Hallway Hangers can make so much money in the drug economy, why don't they make a career of it? All of them understand the risks. Three young men on the fringes of the Hallway Hangers have been killed over the past five years, and the Hallway Hangers themselves have lost their youthful sense of immortality. Many of them have been pushed out of the underground economy by teenagers who are willing to take more risks.

FRANKIE: There's a lotta quick money to be made, so they're cliquin' up, they're becoming cliques, gangs, whatever you wanna fucking call 'em. And, y'know, they don't care about dyin', so they saying. That's the coke talkin', and I know that. But, y'know, it's the image they have to put out.

When Slick dealt full-time, he and his girlfriend, Denise, lived in a condominium. A year later he bailed out because of the risks.

JM: How did you go back to eight dollars an hour if you know you can make . . .

SLICK: Two hundred dollars a day . . .

JM: On the street?

SLICK: Yeah. You gotta remember, you gonna get caught. People, kids on the street, guys, they don't think far enough ahead. They thinkin' for now, "What can I do right now?" Don't forget when you're sixty-five and don't get no Social Security, what you gonna do then, still sell drugs? Sometimes it does pay off, though.

JM: Can it pay off over the long term if you play your cards right?

SLICK: Can it pay off? Yeah, it can. But there's not too many people out there who can do it, y'know? It takes a lot of organizational skills. You can make a go, but then you gotta worry about getting caught, you always gotta be looking over your shoulder. Worry that someone's gonna rat you out. And that's a big worry, believe me, every night. Every time you see a police officer, thinking, "Is he gonna be grabbing me on something?" You always gotta look out. You always gotta worry about it. This is my second son. Before he was born, before I started working steady, I was making whatever money I could, but I knew when to stop, you know what I mean? You can't—I knew when not to go too far, knew when I was pushing it.

Jinx very nearly pushed it too far and, like Slick, hates to consider what that would have meant for his child.

JINX: I was runnin' with this guy. I was sellin' for him. I had five pounds of pot. I had it in three different houses. I would go with him to pick up a kilo of cocaine. Go with him, break it up on the scale into ounces. I was making money. It was a quick cash flow.

JM: During that time, how much would you bring in on a good week?

JINX: On a good week a couple of thousand dollars, easily.

JM: So how would you discipline yourself from getting used to making that kind of money to go back to a steady job?

JINX: See, I got, I got a scare of my lifetime because the kid I was dealing with was with a few other people, and they got arrested for murder. And they doin' big time in jail now. They got convicted. That was enough to put fear in me.

JM: You could've been with them?

JINX: Exactly. Because I was goin' everywhere with this guy. I mean, I was seeing machine guns, hand grenades; this guy had everything. And he would've done anything for me. And I was the same way. I would've done anything for him. So I looked at it as I could've been in that position.

JM: Did you just stop completely?

JINX: Yes, yes, I did away with it all.

JM: Right, and so lookin' back on that . . .

JINX: It's a scary thought, it's a scary thought. I look at it: There was two paths I could've took. I took the right one. If I took the wrong one, I could be dead right now, or I could be behind bars for the rest of my life, never have the chance to see my son grow.

Apart from the risks of violence and arrest, the Hallway Hangers perceive the impact that cocaine addiction had on their profit margin.

JM: What happened with your dealing?

FRANKIE: Well, for one thing, my connection got popped [arrested]. But another thing is that my habit grew. I was kinda losing money cuz I was doing more. And the people working for me, they were coming up with some *serious* stories, y'know, "This happened . . ." Cuz I know today their habit grew.

It became a losing business for me. Just due to addiction. . . . I useta have a quarter gram of coke last me a night. Towards the end, y'know, that wasn't even a hit.

Addiction also cut into Steve's illicit earnings in the cocaine trade.

STEVE: I was sellin' the shit for a while. I got heavy into that.

JM: Just marijuana, or coke?

STEVE: Coke. I got too heavy. . . .

JM: That's where the money is?

STEVE: Yeah, but it's not worth it either. You do more than you sell, for chrissakes. You get caught up in it.

"Getting caught up in cocaine" is a recurrent theme among the Hallway Hangers.

FRANKIE: I got violent, man. And I know today the coke had a lot to do with it. I never really did coke before, cuz I seen what it did. But then I just got caught up in it. It made me violent, between that and the booze. When I useta just drink, I'd get drunk, I'd go home, and I'd pass out. When I drink and do coke, I stay up. I get crazy. And coke enabled me to drink more. It also changed my attitude. You get low on your coke, you start thinkin' where the next shit's coming from. You do anything to get it. Rob, steal, beat the shit outta someone, do what you gotta do. I know that's what I did. . . .

I was all over, man. I tell ya, I'd be in an apartment on Juniper Street one day and I'd be gettin' high with fuckin' two Colombians in the suburbs at four o'clock in the morning the next night. And don't know these two fuckers from a hole in the wall. It was sick. It put me in situations that . . . See, one thing I was brought up, be careful who you're with, keep your mouth fucking shut, and just go about your business. I started doing coke and I started searching for these crazy fucking people cuz I knew they had coke and I knew I wanted it. I was around people I didn't like, man. I knew they were snitches, they were no good; but they had coke, so I would buddy up with them, y'know? Something that totally goes against my grain, what I was taught. So yeah, it fuckin', it even lowered my street values, which is, y'know, pretty incredible. . . .

I know what it is like to be strung out on fuckin' coke and to think—I mean, I've thought of suicide, homicide myself, on coke. . . .

I did controlled thieving and shit like that, y'know? In the end, I'd deal the coke but I'd just deal it so I'd have some for me. I wouldn't deal it to make money. Y'know, I'd go grab an eight-ball off one guy and sell so much and have the rest for me. And then I'd just take it. Fuck up people, y'know? Fuck it. I was entitled to it, so I thought.

Boo-Boo also got caught up in the cocaine racket—with near-fatal consequences.

BOO-BOO: I got caught up in all this bullshit. Drugs and shit, cocaine. I was caught up in drugs from November of '90 til the first of June [1991]. I got caught up in the drugs. I moved to Raymond and I started meeting all kinds of people, cuz my sister lived there. One night, they just come over and they had coke and stuff like that, and they said, "Do you mind?" Cuz they were smoking it.

And a kid come out and said, "Do you want to try it?" And that it would be good. So I did it, and it was, *tsph,* just caught up in it. I was just caught up, I could feel it coming over me.

JM: It's a good high?

BOO-BOO: Yeah. Excellent. So I just got caught up in it and it was, like, an everyday thing. It was like I didn't care about anything. Well, I cared, but that's what I wanted to do almost every day, get high and get high and get high and get high. . . .

I never really had money. I was never really buying it. It was just, like, people coming over, people would ask me where they could get it and I was getting it for them. It was just craziness. . . . At the beginning, it just started off with one day them coming over and they got like twenty dollars' worth of stuff and we sat there and we, like, smoked it, and it just, it just, y'know, they'd come back the next day and they'd have more, and I'd go out and I'd, like, snooze around just to get a little more higher and stuff like that. Sometimes we'd be up all night, 'til the next morning, smoking and smoking and smoking and smoking. Not caring. Just started not caring about anything, really. . . . They'd all come up to our apartment. It was one of the biggest drug streets in Raymond. The people upstairs on both sides, they sold it. They sold it across the street, down the street, around the corner. It was, it was just everywhere.

JM: So were you able to make some money that way?

BOO-BOO: I was making a little bit of money, then one time I got caught up with this guy who gave me some stuff to sell, and I didn't.

JM: Smoked it all?

BOO-BOO: All of it. He tried to shoot me twice. . . . He gave me three hundred and forty dollars' worth of stuff, worth of rocks all made up. He told me I could keep seventy dollars for myself and sell the rest. I said fine. So what I did is, like a fool, I smoked one of them things, and it was history. I sold some, but then I spent that money on more. Screwed up. He almost shot me. Came to my house like three days later with a nine millimeter, and he was gonna shoot me. He had the gun out. I just had to beg him, told him I'd get the money for him. I tried to get up the money. I got up some of the money for him, but I didn't get it all. And then one day I was out and still getting high and he saw me, pulled the gun on me again. I was lucky, man. . . . Drugs will fuck you up.

Of all the Hallway Hangers, it is Chris who most dramatically illustrates how "drugs will fuck you up." Interviewed in 1991 as he awaited trial for three armed robberies, Chris described his tight downward spiral.

CHRIS: It's been crazy. I know it. I can see what I've done to my mom, what I'm doing to myself. I can see it, but I can't fucking seem to do anything about it. I've got the habit and I can't kick it. Freebasing. I'd just do what I had to to take care of business. I'd leave Samantha sleeping in a hallway and go out and do whatever I had to so we could get our next smoke. Break into houses and take money, cameras, VCRs, stereos, mountain bikes, clothes—whatever shit I could find. And then sell them on the street for next to nothing. Cuz these motherfuckers *know* you're desperate. Man, I've taken fifty bucks for a stereo I know is worth more than a thousand. But it don't matter, cuz whatever I got would be smoked up. I stole five hundred dollars out of a guy's wallet. It was on his dresser and his keys fell right by his fucking head. Dude didn't wake up, though. I took his mountain bike—it was right by the door—and rode back to where Samantha was spending the night in this base house. I sold the mountain bike by ten o'clock for a hundred bucks. By noon we were broke. Went through that six hundred bucks in a morning. You do a hit, next thing you know, you're broke. . . . Man, I stole my sister's jewelry, all kinds of shit. Now look at me. No socks, no deodorant cuz I don't have no money. Shittin' in a fucking bucket in here, no lie. What the fuck kind of life is this?

Awaiting trial, Chris has checked into the jail's detox and drug-rehab program, the first move he has made to deal with his drug problem. Even so, Chris speaks with a subdued desperation, has little hope for the future, and feels desperately lonely.

Denied conventional careers, the Hallway Hangers have turned to the underground economy. Peddling drugs holds out the prospect of fast money and respect on the street. But a workplace that offers more dignity than jobs in the formal economy turns out to be fraught with danger. And for drug entrepreneurs, distribution has a way of turning into consumption, especially of crack cocaine. The Hallway Hangers have quit the drug business, but not before some were sucked into a downward spiral fueled by their own addiction, of which

Chris is only the most spectacular example. "Caught up in" the cocaine racket, the Hallway Hangers have generally lost rather than gained autonomy and independence in the informal economy.

The allure of a career in the underground economy makes sense only when measured against the competing option of an underpaid menial job in the secondary labor market. Unemployment is the most powerful incentive. Frankie dealt intensively when he was jobless after returning from out of state in 1988. Laid off from his hotel job, Jinx renewed a friendship with a big-time player in the drug world and began dealing for him. And Slick turned to the drug economy in 1990 when his construction job was one of thousands threatened by the local economy's steep slide. In neighborhoods like Clarendon Heights, there are few career alternatives to crack capitalism.

For the Hallway Hangers drugs are a form of recreation as well as a form of work. Asked about their abuse of drugs and alcohol, Stoney replies, "That's our recreation. Rich kids might go skiing or snowmobiling or go on vacations. We get high." The Hallway Hangers do not have the resources to "get away from it all" through conventional leisure pursuits, so they use drugs to escape the boredom, powerlessness, and despair that poverty breeds.

Stoney implies that the attraction of drugs for the Hallway Hangers can be understood only against the backdrop of class exploitation; Slick makes a similar point from a different angle.

JM: Why did you, not you particularly but the whole group of you, use drugs so heavily? What was the allure of drugs for you guys?

SLICK: Escape.

JM: From?

SLICK: From the way you are. You know what I mean. You use drugs, you get a sense of fucking balls. You know what I mean? You're not yourself. You're somebody that you really want to be.

Drugs, says Slick, promise power and self-actualization, which are otherwise beyond the Hallway Hangers. After five years of living among and learning from crack dealers in East Harlem, anthropologist Philippe Bourgois agrees. Bourgois argues that drugs provide an illusory escape from oppression. "Instantaneously," he writes, "the user is transformed from an unemployed, depressed high school dropout, despised by the world—and secretly convinced that his failure is due to his own inherent stupidity and disorganization."[14] But the "born-again metamorphosis" offered by substance abuse, especially crack, energizes the user for only a matter of minutes at most. And as Slick has learned from hard experience, drugs do not provide power—only a fleeting "sense" of it. Moreover, the dependency and instability that drugs often bring in their wake only compound and thicken the debilitating effects of poverty from which drugs are meant to offer an escape.

Drug dealing is the most popular way of generating income in the underground economy, but it is not the only way. Theft was an important element in the early criminal careers of the Hallway Hangers; they stole bicycles and cars, broke into local stores and factories, and often sold the stolen merchandise on the underground market to pay for teenage necessities like sneakers and six-packs. Chris continued to steal to support his cocaine habit; and Frankie, until he quit doing drugs, would rob or extort money and drugs from younger, less experienced criminals. But the link between drugs and crime works differently for Stoney. Rather than robbing in order to get high, Stoney seems to get high in order to commit mindless robberies.

STONEY: It's the Valiums, man. They make me do crazy shit but I can't seem to leave them alone. I'll do ten or fifteen of 'em and then drink to get the high. Afterwards, I can't remember what I've done, won't remember a thing.

As noted earlier, Stoney was convicted of attempting to rob a convenience store with a tire iron after taking ten Valiums and drinking on top of that. "It's a stupid high; it's a fuckup high," Stoney admits. "It depresses you." Several months after his release from prison, he was arrested again for armed robbery—again, after drinking and dropping Valiums. This was the time he had held up a pizza deliveryman for forty dollars and a large pizza.

By contrast, Boo-Boo turned to robbery for strictly economic reasons, two years before getting involved in serious drug abuse. He was living with his girlfriend, Ginger, and their two children in a dilapidated basement apartment because Ginger had not received a subsidized housing voucher.

JM: When you were unemployed, how would you hustle up the money and stuff?

BOO-BOO: Whaddya mean?

JM: How would you get, y'know, how would you survive?

BOO-BOO: Well, my girlfriend got her check and stuff like that. . . . And me and some friends, we robbed a night deposit thing one night. Made three thousand dollars. Got caught up in that. We did that a couple of times. . . . I did it cuz I needed, our bills were all screwed up and stuff. We were behind in rent, and I needed food and my kids needed clothes, and Ginger wanted all kinds of stuff for the house and stuff like that. So I went, me and this kid, we made good money. . . .

See, any business on this whole street, they always, they hafta, either they have a safe in the store, or they have to take the money to a bank, either way.

So after like seven o'clock or so, you just sit out there, just watch 'em for one week, and then the next week, you go and just take it, and run. It's like snatching a pocketbook or taking a newspaper. Y'know, it's easy.

JM: And you'd have a car nearby where you could get up outta there?

BOO-BOO: No, just run a coupla blocks, hop into a cab [*chuckles*], and go home. I did it twice. One time we went and robbed in Jackson Square and they had these big giant bags with a whole bunch of small bags in them. They were all checks, we had like a million dollars in checks.

JM: Were you able to cash any of them in, or . . .

BOO-BOO: No, we just threw 'em in the river, got rid of them. . . . I got away from that, though. Cuz if you get caught, it's federal stuff. I got away from that.

Boo-Boo has turned to theft when unemployed and under severe financial pressure. Other Hallway Hangers have also chosen economic crime or "off the books" employment when decent, aboveboard jobs eluded them. Some have resorted to dealing drugs after losing legitimate jobs. Others have dabbled in the drug economy to supplement their wages from jobs in the formal sector. In general, the underground economic initiatives of the Hallway Hangers have been undertaken when these young men have been deprived of legitimate economic opportunities.

However, the entrepreneurial criminal careers of the Hallway Hangers have not been governed by economic rationality alone. The Hallway Hangers are not cool cost-benefit analysts. Their actions on the job market, both aboveboard and below, are inextricably linked with their emergent social identities, with their sense of who they are. The Hallway Hangers experienced school together—they developed rituals of resistance, indulged in the joys of alienation, and collectively projected identities they considered superior to those of other students and school staff. In a sense, the street is an extension of their schooling. The underground economy allows scope for collective experience and expression, whereas the new service economy does not. The cultural experience of working in a service-sector job is completely different from the interpersonal dynamics of working on the shop floor in a factory. In the factory, aspects of working-class and street culture are assets. One can afford to be tough, macho, quick-witted, verbally sharp, and resistant to authority; collective identity and solidarity, formed at the point of production, are encouraged and given expression by unions. The Hallway Hangers, in contrast, tend to experience the job structure as atomized individuals. Their work sites allow little space for resistance. Whereas the new service economy pays poorly and severely circumscribes cultural identity, the underground economy pays well and seems to offer scope for collective expression and resistance to authority.

And yet, in reality, cocaine capitalism, far from creating conditions in which the collective identity of the Hallway Hangers can flourish, further fragments their peer group.

JM: You guys used to be tight. Tell me about how that started to change and why.

FRANKIE: You want my theory?

JM: Yeah.

FRANKIE: I believe it was cocaine that separated a lot of us. You start out doing cocaine, y'know, you share it. You start getting a little hooked on cocaine, you start hiding it. You don't wanna be around people. You don't wanna share. It's a sick drug, man. It does a number on you. A couple of people went in and outta jail. So between goin' in and outta jail, and drugs and women. I know for me I clung onto a woman. It's a combination of a lot: between jail and cocaine, I know cocaine definitely separates people. You fucking grate on each other. You begin hating each other, y'know? Between women, coke, and jail. Lotta guys were in jail, lottta guys were just fucked-up, man. People took their outs. A few went jail, some went drugs—that's about the only two routes we went, I guess.

Marginalized more than ever by the shift from manufacturing to a service economy, the Hallway Hangers turn to the underground economy for financial gain and cultural affirmation. They find neither. Drug distribution in pursuit of profit easily turns into costly drug addiction and desperate, self-destructive behavior. Drug dependency also weakens their friendship ties and further dissolves their peer group.

Prison, of course, provides ample opportunity to develop a collective identity around resistance. Chris, Stoney, Shorty, and Steve have been incarcerated for most of the period since 1984, and Slick has also done a stint behind bars. The Hallway Hangers have shared a common experience in prison, which, like school, provides a clear institutional structure to challenge.

SHORTY: We were all up there, man, at one time—me, Steve, and Slick in '87 and '88. Steve's like, "I love it up here." Hell, we were sayin', "If the judges could see us now, eh? We're in here, we're drinking home brew and smokin' dope, getting high. Don't have to pay no rent, no electricity, we have to pay for no food, sittin' here living it up. If the judge could see us now, right?"

The Hallway Hangers were able to create and exploit spaces even within the "total institution" of prison to celebrate their little victories and make life bearable, but the conditions of incarceration remained unchanged, as Shorty articulated in his next breath.

SHORTY: It sucks, y'know, it sucks. You don't like to have someone getting paid eight dollars an hour to tell you what to do. And the screws will fuck you over. Lock you up for ninety days. Locked up all day long. They don't let you out for chow or nothing. They slide your chow under the door. They only let you out on Wednesdays and Saturdays to take a shower—they give you fifteen minutes. . . . I've got sick of doing fucking time. Sick of fuckin' gettin' in a fucking cell. A dog has more room in a fucking kennel than two guys have in a cell. You got two guys in a fucking cell. It's a hundred and fucking eight degrees. Fucking, one farts or something—it smells for twenty-four hours. No fucking circulation in the fucking thing. No AC. Fuckin', in the winter you freeze. All fucking holes in the window. You get some fucking asshole that's working. You wanna make a phone call cuz somebody's sick in your family, and he's being a prick to you, "Fuck you, you ain't gettin' a phone call." You wanna kill him.

The social relations and physical conditions of prison life combine to create an extraordinarily oppressive situation.

Stoney detests prison life. "I hate it, I can't stand it," he declares. "It's the physical aspect and the psychological aspect: I don't know which fucks you up more." However, after six stints in prison, Stoney is becoming "institutionalized"—dependent on prison life. Recall that in 1987 he requested to serve a suspended six-month sentence.

STONEY: It's weird, y'know, when I did these dumb robberies I was high, really fucked-up. But I was also like, fuck it, I'll go back to jail if I have to. It's weird, but I kinda feel safer in prison than out there. It's hard to believe. But that's the way it is.

Stoney's absurdly inept armed robberies may have stemmed from a longing, conscious or unconscious, for the security of prison life.

Shorty thrived in prison, at least from an entrepreneurial point of view. He made and sold knives, peddled drugs, and helped run a gambling operation.

SHORTY: They raided my cell; they thought I had weed. I did have weed, I had twenty-two joints—they couldn't even fucking find it. It was underneath my pail. They took down my curtains, everything. They found sixty-four football cards. I had homemade football cards. They busted me for racketeering. [*laughs*] I had football cards and lottery sheets. I used to take the numbers and run the betting on the games. . . . I know how to make some real nice ice picks. From the headphones of Walkmans, you know the metal piece that goes through there? I used to go to people's cells and rip them off, steal their fucking shit. Take it, rip it apart, get the metal piece and put two of them together, and I'd put tape around 'em. Get tape from either a guard or from fuckin' some of the maintenance workers. Put the tape around it and file it on the ground, out to a ice pick. Some nice ones I made in there, baby.

JM: You'd make money that way?

SHORTY: Yeah. I was selling 'em for five-packs.

JM: Cigarettes.

SHORTY: Yeah, cuz one day we were s'posed to have a racial riot, us and the blacks. It never happened, but I still made a lot of money on them.

Ultimately, the Hallway Hangers are themselves hurt by the racial hatred they sow. But prison is one place where Shorty has actually managed to squeeze some short-term profit from racial antagonism.

Incredibly, none of the Hallway Hangers have been arrested on drug charges since 1984. And although Chris and Stoney have been convicted of robberies, no other Hallway Hanger has been convicted of an economic crime. The Hallway Hangers have been caught perpetrating violence rather than committing economic crime. They have been arrested for assault, assault and battery, assault on a police officer, assault with a deadly weapon, violating restraining orders, mayhem, and attempted murder. This pattern contrasts sharply with that found by Mercer Sullivan in his study of young offenders in three Brooklyn neighborhoods. Sullivan found that white, Latino, and African American men all moderated their street fighting as their careers in economic crime unfolded. Moreover, their forays into economic crime more often resulted in arrest than did their street violence.[15] Why do the Hallway Hangers intelligently and calculatingly bow out of dealing drugs as the risks mount, yet succumb to the temptation of mindless violence? In fact, the violence of the Hallway Hangers is neither mindless nor random. It's not about money. It's about something more important to these young men: protecting and projecting their identities.

PRODUCING THEMSELVES

The Hallway Hangers' violent crimes are tied to their identities as men—specifically, as white men. Street fighting is about maintaining one's status, and for the Hallway Hangers this status is defined in relation to, and usually at the expense of, people of color. Back in 1983 Slick made that connection explicit: "If you have a fight up the high school, you're considered bad . . . especially if he's black, around this way." Eight years later, the Hallway Hangers are still at it—and these incidents involve not just hotheads like Steve and Shorty but Frankie and Slick as well. A telling fact emerges from these incidents: Most of the victims have been black.

Shorty was lucky to be convicted of only disorderly conduct for assaulting two African Americans with a knife.

SHORTY: I got arrested in front of the projects. For disorderly conduct. I was chasing these two black guys—I had 'em in the cellar [actually a large stairwell outside a basement office near doorway #13] with a knife, chased 'em into the cellar. I was about to stab them when all the cops jumped on me and shit.

Slick was also imprisoned after fighting with black youths. "The reason I went to jail," he relates, "was because I threw them two niggers off the porch." Frankie was charged with attempted murder, his victim a Latino youth.

FRANKIE: I almost killed this Spanish guy, I beat him with a baseball bat. I remember sittin' in the jail cell and the cop told me the guy died. It was Martin Luther King weekend, so I had a few days to think about this guy being dead. Then this cop told me that he was okay. He wasn't okay, but he wasn't dead, y'know? He ended up being in the hospital a while, about a month or so. He ended up having a broken jaw, broken ribs, broken eye socket, broken shin. . . . He had bumped into my girl. It was a fight, y'know? He had a knife. I had a bat. He lost. I only got a year's probation cuz he was trying to stab me, too. Hey, I was protecting myself.

Six months later Frankie and Steve were charged with assault and battery, armed robbery, and malicious destruction. Their victim was a Haitian cab driver. Frankie and Steve, both on probation, faced ten years in state prison until the case against them fell apart when the unlicensed driver failed to appear in court. All of these confrontations took place in front of Clarendon Heights.

It appears that the Hallway Hangers, lacking the traditional marks of working-class manhood—blue-collar breadwinning jobs and households of their own—have tried to shore up their masculine identities through highly public displays of violence. This violence is not directed indiscriminately; the Hallway Hangers lash out at those by whom they feel threatened: black men. They seek to regain a sense of male power by asserting their dominance at its most basic level—raw physical violence. In his study of youth unemployment, Paul Willis warns that without the social and cultural identity afforded by a job, young men may resolve their "gender crisis" through an "aggressive assertion of masculinity" and a "physical, tough, direct display of those qualities now 'automatically' guaranteed by doing productive work." Such aggression, Willis adds, "may also deepen some of the brutalities and oppressions experienced by working-class women."[16]

Indeed, some of the Hallway Hangers have directed their animosity and violence toward women. Steve was jailed once for ransacking his girlfriend's apartment and destroying much of her property. He has also been arrested for violating restraining orders and beating his girlfriend. Shorty's claimed conversion to monogamy came not out of feelings of fidelity but out of a fear of AIDS, and his confession of lapses underscores his own frankly exploitative attitude toward women. In contrast to the other Hallway Hangers, Steve admits to carrying on several casual sexual relationships simultaneously. I stayed with Steve for several days in 1991. He was an exceptionally solicitous host, constantly asking after my needs. This generosity contrasted sharply with his attitude toward women. Arriving back at his mother's Clarendon Heights apartment one evening to find the door locked, I joined a teenage girl sitting on the stoop. She was waiting for Steve to return and walk her home. "He's just gone around the corner to call his son's mother," she said, smiling. We waited an hour and then I drove her home. Back at his apartment later that night, I asked him what happened. "Yeah, I was s'posed to walk her home, but I saw Shorty and we went for a few beers and then bought us a couple of gems [crack crystals]. She's pretty fucking nice, though, huh? Only fucking fifteen, though." Then, laughing, "I fucked her on your bed. Sorry about that." Sexual exploitation, underlined by postcoital disregard, seems to feed Steve's sense of masculine superiority and dominance.

Whereas other Hallway Hangers may have physically abused their partners (Shorty is rumored to have beaten his girlfriend), Jinx set upon the police in a public display of violence. When police officers used excessive force while arresting his disabled brother, Jinx "went a little crazy and attacked the cops." Boo-Boo has also been arrested for assaulting a police officer. Taking on the police, potent symbols of power and authority, may dramatically improve one's masculine credibility among Clarendon Heights peers, but it's also the one violent street crime that's unlikely to go unpunished, and most of the Hallway Hangers shy away from police confrontations.

In one extraordinary incident, Shorty managed to combine racial hatred with violence against women and the police.

SHORTY: I lived with this girl, I was with her for about fucking six months, then I went to jail. And she was with a nigger when I come out. I got outta jail and fuckin', I went crazy when she was with a nigger. That was my worst nightmare. I told her, I says, "Hey, I know I'm gonna be away for a while." Says, "Do what you gotta do," y'know? "If you gotta get fucking laid, get laid," y'know? [*groans*] But then when it was a fucking nigger, she's lucky she's livin' and I'm lucky I'm not doing a fucking murder beef. I almost threw her out the third-floor window. Instead, I tore the door off. Took a knife, cut apart the whole power set, tore the fuckin' fridge doors off, threw them out the third-floor window. Threw the stereo, threw the TV, everything out the window. I almost did big time for that. The cops come up sayin', "Shorty, calm down." I said, "Boff [*smacks fist into palm*]. Fuck you." I bit three fucking cops, assaulted about eight of 'em. I was in tip-top fucking shape. I went in jail weighing 238 pounds, I come out weighing 155. The cops all started jumping on me, hitting me with billy clubs. I was still fightin' 'em, kept fucking fightin' and fightin', and then they finally just kept whacking me with the clubs, and I was knocked out.

This incident illustrates the desperation and futility of the Hallway Hangers' contorted efforts to preserve a sense of personal and social ascendancy amid a tangle of racial, gender, and class issues.

Shorty's story highlights the connection between the Hallway Hangers' racism and the imagined threat of black sexual superiority. Recall that in 1983 Frankie concluded that two white girls provided Chris with cocaine because "they want to suck his black cock, that's why." And when Shorty's girlfriend slept with an African American, Shorty seems to have considered it a direct challenge to his manhood and responded with an orgy of violence. For Shorty, this "worst nightmare" represented the most extreme incursion of black power into his world. For the white Hallway Hangers, perceived black ascendancy haunts them in Clarendon Heights, in the underground street economy, and on the legitimate labor market. Now, it seemed to Shorty, blacks were superseding him in the bedroom.

The Hallway Hangers are obsessed with the number of African American residents moving into Clarendon Heights and allegedly taking control of the neighborhood.

JINX: They're movin' more black families and foreign families into this place than white families. A white family moves out, a foreign family moves in. Now you tell me there's no white families out there on the housing list. It's just discrimination. . . . It's been a lot more drugs comin' around here. . . . The violence has gone up around here. I mean, there's been a few shootin's around here.

JM: There's always been shootings.

JINX: Yeah, but I mean the shootings were not people shootin' each other, just, y'know, one black dude shootin' another black dude over a sale or over turf. Now it's over drugs, the shootings out here. Before there was a solid reason behind the shootings. Now they're all out here sellin' the shit. Now it's drive-by shootings. I don't want my kid to be out there.

JM: Who's "they," when you say "they"?

JINX: I mean all the black kids. They sit out here twenty-four hours a night sellin' crack. Now you got black people out here who you don't even know who the hell they are. I don't feel safe at all.

Frankie also contrasts the mythological golden years of Clarendon Heights with the way things are now.

FRANKIE: Lemme tell ya, when I grew up in Clarendon Heights, even though it was a bad place to a lotta people, to a lotta the outside people—even, y'know, cops wouldn't come down there—but within the community we were tight.

Everyone knew their next-door neighbor, everybody looked out for each other. Cuz we were tight. I look at it today and now you've got niggers from the East Side, from Riverside, y'know, niggers from all over. No one knows each other. Before everybody knew everyone, and everybody took care of everybody. Now everyone's out for themselves.

JM: What's the cause of that?

FRANKIE: I believe the fuckin' black culture is a major reason for that. Y'know, I still suffer from Archie Bunkerism, but, y'know, that's just somethin' that's been inbred inta me. But that's [black culture] got a lot to do with it.

JM: Because . . .

FRANKIE: Because they're fuckin', they have no fuckin' values in life. They don't respect themselves, how they gonna respect others? And I honestly believe that. And the reason I honestly believe that is cuz I know. I've seen it. I've seen 'em all my life. I was always brought up to respect women, respect older people, and never rat on anyone. I look at the niggers and they don't respect their own mother. They have no respect, no respect for themselves.

The Hallway Hangers attribute problems that they themselves inflicted on Clarendon Heights for a number of years to new black residents and their friends. Clearly, they feel threatened by the rising tide of blacks in the neighborhood. In fact, the proportion of racial and ethnic minorities living in Clarendon Heights has increased substantially, though not as dramatically as the Hallway Hangers suggest. Whereas minorities accounted for roughly 35 percent of the project's residents in 1984, they made up nearly 60 percent of that total in 1991.

It's not the sheer number of African Americans in Clarendon Heights that bothers the Hallway Hangers as much as the sense that whites are losing control of the neighborhood. To the Hallway Hangers, black youths have the temerity to congregate in front of the housing project and outside doorway #13, hallowed space that the Hallway Hangers inherited from their elders and bequeathed to their younger peers but that is now lost forever to blacks who "don't know their place." The racism of the Hallway Hangers has a strong territorial dimension. Fears of invasion and displacement are powerful themes that point to the role of an imaginary territory in the social identities of these young men.[17]

Shorty's racism and its violent expression are evoked by black challenges to his status and sense of self. He works himself into a frenzy describing how "young, wise, cocky little niggers" around Clarendon Heights fail to show him the deference he deserves.

SHORTY: It's nothing but blacks there [Clarendon Heights], man. Some of 'em have no respect. One night I was there, I was looking for this black kid,

Super. I was gonna buy a couple of lines off him, right? Fuckin' two of them niggers givin' me a hard time, started laughing and shit while I was walkin' away. They were real wise, about sixteen or seventeen years old. I went back there, slapped one of 'em in the face, and said, "Who the fuck you think you're talkin' to?" Y'know? They got real cocky attitudes.

The Hallway Hangers, without the trappings of conventional success, always had their self-esteem invested in their tough street identities, but now even that street credibility is being eroded by assertive young blacks in their neighborhood. The incident recounted by Shorty began with the humiliation of having to search out a black youth to buy cocaine, a commodity whose local distribution the Hallway Hangers had hitherto controlled. Indeed, young African Americans have successfully challenged white control of the drug trade around Clarendon Heights, fueling the Hallway Hangers' resentment of blacks. "I was selling drugs," recounts Shorty. "We stopped sellin' cuz it was gettin' too hot. As you've noticed with all them niggers around sellin' 'em now."

The Hallway Hangers resent black competition in the drug trade but also on the legitimate job market. Chapter 7 explored how the racism of the Hallway Hangers retards class consciousness. Their feeling of being victimized by class exploitation is undermined by their conviction that affirmative action and blacks are the real problems. What begins as a rudimentary but promising perception of their condition is derailed into a strident racism that contributes to the oppression of other members of their social class and, ultimately, to their own continued subjugation. This tendency is even more dramatically illustrated by the recent research detailed here. The Hallway Hangers trace their problems as adults, particularly their employment problems, to "reverse discrimination." Jinx, the only white Hallway Hanger who empathized with blacks back in 1984, takes quite a different attitude in 1991.

JINX: Nowadays, you know who's the minority, right? The white American. You go to find a good job nowadays, you gotta be black, Puerto Rican, Indian, something to get anywhere. You're either overqualified or you're underqualified. And they give it to someone who don't know what the hell they doing. . . . That's how backwards this whole world is. It's so screwed up; you have double standards. That's what this world's full of is double standards. It ain't gettin' any better. It's gettin' worse as years go on. . . . Don't get me wrong, it's not stereotype niggers; it's Puerto Ricans, it's all these immigrants who come over off the boat. They can't speak much English but they can sign their name and get their paycheck every week on a good goddamn job that someone who worked their ass off all their life should be able to get. . . . It's not just the blacks. Minorities are taking over this fuckin' city. . . . I'm a typical American. I get no breaks in life. All I do is bust my ass. Everything that I should have a fair shot at, they say, y'know, "equal opportunity employer." But it's not equal opportunity employer, because they've got standards that say that they have to have so many blacks, so many minorities working for these companies. They have to be promoted before you; they have to get a shot at the job before you. They're entitled to it before you.

For Frankie, the Hallway Hangers are victims on account of their racial and gender identity. They are exploited as white men.

FRANKIE: Well, I look today, and if anyone shoulda had a chance to make it, it's fuckin', it's black people. They got a chance to make it. Cuz there's fucking quotas to be filled. I look today, y'know, I honestly believe the most discriminated person is a fucking white male between the ages of twenty and forty out there on a fucking job. Especially if you want any decent job—post office, public transportation job.

Here Frankie not only scapegoats African Americans, he also contrasts his occupational prospects with those of women.

Shorty takes the New Right rhetoric about white males as the new disadvantaged "minority" and gives it a sharp, characteristically perverse twist. Note the way he moves from seeing African Americans as a neighborhood menace to viewing them as an occupational threat, linking the two with a bizarre theory of impending racial Armageddon.

SHORTY: Those young niggers taking over this place can take their guns and all that kind of thing, none of that shit scares me. I'll stick it up their fuckin' arse. They better shoot me in the head, you know what I'm sayin'? Serious, I hate fucking spooks. I can't stand fucking niggers. I hate 'em.

JM: What does that go back to?

SHORTY: That goes back to like what Charles Manson said, there's goin' to be a fuckin' racial riot, racial fuckin' war, that's what's goin' to happen, believe me. Blacks against the whites, it's happening. We're the minorities now. Can't get a fuckin' job. Fucking all the projects around here in this city, all the maintenance guys, they're all fuckin' blacks and Puerto Ricans. They ain't hiring whites around here; you gotta be black, black or fucking spic. We're the minorities.

In 1984 Shorty was clear about where to lay the blame for his brother's unemployment: "It's cuz of the fuckin' spics and niggers." Seven years later, he traces his own employment problems to the same source: racial and ethnic minorities. And now Shorty, along with Jinx and Frankie, claims minority status for himself as a white man.

In a sense, the Hallway Hangers *are* a minority, not by virtue of their race or gender but on account of their social class. Minority status is fundamentally determined by a lack of power rather than by numbers, and as members of a particularly disadvantaged stratum of the working class, the Hallway Hangers are certainly lacking in power. But the class dimension of oppression eludes the Hallway Hangers. The job Shorty covets is in building maintenance, the lowest rung in the City Housing Authority's vast job structure. Shorty does not resent the virtual exclusion of people with working-class roots from senior supervisory positions and even from middle-level management and social work jobs. But he is prepared to wage war with racial and ethnic minorities, oblivious to the fact that he is fighting fellow victims over virtual crumbs.

Of the Hallway Hangers, now only Jinx explicitly critiques class injustice. He insightfully describes how differences in cultural capital handicap the poor and perpetuate social inequality.

JINX: We have not been given all the gifts we need to live a happy life. We have to get by with what we have. . . . A lot of people from this area are not well-spoken people, their grammar is not great. They grew up in the streets, hanging in the streets. They talk street slang. They don't know how to present themselves in an appropriate way, where people who come from high-class families, they're taught right away, you gotta be, do this, do that, do this, and they get the breaks because their parents know people. They know people, they got connections. That's how they got somewhere. You gotta have connections to get anywhere in life. If you don't know anybody, there's no one out there who's gonna just come to you and say, "Gee, you look like a good kid. Why don't I do this favor for you." It don't work like that.

Jinx recognizes that inequality is formed by the chasm in earnings and experiences between workers and capitalists.

JINX: One of my bosses, when I started workin' for him, he owned three companies. He was part-owning the one I work at. He doesn't never work. All he does all day is sits at his house and picks up the telephone. He must make a hundred thousand dollars a year just on the telephone.

Jinx also resents the preferential status and treatment that his boss's son enjoys at work, an injustice he sees "at my job and everywhere else, and it's just all over the world."

Jinx's comments notwithstanding, the Hallway Hangers generally fail to articulate a sense of class consciousness. Where, after all, would they get the resources to construct a sense of self that highlights social class? Certainly neither mass culture nor the media speak of class, and the Hallway Hangers' own experience of work has failed to instill a class identity. Only Frankie has been in a labor union, and in spite of his humiliating experience working under his boss's son, he fails to consider class injustice as constitutive of his plight. Instead, and against all the evidence, Frankie insists that as a white male he is handicapped by his race and gender. This sort of contorted explanation for the Hallway Hangers' failure to get ahead attests to the utter absence of a class-based ideology in the United States.

The Hallway Hangers' views point to the power and pervasiveness of the achievement ideology—the widespread belief that everyone has equal access to the American Dream. But they also point to the pressure being exerted by New Right ideology.[18] The New Right refrain that "reverse discrimination" victimizes white men meshes powerfully with the Hallway Hangers' sense of territorial displacement. In a way, New Right ideology rescues the achievement ideology. The Hallway Hangers feel exploited. As Jinx says, they bust their ass but get no breaks. But instead of questioning the achievement ideology, they adopt a peculiar version of it: "If only racial bias against whites was removed, then rewards would be based on merit and hard work, and we would prosper." The Hallway Hangers know they are oppressed, but under the combined sway of the achievement ideology and New Right rhetoric, they articulate their feelings of exploitation in the idiom of racial rather than class exclusion.

The Hallway Hangers forge their identities in terms of race and gender. Feelings of racial and male supremacy buttress their sense of self, since the psychological solace of conventional success eludes them. But their racism and sexism siphon off their rage and blind the Hallway Hangers to the reality of class injustice. African Americans are seen as a sexual and economic threat, and therefore as a challenge to the Hallway Hangers' masculine identities. Their male pride already suffering from their inability to secure good jobs and independent households, the Hallway Hangers aggressively assert their masculinity in displays of street violence usually directed against blacks and perpetrated in and around Clarendon Heights.

The African American threat is felt at two levels: at a private individual level and at a public communal level. Frankie tries to articulate a communal identity of white working-class fraternity, of an interdependent, protective community of which he is a part. Violence against blacks shores up the Hallway Hangers' individual masculine identities but also becomes part of an effort to defend a mythological community that they believe is disintegrating.[19] Viewing his girlfriend as an extension of himself, Shorty sees the black man in her bedroom as an incursion into his private territory and also as a threat to his public persona. His violent reaction became a public event, despite the fact that domestic abuse seldom comes to light. Other Hallway Hangers may dominate their partners privately, perhaps through physical brutality. But whereas in 1984 the Hallway Hangers were typically involved in short-term casual relationships, all but Steve and Boo-Boo are now seriously involved in avowed monogamous partnerships. All except Chris are fathers, and four of the Hangers have two children each. For many of the Hallway Hangers, fatherhood has become a key element in their identities.

If the Hallway Hangers have attempted to shore up their sense of self through exaggerated displays of masculinity, fatherhood has pulled in the opposite direction by prompting many Hallway Hangers to rethink what manhood is all about. Jinx lives with Beth, his girlfriend of eight years, and their five-year-old son, Mark.

JM: What was your reaction when you found out you were going to be a father?

JINX: I was shocked. I was seventeen and she was sixteen. The first reaction was she wanted an abortion, but her mother would not let her get one.

JM: What about you?

JINX: Me? I didn't wanna be a daddy either at the time. I knew it would take all my freedom away. But then as she started carrying it, I got more excited about it. I got more and more excited about it.

JM: I notice you spend most evenings with him. Do you get any shit from the guys for doing that?

JINX: No, no. They more or less respect me for it.

JM: Why is it that some people will take that kind of responsibility and others don't? I mean, Steve babysits his kids sometimes, but he doesn't seem to feel much responsibility for them.

JINX: It's like, it's like they try to hide their true feelings that they have in their heart. They have to put out a macho image. It's like they're afraid of somebody actually knowin' what they feel inside.

The tension between their macho street image and the tenderness and devotion demanded by parenthood is felt by other Hallway Hangers as well. Several visits to Slick's home reveal that he dotes on his baby son, and partly because his girlfriend, Denise, has reverted to her cocaine habit since giving birth, Slick undertakes many household and parenting chores.

SLICK: See, my father screwed on us when we were kids. I always said I'd never do that to my children. I like being a father. I love my kids. I love them more than anything in the world. You try to, all you want to do is do the right thing for the kids. You want to be able to hear him say, "Yeah, my dad was there for me." That's it. They don't have to say anything else good. They can say I was an asshole. I don't care about that. I just don't want them never to be able to say that I wasn't there when they needed me. Cuz that's one big thing I hold over my father. I don't believe in a father that's not paying attention to their children. . . . I see my three-year-old at least twice a month, and even that's not easy cuz I don't get along with his mom too well anymore.

JM: Why is it that some people having children will really . . .

SLICK: It tries to make you do the right thing?

JM: Yeah.

SLICK: And some people it just doesn't affect 'em?

JM: Yeah, they don't take real responsibility for the kids.

SLICK: They don't want to get hurt. Who the fuck wants to get hurt? It means turning your life around, and that ain't easy. You're scared of yourself, because you know you can't do the right thing. You don't think you can. Scared of the peer pressure. That you're called a pussy by some of your quote, unquote friends. Wanna know why you're staying home all the time. I got my own brother saying it. But hey, lookit, I got responsibilities.

Embracing the role of father "means turning your life around," a complete reorientation of identity, according to Slick. Earlier in our discussion, Slick catalogued the marks of street credibility—drugs, money, clothes, cars, women— and then abruptly changed tack to undermine their significance and the image they convey.

SLICK: You get drugs, you have money in your pocket. You have money in your pocket and you have women. Gotta have the fancy car, gotta have the clothes. Gotta look good if you're to really be someone. So that's how that goes. That's why everybody's trying to live up—was or is—trying to live up to an image of being a tough person. What I'm trying to say, the whole thing is, the way I try to see it is you can be a tough person but you can also be a nice person. Don't have to be an asshole, goin' around fucking whackin' people to show who you are. You don't need to go through that nonsense bullshit anymore.

In forging his identity Slick is softening up his uncritical affirmation of masculine toughness and molding it into a new form of self-identity with fatherhood at its core. Frankie seems to be undergoing a similar process.

Frankie says that he returned to the city in 1987 and moved in with his girlfriend's family in order to spend time with his baby son, but admits that he "went right back to the boys. Except we were older now. We were barroom drinkers. We moved from the streets to the bars."

JM: Tell me about the impact of fatherhood on you.

FRANKIE: It was '86. I dunno. It was a lotta responsibility. I was confused. It definitely wasn't planned. [*laughs*] It was scary. I was the first one of us to have a kid. It was a lotta responsibility, but I didn't take a lot at first. I was too busy gettin' high. It was different for her, y'know, cuz she had to stay in the house. I wouldn't stay at home. I'd say, "Fuck you, I'm goin' to the bar." Yeah, at first I didn't really take much responsibility. I knew I had a son, this and that, but no responsibility. I mean, I paid my money, but I still went and played my game.

Today, today it's great. Six years ago, I was his father. But until like two years ago I became his daddy because I never spent time with him. But the past two years I have. . . .

I used to be a tough guy back in '84, man. I was the toughest mother-fucker you've ever seen—in my own mind. I look back and I remember that: We were all tough. I believe I'm a tough guy now. Not drinking. Not doing drugs. Being a decent dad.

Frankie and Slick redefine what it is to be tough, and, as with Jinx, their personal reorientation has been largely catalyzed by their experience of fatherhood.

There is no denying the dominance of machismo culture among the Hallway Hangers. Yet under the sway of fatherhood, that dominant sense of masculinity is being challenged. Several of the Hallway Hangers are beginning to define their masculinity in new ways by allowing fatherhood to foster nurturing and caring capacities in them. Like class and race, gender is socially constructed and hence subject to change.[20] Underemployment and joblessness undermine the traditional masculine identities of the Hallway Hangers. Yet as men spend more time helping to rear children in changing economic circumstances, counterhegemonic male identities may be formed. Physical toughness, breadwinning, and the mere fact of paternity are still the most potent symbols of manhood, but it is instructive that even hardened Hallway Hangers are beginning to subscribe to and articulate roles that run counter to male machismo.

Parenthood has certainly wrought changes in Boo-Boo's outlook.

JM: When was your first child born?

BOO-BOO: It was January 31st, 1989, that Natasha was born.

JM: So what effect did that have on you?

BOO-BOO: Oh, I loved it. It was excellent. It was beautiful. She was beautiful. I was there when she was born and everything. It was excellent, it was great. I was at the junkyard and then we moved and I was working for the moving company, so I had money, I was takin' care of business and stuff. I just wanted to be a family man. I stayed home. I'd take care of my daughter while Ginger was out running in the street. I liked it a lot. I was taking care of her more than Ginger. They'd wake up in the middle of the night and I'd be the one to wake up with her and make her bottles, change her, do whatever needed to be done. Jesus Christ, our kids are beautiful.

Boo-Boo has felt the joy of fatherhood, but he has also experienced the pain and devastation of loss. First he and Ginger lost custody of their children. Then came the real disaster. Ginger and Natasha were diagnosed with Acquired Immuno-deficiency Syndrome (AIDS), Boo-Boo and his other daughter, Connie, as HIV-positive. Natasha died in July 1991.

BOO-BOO: I was there in the hospital and everything when it happened. I still don't understand it. I mean, I know she's gone and everything, but I don't understand it. I still see her. I see her in the casket in my eyes. I can see her. I can still see her.

Numb with grief and pining for Natasha, Boo-Boo was struggling to face Ginger's impending death in August 1991. He often traveled twenty miles to visit Connie in her foster home. "In a while," he said quietly but matter-of-factly, "I'm gonna be all alone. Ginger's dying and probably this little girl, too."

Boo-Boo's sense of solitary suffering, of being alone in his affliction, is important. He has no support systems or informal networks to help him cope with either bereavement or his own medical condition. Whereas the gay community cuts across class lines and can flex its financial muscle to mobilize resources and organize support for those who are HIV-positive and have AIDS, those at the bottom of the pile without the wherewithal to tap into those support systems are largely left to fend for themselves. Ginger probably caught the AIDS virus from an infected needle. Drug abuse and AIDS are intertwined killers that hit the inner city with particular ferocity in the latter half of the 1980s and into the 1990s. Alone, AIDS is lethal and drug abuse is dangerous. Linked by infected needles, they have wrought human tragedy on a massive scale. In Clarendon Heights, rumors about AIDS are rife. Before tracking Chris down in prison, I was told by ten people that he had died of AIDS. Like Chris, Boo-Boo was also under threat of another condition that reached epidemic proportions in the 1980s: homelessness. Boo-Boo has no place to go once he exhausts his dwindling welcome at Ginger's uncle's home. Still, he refuses to let hope be altogether eclipsed. "I just need someplace where I can base myself with a job and a place to live. . . . I'm just trying to make it on my own."

Boo-Boo struggles on, as do the rest of the Hallway Hangers. But that is largely what they expected to be doing back in 1984. Whereas the Hallway Hangers were cynical and pessimistic, the Brothers believed in the American Dream and placed their faith in education. Has that faith been rewarded?

NOTES

1. John D. Kasarda, "Urban Industrial Transition and the Underclass," *Annals of the American Academy of Political and Social Science* 501 (1989): 28.

2. Andrew M. Sum and Joseph Franz, "The Geographic Locations of Jobs by Employed High School Graduates" (Unpublished paper, 1990), p. 3.

3. U.S. Bureau of the Census, *Current Population Reports*, Series P-60, No. 146 (Washington, D.C.: Government Printing Office, 1985), table 40. Cited in Loïc J. D. Wacquant, "Redrawing the Urban Color Line," in Craig Calhoun and George Ritzer, eds., *Social Problems* (New York: McGraw-Hill, 1992), p. 13.

4. Kasarda, "Urban Industrial Transition and the Underclass," p. 31.

5. *New York Times*, September 27, 1988. Cited in Thomas R. Shannon, Nancy Kleniewski, and William M. Cross, eds., *Urban Problems in Sociological Perspective* (Prospect Heights, Ill.: Waveland Press, 1991), p. 104.

6. Paul Osterman, *Getting Started* (Cambridge, Mass.: MIT Press, 1980).

7. Paul Osterman, "Is There a Problem with the Youth Labor Market and If So How Should We Fix It?" mimeo (Sloan School, MIT, February 1992).

8. Saskia Sassen, "The Informal Economy," in John H. Mollenkopf and Manuel Castells, eds., *Dual City: Restructuring New York* (New York: Russell Sage Foundation, 1991), pp. 79–102.

9. Andrew M. Sum and Joanna Heliotis, "Declining Real Wages of Youth," *Workforce* (Spring 1993): 23.

10. Andrew Sum, personal conversation, August 1993.

11. Bureau of the Census, Public Use Microdata Sample File, 1980 and 1990.

12. Richard Edwards, *Contested Terrain* (New York: Basic Books, 1979), pp. 163–170.

13. See, especially, Philippe Bourgois's "In Search of Respect: The New Service Economy and the Crack Alternative in Spanish Harlem" (Russell Sage Foundation Working Paper #21, May 1991).

14. Philippe Bourgois, "Just Another Night on Crack Street," *New York Times Magazine*, November 12, 1989, p. 94.

15. Mercer L. Sullivan, *Getting Paid* (Ithaca, N.Y.: Cornell University Press, 1989), pp. 108–113.

16. Paul Willis, "Youth Unemployment: Thinking the Unthinkable," mimeo (n.d.), p. 8. Cited in Lois Weis, *Working Class Without Work* (New York: Routledge, 1990), p. 191.

17. John Dickie first made this point in one of his incisive reviews of the manuscript.

18. For an account of how New Right ideology resonates with the outlook of white, working-class, male students, see Weis, *Working Class Without Work*.

19. I am indebted to Doug Taylor for this point.

20. I am grateful to David Webb for clarifying my thinking on the nature of gender. Webb himself is indebted to feminist theory. See S. Farrell and J. Lorber, eds., *The Social Construction of Gender* (New York: Sage, 1991), and J. Hearn and D. Morgan, eds., *Men, Masculinities, and Social Theory* (London: Unwin Hyman, 1990).

THE BROTHERS
Dreams Deferred

In 1984 the Brothers hoped that by 1991 they would be on the way to middle-class prosperity. Although I considered these aspirations optimistic, I wrote in the first edition that "with a high school diploma, a positive attitude, and a disciplined readiness for the rigors of the workplace, the Brothers should be capable of landing steady jobs." If the Brothers were naive, so was I. My prediction that they would secure decent work was wrong, and so was my assumption that they could cash in on their credentials and attitude. Although they have certainly fared better than the Hallway Hangers, the Brothers have themselves stumbled economically in the transition to adulthood.

SHORTCHANGED ON THE LABOR MARKET

Even more so than the Hallway Hangers, the Brothers have been employed in the service sector of the economy. They have bagged groceries, stocked shelves, flipped hamburgers, delivered pizzas, repaired cars, serviced airplanes, cleaned buildings, moved furniture, driven tow trucks, pumped gas, delivered auto parts, and washed dishes. They have also worked as mail carriers, cooks, clerks, computer operators, bank tellers, busboys, models, office photocopiers, laborers, soldiers, baggage handlers, security guards, and customer service agents. Only Mike, as a postal service employee, holds a unionized position. Although their experiences on the labor market have been varied, many of the Brothers have failed to move out of the secondary labor market. Instead, like the Hallway Hangers, they have been stuck in low-wage, high-turnover jobs.

Consider Mokey. We left him in 1984 as a junior in the rigorous Fundamental School at Lincoln High. His only contact with the job market had been part-time janitorial work with his father. After another summer in Upward Bound, Mokey made the varsity football team in his senior year, worked part-time in a restaurant washing dishes, and graduated in 1985. He was unemployed for a few months before he found work as a stockboy in a large department store. Poor prospects of promotion and a paltry wage of $4.62 an hour prompted Mokey to quit the job and enter a nearby community college in January 1986. He was enrolled in a liberal arts program on a part-time basis for two semesters and then dropped out. "It wasn't doing me much good," he explained. "I couldn't seem to get motivated. I wasn't sure there was going to be anything at the end of the line."

Over the next four years Mokey worked at five restaurants, busing tables and cooking. Two of the restaurants laid him off when business dropped, two closed outright, and Mokey quit one job after getting burned twice in a cramped kitchen. He earned between $5 and $7.50 an hour at the restaurants, which included two exclusive ones. Mokey took pay cuts when he landed subsequent jobs delivering pizzas, stocking the shelves of a boutique, and moving furniture in a warehouse. Derek helped him get a job handling baggage at the airport, but Mokey was fired after a year and a half—unjustly in Mokey's view. When he was unemployed for an eighteen-month stretch, Mokey spent up to thirty hours per week working as a counselor in a youth enrichment program. He supervised children on camping, cycling, canoe, and ski trips, mostly on a volunteer basis. The responsibility, autonomy, and respect he was accorded in his youth work contrasted sharply with his other jobs.

Mokey left several of his jobs when it became obvious that they were not advancing his career. But quitting damaged his prospects even more. Mokey keeps careful employment records and understands that twelve jobs in seven years does not impress prospective employers.

MOKEY: I don't have a good job because I haven't been at a job more than a year. Cuz mostly I'm always leaving or getting laid off. One guy, one employer [said], "How come you haven't been at these jobs over a certain amount of time?" It's just that they weren't good jobs, the ones I quit. And it's not like I can help it when a restaurant closes.

Now, after six years on the labor market, Mokey has come full circle. He has been unemployed for a year, apart from ten hours of cleaning work with his father each week, the same part-time job he held in 1984. And yet his prospects are worse than when he started.

MOKEY: Oh, it's bad, it's bad to try and get a job. Cuz I would look for particular jobs so that I can stay at them. Like my parents told me to go for a job, doesn't matter what kind of job it is. So there was one week that I just said, "Oh, I'll go for anything." So I actually went to anything like gas stations and all different types of jobs, and they still weren't hiring. I mean, I'd go there, I went to a couple of interviews and they never called. . . . It's frustrating. I look it up in the paper, I call them and they tell me to come in and fill their application. I go fill it out and they go over the application and then they tell me they'll give me a call if they're interested. So they don't call because they're not interested. . . . You get frustrated. You're out there and you wanna do this and all these jobs say, "We're not interested." I call places and they've already had someone taken that position. Or when you get there, they tell you someone already taken your position. It's like, "Oh, great. Come all the way out here and you already have the position filled." It is frustrating out there.

Mokey expected that diligent work would be rewarded with increased responsibilities, promotion, and pay raises. That's what the achievement ideology promises. Repeatedly disappointed, Mokey soon discovered that in a recessionary economy he would be lucky simply to keep a job. Now, even with dampened expectations, he can find no work whatsoever.

In contrast to Mokey, Juan has generally stuck with his jobs—but to little avail. For three years he worked at an auto-body shop replacing windows. His hourly wage still below six dollars, he left to enter a community college but could not afford to stay. He worked for three weeks in a department store basement as a stockboy, was unemployed for a couple of months, then took a job at McDonald's. He began at an hourly wage of $4.50, moved up to $5.57 as a crew leader, and after two and a half years was taking home $7.50 as a swing manager.

JUAN: It was all right, but the pay wasn't good enough, for, like, bills. Then they started cutting all the hours off, cuz supposedly they wasn't doin', y'know, that much business. It made it tight for me, so I left there in '89.

JM: Could you move up any further? Or was that really the highest you could go, was swing manager?

JUAN: No, I coulda moved up further if I wanted to. But they wanted more [hours] than what they were paying. They want you to work for salary and put in so many hours if it's necessary, and I couldn't work thirty hours on salary and I get paid for twenty.

Juan painstakingly worked his way up to a salaried position, only to take home less pay for his troubles.

When he quit McDonald's, Juan used Derek's contacts at the airport to get a job as a customer service agent with a wage of $6.87 an hour. He was up to $7.50 when he was fired a year later.

JM: What happened?

JUAN: I came in a couple of times late. And they're very strict on timing. You gotta be there on time. If your shift's at 8:02, you gotta be there at 8:02, period.

JM: Was it a big blow when you lost that job, or . . .

JUAN: Yeah.

JM: How'd you feel about it?

JUAN: I feel bad about it. Outta all the jobs I ever had, it was better because I was gettin' medical insurance in there, y'know? It was better than anything.

JM: Was it your fault you lost it, or was it just the circumstances, or what happened?

JUAN: Well, it was probably my fault cuz, y'know, I came in late a couple of times. Well, more than a couple of times. I came in late three times and I called in sick four other times. I mean, I can't blame it completely on myself, cuz everybody does it, and some of 'em will get away with it. I was doing all right, I mean, everybody lik'ded me and everything, and the only reason was that I came in late three times and called in sick four other times.

JM: During the whole time you were there?

JUAN: Yeah, during the whole time. Sooner or later something would happen, I'd have some kind of incident. And after the seventh time you call in sick or come in late in a year, you're terminated. There's no second chances. Up to seven and you're gone. You're history.

For the past two years Juan has worked at Jim's Tow. The work site consists of a trailer office and a large fenced-in area crammed full of cars, some just towed in, others in various states of disrepair strewn about the lot. I found Juan in the back, amid the rusted shells, painting the front fender of a red Toyota in a shade slightly brighter than the rest of the car.

JUAN: Can you believe this? Look at this, man. I told Jim it was the wrong damn color; it's not mixed right. "Go ahead," he said. "It's close enough. She probably won't even notice." But watch who'll take the blame when she comes to get her car. [*shakes his head furiously and sighs*] If you're gonna do a job, do it right—that's what my mother always says.

JM: [*laughing*] Mine, too.

JUAN: Yeah, well, I guess Jim's didn't. This is just stupid. Now the damn spray gun is clogged all up. I hate this job, can't stand it.

JM: What's the worst part?

JUAN: Always being disrespected. Just treated disrespectfully. My boss, Jim, the owner, he treats me as if I'm like dirt. . . . He said he was gonna give me a raise. He said that six months ago and I still haven't seen the raise, not a penny. Y'know, I'm gettin' paid seven dollars an hour. I deserve for the work here—y'know, I do paint work, I do auto-body work, I do mechanic work, and I do the driving, the towing—I deserve at least nine dollars an hour. But what are you gonna do? Life goes on.

As we talked, as if on cue, Juan was summoned by his boss. Standing on the back steps of the office about forty yards away, Jim bellowed Juan's name sharply several times. "See what I mean?" said Juan with a tight-lipped smile that quickly turned into a grimace. He shook his head and continued to clean the clogged paint sprayer, his back to his shouting boss. Finally, a few face-saving seconds after Jim went back inside, Juan got up, excused himself, and trudged toward the office.

Two weeks later, we talked again on the lot of Jim's Tow, this time as Juan worked on the carburetor of a Chevrolet Caprice. More upbeat, Juan still complained about his job.

JM: What are your hours like?

JUAN: Depends. Depends when he needs me. Last week I worked seven days, put a lot of hours in. Y'know, I need the money. I usually work six or seven days a week. Whenever he calls me, I'm here.

JM: You get overtime.

JUAN: Overtime? What's overtime? They've never heard of that around here. I told you, this isn't the greatest job in the world.

Whereas Mokey changed jobs rapidly in search of a bona fide career opening, Juan has stayed with his jobs. The result has been much the same for both young men: disappointment.

Derek graduated near the top of his class in June 1984. Three weeks later he was married and on his way to boot camp in the navy. After training in aviation electronics, Derek was stationed about a hundred miles from the apartment he rented for his wife, Faith, and their infant son in a working-class neighborhood near Clarendon Heights. Inexplicably, Derek's pay suddenly was cut off for two months. Already disillusioned with the navy, desperate to feed his child, and frustrated at his superiors' inability or unwillingness to rectify the problem, Derek went AWOL. Thus, the promising thirteen-year-old pupil at a posh private school ended up festering in a military prison five years later. Released with a lawyer's help, Derek endured three months of unemployment before finding a job as a ramp worker at the airport. He has been there now for seven years and makes $7.50 an hour.

Derek may not earn much, but he enjoys his job. He interacts easily with fellow workers, having carved out a social space within his workplace that gives him security, autonomy, and satisfaction. Indeed, he often refers to his "niche" in the airline industry.

DEREK: This is really my niche. I love being around airplanes, I love meeting people. I like the prospect of travel and I've been traveling a lot: Every year I take like two or three trips, flying at a great price. . . . I found my niche. I just like being outside, being around a lot of people, having fun, y'know, getting along, doing the job.

Derek's job satisfaction, however, has come at a price. His wage is low, especially after seven years in the industry. He often works the night shift from nine p.m. to six a.m. Almost all of his moves within the company have been horizontal—from ramp leader in charge of loading and unloading the aircraft, to passenger service agent, to team leader responsible for overseeing the routine maintenance of the aircraft between flights, to aircraft cabin cleaner. When I spoke with him, Derek was cleaning aircraft interiors on the graveyard shift. One of the benefits, apart from the hourly wage differential of twenty-five cents, is the scarcity of management. "When I'm on nights, there's really not much management contact except that one supervisor for the total rest of the overnight shift. And that makes a big difference; everything's much more relaxed." Derek was recently offered a management position but refused to sacrifice or diminish his friendships by taking on a supervisory role.

DEREK: Management is very unrelenting. They'll demand that you get down harder on the employee and, I don't know how to explain it, I just don't work well with management because I don't consider management to be people oriented. It's like when I became an agent council representative—that's a person like if employees have problems with other employees and they have problems with management, I become like a middleman and say, "Okay, well, here's how we can work this out," and that was pretty good because it's like I was still one of the agents and everyone looked at me as being an agent and not as a supervisor saying, "Okay, these are the rules; you have to abide by them, otherwise, y'know, you're out." And I enjoyed that a lot. I really enjoyed that a lot. Being a supervisor—that's definitely not for me. The pay really doesn't matter, it's not the most important thing, it's just being with the people, y'know, people who care, that's what it is.

Being a supervisor would divorce Derek from the rank and file and force him to bear down on his friends. He prefers to mediate rather than to dominate, even if it means sacrificing his career.

As comfortable as Derek is in the airline industry, he longs to exercise his knack for mediation as a police officer. "I consider a police officer to be more of a mediator, like a go-between person, you know, trying to resolve problems, and that's something I like doing." In 1989 Derek was offered a job as a policeman in the small town of Avon across the state.

DEREK: Right after I got out of the military I was looking into law enforcement but at the time I needed to make money, so I gotten into the airline industry. . . . The only thing that's ever been on my mind is law enforcement. It's something I've always wanted to get into, like taking the state police test, passed that.

JM: You got a . . .

DEREK: I got a ninety-eight on that, I took the local police test here in the city and I got a ninety-seven on that. I was called for the Avon Police Department. I was, like, this close, inches from becoming an Avon Police because I'd gone through all their screening tests, then all the background checks, their psych evaluations, whatever, but I let Faith and a million other people talk me out of it. They figured you're gonna get shot, this'll happen, that'll happen, nobody likes the police anymore, and y'know, this was like two years ago and I dunno, I just let people talk me out of it. . . . I just always thought being a police officer would be a nice, prestigious career. . . . I want to have some kind of gung-ho career. Yes, that's it. If I couldn't be a marine, why not be a cop or something like that.

JM: The action, the adventure?

DEREK: Yeah, yeah. I like the guns, too.

JM: Now where did that come from?

DEREK: I dunno.

JM: You seem so gentle, y'know?

DEREK: Yeah, I am. My father had an unbelievable collection of guns. I don't know, me, my father, my grandfather, we're all exactly alike. We all like guns. I'm not too keen on the ocean like they are [Derek's father and grandfather were sailors], because I've just got this big fear of this giant shark coming up and eating me [*laughs*], but I'm exactly like they are: I like to travel a lot, I like to meet new people. I mean, I wanna be a world traveler someday, and I will be because I know if I want it *I will get it.*

The same sense of efficacy applies to his police aspiration.

DEREK: I will get into law enforcement. Because it's what I want. I've pretty much taken the stance from now on whatever I want I'm gonna get, no matter what. In fairness, but if I want something I'm gonna get it.

What Derek wanted more than anything else in 1991 was an apartment big enough for his family.

DEREK: Look at this place. It's big enough for two but not four. We knew that when we moved in. But rent these days, it's crazy. Crazy. We're doing okay, though; we're getting along.

JM: It's good to talk to someone who's a success story.

DEREK: I'm not really a success. It's just that nothing bad has happened, and I don't want anything to. I just wanna be in a position to avoid disasters.

More than I do, Derek understands the fragility of his relative prosperity.

In February 1984 James was studying assiduously, making up failed classes after school and intent on designing computer games as a career. The next year, however, he was expelled from school for excessive truancy.

JM: What did your father have to say about that?

JAMES: Let's just say I had a little chat with my father's fists. Then the next morning he woke me up at seven o'clock and put a newspaper in my face, pointing to a little ad. "This is where you're going today, buddy; now move!" It was a free course for a GED.

James enrolled in a class made up mostly of adults for whom English was a second language; he took and passed the test four weeks later, receiving his high school equivalency diploma in the summer of 1986. With the help of a federal Pell grant and $2,500 in student loans, James immediately enrolled in a computer school. "I was lucky," he relates. "My parents paid most of the one thousand dollars that I had to pay. Because the total cost was like seven thousand dollars."

James landed a good job immediately after receiving his certificate in computer programming, although a connection proved as important as the credential.

JAMES: I had a friend who was a security guard at this massive bank, federal reserves, so he got me an interview there like two days after I got out of school. I guess he had a guy in personnel who owed him favors. So they gave me a job as a computer operator there.

James worked nights from eleven p.m. to seven a.m. for an annual salary of close to $17,000. A year later, another friend found him a more lucrative position at Citicorp out in the suburbs, also on the night shift.

JAMES: It was like ten thousand dollars more than I was making, but the only problem was the ride, right, like half an hour ride. I was like, "Yeah, for that much more money I'll take half an hour drive." So I gave my notice in, I went to Citicorp, got a car, and I worked for Citicorp for about one and a half years, and they had a layoff, they closed down my division. So there I was without a job. But Citicorp, they helped me get a job with another bank in the city. Another bank needed an operator, so I got a job there, only I had to take a pay cut of like ten thousand dollars, back down to eighteen thousand dollars a year.

Back on the night shift as a computer operator at a central city bank, James worked for a year before he was dismissed in June 1990. As James tells it, he was routinely victimized by his supervisor. Matters came to a head when he was forced to switch shifts and then was blamed for bungling the new operations he had not been trained to undertake.

JAMES: He just starts ripping into me, talkin' about I'm doing all this stuff wrong, blah, blah, blah, and if I don't like it, I can get outta here. And he's pointing in my face, and he's acting like he doesn't have any sense. So I got ticked off and I left. I walked out, and I said, "Hey, this ain't my shift, man." And I left, I went home. So I came back the next day and they had a book with the rules of the bank there, and one of the rules of the bank is that if you leave work without authorization, then you get fired, so . . .

JM: Have you been actively looking for work since then?

JAMES: Yeah, it's hard. It's been over a year now. Sending out résumés, going to different companies, filling out applications. I've been on interviews to banks out of state. . . . I've sent out an average of twenty letters a month. Nothing. So here I am sitting at home watching MTV.

James's heavy educational investment paid off at first, although he was actually overtrained for all his jobs. Qualified as a programmer, he worked as an operator. "Actually, what I'm doing is nothing—it's not even close to programming," he reported in 1987. "I just sit there, punch a few buttons, get paid." Job satisfaction was low, but pay was relatively high—until the economy began its nosedive. And James soon discovered that as wages shrank, so did job security.

Craig, too, has followed the prescription for occupational success by investing heavily in education. He attended a junior college after graduating from high school and then transferred to a large university. He struggled to pay his bills, and he struggled academically. To make ends meet, he had to work extensively during both academic terms and holidays. He finally graduated in 1989. Craig returned home saddled with over $10,000 in student loans and hoping to land an entry-level job in the business world. He was disappointed. Unemployed for over a year, Craig settled for a clerical job in a large store's credit department where he works the phone trying to recover delinquent bills for an annual salary of $17,000.

CRAIG: I just had to take the best job I could get. After a year, you get kind of desperate. I looked hard for a job in banking, preferably in investment. Nothing. In the end I accepted this sorry job.

JM: Do you use any of the skills you learned in college?

CRAIG: None. I don't know what kind of skills these are—detective skills, I suppose, or psychological skills. Actually, I'm pretty good at it. Half the time you hafta lie. It's just going after deadbeats who have moved out of state, trying to track them down. It's just a Joe Schmo job, but it's all I could get.

JM: Is there any room for advancement?

CRAIG: Not really. I don't see a future in this job. I'm looking for others. Hopefully, this is just to tide me over until I can get a good job. I don't want any old Schmo job.

Disappointed but not despondent, Craig is matter-of-fact about his current job and his continued inability to get a better one.

Mike, the only white member of the Brothers, graduated from Lincoln High School in June 1986 and enrolled in a state college. After several weeks, unable to acclimatize culturally and socially, he returned home. Following ten weeks of unemployment, Mike went to real estate school and got his license but has been unable to put it to use. He also took civil service exams for the positions of mail carrier, post office clerk, and firefighter. Meanwhile, he found a night job as a security guard for seven dollars an hour. Having applied to Eastern airlines for a job as a flight attendant, Mike was flown to Florida for an interview but failed to get the position. In August 1987 he landed a job as a bank teller. Combining a forty-hour week at the bank with twenty-four hours of security work, Mike brought in $550 a week. A year later he quit both jobs to begin work for the post office as a mail carrier and also signed on with a modeling agency. Mike's modeling career began to peter out when he pulled a stomach muscle, stopped working out regularly, and began putting on weight, but in 1991 his total earnings topped $36,000. He has owned a BMW and recently bought a Mazda sports car. "I'm making more money than most yuppies," Mike reports. Indeed, he is on the verge of purchasing a $138,000 house in a working-class suburb as an investment.

Mike is a relentless believer in the American Dream and in individual responsibility. To him, the Hallway Hangers have only themselves to blame for their failure.

JM: Do you ever see Frankie or Jinx or Slick or any of those guys around?

MIKE: No, I never see them. Those guys are fucking rejects. Trash. Fuck 'em. Fuckin' trash. You can make it. You can do whatever you wanna do. If you wanna be trash, you'll be trash.

The irony is that Mike landed the job at the bank only after he and Craig indulged in a little collective use of credentials. They doctored Craig's diploma to make it appear that Mike had received his associate's degree, a foray into white-collar crime about which Mike makes no apologies. "Hey, what was I s'posed to do? Be a security guard the rest of my life?" Mike, it seems, caught the 1980s mood of aggressive individualism and runaway greed. "Hey, that's what it's about. You've got to be cutthroat. You've got to be competitive." Whereas Wall Street bankers made millions of dollars with their scams, Mike made hundreds. When his BMW began to run ragged, he paid four hundred dollars to have it stolen, battered, and dumped as part of an insurance job. And as much as he rails against welfare fraud, Mike himself has continued to live illegally in his mother's Clarendon Heights apartment.

Super is one of the people against whom Mike fulminates for not having made more of himself. Since graduating from high school in 1986, Super has worked at U-Haul putting hitches on cars, cleaning trucks, and filling them up with gas. He moved on to Burger King for a couple of months before landing a job delivering auto parts. Making $4.50 an hour, he worked there for five months before being fired for turning up late.

SUPER: It weren't no good job anyhow. I dunno, man, I just found out real quick after I graduated that unless you go on to college or somethin' you just ain't gonna make it. . . . I just wanna make somethin' of my life, y'know, be a success. Not just be stuck in these dead-end jobs. I'd like to get married and have a family, but how'm I s'posed to do that on four and a half dollars an hour?

Eventually, Super got a job at a grocery store and stayed for three years. He unloaded shipments, stocked shelves, and drove a delivery van for an hourly wage that increased from six to seven dollars an hour.

An hourly wage of seven dollars, however, was peanuts compared to what Super began making in 1990 when he turned to crack capitalism. As Super tells it, his criminal career was catalyzed by the anger and betrayal he felt when the police planted marijuana on him.

SUPER: I was working at the grocery store, I just got my check and I was walking through the park to my aunt's house. That's before all this crack shit came up. People were selling weed mostly. I passed through the park there, at that time the park on Lee Street was kinda hot. A cop said, "Hey, you, come here." And I kept walking. Y'know, I'd seen someone there and I started talking to him. I guess the cop knew the guy was selling drugs. He said, "Stop."

I said, "For what? I'm going, y'know, I'm in a hurry, what you want?"

He just run up to me and grabbed me. "You selling drugs, what's your name, you bought some drugs?"

I was like, "I don't know nuttin'. I just come here, I know the guy from school." Showed him my check.

He was like, "I don't give a shit. If you ain't gonna help me, I'm gonna fix you." Locked me up. Put me in the paddy wagon. I stayed in the paddy wagon for like a couple of minutes and he came back. "See this? This is yours now. You don't want to help me, this is yours." He had come back with a bag of weed. Cops nowadays are crookedy, just like the same as the drug dealers. They arrested me, put me in jail. The cops out there now, they get paid off, sell drugs. The world's crazy now. Anyway, I couldn't believe that happened. I wasn't even thinking about dealing at the time, I just wanted to work, stay out of trouble. . . . I was against drugs and shit. I was against people doing that, y'know? I was on the side with the cops, y'know?

Super's story is credible. Dealing drugs was a radical change for someone who, apart from school skirmishes, had stayed out of trouble. And yet Super may be portraying his entry into the street economy in the best possible light.

Whatever prompted his career change, Super emphasizes that once he started dealing, he was able to advance quickly. The drug economy provided excitement and money, but more important to Super was the promise of promotion.

JM: Tell me about how you got into it and stuff.

SUPER: Well, I got into it, I was so bored, I had no money and just worked my way up. I had no money, was broke, flat broke. So I worked my way up. I had to have money. I worked my way up, worked my way up.

Super started off as a runner, delivering packets of crack to customers. Within a few weeks he was selling on the street, handling the money himself but turning it over to his supplier, who would give him a cut. Now Super works for himself, exploiting the small spaces in the market left fallow by the big dealers, moving from neighborhood to neighborhood and even out of state. For Super, the informal economy provided a far better career structure than the formal economy.

The pay is also superior to what Super could make working a legitimate job. At his peak, Super reports that he could gross up to $3,000 during a good week of hard work.

SUPER: It's some long hours. Sometimes stay up all night. Long nights.

JM: People call you any time on the beeper?

SUPER: Turn it off sometimes, y'know? If I'm real tired, I'll just turn it off and go to sleep.

Super sells powdered cocaine but usually cooks it up into its more marketable crystallized form. Crack is better for business, but Super is haunted by the toll it takes on his customers.

SUPER: Crack. Crack. There's something in it that makes them want it more. That crack shit does it to you. It's a real bad addiction, real bad addiction. It's like poison. I dunno, it just does stuff to people, makes girls do shit they don't wanna do: sell their body, steal from their parents, leave their babies out on the street, all shit.

JM: Now, what about you, do you use the stuff?

SUPER: No, I use no crack.

JM: How do you keep from doing that, if you're around it all the time?

SUPER: I dunno, just be strong inside, hold up. I have people that say, "Try it out." Uh-uh. I see what it does to other people. I really don't want to sell this shit; it's the only way I can make a living right now. Can't get a job, can't do nothing, so . . .

JM: Have you tried, have you been, have you had trouble getting a job?

SUPER: Yeah, I tried, y'know? I don't want to sell drugs for the rest of my life or nuttin'. I just want to try to get myself a job and get myself back on the, back going, try to get myself an apartment, get myself a place . . .

Super is torn by his moral culpability as a purveyor of crack but sees no alternative way of generating income.

Addiction does not eat into Super's profit margin as it did that of the less disciplined Hallway Hangers, who are now largely dependent on Super for drugs. But like his white counterparts, Super is preoccupied with the dangers of the retail drug trade. The police often search him, and he is plagued by predators and competitors.

SUPER: It's not a life to live, man.

JM: What are the biggest risks?

SUPER: Getting caught by the cops, having people trying to rob you, people shooting at you. Stickup people coming round and robbing you. Listen, that happens, happens a lot.

JM: Did it happen to you?

SUPER: People tried a couple of times, got robbed, but they didn't get nothing. . . . I've just been lucky, I guess. Had knives, guns pulled on me. I would just say, "Hey, you got your gun, just go on and use it. If you gonna shoot me, shoot me." Usually it's not worth it to them to shoot you. But as you can see [*grins to reveal several missing teeth*], I've got in some nasty fights. . . . You gotta have a gun, too. You can get busted for that, too, but you have to have one, regardless. If you're selling drugs you hafta have a gun.

JM: What about close calls with the police?

SUPER: Yeah, plenty of close calls. But I never would have nothing on me. They come and frisk me down, never have nothing. All I have is money. Can't do nothing if you don't have it. Cops come over and just grab me. "Which one, is it this one?" I guess they been doing surveillance or something. But they only get me with money.

JM: Do you only deal in the projects or . . .

SUPER: In the projects, all over. It's good to move around, not stay in one spot a lot. I slowed down for a while. I stopped selling for a bit, y'know, and right now I'm not out there like 100 percent like I used to. I'm like 20 percent, trying to slow down. You can't be greedy. See, most guys, especially when they start, they'll be greedy. That's why they don't stay in business for long. I used to make good money when I started off, but now I slowed down cuz it's getting bad out there. Gotta be careful, real careful. Go up to cars, that's one thing you never do. You got narcotics agents out there now, they go and rent cars with out-of-state plates. Driver'll say, "Whatcha got on you? Whatcha got? Whatcha holding?" Soon as you pull it out, boom, you're arrested.

JM: So all you do is hang around and people know you and will approach you?

SUPER: You can tell who smokes and who doesn't smoke.

JM: How can you tell?

SUPER: Easy, by just looking at 'em. You can tell if a person doesn't look right, you've never seen 'em before, or this and that. "Uh-uh, I don't have nothing." Tell 'em I don't have nothing. . . . When you're living a life like this, you can't trust no one.

JM: That must be hard. What about your girlfriend?

SUPER: I trust her, but I can't trust her too much either.

JM: How come, what can happen?

SUPER: You never know, you have an argument with your girl and she'll call the cops. If she knows too much it can hurt ya. Sometimes, y'know, you'll get people, dealers, they'll get mad and call the cops on you, shit like that. Wanna come and rob you. Hatch fights with people, y'know? People that I've known for a long time, arguing with me. I had to hurt 'em, almost. I've had shootouts, got shot at. Haven't been hit yet.

Super has not been seriously injured, nor has he been prosecuted for a drug offense, but he understands that it is only a matter of time. Still, he plows on, longing for a legal job. Over and over, Super underlines how the dearth of legal economic opportunity keeps him in the grip of the risky cocaine trade.

SUPER: Right now I feel myself kinda trapped. I wanna get out of here bad. I just need a job, job paying all right, reasonable money.

JM: What's reasonable money, what would that be?

SUPER: Nowadays with rent, know what I'm saying, so expensive, food—about eight bucks, seven bucks an hour. That means I could get myself an apartment, probably go back to school at night, work in the day.

JM: What do you see as the difficulties of getting out of here?

SUPER: Money.

JM: But you've been making it quick. I mean, do you see yourself being able to work two months for what you can make in a couple of days now?

SUPER: Yeah, I know it may seem crazy, but I think I can do it if I could just make the money. Making my money legit, I don't have to worry about cops bothering me. No one bothering me, I'd work hard for that; no one can take that from you. . . . I don't want to live this life anymore, I wanna try to get a job, I really don't wanna sell drugs to people, y'know, I don't wanna try to make people do bad, y'know, I don't wanna try to down no one or nothing. It's the only way I can make a living right now.

JM: Do you get pressured a lot from other people to stop dealing, or do they just not know what's going on—like family and stuff, parents, your aunt, other people?

SUPER: They know what's going on. They're telling me to stop, try and get a job or something. There's no jobs, y'know, that's the way it goes. They say if I keep doing this, I ain't gonna live that long, usually dealing drugs, living fast life, end up in jail or dead, which is true. I might get robbed, might get shot. What are you going to do?

JM: How long do you think you can keep going this way before you really end up getting, either getting in big legal trouble or getting hurt?

SUPER: I dunno. Never can tell. Chance it every time. Could happen today. Could happen tomorrow. Never know. . . . I just wanna stop doin' what I'm doin', y'know? This life ain't the life to live, y'know? I dunno. I just feel if I keep going as I'm going right now, selling drugs, I know I won't be in jail, I know I'll probably be dead. I know that myself. I try not to think about it, cuz it gets to me.

Although the other Brothers feel less hemmed in than Super does, most of them have found the transition from school to work more difficult than they anticipated. The Brothers, after all, were no dropouts. While many of their peers were dawdling through school days courting girls, playing ball, and getting high, the Brothers toiled in the classroom. And yet rather than question their commitment to school, the Brothers, Super included, reaffirm it.

SOLD ON SCHOOL

All of the Brothers graduated from high school. A high school diploma, they expected, would give them a leg up on the labor market. They had been told over and over by their parents, teachers, and counselors to stay in school, that they needed a high school diploma to get a decent job. This was good advice. As cities in the United States have shifted from producing goods to processing information, jobs for high school dropouts have largely evaporated. As stated earlier, the city in which Clarendon Heights residents work saw a 59 percent drop between 1970 and 1980 in the number of jobs held by those who did not complete high school.[1] And as African Americans, the Brothers would be especially hard-pressed to find jobs as high school dropouts. National data for October 1990 show that among sixteen- to twenty-four-year-old high school dropouts, only 57 percent of the whites were employed. But the figure for blacks is truly catastrophic: Fewer than 30 percent were working.[2] African Americans with little schooling do indeed become ensnared in the web of urban industrial transition. The answer, educators and economists agree, is for blacks to stay in school. And the Brothers, without exception, stuck it out and graduated from high school.

Across the country, more and more African Americans, like the Brothers, are staying in school. Whereas between 1970 and 1990 the percentage of white sixteen- to twenty-four-year-olds not enrolled in school and not high school graduates remained essentially constant (between 12 and 13 percent), there was a sharp increase in school attendance by blacks, for whom the corresponding figure fell from 26 percent in 1970 to 13 percent in 1990.[3] But although blacks are staying in school, their job prospects fail to show a corresponding improvement.

What the Brothers did not realize is that jobs in their city held by those *with* a high school education also fell by 29 percent between 1970 and 1980[4] and has shrunk further in the ensuing ten years, particularly for young African Americans. In 1980 the local unemployment rate for black male dropouts between the ages of twenty and twenty-four was 26 percent. In 1990 the figure was 25 percent for those *with* a high school education.[5] As high school graduates, the Brothers have barely improved their job prospects over those of black dropouts ten years earlier.

There is a large racial gap in unemployment and earnings among high school graduates as well as dropouts. Nationwide, the unemployment rate for white sixteen- to twenty-four-year-olds with a high school diploma in 1990 was 9 percent. For black high school graduates it was 26 percent.[6] If black high school graduates without jobs feel betrayed, many with jobs also feel let down because they earn so much less than whites. In the local labor market for men in 1989, white high school dropouts between the ages of twenty and twenty-four earned $9,294 per year. White graduates made $14,237. Black dropouts of the same age earned only $7,648 per year. And blacks with a high school diploma made a mere $8,856—less than white dropouts. A high school diploma improved the earnings of whites by 53 percent. The return for blacks was a paltry 16 percent.[7] For African American men, a high school education simply does not pay off as promised.

For the Brothers this fact was a rude awakening. Many now feel they were deluded about the value of a high school diploma but trace the delusion back to themselves rather than to a restricted opportunity structure clothed in an ideology of equal opportunity.

MOKEY: My diploma didn't do anything for me, job-wise.

JM: When you consider back to, like, your hopes back in high school . . .

MOKEY: I wish I could start it over. . . . I think I shoulda worked harder in high school. Because in high school I didn't do a lot. I shoulda been at a better college. I just was really lazy about it. . . . I didn't know what kind of major I actually wanted to do. Y'see, when I went to high school, I actually told my parents I didn't want to go on the Fundamental program—that's like college prep—and at that time I thought I was more of, like, a technical person. And they had that Oc. Ed. trade thing over there at the high school. It was more like I wanted, a trade program. I wish I actually went to, y'know, trade classes. My parents, they just wanted me to just learn the education, y'know, and not the trade.

Although he recognizes the limited utility of his diploma on the job market, Mokey still berates himself for being lazy in high school. He also implies that under the sway of parents who advised him to "plan to be a success and reach the highest goal possible," aiming high and undergoing a purely academic course of study may have been a strategic mistake. Channeling students into vocational tracks is an important mechanism of social reproduction. Mokey resisted this process, only to find that the impermeability of the class structure is such that he might have been better off with more modest aspirations and vocational preparation. Super agrees. But Juan does not, for he graduated from the Occupational Education program and contends that his vocational degree has been of little use.

JUAN: High school hasn't really helped me, my diploma. To tell the truth, it really hasn't. I thought for sure I would need my diploma. But who needs a diploma for this? [*turns up his oil-stained hands*] High school hasn't helped me. You're better off to go to one of those, y'know, ten-month trade schools, that's if you've got the money.

The Brothers have discovered that for African American men, a high school diploma of whatever variety often fails to secure even a toehold in the postindustrial urban economy.

When I spoke with a jobless Super in 1987, he was despondent. He felt misled, and like Mokey, he reckoned in retrospect that he should have pursued a vocational degree in high school.

SUPER: I ain't goin' nowhere out here on the streets, man. Nowhere but down. I got to get an education, go back to school. I'm thinkin' about goin' to a community college.

JM: Were you disappointed with the jobs you got after you graduated?

SUPER: Yeah, I found out real quick when I got into the real world that it was gonna be a lot tougher than I thought.

JM: You were led to believe it would be different?

SUPER: Yeah.

JM: Who by?

SUPER: Teachers and stuff, I guess.

JM: Did you believe them?

SUPER: Well, yes and no.

JM: How do you mean?

SUPER: Well, I could see some kids had graduated but didn't get good jobs. But I thought I still might cuz some kids do. But, y'know, those kids did Oc. Ed.—sheet metal or carpentry, like—and their teachers got them jobs in construction or somethin'. Now I see that you can't get no decent job with just a high school diploma. Now, I hear that it's tough even if you go on and finish college to get a job.

It is instructive that Super began by reaffirming his belief in the value of education despite his frustration, disappointment, and confusion.

Super has good reason to be confused. The Brothers entered an educational maze when they enrolled in high school. Whereas middle-class pupils are clued in to where they're going thanks to the cultural capital they inherited from their parents, working-class students are given very little guidance in negotiating critical turning points. How were the Brothers to know whether they would be better off in the Pilot School or the Fundamental School, in House B or Oc. Ed., in a college track or a general one? And their confusion continues upon graduation from high school. Which programs, degrees, and institutions are worthy of investment, and which lead down cul-de-sacs? Pseudocolleges and training programs have become a veritable racketeering industry. Many seem to target very weak students, suck money from them and from federal assistance programs, and spit them back onto the streets without having appreciably improved their job prospects.

In fact, with the exception of Derek, all of the Brothers have pursued postsecondary school education, although only Craig has completed a degree program.

Super studied electronics at predominantly black Rosebank Community College for several weeks.

JM: What happened?

SUPER: I just left it, couldn't study. Couldn't handle it. Too much stuff on my mind. Didn't have no job or nothing. Didn't have no money hardly. Not enough to go to school.

Juan lasted two months at a nearby, mostly white community college before quitting. "It was a pity, y'know, cuz I really enjoyed it. I had to leave to get some money." Mokey attended the same school's liberal arts program for two semesters. As noted earlier, his motivation was sapped because his studies weren't improving his employment prospects: "I wasn't sure there was going to be anything at the end of the line." In fact, a comprehensive evaluation of community colleges finds that there is often very little at the end of the line for students. Norton Grubb's study shows that men enrolled in community college certificate programs fail to improve their prospects, and that even community college degrees yield relatively few benefits on the job market.[8]

And yet Super is convinced that further education is the key to his future, and both Mokey and Juan would like to return to school.

(in separate interviews)

SUPER: I think if I go back to school then it'll help me to get a better job and move on in life. And probably get away from this place. Carve me something out of life. Make me a better man than I am.

MOKEY: I've been accepted to go back [to community college], cuz job-wise, over the last year, it's been really bad, so I was gonna go back to school. I was gonna go into school for electronics, cuz I wanted to go to school for technology and for engineering. But I didn't get my financial aid. Don't know why.

JUAN: If I had the money, I'd go back to school, back to community college. I need to do something. But there's no way now. I've got too many responsibilities.

Super, Mokey, and Juan have always been confined to the slow lane of the formal economy. Now, having stalled out completely, they see further education as the answer. What else could help them?

To be sure, higher education can be crucial for economic success, but high-caliber schooling is beyond most of the Brothers' means. James proved an exception. His parents made a large contribution toward his expensive computer training and supported him financially while he studied. And his schooling paid off handsomely until the economy slid into deep recession. But then, James got breaks that other young blacks cannot count on, as we shall see.

Other Brothers have had the opportunity to study at four-year colleges. The September after his high school graduation, Mike found himself in a rural state college studying management. His fellow students were also white but not of his background, and Mike braved the cultural clash for only a few months.

MIKE: I picked the wrong school. Maybe I should've gone to a junior college to break myself in. The people were different, goddamn airheads. All they could do was go out drinking, come back puking. My roommates were scared of me, so I wasn't that friendly. I kept to myself. And the girls—they were snobby as hell, I couldn't stand 'em. Plus, y'know, I was used to city life and there I was all of a sudden in the middle of the fucking woods, nowhere to go. . . . I just didn't like it. It wasn't me.

As a residential student, Mike found that the college's alien cultural landscape placed too many strains on his identity.

Craig, by contrast, flourished in a junior college. In September 1984 I drove him to a small, rural, two-year college to which he had won a basketball scholarship. He talked apprehensively in the car about adjusting to the new social milieu. But as the star of the basketball team, Craig proved popular among the almost all-white student body. In two years he graduated with an associate's degree and transferred to a large out-of-state university. Yet Craig struggled at his new school. He was granted only a year's credit for his work at the junior college and had to live off-campus. He was cut from the basketball team. And he failed two subjects when a delay in his financial aid caused him to miss the first few weeks of the spring term.

To make ends meet, Craig worked between fifteen and twenty hours each week during term time.

CRAIG: At first I worked at an architecture firm. I messed up that job. It was tough to work it around my schedule, and I ended up not showing up a lot. What happened was I got disillusioned. I was just photocopying stuff. It was just a lot of busywork. I never got a chance to help design at all, never got close to it.

JM: How did you get that job?

CRAIG: Showed them some of my drawings. I guess they thought if I could draw, I could photocopy. [*laughs bitterly*] Architects do a lot of copying. It's not what it's cracked up to be.

Working two jobs, Craig logged up to seventy hours each week during the summers. Still, he could not afford to buy the required textbooks.

CRAIG: Man, some of those books were so expensive it was incredible. I remember one called *Structural Dynamics* went for a hundred and fifteen bucks. There was just no way I could afford that. A lot of books I ended up getting from the library, but then that was tough because they'd be on reserve. You couldn't check them out.

Finding the compulsory physics courses too demanding, Craig switched from architecture to business. He graduated in August 1989 in good academic standing.

Unlike most of the Brothers, Craig now has a stable job. However, it took him more than a year to find employment. And after five years of college education, his annual salary is barely a third of the national median for male workers. Craig's experience notwithstanding, the Brothers retain a deep faith in the ability of schooling to boost their economic prospects. And of course further education does help them. But the effect is often marginal. Having graduated from high school, many have found that their diploma is not worth much on the job market. And this is no misconception. Statistics show quite clearly that for African Americans who have invested in a high school education, the payoff is often scant. Those who graduate from college do much better; but as Craig illustrates, even black college graduates from disadvantaged backgrounds are hard-pressed to parlay their academic credentials into economic prosperity. For Craig, as for most of the Brothers, the gap between aspiration and outcome looms large.

ASPIRATION AND OUTCOME: WHAT WENT WRONG?

The discrepancy between aspiration and outcome is much larger for the Brothers than for the Hallway Hangers. In 1984 the Brothers had hopes of middle-class careers, of happy families, of nice cars, and of homes in leafy suburbs. Eight years later, they are for the most part living at home with their parents and struggling to make ends meet. The first edition of this book could only speculate that the Brothers' aspirations and expectations would be "cooled out" once they experienced the realities of the job market. The critical question here is whether they have begun to question the openness of American society or whether they reproach themselves for frustrated ambition.

Some of the Brothers maintain their faith in the American Dream. Derek does not earn much, even after seven years at his airport job. He and his wife live with their two children in a cramped two-bedroom apartment. But Derek's affirmation of equality of opportunity is still unequivocal. He is particularly vehement when reflecting on those who have resigned themselves to menial jobs or unemployment.

DEREK: If you really want something in life, you gotta go for it because it's really not that hard to make money. If you really want something, you just gotta go for it. Too many people I know don't realize that; it's their own fault, I guess. . . . If these people would really commit themselves, they could have anything they wanted. And I don't know of anyone who could tell me different. . . . There are too many opportunities out there, too many people that are willing to do things for you. Hell, they can even get a federal loan and get something out of their lives, but they don't want it.

For Derek, occupational failure can be attributed to lack of personal initiative and competence.

Mike agrees. "If you dig in, there are a lot of opportunities out there. You just have to go for them," he insists. The Hallway Hangers are "a bunch of lazy, loser, fuckup bums." A friend is also branded a bum, but Mike reconsiders.

MIKE: Bobby, he's a bum. No, that's not true, he's not really a bum. He works hard but he's kinda lazy. He's in a dead-end job. He's not going anywhere.

JM: Is that his fault?

MIKE: Yeah, it's his fault. Who else's fault could it be?

According to Mike, and to most Americans, those who fail have only themselves to blame. There is no publicly accepted idiom that can be invoked to explain failure apart from personal responsibility; a structural explanation is a nonstarter.

Most of the Brothers have tempered their belief in the openness of American society. They blame themselves for failing to get ahead, but the social order also comes in for some criticism. As noted earlier, Mokey chides himself for being lazy, for failing to study hard enough, and for switching jobs too frequently. But he also notes the lack of opportunity.

MOKEY: If I did something for myself, did better in school, I think I woulda been in a better position. But I know friends right now, I mean, they're in the same predicament. One friend, he graduated from Madison College and he's still looking for a job. . . . Looking for a job now is really hard.

Similarly, Super blames himself for his condition but never loses sight of the larger context.

SUPER: I've been moving a lot, man, that's probably the main reason why, you know, I can't get my head straight. It's like when I got out of high school, I had in mind going to school, I was doing good. I just fucked everything up.

(later in the same interview)

SUPER: I know I need to stop [selling drugs], but how can I stop? I mean, I gotta make money somehow, y'know? There just ain't any jobs, no jobs. You know that, right? Ain't no jobs. Y'know, there's just no jobs, ain't no jobs out there.

Super never shirks personal responsibility for his plight, nor does he absolve himself of moral culpability for dealing crack. Still, he understands that he has been constrained by economic realities over which he has no control.

Juan castigates himself. "I really screwed up, I just screwed up, I screwed up my life." And yet he also indicts the opportunity structure. Based on his experience in several jobs, Juan is convinced that the term *entry-level position* is often a euphemism. "They always tell you when you start a job that there's gonna be good chances of being promoted, of moving up. But it never happens."

James knows the vagaries of the labor market. He has tasted occupational success, but he has also been unemployed for over a year, in spite of his eagerness to work, his specialized computer training, and his work experience. His own work history has taught him the importance of structural constraints on opportunity.

JAMES: I've been on many job interviews to this very day that I know I was more than qualified for. They knew that I could do the job, but the way that the economics is, there's fifty other guys that can do the job. The other guy can do that job, his job, six other people's jobs, ten other jobs, he'll work for every day of the week for no pay. It's just, there's too many people without jobs. . . . It's just the economic system is falling apart right now.

James is the only Brother to criticize the economic system explicitly and consistently, and thus to contextualize individual choice within a larger framework. Responding to a question about Super dealing drugs, James sympathizes with his friend's situation.

JM: Tell me about Super. What happened with him? Cuz in high school he never did all that well, but he tried hard.

JAMES: What I can't understand is selling drugs and stuff like that. That never was him. I guess he'd say he's doing what he has to do to get by. Man, a lot of people's doing it. I can't really find fault in them, cuz they doing what they gotta do to get by. They payin' their bills and stuff. And the way that economics are now, man, a lot of people that wouldn't be doing that before, wouldn't do something like sell drugs, or sell stolen goods, wouldn't have done that before, they're doin' it now because, hey, they don't have jobs and you gotta support yourself, you gotta look out for your family, and you gotta look out for number one.

JM: So you don't really find fault with them individually?

JAMES: No, no, I find fault with the economic system. That there's so many people out of work that a lot of people are forced to do that. . . . Yeah, a lot of people are forced into it. They're not just criminals because they want to be criminals. They're criminals because they need some way to survive, and they can't. . . . That's where we go back to the economic system now. Nowadays, if you have a job you're doing good, the way the economics is now. . . .

James is clear on this point: that the lack of economic opportunity more than anything else explains why the Brothers have failed to get ahead as they envisioned. But notice how often James says "now" and "nowadays." He seems to blame the recession, passing economic circumstances, for their situation. This reasoning is quite different from the sociological insight that inequality in the system is structural rather than just temporary, although both types of explanation may be at work in James's statements. Recession may actually mask enduring inequality by making economic injustice appear transitory. Instead of having their faith in the free market pricked, those on the sharpest end of economic downturns simply long for recovery along with everyone else. Unfortunately, the Brothers and Hallway Hangers have rather less to recover than do the rich. In bad times even more so than good ones, it may be difficult to discern that the rules of the game are structurally rigged against the disadvantaged. Clearly James is not alone in emphasizing the current rather than the continued obstacles these men face, and this fact may have important political implications.

Whatever the exact diagnosis, James is convinced that economic realities are at the root of the problem. Still, he does not spare himself.

JAMES: I left the first job that I had. I jumped at the chance to get more money. I was young and I didn't realize if I had stayed at the Federal Reserve until now, I had befriended enough people to go up a level. [*clicks his fingers*] Y'know, I would've been somewhere now.

For James, as for social theorists, both individual agency and structural constraint are required to explain his occupational career, his current unemployment, and what he sees on the street.

Derek and Mike retain faith in the achievement ideology. Mokey, Juan, and Super second-guess their decisions and find fault with themselves but also begin to blame the larger socioeconomic order, a critique that James extends. Interestingly, rather than blame himself or the social order directly for the discrepancy between his hopes and his current situation, Craig critiques the aspiration itself.

CRAIG: I think when you're in college you get really unrealistic expectations of what kind of job you're going to get. You think it will be easy to land a decent professional job in the business world. You think that's what you're being prepared for. But the reality is different. You see, studying is not the same as working. They're two different things. Going to and graduating from a four-year school doesn't guarantee you anything. Every Joe Schmo out there has a four-year degree. That's nothing. It means absolutely nothing. Anybody can go to a little state school and come out with a degree. Everybody's got the degree. And everybody's got a résumé stuffed with decent jobs that's been done on a good word processor with a laser printer.

None of the Brothers would be more justified than Craig in feeling betrayed by the achievement ideology. But rather than complain that the goalposts keep being moved, Craig seems to hold himself responsible for misjudging the situation and nurturing unrealistic expectations. Only now does he realize that with the general inflation of diplomas, employment prospects cannot keep pace with educational qualifications.

Racism

In coming to grips with the disparity between aspiration and outcome, the Brothers do not cite racial discrimination as an important factor. Rather, as we have seen, several of them contend that employment opportunities are constricted. In this the Brothers echo recent sociological thinking that emphasizes factors other than direct racial discrimination to explain the economic subjugation of blacks. Sociologists show how industrial restructuring, for example, has taken an especially heavy toll on the job prospects of inner-city black men, for whom the new information-processing jobs, many of them located in the suburbs, are beyond physical and educational reach. Structural changes in the economy mean that African Americans like the Brothers face a deflated opportunity structure. Most of the Brothers understand this fact themselves.

The Brothers are also aware that informal social networks—connections—are an important occupational resource that they largely lack.

(in separate interviews)

SUPER: Nowadays, y'know, you go to look for a job, you call, they tell you they got a long waiting list, y'know? This 'n' that. Depends on who you know, too, if you can get a job.

JAMES: One thing that I didn't know in high school that I wish I had've knew in high school is that it's not what you can do, it's who you know. . . . If you befriend the right people, you're gonna move up that ladder. . . .

CRAIG: You need to know the right people. That's what I'm seeing. I'm trying to develop some connections because I'm finding that's what you need out here.

After several years of struggle, the Brothers understand the importance of contacts on the job market, an insight that contradicts the achievement ideology they took to heart in high school.

Again, the Brothers are in line with sociological thinking. Studies of labor markets show by and large that people do not get jobs through an impersonal, meritocratic process based on their "human capital"—their educational attainment and prior work experience. Rather, people obtain jobs by exploiting informal personal networks; they learn about jobs through word of mouth rather than from newspaper advertisements or employment agencies.[9] Family, friends, and acquaintances are invaluable resources for learning about job openings and for pulling strings to get hired. Here again we see the workings of cultural capital. Working-class whites are advantaged relative to working-class blacks. The Hallway Hangers have landed jobs through white ethnic networking, but these are networks from which the Brothers are largely excluded. Mercer Sullivan discovered the same dynamic in his study of three New York City neighborhoods: Working-class whites used family and neighborhood networks to get blue-collar jobs, whereas "the minority youths suffered . . . from their lack of comparable job networks."[10] Similarly, young whites in Boston interviewed by Paul Osterman were able to use parents and relatives twice as frequently to find jobs as were young blacks.[11]

Mike actually makes the connection between race and informal social networks. Craig, he says, is without a good job because as an African American he lacks connections.

MIKE: I thought going to college would help Craig. But he came back and was without a job for about a year and a half before he got this job, which is shit. I think he'll be okay when the economy picks up. It's hard, him being black. I think it's because of his skin color. They don't wanna hire blacks. Especially in this city, it's like white kin. Craig doesn't have no contacts. He doesn't know anybody.

In Mike's mind, the fact that Craig cannot exploit occupational connections is racially rooted. The black Brothers do not articulate this link, although their belief in the importance of connections may reflect experiences of race- and class-based exclusion.

Most of the Brothers explicitly discount racism as a handicap in their occupational careers; being black, some suggest, can be an advantage on the job market.

JM: Did you find in the jobs you were trying to get, or in your studying or whatever, that discrimination was a problem? Did being black hold you back at all?

SUPER: No, not really, never look at it thatta way.

(in a separate interview)

JM: Do you think being black has hurt you in terms of getting a job?

MOKEY: I've never felt any problem being a different color to an employer. . . . I really don't think the racial thing bothered, I never been bothered by it. I really never put racial into a job. Going for some jobs, maybe cuz I'm black that would help, like for the police force.

Similarly, Derek rejects any suggestion of racism and indicates that affirmative action can help with public-sector jobs.

JM: Have you ever felt that discrimination has held you back in any kinda way in any of your jobs?

DEREK: No. When I went for the police officer [position] in Avon, I could've gotten it cuz I was black, but I could've gotten it cuz I scored well.

Only Juan speaks of a direct experience of racial prejudice in employment. He takes personal responsibility for losing his airport job but then indicates that racism also played a role.

JUAN: Everybody comes in late, and the thing is, some of 'em get away with it, so I found it discriminating.

JM: Because you're black?

JUAN: I saw it like that, to be honest.

For the other Brothers, racial prejudice played no direct role in their employment or educational histories.

But racism, after all, is often a subtle phenomenon. It seldom rings with the clarity of the Hallway Hangers' vicious denunciations. James alludes to the subtle workings of racial domination, first in his schooling and then in his workplace. In neither case does he view the situation as overtly racist, but both contribute to the subordination of blacks. Within the computer institute James attended, there were two distinct educational tiers. Classes were unofficially segregated along racial, class, and age lines, and James believes that he got a crucial career break when he switched to the more advanced "white" classes during the day.

JAMES: I realized how the business world works because of the fact that when I went to computer school, they started me off at nights, in night school. Night school was all black people. There were no white kids in night school, okay.

JM: Why was that?

JAMES: I guess white guys, they didn't wanna go to school at night. Beats the heck outta me, I have no idea. All I know is that I was way more advanced than most of these guys that were in my class at nights, because I had been working on the computers in high school and I had a computer at home. So I was, like, well ahead of them. I was, like, up there with the teacher. So the teacher said, "Hey, I have a more advanced class in the daytime. Why don't you switch over to day class?" So I did. And, um, well, actually, I do know why most of the people in my class at night—all of them were black, well, black and Hispanic—because they were workin' day jobs and then paying to go to school at night. So he switched me over to the day course with all white kids. They were as young as me, cuz the night class was older people, older black and Hispanic people. The day course was young white kids, but it was, like, young white kids from the suburbs that their parents were paying for them to go to school. But that class was way more advanced than the night class. So we got a lot more out of it.

Unable to give up their day jobs, students of color seem to have received substandard education in the night class. And for James, who could afford to attend during the daytime, direct discrimination would have played a role when "they started me off at nights." The registrar probably did not consider it an act of overt racism when he or she placed James in the night class. On the contrary, based on James's skin color, accent, and posture, it probably seemed a "natural" and "sensible" thing to do. Perhaps it never occurred to the registrar to inquire about James's qualifications and ability. Unconscious discrimination and institutional racism, as much as the outspoken prejudice of the Hallway Hangers, contribute to racial oppression. Although James does not use those terms, he feels privileged to have received the standard of education that his white counterparts take for granted.

Schooling aside, James insists that he felt no direct discrimination in his various jobs but then hints that racial dynamics played a role in his termination.

JM: Were you treated any different in your jobs, did you feel any discrimination on account of being black?

JAMES: No! No. None. None whatsoever.

JM: You didn't feel the last one was racial, that he was up in your face . . . ?

JAMES: No, he was another black guy. I felt from the last job, I felt there was more pressure put on us because our operations department was black. And that's what it was. He didn't want them looking at our department and going, "Oh, these dumb black people, they keep messin' up every time." And that's what they were basically doing, was saying every time something went wrong on their end, on the higher end, like the software technicians and guys like that screwing up, we were the ones who caught the blame: "Oh, no, those dumb guys in operations; they don't know what they're doing."

JM: So did your boss used to say that to you guys?

JAMES: Yeah. He felt a lot of discrimination, and that's basically what pushed him to, that's really what pushed him to firing me.

In a different context, James affirms that "racism is everywhere" and that police brutality against blacks is widespread. Back on the subject of occupational discrimination, James contends that being black can be both a liability and an asset on the job market.

JAMES: There's been so many negative things said about blacks and everything, a lot of people are scared to hire blacks. It depends on what you're doing. There's a lot of affirmative action in different types of areas, like hospital work, in computer work, banks, stuff like that. So, basically, these places have to meet quotas anyway. So they gonna hire you because you're black anyway.

JM: So do you think you might have actually benefited?

JAMES: Because I was black? When I was in computer school, a guy told me that I would benefit more because I was black.

JM: Was he white or black?

JAMES: He was white. He was the director of our school. He said a lot of places have to hire blacks.

JM: Do you think he was right?

JAMES: Yeah, yeah. Most definitely. That's the reason why they hired me at the bank. [*clicks his fingers*] They hired me that same day that I went in for the interview. Then the second job, they hired me right then. They had no black guys workin' there, no blacks at all. They hired me right on the spot because of the fact that I was black.

Affirmative action, of course, seeks to help redress historic patterns of employment discrimination. In both the public and private sectors, affirmative action plans do not involve quotas; even plans imposed by the judiciary in extreme cases require only good-faith efforts to reach hiring objectives and goals. Targeting of this type, which seeks merely to level the playing field for qualified racial minorities, is increasingly viewed as reverse discrimination against white men. The Hallway Hangers certainly subscribe to this notion, and some of the Brothers believe that black skin may be an asset on the labor market.

In fact, affirmative action appears to have done little for poor African Americans. Although studies indicate that the earnings and promotion prospects of middle-class blacks have improved,[12] the situation for black men on the lower rungs of the labor market is still abysmal.[13] This reality is borne out by the experiences of the Brothers. Although some of them believe the rhetoric that all blacks, themselves included, receive preferential treatment via affirmative action, only James is sure to have actually benefited.

Caught in Cultural Limbo

The Brothers are caught between a predominantly white bourgeois culture and a black subproletarian street culture. Earlier, James alluded to the portrayal of blacks and the fears of employers. In the past decade, black youth street culture has been so sensationalized and demonized that young black men are automatically invested with an aura of moral irresponsibility, social unworthiness, and cultural depravity in the minds of many Americans. Like other young black men, the Brothers have become symbols of danger and degeneracy.

JAMES: You walk outside onto the street, racism's everywhere. I see it on the phone. I'm talkin' on the phone with my girlfriend at night, and people lookin' at me, on the phone. It's like last night, I'm on the phone, and a white lady and a white guy, you could look and tell how they dressed they don't live around here, they're from the suburbs or wherever you wanna call it— Beverly, Chester, some uppity rich place, Beverly, Belmont, something like that. And they don't wanna ask me if they can use the phone because of the fact that they sit at home and they watch TV every day and they see how vicious these young black guys are. They just pull out guns and they just shoot people, and they kill everybody and they're robbing babies and they're doing all this stuff—they're selling drugs and all that.

The Brothers do not look like hoodlums. But neither do they look like they belong on the *Cosby Show*. Because they do not immediately convey a mastery of middle-class culture, they bear the public taint of the "underclass," with all the racially coded characteristics that term has come to imply. In the popular mind, the Brothers are morally dissolute and criminally inclined if not downright dangerous.

The irony here is palpable. By any standards of youth conduct, the Brothers were (and with the exception of Super still are) veritable puritans. They have a strong work ethic. They are sexually responsible. They don't smoke. They don't use drugs. They drink only in moderation. They respect adult authority. The Brothers are not angels, but they sometimes seem to be, even in comparison to the well-heeled but hard-partying university students up the street who steer safely clear of the Brothers and their ilk.

The Brothers must negotiate complex racial and class dynamics, not least in relating to prospective employers. In a study of Chicago employers, Joleen

Kirschenman and Kathryn M. Neckerman discovered that young African American men are often considered shifty, lazy, unreliable, dishonest, ignorant, and socially inept. In short, employers view poor young blacks in much the same way as do most Americans. Many proprietors conflate race and class. The owner of a construction firm, for example, observed that for people of color in general, "the quality of education . . . is not as great as [for] white folk from the suburbs. . . . And it shows in the intellectual capability of the labor force. . . . The minority worker is not as punctual and not as concerned about punctuality as the middle-class white." Other employers made class distinctions among prospective black employees. Unless black applicants could somehow signal middle-class origins, they were tagged with the racial stereotypes associated with the "underclass." Home address was also a distinguishing mark to many employers. African American applicants from ghetto neighborhoods, especially those from "the projects," were assumed to be particularly deficient. Kirschenman and Neckerman conclude that although race is of greatest importance, it is often qualified by class and geographical space in hiring decisions.[14]

Caught in a class and racial no-man's-land between white middle-class culture and black lower-class culture, the Brothers face special problems on the job. The new service economy has transformed the social relations of the workplace. Laborers in the old unionized manufacturing jobs could "be themselves" on the shop floor, where they were physically distant from consumers and socially distant from their bosses. Service workers, in contrast, often have neither a physical nor a social space to themselves. This situation places extraordinary demands on young working-class blacks who are constantly rubbing elbows with supervisors and customers. Busing tables in a swanky restaurant, photocopying files in a corporate office, or working the register at a supermarket, young black men like the Brothers must overcome the wariness and unease of their mainly white, middle-class clientele and supervisors. The Brothers are honest, dedicated, and hardworking. But these qualities are not easily projected across the cultural and social divide that separates them from their employers. To their white bosses, they may come off as sullen, inarticulate, and distant. As Philippe Bourgois's penetrating ethnography discloses, the basic subjective job requirement in the service economy—a "good attitude"—conjugates with racism and subtle class dynamics. Skin color, hairstyle, apparel, vocabulary, inflection, posture, gaze, and gait become signs of dissonance and unsuitability. Being looked in the eye can make supervisors nervous.[15] Especially in small firms where control is exercised informally and interpersonal bonding becomes essential for job security, young blacks like the Brothers are at a disadvantage unless they can cultivate a style of social interaction that puts employers and customers at ease.

Some of the Brothers have managed this feat. Derek's hourly wage at the airport may be paltry, but in contrast to the other Brothers, he has mastered the social milieu of his workplace. Between flights, he banters playfully with fellow workers, most of them white—teasing, laughing, winking, jostling. Obviously well liked by his colleagues, Derek has an enthusiastic personality that is given full rein. His job allows him to assert his identity, whereas other Brothers are required to submerge theirs. This includes his racial identity, which comes easily to the surface. I told him he was looking good after we greeted each other at the airport. "Of course, I'm black," he answered, grinning. "Shame about Curt here, though," he said, laughing, jerking his thumb at an older white worker and dancing quickly away.

DEREK: In my workplace I have fun. It's like people will sit there and call me nigger and I'll just sit there and insult their mother. That's how we are, that's our workplace, we get along so well, I know everybody there. We're all friends. I mean, I could walk up to one of my friends' mothers and start tickling them like I do everybody else. See, that's the thing, I treat everybody the same. And that's why I get along so well with everybody.

In contrast to nearly all the other young men in this study, Derek has a job that allows him to be himself.

Of course, Derek draws upon unique resources in order to master his workplace. As a youth, he attended the prestigious Barnes Academy, where he learned the social cues of a wealthy white environment.

DEREK: For the first couple of years I started going to Barnes, it was, like, myself, a guy named Teddy Cook, and one other black student and two black girls. I think we were, like, the only black people that I saw in that whole school—the lower school, the middle school, and the upper, which was considered the high school. And, y'know, that never bothered me, that definitely never bothered me, because if it did I would never have gone to Mexico for two whole summers with Mexican people and white people and sometimes I thought I was the only black person in the country but it was worth it for the experience. . . . I never had any money [at Barnes] but I managed to get along with everybody. I can get along with anybody if I want to.

JM: Right.

DEREK: And it was really different. I mean, this kid—his mother owned seven private schools and they could do anything they wanted, just like that. One time we spent the whole month in Acapulco, at the Princess [Hotel]—like, I think that's the most expensive place—and for my birthday one year we went out on the beach and we went horseback riding, parasailing, and they threw this big cake in my face, burnt my nose, and it was, it was, it was really different. And that same summer we went, we came from Mexico City, we went up to San Francisco for a wedding, and we went to Austin, Texas, for a family gathering they had. Y'know, I really got a look at what the other side's like.

At Barnes Academy, Derek was socialized into affluent white culture. Traveling with rich friends, he learned to adapt to alien and challenging social circumstances. Both experiences, hardly typical for poor young African Americans, have helped him to negotiate and master the complex social currents in his workplace.

James never quite mastered the social relations of his workplace, but he learned to be bicultural: to play the game downtown and to be himself back in the Heights. But he found it difficult to keep his professional and street roles distinct. He was accused of acting white at home; and, conversely, he lost his job because when his boss began to "rip into" him, James failed to batten down his street pride and walked off the job.

JAMES: The environment that you grow up around has a lot to do with the person that you come out to be, but, it's like, I can operate on a street level and I can operate on a professional level. But a lot of people don't differentiate the two. They don't say, "All right, I'm at work now, let me act professional." They go in and they have their same street attitude. Someone from the Heights going in with an attitude like that, you're not going to stay in a job like that, not in a professional-level job. And that's what I've learned really quick. I learned that two days after I started working at the Federal Reserve bank, that I couldn't go in with my tough-guy attitude. Cuz you just can't function, you can't function doing your job. You have to have a professional attitude.

JM: Do you ever let the professional attitude come out here, and then people get on you for acting different?

JAMES: Yes. All the time, all the time. I went with a girl the year before last, she says to me, "If you only knew how white you sound!"

I'm like, "How white I sound? What do you mean, 'How white I sound'? I sound like me, I sound like myself."

She's like, "No, you sound white."

And, like, my girlfriend now, I called her house for the first time, I didn't believe that it was her. She sounds just like a white girl because she has that professional voice. But that's what a lot of black people have to put aside, too. They have to put aside the fact that they think because someone acts professional, they're acting white. If you're acting professional, that's what's gonna move black people to a different level, is a lot of professional-acting black people. Then you won't see on TV, you won't see every day, "Oh, man, these black kids, they're out there shootin' each other, sellin' drugs on the corner, doin' this," because you'll have a whole society of professional people.

JM: Are there the jobs out there that would allow that to happen?

JAMES: Well, the way the economy is right now—no. If there were jobs out there that would allow that to happen, I would have a job. Cuz it's not like I'm chillin' at home, not looking for a job.

James highlights the difficulty of being caught in limbo between black street culture and white bourgeois culture. To many of his peers, professionalism is a betrayal of black identity. But with the eyes of the wider culture in mind, James believes that professionalism will salvage the race's image because it contradicts their stereotypes.

It was only because James swam against the flow of racial and class domination that he learned to act professionally. If he had stayed in the computer class into which he was originally placed, attending evening classes with older people of color who were holding down jobs, he may never have developed the resources to act biculturally. James learned superior skills in the advanced day course with suburban whites, but he stresses the importance of being socialized into "business culture."

JAMES: From the moment that I got into that class, I realized how exactly the business world works. I looked around and I knew I had to develop a professional attitude.

As James himself contends, he was lucky. He was lucky to have been noticed by his teacher and lucky that his parents' financial support freed him from a day job. But why was he channeled into the night class in the first place? The practice of tracking, it would appear, is not limited to secondary school. More insidious still is the extent to which the Brothers have been hamstrung by the discriminatory appraisal of cultural capital in their working lives.

Derek and, to a lesser extent, James have developed personal skills that allow them to cope on the job. But Craig is the only Brother who immediately conveys an outward mastery of middle-class culture. His wardrobe, bearing, and walk prevent him from being instantly stereotyped as a member of the ghetto poor. Five years of higher education have schooled Craig in bourgeois etiquette and deportment. Telephone calls to the other Brothers invariably result in brief conversations with their mothers, televisions blaring in the background. But when Craig is out, the caller reaches an answering machine with a smoothly articulate message sandwiched between bars of soft jazz. And yet despite Craig's bourgeois bearing, Mike insists that one of Craig's problems on the job market is that he will not go further and submerge his racial identity.

MIKE: Craig hasn't got the contacts, but I'll tell ya, another thing is that he acts too black. He hangs out with black guys most of the time; I think I'm really his only white friend. Y'know, he's into black music, black . . . he's just into that black thing.

JM: You think that's hurt him trying to get a job?

MIKE: Yeah, shit yeah. You think the guy's who's hiring, the personnel guy, you think he's gonna be into LL Cool J?

In Mike's view, distinguishing oneself from the stereotyped street culture of the ghetto poor is not enough to ensure a higher rung on the occupational ladder. African Americans like the Brothers must completely abandon their racial identity at the company door if they are to really get ahead.

If Craig has edged in one direction in the bind between a dominant bourgeois culture and a black street culture, Super has moved in the other. Super alludes directly to the cultural clash he felt with his boss at the grocery store.

SUPER: My boss, this lady, I had this lady boss who started getting on my nerves. We couldn't get along. She'd, like, smile at me all the time, y'know, but I could tell she hated me. Man, I didn't really like her either. She was so uppity. Really, she was a bitch. Her boss, the vice president who was cool, understood me, know what I'm saying?

Making his money on the street, Super doesn't have to deal daily with the silent humiliation of his boss's patronizing smile. Now he deals daily with the prospect of arrest, injury, and even death. Super has become enmeshed in a street culture where brutal violence and the crack plague feed off each other and intensify problems of poverty, AIDS, and sexual exploitation, leaving wasted lives in their wake. And yet this is a way of life that Super has embraced not because he is so different from the rest of us but because he is so similar. Super's goals are completely conventional: to have a place of his own, get married, and raise a family. Only he has to resort to criminal means to achieve them. As Robert Merton's brilliant analysis of anomie makes plain, when society encourages everyone to strive for the same lofty goals and then denies the poor the wherewithal to achieve them, criminality is the inevitable outcome.[16] Like the dealers befriended by anthropologists Philippe Bourgois and Terry Williams,[17] Super sells drugs because he is so committed to making the American Dream his own. Even as he despairs of his lifestyle, he is quite clear about its attraction: "It's not a life you want to live, but y'know, you want to be someone, make fast money, have respect."

GROPING FOR THE GOOD LIFE

All of the Brothers, like Super, are in search of respect. But respect does not easily come their way. Juan works but is denied a job description, set hours, overtime, job security, and decent pay. Yet what bothers him most about the job is "always being disrespected." Disdainful of manual work, Juan is unable to generate self-esteem from his employment. In 1984 he longed for a "clean job," a longing he still nurses.

JUAN: I don't like dirty jobs. I'd rather get a clean job.

JM: Whaddya mean, like a dirty job?

JUAN: You got dirt all over you. I mean, at a auto-body shop, you got chemicals all around there. And, like, you get out, your head's all painty, you smell like thinner. If you got to go to an appointment or something, you gotta go home and have a wash, take a shower. At least at McDonald's it's a clean job. A lot of grease, but at least you look a little presentable wherever you go, just about, y'know? Over there, you come out all dirty, pants all ripped, with twenty different colors.

JM: Why do you think that's important to you, y'know, to have a clean job?

JUAN: On a clean job you got a better chance of gettin' promoted. In a dirty job, they just have you there to do one thing and that's it. Who cares? In a clean job, they respect you cuz you look good, you present yourself good.

Again, respect eludes Juan, whereas many manual workers might regard their dirty work clothes as a badge of masculine pride. For them, as for Paul Willis's lads,[18] the "real work" of manual laborers is superior to the flimsy, ephemeral, and effeminate character of mental labor.

Mike is the only Brother who begins to articulate a working-class consciousness, although he earns far and away the most money. Much of his political analysis seems to stem from his union membership.

MIKE: I'm thinking about going to night school, get myself a degree in management, just in case the post office isn't around in the future.

JM: What, you think it might be privatized?

MIKE: Yeah, it could be. Maybe fifteen years or so. I want training just in case. I don't wanna be hung out to dry if they do privatize it. They might, too. I'm tellin' ya, the Republicans are fucking us over. Reagan fucked us over so bad. I'm tellin' ya, it's the blue-collar worker in America who's getting screwed. They don't care. They might hack us up, sell us off, break the union. There goes the working class. They'll sell the post office to their fucking friends is what they'll do. Sell us to their friends and fuck America. I just got a letter from the union telling us how Bush is fucking us up. The Republicans, they hate us.

JM: You're a big union supporter, then?

MIKE: Yeah. Management will fuck you over, I know that much. Unions can do something about that, can protect us. In white-collar work you're fucked.

Mike is proud to be working class and proud to be "making more than most yuppies." But when he's "on the prowl," trying to pick up women, Mike poses as a lawyer. He has a steady girlfriend but often boasts of his nightclub conquests.

MIKE: I just like to go out for a bang, go out to clubs, see what I can find. . . .

JM: What about your girlfriend?

MIKE: Miranda? I'm still with Miranda. We're pretty serious, actually. It's five and a half years we've been together. I'll probably settle down with her. We could be married in a year or two. I won't go out and fuck around when I'm married. There'll be just one woman then. . . . Yeah, I know. It must sound shitty. But hey, it's our nature. All men cheat. Whaddya think? Before civilization, we didn't care about nothing. All we did was run around and plug up every hole we could find. It's just our nature.

Mike's frankly exploitative approach to women is the exception among the Brothers. Craig accompanies Mike on his forays into black clubs, but Craig is usually accompanied by his girlfriend. James and his partner are on the verge of engagement, although he'd like to wait until he's found a job.

JM: So do you ever think about marriage?

JAMES: [*laughs*] The first time I ever saw her I thought about marriage. I've gone out with lots of girls before, and I never thought about marriage. I wasn't the type of person to get married. I never thought about it, it never entered my mind—marrying someone. I liked this girl from the beginning. She's just like, "Be yourself." Cuz all these girls, they want this phony attitude and guys'll walk around like Ice T: "Yo, babe, yo babe." And y'know, that's what I was thinking, "Oh, what if I act like me and this girl doesn't like me? I want this girl really bad, er, maybe I should act like somebody else." She told me to just be myself. She said the onliest reason she wanted to talk to me is because I was looking nervous. Because I just wanted to bust out and talk to this girl. And she said I looked like I had words caught in my throat. Man, I love Tricia so bad. . . . I have had girls that I have treated bad. I treat my girlfriend now like gold, man, cuz she's what I want out of life. If you're brought up the way we were brought up is you treat a woman with respect. And that's how every, to me that's how every man should act towards a woman. Girls in our family are like, if you're a girl, you're a jewel. It's like a diamond, okay. It's like you went to a coal mine and you got a diamond. . . . Yeah, we've been talking about getting married. But without a job, what kind of husband would I be? I need a job, man, I need a job.

For James, as for so many inner-city youths, the economic basis of marriage has been undermined.

The other Brothers are more prosaic about their relationships. Mokey and his partner, together since high school, have also contemplated marriage and children.

MOKEY: I said no. It's not time. How could we? We're both living at home. We can't afford a place, there's just no way. It'd be crazy. But it would be nice, too, though. . . .

Super lived with a woman for two years and was engaged to be married before she left him.

SUPER: She goes with one of my buddies now. I see them all the time. That hurts, man, that does, I gotta admit it, that hurts.

JM: What about Keisha, how long have you been seeing her? Are you two pretty steady or what?

SUPER: Yeah.

JM: But sort of informal, on-and-off kind of thing?

SUPER: Naw, steady.

Most of the Brothers are involved in stable relationships with women. And yet Mike, Craig, James, Mokey, and Super do not have children.

Juan does have children—two baby daughters born five months apart. Juan's pride in fatherhood is overshadowed by regret. There are constant problems with and between the two mothers, one Italian and one of African and Portuguese descent, as they vie for Juan's affection and commitment. Juan supports both children financially and sees them every week.

JUAN: I really screwed up. I just screwed up. I screwed up my life. Two children and two different mothers. Shit. I thought I didn't have much money before. Ha. Now I see life used to be carefree—not so many bills as with my daughters. Now I've got to work every chance I get. Except Sundays, that's my day with my kids.

JM: Were you surprised when you found out you were gonna be a father?

JUAN: It was so unexpected. What can I do? I had no idea, y'know? But I found it can happen. I'm proud of my daughters, I'm proud of them. It's not like I'd ever leave them stranded. They're the first two things in my life, besides my parents, y'know? I don't take no shit from nobody when it comes to my children. They wanna tell me, "Oh, you hafta work on Sunday."

"Uh-uh. Today's my day off, it's for my kids, and I'm taking them out," and out we go, y'know? They try to do that with me, my boss, Jim, does. "Naw, I gotta take off, take my daughter to the hospital."

"No, I need you here today."

"You need me here? My daughter needs me over there." I may not be able to pay my bills, but I feel a lot better being there for them. "You wouldn't want me telling you you hafta work and you can't see your kids, right?" It's just a hassle. You've got to put your kids first, that's how I look at it. I have no choice. Matter of fact, when you think of yourself, you get greedy. I can't think about that. Cuz I got kids. If you think greedy, you ain't gonna think about your kids. Everything you see: I want, I want. But what about your kids, what do they need? . . . Those are my kids. I'm never going to deny them. But like I say, I wish it had never happened. . . . I'm hanging in there. I try not to look at the worst. It could be worse, so you keep fighting, keep a free mind, keep hoping. Sooner or later, someone's gonna do you the favor that you've done to them.

Juan tries to feel buoyant, but he is struggling to stay afloat. Under the combined weight of a job he hates and family responsibilities he can not properly fulfill, Juan seems to be slowly sinking. Hope is the only thing he can hold onto.

JUAN: Things will pick up, though. Things will get better further down the road. That's the way life is: picks you up, puts you down. Things will pick up.

JM: How do you stay so hopeful?

JUAN: You've got to be hopeful. You've got to be hopeful or you wouldn't be able to face the grind, the rat race. You live by the days. If you wake up, you wake up. Tomorrow's another thing. Today's enough reality, I don't need any more. Every day's precious, so you live day by day. Got to, ain't got no choice.

Derek is the other father among the Brothers. He was married in 1984 just before entering the navy.

JM: You got married right out of high school. That always surprised me, you got married that quickly.

DEREK: She was pregnant.

JM: Right.

DEREK: I felt an obligation, a moral obligation. Y'know, if I do something wrong, I have to do something to correct it. I'm not exactly the marrying type cuz I'm still a person that believes I want to get out and do this and do that, but I can't. I don't regret having my kids, it's just I regret not taking more time to have fun and do the things I wanted to do. Cuz I provide for my kids. That's important. I've got saving bonds set up for them that's deducted from my pay every month. I have fun with my kids. We go kite flying, we go to outdoor concerts and listen to jazz music and everything like that, and I feel like I have a good rapport with my kids. Carlton just turned seven and Amy just turned five. We talk and have fun together. I dunno, marriage, that's just not for me. But it's working.

Derek and his wife, Faith, live with their children in a small, two-bedroom apartment not far from Clarendon Heights. Although Faith works at an electronics firm, the family cannot afford to buy a home.

Derek longs for the "good life" he tasted while traveling with his Barnes Academy friends. At the same time, he insists that he is quite satisfied and is adamant that money does not necessarily bring happiness.

DEREK: I've always wanted to succeed, I've always wanted to try and do something with my life. . . . I've had the opportunities to see a part of the good life, y'know? If you want something you go for it, and it made a hell of an impression on me. It's like I've seen everything that there is out there to get and I wanna try and be a part of it before, before too long.

JM: Do you ever run into any of your old classmates from Barnes?

DEREK: As of recently, no. The guy I went to Mexico with, I haven't seen him for three or four years. I know they've gone on to college and they've gone on to whatever professional or nonprofessional jobs that they get along with. But every long once in a while, I'll run into somebody.

JM: Do you ever see people who are on the fast track in banking or something, making lots of money, and think, "I could do that. I have the intelligence, I have the drive, I have the commitment, I have the responsibility," y'know? Do you ever think that or do you . . .

DEREK: No. All the choices I've made in my life, y'know, I'm starting to take control. But I'm not gonna kick myself in the ass because I didn't do something someone else has done. Cuz I know if I wanted to do it, I could just try a little bit harder and do it. So. I'm pretty much happy where I am. Not that I'll change it. Like I said before, pay doesn't matter. What matters is being happy. Happy, happy, happy. I'm meeting my bills. I'm doing it. I just need a house, a better home for the kids. They shouldn't have to share a bedroom at their age.

Although his home is cramped, Derek has at least managed, with his wife, to set up an independent household. Apart from Craig, none of the Brothers have a place they can call their own. Mokey, James, Juan, and Mike live with their parents. Super has no fixed abode; he currently spends most nights on a couch in his aunt's public housing apartment.

JM: You're twenty-four now. When you were back in high school, what did you think you'd be as a twenty-four-year-old back then?

SUPER: Out of college, have a good job, my own apartment. Or probably my own business or something, y'know, doin' good, not doin' bad.

JM: When you look at the other guys you used to hang with—Craig, Mike, Juan, Mokey, Derek, James—how do you think they're doing?

SUPER: Most of 'em, they're doing all right. Y'know, a couple of 'em got apartments, jobs. But they're catching hell, too. A lot of 'em are. Got kids, rent to pay. They're catching hell. And most of those guys are living at home, living with Mommy still. I mean, they ain't teenagers anymore. That's kinda pathetic, when you think about it. But I ain't one to talk. At least the ones that are working, they're making their money legal, not like me. I haven't ate a good meal in a long time. Like, I used to eat every day, y'know, like a home-cooked meal.

Super has money to buy food. What he longs for in his unsettled life are the security and fellowship a family meal symbolizes.

Mokey, James, and Juan cannot afford to live on their own, much less support a family. Only Mike and Derek have health insurance. The signposts that have traditionally marked the transition to adulthood for young men—a stable job, an independent household, the beginnings of a family—have proved beyond the Brothers' reach. Hard as they try, the Brothers have simply not been able to work up a head of steam on the labor market. Unfortunately, their experience is all too typical for poor young adults, particularly African American men. A high school diploma, a bit of college, a positive attitude, and a wealth of ambition do not pay off as advertised. The Hallway Hangers can be dismissed by unsympathetic observers as self-destructive burnouts. The Brothers cannot. The Brothers have made mistakes, but they are generally conscientious men committed to the American Dream. They show quite clearly that our society is not as open as it purports to be. Given the modest gains of the Brothers, who can condemn the Hallway Hangers for turning their backs on a game that is also rigged against them?

NOTES

1. John D. Kasarda, "Urban Industrial Transition and the Underclass," *Annals of the American Academy of the Political and Social Sciences* 501 (January 1989): 30–31.

2. Paul Osterman, "Is There a Problem with the Youth Labor Market and, If So, How Should We Fix It?" mimeo (Sloan School, MIT, February 1992), pp. 14, 51.

3. Ibid., p. 27.

4. Kasarda, "Urban Industrial Transition and the Underclass," p. 31.

5. Bureau of the Census, Public Use Microdata Sample File, 1980 and 1990.

6. Osterman, "Is There a Problem," p. 51.

7. Bureau of the Census, Public Use Microdata Sample File, 1990.

8. Norton Grubb, "The Economic Returns to Post-Secondary Education: New Evidence from the National Longitudinal Survey of the Class of 1972," mimeo (School of Education, University of California at Berkeley, 1990). Cited in Osterman, "Is There a Problem," p. 36n.

9. In this connection, see M. Corcoran, L. Datcher, and G. J. Duncan, "Most Workers Find Jobs Through Word of Mouth," *Monthly Labor Review* 103 (August 1980): 33–36; and Mark S. Granovetter, *Getting a Job* (Cambridge, Mass.: Harvard University Press, 1974), pp. 5–11.

10. Mercer Sullivan, *Getting Paid* (Ithaca, N.Y.: Cornell University Press, 1989), p. 103.

11. Paul Osterman, *Getting Started* (Cambridge, Mass.: MIT Press, 1980), p. 143.

12. Soo Son, Suzanne W. Model, and Gene A. Fisher, "Polarization and Progress in the Black Community: Earnings and Status Gains for Young Black Males in the Era of Affirmative Action," *Sociological Forum* 4:3 (1989): 309–327; William J. Wilson, *The Truly Disadvantaged* (Chicago: University of Chicago Press, 1987), pp. 109–118; Michael Hout, "Occupational Mobility of Black Men: 1962–1973," *American Sociological Review* 49 (1984): 308–322; Richard Freeman, *Black Elite: The New Market for Highly Educated Black Americans* (New York: McGraw-Hill, 1976); Andrea H. Beller, "Trends in Occupational Segregation by Sex and Race, 1960–1981," in Barbara F. Reskin, ed., *Sex Segregation in the Workplace* (Washington, D.C.: National Academy Press, 1984), pp. 11–26.

13. Marshall I. Pomer, "Labor Market Structure, Intragenerational Mobility, and Discrimination: Black Male Advancement Out of Low-Paying Occupations," *American Sociological Review* 51 (1986): 650–659; Soo Son et al., "Polarization and Progress"; Wilson, *The Truly Disadvantaged.*

14. Joleen Kirschenman and Kathryn M. Neckerman, "'We'd Love to Hire Them, But . . .': The Meaning of Race for Employers," in Christopher Jencks and Paul E. Peterson, ed., *The Urban Underclass* (Washington, D.C.: Brookings Institution, 1991), pp. 203–232.

15. Philippe Bourgois, "In Search of Respect: The New Service Economy and the Crack Alternative in Spanish Harlem" (Russell Sage Foundation Working Paper #21, May 1991).

16. Robert Merton, *Social Theory and Social Structure* (Glencoe, Ill: Free Press, 1949), pp. 131–153.

17. See Philippe Bourgois, *In Search of Respect: Selling Crack in El Barrio* (New York: Cambridge University Press, 1995), and Terry Williams, *The Cocaine Kids* (Reading, Mass.: Addison-Wesley, 1989).

18. Paul E. Willis, *Learning to Labor* (Aldershot: Gower, 1977).

CONCLUSION
Outclassed and Outcast(e)

One afternoon, while hitchhiking to the city, I was picked up by a motorist in a BMW. The charitable middle-age man chatted away for an hour about his teenage children. As we drove into the city and past Clarendon Heights, however, he peered at the young men lounging in the project's doorways, shook his head in disgust, and dismissed them as ignorant, lazy losers. That sort of causal simplicity is attractive: Losers lose; wanting individuals lead to wasted lives; poverty is self-generated. What we see on the streets, however, is actually complex. Once we push beneath the surface texts of individual lives, we discover the hard contours of structural inequality.

Our society is *structured* to create poverty and extreme economic inequality. There are simply not enough good jobs to go around. For every boss there are many workers, and the gap in their pay is unparalleled among industrialized nations. Chief executives of large U.S. companies made 160 times as much as the average blue-collar worker in 1989.[1] Indeed, while Juan, Mokey, Stoney, and Shorty struggled to survive on earnings of five dollars per hour, top corporate executives routinely raked in up to $5,000 per hour (including stock options and other income).[2] By 1993 the median pay package for the chief executive officers of the Fortune 1,000 largest companies was worth over $2.4 million. By comparison, the median annual earnings for everyone over fifteen years of age in 1992 was $17,696.[3] Our occupational structure is shaped much like the Eiffel Tower. There is little room at the top, a larger but still limited number of tolerably well-paid positions in the middle, and near the bottom a wide band of inferior positions (with no "positions" at all for the unemployed). This roughly pyramidal structure ensures that even if everyone excels in school and strives ceaselessly for the top, the great majority are automatically bound to be disappointed.

The occupational structure guarantees a vast divide between rich and poor. In 1989, 1 percent of the population owned 37 percent of the wealth and 10 percent of the population owned 86 percent of the wealth.[4] By the end of Ronald Reagan's second term, 32 million Americans were living below the poverty level and the gap between rich and poor was at an all-time high.[5] Consider not only the sheer magnitude of inequality between winners and losers but also the fact that most losers have had to play on a field slanted against them. The pyramid isn't shaken up and recast from scratch for each generation; rather, families tend to occupy similar locations in the social division of labor over time. Families at the top of the class structure can use their superior status and resources to stay there, while other families, low on options, languish at the bottom. We are all born into a social class, and most of us die in the one into which we were born. Although a few working-class individuals with dedication and ability will rise to the top of the heap, most (including many who are just as conscientious and able) will remain close to where they started.[6]

The United States has a remarkably stable class structure, albeit one that is obscured by the rhetoric of classlessness. To be sure, social mobility does exist—just enough to maintain the myth of America as the land of opportunity. Whereas a completely closed society cannot maintain a semblance of openness, a society that allows some mobility, however meager, can always hold up the so-called self-made individual as "proof" that barriers to success are purely personal and that the poor are poor of their own accord. And so most Americans, the denounced teenagers often as much as the denouncer in the BMW, see poverty in purely individual terms rather than as structurally induced.

This book shifts the emphasis from individual deficits to structural inequality. Part One discloses that the roots of perceived individual pathology—unruliness in school, alcohol and drug abuse, violence, and crime—actually lie deep within the social structure. The leveled aspirations and behavior of the Hallway Hangers cannot be understood apart from structural constraints on opportunity that in their cumulative effect are all too forbidding. The Brothers, in contrast, refuse to be cowed by the long odds. Spurred on by the distinctively American language of aspiration that gushes forth from our television shows, our pop songs, and our advertisements, the Brothers lace up their sneakers and "just go for it." But we have seen that schools, even ones as good as Lincoln High, end up reinforcing social inequality while pretending to render it superfluous. The Brothers struggle academically in school and are socialized for positions near the bottom of the class pyramid.

Part Two explores how the Hallway Hangers and Brothers fare in the structure of the job market. The results are depressing. The experiences of the Hallway Hangers since 1984 show that opting out of the contest—neither playing the game nor accepting its rules—is not a viable option. Incarceration and other less explicit social penalties are applied by society when the contest is taken on one's own terms. There is no escape: The Hallway Hangers must still generate income, build relationships, and establish households. The stresses of everyday life have led Stoney to "escape" by choosing captivity over life outside prison. Trapped inside the game, the Hallway Hangers now question their youthful resistance to schooling and social norms. Granted the opportunity to do it over again, the Hallway Hangers say they would have tried harder to succeed.

But the Brothers *have* always tried, which is why their experiences between 1984 and 1991 are as disheartening as the Hallway Hangers'. If the Hangers show that opting out of the contest is not a viable option, the Brothers show that dutifully playing by the rules hardly guarantees success either. Conservative and liberal commentators alike often contend that if the poor would only apply themselves, behave responsibly, and adopt bourgeois values, then they will propel themselves into the middle class. The Brothers follow the recipe quite closely but the outcomes are disappointing. They illustrate how rigid and durable the class structure is. Aspiration, application, and intelligence often fail to cut through the firm figurations of structural inequality. Though not impenetrable, structural constraints on opportunity, embedded in both schools and job markets, turn out to be much more debilitating than the Brothers anticipated. Their dreams of comfortable suburban bliss currently are dreams deferred and are likely to end up as dreams denied.

POVERTY: A CLASS ISSUE

This book shows clearly that poverty is not a black issue. In absolute terms, most poor people are white, although a disproportionate number of African Americans are impoverished. Many of the black poor live in ghettos: urban neighborhoods that are racially segregated, economically devastated, socially stigmatized, and politically abandoned. As government and civic institutions have crumbled and the labor market has declined, the vacuum has largely been filled by "the blossoming of an underground economy dominated by the only expanding employment sector to which poor minority youths miseducated by public school can readily accede: the retail trade of drugs."[7] As a result, these enclaves of concentrated and pernicious poverty have become virtual war zones where terror, despair, and death are commonplace. To much of the American public, however, the state of the ghetto signifies not the gross inadequacy of the welfare state but its overgenerosity to a black underclass that is morally dissolute, culturally deprived, and socially undeserving. The underclass has been twisted into a racial rather than a class formation, and poverty has become a black issue.

By bringing the white poor into view, our story dissolves the mistaken connection between African Americans and behavior associated with poverty—crime, family disruption, substance abuse, and so on. The Brothers and Hallway

Hangers fail to follow the script penned by journalists, academics, politicians, and policy analysts. Because criminality is almost completely confined to the Hallway Hangers, this study debunks stereotypes about the black poor. Even in the case of white youths, what appears to be a tangle of pathology and purely self-destructive behavior turns out to have an underlying social rationality. Far from being a distinctive breed apart, the urban poor are ordinary human beings struggling to cope as best they can under oppressive circumstances. Poverty is not a moral problem, much less a black moral or cultural problem.

The underclass debate in the popular media divides the poor along racial lines, focuses the spotlight on African American poverty, and largely ignores the socioeconomic context in which the drama is set. This book draws the white poor out of the shadows, widens the debate beyond race, and recovers the common class basis of exploitation that bedevils all the urban poor—black, white, Latino, Asian, or Native American.

Industrial restructuring—the decline of manufacturing, the suburbanization of blue-collar employment, and the ascendancy of the service sector—has hit all the urban poor. Real wages and job security have fallen dramatically, as the experiences of the Hallway Hangers and Brothers illustrate. Layoffs, seasonal cutbacks, closings, and abrupt dismissals have been widespread for both groups of men. The economic recession of the late 1980s has exacerbated the instability of the low-wage labor market, and so has the weakening of labor unions and the absence of government regulation—both matters of public policy. It may be that insecurity and volatility are structural features of the new urban economy.

The experiences of both the Brothers and the Hallway Hangers also indicate that "career tracks" are sparse for uncredentialed individuals. The jobs these men manage to obtain seldom lead to a sequence of ascending positions with increased wages, responsibility, and security. Movement, when it occurs at all, tends to be lateral or between firms but not along an occupational ladder. Disappointed, workers like Mokey and Jinx move rapidly between dead-end jobs, a strategy that ends up reinforcing irregularity because they become even less attractive to employers. Contrary to popular perception, none of the Hallway Hangers or Brothers shun employment in low-wage entry-level positions as working for "chump change."

JM: You're looking for a job now?

BOO-BOO: Yeah.

JM: And how's that going?

BOO-BOO: Not that good. Not that good at all. I just gotta keep on looking. I'd even work at McDonald's or something. Just so I can get some money together, just 'til I can find something a little bit better. . . . I'll work at McDonald's if I have to. I need something. Sell newspapers, anything.

Boo-Boo's stated willingness to accept any job is no empty declaration: Among other places, he applied for work at car washes, grocery stores, and fast-food chains. Mokey, Shorty, and Slick echo Boo-Boo's willingness to accept poorly paid menial employment. What they and the others object to are so-called entry-level positions that lead nowhere.

Both groups of men have been stuck in the secondary labor market with low wages, infrequent raises, awkward working hours, minimal training, and high turnover. Only James has earned a family wage, and he was soon laid off. Only a couple of these men have held jobs with basic health and retirement benefits. Most cannot afford to own a car, let alone a home. Stable employment is the crucial pivot for social and cultural transitions into adulthood. Without it, many of these young men have been unable to contemplate settling down, marrying, or establishing households independent of parents. Their physical mobility has been minimal, and they have generally been excluded from leisure pursuits that most Americans take for granted. In short, the lives of both the Brothers and the Hallway Hangers have been severely circumscribed by their subordinate position in the class structure.

RACIAL DOMINATION: INVIDIOUS BUT INVISIBLE

Both the Brothers and the Hallway Hangers are victims of class exploitation, but the African Americans among them have had to cope with racial oppression as well. Sometimes this oppression is brutally direct, as Shorty's and Boo-Boo's contrasting experiences attest. Shorty assaulted several police officers after ransacking his girlfriend's apartment, but he was let off.

SHORTY: I had fucking—I coulda been doing at least twenty years for that, right there. Three counts of mayhem, I had like eight assault and batteries on police officers, each one carries two and a half years to four and a half years. Mayhem alone carries fifteen to twenty. I had three of 'em for biting three cops. Lucky my brothers were cops. If I didn't have no brothers that are cops, I'd be, I'd be doing at least forty fucking years right now.

JM: So no charges were ever pressed?

SHORTY: Yeah, they pressed 'em at first, but then I got 'em all dropped. The judges were pissed off about that; they didn't like that. None of the cops showed up to court. I fucking lucked out big-time then.

Contrast Shorty's experience with that of Boo-Boo when he was stopped by the police for reckless driving.

BOO-BOO: I was drinkin' and drivin'; I was cheatin' on my girlfriend with this other girl, Josie, from the Heights. We were drivin' around. The cops, they beat me up and they called me nigger and black bastard and all this stuff, y'know? It was crazy. And they put me in jail. . . . They broke my nose and cracked my jaw, y'know, and ripped all my chains off my neck and scarred up my arms and all that stuff like that.

Racial domination is seldom as graphic and straightforward as police brutality, although some police officers are openly racist. Standing in front of Clarendon Heights one evening, I was asked by an officer in a cruiser, "Seen a carload of niggers drive by just now?" Doubtless, Boo-Boo was beaten up largely because he is black. Yet there is also a history of police violence against white residents of Clarendon Heights: In the 1970s a white youth from Clarendon Heights was beaten by police in front of the project and died in custody. Moreover, black police officers can be just as brutal as their white colleagues. Even police violence cannot be explained in purely racial terms. Racial oppression, though it often takes the form of direct discrimination, is also more subtly embedded in the social order.

As African Americans, the Brothers are not as connected as the Hallway Hangers to informal networks that can provide access to jobs. Consider a string of three jobs Frankie held when he returned to the area from out of state.

FRANKIE: Then I moved back. I had my son. So I come back down here. I tried a little floor-laying.

JM: How did you get in?

FRANKIE: Mutual friends, y'know? . . . Got the floor-layin' job. That didn't kick out. So I started seein' people, y'know, that I knew, guys that had jobs, and I went on to a few city jobs and state jobs—they were real good jobs, but doin' my drinkin'—like, I had one job as a custodian up the high school, and it was a real good job. And I screwed that up by drinkin'. Y'know, it's a job where you got so much to do and then you can slack. And my slackin', I was leavin' the premises, goin' to the bar and playing the dogs, y'know? I just got in the way of fuckin' goin' to the bar and goin' to the dogs. So I left that. And when I left that I got another job through the same guy—a politician—and I was over to the big convention center and they made me crew chief. I was over there, I was a crew chief, and I didn't have a fuckin' inkling of what I was doin'. They have a cleanin' crew, just Spanish guys. Y'know, they couldn't even understand me. So I didn't show up much, evidently. But I was still gettin' paid. They paid me hours I didn't work. Y'know, I did eighty hours one week, and I was lucky to have worked ten, y'know? These were set jobs. And I couldn't even hold them. I know why today: cuz I was drinking.

Apart from access to jobs, personal connections provided some job security for Frankie. During roughly the same period, Juan, Mokey, and James all lost their jobs on account of minor infractions of bureaucratic rules in their work-places. Frankie's experience also underlines the poor prospects of promotion for people of color. When people like Frankie come in at a supervisory level, people like the Brothers and Frankie's Spanish crew are robbed of opportunities for advancement. It is instructive that Frankie was able to exploit personal contacts to secure employment in the public sector, the area where antidiscrimination policies should most improve the prospects of racial and ethnic minorities. If Frankie can leapfrog over others in government jobs, it is no wonder that industries with informal hiring and training practices are virtually closed to the Brothers. Jobs in construction are a notorious case in point.[8] Slick, Shorty, Steve, and Jinx have all landed jobs in the construction industry through informal social networks. Jobs like roofing are hardly prestigious, secure, or highly paid; nevertheless, they are jobs for which white ethnic networking has given the white Hallway Hangers an edge over their black counterparts.

Their exclusion from occupational networks handicaps the Brothers, but they also have special tensions to negotiate if they do manage to get a job. In the new postindustrial service economy, both the Hallway Hangers and the Brothers are in closer contact with supervisors and clients than they would be in manufacturing jobs. The members of neither group have much social space in which to express their class and cultural identities. Frankie finds it difficult to interact with young, bossy, bourgeois supervisors, gossiping middle-age colleagues, and the upper-class consumers whom his catering job served. But the Brothers must also deal with racial prejudice that stereotypes them as hoodlums. The interpersonal experiences of black jobholders, especially those who do not convey a mastery of middle-class cultural conventions, are a special source of tension in service jobs. Busing tables in a posh restaurant, Mokey will find it more difficult than Frankie to put customers at ease simply because his black skin evokes so many stereotypes.

Whether the result of social tension in the workplace, reduced access to occupational networks, or straightforward discrimination, African Americans fare poorly on the job market. Unemployment is higher and wages are lower for blacks than for whites. Moreover, the economic returns for a high school education are substantially less. The labor market is far from color-blind. And yet the Brothers do not cite racism as a factor that holds them back. Perhaps race is so seamlessly woven into their identities and daily lives that it simply does not stand out. Deeply embedded in their consciousness and inscribed everywhere in the outside world, race is simply taken for granted as a suffusive and ubiquitous fact of life.[9] In this respect, Boo-Boo is the exception that reinforces the rule. For the Brothers, their blackness hardly bears comment. But Boo-Boo, an African American who associated with the Hallway Hangers nearly all of his life, fell in with an exclusively black crowd when he moved to Raymond. For Boo-Boo, race is an issue.

BOO-BOO: It was kinda weird for me in Raymond. All of a sudden all my friends were black. It was weird, cuz they're just, they're more different than white people cuz of the fact the way they carry themselves, the way they dress and stuff, dress and talking, just being black. Like when I go down to see, y'know, say, Chub and all them [in Clarendon Heights], they're like, "Wow, Boo-Boo changed." Then, y'know, I just, I dunno.

JM: Is that kinda hard for you, to balance that out, or . . .

BOO-BOO: It is kinda hard for me. I mean, I been around white people all my life and then for one, for like six or seven months, whatever how long it was, to just, to just change, I changed that quick. And then got caught up in the drugs and all stuff like that. It's just a big change. It was. Big change. . . . I just can't handle, I don't really understand, I don't understand black people at all, really. Cuz I haven't been around 'em. They don't understand why I can sit there and listen to rock 'n' roll, Led Zeppelin and stuff like that, sit in the house and listen to Led Zeppelin and Black Sabbath. Call me white man, Uncle Tom, or something. So that's the deal with it. . . .

JM: You and Frankie and Slick and Steve and Shorty were really tight way back; how did that kinda break up?

BOO-BOO: Well, they'd get to drinkin' and they'd want to fight me and stuff like that. We never got into a fight, but they, like, started calling me a nigger and stuff like that. It didn't really bother me, but after a while, y'know, they're s'posed to be my friends, and all the time we'd been hanging around it had never came to my mind to call a white person a honky. I don't understand that. It's strange to me. I never called anybody anything like that in my life. I don't consider myself a nigger either. I just consider myself as Boo-Boo Taylor. Same as anybody else. So I just broke loose from that.

Having traversed the racial divide and negotiated the tensions on each side, Boo-Boo thinks in racial terms. Of the African Americans featured in this study, Boo-Boo alone emphasizes racial discrimination in the labor market. Asked whether he'd been actively looking for work, Boo-Boo recounted how a friend had directed him to a store that was taking job applications.

BOO-BOO: So we walk up there, and she said, "We're not hiring." And she said it in a bad way where it came down to me like she was prejudiced cuz I was black or something. Cuz why would she say that, why should she lie and say she wasn't hiring?

JM: Has that been a factor a lot, do you think?

BOO-BOO: It has been around here, yeah.

JM: Discrimination, in terms of you trying to get a job.

BOO-BOO: Basically, around here, yeah. It bothers me, but—it's part of life.

For the black Brothers, race is so much a part of life that it figures only tangentially in their expressed worldviews. But to say that race is inscribed in the social scenery is not to denigrate its importance. On the contrary, the experiences of the Brothers and Hallway Hangers since 1984 beg the question of whether race is a more fundamental cleavage than class in American society.

RACE VERSUS CLASS: CAN THEY BE UNTANGLED?

On the face of it, race appears to have taken on heightened importance as these young men have sought jobs. Racial inequality seems to account for differences in outcome both between and within the two groups. Given their ambition, schooling, and skills, the Brothers could have been expected to leave the Hallway Hangers in the dust. They haven't. Indeed, the Brothers are only marginally better off than the Hangers. Moreover, the African Americans within each group have fared poorly relative to the whites. Of the Hallway Hangers, the two black members—Boo-Boo and Chris—are in the most desperate straits. And of the Brothers, the sole white member—Mike—has been far and away the most successful on the job market. Does race matter as much as (or more than) class in determining the economic fate of African Americans in Clarendon Heights?

The race (caste) versus class debate has raged with particular passion since the publication in 1978 of William Julius Wilson's *The Declining Significance of Race.* Wilson's title is misleading, for he argues not that racial-caste oppression has become less significant in absolute terms for African Americans, but that it has become less significant *relative to social class* as a determinant of life chances. Whereas all blacks faced a wall of direct racial discrimination in past eras, a chasm between middle-class and working-class blacks has opened up since the 1960s. The relative success and security of the black middle class contrast sharply with the plight of poorer blacks who are trapped in the secondary labor market and in blighted inner cities. Racial inequality results not so much from direct discrimination as from structural changes in the economy that marginalize the black proletariat. Class, Wilson argues, "has become a more important factor than race in determining job placement for blacks."[10]

Wilson's book unleashed a furious storm of criticism and debate that continues to this day. Sociology journals still feature articles that purport to measure the effects of race versus class. Statistical analyses typically use a complex series of regression equations to discover that black-white disparities in educational and occupational attainment cannot be explained by other variables, and so are vestigially ascribed to race. But the entire quantitative quest to measure the relative importance of race and class is founded on the assumption that race and class can be reduced to one-dimensional, quantifiable factors that can be isolated from each other.[11]

The present study shows quite clearly that neither race nor class can be reduced to abstract forces that mechanically manipulate people like electrons in a charged field. Rather, race and class (along with gender) are interwoven in variable patterns, and the resultant geometry is complex. Class and race work simultaneously, and each can magnify or mitigate the effects of the other. Part One disclosed, for example, how race introduces new structural constraints and serves as a mediation through which the limitations of class are refracted. Largely because the Brothers are black, they accept the achievement ideology and act as if class and racial barriers to success don't exist. And yet for African Americans living half a mile away in a black housing project, black skin becomes a reason to reject the American Dream. Class and race interact with factors like a neighborhood's distinctive social ecology to produce complex patterns that defy quantification.

This ethnography, with its minute "sample" sizes, cannot measure the relative effects of class and race any more effectively than quantitative studies have done. There is nothing to guarantee that the occupational outcomes of the Hallway Hangers and Brothers are representative rather than mere accidents of the job market. What this study can do, however, is explore and elaborate how simplistic and static concepts of class and race can be deepened.

Ain't No Makin' It demonstrates that class and race each have objective and subjective dimensions, a distinction pressed by Pierre Bourdieu and Loïc Wacquant. Drawing upon and extending Bourdieu's theory of social space, Wacquant argues that

> both class and race lead a dual existence: each exists first in materiality, as objective differences that can be observed, measured in the form of distributions of efficient resources and goods; and second in subjectivity, as schemes of perception, appreciation and action, in the form of symbolic distinctions produced and reproduced via socially engrained dispositions.[12]

In other words, class and race introduce objective structural contraints that individuals must face. The bricklayer's child has barriers to overcome that the banker's child need never negotiate. And blacks face limits on opportunity relative to whites. These are real differences rooted in objective material conditions.

On the subjective side, individuals can make of these objective conditions what they will in forging their identities. The bricklayer's son may look across his high school desk at the banker's boy sitting in front of him, shake his head dismissively, and silently wager that the other can't change the oil in his Volvo. Or he may see in the banker's son an effortless ease with girls, grades, and teachers and shake his head despairingly at his own oil-stained fingers. Or he may do both, depending on the context—which peers are around, who the teacher is, and whether the class is algebra or technical drawing. Both attitudes are subjective articulations of class identity that are ultimately rooted in objective economic inequality. But neither attitude can easily be traced to that source. The subjective refuses to be reduced to a reflex of the objective.

There is a real tendency to collapse the objective and subjective dimensions of class into each other. As a youth worker in Clarendon Heights, I had to struggle to make any sense of what I was seeing on the street until Bourdieu, Bowles and Gintis, and especially Willis introduced me to the logic of social reproduction. Seeing how heavily structural inequality weighs on the Brothers and Hallway Hangers, I now tend to analyze the primary material in that light. Thus, when the young men acknowledge constraints on opportunity, I applaud them as "insightful," "discerning," "penetrating." And I judge their subjective interpretations by how closely they point to the objective limitations of social class. There is an implicit yardstick of truth and an implicit politics here, both provided by the social reproduction perspective. Reading the research data along this *evaluative* axis allows an assessment of the truth of individuals' views and of their political potential. If those who are denied opportunities see their condition clearly, they are more likely to kick up a stink and change things. This is a crucial issue, and it deserves to be addressed.

At the same time, the primary data need to be analyzed along a *descriptive* axis that revolves around the question of identity. The task here is to describe the opinions, values, and actions of the men as they seek to make sense of their situations. Leaving aside the sociological accuracy of their views, the descriptive part of my task concentrates on how the Hallway Hangers and Brothers maintain their identities in their distinctive social and cultural contexts. The class identities articulated by the young men in Clarendon Heights cannot be reduced to the question of whether they discern structural constraints on opportunity. The descriptive axis sees class identity as just one more identity, constructed around images of space and common cultural reference points. In this view, there is a class ideology in the United States, but it has almost none of the socialist content and symbolism that working-class identity features in, for example, Europe. The Hallway Hangers' opinions are explained not only by the absence of the good or true ideology that the evaluative axis presupposes, but also by the presence of numerous other ideologies. Class identity is always articulated in historically specific circumstances and always incorporates ideological or imaginary components: a sense of community, status symbols, territories, rituals, and gender and racial inflections.[13]

In combining the descriptive and evaluative tasks, always a treacherous enterprise, Willis is relatively optimistic about the capacity of British working-class culture to penetrate the dominant ideology and to catalyze constructive social change.[14] The Hallway Hangers and Brothers give few grounds for optimism. Given the sway of the achievement ideology, many of their counterhegemonic views are penetrating indeed. But insightful opinions are of little use in isolation; there needs to be an ideological perspective and a cultural context in which their insights can be applied that leads to *positive* and potentially transformative rituals, symbols, territories, and political strategies.

In fact, the Hallway Hangers completely invert objective reality in their subjective rendering of it. Their racial and gender identities as white working-class men are actually assets on the job market, whereas their class background puts them at a disadvantage. But most of the Hallway Hangers see exactly the reverse: They complain not about class oppression but about discrimination against white men. Here again, the views of the Hallway Hangers point to the potency, pervasiveness, and persuasiveness of neoconservative ideology and the historical slough of class analysis in the United States. Perhaps the Hallway Hangers fail to see class as a variable because they grew up so ensconced in their own class culture. Just as the Brothers do not consider race an issue, the Hallway Hangers fail to see class as constraining.

Like class, race has an objective dimension rooted in the structure of opportunities.[15] Educational attainment, annual earnings, rates of employment, and a host of other measures confirm that African Americans are disadvantaged relative to whites. Yet race exists not just in material differences in power and resources but also in its subjective dimension—in individuals' minds as a category that shapes the way they view themselves and the social world. As with class, the subjective articulation of race seldom lines up with its objective dimension. Thus, although race is a central category by which both the Brothers and the Hallway Hangers understand themselves, neither group underscores the objective constraints faced by African Americans. Structural constraints on opportunity, whether rooted in race or class, are largely invisible to the young men in this study. The Hallway Hangers and the Brothers, like almost all Americans, tend to interpret their situation in individual rather than structural terms.

STRUCTURE VERSUS AGENCY: "NO ONE TO BLAME BUT ME"

Every individual in this study holds himself accountable for his condition. Chapter 7 disclosed how the Brothers blamed themselves for their academic mediocrity. The Hallway Hangers were less self-critical but still reproached themselves for screwing up in school. Eight years later, for both groups, the verdict is similar. The previous chapter shows how the Brothers variously chastise themselves for being lazy, unmotivated, indecisive, unrealistic, overly opportunistic, fickle, and generally inept. Juan is straightforward: "I really screwed up." Super is equally succinct: "I just fucked everything up." The Hallway Hangers, it turns out, are also hard on themselves.

(all in separate interviews)

JINX: I could kick myself in the ass, because if I stayed in school, I'd probably have a better job, and I'd be doing better in life right now.

CHRIS: I fucked up. I regret everything. I feel real bad about my mom. I just fucked up, man, fucked everything up. I'd like to regain back the trust of my family. Man, I wouldn't wish this situation on anyone.

STONEY: I was doing good for a while. Running this pizza place over in Medway. He gave me the keys, the boss did. I was running it, doing a good job, too. The money wasn't great but still. I ended up fucking the guy over. He vouched for me when I was in the prerelease center. I burned that bridge. About two months after I got out I said, "Here, here's the key, I'm fuckin' through, I'm sick of this." Shoulda stayed. Shoulda stuck it out. He might've given me more money, who knows? My judgment sucks sometimes.

FRANKIE: I know today I wasted a lot of my life. I had a lotta fun but I wasted a lot of it. Lotta guys went to jail, lotta guys were just fucked-up, man. And I was fucked-up in my own way.

BOO-BOO: I should never have got into drugs. I dunno, if I could do one thing, start all over again, I'd just go right back to school, I'd do my thing, wouldn't get tied up in all this bullshit I got tied up in.

STEVE: I've been fucking up big time, Jay, no lie. Going away [to jail] too much, man. Fighting with my girl. I left her, and she called up and said I was doing drugs and drinkin' and all that other shit. Which I was. Called my probation officer and ratted me right out. . . . I dunno, dude, I guess I've got no one to blame but me.

Both the Brothers and the Hallway Hangers hold themselves responsible for their plight. Like most Americans, they point to personal vices and individual shortcomings to account for their subordinate position in the class structure.

But this is not the whole story. We have already seen that, apart from Mike and Derek, the Brothers blame not only themselves but also the socioeconomic order for their failure to get ahead. James argues most forcefully that the economic system is also to blame. He acknowledges constraints on economic opportunity, holds the government accountable, and sympathizes with those who turn to illegal activity. But James also contends that lower-class culture prevents people from developing proper ambition.

JM: What do you think about the white kids at Clarendon Heights? Steve, Slick, Frankie, Jinx?

JAMES: They, er, gee, what can I say about that? They reached a certain level in their life and then they just stayed at that level. They just said, "Oh well, this is my life. This is what my life's gonna be." But it's all attitude, it's all if you wanna go farther than you are. They're gonna be in the Heights all their life. It's, like, back to, if you grow up in a certain environment, then that's what you gonna live. That's what you're gonna live all your life. That's what you're used to. And that's how their life is. It's the same as the Coopers next door. The Coopers next door are always gonna be the same. They're never gonna change. Fifty years from now a new set of Coopers will be the same exact as these Coopers. Because they've reached a certain level, and they're always gonna be at that level. I'm not down on them, that's all they know. They're gonna just say, "I stopped at that level." But you can't say that. You have to want more for your kids and for your grandkids.

The idea that the intergenerational transmission of poverty is due, at least in part, to cultural attitudes and behavior is also implied by Slick. Like James, Slick points to macroeconomic constraints on opportunity, cultural deficiencies of the community, and individual shortcomings.

SLICK: I feel like I was robbed. I look at people and I say, y'know, I could be doin' what this guy's doing. If I had a college degree or something. But how was I gonna go to college? Know what I'm sayin'? I couldn't afford to go back to Latin Academy. My par—my mother couldn't, because we moved into this city. So that robbed me of that deal, know what I mean? You've just got to deal with it the best way you fucking can. Believe me, I was pissed off about it, and I still think about it to this day. I shouldn't be this dirty. Look at how filthy I am, working with my hands, blisters all over me and shit. I should be working at an office with a tie and nice suit on.

JM: So what do you say to the rich guy who listens to this story and says, "Wait a minute. He wasn't robbed. That was him. He could've, when he came to Lincoln High, he could've made it. It was the people he hung out with, or . . . "

SLICK: Nope.

JM: What do you say to him?

SLICK: What I say to him is, "Come down and learn for yourself, come down and see for yourself what it's like." Because you take it—I was a perfect A student all through my school years 'til I got yanked out of Latin Academy. When I moved here it was like, I ain't never got beat up before. I was into school. I was into sports and shit. I come here, get picked on, get my ass kicked all the fucking time. Finally, I went from being an A student to being, you know, you gotta defend yourself. What are you gonna study, you can't read a book on how to, on how to act like these people do. Y'know, you gotta treat an animal like a fucking animal. That's how it goes.

In the next breath, Slick places the corrosive influence of Clarendon Heights culture within a broader context of class inequality. Slick challenges the apparent superiority of the rich who, he claims, would be lost in Clarendon Heights without the props and symbols of their social status.

SLICK: Tell a person like that to come on down. I'll let 'em stay at my mother's house. The rich people you're talking about. Let 'em stay there with the cockroaches and the junkies shooting up outside and see how they react to it. Without their little Porsches and their little Saabs. Y'know, let them survive for a little while.

Slick's passing reference to roaches touches on an important dimension of lower-class life often missed by outside observers: what Wacquant calls the "demoralization effects" of life in intense poverty and permanent material insecurity. Living in places like Clarendon Heights tends to eat away at a person's energy and insides over time.[16] Slick knows it is different elsewhere and begins to articulate a critique of class privilege. But like the others, he holds himself responsible for his condition.

SLICK: I personally should've finished high school, then went on to some sort of college, any kinda college. Then looked over my options and *planned* on what I was doing. *Planned* on having children. *Planned* on my career. Instead of things just happening.

Like social theorists, both the Brothers and the Hallway Hangers wrestle with the roles of structure, culture, and agency in the reproduction of social inequality.
It should be obvious from this study that all three levels of analysis—the individual, the cultural, and the structural—play their part in the reproduction of social inequality. Had Slick been born into a middle-class family, he probably *would* be sitting in an office with a suit and tie on. Had his peer group been into Shakespeare and square roots rather than beer balls and bong hits, Slick might not be so blistered and dirty. Finally, Slick would be in better shape had he made different choices himself. Although all three levels have explanatory power, the structural one is primary because it reaches down into culture and individual agency. The culture of Clarendon Heights—with its violence, racism, and other self-destructive features (as well as its resilience, vitality, and informal networks of mutual support)—is largely a response to class exploitation in a highly stratified society. Similarly, Slick's individual strategies have developed not in a social vacuum but in the context of chronic social immobility and persistent poverty. To be sure, individual agency is important. Causality runs in both directions in a reflexive relationship between structure and agency. Structural constraints on opportunity lead to leveled aspirations, and leveled aspirations in turn affect job prospects. Contrary to popular belief, structure is still the source of inequality.

Most Americans tend to ignore the link between individual behavior and cultural patterns on the one hand and economic inequality on the other, but neither Jinx nor Frankie fall into this trap. Both contextualize their peer group in a nexus of class injustice.

JM: When you look back on the heyday, back in high school as teenagers and the closeness you guys had, what d'you think brought you together that way, compared to other people?

JINX: Probably because we all grew up together, we were all the same age. We all went to school together. We were spendin' most of our times together as a unit, most of the time in the day. We were spendin' more time together, all of us, than we were with our families. We went through the good and the bad together. Most of the times were bad. I mean, in the projects, it's not everybody's happy-go-lucky. Nine times out of ten you're strugglin' to get what you want. So it makes your friendships bond tighter. Because you gotta rely on other people to help you through whatever it is you need. We didn't have money. So we had to get by with whatever we could. And how I look at it, what we used to get by with was our friendship.

JM: What would you say to those people who drive by and look over and see us. You can almost see it in their eyes, in . . .

JINX: Yeah, they're stereotyping right away: "Yeah, these kids are no good." But they should try to take the time out to understand us instead of right away, "He's a hoodlum because he lives in a project." I mean, there are a lot of people out here who are just like me—hardworkin'. They'll do anything for anybody. All they want is to be treated the way they treat people, y'know, with respect and kindness. They're not out there to screw anybody, but there are a lot of people, "Areas like this bring trouble."

Frankie also refers to class prejudice and, like Jinx, sees their peer group as rooted in the experience of growing up poor in a hostile dominant culture.

FRANKIE: Well back then, y'know, back then we were cool. We hung tight because, I know today, because we were looked down on our whole lives, man. From the projects. I believe, in my opinion, we were never invited anywhere. When we were places, y'know, people always knew: "Those are the kids from the projects." I would say we stuck together just, for a fact that, just, just to prove these people right. "You're right." We were from the fucking projects, and you didn't invite us to your party, so we're gonna come anyways, just to fuck it up. And it was the generation before us, the generation before us, when my brothers and them were growing up . . . it was just our values, man: Stick tight. We were taught that you had to stick together, just from generation to generation. . . . I grew up thinking I was a bad fucking kid. And I liked that. I liked being known as a bad kid. I look back there—there aren't any bad kids—there's a lotta kids that just had a fucking tough life.

Bad kids or bad circumstances? Frankie leads us right back to the theoretical impasse between structure and agency. To what extent are the Hallway Hangers and Brothers victims of a limited opportunity structure, and to what extent are they victims of their own flawed choices?

Is Super, for example, forced to deal drugs because he was born at the bottom of a class society that glorifies conspicuous consumption while denying the poor real opportunity? Or does Super simply choose to deal drugs because he can't be bothered to work his way up legitimately like everybody else? In short, to paraphrase the title of Diego Gambetta's book, was he pushed or did he jump?[17] Is Super *pushed* into crime by the forces of social reproduction? Or does he *jump* as a matter of individual choice? Certainly Super is *pushed from behind* by forces of which he is largely unaware. Super was handicapped in school by the effects of cultural capital, tracking, and teacher expectations. On the job market, Super's alternatives are limited by the sectoral shift from manufacturing jobs to poorly paid service positions and then squeezed further by racial discrimination embedded in the labor market. Thus, Super is pushed from behind by structural forces acting "behind his back" that propel him into the street economy. In addition, Super is *pulled from the front*, as it were, by structural forces that he sees and with which he wittingly struggles. Super is aware, for example, that the economy's recessionary plunge means fewer legitimate jobs are available and that his high school diploma is far less helpful than he imagined. He also believes that cocaine capitalism proffers more of a career structure than do legitimate jobs in the new postindustrial economy. With Super being pushed from behind and pulled from the front by structural forces, his entry into the informal economy is nevertheless his own decision individually taken. Super *jumps* into the cocaine trade because he wants to. Super wants "to be someone, make fast money, have respect," and his decision is intentional and even rational. And yet the decision cannot be understood apart from the structural limitations on his options. In the end, perhaps the fairest account is that Super was *pushed into jumping*.

Structure and agency are inseparable. Individual agents like Super are always structurally situated, and thus human agency is itself socially structured. Social structures reach into the minds and even the hearts of individuals to shape their attitudes, motivations, and worldviews. Structural determination is thus inscribed in the very core of human agency.[18] Bourdieu's concept of habitus captures the interpenetration of structure and agency, but habitus is more a label for a site than an explanation of what goes on within it. Bourdieu neglects the actual process whereby external forces and internal consciousness wrestle with each other. Rather, he seems to imply that agents are unwittingly and unconsciously disposed to adjust their dispositions and practices to the external constraints that bear upon them. In Bourdieu's view, all this happens behind the backs of agents in the sense that it unfolds beneath the level of rationality, conscious deliberation, and intentional choice. And yet while pushed from behind by structural constraints of which they are unaware, the Brothers and Hallway Hangers are also pulled by forces that they actively and consciously manipulate. Although he claims otherwise, Bourdieu's notion of habitus fails to allow space for this kind of conscious, calculative decision-making. Habitus is an ingenious concept, and Bourdieu is surely correct to insist on a dialectical relationship between objective structures and internal subjectivities. However, Bourdieu never makes clear *how* the habitus engenders thought and action, and so his resolution of the agency-structure dualism seems more a sidestep than a solution.[19]

Still, by insisting on the inseparability of structure and agency, Bourdieu reminds us not only that structure is at the heart of agency but also that agency can reach to the heart of structure. The social universe people inhabit isn't simply received as a given from without; rather, it is produced and constructed anew by agents. As Wacquant explains, "The structures of society that seem to stand over and against agents as external objects are but the 'congealed' outcome of the innumerable acts of cognitive assembly guiding their past and present actions."[20] Structures are not fixed, binding, nor unalterable, yet they often appear so. Bourdieu unravels and picks apart the symbolic power that cloaks exploitative and oppressive relationships with an aura of inevitability and renders them fair, natural, and normal.

Now we begin to see why the Brothers and Hallway Hangers give no indication that they might be able to alter the structures that constrain them. Among them there is very little political or collective energy, or even a sense that change is possible. Of the Brothers, for example, James is critical of the economic system and government policy but never suggests an alternative to the policy he criticizes, much less an alternative to the economic system. Neither do the Hallway Hangers envisage the possibility of substantive change. As we saw in Chapter 9, Jinx complains about class injustice in his workplace but feels politically impotent.

JINX: He's a complete moron, and he can do as he pleases because his father's the boss. Because he's got money it makes everything he does right, y'know, whether it be wrong or right. He can't do no wrong. I see it at my job and everywhere else, and it's just all over the world.

JM: But apart from just recognizing that, it doesn't seem to make you that angry.

JINX: It does and it don't. At times it does, but there's a lot of things in this world that make me angry. If I was to let every little thing that makes me angry bother me, I would be upset twenty-four hours a day. I would hate the world. I just try to have a few beers, smoke a few joints, and laugh at the world. It's so fucked-up, it ain't even funny anymore. That's why I try gettin' the philosophy, "Hooray for me, and fuck everybody else." Cuz no matter how hard you try, you're not gonna change it. I cannot worry about every little thing in life, okay, because there's too much out there to piss me off. And no matter what I do, if anything I try, it's not gonna change it. It's not gonna make it a better place for anybody.

JM: Most people say, y'know, this is the United States, it's a democracy. Is it impossible that we could vote into office people that would change things for the better?

JINX: That's my philosophy. I don't even vote because all politicians are crooks. The only thing they can agree on is to give themselves a raise. What about the poor folk? I mean, how many people are out on the streets homeless? They cannot put money aside to help feed them and support them, right, but they can give themselves a ten-, twenty-thousand-dollar-a-year raise. . . . We're in a state of recession, right? Fine, the cost of living goes up. How come our paychecks don't go up? It's just, I look at it at times, the whole world's fucked. No matter what you do, you gotta come out losin'. You can try and try and try and never get anywhere.

These last comments highlight the deeply felt sense of powerlessness among residents of Clarendon Heights. In 1983 Jinx was adamant that personal ambition was pointless: "I think you're kiddin' yourself to have any [aspirations]. We're just gonna take whatever we can get." Now his pessimism extends to aspirations for social change as well. "No matter what you do, you gotta come out losin'. You can try and try and try and never get anywhere."

This is pretty depressing stuff. We might expect those who are suspicious of the chances for individual upward mobility to be disposed toward collective political action to transform society. But when political *and* personal efficacy is judged illusory, then resignation and despair are liable to take over. The human psyche, however, resists hopelessness, and the Hallway Hangers are cast back on individual aspirations to sustain them. Slick is angling to be a supervisor on his roofing crew. Frankie wants to qualify as a mechanical contractor and supervise a building. Boo-Boo still hopes to be a mechanic; and Stoney, to own a pizza parlor. Shorty's aspirations are untempered by reality.

SHORTY: I'm s'posed to be getting my settlement soon, for gettin' stabbed. It's called victim of a violent crime, y'know? And I'm s'posed to get like probably forty grand. I'm gonna give my mother some money, help her out with some of her bills, and I'm gonna go halfs with my brother. We're gonna buy a two-family house and rent it out, the whole thing, and I still live with my mother, y'know? We'll see how that goes, and if it goes good we'll gonna buy another one and then another one, and just keep buyin' real estate, that's the thing to get into. . . . I will make money one of these days. Like to buy a nice fucking condo on Palm Beach. Next to the Kennedys'. [*laughter*] No, I'm serious. I'm gonna make some money.

As implausible as Shorty's vision may be, his aspirations help to keep him going. Whereas the Hallway Hangers previously drew sustenance from their peer group, today they rely on their own individual hopes. The Hallway Hangers have slid into the system alongside the Brothers. Without their tight clique and its own definitions of success, the Hallway Hangers have become much more incorporated into mainstream culture. Far from celebrating their outcast status, they see retrospectively in 1991 that their youthful resistance dug them deeper into marginality.

Frankie articulates this point most clearly. Today, he wants and needs to see opportunity. His recovery program from drug and alcohol abuse is predicated on a sense of personal efficacy, on a can-do mentality that emphasizes control over one's destiny. Given his own recovery, Frankie is preoccupied with the toll that substance abuse has taken on the Hallway Hangers.

FRANKIE: There's a lot of sickness there and I see it. I see it today, y'know. Two years ago I was part of it, y'know, and today I'm not, and I can see. For once I'm on the outside lookin' in. It's changes and it's drugs—there's no other way to put it. That's the bottom line. And I just know that from experience.

JM: Do you see any causes even beneath the drugs? Like, I'm hearin' you say that a lot of your problems during that time and individuals' problems now is the drinking, is the drugs. Are there things, are there other things that have kept people back?

FRANKIE: The economy sucks. It's just bad, a lotta people just don't see a lotta opportunity, y'know? They just don't see opportunity in life, man.

JM: Is it that they don't see it, or is it that the opportunity's not there?

FRANKIE: [*after a long pause*] Back then, I would say it's, y'know, they'd probably think it's not there. I, I, some days I still don't think it's there, but it's there, man. Y'know, you only feel when you stop tryin'. My whole problem is I never began to try, y'know? And I'm sure maybe that's some of their problems, y'know? You gotta be willing to try.

JM: It's interesting to hear you say, y'know, that you gotta try, cuz I remember back then you would look at the black kids from around the Heights—the Dereks and Mokey and . . .

FRANKIE: Your buddies.

JM: Yeah, right. You said they were chumps because they did try, because they tried in school and they were convinced that they would make it.

FRANKIE: Well, I look today, and if anyone shoulda had a chance to make it, it's fuckin', it's black people. . . . But no, I look at it today, y'know, they were probably doing the right thing, y'know? But my motives were different then, you hafta realize. I know I realize that. My motives were fucked-up back then.

JM: Has it paid off for them?

FRANKIE: I dunno. I don't see them. I dunno what the fuck they're doin'. I don't care. [*laughs*] But I dunno. I haven't seen them. I know I wasted quite a bit of my life.

Here Frankie cuts to the crux of the matter. His confession that "my motives were fucked-up back then" sounds like an admission that the Hallway Hangers' resistance ultimately proved counterproductive. Caught in the game and convinced that the rules are beyond changing, Frankie has only one sensible option, to commit himself to the competition. Frankie wants to believe that the future is in his own hands, only "you gotta be willing to try." Otherwise, what is left to hang on to? But the Brothers have always tried, and unbeknownst to Frankie, they have failed to make it. And what does Frankie himself have to show for all his aspiration and application, his job counseling and vocational training, his sobriety and disabled status? Frankie is unemployed. But he is absolutely right to make the effort and seize what little opportunity may arise. What other choice does he have? As Rickey, a street hustler from the ghetto of Chicago's South Side, relates: "You know, like I said, it's a goo' feelin' sayin', 'Hey, you can't make it but you try.'"[21] For Frankie, as for the Brothers, Hallway Hangers, and countless Rickeys across the country, hope flies in the face of crushing odds. The American Dream may be but a mirage. Still, it provides a vision toward which the thirsty may stumble.

WHAT IS TO BE DONE?

The picture that emerges from this ethnography deviates substantially from the myth of America as the land of opportunity in which any child can grow up to be president. American society is not as open as we like to think; the ladder of social mobility is not accessible to all, nor are its rungs easy to grasp. Both the Brothers and the Hallway Hangers testify to the prevalence of social reproduction rather than social mobility. For many of those in the lowest reaches of the social structure, the American Dream is a hallucination.

Such a picture is troubling, for it shatters many of our illusions about the fairness of the American economic and social system. It also demands a political response that goes well beyond the offerings of contemporary American liberalism. Extending the welfare state will not fix the basic problem facing the Brothers and Hallway Hangers. Improving the material conditions under which they live—better housing, health care, child care, and social services, less restricted and larger welfare and unemployment checks—certainly would be a step in the right direction, but such measures leave the basic emotional encumbrance of lower-class life untouched. These boys, all of them, desperately want to be somebody, to make something of their lives. By denying them that opportunity, by undercutting their very aspirations and reducing them to hopelessness at the age of sixteen, or by trapping them in the secondary labor market and leaving them disillusioned but still dreaming at twenty-four, the economic and social system causes untold misery, waste, and despair. The ideology that permeates American society holds out the rags-to-riches story as a valid option, despite the fact that very, very few people can live it out. If the Brothers and the Hallway Hangers are to have the opportunity to fulfill their potential as citizens and as human beings, more will have to change in the American political and social landscape than the expansion of the welfare state.

In short, what is required is the creation of a truly open society—a society where the life chances of those at the bottom are not radically different from those at the top and where wealth is distributed more equitably. Rather than reaching for the dizzying heights of the Eiffel Tower, the occupational structure could be shaped more like an onion. The socialist vision of a transformed class structure that radically reduces social inequality may seem hopelessly out of touch, but there is no denying that the capitalist free market, left to itself, can neither protect the environment nor meet human needs. The market has a major role to play in a decentralized socialist economy—but as a servant, not as a master. A mixed economy combining public power and private ownership can channel market forces so they flow in the desired direction. Competition and incentives do not require capitalism's unconscionable inequalities. Yet the 1980s saw the resurgence of a smug and vainglorious capitalism that widened the gap between the rich and poor to an all-time high. The tide may turn, but Democratic policies tend to tinker with a system that is in desperate need of an overhaul.

Whose Welfare?

For all the public cry for curtailment of the welfare state, the fact is that the United States does not have a welfare system worthy of the name. Public housing is a case in point. Experience has proved over and over again in nation after nation that a free market economy simply cannot provide homes for people on low and moderate incomes. Private developers build for the rich, not for the poor. Yet public provision of low-income housing in the United States lags way behind that in other industrialized nations. In 1980 public housing accounted for roughly 1 percent of the American housing market; in England the figure was 46 percent and in France 37 percent.

Instead of building housing for the poor, the United States has directly and indirectly subsidized homes for the better-off. From 1937 to 1968, 10 million middle- and upper-income private housing units were built with help from the Federal Housing Authority, whereas only 800,000 public units were constructed with federal housing subsidies. Moreover, as Wacquant notes, what little public housing was built consists mostly of cheap, massive, public housing projects stacked in central cities that reinforce racial segregation and the concentration of poverty.[22] The 1980s housing policy was even worse: to cease building public housing altogether. Widespread homelessness has been the result, a condition with which Boo-Boo and Chris are acquainted. And because only the poorest and most troubled families qualify for public housing, even small projects like Clarendon Heights are socially ostracized and physically forsaken.

Far from being an exception, public housing policy typifies America's scant commitment to the poor. Cries for the rolling back of welfare ignore the fact that benefits have already been slashed from levels that were paltry to begin with by international standards. The real value of the standard public aid package has plummeted by half. At the same time, eligibility has been tightened. In any case, only 55 percent of those eligible for Aid to Families with Dependent Children (AFDC) nationwide actually received "welfare" in 1992. Fewer than a third of the jobless qualify for unemployment payments. Job training programs, revenue sharing, and urban development grants were all axed in the 1980s.[23] These government cutbacks, combined with the disastrous effects of deindustrialization, have marginalized the urban working class more than ever.

And still the politicians and the populace clamor for more cuts, claiming in utter ignorance confident knowledge of the world in which the urban poor live. Yet the lives of the Brothers and Hallway Hangers—their youthful passion and desperation as they struggle to cope with poverty and devise strategies to escape its grip—point in a rather different political direction than the nation is willing to look. I read the story of the Brothers and Hallway Hangers as a harsh indictment of American class society and as a sharp spur to work for its reformation.

Better Schools?

In Clarendon Heights I was not primarily a sociologist; I was primarily a youth worker. If sociological study drives us to acknowledge the degenerative effects of gender-, race-, and class-based constraints upon young people, then educational practitioners are left in a quandary: If the problems go beyond the kids, what can we do? "Better schools" has been the standard rallying cry for social reformers concerned about sustained economic inequality in the United States. If only poor children had access to quality education, opportunity for individual mobility would be equalized across social classes and the gap between rich and poor substantially reduced. But the problems with this approach are substantial. First, as we have seen, schools actually maintain and legitimize social inequality. Second, educational reform leaves the underlying structure of economic inequality untouched. Still, though no substitute for fundamental structural change, improved schooling could help countless individuals like the Brothers and Hallway Hangers.

My first recommendation is that the achievement ideology must be replaced with ways of motivating students that acknowledge rather than deny their social condition. When used to cultivate discipline by highlighting the eventual rewards of educational attainment, the achievement ideology is neither effective at drawing obedience and attentiveness out of students nor conducive to the development of a positive self-image among working-class pupils. The familiar refrain of "Behave yourself, study hard, earn good grades, graduate with your class, go on to college, get a good job, and make a lot of money" reinforces the feelings of personal failure and inadequacy that working-class students are likely to bear as a matter of course. By this logic, those who have not made it have only themselves to blame. Because it shrouds class, race, and gender barriers to success, the achievement ideology promulgates a lie, one that some students come to recognize as such. For those pupils whose own experiences contradict the ideology—and in an urban public high school there are bound to be many—it is often rejected, and rightly so. Teachers are left with nothing to motivate their students, and it is no wonder that "acting out," aggressive disobedience, and unruliness predominate. School officials can round up the offending students and label them "slow," "learning impaired," "unmotivated," "troubled," "high-risk," or "emotionally disturbed" and segregate them, but the problem is much more deeply rooted.

Teachers do not promote the achievement ideology because they want to make working-class students miserable. Nor are they intent on maintaining social order and cohesion in the face of class inequality by contributing to the legitimation function of the school. In my experience, most teachers are well-intentioned, hardworking men and women who are striving to do a difficult job as best they can. They parrot the achievement ideology because they think it will motivate students, because it probably does not contradict their own experiences, and because they believe it. Most middle-class Americans do. As Willis writes, "What kind of bourgeoisie is it that does not in some way believe its own legitimations? That would be the denial of themselves."[24] The equality-of-opportunity line of reasoning may have worked in the middle-class high schools from which most teachers hail, but its utility in an urban school serving low-income neighborhoods is diminished greatly.

If students like the Hallway Hangers are to be motivated to achieve in school, it must not be at the expense of their self-esteem but in support of it. Schools serving low-income neighborhoods must help students build positive identities as working-class, black and white, young men and women. Rather than denying the existence of barriers to success, schools should acknowledge them explicitly while motivating students by teaching them, for example, about historic figures who shared the students' socioeconomic origins but overcame the odds. Success stories can be important motivators so long as emphasis is put on the obstacles against which these figures prevailed. Teachers can also strive to include material about which the students, drawing on the skills they have developed in their neighborhoods, are the experts. If the school could believe in the legitimacy and importance of students' feelings, perceptions, and experiences as working-class kids, the students themselves might come to do the same, thereby giving them a positive identity and a dose of self-confidence as a foundation for further application in school.

If such measures were undertaken on a systematic basis, boys like the Hallway Hangers might feel as though they belong in school, that they need not choose between rendering themselves naked and vulnerable by stripping off their street identities or aggressively asserting their street culture in disruptive rebellion. One of the reasons the Hallway Hangers speak so warmly about the Adjustment Class is that in Jimmy Sullivan's classroom they were allowed to maintain their street identities. Even more important, these identities were vindicated and given legitimacy because the teacher himself embodied many of the attitudes, values, and traits esteemed by the culture of the Hallway Hangers. The Hallway Hangers saw in Jimmy Sullivan a bit of themselves and in themselves a bit of Jimmy; because of the status and authority invested in him as a teacher, in addition to his independent financial success, Jimmy Sullivan vicariously defended and justified their self-image.

Teachers need not have a black belt in karate, place a premium on machismo, swear in class, or have working-class roots like Jimmy Sullivan; however, they must be prepared to validate the identities that their students have taken on as part of growing up. Admittedly, this is not an easy task, especially as awareness of class, race, and gender stereotyping should be inculcated by teachers. If part of one's education should involve the confrontation of ingrained sexism and its consequences, Sullivan's class would not receive high marks. There were no girls in his class, and the uncritical affirmation of machismo confronted the observer in every aspect of the room, from the punching bags, posters of Bruce Lee, and *Soldier of Fortune* magazines to the frankly sexist attitudes of the teacher. But easy educational answers do not exist, and we must resist the tendency, all too prevalent among school reformers, to cling to single-solution, essentialist positions. On balance, I consider the Adjustment Class a failure because, for the most part, the students emerged with very few academic skills. Students must still learn the basics.

In my experience, academic rigor itself demands that the curriculum meet the needs and concerns of working-class and minority students. If the curriculum is made responsive to student needs, the gap between academic skill and maturity can be bridged. No one is going to get Shorty to read about the Hardy Boys; on the other hand, his reading ability may not be much above a fourth-grade level. Novels and poignant nonfiction works dealing with the concerns of working-class and minority youth could be incorporated into the curriculum. It is ludicrous, for instance, to expect students in the Adjustment Class to learn about social studies from a sixth-grade U.S. history textbook. Meanwhile, the thirteen-year-old younger brothers of the Hallway Hangers have managed to research prison life through books, movies, slides, seminars, and field trips and to produce a thirty-page anthology of interviews with former inmates, many of whom live in Clarendon Heights. Their achievement, *Behind Bars,* demonstrates what can be gained in educational terms when local history and culture are taken seriously and when students are actively involved in thinking and doing rather than being passively exposed to textbook material. These would-be Hallway Hangers did not memorize rules of punctuation, spelling, capitalization, subject-verb agreement, and other mechanics of grammar. Rather, they used them time and again in the process of putting together their magazine. Connecting the curriculum with the interests of pupils like the Hallway Hangers can be done; it only requires a commitment—both attitudinal and material—to meeting the needs of working-class students.

Material commitment is crucial. Many schools in poor neighborhoods lack the most basic resources: classrooms, desks, books, science labs, photocopy machines, cafeteria furnishings, functioning toilets, and properly trained teachers. Among the member-countries of the Organization for Economic Cooperation and Development (OECD), the United States has the lowest per capita expenditure on primary education. Inner-city schools, segregated by color and class, have been allowed to deteriorate to the point where they are downright dangerous. In this context it is worth remembering that the Hallway Hangers and Brothers actually attended a highly regarded public high school. Even a curriculum reformed along the lines I have outlined would neither dissolve a school's social reproductive function nor directly address the fundamental problem of the transmission of class inequality. Thus, educational reform should be pursued not as an end in itself but as a component of more fundamental change in the social fabric of American society.

The transformation of American class society is currently a political impossibility, and progressive social change is bound to be slow and piecemeal. One way forward is through education that fosters a critical understanding of social problems and their structural causes. As students develop tools of social analysis and begin to understand how class-based inequalities in wealth, power, and privilege affect them, this awareness of self in relation to society becomes a motivating force much more powerful than the achievement ideology. Reflection on their personal and social reality frees learners from the debilitating effects of the dominant "blame the victim" way of seeing the world. Consonant with the praxis of the Brazilian educator Paulo Freire,[25] when learners perceive the structural roots of their own plight, they develop a new sense of personal dignity and are energized by a new hope. Time and again I have seen poor students face up to long odds and vow to overcome them instead of resigning themselves to the marginalized fate of the Hallway Hangers. When their passions and intellects are stimulated by indignation, youths are often moved to challenge the heretofore hidden social, political, and economic forces that weigh so heavily upon their lives. For some, this means an intensely personal drive and ambition. Others begin struggling to create a better world. In still others, these impulses coexist; such youths work for social, political, and economic reconstruction as well as personal transformation. For all of them, in contrast to the boys in this study, education has recovered its mission: It has become emancipatory.

CLASS DISMISSED

The experiences of the Hallway Hangers and Brothers, properly mined, highlight failures in economic, social, and educational policy, and the preceding pages offer a rough sketch of the book's broad policy implications. But this study points an accusing finger at one dominant dogma, itself a major obstacle to political change: the persistent belief that poverty is caused by the personal vices and cultural pathologies of the poor. Distinctively American, this old notion was rejuvenated in the 1960s by Oscar Lewis and Daniel Patrick Moynihan, who argued that a "culture of poverty" characterized by fatalism, family instability, and social irresponsibility promoted persistent urban poverty. Yet both Lewis and Moynihan contended that this "tangle of pathology" was rooted in sustained social immobility and chronic unemployment.[26]

Today, the link between economic opportunity and lower-class behavior has been completely cut in the popular press and the popular mind. Liberals such as Nicholas Lemann, keen to blame the poor for their plight, long to give ghettos an injection of bourgeois mores to cure the cultural malaise that black migrants allegedly brought up from the South, a theory he borrows from Edward Banfield.[27] Meanwhile, Banfield's archconservative heirs such as Charles Murray have set about convincing the public that welfare programs cause rather than contain poverty and that the social safety net should be scrapped altogether.[28] Egged on by Republican and even Democratic rhetoric, more and more Americans bewail the waste of their tax money on "the mythical black welfare mother, complete with a prodigious reproductive capacity and a galling laziness, accompanied by the uncaring and equally lazy black man in her life who will not work, will not marry her and will not support his family."[29] The war on poverty has become the war on the poor.

This book confirms that structural inequality causes poverty. The presumed behavioral and cultural deficiencies of the lower class are the consequence rather than the cause of poverty. Culture of poverty theorists consistently cite lack of ambition as a barrier to lower-class advancement. But the leveled aspirations of the Hallway Hangers can be directly traced to the impermeability of the class structure. Moreover, the ample ambition of the Brothers has been drained away by the tilted playing field under their feet. Over and over we discover beneath behavior cited as evidence of cultural pathology a social rationality that makes sense given the economic constraints these young men face. Born into the lowest reaches of the class structure, the Brothers and Hallway Hangers variously help and hinder the inertia of social reproduction. Their individual choices matter and make a difference, but the stage is largely set. Even the Hallway Hangers, far from authors of their own problems, are victims of a limited opportunity structure that strangles their initiative and channels them into lifestyles of marginality, and then allows the privileged to turn around and condemn them for doing so.[30]

But it is not merely the man driving by in the BMW who blames the victim. The Hallway Hangers and Brothers largely blame themselves for their plight. Schooled in the rhetoric of equal opportunity, the young men themselves confuse the consequences with the causes of poverty. Their self-blame is not total; many of the men in this study feel the constraining forces of social reproduction. But structural insight usually collapses into a feeling of personal responsibility for their failure to get ahead. Both the Brothers and Hallway Hangers see themselves as basically undeserving.

Class is not in the vocabulary of the Hallway Hangers and Brothers any more than it is in the vocabulary of other Americans. And yet class determines the grammar and idiom of their existence, if not the precise syntax. Yes, Frankie and company chose to follow the example of their older brothers and to hang out in doorway #13; chose to smoke and sell marijuana and angel dust at age thirteen; chose to deny rather than defer to teacher authority; chose to apply themselves to stealing rather than studying; and chose to drink and fight and assert their masculinity in displays of street aggression. Just like, as Benjamin DeMott imagines, a boy on the other side of town chooses to follow the example of his father (an engineer) and develop a science hobby in junior high (taking over the basement lounge for a lab); chooses to develop a research focus on robotics under the guidance of his brilliant young physics teacher (who already has two Young Scientist finalists); chooses at MIT to specialize in space robotics; chooses to take the NASA fellowship offer; and so on and on. In the American mind, life is about individual choices; social class matters not.[31]

The Brothers and Hallway Hangers live in a class society committed to the denial of class. Their lived experience attests to the power and pervasiveness of social class, but in the absence of any organizing and overarching ideology, their awareness of class is politically limp and inchoate. Where is such an ideology to be found? Democrats and Republicans fall over each other to please the mythically all-inclusive "middle class." Apart from conspicuously failing to address poverty as an issue, politicians pepper their public speeches with references to the "decent," "responsible," "hardworking" families they are so keen to court. "Symbolically cast out of the civic community," the poor, far from being a viable constituency, have become a political football to be kicked around in the debate about crime.[32] Politicians of all stripes want simply to lock up the likes of the

Hallway Hangers, as if criminality and economic opportunity were not inextricably linked. Once again, social problems are reduced to problems of individual morality and pathology. In contemporary American politics, there is no critique of the class structure; instead, the poor find themselves pushed beyond the political pale.

If the tide and toll of advanced marginality in the United States is to be checked, new organizational forms of popular mobilization need to be nurtured: grassroots organizations, women's groups, community organizing outfits, and coalitions campaigning on issues of health, housing, schooling, child care, crime, and local neighborhood concerns. Political parties and trade unions alone are ill-suited to stop the steady advance of new forms of social inequality.

In many countries, trade unions still carry the cause of workers and promote class consciousness. But the American labor movement has been crippled by red-baiting, right-to-work laws, racism, corporate power, and its own conservatism. In today's postindustrial economy, unions are consumed by the fight for survival, and a comprehensive critique of the class system is far from their agenda. Still, some unions serve their members and instill class solidarity. If it weren't for his progressive hotel and restaurant workers' union, Frankie might still be strung out on coke. Mike, the other union member, makes far more money than the other men in this study. And as much as he rants about welfare cheats and raves about oceans of opportunity, Mike quotes with approval the literature distributed by his postal union about how "the Republicans are fucking us over, selling the working class down the river." Alone among the subjects of this study, Mike speaks of the "working class." And yet he is also the most reactionary, variously characterizing the Hallway Hangers as "fuckin' rejects," "fuckin' trash," and "a bunch of lazy, loser, fuckup bums." Mike has forged his working-class identity by distancing himself from the "lazy" subproletariat. The class solidarity he articulates is defined as much against those below as against those above. Unfortunately, Mike's attitude is symptomatic of a working class that is severely fragmented.

The top tenth of the population owns 86 percent of the nation's wealth. But the rest of the wealth is distributed in such a way as to turn those in the bottom nine-tenths against each other. The working class is divided. White-collar workers vaunt themselves over manual laborers; skilled workers look down on the unskilled; those in low-status occupations belittle the unemployed. For the bulk of the workforce, there are always groups like the Hallway Hangers to whom they can feel superior. And the Hallway Hangers themselves, their peer group dissolved, seek solace and superiority in sexism and racism. They sense that the odds are stacked against them, but under the sway of New Right rhetoric and in the absence of any alternative political philosophy, the Hallway Hangers believe that they are victimized as white men. Victimized they are, but by a class system so clothed in the rhetoric of classlessness that the Hallway Hangers can be persuaded to pitch their tents with the powerful in a circle that excludes the Brothers. That is their tragedy, and ours.

NOTES

1. J. Castro, "How's Your Pay?" *Time,* April 15, 1991, pp. 40–41.

2. "Corporate Executives Go to the Trough," *Dollars and Sense* 138 (1988): 10–11. Cited in Thomas R. Shannon, Nancy Kleniewski, and William M Cross, *Urban Problems in Sociological Perspective* (Prospect Heights, Ill.: Waveland Press, 1991), p. 104.

3. David R. Francis, "Executive Pay in the U.S. Just Goes Up and Up," *Christian Science Monitor,* May 20, 1994, p. 9.

4. Cornel West, *Race Matters* (Boston: Beacon Press, 1993), p. 6.

5. Manning Marable, *Race, Reform, and Rebellion* (Jackson: University Press of Mississippi, 1991), p. 207.

6. Leonard Beeghley, "Individual and Structural Explanations of Poverty," *Population Research and Policy Review* 7 (1988): 207.

7. Loïc J. D. Wacquant, "Morning in America, Dusk in the Dark Ghetto: The New 'Civil War' in the American City," *Revue française d'études américaines* 60 (May 1994): 97–102.

8. See Roger Waldinger and Thomas Bailey, "The Continuing Significance of Race: Racial Conflict and Racial Discrimination in Construction," *Politics and Society* 19:3 (1991): 291–323.

9. Loïc J. D. Wacquant, "Urban Outcasts: Stigma and Division in the Black American Ghetto and the French Periphery," *International Journal of Urban and Regional Research* 17:3 (1993): 366–383. Wacquant refers to the historic all-black ghetto, but his insight also applies to the Brothers in their different context.

10. William Julius Wilson, *The Declining Significance of Race: Blacks and Changing American Institutions* (Chicago: University of Chicago Press, 1978), p. 12.

11. Loïc J. D. Wacquant, "The Puzzle of Race and Class in American Society and Social Science," *Benjamin E. Mays Monograph Series* 2 (Fall 1989): 7–20.

12. Wacquant, "The Puzzle of Race and Class in American Society and Social Science," p. 15. See also Pierre Bourdieu, "Social Space and the Genesis of Groups," *Theory and Society* 14 (October 1985): 723–744.

13. I am grateful to John Dickie for this point.

14. Paul E. Willis, *Learning to Labor* (Aldershot: Gower, 1977).

15. This objective dimension of race has nothing to do with the scientific category of race, which is biologically useless. Race is a sociohistorical concept rather than a biological one.

16. Loïc J. D. Wacquant, "The Ghetto, the State, and the New Capitalist Economy," *Dissent* (Fall 1989): 508–520.

17. Diego Gambetta, *Were They Pushed or Did They Jump?* (Cambridge: Cambridge University Press, 1987). These schemes—of being pushed from behind and pulled from the front—are borrowed from Gambetta but take on a somewhat different meaning in the present context.

18. Loïc J. D. Wacquant, "On the Tracks of Symbolic Power," *Theory, Culture, and Society* 10 (August 1993): 3–4.

19. To be fair, Bourdieu reckons that the structure-agency dilemma is improperly framed and leads to a theoretical cul-de-sac. It would be harsh to fault him for failing to resolve this dilemma, if it were not claimed by others that he succeeds in dissolving and transcending the structure-agency dualism.

20. Wacquant, "On the Tracks of Symbolic Power," p. 3.

21. Loïc J. D. Wacquant, "'The Zone': Le métier de 'hustler' dans le ghetto noir américain," *Actes de la recherche en science sociales* 93 (June 1992): 58.

22. Loïc J. D. Wacquant, "The State and Fate of the Ghetto: Redrawing the Urban Color Line in Postfordist America," in Craig Calhoun, ed., *Social Theory and the Politics of Identity* (New York: Basil Blackwell, 1994).

23. Wacquant, "Morning in America, Dusk in the Dark Ghetto," pp. 97–102.

24. Willis, *Learning to Labor,* p. 123.

25. Paulo Freire, *Pedagogy of the Oppressed* (New York: Continuum, 1981).

26. Douglas S. Massey and Nancy A. Denton, *American Apartheid* (Cambridge, Mass.: Harvard University Press, 1993), p. 5. See also Daniel Patrick Moynihan, *On Understanding Poverty* (New York: Basic Books, 1968).

27. Nicholas Lemann, *The Promised Land* (New York: Alfred A. Knopf, 1991). See also Lemann's "The Origins of the Underclass," *Atlantic Monthly*, June 1986, pp. 31–55, continued in July 1986, pp. 54–68; and Edward C. Banfield, *The Unheavenly City* (Boston: Little, Brown, 1970).

28. Charles Murray, *Losing Ground* (New York: Basic Books, 1984).

29. Rosemary L. Bray, "Growing Up on Welfare," *The Observer Magazine,* January 2, 1994, p. 37.

30. Brian Powers, "Two Tracks to Nowhere," *Socialist Review* 19:2 (April–June 1989): 157.

31. Benjamin DeMott, *The Imperial Middle* (New York: William Morrow, 1990), p. 186.

32. Wacquant, "Morning in America, Dusk in the Dark Ghetto," p. 5.

PART THREE

AIN'T NO MAKIN' IT?
The Men at Midlife

When I stepped off the number 69 bus in front of Clarendon Heights in April 2006, I reckoned I'd made a mistake. I'd been away for fifteen years, and the place was nearly unrecognizable. A macadam courtyard between the six low-rise buildings had been the center of social life, a place where kids played and older people chatted and where teenagers ruled at night. Now it's a street lined with shiny vans and sporty family cars.* Apart from the high-rise building at the back for the old and infirm, the apartments themselves all have separate entrances and their own tiny yards. This was not just another cosmetic makeover. And if the physical environment could be so transformed, how could I hope to connect with the Hallway Hangers and the Brothers after all these years? We have both moved on.

As an ordained minister in the Church of England since 1993, I would return to the United States every year or two with my British wife and three children for family holidays. Seeing my parents and my brother and sister and their families was the priority, and I had fallen out of touch with the younger men in the youth enrichment program as well as the Hallway Hangers and Brothers. Slowly walking up the new street and between the buildings of Clarendon Heights on this sunny spring afternoon, I failed to recognize a single face. But then I turned a corner, and there was Mrs. Carlucci sitting on the sidewalk just as she was twenty-five years earlier when I'd come to Clarendon Heights as a college sophomore. It looked like it could have been the same lawn chair! Westview Press found telephone numbers and addresses for many of the men in this study using the Internet and a security firm, but Mrs. Carlucci proved a better source of information on the whereabouts of the Hallway Hangers. I'd long known that Boo-Boo died of AIDS in 1994, and I discovered that Craig is estranged from his family and living out West. I managed to conduct in-depth interviews with all the other Hallway Hangers and Brothers, having tracked them down in spring 2006 or on subsequent visits during 2006 and 2007.

---

*While city centers pedestrianize their streets, Clarendon Heights has done the opposite, and residents aren't complaining. Realities may change but reputations linger. 29 Green Street is still preferable to 132 Clarendon Heights on a job application.

When I agreed to this third edition of *Ain't No Makin' It*, I did so on the understanding that the new data would be presented as oral histories. For Parts One and Two of this book, I spent months and months poring over interview transcripts and field notes trying to make sense of the material and to create a sociological narrative that was true to the men's lives. I simply did not have the time to do that this time around. So Chapters 12 and 13 are edited transcripts of recorded interviews (except for Chris and Mike, whose words were recorded from memory immediately after the conversations). Some of the original transcripts ran to eighty pages, so I have been ruthless with the Delete key. Material has been moved about to improve the flow of the interview, and I have integrated some comments from less formal conversations with the men.

I also think that presenting the men's stories as oral history is intellectually honest. Before moving from Trinidad to England himself, C. L. R. James (arguably the greatest public intellectual of the twentieth century) distrusted all firsthand accounts of the English, whether offered by professionals, politicians, or professors. But James listened to his cricket-playing friend Learie Constantine because "he had no theory to expound, no abstract studies to square what he saw with his eyes and heard with his ears."* In Parts One and Two of this book, I looked and listened, and I analyzed the stories of the Hallway Hangers and Brothers, using social reproduction theory to help frame the ethnographic material. In Chapters 12 and 13 the Hallway Hangers and the Brothers speak directly to the reader. I serve up raw interviews rather than presenting analysis with supporting quotations from the men. To be sure, I've decided what to keep and what to cut, but you are invited to "do the sociology" as you read, having picked up (I hope) some of the tools of the trade in Parts One and Two.

But the professional sociologist still has an important role here, and I agreed to the third edition on the condition that Katherine McClelland and David Karen would analyze the new data. In Chapter 14 they are charged with doing the "squaring," to offer an analysis of what has become of the Brothers and Hallway Hangers in midlife. Both have been deeply involved in this study from its genesis, McClelland as my thesis adviser and her husband, Karen, as an unofficial mentor. Sociology professors at Franklin and Marshall College and at Bryn Mawr College, respectively, McClelland and Karen teach (among other things) social stratification and race relations. In Chapter 14 they adopt (and adapt) the social reproduction perspective laid out in the first two parts of the book and introduce new frames as well. I myself have learned a great deal from McClelland and Karen's analysis, and I trust that readers will too.

---

*C. L. R. James, *Beyond a Boundary* (London: Yellow Jersey Press, 1963), p. 147.

THE HALLWAY HANGERS

Weeble, Wobble, but We Don't Fall Down

When I spoke with Boo-Boo in the summer of 1991, he was grieving for one daughter and contemplating the deaths of his second daughter and his girlfriend. He didn't say so, but it was clear that Boo-Boo was also facing up to his own fate. Boo-Boo died in 1994, having first buried Natasha, Connie, and Ginger. During the early days of my 2006 fieldwork, nearly every street-corner conversation alluded to Boo-Boo's deathbed courage and to his extraordinary funeral (which featured heavy metal music, songs written by friends, tributes from his family, and a graveside party, which moved to his sister's home and was still going strong thirty-six hours later). Several people on the fringes of the Hallway Hangers have also died, some of them violently, but the rest of the Hallway Hangers survive. Here are their edited interviews, offered without a theoretical framework to conceptualize the external forces that constrain the men. I've been completely out of professional sociology for well over a decade, but that doesn't mean I could return to Clarendon Heights without theoretical baggage. Indeed, some of my questions introduce clunky sociological categories into the interviews. This didn't always make for great conversation, but sometimes it induced the men to articulate their own sociology. Rather than being absolutely raw data, these stories are lightly toasted in the telling but retain, I hope, a freshness for the reader.

FRANKIE

Connected

I was told that Frankie now lives two blocks from Clarendon Heights in a small housing development. The owner-occupied duplex homes are painted in pastel colors that suggest that a slice of suburbia has somehow slipped into the city. In fact, these are HUD homes with federally subsidized mortgages. When I asked a man watering his tiny front lawn where I could find Frankie, he squinted at me and shrugged. Sensing his unease about directing a stranger to Frankie's house, I explained that Frankie and I went way back and that I'd traveled from England. He kept watering the lawn and I waited. Eventually he nodded at the house next door. Before I'd finished knocking, Frankie opened the door and came out on the stoop. His light, wiry hair had thinned but he still moved with an easy lope that contrasted with the piercing eyes and the commanding presence. I stuck out my hand and said my name, and he laughed and gave me a bear hug. "Jay MacLeod. Unbelievable. The hillbilly college kid comes back to the 'hood!" Frankie was heading to work but he introduced me to his bemused wife and teenage son. "Lemme guess," Frankie ventured with a grin after we'd quickly caught up about families and jobs, "you're short of cash and need to do another edition of that book." "Got it in one," I said, laughing. After twenty years of English reserve and reticence, I was caught off balance by Frankie's outspoken perspicacity. So much for my higher motives of intellectual inquiry and commitment to social justice! We arranged an interview for the following Saturday morning. When we sat down at the kitchen table I was surprised to glimpse *Manufacturing Consent* by Noam Chomsky on a side table. I thought the interview went well, but Frankie phoned me a few days later and apologized for the quality of the conversation, explaining that he had worked all Friday night and had been jaded with fatigue. So we met again, and this time his wife and son joined us at the kitchen table for the last half hour. Both conversations figure in the account that follows.

JM: What've you been doing for work since I last saw you?

I worked in the parts department of a car dealer. That was my job to find a job. I had put in for the City, and put in for Housing. The day Housing called me, the City sent me a letter to hire me. I was looking for, like, a career job, so in '93 I went to the Housing Authority, worked there 'til November of last year. Then I went over to Highways.

JM: How'd you get the job at Housing?

Persistence. Just kept calling. Calling and calling. I would call Housing every Thursday at one o'clock and they would say no. And I'd say, "Well, I'll call ya next Thursday at one o'clock." And then they called me on a Thursday at a quarter to one, and they said, "Don't call, come in." During the interview the head of management realized I'm an O'Sullivan. He said, "You want me to fucking hire you?" Just like that. And I said, "Yeah, listen, I never got arrested in Housing property in my life. It's my brothers you're thinking of." And so when they hired me I showed them my record. Now they said, "Hey, you said you didn't have a record." And I said, "No, no, what I said is I never got arrested in Housing property." So I told them, "Call my ex-PO, he'll vouch for me." It was a good job, maintenance. Started at Lipton Park, then went down to Howard's Court, the elderly home, the one over the tracks, and I was there for nine years.

JM: I imagine maintenance was the easiest part. Was it dealing with people as well?

I'm a project kid, and I get along good with everybody. You're in their house because something's broke, so you're the front line. You hafta have some diplomacy, some empathy, sympathy. But a mom with one kid would be bitching and I'd say, "Go get a job." "You don't understand, I got a kid." I said, "Look, you're talking to the wrong guy; my mom brought up eight and worked full-time." At Lipton Park I was a servant of Haitians; the projects aren't what they used to be. A lotta foreigners. And they're dirty, very tolerant of pests. But the elderly home was good. I'm a pretty diplomatic guy. They loved me there. I was there for a long, long time too. And I actually miss it.

JM: So how'd the opportunity at Highways come about?

I applied. You know the way them jobs come, Jack, only one way you get those jobs. You have fifteen thousand applications, they don't just pull your name out. Connections. That's how it works. It's a good gig; I like it. Nights suck. But it'll be a good job. Heavy equipment. Union job. Big money. A little dangerous out in the fucking road with a lot of drunks. We had a guy rear-end us last night. People just don't fucking pay attention. I do a little bit of everything. Run the sweeper, a loader, operate a cone truck, set out cones, block off roads. Usually a crew of four. You have your truck, a backup truck, lot of times you get a statey [state trooper] with you. Depends what you're doing. Like whether we're washing the walls. They do the tunnels by a brush and a front-end loader. Them water tankers follow it. And we do the sewers, clean them out.

JM: Will you have a chance to progress there?

Oh yeah. I'm actually waiting for a job to open up right now. It's like a maintenance manager: greasing the fans, greasing the bearings. They have huge exhaust fans. For that one mile of tunnel we have twenty miles of vent shaft. So I'm waiting for that to kick in, and that's big money there again. I just got my crane license for a rigger's job.

JM: And does this allow you to use your leadership skills, your personal skills?

If I'm on a crew it just seems that guys listen. But as for the foreman, I'm always on punishment just cuz I'll stick up for others. These two guys, they're dicks. They're fresh, one kid grew up in Salisbury [wealthy suburb], and you can tell he had his lunch money taken away from him, and now he's the boss. The other guy's a herder out from, like, Putnoe.

JM: A herder?

You know, herder: a country boy like you. [*laughs*] Now, these guys have some authority, but I'll say, "Fuck you, pal." So I go on punishment. Like last night I was on punishment. They knew my back was bothering me, so they kept me out in the rain last night washing lanes. That's fine. They can't break me. I took it in stride. My back was a little stiff. So he stuck me out in the cold and the rain. But no big deal.

JM: So having a boss like that grates on you, but you've found ways of coping with that, dealing with that.

That's his shit. Those are his issues. I pray for him. Sometimes I pray that he gets hit by a truck. [*laughs*] I don't sweat the small stuff. But I'm still a project kid at heart, and my first thought's still the project thought every single time.

JM: Which is?

Not a good thought: whack him, stab him. But then my God thought comes in and overrides it. I hooked up with a guy a few years back, a guy from the neighborhood, an ex–armored car robber. He taught me that it was okay to do the right thing. I had to delete that old shit. It's all right to be a good guy; it's not being weak. And he got me back into the church. He's a Eucharistic minister. So I read my gospel every day. That's part of the recovery fellowship. The Serenity Prayer: God grant me the serenity to accept the things I cannot change, the courage to change the things I can, and wisdom to know the difference. God is big. I carried a lot of shit through life that I just didn't think I would ever be forgiven. But I believe I am forgiven. And that's made life a little easier. I'm not proud of a lot of the shit, but what happened, happened. What are you gonna do?

JM: When did you first experience this sort of turnaround?

Part of the twelve steps is to find the power greater than yourself. I kind of halfheartedly believed. I believed in keeping clean and keeping sober. But now I know. I don't need to see to believe. I don't hafta feel the hole in his hand. I know he's there, definitely know he's watching over me. He's blessed me with a great wife. Jesus, I'm still alive. If I knew I was going to live this long I would have taken a little better care of myself. [*laughs*]

I know today that I grew up with a lotta stuff. My old man killed himself when I was five. He jumped off the Emerson Bridge. And I didn't deal with that until I got sober. We never talked about it. Growing up I thought it musta been something we did. Today I know that he was an alcoholic and a gambler who was heavy into debt. His option was, "If I kill myself my kids will get my veteran's benefits." Which we did. I dunno. I don't know what one person's thinking when they're suicidal. [*pause*] At some point did I think of that? Absolutely. But knowing what happens to the people left behind, it was never an option. So I dealt with that. I dealt with a lot of shit within the family. It was a crazy fucking house. Stabbing, shootings, and that just was the living room. [*laughs*]

I wrote it down, all my resentments. And then I made my amends. I believe the day I was set free was when I apologized to my brother for stealing off him. He had thought it was my other brother for years. So I paid him, apologized for him thinking it was the other brother. And he turned to me and said, "Well, I forgive you, cuz I'm sure you forgive Dennis." See, my brother Dennis had like eighteen felony convictions under my name. I said, "Forgive Dennis? Fuck him, that motherfucker." So I walked back to the house. And then I thought, "Here I am looking for forgiveness from people, and I'm not going to forgive." Y'know, I trespass against ten people for every one that trespasses against me. And it wasn't until I said, "I forgive everybody," that I finally learned how to sleep without homicidal fucking thoughts at night. I'd got into real stupid shit, too, remembering something that happened when I was like eight, and me saying, "That motherfucker, I'll kill him." It would be my first thought in the morning and during the day I'd kill him a hundred fucking times in my head. I don't have that anymore. I don't have it. It's nice, it's nice to sleep. I have some rough sleep some nights, just from some of the fucking madness back in the house and some of the stabbings that I was involved in. So that bothers me. That's the only thing. I'm pretty good until I get behind the wheel. I still got a little fucking road rage [*laughs*], but I'm working on that too.

I'm trying to deal with this kid. Trying to get him back on track. He's been sheltered, maybe a little too much, y'know? Spoiled. I been trying to keep him away from the shit that I went through. That's my life, y'know: It's him.

JM: Do you see yourself in him at all?

He got my temper; he's got my fucking laziness, procrastination. I mean, he's always had passion. He won a scholarship to Ireland. When they came back and they were looking to do some fund-raising, all these kids had their speeches on paper. I'm sitting there and Darren ain't got nothing written down. He went up there, he killed them. Just off his passion.

JM: That must have been a proud moment for you when he went up to that microphone.

Oh, yeah. When he went for his college scholarship, in the interview they asked him what he'd learned from his parents. He talked about his mom and her commitment, this, that, and the other thing. And they were all sitting at the table and they said, "Well, what's the most important thing your father taught you?" He said, "That's simple: The Yankees suck." [*laughs*] I was a proud dad that day he won the scholarship. For the most part he's a good kid. He's a likable kid. All the kids he grew up with, he was the only one that had both parents. I was the neighborhood dad. This place here, we're all shareholders. It's a co-op. It's run by the tenants themselves. HUD actually owns the mortgage, but we're self-sufficient.

JM: You weren't worried at all about coming back? The way some guys cope is that they move to be away from the neighborhood.

Jay, if I moved, I was bringing me, know what I mean? So I couldn't get away from me. So it doesn't matter where the fuck I lived, I still had Frank. I just had to change Frank. And that's what I try to do. And then there's Carla. She does it all. Girl makes the money. Smart girl. She's a CPA without being a CPA.

JM: So how'd you hook up with her in the first place? That was in your heyday. You were nineteen. It must've taken some charm, y'know, because at that time you were bringing some baggage with you.

Oh, yeah, and I put her through fucking hell the first seven years. And I put her through hell again when I went out and fucking relapsed.

JM: Tell me about that.

I had an injury, fucked up my back, got prescriptions. And got more prescriptions for the opiates. And got a couple of doctors. It was nuts. I'm an addict, and I was the last one to realize I was hooked. I was getting these prescribed, so it was justified, and then the habit kicked in, and after that, you gotta do what you gotta do. I kept doing meetings but I just couldn't get clean. Just couldn't get clean. I just couldn't get rid of the street-corner mentality after I was getting high. I went right back to that. I'm a project kid. I went right back to the project kid in my head even though I was older. Now these fucking young boys are running out there, and I was out there running with the young boys, Stoney's kids, actually. They've been through a ton of shit.

JM: And was there a certain attraction to that, y'know, being back?

No, no. I just needed to fucking play the game to get high. Did I want to be there? Absolutely not. I wanted to be home with my family. Just caught up in addiction. You start networking where I was getting scrips, you start to learn who gets scrips, who's getting it this week: "I'll give you some until I get mine." It's fucking madness, it's just madness. It's a full-time job just getting high. Sucked. I learned from it. I learned that I don't want to go through it again. And just trying a day at a time to stay clean. With God and AA.

JM: How did Carla cope with it all? Did she see you going back to twenty years ago?

Oh, yeah, I put her through fucking hell, whacking fucking ATM cards, getting cash advances. It was crazy, madness. Why she stayed, I don't know. I wouldn't've. But she did.

JM: That was how long ago?

I been clean now twenty-two months. I mean, I was fucked, and she stuck by me.

JM: Affected your job?

Yeah, it affected the fucking job. Some of the old veterans and shit were supplying me. But I've always been a worker.

JM: So how did you get out of that cycle for the second time?

Well, I kept going to meetings. I got hooked on a weird drug for terminally ill patients, the patches with the seventy-two hours. I would bypass that by cutting it open and licking it. And then I heard a kid, he spoke of how he was hooked on it, and what helped him with the withdrawals. I went to my primary care doctor and we set up a game plan. It worked.

JM: When you see the other guys, the ones that have really continued to struggle, what do you think?

I feel for them. I pray for them every day. Fucking addiction. It sucks. They gotta get clean, first and foremost. Gotta get clean. Can't do nothing while you're getting high.

JM: There's addiction, but are there other things that play into it?

Did ya make a fuckin' independent choice to get high? No. You dug yourself a hole, you got a record, it's all built up. It's a bunch of shit. I just don't think they know there's hope. If I wasn't blessed with Carla, I wouldn't be where I am today. God bless her. Growing up, you never lose the project kid in your fucking head. You still have it.

JM: But as a project kid, if you can imagine growing up in a completely different environment, even with your propensity for addiction, would it have been a lot different?

Yeah, I probably wouldn't've had a record. I was always a bright kid. But I was always an O'Sullivan. From first grade, I was just another O'Sullivan. And that wasn't a good thing. Shorty had the same—he was a Flanagan. Steve and them—they made their own fucking reps, where me and Shorty, our brothers made our fucking reps. And when you put fucking Clarendon Heights on a job application, that was a stitch up.

I had to do everything I did to be the man I am today. Am I sorry for some of the shit I did? Absolutely. But I know deep down I was always a good guy. I just did some fucked-up shit. A lotta it is just fear. I know a lotta my aggressiveness was fear, masked fear.

JM: Of?

Just fear. Fear of anything. Growing up in fear. In my house I never knew when I was going to get cracked. The only place I could go to fucking have peace of mind was in the closet. I got cracked in the head just for grabbing an extra scoop of potatoes.

JM: Was there ever a sense, because you were a bright lad—I'm thinking about when you were eleven, twelve, thirteen years old—were you aware then that there was another option: to go for it in school?

No, absolutely not. Not living in the projects. I woulda been looked at different, I wouldn't have been one of the boys. Absolutely not.

JM: Did you ever get fed up with the society that dealt you that hand?

Was I angry? Absolutely. Did I despise fucks like you? Absolutely. Every fucking kid in the projects looked at Barneys, college students—we useta go Barney-hunting. I'd fucking whack guys just for being a college student. I look at that today and that was nonsense. But I was fucking mad.

JM: But that anger, tell me about that.

The anger was just hopelessness, I guess. Always being looked at differently. Knowing. We were the kids who were never invited to your party but we came anyways. We were project kids. And we knew that. And other people knew that.

My perception is that people are looking at me as if I was less than. How do you overcome that? You impose your will upon 'em. All I knew was what I'd been taught. We had four fucking blocks. All I knew was my 'hood. I didn't care about fucking America or any other fucking place.

JM: But when you turn on the telly and you're watching the shows, seeing kids going on holidays, having these things . . .

I would have dreams of not being me. But I was who I was, and I had my boys back then. That was big to me. That was big. That's all I had.

JM: Do you miss that?

No. I feel bad for the boys, though. I feel like I mighta been a part of that, the influence of them fucking up. Like Stoney and Chris, I kinda feel a little responsible for the way they turned out. Because they were very fucking impressionable.

My sponsor, the guy I was tellin' you about, the ex–armored car man, he was the type of guy that we looked up to, growing up. He's taught me that doing the right thing is okay, because doing the right thing definitely wasn't okay back then, it was weakness. You let your guard down, you can open yourself to be hurt, and it's just something you never did. You never accepted help. I look back now at all the programs, all the social workers, all the psychs we've seen, and the walls just went up. That was a defense mechanism.

It's like the hate we had towards James, Craig. It's not like these guys were aggressive, but these dudes were intruding, and how that looks to our crew, you couldn't be weak. Individually, they were pretty cool. But as a whole, listen, those were our basketball courts, those were our parks, that was our project for years. That was ours. It was fought for. It was fought for and won by the guys before us, and it was our jobs to maintain it. That's the way we were looked at.

JM: How do you look at it now?

We had a reputation to uphold, and even though you came across fearless, there was a lotta fear involved. And stuff that I wouldn'ta did straight, with some booze and drugs in me, it very easily became sociopathic behavior, whatever you wanna call it. Because I was an altar boy, I was brought up with values, but in the game we were playing, you couldn't have those. There wasn't room for that. There wasn't room for caring.

JM: But there was a solidarity with each other.

Absolutely. That's what we had. We had each other and that was it. Y'know what I mean? We had each other and that was it, and it was us against the world. We were project kids. We were just always looked down on.

I'm a union man now. There is still brothers and sisters I work with, and it is us against them. Management is up, and we are us, and we stick together, cover each other's back. Someone fucks up, we try to cover the fuckup. We police ourselves. So, yes, it's still kind of that way for me.

JM: Throughout your working life, have trade unions served you well?

Absolutely. If you're a white male, you need to have. If I was a black guy, I'd have a great job right now, no question in my mind. The opportunities are there. But being a fucking working white stiff, you gotta have connections. Like where I am now, these black guys that work there, they got it off the street. I wouldn'ta had a shot at this job off the street, not even close.

JM: The other way to look at it is that you've got access to connections that others don't.

Let's put it this way: White guy trying to become a cop, you better score a hundred or you're not becoming a cop. I still believe the best man should get the job. If I scored a ninety-five and if a black guy scored an eighty-five, he's getting the job today. Does that make it right?

JM: I don't know what the figures are now, but back in 1991, the fact of the matter was that a white high school graduate was making more than a black college graduate in the local economy. So actually, on balance, they're getting screwed.

I find it pretty comical that the American black is bitching about the fucking Asian taking his job. Because that's what I was doing. The Portuguese was our beef: fucking Portegis taking our fucking jobs. Portuguese are saying the same things about the Salvadorans, the Haitians. That's it, we're focusing on us, and not the real issues. The real issue is that not everyone's got a shot in this country; they just don't, and some people are just privileged.

JM: Is that a disparity between blacks and whites or a class thing between rich and poor?

I believe it is a class issue. The rich white guy wants the poor white guy and the poor black guy to not like each other. As long as we're not liking each other, we're leaving them alone. I believe we're in the same boat. But we're just too fucking focused on each other. And the Rothchilds, the Rockefellers, they're getting over. Especially nowadays with Bush in fucking charge, the rich are getting richer. But I have my options. Got my cabin up north, my bills are fucking paid. Leave me and my family alone, we're going to be cool. All I want to do is get my kid educated, leave him some land, because there's a rumor they're not making any more of that. I'm fighting for my family.

JM: Is there no room for fighting that fight but also fighting for other people?

I was a union official. But since the heart attack it's been a little different. I've had five or six guys approach me and ask me to run for steward, but I told 'em, "Look, I had a heart attack, and I just can't do it." I can't get caught up in that, y'know? It takes a fight, and I need to pick my fights a little more wisely because I exhaust a lotta energy in whatever fight I pick. My fights are going to be for my family today. I can't be fighting for everybody. Those days are over.

JM: Could you see yourself in management? You've got the skills.

It wouldn't happen. It won't happen. I'm not management material. I couldn't do it.

JM: Because?

I wouldn't want the responsibility.

JM: What is it about the responsibility?

I look at these managers now, and they're looking at guys as guys. I mean, I'm working with some active dope addicts. Everybody has a wife and kid. Jay could be an asshole. Well, what did Jay's wife and kid do to me? So I look at you differently. And if I was management, I couldn't work that way. I'd have to look at *you.*

JM: Have you been in management in any of your jobs?

No, but just about every crew I've been on, I've just naturally came to the top. At Howard's in Housing, I ran that building, even though there was management higher than me that ultimately was supposed to take the responsibility of running the show. I was a laborer but in actuality I ran the building.

JM: Tell me about the heart attack.

I was up at my summer home last July. And I had some bologna. I had craved for fried bologna, some nice project steak. [*laughs*] And went to bed. Woke up, burped, could taste the bologna. Had this serious burning pressure. Thought I had indigestion. So went back to bed. Woke up the next day, still had it. Drove back down here. Took a nap, woke up, still had it. Went up to the hospital and told me I had a heart attack. Not much damage. They gave me a stent. Good enough.

[Frankie's wife, Carla, and son, Darren, come home, and after tea and coffee are made, they join the conversation.]

JM: [*to Carla*] You've gone through some really rough times and you've stayed with him. There must have been some dark days, and you stuck to it.

CARLA: There's qualities in him that I saw from the very beginning that other people probably didn't see. And I was very naive. I was not a drug user as a teenager. There were probably warning signs that I didn't recognize. I didn't know any better.

FRANKIE: What about my last bout?

CARLA: Yeah, well, then I became quite intelligent. I could do the drug sweep. I could tell each and every time he was high. That set me right off, and then I would tear this house apart. I would go out and tear the car apart, and I'd confront him and I'd confront him and I'd confront him. And he struggled with it, and I guess he had a determination to stop doing it, but I think I had a determination to make sure he stopped doing it. Y'know, he came very close to not being a resident of this household. Extremely close to not being a resident of this household.

DARREN: She kept more faith in him than I did, because she talked to me about it and I said, "Yeah, kick him out," because I was sick of it myself.

FRANKIE: And now I'm trying to tell her to kick you out. [*laughs*]

DARREN: She has more faith in both of us than any one of us have in ourselves, I guess.

JM: Going way back, when you first got together . . .

CARLA: We met at church. [*laughs*] That's what we tell people. It was the railroad tracks behind the church.

FRANKIE: I was drinking behind the church. [*laughs*]

JM: When you look at the way these different guys have ended up, relationships have been crucial. The ones that have developed a relationship with somebody who has stood by them and been a positive influence, that's made a huge difference.

CARLA: And I think that might have made the difference. I didn't have those issues, don't necessarily understand them. My father's an alcoholic, but my mother divorced him when I was very young, five. We grew up alone.

JM: [*to Frankie*] Looking back, one thing I never asked you guys about was domestic violence. Knowing these guys as you did, was that a big thing in these households?

FRANKIE: How many of us actually had fathers? Shorty's old man never was. Stoney had no old man, I had no old man, Chris had no old man, Boo-Boo had no old man, Slick and Sean had no old man. Jinx's the only one that had a father. There was domestic violence in my house. Absolutely there was violence in every home. But moms kicked your ass back then. I can remember times that Bobbie, Jinx's ma, hit me, and if I went back and told my mom that Bobbie gave me a whack, I was getting whacked again because Bobbie didn't whack me for nothing. That's just the way the 'hood was, and that wasn't a bad thing.

JM: One of the Brothers said that's why he didn't get into more trouble, because he knew his dad would beat the hell out of him. Now, without really thinking about it, that's the posture he adopts with his kids. He doesn't beat them but it's based on fear.

FRANKIE: The most intimidating words to a kid should be, "I'm telling your father." That should terrify a kid. You've got to have some kind of control, but how many kids can you use that threat?

CARLA: "I'm telling your father" to him didn't mean a thing! He wasn't afraid of you because you were more like his buddy.

JM: Where did Darren go to school?

CARLA: He went to Dunning. We were coming from Salford and I didn't know any better. I thought you were supposed to go to Hoover. They told me Hoover was full. Then I said, "Well, okay, Dunning." I didn't know he could go to any school in the city. If I had known that, I would have did a little bit more research and—

FRANKIE: Dunning wasn't one of your better fucking schools.

CARLA: And then when he graduated from eighth grade you have to apply for the high school House where you want to go. And House A was the more academic, college-level program, and one kid out of his whole entire class was selected to go to House A, and everybody else was kind of streamed into what they called Fundamental. I had to go up and sit before some people at the high school, then fight and explain to them why I wanted him in House A.

FRANKIE: Like 19 percent of people of color in the city, yet 60 percent of your enrollment in high school is of people of color. For the money they're spending per pupil, it's a madhouse up there.

JM: So how did you get on in high school?

DARREN: Uh, underachiever. I think I'm lazy. I always did well in history.

FRANKIE: Shit that interests him: Che, Chomsky, that kind of stuff.

CARLA: Otherwise he doesn't really apply himself.

DARREN: I'm a militant socialist. It's not that we're talking about a coup but by whatever means necessary.

JM: Why don't we elect a socialist government?

DARREN: I think it's because of a lack of unity between poor blacks and poor whites. In this country everything's brought out to be due to race and religion. The government keeps feeding that to us, saying, "Let's take this white guy and this black guy, and then you're going to go for a job," and sometimes the white guy is going to get the job, sometimes the black guy is going to get the job, whether they're qualified for it or not, because of racial quotas, affirmative action, and whatnot. That just keeps putting poor whites and poor blacks against one another. Race becomes the issue every time, and it's a class issue.

FRANKIE: There's no media outlet for our class. The Jews run the media, and that's just a fact. I'm going to come across racist, but what the Jew media gives to America, that's what we're getting. And if the Jews get the working-class white guy more worried about the working-class black guy, it's easier for them to do what they do.

JM: We were just talking about class, but immediately you draw back in race and ethnicity.

FRANKIE: No, because that's ultimately who runs the media. How is the working-class guy gonna get the word out when the media is owned by people who care less what the fuck you're gonna say? If you gave the working-class guys an outlet and that if we stick together we can actually do something here. Even unions, there's no consolidation, each union is so worried about their own body. There was a early retirement bill coming up in the state-house, so there was a hearing, and in the hearing all the unions had their representations: Teachers union showed up with like twenty lawyers, the police, the firemen. Everybody divvied up and started fighting each other.

DARREN: There's a real lack of solidarity.

FRANKIE: I loved what happened in the WTO [World Trade Organization] in Seattle, but it got washed right under. They're showing the people smashing the windows. The longshoremen had a great rally, the Teamsters had a great rally there; you didn't see any of that on the news. You seen the guys breaking the window, kids throwing paint balloons. Why? Because they don't want you to see that.

What's wrong with this nation is the CEO. What are they making, something like 360 times a laborer? Everything's about the stockholder, so they say. Who's the stockholder? It ain't me. These CEOs are losing billions and still getting their bonuses. The CEO for the biggest refinery in Texas, he's making $850 million off of stocks this year. It's sick. It's crazy.

It's come to the point where it's not even a class issue in America. It's a world class issue because it is such a global economy. We'll outsource it to India. What are you going to do? Unless you get these other countries on board to start making labor laws, we're screwed.

One of your biggest illegals in this state is the Irish. As long as they're hiding out, they ain't got no voice. Business takes advantage of them, puts them in unsafe working conditions. Once again it's the rich getting richer. They ain't paying health benefits for these people. Pay taxes, compensation, insurance on these people, they're not doing that. A guy has either come here legally or a guy who was born in this country got a wife and kids, trying to support himself, and he can't get the job. It's just not right. But it's America. I can't worry about that. Whether I'm giving up or whatever, I believe I'm dealt the hand I'm dealt. We're not in the ideal world and I've accepted that. I got to just take care of me.

CARLA: There's always hope.

FRANKIE: I became morally spent, spiritually bankrupt at one point, and that was my bottom, and now it's new. It's a new life. I believe this is what God has given me, and I'm blessed. A great wife, and I didn't get a bad kid. This was as good as it was going to get and it came because God gave it to me; it was an act of Providence. This is definitely unmerited. Did I waste some qualities that I had, that are just naturally given to me? Absolutely. I maintain the highways. I like my job, I enjoy my job, I'm doing something different all the time. Working nights sucks, but I make the highway a safer place.

JINX

Stuck Around

Jinx is the only Hallway Hanger who still frequents the neighborhood. I found him at his son's Little League game, a few yards from the court where I'd spent so many hours playing basketball with the Brothers. Jinx was leaning against the waist-high center field fence with two workmates, a can of beer in his hand, and the remains of a twelve-pack at his feet. He glanced up and exclaimed, "Hey, hey, look who's over from merry old England. What the hell, the queen kick you out? I heard you were looking for me." He grinned widely, ignored my extended hand, and embraced me. His hair was mostly gray and his grin revealed missing and blackened teeth, but this was the same easygoing Jinx, somehow both spirited and resigned. We watched the game and chatted. When his son Jason turned a line drive over second base into a home run thanks to fielding errors, Jinx led the cheering. And when Jason struck out next time up and trudged out to his center field position, Jinx shouted, "Hey, keep your head up; it was just a good pitch." Jinx's older sister arrived, held up a joint, and led Jinx and one of his workmates over to the trees past right field to light up. "Sorry about that," Jinx said, chuckling, on his return. "Still gotta have my weed. That's one thing that ain't changed." He told me that his twenty-year-old son, Matt, is in jail. Jinx also explained ruefully that he and his long-term girlfriend broke up some ten years ago and that he ended up with her older sister. Jinx now lives with her and Jason in an apartment in Emerson Heights, a public housing development a half mile from Clarendon Heights. Racial tension between the two projects led to street violence in the 1970s and '80s. When I interviewed Jinx at his home, I got the distinct impression that some white friends rely on Jinx to source marijuana and cocaine from the neighborhood rather than relate to black dealers themselves. Back in doorway 13, Jinx was something of a peacemaker between the white and black members of the Hallway Hangers. Twenty-five years later he's still putting his poise and personal skills to use, if not always to good use.

JINX: I work on a crew doing landscape gardening. Just a small group of guys, but we do some big jobs. Japanese gardens, terraced, all on different levels. My boss, the designer, he knows what the fuck he's doing. It's funny, when we start tearing up people's yards, they go crazy, "Whaddya doing?" But when we finish they love it. All the neighbors gather round to admire the work. He [the boss] divides the yard into four or five sections, and in his mind he knows where he's going with it. Two weeks ago that yard had piles of dirt six feet high, a real mess. Now it's beautiful. People hate you when you start but love you when you finish. It's a good feeling when you finish the job and you can see what the fuck you've done. It's not like other jobs. You can see what you've accomplished. It's not a skill or a trade. It's a fucking art form. Our boss, he is an artist. I'm making twelve-fifty an hour, which ain't bad. A couple of guys work under the table and then a few on the books. The boss is actually a decent guy. I work my ass off. It is fucking physical work, bull work. Digging, moving fucking stones, and your body just ain't taking this shit. Running wheelbarrows of fucking rocks and shit up hills. Every now and then you just gotta take a breather, have a cigarette. And he understands that. He'll bust your balls: "Oh, man, what the fuck, you outta shape, fucking weakling?" He'll bust your balls about it, but he ain't mistreating you, he's only doing it to bust your balls. You're being treated fairly. I mean, don't get me wrong, he's making the money, but it's not like he's out making fucking millions of dollars either. He's making his money, but he treats you fairly. I mean, he's a good fucking guy.

Before that I worked at an automotive warehouse. Started out there at eight bucks an hour. The year I left they made a profit of $365 million. They owned thirty warehouses and three hundred automotive stores in the United States. I worked there for four years, made it to ten dollars an hour, got my brother in there with me. But there was double standards, which I can't stand. You're the one busting your balls doing all the work. So I got fired from there because I told my manager to go fuck himself.

JM: What was the double standards?

What pissed me off is I had the key to open the place. When the alarm went off at night, I'd get a call to go shut the alarm off and shit like that. I mean, I was one of the best workers, but there was this girl that was working there who the assistant manager was in love with. She'd come in at nine o'clock, he'd write her in at eight o'clock. She'd leave at three thirty, he'd punch her out at five thirty. I'm getting yelled at because I'm not staying 'til six o'clock. They're not even throwing me a bone. I said, "Go fuck yourself." How can you give 110 percent for somebody who ain't giving it back to you? If I'm going to be treated fairly—like my boss now, nice guy, never had a problem with him—I'll work my ass off.

You remember the warehouse I was working in, the nut-and-bolt place? I was running that place for about five years. I was making fifteen dollars an hour there after fifteen years.

JM: And you started at, when you first went to that place?

Six-eighty. But that was a little family-owned business. I picked up on it very quick, but I had to fight for most of what I got. When I became manager, it just became too much politics. Everything was my fault. There was a lot of stress and aggravation. Plus, I had work to do at home, piecework. I'd bring home three hundred pounds of screws, big boxes, different types of screws and washers, and a bunch of bags with labels on them and sealer. I had my mother doing it, my sister, brother. You had to put five of this, six of that, put bags together, get paid so much per bag, nine cents for every bag you put together. So if you did a thousand bags, you made ninety dollars. Take-home money, under the table, no taxes. I had a digital scale to check every one with because they'd have to be 100 percent accurate. But I got sick and tired of that shit. The boss was selling the company, I was like, "Fuck it, I'm outta here, see ya."

I went to another job, doing quality control with computers, and the guy that hired me, he had a calcium buildup in his calves, so they cut his calf open, so he was out of work for a little while. He worked there for like thirty years; he was making big money. Well, they figured I could do his job after being there a month. And they fired him when he came back to work. I was heartbroken. I had tears in my eyes. He's like, "You know what? It's better you than some fucking foreigner who don't know English that's got my job. Good luck to you. Wish you the best." I was like, "No, this ain't working, I ain't staying," so I gave 'em my two-week notice.

JM: So the actual work at each place, these were mostly desk jobs, in an office.

Yeah, I can play on a computer; I got no problem working on a computer. I've done shipping, check inventory, prices, see how many we're supposed to have in stock. I can do all that. But it was repetitious. I could predict my day. Every day I woke up, I knew what I had to do. That's what I like about this job. I can go in tomorrow, figuring I gotta go do this, but my boss will turn around and go, "You're doing something different." It's not the same thing over and over again. I'm very good when it comes to basic math. I should actually—I thought about it a million times—go to become a bookkeeper or an accountant because I love working with numbers. But I can't sit behind a desk. Believe me, I know there's money to be made there, but it's just too aggravating. I like the challenge now, it's something different. In the warehouse, it's the same thing: You build a wall and knock it down. Stock coming in, depleting your stock, selling the same thing over and over again, constantly loading and unloading trucks.

JM: Any of these jobs, was there ever any benefits, health insurance?

The warehouse job, the company paid my medical insurance. I also had sick days, vacation, shit like that. The last job I had medical, had 401(k). It comes out of your check every week. So I put it into a savings account, then when I took it out they penalized me. Gee, it cost me two hundred dollars to let you hold seven hundred dollars of mine. It made no sense, but that's the way your life rolls. Now this job I got no benefits at all.

JM: Within these jobs has there been any sort of career paths, like any ways you could move up?

If I wanted to be an ass-kisser, a brown-noser, a "Yessir" man, I could've probably eventually gotten a manager job. Being a big corporation, you only got to go so far and you ain't gonna get what you really deserve, no matter what. Big companies, you're just a number. You ain't even a face, you ain't even a name. You're a number. They could give two shits about you. I found out if you work for like a ma-and-pa company, a little family-owned small business, you get treated better. The ideal person you want to work for is somebody who started out just like you did. At the bottom. Was given nothing. Worked his ass off to get where he's at. He's the one that will appreciate you busting your balls more. When you work for a little person like that, he says, "Okay, that's how I was, that was me twenty years ago, busting my ass." So he gives you more respect and takes care of you better than these other people.

JM: Any of these jobs, you ever been in a union?

No. Another job I went for was good money, working the night shift, warehousing. Only I didn't pass the fucking piss test. I'm not giving up my fucking weed, I'm sorry. I can't deal with life if I don't have my weed. When I was in the screw place my Christmas bonus was a two-pound can of pistachios, but I got a week's pay, taxed. The next job I got a candy cane with fucking ten dollars. From a big fucking corporation. If it wasn't for us little fucking peons, down there in the fucking trenches, busting our balls, guess what: You wouldn't be a millionaire. The raises you get—ten, fifteen cents a year—the cost of living is going up more than fifteen cents an hour. Come on, now. I can't even keep up with the cost of living, but I'm supposed to be happy working for you? Nah. Why are all these people millionaires? It's all about their profit, finding ways to cut corners like everybody else is.

JM: Can you imagine a world in which the bigwigs, the owners, the corporate executives are making enough, but the workers are also making a decent wage . . .

It'll never happen. It's impossible; that's a miracle.

JM: Why?

Why? Greed. Bottom line. Greed.

I've been working since I was sixteen, busting my ass on the books, having Social Security taken out every fucking week. Now you hear when I'm ready to retire there might not be no more Social Security. Hello? Where's all the money I put in there for the last forty fucking years? So now I'm going to retire at sixty-five and have nothing.

You look at it, they're cutting everything for the fucking poor. They're not trying to bridge the gap, they're just widening the gap between fucking rich and the poor. They're cutting the poor, cutting fucking Medicaid, spending more on your military budget. You got other countries that got universal health coverage. There is no health coverage. Everybody's scamming everywhere. That's why I never voted in my life and I never will. I'm not even a registered voter, thirty-eight years old and never voted once in my life.

JM: But the gap you were talking about between the rich and the poor. You don't think that voting is a way to—

What, my one vote?

JM: No, you and all the other working-class guys.

I don't need a fucking politician to be a thief taking money out of my pocket. I'm quite good at fucking blowing my own money. I don't need someone else to blow it for me. And that's basically all they are. The only thing they can agree on is to give themselves a fucking raise. Has any politician ever done anything for me? No. My father used to go vote. You know who he'd vote for? Mickey Mouse, Donald Duck, Fred Flintstone. They can talk a good game: Oh, yeah, we're here to help the poor.

I've grown up seeing people die, getting killed, beaten with bats, chains, beer bottles. That was when I was about ten years old. Harry got killed by the police. They had the riots, blew up two cars. They had a big march to City Hall, all the teenagers and everything. And from there, in the projects, in the back area was predominantly black, the white was all up front. Back then, you remember, the blacks and whites didn't hang out together. So every night would be a clash of the teenagers sitting out there drinking. There was one fight and the fight turned into a racial war. Tear gas. Chaos. Back then all the roofs were open: You could run up one hallway, run across the roof, down another hallway into someone's house; the cops would never catch you.

JM: There was nothing else underlying the racial tension, it was just . . .

Teenagers basically partying. You figure, they were busing the blacks into white communities, so there was a lot of racial tension. Now a lot of white people are bitching more about Brazilians and people coming over, because they're willing to work for less money, taking money out of our pockets. It ain't so much about blacks. Now it's about the new group of foreigners coming in who are taking the jobs, willing to work for less, bust their balls. Someone grew up in this country: "I ain't working for nothing less than ten dollars an hour." It's business. Looking at it from someone owning a company, if I can give you five dollars to do the same job I gotta give him ten to do, I'm going to give you the five dollars, ain't I? That's five more dollars every hour in my pocket. That's now where a lot of the racial tension comes from. Ain't black and white no more. I hear a lot of bitching about foreigners coming over, they'll give 'em money to get a house, but you're born in this country, right? You get nothing. That's just the way society is; you gotta take it. You get by. Try the best you can.

When you have a kid, it ain't about you no more. It's all about doing for the kid, make him better, give him more than I ever had. Try like hell. I love my son dearly, but he's just got a lot of anger in him.

JM: Where's that anger come from?

He always was fighting in school, been in every school in the city. Went from there to youth services, put him in all different programs—social services, youth services. He was in the lockup units. Finally got him a job with me. One day, he was supposed to be working, calls me, "Uh, I'm in jail." Lost the job. Shit happens. There's two lives here. I can understand what he's doing because I work my ass off, I got a roof over my head but nothing to show for it. These young kids on the street, slinging their thing, selling their drugs, they got brand-new cars, they got all the women, all the jewelry, pocket full of money. But where's that life gonna lead you? You're gonna end up dead or in jail. But a twenty-year-old kid, I can tell you my advice, but you do what you want. It sucks, it breaks my heart, but it's just the way life goes.

JM: What sort of ways did you, over the years, try to influence him?

I got him a job, I've talked to him. There was one thing I did. He was being picked on by a lot of the kids, always taking advantage of him, using him. Back then I was doing the same thing, sold my shit [drugs], I always had money, so I spoiled him, and his friends took advantage, his so-called friends, and they used to hit him. Well, one day I got tired of it and gave him the Wiffle ball bat and said, "Go downstairs and play with them. First one that fucks with you, crack 'im upside the head with it; he'll never fuck with you again." He sure as much did it. Now nobody will fuck with him. He's to the point, "Worst that can happen, they'll kill me, but I'm not going to be anybody's pansy, I'm not going to let no one shit on me no more." Growing up in the streets, especially in the projects, you gotta have some street mentality. You cannot go around being a little pansy and having somebody turn around and take everything you got or everything you earned, and then running scared from them. I don't care if you lose the battle, you stand up and fight. He ain't going to want to fight you again. Because he'd rather go pick on someone who ain't going to fight with him.

JM: It's a fine line, though, isn't it, because these same kids who at twelve, thirteen, fourteen get that reputation for never backing down . . .

Well, my kid got that now, and nowadays it ain't like when we were growing up. We'd have a fistfight; the next day we'd be sitting there having a beer. Nowadays they got guns, knives. It's nothing to pull a trigger.

JM: So for a kid in the projects, it's tough, because on the one hand he's got to stand up for himself, but as soon as they do that, then they get in that thing where their credibility, their respect, comes from being the tough one.

Right. And they can't turn back. After you put your first foot down, you cannot go back. If you put your foot down and say, "I'm not taking no more shit," and then you let someone shit on you after that, you're going to deal with your friends: "Pussy, you little faggot." It's all peer pressure.

JM: But when you take that dynamic on the streets, and then suddenly when you're in school . . .

It's a fine line. As far as schooling goes, now there are a lot of people who put their minds to school, but for a kid growing up in the projects, what are they looking at? Are they looking at you going to bust your ass to make ends meet, working eight hours a day, coming home tired as a dog, filthy and shit? Every project has their drug dealers with women, jewelry, car, living life large. To them it's an easier way out, but they don't look at the other consequences.

But then how many of them that went to school, got that great-paying job, got the steady career? I'm interested to know. Because I still hear of a lot of people out there with degrees who can't find work. Society has changed, like it does constantly. You gotta find out a field that is on the boom, that is hiring. You gotta follow the fields that society wants. If you're going to go to school, you gotta hit it at the right time in that field, then get that job before society changes, and there's an increase for another field.

It's a learning process. Being a parent is a learning experience. It's what you feel in your heart. There are things I regret, but then there are things I'm glad that I've done. You just hope you do the right thing, but if you don't, you just try to make it go the best way it can. Kids are going to make their mistakes. They're going to screw up. No one's perfect in this world.

Like I tried telling my son, I grew up in the projects, been arrested, never did time in jail. Why? Because I can read somebody. I know somebody is going to get in trouble, I'm walking away before it happens. "See ya later." You can't call me a turncoat, didn't stick up for you, cuz I wasn't there.

JM: Your younger son, how old is he?

He's twelve now. How he's taken care of, as far as the discipline and that shit goes, what goes on in his life, that's her call. Because she don't want me to do what I did with Davey. But he's going through the same things, and me knowing how it is growing up.

Becoming a teenager, now it's time he's going to try solving his own shit. I did the same thing. My brothers, my father used to tell me, "What are you doing? Why'd you do that? You watched your brothers go through it and all, and always got in trouble and got caught, but you do the same thing. What are you, stupid? Hello?" When I was a kid, even though I watched them do it and get in trouble, I had to do the same fucking thing.

There are days I say I should have stayed in school—it's not like I didn't have the intelligence or the knowledge. And there are times I say I should've done what my brother did and went right in the service. Which I didn't do. I made a choice and I lived with it. Davey was born. I had the opportunity to go in the army; I chose not to. I wanted to be around for him, and that was my choice. Things didn't turn out the way I planned, but what can I do? I can't turn the hands of time back. You gotta try to go on and make the best from this moment on. If you sit back and look at all the failures and all the things that happened wrong in your life, you might as well just go put yourself in a rubber room.

JM: What about your relationships with women? Are there things that you would have done differently or regret or . . .

I'll tell you right now: The only woman that I'd ever marry would be a woman like my mother, which I never met. The two I have had, Beth and her, love them dearly, but shit. Put it this way: could be better. Couldn't be much worse. But it's hard to walk away once children are involved. As I say, go with the punches, go with the flow. Like that, weeble, wobble, but we don't fall down.

JM: How's the child-support thing affecting people?

Uhh, well, I don't pay for him. Because on the books I'm not his dad. I been with him since he was born, but my name ain't on the birth certificate. For Michael, I paid for twenty years. Most of the time he was taken away, put in placements, so I was paying child support and going to visit him, giving him money, so I was getting a double jeopardy. I got sick of paying child support, so I stopped. Called them up, said, "Lookit, where's the money going that I'm paying?" In an escrow fund. Hell with the escrow fund. So I stopped paying, but then the IRS screwed me. So I ended up paying for twenty years. They intercepted them every year.

But then it's how you were brought up, responsibility. You have a kid, what are you gonna do? You gonna walk away or you gonna try and stay in his life, or her life? It's choices you make.

I chose to stay here, to stick around. Everyone who's done anything has got outta here, away from here. I hate to say it, but it's true.

SHORTY

All Bull Work

Shorty lives only a few blocks from Clarendon Heights, but it was difficult to discover his address. And I was in no big hurry to speak with him. We'd never related well, and if street gossip was anything to go by, Shorty was still emotionally unstable and prone to fits of violent temper. One Hallway Hanger advised against being in a room alone with Shorty. So when I rang the doorbell at the address his older brother had provided, part of me was relieved when there was no answer. But I was flying back to England the next day, so I kept ringing and knocked and called his brother's cell phone. "He's in there sleeping," I was told. "Keep making a racket. Hell, it's nearly noon; he oughta get his ass up anyway." Sure enough, the door opened, and there was Shorty, wrapped in sheets and squinting at me. "What the fuck?" I reminded him who I was and about *Ain't No Makin' It* and asked if I could come in to talk to him. "What the fuck?" he repeated but held the screen door open and led me upstairs to his tiny one-bedroom apartment. Shorty struggled up the stairs, so much so that I listened to hear his joints creaking. Shorty doesn't have much of a neck, giving the impression that his large, open face rests directly on his compact, squarish body. Shorty apologized for the mess, sank into the couch, and said he had about twenty minutes before he needed to get going. He then spent over an hour relating the details of his troubled life. His account is hardly free from self-delusion (what account is?), but Shorty was far more forthcoming than I had any right to expect.

JM: Can you tell me the sort of jobs you've had?

I've been doing roofing and carpentry. With my son's uncle. He's unbelievable, one of the highest-paid carpenters around. Knows his stuff. I've been outta work for the last year because I get spinal ulcers and separated discs. I'm going back to work with him soon, to save some money up. He calls me a lot, "When you coming back?" He knows I'm a good worker. Like a bull. But I always tell him too, "[If] I come back, I ain't fucking doing all bull work." I like doing finish work and stuff. Doing all the carting and shit like that, digging holes, pouring forms, sledge-, jack-hammering: I don't like doing that no more. Carrying shit up the forty-foot ladder nobody else can carry. "Oh, Shorty will carry it." [*laughs*] Fuck that. Killing my back. My back's gonna kill me the rest of my life. In '94 I got hurt on the job, had back surgery. I got twenty-four grand from the company I worked for and I got twenty-one grand from the government because I went on disability. I tried to go back to work, and I couldn't, so you sign up for disability, and it took them two years to approve me, and that's all retroactive. I got screwed. I had a shitty fucking lawyer. I shoulda got over a hundred grand. I fucking had two back surgeries and then I have back pain for the rest of my life; I got twenty-four grand. The owners were cool about it; they knew it was legit; it ain't like I faked it. Furniture company, I was moving furniture. They owned a bunch of stores. They were very good people. I got hurt, I went back to work, and really I couldn't do it no more, so I went and got the MRI done and all that shit. And they said a herniated disc right on my sciatic nerve. Every time I sat down or got up I was in pain. I couldn't move at all. That's why I had the surgery. And then I went back into construction, after like seven months off. And it just gets worse, carrying fucking bundles that weigh seventy-five pounds, and then rolls of tar paper and all the other shit. I put them all on both shoulders and hug a ladder like that, and fuck, that doesn't help. I already had two surgeries on it, and now they wanna give me another one. I refused it. So I go to physical therapy, get steroid shots, eat medicine. Sharp pains every day, sciatic nerve.

JM: What do you take for that?

Percoset, Oxycodone, but I'm all out. [*laughs*] I got my prescriptions in there. It's very expensive. I got insurance, but sometimes when I get the prescriptions too early, they won't fill 'em. If I need money, I'll just sell some of my medicine. When I go back to work I'll be all right.

JM: The settlement money come to you all at once?

One check came, and then about five months later another check came.

JM: So what did that feel like when you opened the mail and there's a check for—

It was already gone! All the fucking money I was borrowing. I owed like eight grand outta one and ten grand outta the other. From my family I borrowed a lotta money cuz I wasn't working. I haven't been hitting the bars or nothing. I'm a good boy, I'm out of trouble. I haven't been in a bar in like ten years. That was all I used to do when I go to bars was fight all the time.

JM: Do you manage to keep that discipline—not going into the bars?

I know if I go, I go back to prison. I got a kid now. He's twelve.

JM: I heard that. People said I'd catch you at a game in the park where he plays Little League.

He's playing in New Hampshire now. She took him up to New Hampshire. We bought a cottage, a boat, she took everything, lied to me, said she was going to give me custody of the kid, so I didn't fight her in the court. She took my kid up there this last October. I tried to commit suicide. I slit my wrists. I called 'em up to say goodbye, he [Shorty's son] got nervous, told his mother, and she came over here and called the cops. It was pretty bad. I lost a fucking lot of blood. She come up here, and beneath this couch is a puddle. I was in a coma for a day, in the hospital for a month. I was in a state, hearing voices and everything. I just snapped. And I wasn't even drinking when I did this, either. That's what everybody, my family, was asking me: "Hey, were you fucking bombed?" I drank only four beers, I think it was. She took my son. He's my life and she took him away. I was fucking devastated. I was like, "I ain't gonna see him no more, so ain't bother living." That was it.

JM: Did you get any help after that?

While I was in the hospital I seen a psychiatrist or whatever. I came out, and I'm like, "I ain't gonna go." I stopped taking the medicine, everything. They gave me some depressant pills, I didn't take none of it. I just had a bad moment in life. Get over it, move on. I only had one beer in the last ten days, I haven't been drinking at all. I haven't been going to bars.

JM: So when you do drink it will be with friends or at home.

I don't got no friends. I go over my brother's, that's about it. I don't know nobody no more. Steve, nuttin'. I talked to Steve once or twice in the last fucking two years.

JM: Why's that?

Steve does a lot of drugs. There's nobody else around. I don't get along with nobody.

JM: What about through work, you don't meet people?

I don't like 'em. They're backstabbers. One guy at work, I like him, but he drinks a lot. I try not to drink that much no more, getting old. Fuck it, I want to spend time with my son. I don't care about nobody else.

JM: Tell me about fatherhood, what it was like.

It's awesome. To see him. I wouldn't hold him at first, I was scared I was going to drop him. I wouldn't cut the cord or nothing. I was starting crying, I was walking out, I felt like I was high, it wasn't on no drugs or nothing. That was the greatest high ever in the world. He's so small, eight pounds. Plus, he's intelligent. He'll be in Harvard some day. Everything he does, he's good at. He plays the guitar, he played the piano. He's a straight-A student in school. We almost lost him four years ago. From his waist down, all the veins in his body burst, and we're like, "He's got a rash or something." She's like, "You better take him to the hospital." And I took him, they took blood, said, "Oh, boy, he's got HSP." It's named after two German doctors, they got no cure for it. If it gets worse, he starts passing blood, he'll need a kidney. He started passing blood, so that scared the shit out of us. But they give him some steroids, some other kind of medicine to fight the bacteria, and it obviously went away.

She took my son. They told me I couldn't have kids, and I had one. I changed his diapers, everything. I spent more time on him than she ever did. I got out of work before her, I'd go right home, play with him. I spent all the time with him. She leaves him up there now. She works in the city here, comes down. It's like 120 miles. She works until seven at night, he's up there alone. It's boring up there for him too. New Hampshire. She works three days a week down here, and then the other two days she works on the computer at home. Now I only get to see him like once a week, if I do get to see him. I haven't seen him since his birthday, a coupla weeks ago. I'm gonna go up this weekend and hopefully pick him up if he doesn't play his game, because he's playing up there.

He's great. I had two guys from Oklahoma State University give me their card; I lost it. Cuz I took him over to a camp in Salford and he hit forty pitches, seventy-eight miles an hour, at the age of ten years old. Thirty-six of 'em in fair territory. Camp with this guy—he played for the Dodgers and the Rockies. Promised him everything, though, Red Sox tickets. He kept breaking my son's heart, though. I says, "You made my kid cry. Don't you ever promise this kid nuttin." So yeah, scouts were coming there to look at his college students and seeing my kid playing, saying, "How old is he?" And I said, "He's ten year old." They said, "What?!" cuz he can hit.

JM: How's that make you feel?

Oh, awesome, cuz I taught him. His team last year went 17 and 0 and they lost the last game by an error. It was a bummer. Everybody in the whole city: east, west, north. When I went to his ballgame up there, what a difference. They said, "This is the greatest baseball league in the state," and they suck, all those rich kids. They can't play ball like these city kids. I want to get my kid back down here. The fucking team he's on, they suck. He's the only one that gets hits; these kids can't throw, catch, nothing. These city kids are way better.

JM: What was the atmosphere like at the game compared to down here?

It was all yuppies. All white. I just don't associate with nobody, not even his mother. Me, my brother, and my friend, I just stay in the outfield.

JM: But he appreciates you coming?

He was shocked; he couldn't believe it. I had him for like a week, and then I dropped him off. His first game was on his birthday and I showed up. He was like, "Aha, my dad." I bought him these bat gloves, gave him some money, gave him scratch tickets, bought him sneakers. The first fucking game, they stole his bat. I was fucking pissed. He's crying his eyes out. I'm like, "Don't worry, I'll buy you another one." Fucking rich kids. But he did great in the game and everything. He smacked it. It's 220 feet up there, and he's already hit one home run.

JM: So he deals with pressure pretty good with you there in the outfield. How often do you get to see him play now?

I've only saw him once, and he's played three games. I stay in the outfield because he gets nervous behind home plate.

JM: What about his hopes for the future, do you encourage that, or do you say don't get too high a hopes?

No, I encourage it. Stick with the baseball, but stick with the books too, because if not, he wants to be an engineer, an architect. He'll make it in construction if he doesn't make it in sports. Engineering or a fucking architect, like his Uncle Floyd, the guy I work for. He's named after Steve. I don't wanna taint him with my name. See the pictures there? I've got a shitload of 'em. That's my boy.

JM: He's a good-looking kid. How'd that happen? [*laughs*]

I dunno. His mother's a fox. We had a professional photographer come down last year during the All-Star Game. He made the home-run derby. His first home run was off his best friend, and it was a grand slam.

JM: How'd that make you feel?

Awesome. I was so excited, I went out and grabbed the ball. The umpire's like, "Throw the ball back." I threw ten bucks, said, "Go buy another one. You ain't getting this ball."

JM: Looking back, do you think things would have been different for you if you hadn't grown up in this particular neighborhood?

If I'd stayed in school I probably could have had a better job. I hadn'ta been drinking and taking drugs when I was younger, I would've had a better job and my own house by now. Instead of fucking being on subsidized housing and all that shit. School means a lot. I try to teach my son that now.

JM: Where do you think you would be if you stayed in school?

Probably would have fucking took up something where I don't have to be doing labor all my life. Definitely something different. Because this is hard labor, doing all that construction shit. And then when you get hurt, you're fucked. I don't know how to spell and shit like that; I can't go back and find another job, a desk job, working on a computer, shit like that. So I gotta do that for the rest of my life.

JM: I suppose if you're working under the table and you get hurt, it's like it didn't happen, no benefits, no—

Nuttin'. He wants to put me on the books, but if he does, then I lose this apartment; I'll have to pay fifteen hundred for one fucking bedroom. You shitting me? Fifteen hundred? It's unbelievable, the price that they get. Two bedrooms, twenty-two hundred. Ridiculous. That's why we bought the cottage; my plan was moving out there. We rented it for like three years every summer; it was like five-seventy-five a week to rent, and the mortgage is only five hundred dollars a month, and we ended up buying it offa her. You walk from here, out to the front of this house, and there's the beach, a private one on the lake. The cottage is awesome, right off the lake. Not even a minute, and you're right at the water.

JM: And did you have any trouble getting a mortgage?

No, everything went under her name cuz I couldn't have nothing underneath my name because of disability. I gave her six thousand, and she give four thousand, put that down. And that's how I got screwed. I did the roof over, I did the side, I jacked it up, it's like a ranch style now. Winterproofed, everything. A shower, two bedrooms, a big built-in screen porch, L-shape. A big, big dining room and parlor, all opened up. Small kitchen but it's nice. The whole thing was sinking into the ground. I tore off all the siding, tongue and groove, and I went underneath it and jacked it up. I put in new pressure-coated columns, because all the other ones were rotting. It's on wetland, so I packed down as far as I can. I put in new windows and doors. I did most of it myself. I spent a lotta my fucking money, this bitch. The women get everything. My brother lost three, four million dollars in property, he just got divorced. His wife got everything. Everything. I thought I had it bad. But like I said, I wanted my kid. I never fought her in court. I coulda won, but she said she was gonna give me my kid. She said you can have custody of your kid. In October she moved to the cottage. She was living down by the projects in her mother's house, and they wanted fourteen hundred and she was only paying three hundred dollars a month. I didn't know she was gonna move up there 'til the last minute and take my son. She does shit like that. I didn't want to fight her over the property or nothing. I paid for everything on my settlement from my back. The cottage was only worth seventy-eight grand, now it's worth a hundred and sixty-eight, all the work I did on it. And we bought a boat at some yard sale for seven fucking grand, a twenty-four-footer. We go to a yard sale, looking to buy furniture, end up coming back with a boat. She's like, "I want a boat." Drove all the way down here, I borrowed money from my mother because my check didn't come yet, and we financed that. So we gave the guy a seven thousand–dollar check off her credit card, took the boat. I couldn't believe it: cruising around, fishing, waterskiing, the kid loves it. It's awesome. Big boat, bathroom in it. Little bed downstairs. It sleeps six, twenty-four-footer.

JM: You financed it, so you're still paying on it?

Yeah, she is. Well, she claimed bankruptcy. Since the first of January, you can't claim bankruptcy no more on credit cards and shit, but she did it before the deadline. She knows, she's an accountant. That's fucked. But I don't care about the boat or the property; I'd rather have him. Let him go up there for weekends. Then the next thing I know she enrolled him in school up there. I was fucking devastated.

JM: So much of your hope would be not for yourself, but for him, and that must feel good that you care, but does he ever feel any pressure for him to succeed?

No, he's too young to think like that way. He's only twelve. He never misses school, he loves school. He said they're real rich, all the people around him. It's like a real yuppie neighborhood.

JM: You're able to go up there; there's no restraining order or anything like that?

No. I don't talk with her. She went to one game drunk; it was embarrassing. It's a two-hour drive up and a two-hour drive back. I loved it up there, too. Sucked. I'd been with her for like eleven years. Never married her or nothing. We just broke up. I told her I didn't wanna be with her no more, and she fucking screwed me. I woulda took her to court, woulda got half of everythin', because I had been with her for eleven years, and seven years is like common-law marriage. Hell, she fucking screwed me. She's a nutcase. She snaps. A yellow light will turn red, and she didn't make it through, she'll start fucking crying, swearing. I'm talking a big-time manic-depressive. Nothing goes her way, she just snaps. She starts getting violent, she'll throw things. She hit me over the head with a frying pan, the fucking phone, she tried to stab me with a steak knife. Her mother come out and she's like, "Shorty hit her." I just give her a backhand, y'know. He's crying. He used to get bummed out sometimes when I was drinking around his mother. "Dad, stop drinking." When I would fight with her. He useta yell at both of us for drinking. He's a good kid, like I said, everything he does is unbelievable, y'know? She's psychotic. She's been in and outta mental institutions. She's taking manic-depressant pills and everything, but she'll always be like that. She's been through Prozac, Zoloft, all that shit.

JM: I remember you said before that you ended up in the state psychiatric wing.

Yeah, I slit my wrists.

JM: Before that, way back.

When I burnt the cop's house down. I was smoking angel dust. They put me in a state mental hospital for nine months. A lotta fruitcakes in there. I was just there because I was high on angel dust and they said I was crazy. I went there for the psychiatric evaluation and the interviews and they kept me.

JM: Did you get any treatment? Did it help you at all?

Naw, I came out, started drinking again, getting in trouble. But I haven't been in jail since '89. Well, yeah, I was: I was broke, I went to collecting money for people and stuff, and this one guy—I knew him too, I loved his parents, they were all very bummed out at me—but I hadda to do it, five hundred bucks, y'know. He fucking ripped somebody off, told on 'em, ratted 'em out. So the guy gave me five hundred bucks, I went in the store, and I had this big wire filled with lead, and I bashed him over the head, fractured his skull, broke his elbow and everything, and I took off. I dropped that down a sewer; the cops never found that. They held me for thirty days, said I was a danger to society, set a hundred and ten thousand dollars, cash, bail. The trial went on for like a fucking year and a half, they wouldn't drop it—the judges, the DA, they wanted me so bad. My lawyer said, "You're doin' time, you're doin' telephone digits if you're found guilty for this. You extorted money; you not only extorted money, you're like a hit man, hittin' people for money." He [the victim] showed up once to court, but then a couple people talked to him. Little neighborhood store, everybody in there knew me, y'know. Just went in there and whacked the fuck. [*laughs*]

JM: What happened to him? How long was he in hospital?

Not long. I see him now, he waves, I say, "Hey, how ya doin'?" Naw, he knows. A lotta 'em out there, they know. That's why I don't go to bars; I get myself in trouble, shit like that.

JM: Did you go through a time where you were doing quite a bit of that, debt collecting, whatever?

Aw, fuckin' did about four or five of them, y'know? People that owe money to other people. They wanna get it. If you kill 'em, they ain't gonna pay you. Let 'em fucking break their leg or break their arm or something, smack 'em upside the head. Then you'll get their attention; they're scared.

JM: Did you find that hard to do? I mean, what was it like, doing that?

I didn't care. That was before I had my son. I didn't care. Now I'll think before I do something. Because, hey, if I get caught, I'm gonna lose my son. Oh, yeah, actually, it was when I had my son, when he was a little baby and he useta ask me where I was, and I useta tell him that I was working in California. That's right. I think he was like three years old. I got bailed out after thirty days but for ten grand. I came back here, started going to bars, and the first night out, I got in two fights in two different bars. That's fucked-up. My brother was pissed because if I got re-arrested he would lose the ten grand, y'know?

JM: So did he lose it?

No, they didn't catch me, and those people didn't testify. I fought one guy that I knew, this big black guy, and I kicked his ass. First of all, he come and smack me and Steve upside the head—this was earlier in the day—and I says, "Sonny, do that again, I'm tellin' you right now." Me and Steve had him in the car, dropping him off; it was pouring out. I told Steve I was definitely gonna kill him. Steve was driving; I told him to get in the front, the black guy. I had a knife ready. I was gonna stab him. I looked at Steve to get the okay, and Steve was all fucking nervous. I was the one going to kill him. You ain't gonna disrespect me, you fuckin' nigger. He's from the projects. He grew up with us. Anyway, I go back in there later that night, I'm taking a leak, and he smacks my fucking head and it hits the tile, and I said, "I told you, you fuckin' nigger," and *whack.* I fuckin' hit him, and then he tried to throw a punch, and I ducked. He hit the fucking stall, fucked up his hand, and I hit him with an uppercut, and he went down. I just kept kicking him and kicking him. He's laying in a pool of fucking piss and blood. So then I walked out, grabbed my drink, and the owner was freaking out and everybody said, "Leave, the cops are coming." So I left, went down to the other bar, and this guy fucking started saying something in Portuguese or whatever, I dunno, and he put this fucking steak knife in my face, and I knocked him out, one shot. Rescue came and got him. I had to jump outta the bar, hide in the bushes, and I could hear all the cops out there talking, saying, "It's Flanagan, it's Flanagan." He just had a fight in the Parkside, he just had a fight at the Cape. Everybody spread out, and I was like, "Aw, shit." I sat there waiting for a half hour, and I cut through Salford and went to Bromham.

I seen him again a couple days later, he has a big cast on his arm with the wires coming out of it and everything. He walked in the Cape and saw me, says, "Wait for my arm to heal." I pulled out a knife and I stuck it up under his neck, I said, "Sonny, I'll fucking harpoon you, you nigger, you ever come near me again," and that was it. I won't even carry a shank no more, because I know I'll fucking use it. But if he fucks around, I'll just knock 'im around with my hand, the big nigger. I did it once, I'll do it again. I ain't afraid of him. I'd kill that nigger.

JM: What are race relations like now?

There are a lot of blacks around here, but they don't bother me. Kids, like when I was at that age, fighting the blacks and the whites. Not me; I'm forty years old now. Ain't got time to go hanging out outside all night, fucking doing drugs. There's a lot more dope around, heroin and crack. I don't do that shit. I don't really drink that much no more. I had like one beer in the last ten days; before that I probably had like eight beers in fucking two months.

JM: Addiction has never been that big of a thing for you?

Yeah, when I was younger, mescaline and beer. I was always drinking, seven days a week. Now I don't really like the taste of beer much no more. I drink Sambuca; I drink like three, four bottles of that, and I ain't drunk, and I'm talking the big bottles, so it's like a waste of my money now. [*laughs*] Like yesterday I drank three bottles of Sambuca when I was in Bromham. Nothing. Anybody else'd be gone after that fucking first bottle, or half of it, y'know. Three pints, that's a lotta liquor.

JM: And when you see some of the other guys . . .

Steve's all fucked-up in drugs, booze. That fucker owes me big bucks. I got him a job, my boss sent him to use the truck, and he told me he had a license. He didn't have a fucking license, hit two cars, and fucking they wanted to call the cops and everything. "I'll take care of you, please, I don't wanna go to jail. I don't wanna go to jail." I had to say that I did it, cost me thirty-five hundred dollars over five years for insurance. The rates went up and I got to pay for the fucking thing, and I get the penalty on my license now. He's s'posed to pay me back; he didn't give me a fuckin' penny. I told him, "Fuck you." Ain't got no license now, though. I owe on tickets, parking tickets. Soon as I go back to working I'll pay them. Well, as soon as my credit card comes. I fill out a form, they approved me for a ten thousand–dollar credit card; I could pay the tickets with that.

JM: So your bills will be like . . .

I pay fifty-four dollars a month for this. Subsidized. It's a nice, small place. I get a check once a month, six hundred something bucks. I sell some of my pills, I get eighty dollars for one pill.

JM: And then child support, presumably . . .

Disability pays for it, direct deposit. Plus, I gained some money from my settlement. So he has money when he goes to school. But he'll get a scholarship anyways, playing ball.

JM: How have you raised him?

Go to school. Don't smoke, don't drink, none of that stuff. I talk to him about sex. I talk to him about fuckin' drugs.

JM: Looking back, as a kid, what was it like growing up in your household?

Crazy, crazy. So many people in the house. It was just chaos. Eleven of us in a three-bedroom, y'know? Bunk beds everywhere. We were always fighting; you got eight boys together. I spent more time out of the house than I did in it, just slept there, really.

My brother died three years ago. Too much drugs, smoking crack, clogged up his arteries. He was forty-two. My mom died, my brother died, and my father died a week after my brother. Three years ago. My mother died a slow death; cancer ate her all up. She was in so much pain. I felt bad for her; you think what she went through in her life, raising all of us, going through World War II, being raped at nine years old by the German soldiers and shit. My father met her over there; he was in the air force and then the navy for eighteen years. I was upset, cried. Why let her suffer like that? She just kept fighting and fighting; it took her like two years to die.

JM: What do you think the future holds for you?

Doing hard labor, spending time with my son, take it day by day.

STEVE

My Life Sucks

Steve lives with his mother in a small house four miles from Clarendon Heights. When public housing tenants are evicted under the "one strike, you're out" policy, this is where they tend to end up: in working-class suburbs with small-town social services and big-city problems. Steve wasn't home at the appointed time, so I chatted with his mom, who remembered me from the Clarendon Heights youth enrichment program. When Steve finally arrived, he was all hugs and smiles and practically bouncing off the walls with euphoric energy, almost certainly cocaine-induced. He looked fit and trim with a full head of hair and the same cocky gait I remembered. Steve had heard of my own career direction. "So you're a goddamn priest now, huh? How fucking crazy is that?" As I summarized the ecclesiological and theological differences between the Roman Catholic Church and the Church of England, Steve cut in: "I got it. You're the kind of priest that can get laid!" He might have been high but he was still sharp. When the laughter subsided I managed to get Steve to sit down on the back porch for the interview. This clearly wasn't going to be a deeply reflective conversation, but Steve was candid, sliding back and forth between bravado and despair, and easing the strain with humor.

JM: So what have you been up to? In 1991, when I talked to you last, you had been in and out of prison and—

I did Bradford in '92 to '95. A stabbing. We were drinking in the fucking bar there [next to Clarendon Heights]. Me and my brother Slick. I ended up stabbing this kid in the car, my brother's friend. I fucked him up. Ended up getting five years in Bradford for it.

JM: You served?

Thirty-six months on a five-year sentence. Had a fistfight with a cop in jail, prison guard. He fucked with me, so we got into it. [*laughs*] Got jumped by all the rest of the cops. Wanted to give me five more years but I got off that.

I ended up getting pinched again after '95; I went back from '95 to '97. Assault and battery. I didn't do it, but the fucking cops framed me and I got screwed. They took pictures of my hands and shit, right? They said my hands were all fucked-up, right? From the fucking beating I gave to her or something. But I never did. I petitioned the court for the photos, and they ended up saying we lost the pictures before the trial. I ended up back inside for two years.

I went to school in '95, right after Bradford, to be a steam fireman. Got my license, second-class fireman's license. You can operate big steam boilers, those things that run the hospitals and shit. But you need a state license to do it.

JM: Who was paying the fees and stuff?

I paid them; I got a fucking little shit job. I was roofing with my brother. I ended up going to school in the evenings, a twelve-week school. Fucking twelve hundred dollars.

JM: Whose idea was that?

My brother Curtis's. He's like, "Steve, I think it would be good for you; do something with yourself. Get back on the right track." I actually just went back again because I have to take a refresher course every five years. Thirty hours, cost fucking four hundred and eighty dollars. But when you go to get a job, Jay, I'm an ex-felon. They don't want to fucking give you nothing, man. It's hard. It's very hard. Sucks.

JM: Tell me about what jobs you've had.

I've had boiler jobs, painting jobs. Big food companies, laundry places that need the big steam dryers and shit.

JM: How would you get the jobs?

I would apply for them. But I wouldn't say that I was arrested or any of that shit. It was easy back a couple of years ago. But I just went for a fucking steam boiler job and they shot me down because they did a CHR [criminal history record] check and fucking found out I was in jail and shit, because I told 'em I wasn't. I got the job. They had me sign papers and everything. I was s'posed to go in the next day, but they were waiting for the CHR report. They're like, "See ya later." Because of my record.

JM: How did you react to that?

I was fucking pissed. But then again, I lied. Maybe if I told 'em the truth up front, I dunno what could've happened, y'know? So it's been tough. No work. Fucking selling weed here and there. I got an ounce for you right here. [*pulls a bag of marijuana from his pocket*] It's good shit, too. You gotta love it, huh, Jay? [*laughs*]

JM: Same old game. But that's dangerous now, isn't it?

What, the weed?

JM: Selling.

No, it's weed; crack and all that other shit—they'll kill you. You get fucking years for that. Pot, you can do fucking forty-nine pounds; if you get anything over fifty pounds, you get fucked. Anything under, you're fucking good to go, you get like a year to six years.

JM: And what about yourself? You still do the odd hit?

What, crack? Here and there, once in a while. What about you? [*laughs*]

JM: You were telling me about the jobs.

They sucked. Nuttin' steady-like, know what I'm sayin'?
I went to jail '92 to '95, and then '97 to '99. I've been out of jail for ten years. I went away for fucking dumb shit, fighting with my brother and stupid shit like that. But I've calmed down a lot. I don't really beef and all that shit. Remember when we were kids? We used to fucking be in fights all the time. I don't do that shit no more. I got two daughters, Shelly and Kerry, twenty and sixteen, good girls.

JM: And no kids since then? How have you managed that?

Jail. Fucking whacking off. [*laughs*] I've been lucking out. I've been getting blow jobs. [*laughs*]

JM: Was it hard, when you go from the street, messing about, then when you go into the job, how do you cope with that change? You have to be there a certain time every day.

Ya hafta; it's your livelihood. Fucking just do it. Nobody likes taking fucking orders, Jay. I know you don't, I know I don't. But you gotta sacrifice something, to get a little you gotta give a little, right?

JM: You've been hit for child support all along?

They took my licenses for the child support. If you owe back child support, they take your licenses, take your driver's license and your fireman's license. Any license you fucking procure. How the fuck do they expect you to work if they take your licenses? How you supposed to pay child support? How the fuck are you supposed to do it, collect cans or something? I didn't even know I owed the money, because I was paying the fucking broad. I didn't know the bitch was on welfare. I was paying her cash like a fucking idiot. They were taking my money, but they were also getting money from the state, double-dipping and shit.

JM: Do you ever get angry?

All the time.

JM: At who, and at what?

Everything. My life sucks. But you have to cope with it.

JM: What's the biggest problems you've had to overcome?

Financial, I'd say. I ended up getting into heroin, Jay. I got all fucked-up on it. I had everything going on in my life good. I had a Mustang, nice job—flushed it all down the toilet because I got fucked-up on heroin. My kid's mother introduced me to that shit, and she and I ended up getting real fucking sick from it.

JM: Can you describe how that started?

When I got out of jail, I ended up going back with her and she was a user. I never fucking touched the shit. Then one night I fucking tried it. I saw myself doing it every fucking other day. Then it was every fucking day. After that I ended up getting caught up in it. It just spiraled out of fucking control, fast. Fucking seriously. That was the ugliest shit I ever did, Jay. You always lying, fucking making up shit, making stories why you're not at some function. You're constantly full of shit.

JM: Did your family know about it?

Yeah, my mother, everybody knew. You're fucking a mess, y'know what I'm saying?

JM: Much more than with any other drug?

Much more. Crack, I smoked that once in a great while, every now and then, I want to get the feeling. [*laughs*]

JM: Some other guys, when their kids were first born, straightened up. But back in '91, you said, "No, I'm still a kid, really."

I still feel like a kid.

JM: Back then you had trouble with your temper and you got violent with your girlfriends.

Yeah, I feel like fucking them up sometime, but I know the consequences now, and I don't think I want to go through that jail shit. I'm fucking tired of it.

But if it happens, it happens. I don't give a fuck. I'll explode in any given minute. I used to fucking slap the shit out of my chicks. Now I just walk away and get the fuck away.

JM: How did you learn to do that?

I dunno, I just did it.

JM: Did you have any help, like all the time you were in prison, counseling or anything like that?

Nothing. Nothing at all. I don't know, I'm just sick of the consequences. You pay a fucking real fucking high price. Plus, people don't like getting slapped around, and I wouldn't want anybody slapping me around.

JM: Looking back, do you think the problems have been your problems?

I created my own fucking, shit, Jay, yes.

JM: All along the way.

All along the fucking way. Because I could have did things different.

JM: What would you do different?

Everything. I wouldn't have kids. I would fucking go to school more. I'm living with my mother, I'm fucking forty years old, and I'm practically fucking homeless. I would do a lot of shit different. I wouldn't do drugs. There's a totally different ball game, there's a life that you can have, a good fucking life. It's what you make of it. But it still ain't too late for me. I would fucking probably get into property, knowing what the fuck I know now.

JM: So did you guys have the same chances in life that other kids have?

No, probably not, because we were poor.

JM: And how were your chances different?

Well, money gets you the good schools. Money brings you power. If you're poor, when you're a kid—you were around when we were kids, you remember—it was crazy. If you're a rich kid, then you have parents and shit to fall back on, or some sort of stability. There's never been stability, that's what I fucking see.

JM: Your girls are about the same age now as when I first met you.

My daughters, I tell them. Kerry fucking tried weed, thinks she can drink, and I scared the shit out of her. I says, "That's not going to do you any good. It's not going to solve your fucking problems, it's just going to get bigger." So I talk to them as a parent. But I'm open with them, like, "This destroyed me, and this fucking did your mother in, so don't fucking go that road." My daughter wants to be a nurse, and the other one wants to be a lawyer, so I hope something happens good, y'know? They're good girls. I always encourage 'em: "Don't worry about it, something good will happen. Just hang tough. You gotta hang tough. It's all about fucking staying in the game. Something good'll come."

JM: Have there been times where you were having trouble seeing that yourself?

Every fucking day of my life.

JM: Is there anything anyone could have done back then, to make you see—

Yeah, maybe you could have took me on that canoeing trip, or to that fucking baseball game or something, like you did with my younger brother and those kids. [*laughs*] Jay, I love you, man. We fucking go way back, baby. I want a bonus for this, Jay, cuz I'm your most interesting subject, I know that. I fucking know I am. [*laughs*]

STONEY

Saved by the Drum

Stoney lives with his wife and younger brother on the top floor of a ramshackle triple-decker twenty miles from Clarendon Heights. It was wonderful to see Stoney out of prison: lean and tanned, his hair crew-cut and his torso covered with tattoos. Stoney was candid and thoughtful, and I learned for the first time how an eighth-grade prank affected his future. Stoney related how his music and his wife now keep him on an even keel, but I was acutely aware by the end of the interview how precarious his life is. Like many of the men in this study, Stoney had his driver's license revoked because of failure to make child-support payments. Yet he drives forty miles most days to care for his mother-in-law, and a single traffic incident could put him back behind bars. Of more pressing concern to Stoney is the fate of his two sons, both of whom are latter-day Hallway Hangers back in the Clarendon Heights neighborhood. Countering the inertia of social reproduction is a personal priority for Stoney, but he's philosophical about his boys' prospects and his influence on their aspirations and attainment. Both of Stoney's sons were arrested for attempted murder (they got off), and against the background of their chaotic young lives, Stoney seems settled indeed.

JM: Back in 1991 you were in Grassmoor [State Prison].

I was in for four years then, and I actually got out with no probation, no parole, no nothing. I was brand-new fresh, and I had a good girl. I had met Connie in between sentences and she stuck with me. We got a place. Still, I was back in a month. I just fell off the wagon and went kinda crazy.

JM: She must have been gutted. Armed robbery again?

A 7–Eleven. I was smoking coke and robbed the pizza shop that I was working in the night before. Took the money, smashed the register off the wall, told them that two black kids came in and took the money. The next night I ended up robbing a 7–Eleven. Just to get high. Crack—I got grabbed on that. I hit bottom so fast. I went from looking good, feeling good, pretty clean to worse than I was ever before.

JM: So how did that happen?

I dunno. I hate to blame other people, but there were other people involved. And then I started dragging other people down with me. I was just by myself for about a week before I went to jail. Just getting high, making pizza, getting paid daily. Connie was shunning me, didn't want to be around me when I was like that, moved out of that house, went to her mother's house for the last week I was out. Then she was left with the duty of going and emptying out the apartment. Pretty tough times.

They wanted to give me twenty to twenty-five. I ended up getting seven to ten and doing five years. Took parole for two years and I've been out ever since. I think it really had a lot to do with Connie. Having something to push towards. I asked her to marry me and she's like, "I'll tell you what: Why don't you stay out of jail for a year before we even talk about it?" So that gave me some incentive. We got married in '97, just passed our ninth anniversary. It's a good marriage too. She kinda saved me. The one thing about her is her brutal honesty. Didn't think I really ever wanted to get married, but when I met her it was, like, a huge step up and I was psyched. I just held on to it. [laughs] It's like that one time you go out and grab the rim and you don't want to let go. So it was like, I'm not letting go of this. I met her in 1990 when I was in prerelease making pizzas. Met her over one of the drivers' house. She had a killer job: driving a train on the subway. Now she works for an electric company. She was a union electrician for a while, but now she's not in the field; she's an estimator and a project manager. She's doing well.

JM: What jobs have you had?

I worked for my buddy's pizza shop, I worked for his brother for a couple of years at a different pizza shop, I was a laborer at a welding shop. And there was the Harley thing: Soon as I got out I started working at Harley-Davidson in the city. I went to school in Florida, needed a certificate to get a job at the dealership. So we both went down there and that's when Connie's mom had her first stroke, so I came back but I was still able to sneak into Harley and get a job. So I worked there for four years, where I met a guy who was the old drum tech for Joey Kramer from Aerosmith, and he had a band and he wanted me to help him, so he taught me all the tricks to drum-teching.

JM: What's that?

Drum tech: You set the kit up to the drummer's specifics. And while he's playing, you stand behind him and if anything falls over, any microphones you see moving or anything, you have to get right up there and take care of business. It's intense, pretty cool. The drums and the music thing just took off big-time. I've met so many people, worked big shows, hung out with bands, playing in bands. I'm kinda old. I'll be forty in July, but it's kept me out of trouble. I love to see music and kids. Music is just so positive for people. It just makes you feel good. With music, anybody can really do it if you practice hard enough. I was practicing at one point six nights a week.

I do a lot of work now taking care of her mom, who had two strokes in the last eight years. And so where Connie makes really good money, it makes more sense for me not to work and me to distribute medication, take her to doctors' appointments, do her food shopping, and stuff like that. Her mom's from the Filipino islands. We do everything. Connie burnt herself out in the first four years and did so, so much, and she just can't deal anymore. So now I do most of it so she doesn't have to. Makes everything go smoother.

JM: Have you ever thought about kids with Connie?

No. We're all set. She's not able to have them. The boys lived with us a couple times while their mom was going through hard times. She was into the heroin pretty bad and she just called me out of the blue: "Hey, can you take the kids for a few months?" "Absolutely, bring them over." Then one time they ended up staying for a year and a half.

JM: How old were they then?

Fourteen and twelve.

JM: That's not an easy age. How did you cope with that?

I was cool with it. We let them stay in their school. So my wife would drop them off in the morning on the way to work, pick them up, and they come pick me up from work. It was really hard. My kids, in and out of trouble. Same story as me. Maybe worse, starting a bit younger. They both just beat an attempted-murder charge. And my Buddy's back in jail now for fourteen months with probation violation. He'll be twenty-one in November. My son Jamie has diabetes; he's eighteen. They started like fourteen, fifteen, getting in fights, and it was the money thing with these kids. They see the money you can make selling drugs, and they're right in the middle of all of it. They still hang right there by Clarendon Heights. Buddy, my oldest, he's tough. Selling the drugs—that's why he's back in now.

JM: Having had your experiences, how did you raise them? How did you try to motivate them or encourage them? What sort of line did you take?

Connie was big on the sit-down dinner every night. Just consistency with dinner at five thirty every single night. It was tough because they only had one bedroom to share and they used to argue a lot. When it was time to bring the hammer down, she was the one. They would listen to her. They respect Connie a lot. Lead by example. Get up, go to work every day, and come home. Do my band thing. They were really happy about the band thing, even though they didn't like the music very much. They're into the hip-hop. We had family night with TV; we ended up picking South Park as a program that we could all watch. So it turned more into a friendship thing. . . .

JM: So talk to me about what the music has done for you.

I just ran with it. I just started playing the drums and just kept running with it. I'm getting better and better and better. And I'm the type of drummer that has to work for every little thing that I get. If I don't work hard I'm not going to improve, whereas some people, it's just God-given talent. Playing the drums—if you're angry, that's gonna take out a lotta frustrations. It's not like I'm sitting down knitting quilts or something. You're being aggressive. And it keeps me in shape, keeps me from getting fat. The wife loves to come to the shows, my mother comes to shows. It's been a lotta fun. And that's the attitude I try to keep. I'm not going to get discouraged if we don't get radio play, don't get a record deal, or don't put together an East Coast tour. I try not to get discouraged, just keep moving ahead. I was talking to my buddy, the one that used to tech for Aerosmith, and he told me, "You're going to get so many doors slammed in your face, man. Just keep going." Because it is a business too. I mean, we do want to make money at it.

JM: It's interesting your sons are into hip-hop. That wouldn't have happened twenty years ago.

It's changed now. The videos, the girls, the constant sex thing, the constant "get high, fuck this bitch, 'F' that." The kids are feeding into that and they kind of like that. Now the kids that are into rock are your suburban kids, Columbine-type kids, long black trench coats. You go into any inner city, you'll see every kid with his hat on sideways, his pants around his ass, two-hundred-twenty-five-dollar Nikes on, chain. Even my kids used to walk around with their whole getup worth around five hundred bucks. And they don't have a job. They're slinging drugs and hanging out on the corner and treating their girls like shit. I don't think any of these kids know how to treat their girl these days. Like Connie's brother, twenty-one years old, absolutely zero respect for women. The generations are getting worse and worse.

JM: So how's that come about, do you reckon?

I dunno. Do you blame it on parenting? Growing up in a house where your dad's in jail and your mother's got sixteen boyfriends? Because then there's the kids like Connie's brother, where their mother did everything for them, baseball, hockey, soccer, he was in everything. Still a punk. So how do you really determine? My stepbrother and stepsister went through that tough time with my dad and his girlfriend. Both of them, in the years that they would have been in trouble, shined. He tried out for the Tampa Bay Devil Rays, and my sister's a beautiful girl, and they always got top grades in school. And then after that, then they got into their drug thing. But once they started getting into it, boom, your family traits kick in, your addictive personalities. I don't know how much I really believe in any of that. Whether if I'm an alcoholic my kids are going to be alcoholics because of some kind of genetic passdown. Society too: I mean, Connie grew up right in the middle of so much stuff, she's probably seen more people killed than I could ever see in the rest of my life. Great kid, though.

JM: Did you ever get angry that you grew up in a neighborhood where there really weren't the opportunities that other kids on the other side of town enjoyed?

No. Because I got accepted to Barnes Academy, a prestigious school.

JM: Did ya? I didn't know that.

And what did I do? Two weeks later I tripped a teacher at my old elementary school and broke his nose, so they took away my scholarship. I blew that one. Never went. Got my scholarship taken away for getting suspended for injuring the teacher. I was taking clarinet, and he was passing out papers, and I kicked the case out while he was going by my desk and he fell face-first. The school got in touch with Barnes, let them know exactly what happened, and they didn't feel like I deserved it. Said that there was other kids that deserved it, that had the grades and were way less of a problem. I was a clown. My grades were always good. I was bored in school, though. I went to Dunning nine years: kindergarten through eight. It was right across the street from my house. I got suspended so many times, they used to just take me by my ear and bring me right to my mother, just walk me right over there. Wouldn't even call her. Walk me right to the house, knock on the door, and she whipped my ass for a little bit. [*laughs*] Yeah, I blew that. So that's my example.

JM: But yourself and some of the other guys that you were hanging around with, if they had been born two miles up the road . . .

Nah, I don't believe that. I still believe that if you gave ten of the guys from my neighborhood the opportunity that ten of the guys from the rich neighborhood had, 50 percent of them will still drop the ball.

JM: Yeah. I agree with that. But it's the other 50. If you had to do it all over again, what would you do different?

I would definitely have concentrated more on school and tried to run with what academic talent I did have back then because I'm sure the drugs destroyed a lot of that. I probably wouldn't have had children so young. I did have my op-portunities and I blew it. Could have someone been more disciplined with me? Probably not; my mother was pretty strict, she's pretty free with her hands. If you had taken me out of Lincoln and put me in a suburban private school, maybe things would have been different. Maybe.

JM: I guess you're having to go through the same thought process: Is there any-thing I can do with my lads to keep them from having to learn the hard way?

Yeah, I tried. I sat them down, Connie sat them down and talked. "I know, I know, Dad, I know." I try to show them by what we do, with our actions, lead by example. You can't preach at them anymore, we know that. I think everybody has to learn their own lessons in life, no matter how much you put it in their face. I mean, your grandfather's been in jail, your father's been in jail, your cousin's in jail, brother's in jail—how could you not fucking know in your head that that's the wrong path to go? But still you take that path.

JM: Did you ever have a teacher that took a particular interest in you?

Umm . . . no.

JM: Something happened when you went to high school.

Yeah, I went from a school right across the street with twenty kids in the class. If I didn't show it would be obvious, it would be a problem. Whereas in high school: Cappello's not here, Wright's not here, this one's not here—okay, on with the lesson. It didn't really matter. They had too many kids to deal with.

JM: You had no sense like, "Oh, I might be screwing myself"?

I was afraid of my mother, that was about it: "What am I gonna do if my mother finds out?" And then it got to the point where I didn't give a shit, espe-cially once I started getting high and drinking and smoking and doing pills. And it just got to the point where nothing really mattered to me.

JM: How did your mom react to all that?

She got tired of smacking me around. So we got the old "get out of the house" thing; "maybe that will straighten him out." She just got tired of it. Especially when she was going through the thing with my dad. It wasn't like there was much time after what she went through with my father, then I started coming through my stage. "So, you're just like your father," blah blah blah. Sometimes saying mean things, being angry. And then when I found the beatings don't hurt as much anymore, you put your arm up, she starts hurting her hand, she lays back, she's not hitting you as much anymore. Finally she just gave up. You can't keep on smacking around a sixteen-year-old kid. It's way too late for that.

JM: I remember back then your aspiration was to have your own pizza shop, wasn't it?

That went out the window after being in the business for a few more years. Number one: you hafta be there all the time, you can't really trust anybody after I've seen what people do, what I've done to people. And just the public servant thing: I just can't do that. If I have to say, "Can I help you?" to one more mother-fucker, I can't do it, dude. I'd rather make someone smile watching me play drums on stage then have to get them their slice of pizza. There's no progress. Everything is the same every single day. You go in, you make your fifteen salads, you make the same food. It's not like you're building a house and each day it comes together a little bit more and then when you're done you can go: Wow, nice job, y'know what I mean? Same shit every day. There's no sense of accomplishment.

JM: What about the Brothers? They were into school, they graduated and thought that they would get good jobs.

Yeah, it doesn't guarantee you it, though. Even your first four years of college doesn't guarantee you shit. When I was nineteen, working at Carlucci's and making a decent paycheck for a kid, I got a waitress that's standing over there that just did six years in college but she's making fucking twenty bucks less a week than I am. It's like four years of college doesn't get you shit anymore. There's so many qualified people out there that's got their shit on the ball, and the opportunities just aren't there. There's just not enough jobs to go around for all the people who have that drive. I feel bad for a lot of people who spend half their life in college and now they're busing tables or waitressing or whatever, working in that job that I could get just as easily with absolutely no education.

JM: And you had a skill early on that you were good at: making pizza.

Yeah, making the pizza. Saved my ass. Whenever I needed a job I could get it. The education thing, though—it's just like anything else: connections, who you know. You got an uncle that's an executive at IBM, boom, you got the qualifica-tions you need. You and fifteen other guys have the same qualifications, but you know him. So it's kind of a luck-of-the-draw thing.

JM: Frankie had connections to construction and—

City connections. He puts a lotta time in that, though; he's earned that. He stands out there in the rain with that sign when this one's running, when that one's running [for election]. He'll go down, he'll vote every time. I never voted in my entire life. Frankie's not stupid. Everybody likes him because he's a got a way about him.

JM: Frankie's gone through AA. How did you moderate?

I just try not to mess with drugs. I don't disassociate with people who do them. In the last band, a couple of guys, they'd do a line here and there. Didn't even faze me. Did I have to walk out of the room? Sometimes I'd go smoke a cigarette. But I wasn't, like, shaking, "Oh, my God, let me have some of that." I can look at things now and say, "Okay, I can do this, I can do whatever I want, but I better be willing to pay the consequences of what I do." I don't do anything that's going to put me in a situation. I mean, I try. I still drink my beer and smoke a little weed. But no pills, none of that stuff. I try not to be too stupid. Plus, Connie keeps me in line. That's a lot to do with it. She keeps me in line. I know that I'm throwing a lot out the window. Do I want to throw away my marriage and someone I've been with for sixteen years over fucking getting high? That's ridiculous. That's insanity.

I think you got to hit your own personal bottom. I did a program, a Correctional Recovery Academy. They made you go to meetings all day long, to the gym, to walk and run classes, meditation classes. Did I dig it all? No, I hated it. Do I really think that's what helped me? I don't think so. I had just had enough, dude. I just wanted the outside more, couldn't give them any more of my time.

We were in a meditation class, and it had to be forty of us sitting in a circle. And so there's this lady sitting there who's running the class, and she's got no shoes on, and she's rubbing her fingers in between her toes for the first fifteen minutes she's talking to us. So then she proceeds to take a bowl of raisins and pass them around the class and tell us to put the raisins in our mouth, but don't chew them, don't swallow them, just feel the raisin. And so everybody else put them in. I'm not doing nothing. And she's like, "Are you going to be a problem? Aren't you going to put the raisin in your mouth?" I said, "Absolutely not. You just sat there and rubbed your feet for fifteen minutes, then passed these things out." Everybody started spitting the raisins out. [*laughs*] So they pull me down. And so the cop's like, "What happened?" On minimum security the cops tend to be pretty okay. "What happened? You've been doing so good." I told him and he's like, "Fuck that. I would have said the same thing."

It's funny. In there you tend to act like a clown to make time pass by. It was like a whole crew of people doing whatever they could to laugh. At the Correctional Recovery Academy I never was really too interested. Of course my ulterior motive was to get a parole. I earned tons of good time. But as time went on, I got more into it and I ended up being the MC at the ceremonies. When I first got out, I didn't drink for almost two years.

They axed all those programs. They have truth in sentencing now. Just a straight seven to ten. You do seven and see the parole board, ten to wrap. It's way harder. It's strictly 100 percent punishment, no rehab whatsoever. The prison system—the flood is coming and the water is rising up and up and up, and they just keep trying to build the ceiling higher and higher. They're not doing anything to contain the water. No education, no rehab, no programs anymore in this state.

JM: Has it been important to you, not being back in the old neighborhood?

From first coming out of jail and not going back, probably the best move I've ever made in my life. Seems like the older crowd has done worse than us, and they're still all out there. And now you have this next generation coming up that are just totally fucking outta control. You gotta be careful with these kids these days; they'll cut your head off in a heartbeat. It's really vicious. It's worse now than it ever was.

JM: Everybody had their drug of choice back then.

Oh, yeah. I was one of the only ones that was into the downs back then.

JM: So how did that trajectory go? What did you first get into, and how did things progress?

Basically do everything and pick which one you like the best: what's cheaper, what's the best high for the money. How high can I get with this ten dollars? I can get five Valiums or I can get two Valiums and a six-pack. I never really liked uppers too much because I'm already hyper, so any upper just makes me shake and stuff. Yeah, it was definitely downs. Which made a depressing dude more depressing. Then you start feeling sorry for yourself, because those things bring out the retardedness in you. Start feeling bad, just doing stupid stuff, get yourself in trouble on purpose, just to get out of the situation you're in because you think that's the only way out.

JM: I remember when we talked the last time, in '91, you were getting that used to prison. There's a kind of security in that. Because I remember you were in for silly stuff. It was almost as though you were—

Getting in trouble on purpose? Yeah, absolutely. I would definitely admit to that. Now there's the thing hanging over me: If I commit another felony, even if it's fifteen years from now, I could be brought up on habitual offender. I could still end up doing the rest of my life in prison.

The worst thing I probably do right now is drive that car with no license, which I've been doing for a while now. But it's just out of my range to get it back. I drive Connie to work every day to Denton [thirty miles] because I need the car to take care of her mom.

JM: Why did you lose your license?

They took it for child support because all the time I was in jail my bill was pretty huge. And I can't get that cut down at all. When you go to jail you're supposed to get the court to stop the payments for the time that you're in there. And all that would take is a piece of paper in the administrative building: "Anybody with child-support issues see a caseworker." But hell, no. You know how many fucking trips they're going to have to make to the courthouse if they put that sign up? How much that's going to cost them? So they don't tell anybody. Now you can't do anything about it because you didn't go into court and have the payment stopped. So here I am in the custody of the state, and now the state's trying to hit me for child support while I'm sitting in a jail cell.

JM: So while you're in prison, this bill's racking up.

Racking up! It's up around $90,000 now. And it's only like $13,000 in back support. All the rest is interest and penalties. And they send you a bill like a phone bill, "Please pay in full." Fucking $91,800 and something. Are you shitting me? So they suspended my license. And then there's the thing of them categorizing you as a deadbeat dad. Officially, I'm a scumbag. For the last year and a half I had legal custody of Jamie, so all that money should be wiped out. What about the year and a half they stayed with Connie and I? That should be wiped out. But there's a state law that prohibits any judge from retroactively reversing a child-support order. You cannot reverse that order. It had to be stopped while I was in jail. Now it's too late.

JM: No one's ever said this is crazy? They won't look back and waive that?

We tried; they gave us a stack of papers this thick. "Fill these out and come back." Well, can you help me? "No." They discourage you. That's how screwed-up this state is with their whole child-support thing.

JM: That's a lot hanging over your head, because it's not going to go away. Presumably you can't work legally . . .

No. The last ten years, they've been . . . boring because it's a lot of sitting at home, watching TV. I do practice three nights a week. The way I'm running with the band thing is pretty important to me. I've finally progressed in something and not just did okay at it. I'm getting better as time goes on. I don't feel like I'm wasting time. I've met a lot of good people and it keeps me busy. I guess you have to excel at something to really give you that confidence. I think I've learned to think about other people more. I'm really naturally a selfish person.

JM: Most of us are. *[laughs]*

Like the stuff I do for Connie's mother, ten years ago could I have done that? Absolutely not. I would've been too worried about myself, instead of, "How can I make this work for everybody?" That comes with age.

If everything didn't happen the way it did and play out the way it did, then I wouldn't be who I am today. Which isn't a spectacular citizen or anything. But I'm okay. I'm doing good. I got a beautiful wife. I'm content, dude. I don't own my own house, not much of an apartment here; there's no insulation, so it's hell in the winter, unbelievably cold. We don't make a lot of money. But I have my necessities, and I could live like this forever. I don't need that big American Dream. It'd be nice to get it, but does it really matter to me? Naw. It really doesn't. But, hey, we got cable, we got a computer, we got VCR, DVD players, CD players, Bose speakers, nice car outside. After living in a cement block for so many years, I can live just about anywhere. I can live in a car if I had to. It wouldn't be very enjoyable, but I'd survive.

CHRIS

Back Down at the Bottom

I suspected that Chris would be back in prison, and word on the street suggested the same. But he proved difficult to locate. Eventually, an old friend of mine who worked at the county jail made some telephone calls and discovered that a "dope sick" Chris had been transferred to a jail across the state. I phoned the jail, but they refused to confirm that Chris was there. Even if he was, to arrange a visit I would need to be on his visitors' list. How long does that take? "Maybe a month." I wrote to Chris at the jail but the letter was returned with a big red stamp—RETURN TO SENDER: ID# AND UNIT REQUIRED. Frustrated, I phoned the chaplain and introduced myself as the Reverend Jay MacLeod. The chaplain said a pastoral visit could be arranged. Could I fax him a copy of my ordination certificate? The certificate was sitting in the bottom drawer of my desk on another continent. Eventually, I phoned my bishop in England, his secretary phoned the chaplain, and a pastoral visit with Chris was arranged. I put on my clergy shirt and drove fifty miles to the rural county jail. Fifteen minutes after arriving, I had bypassed the visitors' waiting room, negotiated the front desk and the security routines, and was ensconced in a lawyer's cubicle on the inside. I barely recognized Chris when he arrived in the hall with two other inmates to see their lawyers. His hair was long and permed, his face angular but not hollowed, and his frame larger and stronger than I remembered. For his part, Chris was surprised to walk in and find a priest rather than a public defender, and it took him a few moments to figure out who I was. He was happy to hear about the book and to talk, although he occasionally broke down in distress. After twenty minutes or so, we were displaced by a lawyer and another inmate, so Chris and I continued our conversation at the back of the chapel. At the end I was more pastor than researcher and fighting back tears myself.

CHRIS: I remember when you came to see me in Broadbottom. That musta been '91. I was being held for three armed robberies. I ended up gettin' five to eight for each, running concurrently. I've been inside for almost all the fifteen years since then. Another armed robbery and a lotta little shit. Christ, you should see my record. About thirty offenses. Some of it is little stuff. Like I'm being held now for possession of a hypodermic needle and a crack pipe. That's the charge: having paraphernalia. Cop picked me up for that. Same cop had searched me many times and found stuff, but this time he took me down to the station. Actually saved my life. There was a group of us in the little park by State Street, near Pilgrim House and this other shelter. This cop came across nearly every day. Anyway, this time he takes the needle and pipe off me, looks at me, and shakes his head. "Y'know what? I'm gonna give you a little holiday. You look like you need a rest." Took me down to the station. They held me in Carlisle [state prison], then shipped me way the hell down here because there was room. I hate these private facilities. The food is no worse than other places but you only get one helping. One scoop of potatoes, one ladle of gravy, half pint of milk for breakfast. They gotta make money. No gym, no weight room, no TV, nothing. I'm in here with guys on federal charges, guys from immigration, state, county. Just waste away in here together. No way to stay in shape. They only got a bar at the end of the block to do pull-ups. I look scrawny now compared to a few years ago. I was beefed up when you saw me last, yeah? I've hardly been out since then. Been locked up eleven, twelve, thirteen times. Same old shit. Just hanging on, drinking, getting high: coke, crack, heroin. Sleeping in shelters, in the park, outside churches. People come by with blankets but it gets cold out there. I spent a week in the hospital because I couldn't walk—frostbite. Now, that was a holiday. The nurses were nice, tried to get me in different programs. Once I could walk I checked myself out. I regretted that. Once you've had frostbite it gets you all the time. I tried to check in to another hospital. And another. They wouldn't take me. Wouldn't have me. I had no way to pay.

This charge now, paraphernalia. I didn't tell my mom or my sisters. I couldn't admit to them that I was using again. I told them I got in a fight, that I'm in for assault and battery. I doubt they're fooled, though. They know what time it is. Only it's much worse this time because I'm a father now. [*lowers his head into his hands and tries to collect himself*]

There was a stretch when I was doing good. I was out for eighteen months over two Christmases. I'd been through so many programs that no one would take me. I kept applying for all these programs when I was in prerelease. Finally, this Covenant House gave me a break. It was a Christian program, lots of ministers, and I got on real good with one of the counselors. This guy took a real interest in me. So I stuck with it, graduated after six months. With my record it's almost impossible to get a job. Everyone wants a CHR, and even when I level with them, admit I'm an ex-con, explain my situation, tell them I'm in a program, offer to give references, they all say, "Okay, very good; listen, we'll call you." How many times have I heard that? Well, this mobile phone company did call back. I was at Covenant House, and they gave me a chance at their little outlet in the Grassmoor Mall. You know what I'm like, Jay. I'm good with people and I'm good with my mouth. And I've gotten better at listening. I've actually got some gifts when it comes to people skills. It shows in here. I get on with the young guys, the old guys, the white guys, the black guys, the Spanish guys. They'll talk to me. I ain't no counselor but these guys will open up to me. I've got this gift. I'm good with people. Anyway, it turns out that I make a pretty good salesman. I sold a helluva lot of mobile phones. One November I had the company's best sales figures in the state. I was doing real good. Sold 144 phones with a fifty-buck commission on each on top of my wage. Do you know what it was like knocking on my mother's door and offering her a hundred dollars? All those times I'd come round begging or even stealing from her. Stopping by my sister's place and giving her fifty bucks? Not that they'd take the money. But it was a good feeling being able to offer. Going to see my baby and bringing the box of Pampers and bringing a gift for her mom. I was doing good. Word got round the mall about my sales figures. Cingular ended up asking me to manage a tiny unit they opened in the mall. I had some trouble with staff who were fucking up. So I ended up doing it all myself. The shop was open seven a.m. to ten p.m. seven days a week. I'm on the computer dealing with stock and inventory, I'm dealing with customers, dealing with deliveries. It just got to be too much. I was working solo seven days a week, fifteen hours a day. I was bone-tired but it was easier to keep it simple rather than supervise others. But then it got on top of me, and the stress built up. One day this girl Angela turned up, one of my old running buddies. She was fresh out of jail with two thousand dollars in her pocket. She gave me a thousand, and we just took off. Bought a '95 Lexus, looked brand-new. We cruised around, stayed in hotels, living it up. We were living out of the trunk of the car. My whole life was in there. Then I got pulled over for running a yellow light. She was on parole, so she tried to give a false name, but the car was registered in her name and the cop figured that out, so, bang, she was hauled back inside. I got out the next day. They offered me twenty-three hours of community service, so I said, "Fine." I still had some money, so I headed right back into the city and blew it, getting high with the old crowd. Same old crowd. It was a pretty tight downward spiral 'til I ended up in here.

JM: What tends to trigger your downward spirals? What makes you fall off the wagon?

I'm weak. It can be a simple thing, a little setback, and I end up drinking. Once I start drinking, then I want to get high: coke, heroin, whatever. Impatience too. I can't seem to stick with something for long enough. And like I said, I have trouble recovering from setbacks. I don't bounce back the way I should. So I have a few beers, and one thing leads to another and I end up in here.

I fall off the wagon in all sorts of ways. I've been to AA and NA, I've tried to look at my weaknesses, I've tried to avoid getting in situations that will be difficult for me. But I end up back down at the bottom, and it's a steep slide. It's my own fault, I know. I can't blame anyone but myself. You remember when I was a kid I was sick a lot, had these throat problems? A few years ago I finally had my tonsils out. Of course I didn't tell the doctor I was an addict, a recovering addict. He gave me OxyContin, gave me two bottles, and of course I ended up drinking it. Was s'posed to take a spoonful a day and just drank the stuff. Told the doctor that I kicked the bottle over and spilled it by accident. He prescribed another couple of bottles and that was it, I was hooked again. When I couldn't get hold of OxyContin I went back to the heroin and cocaine.

JM: Tell me about your daughter and her mom.

I met Colleen in one of the programs. I look like shit now, with this front tooth missing, but I'm not a bad-looking guy when I have my teeth in. [*takes a retainer out of his mouth, revealing that he has only two top teeth*] So when I'm out on parole and in these different programs, they're all co-ed, and I can sense the girls saying, "Okay, who's this new guy?" There's quite a few of them have fallen for me. This time it worked the other way. I fell in love with her. But I fucked up, ended up dragging her down with me. She got pregnant and I was still using. She said not to bring it in the apartment. She was five months pregnant and was completely clean. One night I came home and she was high. The baby had been lying on her right side on this nerve, and Colleen was in a lot of pain and ended up taking some stuff that I'd left behind. That was it, she was hooked again. Hazel was born about two weeks later. The drugs induced the labor after only five and a half months. She was tiny, smaller than my palm, less than four pounds. That was so hard to take, seeing this little tiny, totally innocent girl, hooked up to all these machines, all these wires going into her. She was born an addict. [*stops talking to collect himself*] She's okay now. Colleen went straight into another program. She had to or social services would've taken the baby from her. It was really hard because they would only let me visit once a month. In this program they don't want the women to have contact with men, they minimize the contact, so I only saw Colleen and Hazel once a month. That was doing my head in. I found that really hard to take. I ended up going off the deep end again. Just fucked up once again. I can't blame anyone but myself.

You don't have any idea how much it hurts when I'm walking through the park and there's a mom and dad pushing their baby on the swing set. I just have to stop and fight back the tears. I just want to cry. Sometimes I do. I want to be a good dad so bad. More than anything. I just don't know if I can. I've been on the inside so much and I've been in so long, it's so hard when I'm out. I know that sounds weird, but it's hard. I believe in my heart that Colleen, because she does love me, I believe deep down that she'll have me back. I don't know that she will but I believe that she will. I'll have to stay clean, of course, but now I've got a big incentive to put away the drink and drugs for good. Two big incentives: Colleen and Hazel. But hell, I might not get the chance. She may not take me back. I don't know what I'd do then. Do you think she'll have me back? What do you think, Jay?

JM: I think you better prepare yourself emotionally for Colleen to want to keep her distance. It's hard for two recovering addicts to be together, and she'll be thinking about what's best for the baby. I dunno. Maybe you could prove that you're serious about changing this time by staying clean for six months or something and then trying to get back together. You'd have to stay faithful, though. Does she know about this other woman, y'know, the one on the Lexus spree?

Yeah, she knows about that. But she also knows how much I care for her and Hazel.

JM: Any chance of treatment in here?

Naw. All that stuff has gone by the wayside. Money, my man. The regime in this state has changed big-time since I saw you last. This place here, they got a chain gang, just like in those old films. Plus, I don't make it easy on myself. I won't back down to a cop. I'm always getting into beefs with the cops in here, the screws. They put me in the hole but I've done enough hard time that it don't bother me that much anymore. Fuck 'em.

JM: Is there racial tension in here?

Yeah, out here in the boondocks most of the cops are white. Things heat up between us and them, and between black guys, white guys, Spanish guys. It gets rough. They useta take some care about who they put together in cells. They put any two in a cell, not like two black guys together. Now they don't care. It's black with the white, with the Spanish, whoever: First come, they're in the empty cell, that's the way it goes. It's better than Butler, though. I had to share a cell with two guys there. Cells built for one with three guys living in it. It's wild. They took out the desk where you write your letters and put in another bed. You gotta sleep one way or you keep getting your head kicked all night. Fucking joke. But you get a television in your cell there to compensate.

I've had enough of this, I can tell you. Truthfully. I'm almost forty years old, and I don't want to come back in here. If I do something I'm going away for a long, long time. Another armed robbery and it's thirty to forty years. I mean, I'm stupid, but I'm not *stupid*.

In a way I've been luckier than many. Lotta guys are dead. I'm lucky I don't have AIDS. The last test I had was eight months ago, but you never know, you never know. When I'm out there using, I'm not too cautious. Not too cautious with needles.

JM: Hazel is your only child?

Yup.

JM: So you've been responsible sexually, then.

[*laughs*] Yeah, I have. It's called jail, Jay! That's my contraceptive of choice. I've been inside, man. I've been locked up most of the fucking time. Shit.

You've seen the other guys? They're not doing too great either, huh? I'm not the only one who's fucked-up. Frankie's doing okay but the other guys—Steve,

Shorty, Stoney—I guess they're doing better than me, I hope they are anyway, but they've screwed up too.

JM: I'm going down to the South to see Slick. I think he's got his own roofing company.

Damn! You're gonna see Slick? He's on the run, right? I thought he was on the run. I hope he has done good. Slick always had that in him. I'm glad he's got out. Frankie—his faith helps him. We useta joke about it: Here comes the preacher man. I ain't laughing now. In the recovery programs they talk about how you can't do it alone. The first step is to understand that there's a power greater than yourself. I believe in God, and I think he's going to help me get through, I hope so. I hope he is. I hope there's more to life than this. At Covenant House I used to read my Bible. I only applied to that program because I'd been rejected by all the others. But when I was there it began to mean something to me. I try to read the Bible but it's easy to get bogged down.

JM: Try the Psalms. They're songs of praise but also of protest and pain. The author is just honest before God. When you talked to me back in '91, I thought of the Psalms. You were really despondent and some of the things you were saying are echoed in the Psalms.

Have the Psalms helped you?

JM: Yeah, very much. They taught me that God doesn't want me to pretend to be humble and thankful and holy if I'm actually fed up to the back teeth and need to shake my fist and shout at God in anger. The Psalms make me more honest with myself. And that's not easy to do.

You're tellin' me. So how does that work for you?

JM: If we know in our gut that God is merciful, that he accepts me just as I am, the real me, the me that's selfish and impatient and full of pride and vanity and ambition, then I don't need to deceive myself. I can face up to the real me. I can put away all the masks that I put on for other people. I can begin to deal with my sin, with my faults and failings.

In my case that's a lotta shit to deal with. [*laughs*] Fuck.

JM: I reckon God can deal with it. When Jesus was arrested and whipped and mocked and spat on, he didn't say, "Fuck you." He said, "I forgive you." The forgiveness we're talking about didn't come cheap: God suffering on the cross, reaching out to forgive you and also to give you strength.

It's hard, though. When you fuck up, you're not just screwing yourself. I see that now. I'm not just letting myself down. I'm letting down my daughter, my girlfriend, my mother, my sisters, all of 'em. My kid sister Kerry, she's been incredible. She was going to visit Hazel regularly. Kerry has been big, really big. And that counselor I was tellin' you about? That guy really was in my corner. I know now, when you get those breaks, you gotta take them. These days it's hard to catch a break if you're coming out of jail. Ain't many employers gonna take a risk on me. The phone guys cut me some slack but there ain't that many people out there these days who are going to do that for you. I've still got hopes for the future but they're pretty thin.

SLICK

Head Up High

When Steve and I finished our interview and I was saying goodbye to his mother, Steve handed me a phone. It was Slick in the South. "Why don't you come down?" Slick asked. "I'll take you fishing." A week later, there I was on Slick's twenty-four-foot boat, the Gulf of Mexico stretching out before us under a cloudless sky. Fifteen years earlier I'd gone to interview Slick in his cramped, chaotic apartment and he'd wondered how he could scrape together enough money for his son's christening. The contrast was surreal. We didn't catch many fish but the interview was productive. Slick finds success bittersweet. This is, after all, the man who'd favorably contrasted Clarendon Heights with a Sun Belt city twenty-three years earlier: "You cannot find better friends because everybody's in the same boat" (see page 36). Back on land, we stopped off at a construction site. This turned out to be Slick's new home—five thousand square feet complete with split staircase, "cathedral" living room, game room, and a walk-in closet bigger than my son's bedroom. I joined Slick's family for a late-evening meal at an Outback Steakhouse and spent the night at their "old house." With his strong, wiry frame and tanned, weather-beaten face, Slick carried himself with an air of authority in public but at home relaxed into easy banter with his kids. I was first up the next morning, but the household was far from quiet: Three television sets were blaring, Slick was crashed out on a couch in the living room, and the girls were sleeping in yesterday's clothes on a sheetless bed. It felt like a slice of Clarendon Heights in the suburban South. To be fair, the household was disrupted both by my presence and by packing for the move to the new home, and maybe my unease betrays my own middle-class sensibilities. In any case, an hour later the three children lined up at the kitchen sink to brush their teeth under parental scrutiny before heading off to school. Slick caught my eye and his grin said it all: Here is one project kid who has made it on his own terms.

JM: 1991: You were living on the other side of town.

I had two sons at the time, Brad and Tyler. Brad, I was not with his mother any longer, and Tyler was a newborn. And my grandmother was diagnosed with cancer, my mother's mother. She's the one that I always cared about the most. Things were what they were in the city, except there was an escalation of trouble: not so much doing drugs but selling them and dealing with the element that you're selling to, not the most upscale of customers. [*laughs*] I was still doin' the roofing gig, but we were in the process of moving [to a working-class suburb]. Prior to that, my brother and I went to pick up some money for a guy, my brother ends up stabbing this guy, almost killed him. Both of us got arrested for attempted murder. This was not a planned thing. This was something he just did, without any knowledge. That caused a lotta friction because, number one—you don't do something like that without telling somebody, and number two—the guy never did anything wrong to anybody to deserve that. So I'm waiting for Steve to do the right thing, which is tell the police that he had did it because there's no sense in someone that didn't have nothing to do with this going to prison. I didn't want to go back to prison because, what the fuck, I had already done a year. Anyways, waiting for Steve to do the right thing. That never materialized, so that entire year, '91 to '92, was real stressful.

JM: They charged you both?

Charged us both with attempted murder. It went all the way to trial. What happened was, roughly, when we went to trial, the victim got up and said, "Slick had absolutely nothing to do with this." That's the only reason I didn't end up going to prison for it, would've ended up doing about seven years in jail. Like Steve did. I ended up getting a three- to five-year suspended sentence for doing nothing.

That's when I realized that if I continued to stay, I'm only gonna continue to get in more trouble. Like I said, the violence, it didn't seem like it was decreasing, it was increasing. In severity.

JM: What was causing that, that increase?

You're not a young kid no more. Now you're an adult, doing adult things. I was never really much into guns, but guns were there, drugs were there, more serious consequences for what you're doing. I was getting into more and more fights. Two guys pulled knives on me in bars. I kicked the shit out of both of them. I mean, I beat them severely, one of them to within a few inches of his life.

JM: So what was going on with that? Why was this happening?

There was always a good reason at the time. [*laughs*] Seriously, I was always provoked. It wasn't always strictly self-defense, but it wasn't a situation you could walk away from and hold your head up high. I felt like I had to fight. Once I was just going to pick up Denise and my mother-in-law, for chrissakes. It was like two in the morning and I walk up and this guy says, "Is this him?" And he bust a bottle in my face. See this scar over my eye? That's where he hit me. We fought for like a full fucking hour, right in the street; it took the fucking cop ages to come. I was on my knees but the other guy was laid out flat. The cops said, "What happened here, Slick?" I says, "I think he fell over, and if you'll excuse me, it's late and I need to get my mother-in-law home." Denise and her mom got pretty good at applying the old butterfly stitches.

I had a guy come up wanting to stab me. He didn't do too well. I beat the shit out of that guy. And I said, "Fuck it, I'll tell you what, I'm ready, I'm getting out; my next chance, I'm outta here."

When I moved, I got a job at a roofing company. My grandmother had just passed away. The roofing company says, "Listen, we gotta go down south; this is right after Hurricane Andrew. We're going down to the Sun Belt, you wanna go?" I said, "Well shit, it's already November, and I know everybody's gonna get laid off up here." I said, "Yeah." So I told my wife, "I'm going down south to work." When I was down there, that's when I made the decision. I called her up and I says, "Listen, when I come back up for my sister's wedding, have the house packed. We're moving." That's what I did. Moved.

JM: Was it a tough decision or was it easy?

It was an easy decision to make; it was a tough decision to stay away, from going back. It wasn't easy, because down here you don't know anybody, you're leaving your entire family, you're leaving the people that you grew up with, you're not so much of a big fish anymore. A lot of adjustments.

I always had the belief, though, when I was a kid, and I think I got this from my grandmother, that if you work hard at something, good things will happen outta it. Good things will transpire for you. And I never lost that, even though when I was in the projects, I swayed from it a lot, but it always was something that stuck in my head. Always.

Once we got down here it was a hard adjustment. You gotta remember, you're a person from an area that requires you to be on the offensive a lot, and then when you're down here with normal people it's almost like you're an animal out of the cage. It's a hard adjustment to make. It's not easy. I couldn't believe that people would wave "hi" to ya, that don't even know ya. "Hey, how you doing?" I thought they were giving me the finger when I first got down here. I turned my car around, "What? Oh, no, just waving, Hi." [*laughs*] I couldn't believe how nice people treat you. It's not that they're trying to suck you into something, they're just genuinely being nice.

It was a really, really big adjustment. Shit, I rented my first house down here, right when I got here, and I was shocked that you can rent such a nice house; it had bedrooms and a living room and a dining room and all this shit, had a pool. It was a big swing of things for me.

When I first came down, you miss the action of being back home because everything can change in a second. Everything is so quick-paced.

When you sit back and you've got time to think, you look back on what you did when you were a kid, going from adolescence into a young man, and you think, I shouldn'ta let my surroundings interfere with my goals. I shoulda used my head more than for just trying to be a tough guy. I should've went against that, been strong enough to say, "No, this is what I'm gonna do. I'm gonna turn around this way, instead of getting in so much trouble." Thirty-two years of your life, you're that person. It's difficult.

I've made a lot of really, really great, great friends down here and everything. They ask about your background; I explain to them, I make no apologies for my background, for anything that I've done. I've done things that I'm not proud of. But I'm definitely not ashamed. I never did anything wrong to kids. I never violated women in any way. I did what I did, and whatever crimes I committed, I paid for one way or the other. I'm forty years old now, and I'm just happy that I left there and I'm alive. Because when I was a kid, I didn't think I'd live past thirty. That's a fact.

JM: Why was that back then, even for someone like yourself?

Because of the way that we lived. You lived dangerously, the element of people you're around, you being part of it, you're into full survival mode no matter what you're doing. Whatever you hafta do, you'll do. And whether it means hurting someone physically, to the point where it's either you die or they die, your mind is to not be the one that's dead.

I tried not to let those people influence what I did, ever. That's why I spent so much time trying to get out of there, by going in the marines, moving down here. I always knew I didn't want to stay there. It was just a matter of "how the hell am I going to get out of here?"

JM: How did your family react to the news when you said, "Get the house packed, we're coming down here"?

My son was only fourteen months old, so he didn't have really much to say about it at all. [*laughs*] My wife didn't wanna leave but she knew that in order for us to be a family and to have the right things for him and whatever other kids we had, we had to leave. We just had to. We weren't in trouble with the law at that time. It was just you're still right in that environment, and we both knew that we just had to get the hell away from it. Or, as your research is showing you, prospects wouldn't have been looking good. I know for a fact that I probably would be either dead or in jail if I had stayed.

The kids in this area have all these great advantages, they're living at the Gulf of Mexico, they're in a suburban setting, most of them in two-parent households, and you see the kids screwing up, their versions. They get into burglary, robbery, drugs, and I just don't understand why they would take that avenue when there's no need for it here. This is suburbia. Everybody's in a pretty nice place; even the shitholes are nice. [*laughs*] It's not easy to be able to tell these kids something. I'm involved with the football and cheerleaders association, we got like 250 young people involved. I'm actually the chairman, and I try to tell the kids but it's hard because they don't know that part of me.

JM: Comparing what it's like here for kids growing up and what it was like back in Clarendon Heights, what are the factors that—

Factors why we did what we did? The single biggest factor, in my opinion, honestly? Parental figures in the household. Almost everybody that I hung around with, probably 90 percent of us came from single-parent households. And that's basically fathers not accepting responsibility, mothers settling to put a roof over the kids' heads, settling for the projects. Nobody when they move to the projects thinks it's going to be a lifetime thing. They all say, "Yeah, we're only gonna be here a year, we're gonna be here six months until we get straightened out," and blah, blah, blah. And then they fall into a rut. There's nobody to guide anybody. It's basically a guideless place. When I'm talking to my son, I find myself thinking, "I wish when I was fourteen years old somebody took the time to talk to me; maybe I wouldn't have chosen this path to go down." That's the single biggest thing.

The second biggest thing is, as you get older in that environment and the repercussions from your choices become stronger, penalties become more severe, such as going to prison. At some point you need to take a look at yourself in the mirror and say, "What do I actually want to do? I've already lost my entire youth to this shit. What type of person am I going to be when I'm forty years old? Do I want to continue this?" And in order to not continue it, they need to get out of it, and a lot of them don't want to get out of it. Even though they're very tough guys, mentally strong, they're really not because they're staying there. Everybody has a choice. Everybody can get a hundred dollars, get on a fucking bus, get the hell out of there, know what I'm saying?

If you're away from there, then that's half the battle. Next thing is to stay away from there. When you're trying to be a regular citizen and you can't make your electric bill, you can't make your water bill or whatever, that don't mean you run back home. You gotta deal with it, boom, take the pain. It's real tough; it's tougher being a regular person, paying your bills, feeding your kids, accepting responsibilities, getting up at five in the morning, going to work every day, climbing these roofs, staying out in this hot sun, than it is to be a fuckup. Anybody can go out there and sell drugs. That's the easy part. Hard part is making your bills, making sure your kids eat. That is no joke. It's still no joke. Got to accept responsibilities, and that will break the cycle of it all.

JM: What about addiction?

I wasn't addicted to anything. I never let drugs really take control of me. [*a long pause*] Well, no, it was a problem because, I look back on it, all the trouble I got into, it started with drinking. When I got into a lotta trouble, it's because I was out drinking. But you're drinking down there to forget things, to get away from reality. Drinking or drugging. But like I said, you better know when the party is fucking over. You gotta take stock in yourself and say, "I'm thirty-five years old; I'm living with my mother. Maybe I'm doing something wrong here." I mean, you gotta be honest with yourself.

But when you're in that environment, there is no relaxing. Your relaxation is getting beer, getting drugs—that's the relaxing part. Like I said, you're on the offensive all the time. You're not on the defensive. Offensive front all the time, you never know what's coming at you at any point during the day or night. That's just a fact. You can't just say, "Hey, fuck it. I'm going down to the river to kick back in the sun." You don't appreciate those things. You don't appreciate the little things like that. You don't know you can take the bus from the projects all the way out to the beach for a dollar.

Getting high was our recreation. We were fourteen-year-old kids living as adults. None of us had to be home at a certain time, predominantly. Some of us were questioned when we got home, yeah. We didn't have to answer to anybody. There was no keeper.

JM: What about your mom?

She tried until I was like fourteen years old. Like I said, a one-parent household—how much authority do you think a woman who is five foot three inches high has over a boy, a guy, a young guy that wants to do what he wants to do? Absolutely none. There's nobody to tell you, "Hey, you can't stay out until one o'clock in the morning at fourteen years old."

JM: There was no teacher that took an interest in you?

Not that I'm aware of. If they took an interest, they didn't tell me much about it. Prior to the projects I was in a school called City Latin, which is one of the premier schools in the country. To get in there, you enter into a test program. Well, I got into that school, did a year in that school, and my mother decided to move to the projects [in a neighboring city]. I used to get up at five thirty in the morning, get myself dressed, feed myself breakfast, get on the bus all the way to City Latin, get to school by seven thirty, come back home. Until they noticed that I was starting to get tired. "What's the matter?" I said, "Well, where I moved—" They said, "Where'd you move to?" When I told them, they said, "We have to charge you an admission because you're out of the area." Obviously, my mother couldn't afford it, it was a heavy number back then, maybe two thousand dollars. Anyway, she couldn't afford it, so I went from there to Lincoln High, and that's when my change came about, when I was thirteen years old.

When I went to the projects, then Lincoln High, I was still highly intelligent, but no big brothers, no father figure, no uncles, no nothing in that project. I was a young, skinny, smart kid in the projects; I wasn't getting too much respect, y'know what I'm sayin'? [*chuckles*] I had to make a big decision, because I had younger brothers and sisters: "Am I gonna get my ass kicked every day," which is what was happening, or was I gonna do what I gotta do, so that way this won't happen to them? And that's what I chose to do.

JM: Why did your mom feel the need to move?

I don't know why; you'll have to ask her that. Never got a good answer. Alls I was told was, "Unpack those boxes; we're only going to be here for about six months to a year. Living close to your grandmother, so we can help her out."

JM: There was no man in the house even if it wasn't your dad?

At that time my mother was going out, bringing home strange guys. It was a terrible existence.

JM: Did you see your father at all?

When I was like eight years old, and I saw him once when I was thirteen or fourteen. And then I haven't seen him since. Shit. But in the last three years my wife actually tracked him down for me on the Internet. We had a friend in the Registry; she says he moved to Las Vegas. She found thirteen Richard Millars in Las Vegas. She said, "One of them gotta be him." About the seventh call, some guy answers the phone, and I know it's my father's voice. "Yeah," I said. "Is Ricky there?" He says, "Yeah. Who's this?" I says, "Ricky Millar." He goes, "All right, wiseass, enough with this." I said, "Oh, you never thought you'd get this fucking phone call?" He says, "Who's this?" I said, "Well, let me take you back a few years, about twenty-five years. You left, you never came back, you left us in the fucking projects. Now you remember who I am?" And there was dead silence for about—it seemed like an eternity—but it was only like a minute. And he goes, "Listen, I left." I said, "Yeah, you did." He says, "I had to leave." I said, "I understand you had to leave. You had to leave. You didn't have to leave us, though. Four fucking kids in that environment." He tried to say something negative about my mother, and I said, "My mother's got her problems, but you know what, she coulda left too, but she fucking stayed. For all her craziness, she did stay." So anyways, I let him know, I said, "Listen, I'm not trying to bother you for anything, I don't need anything from you, I just wanted to see if you were alive or dead, obviously you're alive. So here's my phone number. If you ever feel like calling me, give me a call." It was a pretty quick conversation, lasted about five minutes. And he called about two weeks later. My wife calls me at work, "You gotta get home, you gotta get home." I says, "For what?" She says, "Your father called. He wants to talk to you." So after the second conversation—I'll be 100 percent honest with you, Jay, that's the second conversation I had with that man—it felt like ten thousand pounds had been lifted from my shoulders. I mean, instantaneously, gone. Like a lot of aggression, a lot of, a lot of shit just left me that day. Anger, stuff that I had for one reason or another in me for all those years, just completely left my body. It was odd. It was like instantaneously. He didn't say anything fucking profound, he didn't say, "I'm going to send you a million dollars," or nothing like that, and he didn't say anything that I really particularly cared to hear. It was just the fact that I had talked to him in a civil tone, and I just felt like everything—honest to God, I just felt like a whole load of shit had flown off my shoulders, and it's remained that way ever since.

JM: How widespread was domestic violence in the homes of the guys in the book?

Are you kidding me, man? It was epidemic. Ninety percent of those guys were dealing with that. It sucked, I can tell you. And it's strange what it does to you, seeing that as a kid. You'd think that you'd be like, "Wow, I'm never gonna treat someone like that, I'm never gonna be violent with a girl, I'm never gonna dominate someone." But that ain't the way it works. No, instead you end up thinking, "I'm going to stay in control of my girl, I'm gonna be in charge, on top, do whatever it takes to dominate." You say to yourself, "I ain't gonna take any shit from my woman." It's fucked-up. Then in your own life you eventually realize, man, you can't treat your girl that way, that these are human beings; these are human beings with needs and feelings just like you.

Growing up in a household where it's chaos most of the time is tough. It's bad when your dad beats your mom. But it's really fucked-up when you don't even the know the guy that's just hit your mom in the next room. And this same motherfucker is telling you two days later that he wants to adopt you. "Yeah, right, buddy, you fuckin' prick. Who the fuck are you, you fucked-up piece of shit?" So yeah, domestic violence took its toll and that was something a lot of us were dealing with. Either seeing it or getting the shit slapped out of us ourselves.

I've been blessed with my wife, my kids, a good family. Lemme tell you the hardest thing that ever happened in my life, Jay. We hadn't been down here for long, and my wife, Denise, was seven months pregnant, and I took her out to dinner, and she went into the restroom and had what they call spotting. So I took her to the hospital and the doctor comes out and says, "I've got some really bad news for you; your baby's dead." I was like, "What the fuck? What do you mean my baby's dead?" I was devastated. And of course she was just beside herself. And she had to go through labor, she had to push and everything, and the baby's dead. Denise was a wreck and so I'm getting her in the car to take her home, and these fucking security guys come chasing after me, saying I can't leave, there's stuff we've got to attend to. Denise's in no state to attend to anything, so I promised these guys I'd come back. So I get Denise home and into bed, then I went back to that fucking hospital. It's the hardest thing I ever did. I held the baby, I named the baby, I buried the baby. I called her Angel, and that's why I've got this tattoo. I've been through some shit in my life, but that was the hardest thing I ever had to do.

JM: Tell me a little about your approach to raising your children.

Tyler, I try to tell him to grab the opportunity, be motivated a little bit, you know? I'm very short with him sometimes because I feel like he takes his life for granted. I don't know if it's jealousy or what, but I find that he doesn't try to do more with what he's been blessed with. But I can tell you this: He's fourteen going on fifteen, and he has not touched the fucking drugs. That's not to say there hasn't been challenges out there already. But I can honestly say that he's pretty much a good kid. He's good with his sisters and everything. He's an average kid in school and that's something that him and I have issues where I'd like to see him doing better, but he's always willing to try, which is a good thing. That's one thing I really admire about him. He's not intimidated, he's not afraid to try anything, which is a really good quality to have. I try to talk to him every day as a dad. There's temptations out there, and don't be afraid to talk to me about it. And then you also gotta know when to cool it, give them a little slack to make his mistakes. I just don't want him to make the mistakes I made. Because then I would consider myself a failure as a father. There are two people in his life that deeply care about him, that love him to bits. But right now he's entering that last phase of boyhood going into teenagerville, full-blown. He plays high school football, he's done some boxing. He gets into his troubles in the school, he's had his fights, like every boy does. And when he likes to test the waters to go over the edge, when I see him going to the dark side a little bit, I crack down on him a little.

And my little girls, they're cute, absolutely gorgeous; they're great. Nine and eight years old, they're both straight-A students in school. I tell you something, I love them. The way I raise my son, I try to tell him to treat everybody with respect, everyone, especially women. Because what you give is what you'll get. In the long run, that's true. As far as my own daughters, let me put it to you this way. Nobody will be treating my daughters the way I treated others. Because if they do, that little project devil is going to come out. And that's just how it's going to be.

JM: Tell me about your work down here, how one thing led to another and you worked your way up.

I was doing the roofing down here. I had done it back home, so I kept doing it down here. I built swimming pools for a little while through my wife's father. But I was working for this big roofing outfit for about three years. And one day I came home, and she said, "What are you doing home so early?" I said, "I quit." She says, "What do you mean, you quit?" I said, "I can't work for anybody anymore. I can't do it." I says, "I'm all done. I'll either do it for myself or I don't fucking work at all." That was in 1995, eleven years ago. And ever since then, I've never worked for anybody.

JM: What prompted that?

It was right around Christmastime. I was in charge of a little crew, and I was always good at marketing, selling, making extra money for the company. I had gotten all this extra work to keep my guys going through the holidays, nobody gets laid off, everybody's getting fifty or sixty hours of work, which is good. So we had a meeting in the office with a couple of the other guys that ran crews and my boss says, "Ricky, what we're going to do is give them some of the jobs that you got, so that everybody will average forty hours." I said, "What the fuck does that do for me and my guys?" I said, "Fuck that. I'm the guy that busted my balls to get the extra money for this company. You promised me a certain thing, and you're saying no to that, and I'm telling you, 'Go fuck yourself.' I'm done. Have my fucking check ready in two days." I left. They called me up, "We don't want you to go; we'll give you more money." I said, "It ain't about that. It's about the fucking principle of it. What am I going to tell these guys now? They're expecting sixty hours; Christmas is coming."

JM: Was it tough setting out on your own?

No, actually, right after this I went down to see my wife's family for a week, and I'm sitting on the beach reading the newspaper, and I saw an ad in the paper and got in touch with this guy who was looking for his own roofing guy to do some apartments that he owned. I answered an ad in the newspaper, and I made like forty thousand dollars in four months. I did all the work all by myself without a truck, without anything. Did it out of a sports car, swear to God. I would order all the materials from roofing supply companies, they would deliver 'em up to the roof, and I did it all, all by myself. Ever since then, I would sell the jobs, set the jobs up, complete the job, clean the job up, get more jobs.

Now I have guys working for me, but we're goin' through a drought here right now in this area. There's not a lot of roofing work around. I gotta go farther south; that's where all the work is. I try to give anybody a chance who wants a fucking job. They're working with me, they gotta work hard, though. I'm extremely hands-on. I know all the shortcuts, what you're trying to do, how you're trying to smooth over something you've fucked up.

JM: How do you get on with the Mexican workers?

I don't hire them.

JM: Why's that?

Number one: I don't like 'em. Number two: They're taking away from people who pay taxes in this country. There's no unions or nothing down here. This is a non-union, right-to-work state. So they got guys down here in Florida, they get up on a roof, nine dollars an hour now. You got a guy who's trying to feed his family, if these other contractors are hiring Mexicans, all of them on seven dollars, eight dollars an hour, how you gonna feed your family?

I try to pay everybody good; I always have. I've been on the other side, right? Some of them appreciate it, some of them don't. Pay well and you should be able to get better work out of them, but that is not necessarily true, though. [*laughs*] You always got guys that are bitching, they want more money for less work. Y'know, that's the nature of the beast. One time I hired a crew, I useta have to wake them up at the fucking hotel rooms, right? One of them pulled out a knife on me. This was about four years ago. White guy, redneck. Pulled out this knife, and I says, "Well, here's the thing, my friend: Now that you got it out, I hope you're intent on fucking using it, because I'm going to beat your fucking ass." He ran like a motherfucker. [*laughs*] Like I tell everybody, I only live here; I'm not from here. So you always have that little edge every once in a while that comes out of you, even if you're not still there.

JM: Is that a good thing?

Sometimes. It just comes out, part of your built-in personality. Sometimes it just comes out. It's just part of who I am.

JM: Tell me about the progression of jobs you had since you came down here.

Tell you what, I'll be honest with you: When I got out of the marines, one guy gave me a job, an Irish guy. I didn't know him; he didn't have to give me a job or nothing. He gave me a job. Taught me all about this roofing shit. I worked with him for four or five years. I learned everything I know from him. Roofing is a tough job, but I owe everything I have to him. And I called him up, about three weeks ago, I got his phone number. He's a real nice guy. I said, "I just wanted to let you know something." He said, "What's that?" I said, "I've been trying to call you for years." He got divorced or whatever, changed his numbers. I called him up to say thank you for taking the interest in me when I was younger, to show me some shit. I've been down to St. Thomas doing this roofing shit, Puerto Rico, all over the country. So he said, "Well, Ricky, you've always been a hard worker." So it was nice to be able to say thank you to somebody who took some time for me.

JM: But when you first came down here . . .

Just applied for jobs. I was making nine dollars and fifty cents an hour when I first got down here. And I'll tell you what, I'll be honest with you: Anything that I've done, that I've accumulated—boats, houses, trucks—my wife has lots to do with that. She can see a goal and have the visualization towards how to achieve it. I don't have that vision. I can get there financially because I can provide, but I can't look at a piece of property or a house and say, "I can do this to it and it's going to look beautiful." She's very good at that. Early on, she saw something, she says, in me that I didn't really truly see in myself, that I could do things, accomplish certain things. I never knew I could. And she pushes me. In the new house, I'm the type of guy to have a counter, but for her it's got to be a granite counter. Sometimes she pushes too hard and too high, but she's good that way. She's a great mom, very good with the kids.

Denise has a good eye for real estate. It's not that tough to make a few bucks with property, buying and selling. Look for a plot of land with water nearby, at least a coupla acres. Get on the computer, get online, and do some research. See what someone paid for a property—maybe two thousand bucks twenty years ago, so you offer them forty thousand, and believe me, they are tempted. I bought one piece of land off a guy for forty thousand dollars, put a sign up, sold it for fifty-seven grand a few days later. We've done a couple of those deals.

JM: When you're on your own roofing, what would a typical day be like?

Get up at six in the morning, up on the roof at seven. Soak through all your clothes by eight thirty with the sweat because of the humidity down here. Change into another set of clothes. I would bring three sets of clothes a day. It's extremely physical. You're ripping part of the roof off, you're sweeping it up, patching it in, water testing, make sure it's not leaking before you go on to the next section of the building. It's a very physically demanding job. And when you're doing it by yourself it can be very mentally challenging. You got to be disciplined enough to stay up on the roof to work. Mental discipline to stay up there when it's hot. Sometimes I would work twelve hours a day. Work through lunch, all sorts of crazy shit. And then when you got paid it was like, "Wow. This working probably ain't a bad deal." [*laughs*] If you can keep it going. There's serious competition: sixty-five roofing companies in this area alone. We're all competing for the same stuff. I do good work and most of the jobs that come to me are word of mouth, probably 80 percent of my work. I prefer repair work. I'm doing a job right now, I'll finish it tomorrow after you take off. I'll finish it myself, and that'll be two thousand dollars just in a few days' work. Not net: two thousand profit. Materials only cost about 250 bucks. That's why I like to do repair work better than full roofs; repairs have way higher profit margin. It takes its toll, though. Both of my knees are gone. My shoulders are bad. I can't move from time to time, feels like I got bones rubbing on bones.

Going back to the projects, another fucked-up thing is the guilt. After you leave the projects and start your life over, you carry around a sense of guilt for any success that you've achieved. Like, here we are out fishing, relaxing in the sunshine in the Gulf of Mexico, and meantime your friends, your brother, all those guys from the projects, you know that they're still messed-up. You are successful but you feel guilty. It's a bit like what they call survivor's guilt, I guess. You're the one that got out. But you left people behind. They tell me I'm doing the right thing, all the guys back home, that they're happy for me, but you still feel bad.

Clarendon Heights—there's too many people who look at that neighborhood and think these people are fucking losers. You know what they are?

They're people that don't believe they have futures when they are entitled to have one. Okay, they're people who made bad choices; they had nobody teach them how to make the right choice whether you're black, you're white, you're Puerto Rican, it doesn't matter.

That's one thing I feel bad about, the way we treated Chris and Boo-Boo in our little crowd, and how we fucked with Mokey and all them. They weren't bad kids, and we might've been friends if the circumstances had been different. But the whole black/white thing was so big back then, and it felt like our neighborhood was just being taken over, which it has. The city was so polarized—still is, I guess. It's just one more thing that we accepted growing up, them and us. It's not something I'm proud of.

Back home, you're aggressive. Always on the offensive. It's stressful. Life feels like a constant battle. But the bonds that you form with people, those bonds were so strong. So, yeah, I do feel a sense of guilt. We were always there for each other. Don't get me wrong: I've met great people down here in the nine or ten years that I've known 'em. Y'know, I run the police association's football and cheerleading program. But there's not the same bond as with kids I grew up with. I still feel like an outsider here looking in.

The day I went home was the worst fucking day of my life. It was so depressing, everybody still strung-out. You got generations, fathers, grandfathers, and their kids and their grandkids that are fucked-up. Fucked-up on heroin and fucked-up on everything else. The cycle is not ending, and that's what's saddening. It's terrible. They gotta trust in themselves to make that break. Everybody says, "I want a house, I want a family," but they don't know how to get there. These are fucking people that got perfect credit scores, and they don't know how to get a loan. They don't know the importance of credit, they don't know how to do this shit, stuff that a normal person that goes to college takes for fucking granted, you understand? It's fucking—it's so pathetically ridiculous, it gets you angry

JM: Because . . .

Just the waste, man. You're looking at people you know yourself; these are not stupid people. Yet it's like they wasted their entire lives, myself included when I was young. Nobody grows up in there and says, "Hey, I want to be a junkie," or "I want to be a fuckin' jailbird," or "I want to be a murderer," or "I want to be a rapist," or "I want to be a dick-sucker." We all grow up saying, "I hope I don't end up like that guy, that guy in the hallway, that guy in the projects, that guy who's fucked-up every day." But as you grow older, well: "That guy's pretty cool, he just got out of jail, that guy's a gangster, watch out for him, you gotta respect him." Your role models are different. That's what's actually terrible. It's fucking pathetic, man. Now some of those guys at home are so fucked-up on drugs they ain't never coming out of it, never. Some of these people you talked to, this will be the last time in their lives you will talk to them, because within two, three years, I'm sure some of them will be dead. And we're not talking about elderly people, we are talking about people that are forty fucking years old.

It's fucked-up because you know that they can do it, if they put their mind to it, they marshal their resources, try to make a decent living. It's just really sad. When I went home that time—and I'm not a very emotional guy—but when I saw my friends so fucked-up, it was terrible. Guys hanging on the same fucking corner, guys without a home, guys without teeth.

JM: To what extent are they, the individuals, responsible for what happens to them and to what extent is it the society and the opportunities available to them?

You can blame society only so much. You gotta fucking take responsibility for yourself. Okay, in the projects, no question, you're dealt a shit hand. But you still gotta make it work somehow. I mean, do you blame your mother for picking the wrong guy to marry? Do you blame your father for marrying a woman who has no concept on how to raise kids? Do you blame your grandparents for moving here? I mean, you gonna blame the kids you were growing up with, the older guys you were lookin' up to that were fucking people up, doin' crazy shit? I mean, blame can be endless. C'mon, you're fuckin' forty years old, it's time to take some responsibility *yourself.*

In the end everybody is responsible for themselves. But in this particular area we're talking about, you've got two of the most major, highly influential universities in the entire world, right? None of those universities have ever delved into that surrounding community and really tried to help, give the people hope, give them education, take an interest in them. They'll take interest in the people that got money. But those motherfuckers don't need the help. It's those people that are poor that need the help.

JM: When you meet people who have never worked a tough job and don't have as much drive and guts and smarts as some of those people back in Clarendon Heights, and these corporate executives are making five hundred thousand dollars a year, does that ever get to you?

No, not now. Because I make more money than corporate executives, legally. I make a good amount of money. This boat isn't free. The house I'm having built ain't fucking free. Nobody gave me anything. This is not on loan from anybody, you understand? When they see me in my work clothes and I look like this, don't judge me from what I look like, motherfucker, because I got just as much if not more than you now. See, we're equal. It may not look it, but we are.

JM: Are you equal in their eyes?

Maybe, maybe not. I don't give a fuck how they feel. I know where I'm at, I know where I came from, and I know where I'm going. And I could lose it all tomorrow, all of it, be dirt fucking poor, and go back to the projects. I'm gonna live still, I'm gonna be all right. That five hundred thousand–dollar executive, that motherfucker loses it all tomorrow, he's gonna throw himself out a fucking window or shoot himself in the head. That's the difference, point blank.

Whether guys at home have been a success or a failure, I look at guys I grew up with, I look at them with level eyes. I know I ain't no better than them, and I don't look down on them.

13

THE BROTHERS
Finally Finding a Foothold

In 1984 the Brothers were buoyant with hope. In 1991 most were deflated. In 2006 the picture is mixed. I traveled by train across two states to see James and flew to Utah to speak with Derek. Craig seems to have left his wife, cut ties with his wider family, and found work on the West Coast as a personal fitness trainer. I discovered on the Internet a workout videotape that features Craig, but that's as close as I got to him. In tracking down Super, I put on my clerical shirt and collar again before knocking on his mother's door (the first time was to visit Chris in prison). Like the Hallway Hangers, the Brothers related to me as a friend and sometime sociologist but were also interested in my job as a parish priest. It was wonderful to catch up with the men and to help Derek and Mokey renew their friendship. Here are edited interviews with all of the Brothers apart from Craig. The emphasis is on their jobs and their families, although I sometimes probe their feelings or invite them to step back and look at their lives through a sociological lens. Like the Hallway Hangers, the Brothers want to understand the world and to be understood themselves. As in the previous chapter, we start with those living closest to Clarendon Heights.

MOKEY

Manager

One of the first people I'd met in Clarendon Heights was Mokey's mother, Mrs. Moore. Her younger son, Sammy, was in the youth program, and their apartment had been a refuge for me. When I visited the neighborhood in the 1990s, their door was one of the first I'd knock on. But like almost all the families in this study, Mokey's had moved from Clarendon Heights by 2006. No one in the neighborhood had any idea where Mokey might be found, but several people thought Mrs. Moore had moved to Emerson Towers. I knocked on many doors there, spoke with lots of residents, and sought out neighborhood activists and social workers. I left my cell number with everyone I met. One of those encounters paid off, because a week later Mokey's mom phoned me, and later that day we were sitting in her kitchen swapping stories about our jobs and families. She showed me a photo of Mokey's girlfriend and their son. "She's Irish, and you won't believe where they're living—Dover Plain! I was so worried about him living there, but he says it's changed, and I guess it has because he hasn't been stabbed or shot. Yet!" Dover Plain is a white neighborhood with a lingering reputation for virulent racism. Mrs. Moore gave me Mokey's cell phone number. He was keen to meet up but not at their apartment, so I picked him up from work in the city center and we talked for a couple of hours, first on a park bench and then over lunch. Stocky but not overweight, Mokey was his old animated self. This must have taken quite an effort, because the dark circles under his eyes were probably evidence of chronic fatigue. Mokey is a night-shift manager who routinely stays at work through the morning to sort out any snags. He doesn't like to think of his life as a struggle, giving the impression that to accept any degree of victimhood is to cede hard-won ground.

———

JM: Back in '91 you were back working part-time with your dad, I think.

I was still cleaning. Ski instructor during winter, with the YCP [Youth Challenge Project] guys. I was getting paid. I was kinda like a YCP kid. Learned to ski with them in high school, ended up all over the East, teaching. Kept going for a long time. I moved out to Colorado, working in ski rental shops in Boulder, Colorado, and then Steamboat. Did lots of skiing. It was fun.

JM: What prompted the decision to go to Colorado? That must've been a big change.

One of my friends, Eduardo, was living out there, and I moved into his house with him, worked with him for a while. He was the manager of the ski shop. I went on a ski trip one day to Steamboat, had a bad time because I didn't know how to snowboard. So my deal was like, "I'm gonna come back here next season and learn how to snowboard and work that whole season." It was fun. Very, very challenging, too.

It was hard, but it was an interesting thing to do, though, on my own. I took the train all the way, straight through, all by myself. Meeting, talking to a lot of people. Being on my own was kind of weird, without family members being right there. Actually on my own. Really far away.

JM: Gave you confidence?

Yeah, definitely. And then looking to do other things. I wouldn't mind moving back there. It's a lot more mellow, not so fast-paced like right around here. It was fun. But then after that, come back to my job, every six months, and they had my position still there.

JM: This was the cleaning?

Part cleaning and part with the company I'm working for right now.

JM: Tell me about that, how you got involved with this company.

I started there as regular operator, QCing documents. It was called Legal Documents. They take on documents from lawyers and produce them. I was the person that QCed the document. QC: quality control. So I went from QC to a document specialist, handling all the documents, and then after that I got into management. I've been more involved in management for the last six years.

JM: What does that involve?

Really running the show, running the shift. Giving out jobs. Taking in calls from clients, dealing with the sales team. I've been on different shifts. We run a twenty-four-hour shift. Been on first, second, and third. Right now I have eight employees, but I can work with up to eighteen on a shift. I work with a large volume of people. And a large volume of paper. It's a good job. It's fun. Right now I'm manager of third shift: eleven to seven. But I never get off at seven. [*laughs*] Today it was noon, and that's typical. I don't like leaving until I feel comfortable. I like making sure everything is done. People doing all their paperwork.

JM: How did you land the initial job?

Through another friend that was working there, Arnie. You remember Arnie, used to hang out with him over by the park. He was working there, told me about it, and I came in and got the job.

JM: What was the starting wage way back then?

Five bucks or so.

JM: So how did you manage to work your way up?

Just doing a good job, really paying attention, doing what I needed to do. One of the guys really saw something in me, so he brought me on, showed me a lot of things.

JM: Tell me a bit about him.

Guy named Miles, one of my good friends. He's now ops manager for the East. We hung out together, shared a lot together, and he really showed what you need to do to move up. So I followed all those things, and here I am. He just said, "I know that you can do a very good job, and I want to see you doing it." He'd teach me a lot of things. I just followed it and kept on going with it. The managers above him saw what I can do. I've been working for those guys, it's been a long haul: up and down. My opportunities were lost sometimes because of things I was doing. They felt that I wasn't ready for a bigger position than where I'm at now. When I should have been ready at that time.

JM: So tell me about some of the ups and downs.

I had the regional manager come in and say, "All right, we'll follow up with you at a later time." Never get that follow-up. Those are the frustrating thoughts. When people come up and say, "All right, we're going to do this with you." Never happens. My biggest deal is that I never speak up, say, "When are you going to come back and tell me?" One manager really saw something in me, just gave me my chance. This is my opportunity that I got now. I've been running the third shift for over a year and a half, so I'm doing very well. To take on my own shop, I would need to be on first shift so I can deal with the sales team a lot more, because then the regional manager can see what I can do.

JM: This is a big firm?

About sixty-five people, that's including production and sales. We have different divisions—machines and repairs. We have a bunch of offices in New York, pretty much around the whole world.

JM: Did you see straightaway that with this firm, contrasted with the other jobs, there just might be possibilities for advancement? Or wasn't it obvious then?

It was surprising for me that Miles actually saw something in me. I was kind of skeptical about it: taking on a new role, supervising the people that you work with, trying to manage those people around you. Those were things that I had a problem with when I first got into that role, trying to manage your old peers that you used to work with, now you're a manager.

JM: And what particularly was difficult?

Those guys were there before I got there. And they see a guy that came in lower than them and now he's a supervisor. It's kind of hard for them to deal with. And it is hard for me to deal with too, because that did happen to me with other managers, where it was a struggle and where there was jealousy. I was having one struggle with a girl. She was first shift, and I drew third shift. At our transition we were having these big discussions. It was like having this big battle. We had a sit-down with our manager. Over the years we worked things out. She's moved on to doing better things right now.

JM: Are there other struggles at work?

I see a struggle where I want to advance, and one of the things that's holding me back is my shift. I got a team that doesn't want to go any further where they're at right now. There's not really any motivation for them. My manager is saying, "You gotta figure out a way to motivate them, man, get them moving." What it is, I don't know how to get them to go. The people that do want to work, I can get them to go. My people will work to a point, will get the jobs done, but they don't want to work any further than where they have to. Do their eleven-to-seven, "See ya later."

JM: What sort of work are they actually doing?

They're pretty much by a machine, scanning for seven and a half hours. Producing the documents. We're into the digital things right now, so they're sitting in front of a screen for the time that they're at work. And then dealing with the documents at the same time. I want to get into the ops manager's position. But being on third shift, where I'm not producing as much as I want to, with the people that I have, it's so hard to move forward. With the crew that I have, we cannot produce the revenue that we need to. Where it be first and second shift, they have tenured employees. They've been there for a length of time, probably eight years or so. The people I have have been there probably four years, but we have temps come in. So I have five employees with my five temps, so my labor actually goes up higher, because we're spending more on them: twelve or thirteen dollars, just to have the temps in there.

JM: Why doesn't somebody hire them full-time?

Procedures. We try to teach them. The other part is the language barrier. We have a lot of Chinese, and they can't really speak English that well. That's one of the things that I have to deal with that's difficult. It's so hard to keep these guys here, because as they come in, they're also leaving. The temps don't stick around as long.

JM: So how does having them temp help the company?

We don't have to pay them benefits. And if it doesn't work out, it's easy to let them go.

JM: What were the racial dynamics like in the office?

It's really balanced out. We have a Chinese, two Africans as well now.

JM: The guy who took an interest in you . . .

He's black.

JM: The woman you had difficulty . . .

She's black.

JM: Did you ever have difficulty as a black manager with some of the white staff underneath you?

No, it's been pretty good. We never had any racial issues of any kind. Nothing like that.

JM: That must have made a bit of a change for you, after growing up in Clarendon Heights and different hassles.

We never had that many racial issues, like with Shorty and Steve, those guys. I mean, there were some issues, but never any craziness where we had a big huge fight. They respected my brother and I, so that was a good thing about it.

JM: Can you tell me about the benefits that you get with your job?

After working for a length of time, probably six months, if I recall, then you get some protection. When we were sold to a bigger company we had the 401 come in. That was a big benefit for us. Retire thing, pension plan. It's gonna help in the long run.

JM: Do you get health insurance?

Yeah, but it's expensive. I pay probably four thousand a year.

JM: Are you paid by the hour or are you on a salary?

They put me on salary. It's been about a year now.

JM: What were you making an hour?

Close to fourteen and half or so, but I was killing them on the overtime. Now I'm on salary it actually goes down as I work longer. [*laughs*] But the bonuses come through, so it just balances out. It's pretty good. I'm pretty much carrying the whole family because Karen's not working right now.

JM: Have you ever had trouble balancing the books, getting into debt, that sort of thing?

[*laughs*] Oh, yeah. Finances is my worst thing. It's my nightmare. My first car got repoed back in '86. I never was able to control my banking, keep track of finances. I put myself in a situation when I bought a brand-new car; that put a burden to our finances. For some reason I just wanted to go out and spend money, buy things, and not try to keep up with my debts. That was one of the problems that I was having, not being able to keep up with my debt. After I got my credit back, I was fine.

JM: How long did that go on for?

Right now it's an issue. I mean, we're keeping up with the payments, but we're looking for a used car right now.

JM: So tell me about your family.

We're not married but we've been together so long. We met through a nightclub. Out clubbing. That was fourteen years ago. We moved in together nine years ago. The second time I went to Colorado she came with me, just after her graduation from Central State College. Her degree is in teaching, special educational needs. After Colorado we lived in the city but we had a bad landlord, which was really troubling. Then we moved way out of the city into my aunt's house. She passed, so I asked my mom and my uncle if we could move in and fix up the house. Lived there for about two and a half years but then there was a big problem. It was a family thing, turned into a legal thing with the other sisters and we had to leave. We lived in a nearby rental, which was pretty nice. After that we moved up north out of state for eight months. Her sister was offering us a room in her house and Karen wanted to move, so I was commuting to here.

JM: That's a long haul.

About an hour and forty-five minutes, driving fast. I was doing that on a daily basis. I didn't mind doing it. I like to have relax time. She was working in a house for the handicapped part-time. She worked there until her pregnancy and she couldn't stand the lifting and stuff like that. Then we got an apartment in Bristol, which was a bit closer.

JM: Bristol's not that racially mixed, is it? Or has it changed a lot?

You see a couple of Mexicans there.

JM: Karen is white?

Yes.

JM: Have you ever had any difficulties, the two of you, with that?

No. I don't let that bother me. If anybody said anything, it's just never really bothered me. My first couple of months with her was pretty scary for me, because I was coming down the street and a bunch of kids come walking up the street, and they just crowded the street. But other than that, no problem.

JM: What prompted the move to Dover Plain? It can't be the easiest place to live for a mixed couple.

We needed to move closer to the city because I had a brand-new car and was just running up the miles. It's a very small place, one and a half bedrooms. Like two hotel rooms: that's how little. Rayford's room, it's not that big, but his bed's in there. Doesn't like sleeping in it. [*laughs*] Our space is pretty small. It's just so expensive in the city. We've got a good deal. We're paying 630 a month with cable. We're paying for the heat and stuff like that, but with cable it's great. You can't find anything like that in the city. We're living in a family house, that's the reason why. It's her sister's house and she rents the apartment out to us.

JM: Have you thought about buying a house?

We're planning on doing that. That's our next plan. It's trying to work through our credit. Trying to set some budgets down. Karen's not working because she had a car accident. She was hurt and can't work right now. Plus we had Rayford in school for a while. That was too much because I was on third shift, and she was doing the waking up at seven-thirty, getting him to school, and then trying to get to work on time. It got too much on her, so she was like, "I can't work anymore." Also, she wanted to be with him, cuz she is a teacher, and Rayford is very, very smart. He does a lot of things I wouldn't have expected.

JM: Tell me about what that's meant to you: fatherhood.

Oh, man, it's great. Totally. And it changed me. I don't drink anymore. I drink, but it's a casual thing. It's not going out drinking with the buds anymore and then coming back all busted up. Naw. We're closer now, so it's good. Not spending a lot of money, drinking, breaking the bank.

JM: At what point did you get into that, drinking more, even if it was just socially?

Back in the days that Miles and I worked together, after work we just went out to have drinks with the whole team, just go out partying. Out with the fellas. On Thursday go out, Friday we would go out. Same thing, every week. That wore on Karen too. Where Rayford was born, three years ago, it stopped. Slowed down. When you go out, you want to enjoy it, make sure everybody's having a good time. And that was paying. And if I didn't have money, they're paying for me. Other than that, being Dad is very good. I get to play with him when I get home. We just play in the house, play with the toys. He's just getting into the bike now, so I'm going to start going out biking with him. I enjoy him very, very much. He's learning a lot. He watches a lot of TV, which I'm trying to stop him doing, but it's pretty much cartoons and stuff. He's really into Power Rangers. He's a very, very physical kid, jumps on you and grabs you, puts a hold on you and does a job on you.

JM: Looking back, growing up in Clarendon Heights, seeing kids who haven't done well, what do you think about that? Having yourself struggled for a period but now having done quite well for yourself?

I don't define my life or my family's life as a struggle. We were just living our lives.

JM: In '91, you were a little disillusioned. In seven years you'd had like twelve jobs. It wasn't what you thought. You'd completed high school, done a bit at junior college, and it didn't seem to have paid off for you.

You're right. I expected to go to a big school, doing all the sports. But I never got to do it. When I was in high school my mom and dad wanted me to do the educational-type things; I wanted to be the technical person, like going into fixing cars and stuff like that. They didn't want me to do that. Now I'm very good at it: I can figure out how to work on cars, on computers. I feel very comfortable. When my mom calls me up, "Hey, can you fix this?" They're very surprised that I can do all those things. The things that they didn't want me to do— they're very happy that I can do it. [*laughs*]

JM: They pushed you into the Fundamental School?

Uh-huh.

JM: And you really wanted to go a different route?

Yeah, I did. Yeah.

JM: Did they ever realize that maybe they made a mistake there?

I think they still made the right choice of me going to Fundamentals. That was what they wanted, and that's what I did. But my junior and senior year I saw these different courses, these electives like automotive, drafting, photography, and stuff like that, that I really wanted to get into. And that's where they were saying no.

JM: Looking back, is there anything that you would do differently?

Actually go to a four-year school, study civil engineering. Or more business education. I just lost it. When I was at the community college and I seen all my friends from high school, and it didn't seem like it was working for me, so I said, "Aw, forget this, I'm just gonna go work." So that's where I was going through all those different jobs at that time. If I had a second chance, I'd definitely go to school. I didn't take those opportunities, that's the thing.

JM: Have you ever been in a trade union?

No.

JM: Will you take any particular approach with your son in terms of encouraging aspirations for him? Do you encourage him to dream as big as he wants, or will you be a little worried that you don't want him to be disappointed if he sets his sights too high?

Right now I just want him to enjoy what he has. Just learning and having fun. In the future, my biggest deal is respect. For education, I don't feel safe for him to go to public school right now. Maybe some private school. From that point on, I just want to be there for him, whatever his needs are. Like, after I figured out I can go out and travel to Colorado and learn different things, I would want him to learn these things. I don't want to hold him back from something he wants to do, like my parents did. If he feels that he wants to try to be a mechanic, I'll help him to be a mechanic.

SUPER

Hustler

I could not find Super in the spring or summer of 2006. I feared that he was in prison or dead. Nor could I locate his mother or sisters. After chasing several false leads in August 2007, I was given an address for his mother in a largely Latino quarter of a neighboring city. I put on my clerical shirt and collar, borrowed my parents' rusty sedan, and followed the Googled directions. I ended up in a small public housing development, and the assembled teenagers tried to stifle their laughter when a priest climbed out of the clapped-out car. Three women chatting on a stoop directed me to a second-floor apartment. I rang the bell and waited. There seemed to be movement behind the peephole. I rang again. And again. Finally, an uncertain voice came from within—"Who is it? What do you want?" in a telltale southern accent and lilt. I tried to explain my interest in Super and suddenly realized how unlikely the story sounded. I'd met Super's mother only fleetingly twenty-five years ago. The door would stay closed, dog collar or not. She couldn't say where Super lived or how I could get in touch with him. I scribbled my cell number on the back of my calling card and pushed it through the mail slot. "Ma'am, I would be very grateful if you would give this to Super if you see him." Against all odds, Super phoned late that same night. He was curious: "Who *is* this?" I explained. The "Reverend" and the British address on my card had thrown him, but he eventually remembered me. Super must've had instructions from his mother to apologize profusely if the white pastor turned out to be bona fide, because he took pains to explain that she had been warned against con men impersonating ministers. Super and I arranged to meet the next day near the city center. I waited at the appointed street corner and Super nearly passed by before I recognized the heavyset, balding man walking with a limp. We shook hands and found a quiet bench in a nearby park for the interview.

I worried back in 1991 whether Super might have made up the story about the police planting drugs on him. He cited the incident then as a turning point that helped explain his entry into serious criminality. If it was a fabrication, he might be less likely to mention it again. To be sure, lies (or at least elaborations on the truth) can become part of our personal narratives and eventually even believed by the teller. But to recall the same specifics after sixteen years would be unlikely if the story was spurious. So I smiled inwardly when Super brought up the incident himself, complete with corroborating details. Only this time the story is told as evidence of his own stupidity and naïveté as well as of a corrupt world. Like most of the men in this study, Super occasionally points the finger at others but is hardest on himself.

JM: If you can just catch me up; if you wanna, you can go right back to when you graduated from high school.

Since then I got three kids. My son is the oldest. I got married, ended with a divorce; me and the wife didn't work out. My daughter's mother, she had the drug problem. I ended up falling in love with her, but it just deteriorated from the drug problem. She stole my money, stole my car, stole my drugs. She did a lotta wrongful things. Cheated on me. I couldn't take it no more. We had an on-and-off relationship for like ten years. Finally, I couldn't take it no more. She's in jail now. I met my other daughter's mother when I got out of jail and we ended up separating.

JM: Tell me about your oldest.

I met his mother when I was hustling, selling drugs. She told me she couldn't have no baby and all of a sudden she's pregnant. It was my fault in a way cuz I did not use protection. I wasn't ready for a baby, but once a woman gets pregnant, nothing you can do, it's her body. So I ended up getting married. The whole situation just went wrong. She was lying and making up all these stories. Now she don't even have custody of the kid; her mother does. They won't let me see him. I wish I'd seen more of him. He has serious problems now. I try to talk to her mother, and she's tellin' me she needs a DNA test, that maybe he might not be my kid. I call him "son." He still thinks I'm his dad. Now she's telling me that he might not be my son. It's just a lotta headaches; the whole situation is just crazy. I got caught up, not using my brains right, running wild, drinking and partying, and that's what happens. I got to get a lawyer but I can't do that until my money situation gets right. It's just kinda hard for me. It took me a long time to get this job. I'm working for a moving company right now. Moving furniture. I feel like I deserve better, but nothing I can do. I'm making eleven bucks an hour. The guys are all right, a lot of Mexicans and El Salvadorans, and the guy that owns it is Israeli or something like that. I don't really care for the job too much, but I got to deal with it and work. I'm not happy with a lotta things going on. I seen a guy get fired. I think, "That's not fair." But I keep my mouth shut. It's not my business. I seen another guy got fired, which is wrong. Then he puts me in a position as a foreman and won't give me another dollar more. He won't pay me, says, "You're in training." This is bull.

JM: Is it all above the table?

He pays you by check, so he does it on the books. He gets your name and everything and gives it to the IRS. He reports everything, so you got to pay your own taxes and all of that at the end of the year.

JM: Do you get overtime?

Naw, he don't pay overtime. Pays us by the hour. We work as many hours as we can. I get paid every two weeks. I got a hundred hours now because I've been working a lot the last coupla weeks. It picked up, people starting to come back to school. It's going to get busy. "After September it's going to die down," he says. "I probably won't be calling you too much." So I try to make as much money as I can right now. I need to look for another job. It's hard for me to find a job. I've been to places and filled out applications and my CHR is just killing me. Y'know, my past.

JM: Do you tell them straightaway that you've got a record?

Sometimes. Sometimes I don't tell, just don't mark nothing. Few times I got a job and started working, they found out. They did the CHR and they told me they don't need me no more because I got a record.

JM: When was your first run-in with the law?

When I had a scooter. Cop said the scooter was stolen. I had all my paperwork, showed him I bought it. Honest money; I wasn't selling drugs then. I worked and bought that. He told me I didn't have a permit. I went to court and they gave me a fine. Ever since, it seemed like I been having bad luck.

JM: What was the next run-in, legally?

I gave this cop a lotta lip. I still remember the cop right now, through the days. I'll never forget his face. He grabbed me and put a dime bag of weed on me because of my mouth, cuz I talked too much. I end up going to court. I was stupid, I didn't know too much, I had a lotta mouth. If I knew what I knew now, it wouldn'ta happened like that. That was my second arrest.

JM: Was there any racial element there?

No, the cop was black, but he was a dirty cop. World's crookedy, you know. He knew I didn't have a record, only thing I been locked up for was the scooter, and he knew I wasn't bad. He knew that.

JM: So this had quite an effect on you?

It had an effect on me. I sold drugs through the years: If I got busted, I admitted to it, plead out. But this cop had put some weed on me. I was mad about it for a long time, wanted to get even with him. I wanted to kill him. After a while, he left me alone. Maybe they moved him to another area.

JM: But how did you get into the dealing and that sort of thing, because through high school you stayed away from that.

I know. I seen a lotta people making fast money. I was hanging around with a lotta guys, playing ball, and they started. I wanted to try it out, see how it'll work out.

JM: Was there anything that triggered you hanging out with these other guys?

It was the money that I seen these guys getting. I was like, "Wow, this is easy money." I was working, but the money they was getting was just too easy, the things they had, new stuff all the time, big money, and I just got addicted to it. I seen it and I wanted it and I got caught up. It's a bad decision. I started with the weed and then the coke.

JM: Was this using or selling?

Selling it. I didn't use it at all for a long time. I knew a lot of people that did drugs, like Chris and a lotta those other guys—Slick, Steve, Shorty. I sold to them, and they told their friends and a lotta guys came to me, so I made money. In the neighborhood at night. They didn't have to go nowhere. That was my spot. After a while I expanded, going different places. I end up selling cocaine, powder, then rock. Whoever wanted it, I had it. They call me up, and I delivered to them. I expanded, ended up going to different places, then I met a few people and I started selling out of a couple of houses. I met this lady; her sister lived in Clarendon Heights. I ended up going to her house. She had a lotta hookers and stuff like that coming over, young girls selling their bodies. Guys come over there and getting high and smoking. I ended up going over there and giving her some shit, y'know, giving her some crack, for letting me sit in there and make money in there. I won a spot there. There were a lotta other spots that I useta go to and neighborhoods where it's basically the same thing.

JM: It was relatively safe because you knew the people.

I knew the people. You get some people in there that's kinda shaky, but I had protection, so I didn't worry about it. I carried a gun on me. Eventually I was selling downtown for a while. More money, faster pace. It's still like that now. Sometimes I get the urge to go down there and see how things is, check it out, but I don't. It took me a long time to get out of that. In the back of my mind, I know the consequences: It's going to lead me into jail. Someone telling me when to wake up, when to take a shit, when to eat. I'm done with that. I didn't care back then. I was more wild. The way I was living my life I didn't really care if I died or if I didn't die. I was living my life like a time bomb.

JM: Were you working for somebody else?

No, I was working for myself.

JM: How much would you bring in on a good week?

Back then I'd bring in good money, a thousand dollars or more, but I'd spend a lotta money too. I even had an apartment, paying my rent, hanging out, flashing, buying clothes, car.

JM: Tell me about how you went from selling to starting to use. What was the attraction?

My second baby's mother, she had the drug problem, off and on. She was living with me and we's hanging one day and we's in the house, and she wanted to get high, so I said, "Lemme try this." It was my fault. I can't blame her. She told me, "No, it hurts." But I ended up doing it anyway. And once I did it, she was kinda happy, know what I'm sayin'? I started with the sniffing thing, and then I started with the crack. It wasn't me. I can't make nobody love me. I can't fall behind nobody because they have a problem habit. I learned that through experience. It took a long time learning it, but I learned it. I made mistakes.

JM: What was the first time you ended up doing time?

It was drugs or driving with suspended license. Because my license got suspended every time I got caught with drugs. Go to court, they suspend your license, that's how they do it here, that's the law. I get caught with the drugs and my case is still pending and I get caught driving. So one of the two. It was a few months in South Street [the county] jail.

JM: And how did that affect you?

It affected me, but I was younger then. Part of the routine, it comes with it. Time goes on, doing a couple of other bids. I got set up. Undercover.

JM: How did that work?

I was going to give this guy something to sell; I didn't want to do the hand-to-hand because I didn't trust them. He said he knew the guy and he wants three for fifty. I gave him two and he went around the corner and he was taking so long, so I went around the corner, me wanting to know where my money's at, and he's arguing with the guy. "Just take two." "No, I want three for fifty." I look at 'em, I'm, like, grumpy. I took my chances and split out another one. The guy gave him the two and I gave him the one—cops everywhere. They got me. Just being greedy. Greed got me. I went to court for two years on this case. I was trying to see if I could get it dropped down because they was trying to give me eight to ten years. I was fighting with my lawyer; he was telling me, "They're going to give you the time, why don't you take it?" And I was like, "Nah, I'll take it to trial." Then he told me, "You might be able to get it dropped down with the right judge." Finally we get the right judge and the right DA and they offer me a deal again. I think it was seven and another one was five, and I wouldn't take it, and they finally came with the two and a half years, so I took it. That was the new county jail, state-of-the-art new building. And that's one of the roughest places in the state. It had a lot of incidents about the COs [corrections officers] impregnating women, beating up guys, and couple of guys got killed over there. It was a rough experience there. That one changed my mind. Just so much stuff: coming in your room, waking you up, making you strip naked when they have shakedowns. Cops coming in with attitudes and talking to you any kind of way. You can't do nothing or you'll go to the hole or get beat up. Seeing guys get beat up for no reason. There's a lot of things I seen. It ain't for me no more. I never been upstate yet, but next time's gonna be a lengthy one, double digits. And they'll hit me with a habitual offender.

JM: So when you got out, what was that like?

Couldn't find a job. It's hard for me to get a job anywhere now because of CHR, a new thing they use against you since the 9/11, so it's hard for anybody with any kind of criminal record to get a job. You can get a union job if you know somebody. There's not too many jobs that don't do CHRs now. Everything does. McDonald's, supermarkets, city jobs. My record got a lot of violence on it. Little incident with cops, fighting with them. And a gun charge, few of those. Kidnapping charge. I had an incident a long time ago, and it led to all these charges. I was messing with some younger girl then, I end up seeing her fucking somebody else. I always get chicks that fucking cheat on me—how do you deal with it? And I end up going over there with my buddies, kicked the door in, grabbed her, put her in the car. Her parents had me for home invasion. That was, like, one of the first times I got locked up.

JM: When do you hope to get your license back?

A few months. I already been to the registry.

JM: That'll be the first time you'll be able to drive legally since . . .

A long time. Probably ten years or more. I've been driving illegal the whole time. Taking my chances through the years. Trying to do the right thing, take the bus. Soon I'll be legit.

JM: What about the different places you've lived at?

I lived in a lotta rooming houses, I lived in an apartment. I lived with my aunt when I got out of jail for a little while.

JM: What about girlfriends?

I never really lived with a girl. Only my wife. Girlfriends lived with me when I had a room. Rent's pretty high here. A one-bedroom, you're looking at twelve hundred. It's kinda hard, you need a good job, and making eleven, twelve dollars an hour is not hitting it, y'know? Now I'm staying with my youngest sister, temporary. She's not too good. Something happened to her, like a rape, and it traumatized her. She's not had a stable mind. I'm trying to help her out with the bills and stuff. But I need my own house. I'm tryin' to get my license back. I'm tryin' to get my life back on track. I can't get a good job. I don't wanna go back to selling drugs because I've been to prison, and I don't want that life. I'm too old now, and my health's deteriorating. High blood pressure runs in the family. My uncles all had it. I think one died like maybe fifty, but the most-jority of 'em died in their forties.

JM: Have you ever had a connection, like with a union?

Yeah, I had a connection with the union. I was working with my father, but I messed that up, not going to work and going to jail.

JM: What was the job? Construction?

Yeah. I was making good money, like twenty-one [dollars an hour].

JM: So how long did you stick with that?

Through the years, working off and on, even when I was selling drugs. The last time I got locked up, I was doing it then. I didn't pay my dues, and I just tried to get back in now, and they're giving me a hard way to go. Everything's changed now; it's not that easy to get back in like you used to. Now you got to go to school. It ain't like it used to be. Now I know through my experience: Be good. Or you ain't going to make no way in life. Dead or in jail. It took me a while to figure it out.

JM: Having now figured it out, what are the obstacles that you face?

Trying to get back a good job, trying to get back into the hall, some kind of union job. Get my life back on track and try to make the best of it. I'm not getting no younger, I'm getting older.

JM: Your dad works in construction?

Yes, he's been in there forty-some years. He know the guys there, but I guess he kinda gave up. I don't even bother to ask him no more. He's about to retire. It was my fault. I got to try to do it on my own. You remember Dad, we had our problems through the years. Mom, I really didn't want to get her too much involved. It was on me. Every time I did my bid, my family didn't come and visit me. Everything was on me. I was a man, I did what I did, had to pay the consequences and deal with it. That's how it is. My mother never did drugs or none of that, neither did my father. They're still together. All these years, still together. My mother just don't want nothing to do with it. She know I made some bad decisions. Even when I was back in Clarendon Heights, started hanging with new guys, she said, "Why are you hanging with these guys? These guys are bad." Maybe if I listened to her, my life would have been a little bit different. I would have went in a different direction. I planned on becoming a cop when I got out of high school, but it didn't work out.

JM: What about, through all this, friends, colleagues—did they ever stand by you?

Not really, rarely, because when you're in drug business, it's hard to trust anybody. A lot of shaky people. I wish I hadda kept the union job and didn't mess that up. Now I'm trying to get back in. Something legit, legal, what I can count on, and have annuity and have insurance and all that. I need all those things now.

JM: Tell me about your health worries.

I got high blood pressure, high cholesterol, asthma: Health through the years has deteriorated. I'm trying to watch out for my sugar. My mother and my aunt are diabetics; they take insulin, shoot it up. My heart's all right. I had a few incidents, an irregular heartbeat, diverticulitis, been in the hospital. I'm taking pills for my heart, six pills.

JM: Looking back, Super, have you had to deal with racial prejudice along the way?

Yeah, I had to deal with a lot of that, coming up from a younger age. Even right now, my girlfriend's mother is kinda, a little, y' know, not really care for blacks, because she's white.

JM: And the mothers of the kids, the other people you've been in relationships with, have they tended to be white, black . . . ?

My son's mother, she's white. And my middle child, her mother's mixed: Her mother's white and the father's black. And the baby, her mother's black. I been with Spanish girls before. A person's race doesn't make how I feel in my heart toward the person, y'know what I'm sayin'? Color doesn't matter.

JM: But does everybody think that way?

No, people don't think that way, I know that since I was a young kid. There's a lot of ignorance. I dealt with a lot of racism, even before I moved to Clarendon Heights, I dealt with it.

JM: How do you cope with that, what's your strategy?

I just leave that behind, don't think about that. Every day's a new day, I try to move on. That's the past. I can't dwell on the past and say, "Yes, that's how white people, they . . ." You're going to meet ignorant people in life.

JM: The two younger children, do you see them at all?

Yeah, the two youngest children are with my mother, so I see them all the time.

JM: She's got custody?

Yeah, she got custody of them. Because my daughter's mother was on drugs and in jail, so they had her since she was the baby and all. Now she's eleven. And the baby, her mother didn't have a place she could take care of her, so we have her. Her mother knows she's in good hands, so she just leaves it alone. I haven't seen her in years. She hasn't seen the baby in years. I don't even know if she's alive or dead.

JM: So your mom's basically raising the two.

My mom, my sister, I help out too. Even when I was hustling, I help out. My mother was there, she raised them in the house, she watches them and takes care of them.

JM: Was she working during this time, your mom?

No, she stopped working. My mother's health is kinda shaky, she's got a lot of problems. My sisters helped out. None of them ever been to jail, never locked up, they don't do drugs. I'm the only one in the family that's . . .

JM: Tell me about the addiction, then. Is that something you still have to cope with? The attraction? Are there times when you feel down or depressed and . . . ?

Yeah, but I know, even though I'm down, depressed, if I do drugs, you end up with no money at all, blow all your money. Someone will rob you and then you'll just be more depressed. It's like a no-win situation. It's just evil. It's evil.

JM: What are your hopes for the future?

The future for me is to get a decent job, to buy a house, help my daughters out, visit my son and get to know him and help him out with school. Y'know, want the best for them.

JM: How will you approach that? Your son, even though you don't see him much, is the age you were when I first knew you, so how do you influence their aspirations, their hopes for the future?

I will try to talk to them and tell them about my life, and how my life went. "Learn from me. I want the best for you." Tell them what's right from wrong. Be honest with them.

JM: What lessons would you hope that they would learn from your experience?

To go about doing things the right way, don't go on the way that I went. Take the right choices, don't take the wrong choices. Wrong choices will leave you like I am. I don't want them to go through the things I went through.

MIKE

Buyer and Broker

In 1991 Mike was ambivalent about being in this book, and he feels the same way now. Instead of digitally recording an interview with Mike, I had long discussions with him on two evenings and wrote up the conversations verbatim afterward. I discovered back in 1983 that one can recall a great deal, provided that the interview is written up immediately and before having even a brief conversation with anyone else. Mike lives with his girlfriend six miles from the city but has a small real estate office within walking distance of Clarendon Heights. Mike has aged well: still strong and stocky with jet-black hair. He picked me up in his white Lexus and took me to a neighborhood bar and restaurant. A few weeks later we went to an Irish pub for dinner. On both occasions he answered my questions candidly, and he in turn probed my faith and politics. Mike talked and listened with an eager intensity that suggested such conversations are a rarity for him. He reluctantly agreed to being included in this edition as a personal favor to me. Mike did me another favor as well but never said anything about it. He knows Shorty's older brother from a real estate deal, and when I mentioned in passing that I couldn't locate Shorty, Mike must have swung into action. A few days later I received a voice mail from Shorty's brother with Shorty's address. His mixed feelings about *Ain't No Makin' It* notwithstanding, Mike worked behind the scenes to ensure that my research would be successful. That research, after all, began unexpectedly in my college dorm when Mike started talking about his aspirations as I helped him with homework in 1983. Mike seems aware of the tension in our relationship (is he my peer or my research subject?), and his help in locating Shorty may be a way of asserting our collegiality.

In any case, I am grateful for his help.

———————

JM: What do you think made the difference for you and set you apart from the other kids from the projects and set you on the road that you're on now?

I guess it had a bit to do with parental support, the way I was raised, my mom and grandmother. And luck. Luck played a big part, to tell you the truth. I was lucky. I was working at the university mail room for a summer, I was sixteen or seventeen, and this old guy who worked in there, he said to me, "We're going to take the test for the post office. Why don't you come along?" I said, "What?" He said, "Yeah, come on, it won't hurt. They make good money at the post office, I'm tellin' ya." So I went. Ended up taking the tests for the fire and police, too, and scored good on all of them. These weren't tests you had to study for. They were aptitude tests.

The post office called me. I was like eighteen. It was after I dropped out of college and was working as a bank teller. The money was shit there, at the bank, and I had to lie to get that job. Told 'em I had an associate's degree and they never checked. I'm not proud of it, but that's what I did. When you're desperate for a job, ethics go out the window. Anyway the post office called, and I went to work for the post office. It was good money I was making, especially for a kid. I never liked the work, though. It was boring. Carrying mail and driving the truck. I don't like labor jobs. I like to use my head, not my body. I'm not a donkey, just carrying the mail. I knew I could do better than that.

It was when I was at the post office that I started to get into real estate, bought my first properties, and bought at the right time, too: early '90s. Anyway, one day the fire department called. Said they had a job for me. I knew the guy, so I told him, "Look, I'm not actually a minority. I'm half Portuguese but that doesn't count as a minority. I'm not actually Hispanic." It was bothering me, so I told him. The guy says, "Don't worry about it. I'll make sure it's not a problem. Don't say anything." So I got the job. Jay, those were, like, the worst two years of my life. All the guys were Irish and Italian. I had, like, no friends, I was totally isolated, practically ostracized. There was one other guy I got on with—Enrique. And this white guy, Bob. But that was it. The others just cut me out completely. I got a taste then of what it feels like to be a minority. It was hell.

I decided to go and work for myself. And I've never looked back. Working for any organization—private company, government agency—they screw you. You're treated like shit. It's like a game to them, and you're just a pawn in somebody else's game. And they won't think twice about sacrificing you. Moved around, traded, wiped off the board.

See, after I bought the properties in Raymond during the post office days, I got to know some of the real estate brokers, and I began to see how much money they were making. I got to be friends with one or two. I used to go out for meals with this one guy, he says to me, "Why don't you get into this, man? It's the best thing in town. All you do is work for a couple of years with someone else and then get your license. It's a license to steal." I remember him saying that: "It's a license to steal." So I went for it. It wasn't hard.

I worked for this crazy guy, Dennis. I mean, he was unhinged, but he was a good guy. Larger than life, about six-four, big gut. Really gregarious. Crazy as hell. Spent his money as fast as he made it, and he made some, all right. I actually learned a lot from him. The only thing was, he was a crook. Stole people's money. All their deposits. They'd come in the front door and I'd look up and Dennis was gone. Out the back door. They caught up with him in the end. Lost his license. He's in a bad way now. Nearly drunk himself to death.

I was drinking heavy for a while. Back in the '90s when I was making money hand over fist, I'd go out for these liquid lunches. Spend fifty bucks on lunch, drink a lot. It started to get the better of me. So I stopped. Just like that. The guy in the office couldn't believe it, that I could just stop drinking just like that. But I needed to.

Back in the late '90s I was making a couple of hundred thousand a year, just from my renting and selling, leaving aside the properties. Now I just make fifty to sixty thousand each year on the real estate side, but I still do quite well out of the properties. I sold my properties in Raymond and needed to buy elsewhere or pay the taxes. I was running out of time, and it looked like I'd just have to swallow the taxes and take the money. I'd looked at a few places but the numbers didn't work. Then I was talking to a friend, a bartender at the Cape, and he told me that John Flanagan was looking to sell a six-family dwelling. See, this is where luck comes into it. Anyway, John was going through a really bad divorce. I mean, he fucked up and got caught, and it was his fault. But his wife made him pay, I mean really pay. So he was desperate to unload this building, and it turned out to be a really good opportunity for me.

I'm glad I sold those places in Raymond. I was getting to be like you: a social worker dealing with everybody's problems up there. It started to get hairy. I had one tenant who got her Hells Angels boyfriend to come up to my office with one of his cronies. I actually had to get a shotgun. They knocked on my office door and I cocked the shotgun real loud so they could hear, and said, "Come in!" They hit the road, never said anything. I could hear 'em going back down the stairs.

I got pretty good at knowing who was a deadbeat, a bum, and who was for real, who was a hard worker. I've developed this gift, this ability to tell if someone's being truthful, and it's saved me a helluva lot of money. I can read people pretty well, and that's one of the reasons I've done quite well professionally. Being able to judge people has helped me a lot. Dennis, that crooked broker: He was actually a decent guy, really. I learned a lot from him, y'know, really learned the ropes. Anyway, he also had a little property management thing going, too. Evictions and that. He asked me to sort out an eviction from one of his properties, and I said, "I'll take care of it." And when I give my word, I mean it. Well, this family weren't deadbeats. They were just down on their luck and needed a bit of extra time to scrape the rent together. And I knew they were good for the money. I mean, the guy would get his money. But he told me, "No, I want them out of there." "But—" "No," he said. "They're out!" I couldn't do it. I couldn't actually put those people out on the street. We're talking about a family here. They had issues but they were trying to sort them. I can tell the difference between a scumbag and a decent person, and these were decent people. It really got to me. In the end I told Dennis I couldn't do it. He was okay about it.

It's a cutthroat business. That's the way all business is, let me tell ya. It can be cruel, really cutthroat. Dog eat dog. Survival of the fittest; the weak get left on the wayside. You gotta watch your back all the time. I learned that back working with Dennis. There's some double-crossing people in the real estate business, lemme tell ya.

One thing I find, and I'm a bit embarrassed about this because it's going to sound anti-Semitic, but I sometimes find it difficult to deal with Jewish brokers. It's just the way I am. I hate being nickled and dimed. You do a deal involving hundreds of thousands of dollars, you don't need to be quibbling about fifty bucks here or fifty bucks there. Some stereotypes have some truth in them, y'know? Some stereotypes. That's how the stereotype got started in the first place, y'know? Anyway, it's not something I'm proud of, but I rather not do business with Jews. Some black guys have a chip on their shoulder, even in business, and that can be tough too. I know I'm generalizing but it can make a difference. I like doing business with Irish people. Y'know, easygoing. They're good people, easy to get along with. Seal a deal over a pint of Guinness.

I'm conservative when it comes to this stuff. I'm no bleeding-heart liberal like you. We've got to close the borders. Otherwise there's gonna be another big attack in this country, worse than 9/11. I know the danger doesn't come from Mexico, it comes from the Mideast and South Asia. This time it could be a nuclear device. You know how many small nuclear devices and high-grade uranium have gone missing from Russia? It's scary. And Muslims are more violent people; it's different from Christianity and Judaism. It just seems like they're always ready to take up arms—a first resort rather than a last resort. Muslims hate Jews, and that ain't gonna change for a while. Israel stomped all over them in the 1967 war, took their land, and people have long memories.

We need to tighten the borders. There's too many illegal immigrants, and they're climbing up the ladder faster than black people. Blacks are getting pushed lower and lower.

This country was built by Europeans. And it was on the backs of black people who were slaves. Now those coming over the Mexican border are going to change all that. You need to assimilate. Everyone else came here and they wanted to learn English. Now everything's in Spanish. It gets up my nose that, every time I ring a number: "Push 1 for English and 2 for Spanish." I guess I just like things the way they are. I don't want things to change, that's all. Those coming to this country need to change, not us. I don't want to have to learn Spanish. Don't get me wrong, we need the immigrant labor, but it should be controlled. We should know who's coming in and for how long. Let them come and send their money home, but it needs to be tracked.

I'm worried about America. I do worry. Radical Islam. These slick neoconservatives who only make matters worse. I'm ashamed I voted for [George W.] Bush twice. Jesus, he's just not up to it. Look at this war in Iraq. It's draining the country, going to bring us right down. Bush doesn't have a clue. The world's too complicated for him to get a handle on. He should've listened to [former Secretary of State Colin] Powell about Iraq, how hard it would be. But these damn neocons—Wolfowitz, Perle, Cheney—those guys got their own agenda, and they've put this country in a mess. I wish I didn't vote for Bush. But I mean, Kerry? Give me a break. The guy's all over the place. Who's gonna vote for him? You could see it in the debates. At least Bush talked straight. Kerry was flip-flopping all over the place, wishy-washy. Typical politician. Let's face it, they're all corrupt. And usually incompetent. George [W.] Bush never made a decent business decision in his life. Invested in the Texas Rangers, that was the only good move he ever made. Most of his decisions would have ruined a business; he was an abject failure as a businessman. So, yeah, I worry about the country.

To be honest, luck had a lot to do with why I'm here and why some other poor slob from the neighborhood is in the gutter passed out from drinking. My mom and my grandmother, they looked after me. I don't want to talk about my dad. And I had that Big Brother, part of that program to give boys a positive role model. That made a difference. I got hooked up with him when I was just a kid. He came from a big family, big Irish family. They took an interest in me and supported me. That was good. My Big Brother's dad gave me a chance to get in the electricians' union. I decided against it but it was really good of him to offer. Family is so important. It's something I feel strongly about. I think it's from being raised without a dad myself. I see so many broken marriages. A mother and a father is definitely the way to go. That's one of the reasons America is going down the tubes. Especially the black community.

I've been with Rosa for fourteen years now. We're not married. I dunno, maybe I'm afraid of commitment. Her youngest daughter, she's quite bright, got a good head on her shoulders. I didn't realize how smart she was. Then she took the PSATs, scored about 1500. I said, "Whoa." It made me sit up. I told her that she could get into anywhere with those scores. All those soppy liberal schools will love her: Hispanic minority, she should land a scholarship, go for free. The older daughter, it's real tough, she got lead poisoning as a child, and it affected quite a bit of her brain lobe. She's okay, she's got a level of independence, but it's not easy for her.

The youngest one, I put her through private school. Not the big, fancy, twenty grand–a-year ones; I can't afford that. It's a Roman Catholic school, about seven thousand dollars a year. It's a good school. She started in sixth grade. It's just something I wanted to do. I hope it's given her a good foundation, something that will stand her in good stead for the rest of her life.

The public schools where we live are shit, they really are. Part of the problem is the unions. I'm sorry but if you're a lousy teacher, you gotta go. If you can't teach, you're gone. But the unions protect those deadbeat teachers. I seen it in the post office. The union, there's good things about it, but the ones it really helps are the lazy bastards who aren't going anywhere. They don't care about the quality of their work, they don't take pride in what they're doing. Unions are a good idea but in practice they don't work and they get in the way of progress. Plus they're sometimes corrupt. Not as bad as cops, though. I don't like cops. Maybe it's cuz of when we were kids. There was this real sadistic bastard on the beat. Used to harass us, liked to knock us around. He was a real bastard. Corrupt as they come. A lot of cops are corrupt.

I know now that we had it rough growing up in the projects. It was tough with the poverty, all the shit happening. I can see that now. You can't really blame those guys who lost it. You see them now, strung out, deadbeats. I don't have that much sympathy for them, but looking back, it was tough. A kid from a poor neighborhood can make it, but he has to struggle more than a rich kid. A rich kid can't coast these days, but he'll get a few more breaks than a poor kid.

I almost went off the rails myself. I got kinda crazy in eighth and ninth grade. Went through a tough patch. My mom got my uncle to come in and straighten me out. I guess it worked. Maybe it was good I got it out of my system when I was young and it didn't really affect my future. I was lucky, you know? It's funny: My uncle works for me now. He's handy with the tools, does some building work. He's retired, but I gave him a call, asked him if he wanted some work up in Raymond. It works good.

I had a big scare that put things in perspective. My girlfriend and I went on vacation to Brazil. Actually, I nearly died down there. I ate some seafood and had an extreme reaction. My throat constricted and I went into shock. I was scared, man. I thought that my time was up. This is it. Is this it? Is this life all there is?

I see now it's not all about money. There's more to life than making money. Up 'til now that's been my main concern: making money. It might come from my childhood, growing up in the projects, my mother and grandmother, getting knocked around by the cops. I guess I craved security and that's what money has given me. But now I see that there's more. I actually like helping people. Like your job, you don't make squat but you get fulfillment. So I may be looking for something else. But I damn sure will make more than you! A Rhodes scholar making like twenty grand a year—what a waste. Who knows, though? Maybe I'll take a leaf out of your book.

JUAN

Mechanic

On the inaugural day of the Clarendon Heights youth enrichment program in July 1982, Juan's younger sister Maria was dismayed by my ignorance of the upcoming wedding between the Prince of Wales and Lady Diana Spencer. Twelve-year-old Maria and her clique of mostly Latina girls would gather round the latest glossy magazine, enthralled by Diana's beauty and the romance of a royal wedding. Maria reminded me of that as we reminisced in her Clarendon Heights apartment in April 2006. She smiled ruefully and her eyes filled up. Were these tears about the demise of Diana or of Maria's own dreams? It was a heartbreaking moment. We had spoken about Juan's struggles, and Maria's own trials were evident: A teenage daughter was trying to round up two younger children scrambling over broken furniture, and a naked toddler started to whimper. Maria, heavily pregnant with her fifth child, got up quickly to soothe the two-year-old so he wouldn't wake her sleeping boyfriend in the next room. I was struck forcefully by the challenges of Maria's daily life and how they mirror those of her mother thirty years ago.

We phoned Juan from Maria's apartment, and a few days later I drove up to see Juan and his fiancée, Brenda. They live in an old mill town thirty miles upstate. Juan must have been looking out for me, because as soon as I pulled up in front of the house, he emerged to greet me. Juan has gained weight and lost hair but the same plaintive smile often creases his face. He is the father of five children he sees regularly, but he and Brenda live with her four children in the home they have bought together. Juan has fulfilled his dream of home ownership, and his pride was evident throughout our interview. The small, single-story house is located on what a real estate agent would consider the wrong side of the railroad tracks and the river. The mortgage required no down payment, and when I spoke with them, Juan and Brenda had met the payments for the first nine months. As we talked, and especially as Juan related the positive impact of home ownership on the children's futures, a depressive unease crept up on me, perhaps imported from Maria's apartment. I hope and pray that Juan and Brenda still own that house, but I fear that the bank does.

———————

JM: I'm catching up with as many people in the book as I can, asking them to talk to me as honestly as they can. The idea is to find out what you've been up to since 1991, which is the last time I talked to you. If you talk to me about your work to start off with.

Compared to the year you met me, I am doing a lot better today. I'm happy. I've mostly been at Jim's Tow since '83, when I finished high school. Mechanic.

And driver: towing for the city, other towns, colleges, snow removal, all sorts of things. Private property: people that park in no-trespass areas.

JM: So you have to have pretty good people skills for that.

You gotta have a lotta people skills. People that are mad, want to fight you. You can't get mad. You gotta remember you got the system backing you up. You get mad, you lose control. You gotta know when to be aggressive, because you hafta be aggressive sometime, same time as be professional.

JM: Are those skills you've always had or did you need to develop those?

Those you develop. Because every day's a different day. Every customer's a different personality, different attitude. God knows where they're at when you talk to 'em. Maybe a guy's been having a big argument with his ex-wife, and now you're towing his car. As time goes by you learn how to talk to people. You can judge 'em by the way they walking towards you. Every day's different and it's a constant battle. My job as a tow truck driver is like a war that never finishes. I'm looked at as enemy. But when the car breaks down we are their best friend. So it's fun. And I'm still there.

JM: And are there any routes for progression or have you gone as high as you can or . . . ?

If you have a regular license, only certain kind of truck you can drive. CDLs [commercial driver's licenses] get you in a higher level in the company; you can drive a big truck. And you might get a job to go to New York or Miami. And even me, I have a regular license and there's places I've seen that I never thought I'd be. The furthest place I've been to was outta state, took almost three hours to find the place itself. So it's interesting cuz you don't hafta put up with the traffic, clients yelling and screaming or whatever. It's good.

JM: How's the pay?

I can't complain. Based on your performance they give you a pay raise. If they see you're very responsible. Plus I can take a vacation any time I want. I can take an option of leave, and I still got my same pay and my same hours on my job.

JM: What sort of hours do you work?

In the body shop it's eight to five. And Saturday if I want to. In the towing part I useta work any hours. Let's say they schedule me eight to six. "Juan, can you stay a couple hours?" I wind up staying 'til nine o'clock, and that was on a constant basis. So Monday through Friday I was working well over fifty hours.

JM: Do they pay overtime?

No. They can't afford it. And the way they pay us we gain in the long run. Forty hours a week and then the rest in cash. You got the extra change cuz nowadays rents is too high.

JM: So are there any times when you've had a bad day and you're driving back and thinking, "I wish I was doing something else"?

Yeah, a lot.

JM: What would that something else be?

That something else be more in an office. I like clean job. A sharp-looking person is a very respectable person and people judge you by the way you look. In office you wear a suit. I have my high school degree. I have six months of college. I think I got pretty good communication skills with customers. I been with Jim's and we just became one whole big family, almost. My father was one of their customers back in '83. He got me the job because he had cars he took in over there to get repaired. I have no complaint with them.

JM: So is that quite important to you, the friendships you have there?

To me it is important because to get another job someplace else is not as easy unless you know somebody from within the company. Even if you can get in the company then you got all these other individuals there; they don't even know you. Now they feel like they being stepped on, because they hired you or you're doing too good, you the boss's pet. So friendship is very important to me in a job. In my job I already been there. These guys already know what I'm about, they know what I'm made of. So they don't judge you.

JM: So tell me a little bit about your family during this time. Because I remember you had children when you were quite young.

Yeah, I was twenty-three when I had my first daughter. She's fifteen now. That time was my young, stupid age, acting stupid in the street. Her mother left the state to Florida. So I started acting stupid, thinking I was mack daddy in the street. That took a bad course because when she came back I found out she was pregnant, six months down the line. And then that's when I found out another woman was pregnant too. I was confused—where I want to be, what I want to do, where I want to stay. I was looking for a shelter in terms of who really wanted to be with me. And so I was playing blackjack, [staying with] who treat me the best. I was being ignorant.

JM: How did you get through that?

My father and my mom took me out of state for two and a half months. Back to the Dominican Republic. It didn't solve the whole problem but it picked me up a little. I was born in the Dominican Republic, lived there 'til I was five. My real father's still there.

JM: Did things improve a bit when you came back?

My girls were born six months apart. So it was difficult. You try to fulfill a child's need, and the other one would get mad. It was taking a beating on me. I can say it was my past haunting me for my stupidity. I broke up with my baby's mom, then went off on my own, support my kids, have them when I could. I was living with my mom in Clarendon Heights. I didn't leave my mom's house until she passed away.

JM: How did you cope with her death?

It was tough. She died young. In her forties. She had cancer, so the radiation and the cancer were just destroying her by the inside. That was thirteen years ago. I was seeing counseling about it. I couldn't deal with counseling. It doesn't work with me. Because when it comes to desperate measure when you really need 'em they're not really there. I don't believe in counseling. I had counseling because I tried to commit suicide back in '92. Because my baby's mom tried to take my daughter away from me. So that's when I actually, I started really drinking. I couldn't get in to see my daughter. I feel proud of my daughter. And I guess my mind just freaked out one day. They took me to a clinic; I was there for about six months and then they had me see a counselor on a constant basis.

JM: That must've been really tough.

Living in the project, man, it's not the best place to live in. I always say I want to buy a house because I don't want to see my kids grow up in project. There's so much in project there waiting for, wanting for you to make a bad turn. It's so easy. If your parents has their own house, your kids follow you in the future. My parents didn't have their own house. So it was taking a course where I'm working hard like an animal, but the minute I walk into my house I bump into some crackhead around the corner. It was a lot of in the Heights back in the '80s. This is what I had to deal with. The people who lived on the floor below me. The drugs and the sexual activity. I hated it. I was hoping when I open the door to the hallway there was nobody there. None of them living below us worked. Just drinking and drugging. A lotta times I bumped into this stupid thing. I was young, but they were like, "You want a piece, you want to try it?" You say no, but it can play with a kid's mind at that age.

JM: Back then, in the lowest times, what were the different things weighing on you that made you feel trapped?

I feel trapped because my mom wasn't there no more. I didn't have my mother's love there, that support. My father was working with me but it wasn't like a father-and-son relationship after my mom passed away. Because he made his own life after that. I seek love in a lotta places, and I couldn't find it. I had to get a roof over my head. When I moved out of my father's house I didn't want to go back. I didn't want to live at my sister's house. I lived with a girl; it was not a perfect relationship, but what I saw was a roof over my head. Then in '98 I got married to a friend of my sister, but I got married too quick, less than six months. I wasn't ready for marriage. So it was not even a year before things started caving down again.

JM: Where did you go then?

I got involved with another lady. I was over my sister's house. I was house-hopping. For three years I didn't have an address, a place that I can call home. I lost a lotta opportunity in life. I didn't believe in housing, welfare, unemployment. I have a high school diploma. I ain't stupid. I can get a better job. Why I want to waste my time like some of these losers? What am I going to do with my life? I don't wanna live off a check they pay you every two weeks and just hang around. I just cannot stoop myself that low. I don't believe in Section 8 housing. I don't believe in welfare. I believe I can do anything on my own.

JM: Why do you think that was? There's a lot of people queuing up for these things.

I saw a lot of people that lived on welfare. They didn't worry about tomorrow. I always worry about tomorrow. Tomorrow is important. Today is gone. Back in Clarendon Heights in the '80s—I couldn't see myself in that place. So I always say I would never be in subsidized housing, especially welfare.

JM: So you're quite a proud person.

Yeah, I have a lot of pride in me. [*laughs*] I got high standards. Even though I can't see myself no lower than where I am now. I have to go up. Doesn't mean I got to be rich. I just like to be recognized that when you see me coming you say, "Here comes Mr. Juan." I'm not that loser. Or here comes a drug dealer or the crackhead or the alcoholic. You ain't gonna call me that. I cannot say I had a bad childhood. My parents never really let me hang out on the street, which I thank them today for it. I never lived a high school teenaged life: hang out today after school, play basketball, drink some beers. Mine was school, straight home.

JM: And how have you tried to influence your own children in the way they've grown up?

I've tried to teach them things from my past experience. Because I started drinking the age of twenty-one. And my first drinking and driving was at the age of twenty-two. But then I attempted to ignore it. I kept drinking. I try to influence them even though I was having my defect that I still was getting drunk when I had the chance. But I talked to my kids about my sister, not being a high school dropout, about my aunts, me, not being a high school dropout. How important a high school diploma is. About my aunt, one of them that finished university.

JM: So you drank quite heavily from twenty-one?

Yeah. It wasn't like I was born alcoholic, because I was able to keep my job. Some of them call it an alcoholic, and some people call it "Hey, he's had a bad turn that weekend. But Monday through Friday he's here doing his job." So I don't know where the line of an alcoholic is still. I can have a beer in my house and I can say I don't want to drink it. I can still say no to the alcohol. It's just I refused to say no to it. Like if I go to a party I have beer, then I may have a couple shots of Jack Daniel. But the only problem alcohol had given me was drinking and driving because unfortunately I was like some typical rich kid. Money, good job, car. All those three together, it's going to lead you to trouble, because I kept putting alcohol into the mix. After work, let's go out and have fun, and it's drinking. It kept leading me to trouble. Before I got married I was arrested and had to spend a week in jail for my drinking and driving. And so they put me house arrest for a year, and that was my third offense. Because I just got my fourth offense two years ago, another incident for my stupidity drinking. I'm driving a company's truck and I'm drinking and I swiped out about six cars. And that's when my life took a whole different change. I was arrested. They wanted to give me five years.

JM: Was anyone hurt?

No. Thank God nobody was hurt. But this was the fourth one. And it was hit and run because I wouldn't stop. When I hit the cars I knew what I was doing was wrong, but I didn't want to acknowledge that it was wrong right there and then because I was getting a rush—"I gotta get away from here." And then when I got to my job they arrested me for drinking and driving, hit and run, leaving the scene of an accident, and damaging private property. In the process of being incarcerated I let the system do its job. My boss, since I'd been there so long, he asked me if I wanted a lawyer. And I refused him. Obviously, I'm being too ignorant to acknowledge that drinking's going to kill somebody. And I said leave the system do its course. A good lawyer would probably get me two years' probation but no time. And I said no. So I did a year in the county jail. And I learned a lot. This is a one-way in, but this one has a back door and I ain't coming back. And I'm going to do whatever it take to stay out. When I came out I went to my old habit because I didn't have a place yet that I could call home. And then I got involved with my fiancée here and started breaking ties in a lot of different places cuz my daughter moved in with me and I was forced to look for a safe environment. This is my second daughter, Jasmine. She's fifteen. So I had to find a safe environment where there ain't no yelling, screaming, cursing, drinking, because where I was living that's how it was. The weekend comes, "Let's go get a six-pack, a twelve-pack," next minute we all drunk. I'm not going to pull another person into this mess who is innocent. And that was my daughter. I was living in Clarendon Heights still with an ex-girlfriend I was going out with. I was there for the convenience until my daughter moved in with me. And then I looked for a place more aggressive, spoke to my boss, and he had a place where I could move in. Rented that for a good price, and I been on the right track about a year now. My fiancée, we bought a house about six months ago. I give her a lot of credit; she put up a lot with me. Our relationship was touch-and-go. I wasn't ready to make a commitment but she fought for the relationship. And after I came out of jail we had a certain altercation and we crashed in a way that we decided to make it together based on her past experience and my past experience. And like I said, I'm doing good, I think. I mean, I own a house. I did complete something I always wanted, something I said I was going to do. It was to buy a house. Some people in the court system don't believe that I am involved with a house. They say, "Wow, you came out of jail and you already own—you're already involved in a house?" Because I didn't want to accept that alcohol was getting me in trouble, especially on the weekends.

JM: So throughout this time, the time you're in jail, or as part of the sentencing from before, or the time you attempted suicide when you were in the hospital, did you ever get any help for dealing with alcohol?

It's funny you ask me that question, but, you see, only you can help yourself. Because you can be telling these people your past so they can try to lead you some way. I respect their profession, but I find them somewhat hypocrite. Because when I really needed it, it wasn't there. I've been in the hospital and they say, "Oh, yeah, we're going to talk to you in a few minutes, give us a second." And I walked out because I was in there for about an hour. I have an appointment at one o'clock; why I'm here until two thirty waiting to see this counselor? Now this is stuff that's playing in my head. So now I'm thinking, "Should I walk away? This counselor ever really did anything to me?" Some of them, they tend to downgrade you in the process of trying to teach me where I did wrong.

JM: Yeah. But quite a few people discover they couldn't do it on their own. Like with AA, the twelve-step program, you get support not just from professional counselors but from other people who've been there.

Yeah, I'd rather listen to people. But in an alcoholic or drug-abuse program, they downgrade you. They look at you like you're a loser. And like I said, I have too much pride.

JM: What about your friends during all this time? Did you get any support, any help from them?

Y'know, in a time of need you don't have a friend. I was in jail thirteen months, and not one friend visited me. And that's one thing that has changed— choosing my friends. Doesn't mean I have to hate them or avoid them, but be more careful who I choose for a friend now. Because I did thirteen months and I didn't have one visit or even a postcard. And it felt lonely, because, wow, when you were there drinking and partying with these guys, they were all your friend. And then it's me talking to my own conscience in my own self. What you have in this cell? Nobody but me and your conscience. But to find out who your friends are you hafta go to jail? That's an ugly way of finding out. You don't know who your friends are until you run into trouble. So I'm happy with my fiancée right now. Because my worry is what's in my ring. What's in my ring is what is in my castle, my kingdom. My house, this is mine. My worries are only you guys. Out of this door, what happens out there, is none of my concern, none of my business.

JM: Is it four or five children that are yours?

Five children. Three boys and two girls.

JM: What sacrifices have you had to make to buy the house?

The money we make is enough to cover this mortgage. Certain expenses we got to cut out. We can't afford two cars. I had to get a major pay cut since I lost my license in 2004 for ten years.

JM: Because you're not able to drive, you're restricted to the auto-body shop and don't get the overtime?

Right. The shop is eight to five. Before, I could work until eight to five and go to the tow yard and work four hours. Now it's eight to five with no exceptions. So I took a pay cut on that. And that's cuz of my negligence.

JM: You still drive a bit?

I'm not going to lie: I do drive a little bit. Because I try to help her to drive when we go from here to the city. But she does most of the driving. I'll just do the highway driving. There's a chance of an accident. I'm always trying to keep my eyes as open as I can. It's unfortunate. It's like the system is there to break you. I got my errors, but you take my license away where I live off. They took me in for a year, then they're going to take my license for ten years. Might as well just kept me in there for ten years, because what good am I going to be out here if I can't drive?

JM: Is that automatic, the ten years?

Fourth offense is ten years. Automatic.

JM: Over the years, right from way back when I first knew you, have you had difficulties with racism—problems, hassles?

I had a little bit in the Heights. During high school there was a lot of racism. But I always kept to myself. Once my friend and me were over the tracks behind Clarendon Heights and a couple of white kids that were passing by in cars, and one yelled out, "Nigger." We were young and stupid, so we started running. They chased us to the railroad track. We said, "Well, if they want a fight they're gonna get a fight." We had rocks, so we started throwing rocks. I ain't gonna back down, I ain't gonna let nobody push me around telling me, "You're a stupid nigger." It was two white kids that went to the high school; they were probably Shorty's friends. I ran into a problem with him when he hit me one day. I was like 110 pound versus a 200-pound guy, telling me, "You fucking nigger, I'll beat you with a belt." I said, "You gotta be kidding." My friend Derek told me, "Don't bother; he's going to stab you right where you are." You had to be careful where you be walking around that neighborhood because there were lots of racial fights. I had a friend who was jumped by white kids, and they almost killed him. They sliced his head open with about twenty different slices on the head. He's alive today, but he walks with a big stick. He lived in the same building that I lived in in Clarendon Heights.

It was weird. Chris, we called him a wannabe because he was black, but he gets along with the white boys. We called him a wannabe cuz whatever the white boys tell him to do he would do. Boo-Boo, he knew how to stand his ground. He would go up and up with anybody even though he hang around with these white kids. But Chris, he was like a toy to them. With us he'd say, "What's up, nigger, you losers." I said, "Chris, why you want to talk to us like an ignorant white boy that you hang around with? Why you talking like that?" I actually saw him in jail. He's a big boy in there.

JM: The children here in the household, your children as well as Brenda's, are starting to face some of the same situations and pressures that you would have faced when I first met you as a teenager. How do you feel about their futures?

Well, my kids have a house, so I think their future's all set. They're not in the middle of the environment where there is drugs, alcohol—the minute they walk in the door that's what they see. That's what I used to see. You find a needle in the hallway. I will do whatever it takes for my kids not to see that. Yes, it will happen. There is drugs everywhere. But as long as I can fight that battle that can keep them in a positive attitude, I'm going to do that. And hopefully through my experience and directing them, hopefully, the right way, they can learn more about life than trying to become a loser.

JAMES

Programmer

I interviewed James in New York City. I've loved the place ever since we brought thirty-two Clarendon Heights kids there in August 1981. It was the finale of the first summer's youth program. We were to sleep on a church floor, so we made the children walk most places and tried to tire them out in a game of Capture the Flag in Central Park. It didn't work, of course; no one slept much anyway. James's younger brother Junior had been on that trip, and it all came back to me as I waited for James on the sidewalk outside his workplace. He burst through the big revolving door like a kid himself. Just over five feet tall, James still walks with a bounce. But I suspected the baseball cap was covering a bald patch. We walked to Central Park. It was a beautiful April afternoon, and the recording of the interview features background music provided by a chorus of birds and a saxophone solo. It proved a fitting accompaniment to what James had to say. At the end he speaks poignantly about the death of his mother, but almost everything else is buoyant.

———

JM: Back in '91, you hadn't worked for about a year, you were living at home, and you were sending out loads of résumés, so take me from there.

I worked for a temp agency, doing computer stuff at a bank. It was three days a week, Monday, Tuesday, and Wednesday, seven a.m. to seven p.m. I was making like six-fifteen an hour, some ridiculously low amount of money.

JM: You did that for how long?

Two years. I was tape librarian. One of the tape guys would call for tape 99. My job was to go in the back and find tape 99, load tape 99 up, sit there, wait until that tape ends, wait for them to ask for another tape, go in the back, load that tape up. That really got tedious. What really made me not like the temping was we had signed a contract that said that you couldn't apply for a job at any of the companies that you were temping at unless it was through the temp agency. So they had two operations positions open there that paid good money. So I went to the temp agency and I said, "They got two jobs open there, the manager likes me, he said he'd hire me." The temp agency said, "Nah, we can't do that. They're not offering enough money." So the manager said, "The temp agency asked for six thousand dollars more than what we're paying, to pay them to hire you. We can't do that." I went back to the temp agency and said, "Listen, I'm trying to work. I'm trying to get a full-time job. I don't want to be stuck temping." They said, "Unfortunately, that's how we make money; we make money from you temping."

I came on a trip to New York and met my wife. My cousin was going out with this girl who was cousins with my wife. She was trying to set her up with my brother Junior. I had a car and Junior didn't. So I said to my cousin, "Listen, if I start dating her and coming down here, then you can come with me and see your girlfriend for free." So he calls his girlfriend: "Listen, I know you want to hook up Junior with your cousin, but if you hook up James, I can come see you all the time." She's like, "Yeah, okay." When I had met my wife, she heard all these stories about me dating all these different women. And I was like, "Well, I'm not dating them anymore." And she says, "When did you stop dating them?" I was like, "Right now. If you go out with me, I'll stop dating them right now." So I called them and told them. I've been married now for fourteen years. I got married a year after I met her.

Her job had a company back home in the city, and she was going to transfer up there, and stay up there, and then her grandmother got sick, and her grandmother helped raise her. She's an only child, and I really liked her grandmother, so I was like, "You know what? I'll find a job out there." So I started looking for a job out here in New York, and her uncle said, "My company's got a computer job open." I put my résumé in, put down her Uncle Bob as a reference, fifteen minutes later they called me, said Bob had talked up a storm about me, I'm his niece's fiancé, and when can you come down for an interview? And I said, "I can come down tomorrow."

I got in my car and drove down and was interviewed by this guy Tim. He looks over my résumé and we end up talking about the Knicks. He says, "I see that you worked on the AS 400, an IBM computer system. If you needed to do something on the AS 400, how would you do that?" I'm standing there, getting nervous. He goes, "Better yet, because I can tell that you're nervous right now; instead of telling me, why don't you sit down at the computer and show me." Click, click, click; he's shaking his head. Says, "I want to know how much memory I have on the machine." Beep. "One more question: Can you start tomorrow? I've interviewed twenty people; none of them could answer those questions, and that's basic AS 400 operations." He said, "I'm looking on your résumé and I see that you was working a temp job in the tape library. How did you know all that stuff?" I said, "During my lunch break I would just sit there and watch everything the operators did." He shook his head, said, "That's how you learned all that stuff?" It's funny because at my job today I stayed late because one of the guys got a new server in and he's opening up the server, showing me, and one of the guys is looking at me like, "Dude, why do you care about what's inside the server?" I'm like, "I just do. I dunno, I just do." I remember all the stuff.

And so Tim hired me, and a week later my wife and I got married. I go to my boss, "Can I have Monday off?" And he says, "Yeah, not a problem." So I take Monday off, come back, and he sees a wedding ring on my hand, says, "James, you got married Saturday, didn't tell anyone, and the onliest day you wanted off was Monday?" I said, "I figured you just hired me; you didn't want to give me a whole bunch of time off." He was like, "James, go home right now and come back next week." I'm thinking, "Aw, man, a whole week without salary; I just got married." I said, "I can't afford that." And he says, "Do you think I wouldn't pay you for your honeymoon? What are you, crazy?" So I'm leaving, going out to my car, and one of the girls that I work with pushes this shopping cart filled with silverware, plates, and pans over to me. She's like, "Here, you're going to need all this stuff; you just got married." So I get home with all this stuff, my wife says, "What are you doing home?" I said, "They told me to come home and gave me this stuff." She's like, "They gave you a shopping cart full of stuff and told you to go home?" She was like, "You sure you didn't take anything, and they told you to go home for good?" [*laughs*] To this day we still have 90 percent of the stuff that they gave me that day.

I worked there. Then they moved from Mount Kisco to White Plains and had a big layoff, and my wife and I were having my first son. I was worried. They called everybody in the room and said, "We're going to lay the whole IT department off, but we're going to give you $10,000 on top of your severance pay, and you will be able to go and get unemployment immediately. We're going to keep one person: Sadé." Now, Sadé's not hurting for money; her mom was, like, president of the bank in Mount Kisco and her husband owned his own business. So this lady said, "I feel really bad, you're just having a baby, and when they offer me the job, I'm going to tell them no and to hire you." And I'm sitting there going, "Yeah, right." They call me into the HR department and say, "Sadé told us that she doesn't want the job and she suggested that we take you instead of her because you know more stuff than she does." Which was the truth: I did know more stuff, but I had a bad attitude. I had a really shitty attitude. So they were like, "You're going to have to calm down your attitude, though."

So I went to White Plains and worked there. About two years into White Plains we used to run these reports, and the reports basically told how much money the company was making. So when the company was losing money, I always knew, because I was the one that ran the report. So I looked and seen the company was losing all this money, just kept losing money, kept losing money, kept losing money. Two of the guys that I had worked with went to Calvin Klein in the city, and they're making like ten, fifteen thousand dollars more, and my best friend was, like, the manager there. He's like, "As soon as they lay you off, call me because I'll hire you at Calvin Klein." So I start working at Calvin Klein but in a different building than my friend and with a different boss. This boss, the best boss I ever had in my whole life, but when I went on the interview, I hated his guts. I couldn't stand him. The first night I'm working something goes wrong with the system and I get on the phone with IBM and take care of it. The boss comes in the morning, he says, "Come in my office. Your supervisor, I've promoted him, and his job is going to be open in the daytime. The way you handled stuff last night, I would rather have you on the day with me. The oniliest reason I put you on night is when I interviewed you, you seemed really uninterested with a really bad attitude. I put you at night because I figured you were better off working by yourself."

JM: How did you get these reputations for these attitudes?

I would tell people off. My best friend now, the one who got me the job at Calvin Klein, when I first met him I hated his guts, and he's black. I couldn't stand him. I thought he was such an ass-kissing Tom. I was like, "Look at this guy, he's just like, 'Yessuh, I'll do whatever you wants me to do.'" Because I just had that mentality. I really didn't like being here in New York. I didn't want to be here. I didn't want to be away from my family, and I was mad about it. How we got to be friends, we were talking about basketball and I said, "You fat bastard, you probably can't play basketball for shit." He said, "Why don't you come down to the park and play?" So we start playing, and I'm blowing him out at first. We're playing a game to 11, and the score's 11 to 11, 12 to 12. I'm wondering why this fat guy isn't falling out yet; turns out he played football in college. We ended up playing to like 36 and we're both panting, and he says, "Why don't we just call it even? You wanna go get a beer?" And he's been my best friend since then. But he got laid off, ended up being laid off for almost three years.

JM: How long did you work for Calvin Klein?

Maybe six months. I got offered a position at a newspaper company closer to my house. I woulda stayed at Calvin Klein, but there was rumors of a merger, that there was going to be layoffs. I had been laid off before, and I had a child now. So I tell my boss and he said, "What do you need, more money?" I was making twenty-seven or twenty-eight [thousand] there. And I said, "No, actually I need assurance that next year I'm going to still have a job." And he said, "As much as I like you, that's one thing that I can't assure you of."

JM: Back in '91 you talked about how you had to cultivate a professional attitude at work versus a street attitude, how you had to hold that line. It sounds like that was a struggle for you, that it's not easy to do.

Absolutely not. Now I work in the City. You have to have a professional attitude. I look at myself now, and I look at myself when I was younger, and they would have locked me up. The attitudes here don't coincide with the street. If you put Frankie O'Sullivan at my job, he'd last fifteen minutes. The minute they asked him to do something the wrong way, he'd tear their head off. And that was kinda my mentality. I'll give you a prime example: There was a lady today, when I was talking on the phone to my wife and reading an e-mail about some problem that I have been resolving, and this lady came and just interrupted me, asking me about something that had absolutely nothing to do with me, then stomps off and sends this e-mail to my supervisor to get me in trouble. If this was '91 I would have probably got up and beat her with my phone or something and gotten fired. What she did was really unprofessional and the sad part about it is this: If that was me acting like that, somebody would have said something.

JM: The dynamics in any office are often complicated. Looking back over the course of your career, are there any particular issues apart from personalities that come up? I mean, has race played a factor or is it just personalities?

Race plays a factor in every single thing that happens every day. Race plays a factor in how people react to me at work, like how she reacted. She probably doesn't know any black people, she doesn't have any black friends. And if you don't interact with any other races, you have this mental picture of how they act, how they're so aggressive and everything, and, to me, that's how she took it. She took it as me aggressively saying to her, "Get away from my desk. That aggressive black man, he's acting up." I'm like, "Whatever, man, that's you. That doesn't have nothing to do with me."

JM: Does it get to you?

When I was younger it would get to me. When you're younger you're less tolerant of petty ignorance. Now that I'm older, what am I gonna gain, if I got up and started arguing with her, except for I'd look as stupid as she looked?

JM: Tell me about the effect that the family has had on you.

A major effect on me. When my oldest son was born, my whole life changed. Before I got married, I used to go to clubs, fights would happen, shootouts—I'd go see who's shooting. Now I have kids and a wife and I'm responsible for them; I can't put myself in that situation. My wife is a preschool teacher. When I had my son I realized that there was a lot of things about my attitude and my mentality that had to change because I had to be responsible for this little being.

And my kids help me deal with my relationship with my father. When I grew up I couldn't stand my father. I thought my father was terrible, the meanest father in the world. I was like, "This guy's just mean for no reason, always on me about nothing." Now I see why my father was the way he was, because he was like me. He wanted the best for his kids. He didn't want to be going to Bradford prison to visit his son James, who is doing twenty to life. He wanted me to be a lot better than he was. Like my son now, the twelve-year-old. He got a bad report card the other day and I didn't really spaz out on him, but he and I got into a little conflict. I had to actually laugh because it reminded me so much of me and my dad. I was just like, "Hey, I've been here before. Wait a minute." I'm just sitting there looking at my son. My son's upset. And I busted out laughing. He's like, "I don't understand what's wrong with my father. Is he losing his mind?" "The hell I am, dude. I've had this argument before, this same exact argument, and I wish I could explain to you how it went." It's because you want better for your kids. My father is almost seventy years old now, and I'm forty in January, and my father still worries about me, calls me every other week to make sure I'm doing okay. Since I have kids of my own I can understand: I guess you just spend the rest of your life worrying about your kids.

JM: How did your parents try to motivate you to do well in school and all that?

My father beat the hell out of me; that's how he tried to motivate me. With my son yesterday, I was like, "Dude, you're getting upset because I'm yelling at you." My father pulled out the cord and whipped us. That's how we got motivated. We didn't get the motivational speech.

JM: But did it work?

I hope it works a lot better for my son than it did for me. I had a hard edge. When I was young and acting up, I didn't learn nothing. My father would say something, it would go in one ear and come out the other ear.

JM: So how do you try to motivate your kids?

I'm lucky in the sense that one of my sons, all I have to do is yell. My youngest son, he's eight, he's just amazing, there's nothing I can say that scares him. He's as bad as me. He's exactly like me.

JM: The twelve-year-old, is he beginning to understand that there is a connection between what he is doing now in school and his future?

When I started laughing the other day, that was the point I was trying to make, that if you get good grades now, you can go to school, you can go to a good college, like some people that I know, you can go to Oxford, like some people I know, and you can write books and do all kinds of stuff. But he's still young and he doesn't get it. I didn't get it because I didn't care. But my son is so much more talented than I was; that's what makes me want to motivate him. His bad grades isn't because he doesn't care. He has bad grades because he becomes bored very easily. He'll be interested in that flower right there for about two seconds. Then he'll look over there and he'll see those flowers and be interested in them for about three seconds, and he'll see all the cars up here and he'll be interested in them for about ten seconds. He can't focus on one specific thing. He wants to do everything in the world, so he'll do a little of this, a little of that, a little of this, a little of that. But I'm trying to explain to him, "Dude, when it comes to schoolwork, you can't do a little bit of this, and a little bit of that, and a little bit of this." My son went from straight As to Cs and Fs, and every comment is "not paying attention in class." Knowing my son the way I know him, I know he's not paying attention in class. He does it because he's not interested. I'm like, "You don't have the luxury of just applying yourself in what you're interested in, unless you're rich."

JM: You had a real interest in computers, like when you were doing that tape job you were actually watching these guys. Now, was that because you wanted to get ahead at your job or just because you loved the computer?

Because I loved the computer so much.

JM: Have any of your jobs actually challenged you, pushed you, given you that satisfaction, or have you always been doing stuff that was beneath you in terms of your computer ability? I remember way back, you said, "I should be programming, not processing; I'm just typing stuff in, I'm not programming." Have any of your jobs actually challenged you?

My job right now, that's it, and when I worked at the newspaper.

JM: Tell me why it's more interesting, more challenging, more enjoyable?

I got promoted twice since I been there. It's more stressful, but they promote you, depending upon your work. If you show them that you're motivated to do something else, they'll move you into that. I started off as their computer operator at night. A lot of things happened at night that they never had anybody there that really wanted to grasp, to take care of. I was doing computer operations, but I was doing a lot of stuff for the warehouse, running a lot of warehouse reports and different things like that. Sometimes I would have to go to Queens, if the system went down there; I would bring the system back up, restore the backup and stuff, and they saw how good I was. So after a while, my first review, my supervisor said, "What do you want to do, because this isn't the job for you. You're really good at it but you can do a lot more." And I said, "I'd like to do help desk, working with the hardware and the servers and stuff." And he said, "If I keep you here in the mornings on Friday for an extra two hours, you'll be paid, and we train you for help desk, working with the hardware and stuff, would you be interested in doing that?" I said, "Yeah, absolutely." I been at so many jobs where they told me that same crap. But I get home that day, I get a e-mail on my pager. It's from my boss: "Next Friday you're going to start staying over two hours so you can learn help desk." So I stayed three Fridays in a row. So my boss calls me one morning, says, "I need to speak to you." So I'm like, "Aw, here we go again; they're going to lay me off." He said, "Nick resigned, so his job is open, and I want to offer it to you." I said, "What?" He goes, "Nick resigned this morning, and I want to offer you his job." I said, "Doing the help desk?" He said, "Yeah, what did you think I was training you for?" The next Monday I go in, he's like, "Come into my office." They got the lady from HR in there, got all the paperwork in her hand. She says, "This is what your salary was, this is what it's going to be now. In two weeks you're going to start on day shift." I'm like, "I don't believe it." He said, "Why is this such a shock to you?" I'm like, "Okay, whatever."

JM: So why was it a shock to you?

Because I had had people tell me so many times before. At the newspaper my boss was going to train me to be a programmer. Guy gets a job in California and leaves. My new boss tells me, "You don't have to keep studying. I'm not going to have you as a programmer. I don't want you as a programmer. I don't need you as a programmer."

JM: Any reasons?

Yeah, he was a prejudiced asshole.

JM: How did you get the job at the newspaper?

Now, this wasn't a guy that knew me. I saw it in the paper, so I sent my résumé. Guy tells me to come over, starts asking me stuff about the AS 400. He has this deep, deep southern accent. He was from, like, Kentucky. I said, "Aw, damn, he ain't hiring me." My whole attitude had changed. I was like, "Yeah, whatever, buddy; yeah, I got extensive background on the AS 400; no, I don't have a problem with working at night." He says, "Come in here. I want to have one of my staff members show you around." I go in there, and I'm looking, I'm like, "What the fuck? This southern-ass guy got all these black people working for him." I said, "He probably ain't paying nobody shit." So I go in there, meet one of the guys that I was to work for, great guy. One of the smartest guys I ever worked with. If you looked up *nerd* in the dictionary he would be there, his face would be there. His name is like Harvey or some shit; I mean, he had a nerd name, everything. And we immediately hit it off. Boss comes back, says, "We're going to set your drug test up for two thirty this afternoon, and then we'll talk money and everything. I don't know what you said to Harvey, but he said to hire you immediately and don't get too comfortable on nights because you're not going to stay on nights too long."

JM: The southern accent: Your parents' roots were in the South?

My mother's from Delaware, my father's from Georgia. And when I was in high school I had an incident with a janitor that had an accent like that. So I immediately equated it to that. And it wasn't like that. He got along with black people better than he got along with white people. I was just like, "Whoa, were you black in another life or something?"

A friend of mine, Jacob, left there and calls me about three months later: "Listen, I'm a manager now at this company out in Jersey. What would it take for you to come out here and work with me?" I said, "Seventy-five thousand dollars," joking. He said, "What would you say to sixty-five thousand?" So I took a ride out there to see where it was. It was real far out in Jersey. So I went home and told my wife. My wife was like, "I'll move anywhere, but I'm not moving to Jersey."

I went to another firm from the newspaper after the Kentucky guy that was training me to be a programmer left. A friend of mine was a consultant and he was working with this lady who places people at this firm, so I got an interview with this guy Pete. It's right across from Grand Central, so I get there and before we go upstairs to Personnel, there's these guys talking about the MTV awards the night before. So we start talking and I'm telling them about the show and everything. So I get my coat to go up to the seventh floor for the interview and Pete says, "Just fill this out. When can you start?" He said, "I don't care what you know. If you can get along with those two guys, you're hired."

First day I'm there, he gives me a thick pile of papers and says, "Read those instructions and set up your machine." "Myself?" He goes, "Yeah." So I set up the machine, turned it on, and it wouldn't come on. So I opened it up, looked inside, seen what was wrong, and fixed it. So I'm on the Internet. They're sitting there looking. They're like, "James, what are you doing?" I said, "I'm on the Internet." They're looking. They said, "That was a joke. This is your machine," and they pulled a brand-new machine out of a box. "You fixed that machine? We thought you'd try to turn it on, then you'd come to us and say, 'Yo, the machine doesn't work.' And we're sitting here thinking, 'What's going on?'" They see me typing on the computer and they're like, "Is he pretending that he's doing something on the computer?"

JM: So you're a bit of a whiz with the work, everybody's consistently surprised at the quality of your work, but as important as that has been your relationships, your being able to get along with people.

Absolutely. But earlier in my career I couldn't get along with nobody.

JM: Tell me about your current job.

I'm help desk administrator: hardware, installs, everything for this hotel chain on the corporate side. Anything goes wrong with the computers there, we take care of that.

JM: How much are you making now?

Fifty-two thousand dollars, something like that.

JM: Full benefits, health and dental and all that?

Yeah, yeah.

JM: Back in '91, we were looking at some of the other guys, like Super, who was really struggling, and you were pretty clear that whereas in 1984 you might say they just didn't get their act together, in '91 you were saying, "I can't really blame them; they haven't had the opportunities." How do you feel about that now? The kids who haven't made it the way you have, is it their fault or is it the system's fault, they've not had the opportunity?

I think about that sometimes, and I never noticed until I was older that I had two parents. I had a mother and father that both worked. They tried to keep me on the straight and narrow, and a lot of these people, they don't have parents. Some of them got parents that are just adolescents. I mean, the cards are kinda stacked against you. The deck's kinda stacked against you.

See, my cousin, I used to hang out at the bars with her. Both her kids have been in jail. But if you look at the mother, can you blame them for not knowing how to act? If you don't know how to act it's because of your parents.

If you hang out with a whole bunch of drug heads, you're probably going to end up being a drug head. Me and Junior had this discussion the other week where we went through all the people that we knew that had served time in prison. And Junior said that if one of us had gone to jail, my father would have bailed us out of jail and then killed us. It's a joke amongst us now. He would have bailed us and shot us right in front of the jail.

JM: How did you cope with your mom's death?

Badly. Everybody coped pretty badly. I really cared about what my mother thought about me. My son was just born and I knew she wouldn't get to enjoy him growing up. I think of all the stuff my mother did. I mean, right when she gets to the point in her life that she's been striving to get to for the longest, that's when she dies? She was just getting ready to retire. She had a brain aneurysm. That was the first time she seen my son. So we're there and we're getting ready to go home, and she had this really bad headache and then she just falls out. We call the ambulance and they come and get her. The worst part of that whole incident was having to call my father and tell him. My father never had to deal with nothing. The onliest thing my father ever did when we were kids was beat us. Beat us and buy us stuff. My mother did all the rest. It's just like in my house. It's funny because my life is kind of paralleling my parents' life. My mother was, like, the diplomat, she was the one who remained calm, and he was, like, the guy in the background, Vito the killer. You go, "All right, no more talking now; Vito, choke him." Same thing with my wife. My wife's like, "No more talking now; Vito, choke him." [*laughs*]

DEREK

Trainer

Derek moved to Utah in 1996. He is a lodger in the basement bedroom of a small house in a working-class neighborhood. The single-story house is as non-descript as they come but the surroundings defy description because of their natural beauty. I arrived at Derek's home on a crystal-clear May morning. The temperature was nearly seventy degrees but the valley was still surrounded on three sides by snow-capped mountains. It's difficult to put into words, but the air tasted different and the light looked different than in Clarendon Heights, and the setting somehow suited Derek. So far from home, a black man in suburban Utah could easily feel out of place. But Derek is skilled at adapting to new surroundings in a manner that doesn't compromise his identity. He was clearly at ease in the neighborhood as he led me to a small park where we sat at a picnic table. His eyes sat more deeply in his face on a bed of tiny wrinkles, but Derek was still Derek: insightful, grounded, big-hearted, humorous, and still plowing his own unique furrow.

JM: In 1991 you were . . .

I was married with two children, working for Commercial Airlines [a pseudonym for a major airline]. Me and Faith got divorced in '96, I transferred out here with Commercial Airlines, and now I work for Travel2.com. I'm the main trainer. It's so different here. No Dunkin' Donuts, no state lottery. Food is horrible, so bland. Back home you've got Jamaican, Portuguese, Italian, Russian, whatever. You don't see that here. You have to have a membership to get into a bar. Utah is Latter-Day Saints, Mormon. Surrounded by blonde, blue-eyed women, just freaky. When I came here, you walked in a store, they'd hold the door open for you, they'd say good morning—it just freaked me out. People are very, very guarded. If you're not a part of the church, you're something else. Everything in this state is hidden. This is the methamphetamines capital of the world. There's not five blocks around here where you won't find a meth addict. This is such a repressed state, where I don't think people can really express themselves without feeling that there will be repercussions. But they've been averaging one adult a week getting arrested for trying to entice a minor for sex over the Internet. It's an epidemic here. Sometimes I miss home, but I like the fact that it's so open, and it's clean out here. You'll hear birds in the park. Even their traffic jams aren't bad. You'll see snow on the mountains until June. If I could talk my sister or my mother into coming out here and spend the rest of their days, I would, just because it's so nice and pleasant.

My move out here, it was really hard on Faith and the kids, but I needed to get away. I needed a change, a slower pace. Growing up I had always been the one worrying about everybody else. Helping to try and fix things. I just needed this for me. So it was selfish, but I'm over it.

Gary Santa, in February of '96, called me and said, "I'm getting married." So I came out here, saw that Commercial Airlines was out here, and within a month I just transferred out here. The only opportunity was reservations. So that began my other career as customer service. I think I'm good at it. I like people and they hear it from the tone of my voice.

JM: What was the working environment like?

It's a gigantic office off the interstate, gated entryway. A giant call center. You have your own desk, at least during the day.

JM: For someone who's used to doing ramp work, messing about with your colleagues, was it quite different sitting at a desk and dealing with somebody else on the phone?

It's a completely different environment, more subdued, more safe. There was a lot of internal customer service training: how to treat each other, how we react, how to be respectful, how to show empathy, all of those things.

JM: Tell me about your career with Commercial.

I had started in '87 at $6.37 an hour. By the time I left Commercial in '97, I was making twelve something an hour, with flight benefits. At Commercial I worked the ramp, the ticket counter, training department. The ramp was a great job because you had a team, but you could do what you wanted, so long as you handled the flights. And it was a great working environment with all the Italians, Irish, Portuguese, and Polish.

JM: Have you found in your working life that race has been an issue?

Not for me. Some black people, their mentality is to use that race card to my advantage, and I've never done that. I've always loved people. Going to a private school and just accepting that I wasn't necessarily a part of them.

JM: Are there times when other people's prejudice has affected you?

If you're black there's definitely that silent prejudice, and it will be there for the rest of our lives. I accept it. I have better things to worry about. The majority of my friends all of my life have been white. I don't care what your skin color is. Here, if you're black and part of the church, then you're accepted. If you're not, you feel as though you're being pushed away or they'll watch you a little bit more. But this is where I want to live. It's comfortable, I feel at home, except for the church oppression.

JM: Were you always paid an hourly rate at Commercial or were you salaried?

Always hourly rate. If you're working salary you're at their beck and call. With Travel2 I'm the trainer. The previous trainer left and I jumped into the role. They kept asking me and then I decided it was a relief to get off the phones. I like to talk to people, I know what makes people click, so why not a trainer? I train all the new hires, eight to twelve people, for at least four weeks, teaching them the basics of the computer system, their customer service skills, just how to talk to people.

JM: What's the starting wage for somebody just coming on?

Nine dollars an hour, depending on experience. It can be up to as much as twelve dollars an hour.

JM: What do you make now?

I'm at $11.50, and that really burns me, because I volunteered to become the trainer. I have great people skills, I'm very dependable and dedicated to the job. I like the people I work with, I like my job, but there's got to come a time where I flat-out say what I deserve.

JM: Were there opportunities for promotion at Commercial?

Yeah, to become a ramp supervisor or go up and work the ticket counter, the gates: There were always opportunities. But I've always wanted to be just one of the little guys. To be a part of the minority that's able to voice your opinion without repercussions.

JM: Did bosses at Commercial try to put you in positions of authority?

Absolutely. But they knew I just like being a part of the little people that actually make things work and make a difference, even if it's only internal. If the rest of the world doesn't see it, I don't care. I'm not a glory hound. I just like being one of the small people.

JM: Where do you think that comes from?

From the fact that growing up we had to struggle so much. The race wars in the '70s, me and my brothers having to be the fastest-running kids in the neighborhood. I mean, I loved our childhood. People loved us and hated us. Being black in a predominantly white neighborhood. Growing up, it was like you had to prove yourself. Prove that you weren't weak, that you had some type of integrity. That you were going to stand up for yourself, stand up for your family. It didn't matter if it was the toughest group of people around. So it was definitely hard. There was Frankie and Shorty, the ones who sold all the drugs, had their older friends beating people up. It was the early '80s, we had finally gotten to the point where we just had enough. And we just said, "Anybody who wants to challenge our manhood, whatever, bring it on. It's going to be them against us." It just all stems from being black in the '70s. I remember when we used to live in the big building, and one night we were looking out the back window and there was tear gas everywhere, and all you could see is the police chasing different gangs down the streets. We just grew up through it.

Our older brother, Blade, hated Boo-Boo. He thought Boo-Boo was just too white. Boo-Boo listened to rock music. In high school he went to Occupational Education, got to do mechanics. Blade thought he needed to be more black. They were always fighting. Blade thought he could be the father figure. It caused a lot of stress between the family. Now we're internally fighting, not to mention other races didn't like us.

JM: And then you had the whole experience of going to Barnes.

That was just overwhelming. I went to school where these kids would come to school every day in Audis or Mercedes. But the private school was great. There was safety there. We didn't have to worry about somebody opening up with an AK-47 or bringing a knife to school or anything like that. It's all these nice, wholesome people protecting their own. You know, their fortunes and building a future for their kids. They had money, serious money.

It changed my life because I've never done drugs, never smoked a joint. I saw what it did to everybody else: my mother, my sister, my brothers, all of them. Right on the other side of town is the good life, so am I going to jeopardize that just for a cheap thrill? No, no, no. But Barnes, it showed me that if you really want to succeed, you've got to make it happen. But as well it showed me politically, it's who you know. If you know someone, you can make things happen in your life, in your favor. I didn't want to be a part of that either. So high school, I went back to Lincoln, right back to my roots. The blacks, the Portuguese, the whites—everybody integrated into one school, and I loved it. Four of the greatest years of my life, absolutely. Juan and Mokey, all of us running around the school together, just being ourselves, and enjoying our lives. There was that comfort level. That's what I needed.

JM: What prompted you to come back?

I just had enough. They [Barnes] were controlling. You had to learn French; there wasn't any Spanish or anything. You had to learn things like Greek history, which really has no relevance in my world. A controlled curriculum where you didn't have any say. But my freshman year in high school, I could dictate where my future lay. What path I wanted to go on. It was refreshing.

I always felt that their only concern was numbers, racial harmony. I just felt as though I was a number there. I go back to the public schools, and I've got my friends, more acceptance. Even the teachers were supportive; they were friends, people you could actually talk to. In the private school, even though I did it for five years, I didn't feel that I was a part of it.

Academically it's weird, because I had gone to the private school simply because of my grades. From fourth grade, I was doing math at an eighth-grade level. My deductive reasoning and things like that, they were impressed by that. God, I should have been a lawyer

JM: Could you go back and tell me about your relationships a bit?

There was Faith. We had been together since high school. That ended in '96. Carlton was twelve and Amy ten. We're still friends; that will never change. She still sends me Portuguese and Italian cookies every couple of months. Then I met Nicki at Commercial, moved down to Turvey, lived with Nicki for two years, me and her and her daughter. We still e-mail each other every week. I'll call her every now and then. If I get back to the city we'll go out to eat. She's one of my best friends in the world. And she's friends with Faith, so do you see my pattern? They're all friends; it's the freakiest thing on this planet. When I came out here for Gary's wedding, I met Kelly, and so I lived with her for about four months down in Orem. That was very much a wrong decision. I was thirty, and she was only nineteen, wanted to hang out with all the college kids, go out and party. But the Mormon side of her, every Sunday she had to have dinner with her family.

JM: How did they cope with you guys living together?

It was definitely difficult; they were always inviting me to go to church, and I never wanted to go, and I hung around with Gary Santa, and he was, like, the resident alcoholic. But her parents were always very respectful, very, very nice.

From Kelly it was Hannah, another girl that I met in Commercial that everybody loves; I don't know why I broke up with her. She was one of the greatest women I ever met in my life. I was with her for three years, living together. I have never not been in a serious relationship up until three and a half years ago. I had never not lived with someone since I was married to Faith in '84.

There was Winnie, the mother of my three-year-old and five-year-old. Aahh. She irks me. She's one of those weird cowgirls that cares more about animals than people. I tolerate her because she's the mother of my children. We lived together and then I just finally had it. I moved out. She was irresponsible, her priorities were way off.

JM: Were the children a conscious decision, or just sort of happened?

Just happened. We had five-year-old Cole back in 2001. Then we had Corey. Winnie had a toothache, took a pain tablet, and I guess it nulled out her birth control pills. But even before he was born we were on the outs. Me and her, we just don't mesh. We got into an argument this morning because the kids want to come live with me. We have joint custody; she has them during the week, I have them on the weekends. She also has Colin; he's nine years old. He's my buddy. Cole is like my little best friend. I like the look in his eyes when he's happy or I know when he's sad. It's hard because I have the other kids 2,400 miles away and my daughter hates it, because she doesn't get the attention that Daddy should give her. I offered for her to come live out here with me. Y'know: Life will be easier, you've got friends here from when you stayed the summer, you can get a job, Dad'll help support you. She didn't want to do it. What happens? She gets pregnant! Thank you, God. [*sarcastically*]

JM: So your kids now are aged twenty . . .

Carlton's gonna be twenty-two in August. He's into economics and business, wants to go to school in New York by September. Amy is nineteen, she has a three-year old boy as well. She wants to go into nursing.

JM: How did you react when you found out she was pregnant?

They didn't tell me until she was like five months along. She's already feeling guilty. I'm not going to pressure her. She doesn't need that. It was by a twenty-two-year-old guy that got another girl pregnant at the same time. When my daughter was about eight months pregnant he just stopped seeing her. You learn from your mistakes. There are repercussions, obviously, but what can you do? She's doing fine, lives with Faith, but planning on moving out next month.

I'm very positive, probably the most chipper and positive person you will meet in your life. I can bring light to a situation. We have a thirty-four-year-old girl in work who was just diagnosed with cancer. Me and her kids, we went and got some glow sticks and we put them around her, and she's like, "What are you doing?" And then we turned off the lights: "Hey, you're glowing from the radiation therapy." Little things like that.

If you don't have your family and your friends, if you don't have positive things around you, you're just going to be depressed, you're going to be alone, and you're not going to go anywhere. You're going to be in a dead-end job, just doing nothing. Me, I've done almost everything I've wanted to do with my life. If my kids want to do something, Carlton is like, "Me and a girl from college, we're going to Europe for the summer: Do you have any money to help me out?" He's got his money.

I always save for a rainy day. Always, always, always. Because I know it's going to happen, something will always happen. That's why I live in a basement apartment in a small house, because I don't care about all of the creature comforts. I have my stereo, my PlayStation 2, my twenty-seven-inch TV, but I have my kids and my friends. So that's all I need. I don't need anything else. My ex-girlfriend had told me that this lady had a room for rent, so I'm renting from her. She can't cook. I cook better than she does. That's scary. It's very inexpensive. You've got to be positive, you've got to be supportive. I go and mow her mother's lawn or shovel her walkway when it snows. In the back of my mind I'm always thinking, "Just in case." I don't expect something back in return for doing something, but I like people to know that they can depend on me, that I will always try and be there. And I love people. I do.

JM: You're very good with people, and I imagine you're a very good dad. Are you sometimes surprised that your relationships haven't always worked out the way you would have hoped?

I think it's me. It's definitely me. I get bored. It's not that I get bored of people, but I need something to stimulate me. Faith was a great wife, she's still a great friend, but I had known her from high school. All of the women that I've been with are great women, great providers, great family people, but sometimes I just need to be alone. I haven't been in a serious relationship since me and Winnie broke up. It doesn't bother me because if I'm feeling lonely, I have friends. I need my space. When I'm at work, I am the social butterfly. I'm the positive one, just way-too-chipper one.

JM: It takes a certain amount of emotional energy to be positive all the time. Do you ever have dark moments yourself?

There have been times in life where I've been depressed, where I'm like, "I don't want to grow old alone." It's weird because there's a girl right now who would give up her life for me. Really nice girl, thirty-four years old, my kids love her to death and everything, but she has drama in her life, and I don't like drama. Part of it is very selfish. I don't like drama, but there are times where I am absolutely lonely. Where it's like, "What am I doing with my life; what's really going on?"

JM: Had there been a lot of drama in your own upbringing?

Absolutely. Growing up in the '70s, everybody did drugs except me. Being black in a white society. My brothers were at odds with each other a lot. My sister needed a lot of support, somebody to be there for her. When I went to Mexico in 1980, I came back, my father was gone. He went back to his family in Baltimore. So I step into the role of helping my sister. Me and Molly were his kids. Blade and Boo-Boo were by a different father. He treated them completely different. His mother treated them completely different. Boo-Boo had driven down to Baltimore one time with his girlfriend, and my grandmother wouldn't accept them, wouldn't even let them in the house. So, from that point, I stopped dealing with my grandmother. I can be a very cold person. My father, I talk to him probably once a year. I can hold a grudge. My mother, I don't know if she had a nervous breakdown or whatever, but she was doing her own thing. As far as drama goes, I understand people get into situations. But if you can't, for the sake of your family and the people you care about, if you can't take the time to find a way out of it, why would I drag myself down too? I have to keep a positive attitude. Everybody knows I am always a happy guy.

JM: So how do you manage to be so upbeat all the time?

I like my life, even though it's been difficult at times. I'm turning forty in a month, and it's like, "Where has everything gone?" I'm very grateful for you coming because that's allowed me to get back in contact with Mokey. He's laughing away, "What, you have more kids?" I'm explaining what's been going on in my life, and he is so shocked that Carlton is in college. He's like, "We have missed so much." And we have. But we've enjoyed our lives, we've done what we wanted to do, we've never let anybody hold us back, we've never hurt anybody on the way. Looking back, if I'd have been a cop or joined the fire department, that would have been one of the best things for me. I skydive now, I'm scuba certified, I do all those little extracurricular things, but it's just wasted on recreation. Not that it's wasted, but I could have done more. Maybe instead of going into the navy in '84, I could have gone into the army or something.

JM: If you could just tell me about your time in the service . . .

My grandfather was in the navy, my father was in the navy. Both of my brothers were in the army. In '84, before graduation, I didn't know what I was going to do with my life. I wanted to be a soldier. The navy disappointed me. I should have joined the marines or the army. I regret that. I wasn't getting paid and it was just stress, stress with Faith's health, and I went AWOL. I was young and stupid, and I just decided, "What the hell." If the military wants me they can come get me. Which they did. [*laughs*] About six months later the local police come to the house, brought me down to the police station, and held me there until the military police came for me. So I called Faith and got to see her for about an hour, and they flew me out to Chicago to the military base. Had a hearing before the judge advocates general. Confinement for two months. It was really hard. I'm a grown man, but I cried. I'm like, "How could I be so stupid to get myself in such a position?" Being part of a prison gang. The military is a piece of cake compared to regular prison, but I'd never want to do it again. I was put in the brig for two months and then I was let go. Originally it was a Dishonorable discharge, but then it was upgraded to an Other than Honorable discharge. I was in the reserves. I regret that I did choose the wrong branch of service. If I had gone army or marines, I'd have probably been a lifer.

JM: Financially, supporting the children . . .

I've paid child support since 1996, and it's been obscene. Sometimes it's been up to more than 500 dollars a month. So if you're not working overtime, taking home 350 dollars every two weeks, that wasn't cutting it. It's hard, but you reap what you sow. I don't spend a lot of money. If the people I love are taken care of, that's all that really matters. It's not so much an issue here with the cost of living. For this basement apartment I'm only paying 200 dollars a month. Back home, studio apartments start at 1,000 dollars.

JM: So before Carlton went to college, you were supporting all four . . .

Yeah, so thank God for overtime. I was actually going to get a second job, but I just have so much energy. Before I started working for Travel2, I actually worked at a car wash. Inside the car wash was a bakery, a little sandwich delicatessen place. I worked in there for $6.25 an hour.

JM: And what was that like?

I'd look at my paychecks: "Oh, my God, I'm not making anything!" But it made me happy. I was frontline customer service, right there interacting with people. It was a great environment, all the clientele were really nice, treated you like family. But then reality sets in: "I need to make money, I'm getting too old to be doing this."

JM: You told me a bit about your wages. What about benefits in the various jobs?

Commercial had flight benefits, of course, and you pay your medical and dental. I went to work for Diamond [another national airline] for two years, and it was free health insurance, but now my friends that work for Diamond have had a 25 percent pay cut, plus they're just like everybody else in the world now: They have to pay for their own medical and dental. At Travel2 I have to pay for my medical and dental, but they also give us a [discount] travel card.

JM: Tell me about the time at Diamond.

Diamond was different, in that management sucked. They didn't care. You were a number. They cared whether you had good phone stats, if you came to work on time, if you were at work every day. Granted, the benefits were great, but I wasn't happy there.

JM: "Phone stats," what's that mean?

On reservations, your calls had an average handle time, and there are numbers that you have to produce: for instance, eight and a half minutes on every call. But it just didn't feel like home. Commercial was completely different. People said hi to you in the morning, invited you to parties. Outside of work you could actually be yourself, and inside of work you get your job done. Diamond was just, "You have to produce. Come here, do this." And I didn't like that. At Commercial it's open-door policy; you can come in, say hi, sit down at his desk if he's not busy. I never felt that at Diamond. Other than the benefits, there was really nothing to keep me there. The pay was nine bucks an hour or something like that.

JM: Why was it that you needed to retire from Commercial, take early retirement?

I had transferred out here, and then Faith got sick. I was trying to be there for the family, trying to be there to support her, so that she didn't have to do it all alone. She had cervical cancer at the time. I couldn't get back into the city, because there were no positions open. So I transferred to Newark and was commuting on a daily basis from the city to Newark. I was living with my sister in the city, working on the ramp in Newark. I would take the first [air] shuttle out of the city and one of the last shuttles back every single night. If there's no free seat, and you don't know one of the flight attendants where you can sit in that jump seat where the kitchen is located, you can't get home. So I'd have to sleep overnight in the airport and then work in the morning and then try and catch the next flight out home. It was horrible. I did that for about two months, then I came back out here. But things were still bad with Faith. Her health was just horrible: rheumatoid arthritis, lupus, cervical cancer. So I just left Commercial altogether and had gone back to the city. For three or four months I wasn't working.

JM: Commercial couldn't find you anything back home in the city? And they wouldn't hold your position here?

No. It was weird. There's my family; maybe I should go back and just stay in the city. It just proved to be a wrong decision. Financially, it was definitely a wrong decision because I had a stable job, steady income, benefits which the family can take advantage of. I'm still regretting it to this day. I felt I needed to be there more for the family. I needed to be around. Hindsight, Faith recovered and everything. It was a good thing to do for the family, but careerwise it was a devastating blow. I was making good money in a job where I knew it could be a career for the rest of my life. I loved the job, I loved the people, and it's just really too bad. Because I wish I could go back to Commercial, that's where all my friends are; it's the life that I know. But at least I've made new friends in Travel2, been there a year, and plan on being there for a while. It's kind of strange, my being out here in Utah. It's so different and so far from everything. Other than the fact that I have the two boys, I probably wouldn't . . . It's going to be ten years next month. In ways I feel isolated, just like when I went to the private school.

JM: Tell me about losing Boo-Boo.

Him and Ginger and the girls they had together, all died of AIDS. He had AIDS, and I just saw him slipping away, and I couldn't handle it. Nothing but skin and bones, literally; his muscles were gone, his skin was just laying there. I would go and visit him and I'd just see him laying there in bed, his eyes just so stressed, and he knew he was going to die; it was just a matter of time. He was bedridden, he couldn't eat by himself, he couldn't get up and go to the bathroom. It was really, really sad. But then we get to the funeral—oh, my goodness. All his friends, they had written songs, all these people turned it into a party, and it was fantastic. Even when we went to the cemetery, they poured beer on the grave, just sat there and smoked joints. It was the funniest thing in the world. Then we all went back to my sister's house, and we had the party there. And these people didn't leave until Sunday. The funeral was on Friday. My mother finally had to say, "Okay, everybody get the hell out. You can come back next week and visit, but you all got to leave." I still dream about Boo-Boo very vividly, all the things that we never did as kids, because I miss him.

JM: What do you think the future holds for you?

I'm going to become a helicopter pilot in the next year. I'm comfortable where I am, doing customer service. I'm comfortable being a part of a team, I like the people in my life, I love my family. I fly small planes. I took the kids to Yellowstone; we flew from here to Yellowstone last year. Damned expensive. My biggest mission is to make sure my kids are taken care of, because I don't trust the world. Sorry, but I don't. I want to make sure they're taken care of. I don't need anything; I've done everything I've wanted to do in life. If I find that one person that I settle down with. It'll be hard to tackle me because I'm just so fickle, frugal, freaky. We'll see.

I will always try and be there for other people, so I think that gives me inner happiness. My friends, if they don't have anybody to help them, they will call me. Guys, girls, whatever. If somebody needs someone to talk to, they'll call me and know that I'm not going to judge. I wasn't put on this planet to judge; I'm on this planet to be a friend.

REPRODUCTION, REDEMPTION, AND RESPECT

Introduction *by Jay MacLeod*

Returning to Clarendon Heights in 1991 was a depressing experience. Both the Brothers and the Hallway Hangers were struggling, and their young lives suggested that social inequality is more entrenched in the United States than I'd thought. Thankfully, the picture in 2007 is brighter. The majority of the men may still be mired at the bottom of society, but some have achieved working-class stability and even penetrated the middle class.

I was explaining this to Isaac when we met up for a lunchtime reunion after twenty years. Isaac grew up in the nearby Emerson Heights housing project and was enrolled in our youth program for three summers. When the crack epidemic devastated his neighborhood and many of his friends went to prison (including his brother on a life sentence), Isaac managed to finish high school, graduate from college, and work at the statehouse. He now runs a health initiative for African American men and is an elected member of the municipal school committee. Isaac read *Ain't No Makin' It* in college and was eager to hear how the men have fared, some of whom he knows personally. When I told him that the picture in 2006 was more positive than in 1991 and that some of the men had even broken into the middle class, Isaac stopped me. "What do you mean, 'even'?" I looked at him blankly. He continued:

> Is it such a great achievement that two or three or four of your guys have made it 'even' to the middle-class? Hell, some of those guys have the smarts and social skills to be running a company or a college or a country. [*laughs*] Look at the

clown who's running this one now [George W. Bush]! Seriously, Jay, now that I've been around, been to college, and gotten politically active, I can see. Those guys that I grew up with that are now in prison, living on the edge, some of them dead: Lots of those guys were bright, real bright. I'm not just talking about street smarts. A lot of them were academically gifted as well, or could've been. It's such a loss, for them and their families but also for this city and this society. It makes me sad and it makes me angry. I look back and I know I've been really lucky. Avenues opened up for me that could easily have been shut down and blocked off. Now people use me to deflect criticism away from the system, suggesting that if Isaac from Emerson Heights can make it, anybody can if they have the smarts and the drive. We're back to blaming individuals rather than looking at the environment and the society. Your book taught me to resist this individualistic way of thinking that comes so naturally to most people. You haven't forgotten the lessons of your own book, have you?

Perhaps I had.

It will be easy for readers to fall into the trap of understanding Chapters 12 and 13 in purely personal terms without considering structural constraints on opportunity. My decision to present the new data as raw oral history contributes to the problem. This chapter is the solution. It is written not by me but by Katherine McClelland and David Karen—friends, colleagues, and advisers of mine since 1982. It may seem an odd abdication for an author. But I am a parish priest, and I simply do not have time to review the new literature on social reproduction, to dust off and sharpen up my tools of social analysis, or to sift endlessly through the interviews in search of patterns and meaning. All scholarship is collaborative, and in sociology there is a long tradition of data sharing, in which collectors are not the sole analyzers of their data. Extending that division of labor to ethnography is unusual, but in a sense, I've simply asked McClelland and Karen to take the first crack at secondary data analysis. Fresh eyes and ears have brought some fascinating insights, and I am grateful for their work.

Analysis *by Katherine McClelland and David Karen*

Twenty-four years—almost a quarter century—have passed since we first met the Hallway Hangers and the Brothers. We have seen them finish high school (or not), get further education (or not), and move into the labor market— primary, secondary, and informal. Their challenges have been pressing and varied: finding a job; keeping a job; pursuing additional training; negotiating fatherhood and, for some, marriage; coping (or not) with drug addiction and alcoholism; learning to deal with a white-collar workplace; surviving prison and managing life on the outside; learning that CHR (Criminal History Record)* spells "N-O" for stable jobs in the primary sector of the economy; and surviving on the street. We have said goodbye to Boo-Boo, one of the two black members of the Hallway Hangers, who died from HIV/AIDS in 1994 following the tragic deaths of his daughters and common-law wife. (Yet, as his brother Derek recounts, the funeral was oddly joyous—perhaps reflecting the shared understanding, even among those without much in the line of conventional religious faith, that Boo-Boo had indeed gone on to a better place.) And so we come, now, to the Brothers and Hallway Hangers at age forty.

In the previous two chapters, you heard the men tell their stories in their own words. Here, we present a descriptive and analytic account of the impact of social class and race on their life trajectories. During the course of this chapter, we will summarize what has happened to the Hallway Hangers and the Brothers since 1991 and, by focusing on a set of themes, provide an analysis of the forces that have shaped this period of their lives. However, this effort should not be regarded as the "final word" on the fate of these men. What this book so clearly illustrates, as we follow the varied and at times unpredictable paths of these men's lives, is the necessary arbitrariness of any end point. Although starting points matter, and early decisions do have an impact on later ones, the particular ways in which both structural and individual factors matter and affect each other vary at different stages in the life course. Thus, while our analyses here extend the theoretical frames MacLeod developed in the first two parts of the book (as discussed below), we will also introduce new frames.

As we observe the middle of the men's life courses, we enter a zone where patterns of movement are much harder to discern and compare. Schools impose an institutional structure on young lives that limits the number of possible pathways. Because the decision points are more clearly marked, it is thus simpler to

---

*Criminal History Record, or CHR, is a designation the FBI uses to refer to an individual's criminal "rap sheet." To preserve anonymity, we have adopted this name to stand for the acronym used for the parallel set of records maintained by the state where Clarendon Heights is located.

identify and analyze the factors that influence success or failure in this domain. By contrast, the "labor market" is not a formal organization. There are multiple pathways in and out, many possible branches, myriad decision points. Sociologists typically identify patterns of attainment and mobility based on bundles of attributes of individuals—in mobility tables, path diagrams, or regression equations. And in those kinds of analyses, we don't begin to understand the *dynamics* of starting, stopping, starting over, succeeding . . . we don't get at the *texture* of people's lives. But from these studies, we do know that social class of origin retains a significant impact on destinations, though it is not the only influence.[1] As noted in Chapter 11, a study such as *Ain't No Makin' It*, with its small and deliberately nonrandom sample, can't speak directly to the relative magnitude of the effect of social origins or race on outcomes, but it can show us something about how this impact is transmitted, what factors exacerbate it, and what factors reduce its influence. And, through the voices of the Brothers and the Hallway Hangers, it can show us something that quantitative studies cannot: what it all means to those who are experiencing those changes.

The interplay of structure and agency looks different in midlife, but the dynamics of social reproduction are clearly visible. Through the stories of these men, we see how social structures shape available opportunities, and how their various stores of capital (cultural and social) and their habitus importantly direct their choices. Agency also shapes structure: Among those who move away from Clarendon Heights, we see how a new set of opportunities appears and new choices are possible.* Yet we also see, as Frankie recognizes, that even when you move, you take yourself along; in Frankie's words, "I couldn't get away from me." Culture** mediates between structure and action, as the search for respect in the construction of self, already evident in the teenage Brothers and Hallway Hangers, assumes even greater prominence in their lives and decisions.

Our argument about what happened to the Brothers and the Hallway Hangers has two levels. The first level addresses the specific factors that seem to have mattered most in explaining the current social locations of the former Clarendon Heights residents. The second level attempts to provide an understanding of a motivational substratum for the activity that takes place above. The bottom line is that social reproduction marches on. Of the thirteen subjects MacLeod reinterviewed, only one has experienced long-distance income mobility, and this was a Hallway Hanger (Slick). Two others appear to have attained a middle-class lifestyle in white-collar jobs (Mike, James), and another (Frankie) has been able

---

*In Chapter 11, MacLeod reminds us how Bourdieu's notion of habitus as a "structuring structure" overcomes the structure-agency dualism (see especially page 258).
**Especially, when conceived as a "cultural toolkit." See Ann Swidler, "Culture in Action: Symbols and Strategies," *American Sociological Review* 51 (April 1986): 273–286.

to achieve stability in a working-class union job.* Many, however, are still on the margins of poverty or worse. On the whole, the Brothers have succeeded a bit more than the Hallway Hangers. One can probably point to their different starting points and different aspirations as factors in understanding these outcomes, as MacLeod explained (see pages 129–135). We will point again and again to the importance of social and cultural capital—with a focus on *both* their constraining and liberating potential—in explaining the forty-year-olds' current situations. In addition, we find a striking effect of physical relocation on the men's habitus, structure of opportunity, and ultimate outcomes: under the right circumstances, *moving matters.*** Underlying these patterns—the second level—is the men's motivation *to gain respect:* to receive recognition and *be seen* in a world that has made this a scarce resource, indeed.[2] We find that the men's resources and opportunities shape the *ways* they pursue and conceive of respect and that these specific pursuits and conceptions often lead them to disqualify themselves from certain opportunities and to reproduce their original social positions.[3]

The Organization of This Chapter

Our analysis begins with a summary of "who is where" for each of the men in 2007, and a consideration of the larger structural context within which their journeys have taken place. We continue with an examination of how the structure of opportunities and the men's social and cultural capital, through their habitus, shaped the occupational trajectories of the Brothers and Hallway Hangers.*** These trajectories are also importantly shaped by other factors, and we turn next to a brief consideration of these in the context of the social reproduction framework: substance abuse and crime; race and racism; family; and relocation. We then move to a consideration of the meaning of the narratives themselves, and the issue of how these men understand and "explain" the course of their lives thus far and, in the process, articulate who they are to the larger world. By examining their

---

*We will avoid a detailed set of class definitions. We label the jobs as working-class or lower-middle-class because none is based on traditional educational credentials, which usually provide security because of their convertibility. Some of the jobs do include median (or close to median) incomes and benefits packages.

**It is important to see "moving" not as a verb that someone can simply *do* to turn one's life around; it is not a matter of simple agency. It is probably better to say "having moved matters." We wish to see moving as part of a larger process of interaction among individual agency, habitus, and structure of opportunity.

***We employ MacLeod's conceptualizations of cultural capital and habitus in this analysis. Our conceptualization of social capital is given below.

stories of social mobility and immobility, "class consciousness" (or, more precisely, its absence), and personal redemption, we see how their search for respect as men from "the projects" has animated and informed their actions and shaped their habitus, and how this process differs for the Brothers, who began as strong adherents of the achievement ideology, and the Hallway Hangers, youthful rejecters of the same. Finally, we conclude by examining the fate of the next generation: What has happened, and what seems likely to happen, to the children of the Brothers and Hallway Hangers? We can already see evidence that social reproduction continues into the next generation.

As we reflect on the interviews, it is helpful to keep in mind Erving Goffman's[4] observation that we are all constantly engaged in the process of constructing our own biographies; we engage in a continual process of making sense of our past in terms of our present. Interviews such as these offer their subjects a unique opportunity to refine and present themselves to someone who knew them "back in the day." These men vary greatly in their apparent degree of self-insight and in the extent to which they have thought through the issues we are interested in. Some already use frames for their stories that fit comfortably with a sociological analysis; some do not. Some are given to introspection and others are not. As is the case in any narrative, almost all these accounts contain contradictions. But from a sociological perspective, these contradictions are as interesting and "true" as the facts that fit. They are part of the real story of these men's lives and indeed are central to its meaning. MacLeod's long relationship with the Brothers and Hallway Hangers makes these stories even more compelling. The interviewees trust MacLeod to tell their stories but they know they can't tell him just *any* story; indeed, they must be "true" to who they are, who they were, and who they still aspire to be.

SO . . . HAVE THEY MADE IT?

The post-school careers of the Brothers and Hallway Hangers now span approximately two and a half decades and a host of larger structural trends in the occupational, legal, and social welfare spheres. How have these changes impacted them, shaped their aspirations, and/or constrained their choices? In the lives of these men, we can clearly see how social structure and individual agency intertwine in midlife.

The interviews preceding this chapter present these men's experiences and worldviews in their own words and in considerable detail. They contain sufficient data to construct a brief capsule of each man's current social location. To facilitate our analysis, we will begin with a summary of where, in general socioeconomic terms, each has ended up at age forty. (More details on their current situations can be found in Appendix 2, which contains brief biographical sketches of each man.)

Beginning with the surviving members of the Hallway Hangers, we see that **Slick** has effected a dramatic turnaround in his life. He moved to a southern state in the early 1990s with his wife, Denise, and son, Tyler, and found steady work as a roofer. In 1995, after a disagreement with his boss, he struck out on his own and has been self-employed ever since. In 2006, we find him still with Denise and Tyler and now the father of two daughters, with his own fishing boat and a large house under construction. **Frankie** is also a success story, though a more modest one. Choosing to remain in the community surrounding Clarendon Heights, he lives with his wife, Carla, and son, Darren, and has been steadily working union jobs for the city and state for the past thirteen years.

Far less successful, but still hanging on, are Jinx and Stoney. **Jinx** has managed to remain steadily employed in a series of blue-collar jobs; none was union work and several paid him under the table. His current job, working on the crew of a landscape gardener, is his favorite. He lives near Clarendon Heights with his girlfriend and their child. **Stoney** has turned his back on the pizza industry and discovered his true vocation, as a drummer in a rock band; however, this is part-time work at best. He lives in a working-class town twenty miles from Clarendon Heights with his wife, Connie, who supports the family.

Shorty, Steve, and Chris are in much worse shape. **Shorty** is trying valiantly to turn his life around for the sake of his son, who lives in a nearby state. He struggles with work-related injuries, sustained through years of heavy lifting in moving and construction jobs. Although he is on partial disability, this does not provide sufficient income, so he works when he is able at the same types of jobs that crippled him in the first place. **Steve** is currently unemployed, lives with his mother, and deals marijuana on a small scale. At least he is out of prison. The same cannot be said for **Chris,** who, since 1991, seems to have alternated prison terms with stints of homelessness. 2006 found him once again behind bars, this time for possession of drug paraphernalia. As Chris tells it, the arresting officer was doing him a favor by bringing him in off the streets and giving him another chance to get clean.

In 1991, none of the Brothers could be said to have "made it" by the conventional standards they set for themselves in high school—a stable job, an independent household, the beginnings of a family. By 2006, life has improved for many of them. Married or in a long-term relationship, with seemingly stable jobs and homes in the suburbs, James and Mike have realized all three components of their measure of success, though they certainly hope there's more in the offing. **James's** computer career finally took off after he left town to be with his girlfriend; he is now working the computer help desk at a large downtown corporation in another state and living with his wife and son in a middle-class suburb. He states that he earns $52,000 per year with full benefits—more than two and a half times the official poverty line for a family of four in 2005.* Although we don't have an exact

---

*This would be close to what the U.S. Bureau of Labor Statistics used to call its "medium budget" line. A household at this level would own its own home, have fifteen years left on its mortgage, and make do with older cars, appliances, and electronic gadgets. Stephen J. Rose, *Social Stratification in the United States: The American Profile Poster* (New York: New Press, 2007).

figure for **Mike**'s most recent earnings, it seems clear that his real estate career has provided him with a fluctuating but at least median income since 1991. He now lives in the suburbs with his girlfriend and her daughters, whom he is able to send to a Catholic (but not a "big, fancy twenty-grand-a-year") school.

Mokey and Derek are not as successful but are getting by. **Mokey** is now a manager at the copy service where he's been employed for a number of years; though he notes that this promotion actually meant a drop in his income (due to the loss of overtime), he is pleased with it nonetheless. **Derek** moved out West several years back and is now employed as a trainer for an Internet firm at $11.50 an hour. Despite these successes, neither Mokey nor Derek has been able to purchase a home: Mokey and his family live in a cramped city apartment and Derek rents a basement apartment in someone's home.

To different degrees, Juan and Super are still struggling. Despite his aspirations in 1991 to move on to a "clean job," something worthy of respect, **Juan** is still working at Jim's Tow. However, he is proud that he has managed to buy a modest home in a nearby working-class town with his fiancée, Brenda. But as MacLeod notes, it seems likely that this was made possible with a subprime mortgage, as Juan stated that he made no down payment; thus, Juan and Brenda, like so many others in 2007, may well have already found themselves in default. **Super** has finally turned his back on the drug trade, having served several terms in prison. He is now clean but has not yet found a steady job; he gets some work with a moving company and lives with one of his sisters to help make ends meet.

If we array these men in a line, from least to most successful in conventional terms (weighting economics most heavily, but including family and social stability as well), it would look something like this:* Boo-Boo (black Hanger), Chris (black Hanger), Steve (white Hanger), Shorty (white Hanger), Super (black Brother), Stoney (white Hanger), Jinx (white Hanger), Juan (black Brother), Mokey (black Brother), Derek (black Brother), Frankie (white Hanger), James (black Brother), Mike (white Brother), Slick (white Hanger). Had we tried to predict this in 1983, no doubt we would have come up with a somewhat different ordering. The predominance of Hallway Hangers at the bottom is not surprising, but their presence near the top is. The four most successful among this group—the only ones to have attained the key components of their definition of success**—include two Hangers and two Brothers; three

---

*The reader may disagree with this ordering, as might the Brothers and Hallway Hangers themselves. "Success," as Derek's interview illustrates, can be defined in many ways; in this ranking, we are relying on the conventional socioeconomic indicators—wealth, income, housing, stability/security of housing and income, benefits, etc.

**As stated earlier, this would be defined as a stable job, independent housing, and the beginnings of a family.

are white and only one is black. The two who have fallen completely out of the race—Boo-Boo and Chris—are the black members of the Hallway Hangers. Though this group of men is too small to constitute a sample in any statistically valid sense, it is still striking that here again, at midlife, there is no gainsaying the influence of race on outcomes.

It is also interesting to look at the two sibling pairs, one white and one black, and how differently they have fared. Boo-Boo and Derek seem to have played out their lives in ways close to what we might have expected based on their peer group associations as teens. Derek, who as a youth was marked as academically talented, is making $11.50 an hour at a relatively stable job, and Boo-Boo, who maintained his Hallway Hanger rejection of the traditional path to the American Dream, is dead. But Slick and Steve, both Hallway Hangers, have ended up in very different places as well. Slick is the successful roofer down south, and Steve is the license-suspended, marijuana-dealing steam fireman still living in his mother's home. Of these four, Slick is the one whose outcome is surprising. When two people reject traditional routes of mobility, we expect, racial exclusion being what it is, that the black man, Boo-Boo, will pay more than the white one, Steve.* But why didn't Slick pay the price as well? It is worth noting that within each of these pairs, the sibling who left town is the one who prospered. Derek, who graduated high school and left the city, moved into a white-collar occupation that provides an income just slightly above the poverty line.** Slick, with a concrete skill acquired through networks, left town as well and eventually developed a successful business. So the two siblings who were able to escape the "penalized spaces"⁵ of the old neighborhood avoided the fates of their siblings. And the white Hallway Hanger Slick, who spent his youth rejecting school and imbibing beer balls, ends up doing a lot better than the black Brother Derek, who had originally been committed to his educational journey. There is more to this story than race and geographic location, of course, but the connection is important; we shall explore this further below.

Given the failure rate of small businesses, it is somewhat striking that the two most successful members of this cohort (Slick and Mike) are self-employed.

---

*Indeed, it is striking that Boo-Boo and Chris, the black rejecters of the achievement ideology, end up much worse off than everyone else. It appears almost as if one can survive youthful rejection of mobility if one is white but not if one is black. The paths of the Hallway Hangers were bleak; coupled with racial exclusion, Chris's and Boo-Boo's habitus could not be restructured, and the double-sided rejection (of society's valued pathways by Chris and Boo-Boo; of Boo-Boo and Chris by the opportunity structure) proved impossible to surmount.

**At $11.50 per hour, Derek is pulling down approximately $23,000 per year (assuming forty-hour weeks and fifty weeks worked per year—somewhat bold assumptions in this part of the labor market).

This speaks not only to the opportunities still present in this sector of the economy, but also to the paucity of alternative routes available to those who start at the bottom. By becoming entrepreneurs, Mike and Slick created their own paths to success. They did not have to worry about CHR checks, unsympathetic bosses, or corporate hierarchies. As we will show, both were able to use their stock of working-class cultural capital to their advantage, rather than hauling it around as a handicap. It should be kept in mind, however, that in an advanced capitalist economy, individual entrepreneurs' small businesses—especially as they depend on the boss's physical health—are always in a precarious position. The current slowdown (circa 2007) in the real estate market that initially buoyed Slick's and Mike's fortunes may yet take its toll.

Most of the Brothers have proven capable of landing, and holding, steady jobs. But it took more than the right attitude to get there. Their faith in school, at least as a means for acquiring skills and credentials that could be leveraged into middle-class status, seems misplaced. Only James has attained success via this route, and even in his case, it took a combination of a proprietary school certificate and a demonstrable skill (fixing and maintaining computers) to open the right doors. Their dreams are no longer completely deferred; rather, for most they have been modified. Mokey is pleased to be making progress at last, having moved into management. Even though it meant a cut in pay, being a manager fits more comfortably with his middle-class aspirations. Yet he lives with his wife and son in a cramped one and a half–bedroom apartment in the city, juggling bills and trying to work out a savings plan so they can eventually afford to buy a house.* Derek professes no interest in the material trappings of middle-class status (a good thing, since he doesn't have many), and defines himself as successful based on his friendships. Only Super and Juan admit to dissatisfaction and disappointment with where they've ended up, but each places the blame on their struggles with alcohol and drugs. Super still has faith that he'll be able to turn things around; Juan, whose fall was less dramatic, and probably more tied to the failure of the traditional path to bring him success, is less optimistic.

Arguably, the Brothers have risen just high enough above the Hallway Hangers, and the Hallway Hangers have fallen low enough, to legitimate the basic tenets of the achievement ideology. But the achievement ideology would not have led us to predict that two of the four most successful would come from the peer group that rejected the standard path to the American Dream, or that three of the four would be white. Nor would it lead us to expect that the most successful Brother, Mike, would have had the kind of career he has had—moving out of potentially stable union jobs with the post office and fire department and

---

*We estimate that he's making approximately $28,000 per year, based on a $14 per hour wage rate (again, assuming forty-hour weeks and fifty-week years).

into the more volatile real estate market (where Mike's self-reported income from property transactions has declined to $50,000 to $60,000 per year from "a couple of hundred thousand a year" a few years ago). The traditional formula for success—"to get a good job, get a good education"—has not worked for these Clarendon Heights men.

The career trajectories of the Brothers and Hallway Hangers need to be understood in the context of the economy (national and local), for this determines the structure of opportunities within which the men move. In the 1991 follow-up, we saw the impact of the economic downturns of the 1980s on these men's early careers. The period from the mid-1980s through 2007 includes moments of economic expansion and contraction but has generally been seen as a more favorable time. Yet it is worth noting that the real value of the minimum wage declined between the time MacLeod first encountered the Hallway Hangers and the Brothers and the recent interviews: In 2006 dollars, the minimum wage was $6.38 in 1983 and $5.28 in 2005.[6] A forty-hour-per-week, fifty-weeks-per-year worker would earn less than $11,000 at the 2005 minimum wage, well below the $19,350 poverty line for a family of four.[7] According to many observers, however, the poverty line doesn't indicate very well how much it would cost to meet basic needs.[8] One estimate of a basic family budget for a family of four living in Baltimore in 2000 was almost $35,000, a budget that did not include fast-food meals, vacations, movies, or any savings.[9]

Yet in good times and bad, this was also a period of increasing income and wealth inequality.[10] According to the latest edition of *The State of Working America,* "Between 1979 and 2000 . . . the real income of households in the lowest fifth [of the income distribution] grew 6.1%; the middle fifth was up 12.3%; the top fifth grew 70%; and the average income of those in the top 1% grew by 184%."[11] In terms of wealth inequality, the ratio of the wealth holdings of the top 1 percent of wealth holders to median wealth was 131:1 in 1983, and it had increased to 190:1 by 2004.[12] This was also a period of unionization decline: More than two-fifths of blue-collar men were unionized in 1978, compared with less than one-fifth in 2005.[13] Even in the period that was probably most advantageous for workers in the bottom half of the wage distribution—from the early 1990s until about 2000, a period characterized by low unemployment and a rising minimum wage—low-wage workers only kept up with the median-wage workers.[14]

In *Chutes and Ladders,* Katherine Newman examines the fate of low-wage workers in an expanding economy. She finds some evidence to support the proposition that "a rising tide lifts all boats"; her Burger Barn employees fared better in the 1990s than they had in the 1980s, with fewer bouts of unemployment and higher wages.[15] Neither the Brothers nor the Hallway Hangers are in this segment of the labor market, yet their experiences in the 1990s also reflect the influence of an expanding economy. Slick's roofing business took off in the superheated Sun Belt economy, with its expanding and increasingly affluent population as well as its vulnerability to hurricanes. Mike has made a successful career in real estate in a state where housing prices rose steadily through the 1990s and into the early years of the twenty-first century. Frankie's job in the public sector is made possible by an expanding (or at least, not contracting) tax base in a high-spending state. Mokey has finally landed a stable job, with benefits, in the service sector. Only James has had to contend with layoffs, due to the volatile nature of the information technology (IT) field during this period. But as the industry recovered in the early twenty-first century, so did his career.

Thus, in the generally more favorable economic context of the 1990s and early twenty-first century, several of the Brothers and the Hallway Hangers have experienced some degree of success, or at least greater stability. What factors account for the differences in their outcomes? There are many frames through which we can examine these men's careers. In the account that follows, we will focus primarily on those that have shaped the analysis to date—the social reproduction framework (with its attention to the importance of structural factors, race and class, and the various forms of capital) and the impact of drugs, alcohol, and criminal careers. We will also discuss the role of families (both of origin and of procreation) and geographic relocation. Finally, we will turn to a discussion of identity, culture, and meaning, especially the role of culture as mediating between structure and action.*

CAPITAL ON THE LABOR MARKET

How do you get a good job in America today? For the best jobs, the starting point is clear: Get a good education, and lots of it. Doctors, lawyers, accountants, architects, engineers—even, in the post-dot-com boom era, computer jobs—generally go to those with educational credentials beyond a bachelor's degree. Clearly, the Hallway Hangers have excluded themselves from such jobs on the strength of their poor performance in high school. But what about the Brothers? Here is where their failures in school, and in particular their inability to complete college, come back to haunt them. The only Brother who is able to use his education on the job market is James, whose high school career ended

---

*This analysis could also be framed within a life-course perspective. For the sake of simplicity and unity of focus, we have not drawn all of these connections. But the emphasis within the life-course framework of the ways in which multiple interlocking contexts influence life trajectories is compatible with the analyses set forth here, and we have drawn selectively on the literature in this area to provide additional context for our findings. For an excellent overview, see John H. Laub and Robert J. Sampson, *Shared Beginnings, Divergent Lives: Delinquent Boys to Age 70* (Cambridge, Mass.: Harvard University Press, 2003).

inauspiciously with his expulsion from Lincoln High for excessive truancy. But his father's refusal to accept this as an end point led to his acquisition of a GED and his subsequent enrollment in computer school. Here again, however, he was at risk of being wrongly tracked, but by switching from evening to daytime classes, he was able to acquire a credential that, though not a traditional degree, was at least able to open some doors for him on the labor market. His current position, working the computer help desk on the day shift at a large corporate headquarters, makes him the only Brother to have succeeded in the field to which he originally aspired. And he is the only one of either group to have used an educational credential to get where he is now.*

But even James found that his computer degree alone was not sufficient to move him into the type of job for which he was trained. His first jobs in the field were not as a programmer—the job for which he was trained—but as an operator, usually on the less busy (and much less visible to supervisors, who might notice his talents and promote him) night shift. And even here, his jobs were usually obtained with the assistance of a contact; although he has been working in the IT field for almost twenty years, James has obtained only one job "cold," by answering an ad and sending in his résumé. Thus, even for the Brother with the strongest educational credentials—the best signal of accumulated human capital**—*social* capital has been at least as important in obtaining work.***

The importance of social capital in the labor market has long been recognized,[16] but only recently has it been seen as critical in studies of movement out of poverty. Wilson pointed to the significance of the lack of economically valuable social ties in the lives of impoverished inner-city African Americans in the late 1980s,[17] giving rise to a range of other studies that have reinforced and extended his conclusions.[18] The role of social capital in the larger process of social reproduction is more complex than that of human or cultural capital, and it interacts with other forms of capital in various ways. But its role in the work careers of the Brothers *and* the Hallway Hangers is clear, even in midlife.

---

*If James had been from a middle-class environment, one could imagine that his strong attraction to computers and evident talent in working with them might have led him to MIT or some similar institution, and from there to a career at the forefront of the IT industry.

**We accept that training in a computer field confers specific knowledge that may be attractive to employers and that may, indeed, be useful on the job. We insist, however, that there are signs of cultural capital that are important in this process as well.

***Portes provides a useful elaboration of Bourdieu's concept of social capital. Following Bourdieu, we think of social capital as the access to resources provided by one's social networks. Obviously, those networks may differ enormously in the amount and quality of those resources. See Alejandro Portes, "Social Capital: Its Origins and Applications in Modern Sociology," *Annual Review of Sociology* 24 (1998): 1–24.

The value of "contacts" is recognized by almost all of the Brothers and the Hallway Hangers. Returning to James, we recall that his first job after graduating from his computer course, a "good job" working nights as a computer operator at a bank, was obtained with the help of a friend who worked in personnel at the same firm and was able to call in a favor. A year later, another friend helped him get a better job at a large corporation in the suburbs. Company restructuring and his own admitted lack of professionalism caused him to be fired in 1990 (see p. 206), and when MacLeod caught up with him in 1991, he was working part-time as a tape librarian and had been looking for work for the past year, fruitlessly sending out résumés. Things finally broke for him a year later, when his fiancée's uncle told him of a computer job open in his company, located in another state; James put in for it and, with the uncle as a reference, received an interview the next day. The interviewer gave him the opportunity to show what he could do and he was hired, but without the activation of his newly acquired social capital, it seems quite unlikely (given his past experience) that the interview would have taken place. Though initially hampered by a lack of cultural capital—the residue of his "street persona," which we will discuss further below—James continued to build social capital at this job and was able to parlay his contacts into continuous employment and upward mobility through several companies, until he finally arrived at a job he enjoys, that pays a good living, has full benefits, and that more fully utilizes his talents and skills. Only one of the jobs he's held over the past fifteen years was obtained without the assistance of contacts, and at this job, he acquired a "fresh" contact who helped him obtain the next job. And as he's moved up in the industry, the depth, breadth, and value of his social capital has increased. Although his first contacts were personal (friends and relatives), his subsequent contacts had first-hand professional experience with his work, as coworkers, supervisors, and mentors. They not only inform him of openings, but they also are often in a position to actively recruit him. Of such social capital are white-collar *careers* built.

Social capital works in the blue-collar world as well. The most profitable line of work that has come down the pike for most of the Hallway Hangers is roofing, and as noted in Chapter 9, it was Slick who got them started in it. Slick's entrée into roofing seems somewhat more random. As he tells the story today, his own mentor was not someone he'd previously known. Yet this contact blossomed into a career for Slick, leading him eventually to a very comfortable life down south. None of the other Hallway Hangers was willing, or able, to stick with the trade, however, and arguably, Slick's success is intertwined with his move to the Sun Belt, where, as explained, a more or less perpetual building boom, coupled with the warm climate and occasional hurricanes, has kept the roofing business profitable year-round. But roofing still provides occasional work for Steve and several of the other Hallway Hangers.

As Small points out in his ethnography of a poor/working-class Puerto Rican neighborhood in Boston, even impoverished communities can be rich in social capital.[19] The question is: Where do these social networks lead? Shorty has spent his life doing "bull work"—hard, physical labor in which his brute strength is an asset and his temper and substance-abuse problems are minimal liabilities. In the course of this work, he has acquired social capital that is rich enough to provide him with work—but only of a certain type. Partially disabled by a herniated disk in 1994, stemming from an on-the-job injury that happened while he was working for a moving company, Shorty has been plagued by periods where he is physically unable to perform the work to which he has ready access; he is currently unemployed and, though his old employer keeps calling him, he is holding out for a promise that he won't have to do "*all* bull work [emphasis added]." So far, the promise has not come and Shorty knows that before long he'll be back on a construction site, pain or no pain. Shorty is well aware that his current lack of human and cultural capital bars him from desk jobs ("I don't know how to spell and shit like that . . . ") and has resigned himself to a life of hard, manual labor. His social networks, it appears, provide no hope that this situation can be rectified.

On the other hand, his social capital has helped keep Shorty out of prison on at least two occasions. After stabbing a boy in the stomach and sending him into a coma, Shorty was charged with attempted murder; when the boy regained consciousness and realized that Shorty was a distant cousin, he dropped the charges. More recently, during a stint as a debt collector, Shorty beat up someone from the neighborhood and was charged with the crime. The police and prosecutors, eager to put him behind bars, dragged out the proceedings, but in the end, after "a couple of people talked to" the victim, the charges were dropped. The way Shorty tells the story, there were no hard feelings, or at least none that the victim wanted to acknowledge (perhaps out of fear): "I see him [the victim] now, he waves, I say, 'Hey, how ya doin'?'"

The Hallway Hangers' social capital, then, is convertible in certain arenas and not in others. Frankie, the only one of either group who has attained a stable working-class existence on the strength of a union job, is a good example. In recounting how he started working for the City Housing Authority, Frankie notes that he was unable to draw upon any connections; thus, it was only through sheer persistence that he was eventually hired: "Just kept calling. Calling and calling. I would call Housing every Thursday at one o'clock and they would say no. And I'd say, 'Well, I'll call ya next Thursday. . . .'" But his efforts almost came to naught when, after he finally got an interview, "the head of management realized I'm an O'Sullivan. He said, 'You want me to fucking hire you?'" After claiming that "it's my brothers you're thinking of," Frankie finally got the job when he asserted that he'd never been arrested on Housing property—a claim that, though literally true, neatly skirted the issue of the rest of his criminal record. After a CHR check turned this up, Frankie was hired only after vowing that his parole officer would speak to the sincerity of his reformation (remember, this is the twelve-step Frankie, who'd sworn off drugs and alcohol and had been clean, if only marginally employed, for several years). He took a job in maintenance on city housing projects, a position he stayed in for thirteen years. Recently, however, he has moved over to a more lucrative union job in Highways. How was this move accomplished? "Connections," explains Frankie, "only one way you get those jobs." Persistence, then, gets him only so far; after that point, connections are required.*

MacLeod observed in 1991 that the Hallway Hangers were more likely to draw upon social capital to find employment than were the Brothers; this pattern has continued into midlife.** With their criminal records and spotty employment history, social capital is often the only way the Hallway Hangers can find work, and as other researchers have found, networks play a major role in hiring decisions in the secondary labor market.[20] Trust is particularly important when payment is under the table—a situation in which the Hallway Hangers have frequently found themselves. Yet these social networks both limit as well as provide opportunities, as Shorty's case illustrates.

Connections are also important in the primary labor market (as James's career in computers suggests) but the Brothers' social networks don't extend very far into this realm. Indeed, the setbacks the Brothers experienced in their early careers (James's initial difficulties finding work that used his skills; Mokey's twelve jobs in seven years; Craig's inability to find employment commensurate with his bachelor's degree) are no doubt linked to this. Though unfavorable labor market conditions contributed to these problems, the lack of the right connections—no one to speak for them, to hire them directly,*** or even to offer

---

*One must wonder, based on Frankie's account, whether this persistence, in fact, created a bond with the person at the Housing Authority. Indeed, what we call "persistence" in these situations can be seen as an attempt to accumulate a very specific form of social capital—a tie to someone who can help you get a job. And the person who had the power to grant an interview felt that he could recommend Frankie as someone who is "very persistent."

**Smith suggests that African Americans are less likely than whites not only to have social capital (e.g., to have contact with those who know of jobs) but also to activate social capital (e.g., to have their contacts make the recommendation). See Sandra Susan Smith, "'Don't Put My Name on It': Social Capital Activation and Job-Finding Assistance among the Black Urban Poor," *American Journal of Sociology* 111, no. 1 (2005): 1–57.

***Connections *can* lead to this or that roofing or contracting job. Contrast this, however, with other places in the class structure, where family members are CEOs or high-level managers. Given the articulation of race and class in the larger society, this lack of access to social capital (especially through its relationship to wealth) is even more strongly felt among blacks. See Thomas M. Shapiro, *The Hidden Cost of Being African-American: How Wealth Perpetuates Inequality* (New York: Oxford University Press, 2004); Sandra Smith, "Mobilizing Social Resources: Race, Ethnic, and Gender Differences in Social Capital and Persisting Wage Inequalities," *Sociological Quarterly* 41, no. 4 (2000): 509–537; and Sandra Susan Smith, "'Don't Put My Name on It': Social Capital Activation and Job-Finding Assistance among the Black Urban Poor,"*American Journal of Sociology* 111, no. 1 (2005): 1–57.

them meaningful career guidance—was clearly an exacerbating factor. Juan says as much in noting that, despite his satisfaction with the friendships he's formed at Jim's Tow, he would still prefer an office job—a "clean job," where he can be a "sharp-looking person . . . a very respectable person." With a high school degree and six months of college, he implies that this should be possible, but then he notes that "to get a job someplace else is not as easy unless you know somebody from within the company." Lacking such contacts, he remains at Jim's Tow, in his work clothes, dirt on his hands at the end of the day.

Social capital is useful for getting one's foot in the door, and it can help convert accumulated cultural capital. A sponsor within an organization can help one negotiate a tricky internal labor market. Yet to obtain the necessary educational credentials for white-collar jobs, and to succeed in many blue-collar jobs as well, the right cultural capital is also required.* Arguably, it's their lack of middle-class cultural capital that causes such difficulty for the Brothers, who as high school students were devout believers in the achievement ideology yet struggled to earn the credentials that, they hoped, would be the keys to success. The Hallway Hangers' lack of socially sanctioned cultural capital not only hurt them in school,** but it also disadvantaged them in the labor market. Their "street personas" were mainly useful in the informal economy and the world of crack capitalism. But as even those involved with it recognized at the time, such work leads to nowhere but prison (Chris, Steve) or the grave (Boo-Boo), and those who survived were those who got out. Once they were out, however, the question of how to adapt to the social and cultural demands of a steady job and "normal people" (in Slick's words) presented itself. All of the Hallway Hangers recounted struggles with this problem, regardless of whether they had completely left their pasts behind. As Steve put it: "Nobody likes taking fucking orders, Jay. I know you don't, I know I don't. But you gotta sacrifice something, to get a little you gotta give a little." Even Frankie, now "reformed," still struggles with authority on the job; he notes that "I'm still a project kid at heart," and his first response to a conflict is "not a good thought: whack him, stab him. But

---

*Bourdieu's "cultural arbitrary" helps us understand what kind of cultural capital will be most attractive to and convertible among societal elites. The Brothers and Hallway Hangers have what Prudence Carter (2003) has called "non-dominant" cultural capital, which is potentially convertible in non-elite spaces. See Prudence L. Carter, "'Black' Cultural Capital, Status Positioning, and Schooling Conflicts for Low-Income African American Youth," *Social Problems* 50 (February 2003): 136–155. Essentially, we are arguing that these men have a set of tools in their cultural toolkits that apply only to a specific range of conversion sites. See Swidler, "Culture in Action: Symbols and Strategies," *American Sociological Review* 51 (April 1986): 273–286.

**Though one could argue that lack of cultural capital was the least of the Hallway Hangers' academic problems.

then my God thought comes in and overrides it." Not always in time, however; he notes that when a foreman is around, somehow "I'm always on punishment, just cuz I'll stick up for the others."

Though Shorty seemed to have adapted reasonably well to his life in construction, his lack of middle-class cultural capital became a problem when his son's mother moved herself and the boy to a middle-class community in a nearby state. Shorty, who sees himself as a devoted father, was then forced into close contact with the middle-class world. He describes his son's friends and teammates as rich kids, and their parents as yuppies. The picture is not a flattering one: They can't play ball and they steal his son's equipment. Clearly, Shorty does not feel comfortable there, and one senses that he is concerned as well about how he will be viewed by his son's new friends. When he goes to his son's baseball games, he reports: "It was all yuppies. All white." (Given Shorty's own racism, this comment is a particularly interesting race-class juxtaposition.) "I just don't associate with nobody, not even his mother. . . . I just stay in the outfield." He's also embarrassed by his son's mother, whom he characterizes as a "nutcase" who came drunk to one of their son's baseball games.

It is not only the Hallway Hangers who have struggled with these issues; most of the Brothers have as well. James, as noted above, is a good example: Despite his credentials and evident skill with computers, his first jobs at a new company were usually on the night shift, where his "attitude problems" would be less noticeable. He admits that he's had to work hard to develop a "professional attitude" and asserts that "if you put Frankie O'Sullivan at my job, he'd last fifteen minutes. The minute they asked him to do something the wrong way, he'd tear their head off."* Mokey notes that his rise at his current job has been slowed "because of things I was doing"; indeed, he expresses some surprise that his mentor, Miles, "actually saw something in me" and encouraged his rise. The "soft skills" tasks required of a manager are challenging for him, and he admits to difficulty in getting his workers motivated: "I don't know how to get them to go."

But depending on one's line of work, being able to switch to a street persona can be helpful. Indeed, both Mike and Slick, the two biggest success stories, have occasionally found their "old selves" to be an asset. As a landlord, Mike has had to deal with all kinds of tenants.

I had one tenant who got her Hells Angels boyfriend to come up to my office with one of his cronies. I actually had to get a shotgun. They knocked on my office door and I cocked the shotgun real loud so they could hear, and said "Come in!" They hit the road. . . .

---

*That developing this "professional attitude" has been a long struggle for James is evidenced by the similarity of his comments on this point in his interviews in 2006 and 1991. Though he felt that he'd solved the problem in 1991, it seems as though he still had a ways to go.

In his interview, Slick recounts how a member of his roofing crew, a "white guy, redneck," once pulled a knife on him:

> I says, "Well, here's the thing, my friend: Now that you got it out, I hope you're intent on fucking using it, because I'm going to beat your fucking ass." He ran like a motherfucker. [*laughs*] Like I tell everybody, I only live here; I'm not from here.

Because they are self-employed, neither Mike nor Slick needs to worry about winning the approval of their supervisors. Social capital is still important—especially to Mike's career in real estate—but they have more leeway to tailor their work to the social and cultural niches in which their capital is most effective and convertible. Slick obtains most of his work from referrals and, as a craftsman, the outcome of his labor is observable; his customers are firsthand witnesses to his skill and diligence. Whether he's "rough around the edges" matters less than whether he can deliver what he promises for a good price in a timely fashion. (Indeed, one could argue that in the world of blue-collar contracting, workers are expected to be a little "rough and ready"; Slick's persona may well add to his credibility rather than diminish it.) Mike has no doubt had a greater need to learn and display the trappings of middle-class cultural capital in his business dealings but, as everyone needs housing, real estate agents and landlords deal with all parts of the class spectrum.* Thus, it is no accident that the two most successful members of this group attained their success as independent proprietors. The petty bourgeoisie,** though always subject to the vicissitudes of the market, are not on the receiving end of the relations of authority and exploitation that are attendant to most other places in the social structure. Witness the Brothers, who were initially diligent in their pursuit of human and cultural capital in the traditional arena in which it is offered—the educational system—yet still found it difficult to attain the credentials, contacts, and cultural skills necessary to climb the conventional middle-class ladder to success.***

In another era, unions might have helped members of both groups compensate for their lack of middle-class cultural and social capital and take the first step up out of poverty. And unions were an important part of the success stories of Mike, Frankie, and Derek, albeit differently for each. Mike and Derek obtained

---

*Although we don't wish to minimize the stratified nature of the real estate industry, it is worth noting in this context that a real estate license is one of the few state licenses that can be acquired without much traditional educational and cultural capital.

**Marx's term for the self-employed.

***This is not, of course, to minimize the difficulty for students from a low-income housing project of succeeding in an educational system that rewards dominant forms of cultural capital. Children from this background are thus doubly disadvantaged, facing barriers in school and, later, on the job.

union jobs early in their careers, though neither stayed with them. Frankie is the only one who clearly ties his success to unions: "I'm a union man now. There is still brothers and sisters I work with, and it is us against them." Indeed, it's clear throughout his interview that Frankie has transferred the loyalty he once granted to his friends to his coworkers in the union, a point we will return to below. Through his father, Super was able to join a construction union at one point, and this was the source of his highest-paying legitimate jobs. But, for reasons that are unclear, his dues lapsed, and with his criminal record and spotty employment history, his efforts to get back in have thus far been stymied.

Jinx notes that he's never had a union job, and indeed it's likely that he'd never pass the drug test: "I'm not giving up my fucking weed, I'm sorry. I can't deal with life if I don't have my weed." Slick presumably had the opportunity to join a roofers' union but passed on it, and he has clearly done quite well without it. Beyond this, none of the others even mentioned the possibility. This is confirmation, then, that the time of unions as a *major* avenue for upward mobility has indeed passed, at least in these sectors of the economy in this region of the country. And as suggested by these stories, there is really nothing else to take their place.

Thus, we see that both social and cultural capital have played important roles in shaping the careers of the Brothers and the Hallway Hangers. However, the point at which each becomes critical is different. The key turning point for the acquisition and initial conversion of cultural capital comes in school. By rejecting this pathway, for reasons discussed in Parts One and Two of this book, the Hallway Hangers effectively cut themselves out of the race for most middle-class jobs. The two Hallway Hangers who succeeded did so via what may be the two main alternative routes, neither of which is particularly wide: unions (Frankie) and self-employment (Slick). The Brothers, on the other hand, struggled through school because of and despite their cultural capital handicaps, which significantly impeded their progress and thereby channeled them out of the race for the most secure and lucrative white-collar jobs. But those who stayed the course managed eventually, for the most part, to accumulate enough middle-class cultural capital to succeed in lower-level white-collar jobs, though this was often a slow process that extended beyond school (James, Mokey). And the most successful among them, Mike, like Slick, took the self-employment path, thereby minimizing the impact of his poor start in the race to accumulate cultural capital.

By contrast, there seems to be no single turning point for the acquisition and conversion of social capital; it can be developed and deployed at any stage of one's career. The right social capital can help students make good decisions in school, and even open doors to the next level. (Stoney's story illustrates the flip side of this: Had he had an advocate, someone in the school to speak for him, perhaps tripping his teacher would not have scuttled his chances for the Barnes scholarship.) But it is equally, perhaps more, important in the labor market. Contacts are how you get jobs; mentors help you move ahead. This seems to matter both in white-collar and blue-collar jobs. And like cultural capital, social capital comes in different types and leads to different outcomes. This is one of the key points at which the two types of capital interact: Having middle-class cultural capital opens the door for opportunities to acquire middle-class social capital, and vice versa. The same is true for working-class forms of capital.

However, it is also clear from these stories that having the right cultural and social capital is not always sufficient to open the doors to middle-class success. The timing of the activation of this capital has everything to do with the individual's habitus, which includes most critically his perception of how and where he fits in relation to the barriers and opportunities available in the social structure. All of these factors matter: Two men with a similar habitus and similar resources may end up in very different places due to small differences in opportunity at a given time. Slick's unwillingness to kowtow to authority led him to a life of entrepreneurial success; Stoney's unwillingness to kowtow to customers led him out of the pizza business (and into various forms of instability). Derek chose, at several points, to move away from the path to upper-middle-class success, on which his early academic achievements had placed him—when he transferred from Barnes to Lincoln High after eighth grade; when he chose not to attend college; and when he turned down opportunities to move into supervisory work in his early career. Yet in each case, his choices were constrained by the available opportunities and, through them, and in more complex ways, by his habitus. For instance, his failure to attend college was linked to Faith's pregnancy, which resulted in an early marriage (rather than an abortion, as might have been the choice of many middle-class couples in this situation) and fatherhood. The articulation of one's capital with the available opportunities as refracted by one's habitus is the key to understanding these outcomes. Consider, for example, how an upper-middle-class Derek or Stoney might have played out his dilemma. Located in a more advantageous situation with more resources and a very different outlook on the future, their families would not have allowed the kind of meandering and instability that Derek and Stoney "chose."

THE PATH TO DOWN AND OUT: DRUGS, ALCOHOL, AND CRIME

The value—actual and potential—of whatever forms of capital these men possessed could be nullified quickly by two key factors: substance abuse and a criminal record. It's hard to say that they weren't warned; even in high school, both the Brothers and the Hallway Hangers understood that drinking, drugs, and crime were not the route out. Committed to upward mobility, the teenage Brothers resolved to turn their backs on these temptations; rejecting the achievement ideology and with pessimistic views of the future, the Hallway Hangers embraced them.

It is difficult to hypothesize exactly how drugs and alcohol fit into an understanding of the relationship between habitus and resources, on the one hand, and the opportunity structure, on the other. For some of these men, the lure of narcotizing spaces was too enticing to resist, especially given their perceptions of the opportunity structure, but this was not true for all. Of course, the physical and genetic nature of addiction may explain why some must wage a lifelong struggle while others are able to put drugs and alcohol behind them, or never turn down that path in the first place. Nevertheless, both drugs and alcohol are important factors in understanding the men's trajectories. Drugs differ from alcohol insofar as they offer the potential of alternative sources of income, at the price of a criminal career.

Given the divergent starting points between the Brothers and the Hallway Hangers vis-à-vis drinking, drugs, and crime, the lapses several of the Brothers experienced are noteworthy. Only Derek appears to have stayed completely on the straight-and-narrow path—yet even he had a brush with the law after going AWOL from the navy when his paychecks to his family were inexplicably cut off. Super represents the other extreme: After his own brushes with the law, he dove into the underground economy and was soon swallowed up by it, following the path already being trod by several of the Hallway Hangers, addicted to the drugs he sold and eventually unable to sustain his habit. The story of his descent into the underworld echoes the archetypal theme of the lure of seemingly easy money, made more potent by his lack of success in the formal economy and his youthful sense of invulnerability. Older and wiser, he now reaffirms that drugs are "just evil" and is resolved to stay straight and get back his union card.

Although Juan avoided the drug underworld, he has struggled with alcoholism. He hesitates to define himself as an alcoholic, but only a steady job with an employer who trusts him has kept him gainfully employed through four DUIs, the last of which occurred while on the job and led to a year in jail. He is now determined to "do whatever it takes to stay out [of jail]." He sees this as a struggle that he must wage on his own; he is not fond of alcohol- and drug-abuse programs where "they downgrade you. They look at you like you're a loser." He has "too much pride" for that.

Though they avoided the pitfalls of addiction, Mike, James, and Mokey each mention drinking and "partying" in their interviews. Mike noted that he began drinking heavily when he first started making money, in the 1990s; James liked to frequent clubs where "fights would happen, shootouts"; Mokey enjoyed drinks after work with his colleagues. All, however, claim to have given up these habits. Mike notes that he stopped drinking "when it started to get the better of me," though he does not report this as an ordeal. James and Mokey both quit after they became parents.*

Already experienced drug users at the start of this study, as adults the Hallway Hangers have struggled to master their addictions. Doing so has been a prerequisite to any type of stable lifestyle, and it's clear as well that the attainment of this

---

*Compare the findings of Edin and Kefalas, who found that many of the low-income women in their study reported that having a child "saved" them. See Kathryn Edin and Maria Kefalas, *Promises I Can Keep* (Berkeley: University of California Press, 2005).

stability also acts as an incentive to stay straight.* Frankie and Slick each claim to have beaten their drug and alcohol habits, though Frankie is much more candid about the challenges of staying clean. Their success at building and maintaining a stable working-class (Frankie) and middle-class (Slick) existence suggests that they have indeed left the worst of their addictions behind. Stoney and Jinx maintain their "recreational" drug habits, though they now limit themselves mainly to marijuana; their economic success is less than that of Frankie and Slick, but they enjoy a degree of stability beyond that experienced by their Hallway Hanger peers—Steve, Shorty, and Chris—who are still enmeshed in more serious drug and alcohol use.

That addiction hampers economic success and stability is no surprise; what is more noteworthy is the extent to which a criminal record has hindered the efforts of so many of these men to turn their lives around. With the important exception of those who are self-employed, all who have spent time in prison have struggled to find a way out of the catch-22 the penal system sets in motion. CHR, shorthand for the Criminal History Record (aka a "rap sheet") appears again and again in their stories, a barrier they fruitlessly try to hurdle. Instituted in the 1970s in the men's home state, the CHR system was originally intended to provide information on criminal offenses only to criminal-justice agencies. As part of the "tough on crime" stance that has increasingly dominated public and political discourse, however, access has been granted to more and more agencies (more than ten thousand in this state alone) and is even available to members of the general public who can demonstrate a compelling interest. Indeed, employers seem to have little trouble obtaining criminal-records checks through this process; though they require an applicant's consent in some cases, most applicants do not seem to realize that they are allowed to refuse. In an analysis of the law's effects in one state, Winsor notes the multiple ways in which this system of access to criminal records disadvantages those affected and inhibits their efforts to go straight.[21] These include delays in the application process, which may cause applicants and employers to give up and look elsewhere; misinterpretations of the information provided, which often includes multiple records of the same crime and thus appears to reflect more criminal activity than actually occurred; inaccuracies in the records, which may take years to uncover and fix; "leaks" of information to unauthorized parties; and the stigmatization of ex-criminals who have truly mended their ways. The penal-industrial complex seems to ensure that "past is prologue" for these men.**

---

*It could also be argued that some modicum of stability was necessary to kick the habit; even at the individual level, it is difficult to disentangle the web of causality between stability and addiction.

**The notion of a "prison-industrial complex" (Davis, 1995) was initially focused on the outsourcing and privatization of the construction and running of prisons. See Mike Davis, "Hell Factories in the Field," *The Nation* 260 (February 1995): 229 ff. Here, we see how this complex has been extended not only to controlling the poor inside prison walls, but outside as well. Bruce Western considers these issues in depth. See Bruce Western, *Punishment and Inequality in America* (New York: Russell Sage Foundation, 2006).

Thus, CHR looms large in the lives of these men. Each one who has spent time in prison mentions it. Some simply lie on their job applications. Occasionally, they can talk their way out of it when it's discovered (as in Frankie's legalistic defense that he'd never been arrested on city *housing* property), but most simply hope that employers won't check. When they do—it's one more job down the tubes. Others, such as Stoney, Shorty, and Steve, seem to have given up and accepted their fate on the periphery of the labor market.*

Child support payments are supposed to be suspended while the payer is in prison, yet this did not happen for most of these men. Steve and Stoney both racked up huge debts in back child support while in jail—debts that continue to haunt them both economically and personally. As with CHR, the consequences seem to multiply. Those who owe back child support can lose their driver's and professional licenses, as happened to both these men. The catch-22 is evident to those in this situation, if not to the general public; as Steve puts it, "How the fuck do they expect you to work if they take your licenses? How are you supposed to pay child support . . . collect cans or something?" No longer seeking legal employment, Stoney still needs to drive to take care of his mother-in-law; he does so knowing that he risks fines and prison if he is discovered. With over $90,000 in back child support owed, Stoney seems to have given up on paying it back.

The emotional consequences are also significant. As Stoney notes, "Officially, I'm a scumbag"—a deadbeat dad, and this despite the fact that he has been a relatively involved father, informally assuming primary custody of his two sons for a year and a half. Still, he's fairly laid-back about what could be a very difficult situation. Steve has far greater anger and one wonders how—even whether—he can keep these feelings from damaging his relationship (such as it is) with his daughters.

That the Hallway Hangers are now dealing with the consequences of past offenses, rather than committing new ones, is not surprising; as they move into middle age, they are moving into a period of the life course where criminal offenses typically drop off sharply, even among "high-risk" groups.[22] And in reading their stories, we can see some of the reasons why. Fatherhood, fear of prison, greater feelings of vulnerability, and deteriorating health are all contributing factors. But just as important is the shift in habitus that has taken place.** Seeing

---

*Western reviews the labor market consequences of incarceration. See Western, *Punishment and Inequality in America*, pp. 103–130. With compelling evidence, Pager (2003) demonstrates strong effects of a prison record on the likelihood of being hired. The disproportionate effect on African Americans is a consistent finding. See Devah Pager, "The Mark of a Criminal Record," *American Journal of Sociology* 108, no. 5 (March 2003): 937–975.

**Though the habitus is very connected to one's social class of origin, Bourdieu sees it as an "*open system of dispositions* that is constantly subjected to experiences [emphasis in original]." Pierre Bourdieu and Loïc Wacquant, *An Invitation to Reflexive Sociology* (Chicago: University of Chicago Press, 1992), p. 133.

what has become of themselves and their peers, they realize that going out in a blaze of glory is not in the cards; the far less romantic reality is a slow and steady slide into isolation, instability, and (for those like Chris who continue on the path) the street. Further, the peer group that once supported them is gone, and with it the sustaining counter-ideology. Those who have found something to hold out for—Frankie and Slick, with their families, careers, and status in the community; Shorty, with his son; Stoney, with his wife and his music—take strength and direction from that. For the others, the present is made bearable only by contrast to the past—it's preferable to prison.

To be clear, all of these problems—drug and alcohol addiction, criminal records, unpaid child support—are of the men's own making, in many respects. And to varying degrees, the Hallway Hangers recognize this. Yet the holes they have dug for themselves have become so deep that, at times, the task of pulling themselves out seems hopeless. However many obstacles they faced as teenagers, they confront far more now. It's not surprising that some have given up. But at the same time, it would be overly simplistic to say that any of these factors (drugs, alcohol, and crime), alone or in combination, predetermined their outcomes. What of Frankie and Slick, originally the two ringleaders, now reformed and successful? Or of Super, who started out on the high road, then fell off, but now seems determined to get back on? Frankie's case demonstrates that the process of recovery can be leveraged into employment, given luck, pluck, and, especially, opportunity. Slick was able to capitalize on his second chance by working off the books and eventually going into business for himself (possible only because of the skills he had already acquired in an industry with low capital barriers to entry). And even after we've accounted for every relevant individual factor, we still must factor in the larger social structure, which has dealt all of these men a very bad initial hand. Again, consider the resources more affluent families might bring to bear in helping their sons surmount youthful problems with substance abuse and delinquency; the Hallway Hangers and Brothers had none of these and were left to struggle on their own.

RACE AND RACISM

Compared to the "old days," race is no longer a major lens through which the Hallway Hangers view the world, at least as far as their place in it is concerned. Only Shorty and Frankie specifically mentioned blacks in their interviews, Shorty noting of his current neighborhood that "there are a lot of blacks around here, but they don't bother me." Frankie's views are complicated; to a limited extent, they mirror his previous whites-versus-blacks stance, but the level of antagonism is far lower, and leavened with a more clearly articulated class-based analysis, discussed at greater length below. When prompted, the others will talk about race, but even their discussions of the past, their current views on "what was up" back then, are hazy and unfocused, phrased in clichés about "dumb kids." This may be due, in part, to the fact that as adults, most are no longer part of a racially integrated community; hence, out of sight, out of mind. Yet most have served time in prison—a congested environment in which race is a significant marker of identity. Why didn't this have an impact on their beliefs? One could certainly come up with possible reasons—that the prison environment provides fewer valued resources over which to compete, that the black men they encountered in prison shared the Hallway Hangers' oppositional ideology, or simply that their stints in prison were a while ago—but the interview materials offer no clue as to which comes closer to the truth. Only Chris, the surviving black member of the Hallway Hangers and the only one still incarcerated, makes direct mention of the racial tensions in prison, but asserts that because of his "people skills," he has not been troubled by them.

To a certain extent, resentment over immigrants has taken the place of racism directed at African Americans in the Hallway Hangers' worldview. These comments, however, contain none of the vitriol these men used to direct at blacks. Slick claims that he "doesn't like" Mexicans and won't hire them, because "they're taking away from people who pay taxes in this country." In discussing his first maintenance job with the city Housing Authority, Frankie speaks negatively of the Haitian residents: "They're dirty, very tolerant of pests." The connection he draws, however, is to their immigrant status—"a lotta foreigners"—not their race. Jinx notes that it "ain't black and white no more. I hear a lot of bitching about foreigners coming over." Yet he distances himself somewhat from this view, noting that these foreigners are "willing to work for less, bust their balls" for low wages, while native-born workers are not; thus, their attractiveness to employers is understandable.

The contrast between these latest interviews and the initial ones when MacLeod first met the Clarendon Heights teenagers is revealing. Located in the same housing project, assigned to the same local public school, on the precipice of adulthood and its attendant challenges and responsibilities, the Hallway Hangers expressed virulent racism toward the Brothers. A couple of decades later, with the men scattered, and apparently no longer competing for the same resources, the passionate animosity toward African Americans is much less obvious. Have the Hallway Hangers truly become less racist, or have they simply disengaged from the larger world and ceased to pay attention to the racial politics around them? Frankie's example is instructive here, coupled with that of Mike, the white member of the Brothers. Both are among the success stories, and both remain involved with the world around them. Frankie is deeply invested in his union and to some extent adopts its view of the world; though there are racist elements here—"whites need unions"—with minor prodding from the interviewer, a rudimentary class analysis can also be elicited. Yet Frankie has a hard time staying this course; in response to his son's analysis of how racial antagonism among the working class benefits the upper class, he blames the Jews who run the media for not telling the working man's story, before ending with a general condemnation of CEOs and the global economy.

Thus, racism is still present, but no longer center stage in his worldview, having been eclipsed (but not entirely overwritten) by his union perspective.

Mike's views on race have become more complicated and contradictory. As the only white member of the Brothers, he associated intimately with blacks as a teenager, and he remembers these friends fondly. His girlfriend of fourteen years, with whom he lives and whose daughters he is helping to raise, is Hispanic. Yet he lives in a mainly white suburb, and his interview is sprinkled with anti-immigrant and anti-Muslim comments that could have come straight from Rush Limbaugh (and indeed, may have; Mike's interest in politics could well have led him to talk radio). At the same time, remembering his days with the fire department, he blurs the lines between white ethnicity and race, noting that he was "totally isolated, practically ostracized" by his Irish and Italian coworkers; his only friends were Enrique, and "this white guy, Bob." (Bob is white in contrast to whom: Enrique? The Irish and Italians? Or Mike, who is part Portuguese?* It's not clear.) In that job, "I got a taste of what it feels like to be a minority. It was hell."

In some ways, it's not surprising that Mike hasn't formulated a coherent racial ideology; he's had a set of experiences that are unusual in America today, and there is no ready-made set of beliefs to fit it. Like Slick and Frankie, he is successful enough that he can afford (perhaps, even needs) to sit back and reflect on his current situation and how he got there. When he does, his ambivalence shows through; though he still does not have much sympathy for the "deadbeats" from the projects who "lost it," he now acknowledges class-based barriers to success. But that's as far as it goes. If he sees race as a factor that helped him, while holding back his less successful friends, he gives no evidence of it. Perhaps, at some level, it is slightly threatening for Mike to consider the possibility that he might have been the beneficiary of race privilege.

There has been less change in the attitudes of the black members of the Brothers with regards to race, and not surprisingly, their views differ from Mike's. Although their attitudes and experiences vary in key respects, there is general agreement among them that (a) racism and prejudice are real problems for African Americans; (b) they have seen this firsthand; but (c) they've learned to deal with it. James's is the most expansive view of the significance of race; he notes that "race plays a factor in every single thing that happens every day," including how people respond to him at work. Though he does not explicitly make the link, the "attitude problems" that held him back for years are likely both cause and consequence of these experiences. Derek, while stating that racism has not been an issue for him personally, attributes this to his love of "people" and the fact that he never plays the race card. Still, he accepts that "there's definitely that silent prejudice, and it will be there for the rest of our

---

*An ethnicity that has never seemed a significant part of his identity, though he may have claimed it in his youth to help get a job.

lives." Super says that "coming up from a younger age" he dealt with a lot of prejudice and that even now, his white girlfriend's mother is not thrilled that Super is black. He deals with "a lot of racism" by trying to "leave that behind. . . . You're going to meet ignorant people in life." Only Mokey steadfastly denies that race has been a problem for him, either at work, with his white girlfriend, or (after an initial adjustment) in the white neighborhood where he currently lives. The accuracy of his perceptions, however, is called into question by his assertion that race was not an issue for him while he was living at Clarendon Heights, either, despite the fact that there was no evidence at that time that he received any better treatment at the hands of the Hallway Hangers.

Examining the job histories of the Brothers and the Hallway Hangers, we can still see the footprint of racial domination, though in somewhat muted form. As already noted, the Hallway Hangers have more frequently drawn upon social capital to get and keep jobs. Once a person is hired, race seems to continue to play a role in hooking up with mentors. Though Juan has clearly gotten some breaks from his employer, Jim, these have been useful mainly in keeping his job (not an insignificant feat, given his problems with DUIs), not in advancing, and they came only after he'd accumulated years as a loyal employee. One could certainly argue that these are breaks he's earned. Mokey's mentor at Legal Documents— Miles, the manager who took an interest in him, somewhat to Mokey's surprise— is black.* The network of contacts and mentors James has finally cultivated is, we think, disproportionately black. And it's taken him a long time to develop. Contrast this to Slick's almost fortuitous encounter with the "Irish guy," a stranger, who taught him the roofing business, or Mike's relationship with Dennis, the shady real estate broker who showed him the ropes in that business, or Frankie's extensive network of union contacts. One wonders if any of these white mentors would have "picked up on" the talents and potential of the black members of the Brothers.

The racialized nature of the criminal justice system[23] is evident here as well. Several of the white members of the Hallway Hangers have virtually gotten away with murder; though all have served at least some time in jail, they are all free today. Is it simply coincidence that the single surviving black Hallway Hanger, Chris, is the only one still in prison, or that the only fatality, Boo-Boo, was the other? The ratio of convictions to criminal acts seems much lower for the white members of this group than for their black peers. The only two Brothers to have broken the law—Super and Derek (when he went AWOL from the navy)—both served time for their offenses.

Thus, for criminals and the law-abiding alike, race has left its mark. The most successful members of both the Brothers and the Hallway Hangers are

---

*This relationship may be gendered as well; Mokey notes, in response to a direct question, that the longer-tenured peer who gave him grief over his promotion was a black woman.

white; those who have fallen the farthest are black. The Hallway Hangers, recipients of the racial advantage, still fail to recognize it; though racism is no longer as central a component of their worldviews, this seems more related to their general disengagement from the world than any genuine change of heart in their racial attitudes. Other than Slick, Frankie, and to a lesser extent, Jinx, the Hallway Hangers seem relatively unconcerned with anything that doesn't directly confront them day-to-day; they expect little from the larger world, and thus the energy that fueled their youthful racism is largely banked. The Brothers, now more aware of the impact of race on their lives than they were in high school, have moved to a stoic acceptance that racism is out there, and it affects them, but it can be handled. But handling racism on an interpersonal level, as prejudice, is one thing; handling, or even recognizing, its structural aspects is something else entirely. To do so would entail calling into question key components of the achievement ideology that the Brothers have built their lives around. There is not much evidence that this has, or is about to, happen.

FAMILY: SETTLING DOWN AND MOVING OUT

In Part One of this book, MacLeod discussed the role of family of origin, through its influence on habitus and cultural capital, in understanding the dynamics of the young men's lives. In midlife, we can see the importance of the families these men have formed as well as the continuing influence of their families of origin.

Though middle-class children can often count on the continued support of their families in a variety of ways (thanks to stocks of social, cultural, and economic capital) as they transition from their teenage years through young adulthood to midlife, this is less likely to be the case for poor children. Yet, though dysfunctional families still feature prominently in the Hallway Hangers' understandings of why they "screwed up" in their youth, and why their peers did, a surprisingly large number of them mention their parents in positive terms today. Jinx says he never married because he never met a woman who could measure up to his mother, and he remains close to his siblings. (If MacLeod's encounter is any indication, they may not always be a positive influence; still, siblings, like friends, keep one anchored to a social network, which has positive emotional and psychological value.) Steve's family has not given up on him. He still lives with his mom; without her, it seems quite possible that he'd be on the street. MacLeod also notes that Steve's younger brother is still trying to help him straighten out his life, though his older and far more successful brother, Slick, has not been able to do much for him. Super's mother also stood by her son and is now raising his children; Super does his part by living with his emotionally fragile sister. Thus, although these families don't have much in the way of financial resources to offer their struggling sons, they do what they can. Even for those who have achieved stability on their own, relationships with parents have a symbolic importance. Frankie and Slick, both of whom had problematic relationships with their fathers when they were young, mention reconciliation with these men as important components of their own maturation (though for Frankie, this healing only came years after his father's death).

More notable is the role played by the families these men have formed (or not) as adults; yet the association between their family status and outcomes is not a straightforward one. On the one hand, of those who are economically stable, all but one (Derek) are in long-term relationships with women. In several instances, these women provide significant economic and cultural resources to the family. Mokey and James are involved with teachers; Stoney's wife, Connie, works for the electric company and has been promoted into management as an estimator and project coordinator. Though he is not specific about her occupation, Frankie readily acknowledges Carla's role as one of the family breadwinners: "She does it all. Girl makes the money." Perhaps even more important is her continued faith in him (a theme echoed even more strongly by Stoney about his partner, as we discuss below).

Stable relationships are less common among the men who are still struggling. Super, Steve, and Chris have not been able to maintain long-term relationships, and in their narratives we see former girlfriends as contributing to their drug dependencies (though none lay the blame for their problems completely at these women's doors). Shorty married an accountant, and their relationship produced the son around whom his life is now oriented; however, his wife's emotional instability (perhaps mirroring Shorty's own) brought an end to their marriage and incipient middle-class life, and left Shorty back in Clarendon Heights.

Yet there are also exceptions to this pattern. Boo-Boo's demise was linked with that of his girlfriend, Ginger, and their family. Among those with relationships and who are on the margins of making it, one—Juan—says almost nothing about his fiancée, Brenda, and another—Jinx—has been in two long-term relationships (with women who are sisters) but does not have anything positive to say about either woman. Among the success stories, Mike is involved in a long-term, stable relationship with Rosa but he seems much more focused on her daughters, saying more about the girls and much less about their mother in his interview. Slick's case is even more complex: His wife, Denise, shared his journey from the projects to the suburbs. In 1991 she seemed to be struggling with the same issues he was. Yet somehow they made it through together, to the point where today, her "eye for real estate" and interior decorating skills are part of Slick's success story.

Derek is the most telling exception. It was out of concern for whether his family could function without his paycheck that he went AWOL from the navy all those years ago, ending up in the brig. And it was because of Faith's pregnancy that he left the track to college and enlisted in the first place—to provide support for his child. Arguably, his family of procreation has held him back.

The relationship between economic stability and family formation, then, is complex. Stable relationships are associated with positive outcomes, and their absence with negative outcomes, under some circumstances, but not all. Sometimes, as with Boo-Boo and Ginger, a committed couple spirals down in tandem. And sometimes, as with Slick and Denise, they conquer their problems and rise together. The social reproduction framework can certainly account for some of these variations—resources (cultural, social, and economic capital) matter—but the emotional elements complicate the picture. Recall, for instance, Slick's moving account of the stillbirth of his daughter, an event he recounts to MacLeod as "the hardest thing that ever happened in my life" and which he implicitly offers as evidence of his having successfully assumed responsibility for himself and his loved ones. The impact of family is much more than simply having been "saved" (or not) by the love of a good woman or the birth of a child. Arguably, it is via one's daily involvement with family that the most difficult struggles are fought, as well as (when things go well) where our most valued rewards are won. As Slick notes, taking responsibility is not a decision you make just once, but a struggle that you must wage every day—and nowhere is this more evident than in our intimate relationships. A detailed analysis of these nuances is beyond the scope of this chapter.

Similarly complex is the role of relocation in understanding these outcomes. Previous work on upward mobility out of poverty has cited the importance of "moving out,"[24] and we see evidence of this among several of these men. Derek, James, Slick, and Craig all moved out of state, and Mike moved across town to a middle-class neighborhood, and they are among the most successful.* Indeed, Jinx observes that "everyone who's done anything has got outta here." But these men aren't the only ones who moved during this period—almost all the others had left town at one time or another, for periods of months or even a year or more. Thus, not all relocations provided a "lift" for the men who undertook them. And finally, we have Frankie, the "project boy" who moved up the street, yet was able to defy the conventional wisdom and "make it" right in his own backyard. Looking more closely at the circumstances surrounding these moves, we can gain some insight into *how* moving matters for those who start at the bottom.

Relocation makes a difference if it means gaining access to an improved market for one's skills. This is most likely to happen if one possesses a stock of transportable capital (such as human capital), and less likely if one's capital is primarily social and locally rooted. For example, Slick and James both had transportable capital, in the form of skills (both) and credentials (James); they

---

*Although personal contact with Craig was not reestablished, MacLeod did discover on the Internet a workout video that features Craig as a fitness trainer. Thus, the pattern seems to hold for him as well.

were able to use these to secure employment in a more favorable job market. Shorty, Juan, and Frankie, by contrast, relied on local social capital to get and keep their jobs. With their histories of violence (Shorty) and alcoholism (Juan), how many employers would be willing to take a chance on these men as new employees? One can easily envision both men out on the street after a very short while if they tried to start over in a new town. Frankie's carefully cultivated network of contacts in city and state government and the union cannot be uprooted and moved to a new location; it is of use to him only so long as he remains in the area.

Relocating to an area where the cost of living is lower also makes a difference, an obvious fact that can be easy to overlook. Derek is able to survive on a relatively low wage because he's moved out west, to an area where his salary stretches far enough to meet his modest needs. By contrast, Mokey has remained in the East Coast metropolitan area where Clarendon Heights is located, and he struggles to make ends meet on a salary that is slightly higher than Derek's. Even as a successful roofing contractor, Slick would not earn enough in the Clarendon Heights region to pay for a boat and a 5,000-square-foot house.

Finally, moving is most likely to make a difference if it is used as an opportunity to reinvent oneself, and thereby to significantly alter one's habitus. Slick presents the most dramatic illustration; it appears that the new opportunity structure—not only for his roofing skills but for the new social networks in which he became embedded—made it possible for him to become a "new person." In Clarendon Heights, it seems quite unlikely that Slick could have conceived of himself as president of a football/cheerleading club . . . maybe not even of the beer-ball club. In his new situation, his status elevated with newfound economic and social capital (and even an appreciation for his form of cultural capital), he can become a civic leader. And, equally important, those around him can easily see him in this light; thus, his claims to this new identity are validated. Slick did not need to completely cut his ties to Clarendon Heights to enable this to happen,* but it did help enormously that demands to be the "old Slick" were not experienced daily. To a lesser extent, we see this in Mokey and Derek as well, who both note that through their travels, they gained a vision of possibilities that were not evident in Clarendon Heights.

Frankie's case is the exception that proves the rule. Although he did not relocate permanently,** he was nonetheless able to cultivate a new network of social contacts (thus, a different kind of social capital), a process that began through his involvement in the twelve-step programs that helped him conquer his addictions. Through this program and these contacts, over time he effected a transformation of his identity (becoming "the preacher," as Chris notes) that transferred to his old networks as well. He remade himself, in place—a much

---

*Though it seems that Craig may have felt he had to.
**He did move away for a time with his mother in the late 1980s.

harder feat to pull off, as it requires changing others' already settled views of self and resisting the pull to return to one's old identity. Moving matters, then, because it has the potential to change the set of opportunities one faces and facilitate the process of identity change and habitus transformation, through its impact on social and cultural capital.

Having examined the social and structural factors that have shaped and constrained their occupational trajectories, we move now to a consideration of the ways in which the Brothers and Hallway Hangers have made sense of their lives' journeys to this point. We begin this section with an examination of how social mobility is understood and experienced, focusing primarily on the narratives of three men who have achieved some degree of upward mobility. In the next section, following MacLeod's focus in Parts One and Two, we look specifically for evidence of class consciousness in the narratives; have any of these men achieved more than a "partial penetration" into the structural constraints that shape their lives? We follow this with a discussion of what turned out to be the most prominent theme that emerged as these men told their stories: redemption.

THE MEANING OF (IM)MOBILITY

"I only live here; I'm not from here." Quoted earlier, these words represent Slick's solution to a struggle all of these men who have tried, successfully or not, to cross class boundaries have experienced, at least to some degree. As Ogbu and others have noted with respect to race, negotiating a bicultural persona is not a simple matter when the lines one is crossing mark borders between "right" and "wrong," rather than merely boundaries between different worlds.[25] And it is all the more complicated when the borders are not visibly marked, as by race. The achievement ideology and its adult manifestations (twelve-step programs and the like) provide one solution: Discard the past as harmful and wrong, and move into the present, having seen the light. But this mantra is most successful when the issue is substance abuse. There, as difficult as it is to implement, it is hard to dispute the claim that there is nothing of value in the dark past, and thus you have nothing to lose and everything to gain by turning your back and moving on. Class cultures, however, are not so easily painted in black and white. Slick and Mike have moved the farthest, in economic terms, from their origins, yet they frame their experiences in very different ways. Derek, who has done less well than either of them but who had, at the outset, probably the best mobility prospects, brings yet another set of issues to the table as he thinks back on his life's journey.

Slick is quite clear that when he moved south, he moved to a different world; indeed, he has thoroughly (and perhaps deliberately) conflated his physical and social relocations. His account of the adjustment he went through morphs back and forth between several metaphors. First, it is the story of how he learned to live with "normal people":

You gotta remember, you're a person from an area that requires you to be on the offensive a lot, and then when you're down here with normal people it's almost like you're an animal out of the cage. . . . I couldn't believe how nice people treat you.

Yet a few sentences later, he acknowledges the real and strong bonds he formed with his childhood friends, and affirms that he is not ashamed of who he was, even though he is glad he has moved on:

I make no apologies for my background. . . . I've done things that I'm not proud of. But I'm definitely not ashamed. I never did anything wrong to kids. I never violated women in any way. I did what I did, and whatever crimes I committed, I paid for one way or the other. I'm forty years old now, and I'm just happy that I left there and I'm alive.

The head of the police association's football and cheerleading program no doubt feels the need to come to some sort of terms with his criminal past. It is notable, though, that this is a desire, a wish, not an absolute necessity: Since he is self-employed, Slick need not fear a CHR check that could mean the end of his job. (Though one wonders whether at some point, he will need to submit to a similar background check to continue his volunteer work with youth; many organizations have instituted policies requiring this. If Slick has indeed been as open as he claims, at least this would come as no surprise to his fellow parents.) And Slick has drawn his own lines (not arbitrarily) about what constitutes truly criminal behavior and has his own theories about what causes it, at least in his case; we will return to this point.

Later in the interview, after Slick recounts his experience with the knife-wielding crew member, he goes on to note that "you always have that little edge every once in a while that comes out of you, even if you're not still there." Asked if that's a good thing, he replies, "Sometimes . . . It's just part of who I am." That part of himself is something Slick does not want to give up. It is what connects him to his past, but also to his present—his family and friends who are still in Clarendon Heights. Slick is very clear that it was only by leaving home that he was able to succeed, and since returning home, he has suffered from (in his own words) "survivor's guilt":

The day I went home was the worst fucking day of my life. It was so depressing, everybody still strung-out. You got generations, fathers, grandfathers, and their kids and their grandkids that are fucked-up. . . . You're looking at people you know yourself; these are not stupid people. Yet it's like they wasted their entire lives, myself included when I was young. . . . When I saw my friends so fucked-up, it was terrible. Guys hanging on the same fucking corner, guys without a home, guys without teeth.

Though Slick does not absolve his friends and family (including his brother Steve) from responsibility for their plight—after all, he escaped, which raises the possibility that they might have as well—he refuses to cut the emotional ties that bind him to them. He is still, at some not insignificant level, one of them. His work is physically demanding blue-collar labor. He gets tired and dirty at the end of the day and must draw upon "mental discipline" to stay out under the hot sun, sweating through three sets of clothes in one day, wearing out his knees and shoulders. This is clearly a source of pride for Slick, as it should be: "I make more money than corporate executives, legally. . . . We're equal. It may not look it, but we are." Would they agree? Slick professes not to care; he's got an "edge" that none of them do, an inner resilience that comes from crossing borders his white-collar peers have never even glimpsed:

> I could lose it all tomorrow, all of it, be dirt fucking poor, and go back to the projects. I'm gonna live still, I'm gonna be all right. That five hundred thousand–dollar executive* . . . loses it all tomorrow, he's gonna throw himself out a fucking window or shoot himself in the head. That's the difference, point blank.

And in the end, Slick refuses to call himself better than those he left behind:

> Whether guys at home have been a success or a failure, I look at guys I grew up with, I look at them with level eyes. I know I ain't no better than them, and I don't look down on them.

It is a balancing act that can be hard to maintain—acknowledging both the past and present selves as legitimate, attempting thus to bridge a chasm for which there are few models. Not much has changed in this regard from the world of the upwardly mobile studied by Sennett and Cobb in the 1960s.[26] As with race, border-crossing by class is difficult.

Mike experiences these issues differently. As a member of the Brothers, he has had less of a bridging act to perform. The Brothers always bought into the achievement ideology; they did not romanticize crime, drugs, and life on the street (as the Hallway Hangers now acknowledge they did). And indeed, as he recounts his work experiences since high school and his rise through real estate, Mike does not talk of conflicts between an "old" and a "new" self. There's just Mike, making out the best he can. He reports more discomfort as one of the few non-Irish, non-Italian firefighters in his two-year stint with the fire department than he does with his life in the middle-class suburb in which he currently lives.

---

*It is worth noting that in looking at executive compensation, one must get to the 476th CEO on the Fortune 500 list to find one making under $1 million. Slick's (and MacLeod's) perception of the very top of the income distribution is quite understated!

Yet his view of the past has tempered somewhat over the years. While in high school and the years immediately after, he had nothing but contempt for the Hallway Hangers and their ilk; today he acknowledges that "we had it rough growing up in the projects." At the same time he professes not to "have that much sympathy" for those left behind, he acknowledges that "a kid from a poor neighborhood can make it, but he has to struggle more than a rich kid." Mike does not dwell on his own struggles, and perhaps because he sees the past almost entirely in negative terms, he has no problems embracing his present economic and social world, which he has worked hard to attain, even as he recognizes, on many occasions in his interview, that he was "lucky." That the uncle who was called in to "straighten [Mike] out" as a teenager now works for Mike is "funny," no more. "He's handy with the tools, does some building work." The contrast between this and Mike's own proclamation that "I don't like labor jobs. . . . I knew I could do better than that" does not seem to produce any dissonance. He saw how the game was rigged: "Working for any organization . . . they screw you. . . . It's like a game to them and you're just a pawn." The only logical solution is to work for yourself, which is what Mike did. That the system might be changed, could be different, does not occur to him; you either eat the bear, or the bear eats you.

It is notable that, even as Mike expresses confidence in himself and pleasure about his success, there's an underlying insecurity in his interview that is palpable. With his resentment toward Jews, Muslims, Mexicans, unions, public schools, and cops, Mike can be seen as a lone cowboy who can't work for any organization, and who must send his Latina wife's daughter to a Catholic school so she'll get "a good foundation" and, he hopes, as a "Hispanic minority . . . go for free" to one of those "soppy liberal schools." Even as Mike admits that he "craved security and that's what money has given me," he may recognize that in the end, he's not all that secure (witness his dramatic fluctuations in income) and that there was just way too much luck involved in his success for him to feel that he has simply played out the achievement ideology.

Derek's thoughts on social class and mobility reflect a different set of experiences, and a different resolution. More so than any of the others in this group (and far more so than most Americans), he has firsthand experience with both the top and the bottom of the social class structure in America, and his thoughts and choices are particularly interesting in this light. His years at Barnes Academy exposed him to life at the top of the social class pyramid; the five hundred thousand–dollar-a-year executives who exist mainly as metaphor for Slick were the parents of Derek's Barnes friends. Although he himself declined to follow the path to college and upper-class jobs laid out for him there, transferring to Lincoln High in ninth grade, he acknowledges that his years at Barnes were critical ones:

> It changed my life because I've never done drugs, never smoked a joint. I saw what it did to everyone else: my mother, my sister, my brothers, all of them.

Right on the other side of town is the good life, so am I going to jeopardize that just for a cheap thrill? No, no, no.

But the good life he glimpsed at Barnes came at a price—a price Derek was not willing to pay. Although he claims (with some support) that race has never been an issue in his work or personal life—he doesn't use the race card, he has "always loved people"—in the next breath, he implies that his success at Barnes was predicated on "just accepting that I wasn't necessarily a part of them." Later he returns to this theme:

> I always felt that their only concern was numbers, racial harmony. I just felt as though I was a number there. I go back to the public schools, and I've got my friends, more acceptance. Even the teachers were supportive; they were friends, people you could actually talk to. In the private school, even though I did it for five years, I didn't feel that I was a part of it.

When he returned to Lincoln, he went "right back to my roots. The blacks, the Portuguese, the whites—everybody integrated into one school, and I loved it. Four of the greatest years of my life, absolutely." But race was not the only issue at Barnes; there he also caught a glimpse of how the upper-class world operates: "It showed me politically, it's who you know. If you know someone, you can make things happen in your life, in your favor. I didn't want to be a part of that either."

Connections matter; social capital greases the wheels in the upper class as well as the lower, and people become a means to an end. Is that reason enough to turn away from the path to the top? It is clear that Derek made that choice. And he does not regret it; speaking of his reconnection with Mokey, he asserts, "We've enjoyed our lives, we've done what we wanted to do, we've never let anybody hold us back." What Derek claims he wanted to do—and has always wanted to do—is "to be just one of the little guys." The little people, to Derek, are those who can "voice [their] opinion[s] without repercussions"; they are the people "that actually make things work and make a difference." And as he reflects on his jobs over the years, it is the connections to others that matter most to him. He was happy in his first job at the airport, doing ramp work, as we saw in Chapter 10. He built a comfortable and genuine rapport with his fellow workers and resisted attempts to be promoted into management. He left Diamond Airlines because management "didn't care. You were a number. . . . It just didn't feel like home." By contrast, the work environment at Commercial Airlines, his previous employer, was "completely different. People said hi to you in the morning, invited you to parties. Outside of work you could actually be yourself, and inside of work you get your job done."

Yet when it came to the bottom line, Commercial was still just an employer; when his ex-wife, Faith, became ill, he was unable to transfer back home to help take care of her and their children. After several months of haphazard commuting from a distant city, and still no prospect of a job closer to home, Derek quit.

According to Derek, Commercial, the good employer, was unwilling even to hold his original job for him. Reflecting on this, Derek can say only that it was "weird." Although he does not regret the decision he made to be with his family in a time of crisis, he acknowledges that "careerwise, it was a devastating blow." He still wishes he could return to Commercial—"that's where all my friends are; it's the life that I know." But he knows that ship has sailed.

Derek defines his life, and his success, in terms of his relationships and connections to others. He does not do so in a conventional, middle-class way; family is clearly a top priority, but he is not currently married to the mothers of his children, although he is an involved father in all respects (financially and socially). His other friendships seem just as emotionally significant; he speaks movingly about his coworker, recently diagnosed with cancer, and how he and her children used glow sticks to perform an impromptu "radiation therapy" ritual. In his own words:

> I will always try and be there for other people, so I think that gives me inner happiness. My friends, if they don't have anybody to help them, they will call me. . . . [They] know that I'm not going to judge. I wasn't put on this planet to judge. I'm on this planet to be a friend.

Derek has seen life at the top (at Barnes) and life at the bottom. He sees the problems with each and seems to have resolved the challenge of these extremes by aiming resolutely for the middle.* To be at the top—to enjoy the power and money to do what he wants with his life, take care of his family and friends—one must pay a price, in terms of one's connections to others. But, to Derek, those connections are what make us human, what make life worth living. Alienation from one's fellow humans, from the productive labor that connects us to one another, rather then setting us against each other, is a price he is not willing to pay. Though it is doubtful that he's ever read Marx, Derek is speaking directly to the critique of capitalism Marx set out 150 years ago. He has seen the spiritually and socially impoverished life capitalism offers to those at the top *and* those at the bottom, and he does not want either. Lacking any clear vision of an alternative, he accepts the compromises that are necessary to stay in the middle, though these compromises have led him to drift more toward the bottom of that middle. Forty

---

*By describing Derek as aiming for the middle, we hope to provide insight into how his habitus is constructed. One can readily see how this aspiration emerged from the structure of opportunity he faced, given his social origins. We also wish to acknowledge as a part of habitus the conscious strategizing of one's social position. See Bourdieu and Wacquant, *An Invitation to Reflexive Sociology* (Chicago: University of Chicago Press, 1992), pp. 136–137; David Swartz, *Culture and Power: The Sociology of Pierre Bourdieu* (Chicago: University of Chicago Press, 1997).

years old, with "great people skills" and a positive attitude, he is making only $11.50 an hour at his current job; he admits that "that really burns me." Yet because he has defined his material needs quite modestly—a basement apartment, some electronics, and time for his family and friends—he is content. "I don't care about all of the creature comforts. I have my stereo, my PlayStation 2, my twenty-seven-inch TV . . . and my kids and my friends."

Derek describes himself as "probably the most chipper and positive person you will meet in your life," and in many respects, that is exactly what he is. Yet at the same time, there is a deep ambivalence running through his interview—precisely the kind of ambivalence one might expect from someone who loved his job at Commercial but who watched that job disappear when his ex-wife became ill. The compromises he's made have not been easy and are not what the achievement ideology led him to believe would be the case. He loves people and he likes being part of a team, but at the same time he notes, "I don't trust the world." At some level, it would seem, though he still holds faith with the core notion that life *should* be fair, that it *should* be possible to make a good living in a fulfilling career without compromising one's core values, he has adapted to life in *this* world—one in which neither notion holds true.

CLASS CONSCIOUSNESS?

Derek is not the only member of this group who has expressed ambivalence about the class structure; his concerns are notable primarily because they come from one of the Brothers, a group that, in high school, enthusiastically endorsed the value of hard work and minimized the obstacles in their way. The Hallway Hangers, already closer to an oppositional class consciousness at the outset, to some extent still use this as a filter for their experiences. Yet it remains, in Willis's terms, only a "partial penetration," as seen most clearly in Jinx's interview. From the start, Jinx was one of the least racist, and more politically reflective, of the Hallway Hangers, and this hasn't changed. As he talks of the jobs he's held over the years, his stories are full of accounts of bad supervisors, employers who take advantage, and raw deals. He has worked behind desks and doing manual labor in a series of jobs headed in no particular direction. It appears that he's managed to be employed most of the time, something many of the other Hallway Hangers couldn't claim. Yet he never moves up. Why? For Jinx, moving into management would require becoming an "ass-kisser, a brown-noser." In big corporations, "you ain't gonna get what you really deserve, no matter what. Big companies, you're just a number." He recognizes that it is the workers' labor that creates the wealth millionaires live on, sounding almost as though he is quoting Marx. Yet when pushed to think about a more egalitarian world, where workers can make a decent wage, he flatly asserts, "It'll never happen." Why? "Greed." Those on the top won't give it up, and no one can make them do it. Politics is not the answer, according to Jinx, because the politicians are just as bad as everyone else:

They're cutting everything for the fucking poor. They're not trying to bridge the gap, they're just widening the gap between fucking rich and the poor. . . . Everybody's scamming everywhere. That's why I never voted in my life and I never will.

With no faith in corporations, politicians, or the political process, Jinx's cynicism runs deep. The only person he would trust, the ideal employer, is someone "who started out just like you did. At the bottom. Was given nothing. Worked his ass off to get where he's at." It's a version of Derek's ideal solution and Slick's actual one. Only Jinx does not imagine himself as a middle manager or an entrepreneur; he is simply a worker looking for a decent shake. The only job he speaks of in uniformly positive terms is his current work on a landscape gardening crew. He likes his boss: "He's making his money, but he treats you fairly." But even more, the work provides something more than a fair wage: a sense of satisfaction, of accomplishment that has been absent in his other jobs, bagging screws, checking inventory on a computer, or moving stock in a warehouse. "Two weeks ago that yard had piles of dirt six feet high, a real mess. Now it's beautiful. . . . It's a fucking art form." On this job, Jinx feels he is given the opportunity to do "real" work, work whose results he can see and appreciate, work that connects him to others (his fellow employees, his boss, even the people who contracted with his boss: "People hate you when you start but love you when you're finished"). This echoes, once again, Derek's experiences and his hopes for a human connection at work.* And like Derek's, Jinx's critique stops well short of any understanding that would lead to action. He accepts that he made choices, not always the right ones, but he doesn't see any other options: "Things didn't turn out the way I planned, but what can I do? I can't turn the hands of time back." The only alternative, as he sees it, is "a rubber room."

Stoney has a similar story. Back in high school, he was the only one of the Hallway Hangers with a clear career aspiration: to own a pizza shop. Yet in 2006, he reports that he has long since turned his back on that plan. His experiences as an employee taught him that "you really can't trust anybody"; thus, a small-business owner has to work long hours to protect himself. Further, after years in the business, Stoney has discovered that he can't hack "the public-servant thing. . . . If I have to say, 'Can I help you?' to one more motherfucker, I can't do it, dude." He also notes that there is "no sense of accomplishment" in food service: "You go in, you make your fifteen salads, you make the same food. It's not like you're building a house and each day it comes together a little bit more and then when you're done you can go, 'Wow, nice job,' y'know what I mean?"

Stoney has not worked a steady job for the past several years, due to the loss of his driver's license and the wage garnishment he would face for unpaid child

---

*As we suggested at the beginning of this chapter, Jinx, Derek, and the others are looking for respect; they want to *be seen*.

support (which, as noted, racked up a tidy sum while he was in prison). But he has found fulfillment in a different type of endeavor: Stemming from a contact he made while working at a Harley-Davidson store, he has become a drummer for a rock band. When he talks about his music, it is in stark contrast to his thoughts about work: "Music is just so positive for people. It just makes you feel good." It's hard work; Stoney acknowledges that he's not a natural, that he has to "work for every little thing I get." One senses that he's even a little surprised to be discovering himself as a musician in midlife. But it clearly provides him with a sense of satisfaction, accomplishment, and connection with others that his past jobs never did—not surprising, given the meaninglessness of many jobs at the bottom of the economy. And as a consequence, it affords him a measure of respect that work in food service did not.

Only Frankie has developed something like a trade union consciousness. He sticks up for his crew with the foreman; he has stayed close to Clarendon Heights, rather than moving away (in part because the twelve-step programs have encouraged him to believe that he is the source of his own problems, not his environment). The solidarity he felt with the other Hallway Hangers is connected to the solidarity he feels within his union; the Hallway Hangers helped one another survive as white youths in the projects, just as the union helps white men survive on the labor market. The racism he still harbors continues to limit his understanding of the situation: Whites need unions but blacks don't, because they have affirmative action. Yet in response to MacLeod's suggestion that class might be more of an issue than race, Frankie readily agrees, even going on to assert that racial antagonism among the workers only serves the interests of the "rich white guy." (This is a perspective that his son, a self-described militant socialist who reads Chomsky, also adopts; it's not clear who introduced this idea to the household. Perhaps it was imported from Ireland.) Frankie also speaks with approval about the World Trade Organization action in Seattle, although his interest is in the union protests, not the smashed windows and paint balloons that were shown on the news. Even still, as one might expect with trade union consciousness, Frankie seems to accept much of what is given in the current class structure. Unions can help the worker make the best of a bad situation, but they can't change the system.

When the Brothers and Hallway Hangers were teenagers, MacLeod analyzed their worldviews with respect to their adherence to, or rejection of, the achievement ideology that dominated their academic lives. The contrast between the two groups' perspectives was stark. In midlife, the differences have blurred somewhat. The Hallway Hangers acknowledge the poor choices of their youth and for the most part now assert that they would have been better off applying themselves in school.* But is this anything more than an acknowledgment that

---

*It's unclear exactly *why* they now think they should have focused more on school. Would they have acquired specific cognitive skills? Noncognitive skills? A credential? Would they have appreciated the kind of schooling MacLeod advocates on pp. 263–265?

the system is stronger than you are—so in fighting it, you're fighting a losing battle? You can drop out of school, but short of the grave, you can't "drop out" of the rest of your life. The only alternative to resigned conformity—take a stand and fight—is not visible to them (except perhaps, through his union, to Frankie). As one might expect in this individualistic society, there is a relentless push to blame oneself and not the larger system. In some interviews (Jinx, Slick, Frankie) there is evidence of this tension, but it surfaces only rarely. For their part, the Brothers are now more ambivalent—the sky is no longer the limit. Most have not attained the white picket fence in the suburbs, and those who have come close cannot point to educational opportunities as the path that led them there. In general, the Brothers recognize the broad impact of racism but assert (in a way that reproduces and legitimates the system) that as individuals they can get around it. And they remain largely blind to the impact of social class. For the Hallway Hangers and the Brothers, then, neither class nor race are the primary prisms through which they see the world; indeed, race and class seem quite distant as potential sources of mobilization.

SEEKING REDEMPTION

As the Brothers and Hallway Hangers reflect on their lives' journey thus far, individual redemption emerges as one of the strongest themes in their narratives. As already noted, even the Brothers acknowledge failures in their past—bad choices, personal faults, that led to their not taking advantage of the opportunities presented to them. And for the Hallway Hangers, who early on rejected the achievement ideology and in many cases expected to go out in a blaze of glory, redemption narratives are key to their understanding of how and why they are still standing. Central to these stories is one core question: Do we redeem ourselves—or must we be saved by someone, or something, else? The achievement ideology points to the first; but other currents in American culture highlight the second, and ideologies such as those promulgated by twelve-step programs attempt to combine the two, however awkwardly. (The first step is acknowledging that you are powerless before your troubles, but all the rest of the steps tell you how to conquer them. Waiting for God, your wife, or your parents to do it for you is *not* in the program.)

Several redemption narratives are evident in these interviews, and in most of them, several threads are interwoven. Frankie exemplifies the twelve-step approach; Stoney, the path through love of a good woman; Shorty, redemption through fatherhood; and Slick, the bootstrap story.

Much of Frankie's interview could be nestled into a promotion for any twelve-step program. This worldview still fits Frankie's life as well as it did in 1991; even his relapse did not cause him to question it. Frankie sees his life as a constant struggle against his demons—drink, drugs, and his own temper—the "project kid" within. Yet his temperament inclines him to embrace this in a positive way, focusing on his victories rather than his defeats. The twelve-step programs, with their emphasis on each day a new chance, articulate well with this outlook. This, coupled with ample credit given to his wife for "putting up" with him and having faith in him when he slid from the path, is how he accounts for his victories over his demons. The mix of fatalism and personal responsibility fits well within his habitus; it affords a positive window on his struggles and strong reinforcement for his triumphs.

Stoney went through a drug treatment program in prison and, though he went straight after his release, he denies that this was the cause: "I had just had enough. . . . I just wanted the outside more." He clowned around in the Correctional Recovery Academy but admits that he then "got more into it" and was eventually master of ceremonies at the graduation. Although he stops well short of Frankie's enthusiastic endorsement of the twelve-step approach, Stoney implicitly admits that this program helped him when he condemns the state for "axing" all rehabilitation programs: "The flood is coming and the water is rising up and up and up, and they just keep trying to build the ceiling higher and higher. They're not doing anything to contain the water."

What "contained the water" for him was his wife, Connie: "She kinda saved me." She has been a mother to his children; he has given up drugs and drinking for her. Indeed, it seems as though his life today is built around his family and his music, in equal parts. He risks jail for driving without a license, because without a car, he cannot care for Connie's mother while Connie is at work.*

For Shorty, the birth of his son is recounted as a transcendent moment: "I felt like I was high, it wasn't on no drugs or nothing. That was the greatest high ever in the world." As Shorty tells it, much of his life since has been spent caring for his son as best he can, and striving to be worthy of him. His descriptions of his son are bathed in the glow of fatherly adoration: "Everything he does, he's good at." This is in marked contrast to Shorty's view of himself; when his son was born, Shorty named him for someone else because "I don't wanna taint him with my name." Nonetheless, Shorty has cut back on drinking, drugs, and illegal activities in an effort to remain close to his son: "Now I'll think before I do something. Because, hey, if I get caught, I'm gonna lose my son." He goes on to note, "I don't got no friends. . . . I want to spend time with my son. I don't care about nobody else." When his son's mother moved and took him with her a few years ago, Shorty could not go on: "She took my son. He's my life. . . . I was like,

---

*The irony is that he lost his license for failing to be a responsible parent by not paying child support while he was in prison, as already discussed. This is the sort of bureaucratic snafu that can befall anyone but that has particularly disastrous consequences for those who live on the edge and lack the resources to fight it or to cope. It is parallel to Derek's situation when his navy pay was cut off; unable to correct the problem, he went AWOL so he could care for his family.

'I ain't gonna see him no more, so [I] ain't bother living.'" Shorty was saved from his suicide attempt only when his son, realizing something was wrong, told his mother, who called the police. When asked what the future holds for him, Shorty responds: "Doing hard labor, spending time with my son, take it day by day." It is clear where the only joy in this picture lies.

By contrast to these stories, Slick explains his remarkable rise with a modified version of the "pulling himself up by the bootstraps" narrative. While hardly the classic Horatio Alger tale—Slick's past is too checkered for that—Slick "always knew I didn't want to stay [in Clarendon Heights]." He sees his current suburban residence as some kind of nirvana compared to the old neighborhood, where "you're into full survival mode no matter what you're doing. Whatever you hafta do, you'll do. And whether it means hurting someone physically, to the point where it's either you die or they die, your mind is to not be the one that's dead." Slick feels that "everybody has a choice. Everybody can get a hundred dollars, get on a fucking bus, get the hell out of there." Getting out is only "half the battle," however; then you find out that "it's tougher being a regular person, paying your bills, feeding your kids, accepting responsibilities, getting up at five in the morning, going to work every day, climbing these roofs, staying out in this hot sun, than it is to be a fuckup." That's a struggle that must be waged every day.* So Slick made it, feels anyone can make it, but staying the course is not easy. And though "you gotta take fucking responsibility for yourself," he also acknowledges that "it's those people that are poor that need the help." Slick clearly acknowledges the importance of the help he had from others, most notably his wife, Denise, who shared his journey: "I'll be honest with you: Anything that I've done, that I've accumulated—boats, houses, trucks—my wife has lots to do with that." He also credits his grandmother (MacLeod notes that Slick didn't leave Clarendon Heights until after her death), noting that he's been "blessed" with a good family, as well as the Irish roofer who gave him his start. Thus, Slick's bootstrap story is leavened with an understanding that some have a tougher road up than others and that a helping hand often is necessary; as noted earlier, he clearly has compassion for those who are left behind, and his words imply a recognition that the right attitude is a necessary, but probably not sufficient, condition to make it out of poverty.

Through these stories of mobility, class consciousness, and personal redemption we see how the Hallway Hangers and Brothers have come to understand their individual struggles and triumphs. With their focus on the individual, and how one can overcome personal flaws and barriers on the way to success (or perhaps just survival), the lens produced by these narratives undercuts the development of a more sociological awareness. At the same time, they offer windows into the habitus of these men. And that habitus, as we've seen, is a reflection of

---

*Though he is not a twelve-stepper, there are clearly parallels between Slick's philosophy and the ongoing struggle these programs recognize.

the dialectic between an individual's (evolving) position in a social structure and his (evolving) disposition toward that (evolving) structure.[27] The habitus of each of the Brothers and Hallway Hangers has changed since we first met them, yet, no matter how far the individual has traveled, the marks of Clarendon Heights are indelibly present. Whether we're looking at self-employed Slick or prison-resident Chris, we can see the influence of their "street habitus"[28] in the decisions they've made at key moments. Individual agency is, indeed, important; these men have made very different decisions at key points in their lives. But at the same time, we can see that the choices are highly structured by the social environment in which they find, and found, themselves.*

THE NEXT GENERATION

With the updated interviews, social reproduction can now be examined for the next generation. All these men are now fathers. Their relationships to their children, however, vary dramatically, sometimes even within the same family. And the paths these children have followed vary as well. Overall, as one might expect, it seems that the fates of these men's children are most directly linked to their current class location; those whose children are growing up in Clarendon Heights, or similar environments, are finding that their children face challenges similar to their own youthful experiences. More than one of these men see themselves in their children, and not always in a positive way. And they feel just as helpless to do anything about it as their own parents were.

Stoney reports that his two sons are "in and out of trouble. Same story as me. Maybe worse, starting a bit younger." Both hang in Clarendon Heights, as Stoney did; both have been in trouble with the law, and one is back in jail for violating his probation. Both have dealt drugs. The best he could do for them, it seems, was to offer up his home when needed (up to eighteen months at one stretch while their mother was coping with her heroin addiction), and his wife, Connie (not the boys' mother), as a role model and stable influence. He himself is more like a friend than a father, sharing his music (which he says pleases them, though they prefer other styles) and watching *South Park* together for family time. He says he's tried to talk to them but has concluded that "everybody has to learn their own lessons in life, no matter how much you put it in their face." If, looking at their own family history, his sons do not understand that crime and drugs are the wrong path, then what else can you say? His own mother had tried beating some sense into him as a child, but that didn't work. Stoney seems resigned to the fact that he can't force his sons to make the right choices, so why not just be friends?

---

*See MacLeod's discussion about the relationship between structure and agency (pp. 252–261); it is very apt here.

Steve has two daughters, whom he describes as "good girls,"* though he appears not to be very involved in their lives. He says he has tried to urge them to stay away from drugs: "This destroyed me and this fucking did your mother in, so don't fucking go that road." However, he admits that despite this warning, his oldest has "dabbled" in drinking and drugs. He notes that one of his girls wants to be a nurse, and the other one a lawyer, but the most he can offer them is general encouragement to "hang tough. . . . It's all about fucking staying in the game. Something good'll come." He seems to be speaking as much to himself as to them, however, and he admits that he has a hard time believing it.

Jinx, father of two, notes that his older son has "got a lot of anger in him." He does not have much that is positive to say about the mothers of his boys (he "love[d] them dearly" but they "couldn't be much worse") but feels an obligation to stay involved for the sake of his sons. His older boy, Davey, was the beneficiary of several life lessons from Jinx, most notably the importance of physically sticking up for himself on the street. "You cannot go around being a little pansy and having somebody turn around and take everything you got." He seems proud that his son learned this lesson but also acknowledges the difficulties it has led to, including repeated stints in the custody of youth services, eventually lockup in another juvenile facility, then finally jail. But Jinx can't really condemn his choices: "I can understand what he's doing because I work my ass off, I got a roof over my head but nothing to show for it." The best he can offer is the hope that his son will learn to "read people," as Jinx has; this is the key to remaining out of prison. He remains skeptical that schooling can offer better options: "I still hear of a lot of people out there with degrees who can't find work." Thus, Jinx's older son faces much the same world his father did (maybe worse, according to Jinx), and with much the same attitude.** The mother of Jinx's younger son, wary of the object lesson that is his older brother, seems to be trying for a different outcome, but Jinx is not so sure it will work: "He's going through the same things. . . . Becoming a teenager, now it's time he's going to try solving his own shit."

Juan and Super each have several children with different mothers, and their circumstances vary. Super's oldest child, a son, was born while Super was still in the drug trafficking business. He notes that the boy is now being raised by his

---

*Although we won't explore it here, there is a gendered aspect in the way these men (both Hallway Hangers and Brothers) view their children and their prospects for the future, particularly in school, that parallels the "gender gap" in academic achievement. Their daughters are disproportionately "good girls"; their sons, even those of whom they are justifiably proud, always seem to have at least a bit of the devil in them.

**It's almost as if Jinx fears that his son not only faces the same opportunity structure that Jinx did as a kid, but also that he will adopt (if he hasn't already) the Hallway-Hanger orientation to the world.

grandmother and that he has "serious problems"; however, the mother and grandmother won't let Super have contact with him and are now disputing whether Super is really the father. His two youngest children are being raised by his own mother, in the same environment in which Super grew up. He is grateful for her involvement and assistance, and seems pleased that he is able to see his girls "all the time," yet he has little to say about who they are and how they are doing. His hopes for their future are to help them avoid the mistakes he made—to "take the right choices, don't take the wrong choices"—but it's not clear how he intends to do this.

Being a father has been very important to Juan. Although he is not proud of the fact that his first two daughters were born to different mothers, and only six months apart, he remained involved with both babies, providing financial support and taking them when he could. He tried to commit suicide in 1992, when one daughter's mother tried to take her away from him, and "that's when . . . I started really drinking." Later he moved away from Clarendon Heights when the other daughter, now fifteen years old, came to live with him: "I had to find a safe environment where there ain't no yelling, screaming, cursing, drinking. . . . I'm not going to pull another person into this mess who is innocent." He attributes many of his own problems to having grown up in an environment where "there's so much . . . waiting for, wanting for you to make a bad turn," and he hopes to spare his children this. He worked hard to become a homeowner, an achievement of which is he rightfully proud. Asked about his children's prospects for the future, he replies: "Well, my kids have a house, so I think their future's all set. . . . They're not in the middle of the environment where there is drugs, alcohol—the minute they walk in the door." Although this is clearly a key step, it is telling that Juan goes no further in discussing his children, their current situation, or his hopes for their future. Getting them out of the projects and into their own house was enough for him (of which we will say more below), but will it be enough for them?*

Frankie's decision to turn his life around while remaining connected to his roots meets its critical test in his son, Darren. And it seems, from what we see here, that it's been a qualified success. Frankie describes himself as the "neighborhood dad," noting that his son grew up with the only two-parent family in the neighborhood; he implicitly presents himself as a one-man reform project, attempting to turn the block around by his own example and involvement. Yet when it came to Darren's schooling, Frankie and his wife were still somewhat handicapped by their lack of middle-class cultural capital. Both agree that they

---

*Juan's description of how he's raising his children is an excellent example of Lareau's concept of "accomplishment of natural growth," a child-rearing approach she suggests is most common in working-class and poor families. See Annette Lareau, *Unequal Childhoods: Class, Race, and Family Life* (Berkeley: University of California Press, 2003).

would have made different choices about their son's education had they better understood how the public school system worked; this echoes Lucas's conclusion that the myriad choices made available to parents in many large public school districts require a substantial degree of expertise and middle-class cultural capital to navigate optimally.[29] Still, Darren clearly takes school, and intellectual and political pursuits more generally (witness the Chomsky text lying among the books in the kitchen), more seriously than his father did at the same age; although he is currently a college dropout, at least he got his foot in the door. Frankie describes him with a mix of concern and pride. He notes that Darren "got my temper; he's got my fucking laziness, procrastination," but also suggests that he has "passion." Frankie talks with justifiable pride of how Darren won a scholarship to go to Ireland, and on his return wowed the audience at a fund-raiser with his impromptu speech about the experience. Though Darren's story is still unfolding, it's clear that he's had a much better start than Frankie did, and seems to have avoided most of the problems his father faced (or, as Frankie now suggests, created for himself).

Derek has two sets of children: a grown son and daughter with his first wife, Faith, and two young sons with his most recent girlfriend. Carlton and Amy stayed back east with Faith when Derek moved away and, though he has provided emotional and financial support, he was not a daily presence during their teenage years. They grew up in working-class neighborhoods near Clarendon Heights, though not in the projects themselves. Both have professional ambitions (Carlton in economics and business, Amy in nursing), but Amy had a child out of wedlock at age sixteen. She and Derek's grandchild have been living with Faith, though they plan to move out next month. It's hard to say what her prospects are, but her brother, Carlton, is in college—a step beyond Derek already. Derek's other sons are three and five, too young for any confident predictions about their futures. Though he did not marry their mother, Derek has joint custody of them and seems to be a loving and involved father. And clearly they are being raised in an environment far away from the projects of Derek's youth.

Those who live in the suburbs, or who can afford to send their children to private schools (and via these two paths, select a different social environment for their offspring), seem, overall, able to produce better outcomes than their peers who remained in Clarendon Heights or similar locales. It is also noteworthy that, with the exception of Frankie, these men are the only ones who are raising their children in a two-parent family; thus, the influence of family and neighborhood cannot be disentangled here. Mike is able to send his academically talented stepdaughter to a private Catholic school, thus avoiding the public schools in their area, which he characterizes as "shit" because "the unions protect those deadbeat teachers." With his stepdaughter getting a 1500 on her PSAT and having a Hispanic heritage to boot, he sees the world of colleges as wide open for her, and with the assistance of a good college guidance counselor (which, hopefully, the Catholic school will provide), he may well be correct.

(His older stepdaughter, however, suffers from lead poisoning, a syndrome linked to urban poverty, which seems likely to limit her prospects.)

But there are also hints that the next generation will continue to be handicapped to an unknown extent by their parents' lack of middle-class cultural capital. James's description of his son's academic difficulties, for instance, sounds to any middle-class parent like ADHD (attention deficit/hyperactivity disorder); yet for all his concern and involvement, it seems that James has never investigated this. James is aware that his son's ways have to change, but (interestingly, given the racial lens through which he views his own experiences) attributes his greater risk factors to class rather than race: "You don't have the luxury of just applying yourself in what you're interested in, unless you're rich." As an African American boy, James's son runs the risk of being classified as a behavior problem—being produced as a "bad boy"[30]—even in his suburban school.

Shorty's son is now living in a middle-class community in a nearby state, and Shorty has high hopes for his future prospects. He's an ace baseball player and a straight-A student. Shorty strongly encourages his son's ambition, but these aspirations are a mix of blue-collar dreams (professional athlete, construction) and middle-class goals (engineer, architect). It's not clear whether Shorty understands how to navigate a path toward these outcomes, but it is likely that his son's teachers, friends, and friends' parents do. And if Shorty is correct in his assessment of the yuppified nature of the community, with luck his son should be able to avoid the pitfalls that befell Shorty and his friends.

Slick's son, Tyler, was fourteen months old when the family moved down south.* Now he's fourteen years old, and coming into his own. Slick has seen the downside of the suburbs; he knows that kids can (and will) find a way to "screw up," even there, "where there's no need for it." But his own children seem to be doing well. He keeps a close eye on his son, but he recognizes that he must give him "a little slack to make his mistakes"—as long as they aren't the same mistakes Slick made. Although he seems somewhat disappointed that Tyler is only an "average" student in school ("I'd like to see him doing better"), he is "pretty much a good kid." Tyler evidently has had some trouble in school, some fights, but Slick accepts that as typical for a boy. Although this is clearly a gendered perspective, there may be some class elements here as well. Would born-and-bred upper-middle-class, professional parents regard it as "natural" for their sons to engage in physical fights? Tyler's race and current social class may protect him from the worst consequences of such physical "acting out," however. By contrast, Slick's two daughters are "cute, absolutely gorgeous," and "straight-A students in school." Slick stands ready to ensure that they remain that way, noting that "nobody will be treating my daughters the way I treated others. Because if they do, that little project devil is going to come out." This may well depress his daughters'

---

*Slick also has an older son, Brad, with a different mother.

romantic prospects in high school, but it is unlikely to have any negative impact on their academic careers. Slick's parenting style does not seem to be the concerted cultivation practiced in many middle-class households;[31] it has much more in common with the "accomplishment of natural growth" approach of the working class. (Indeed, James and Mokey seem closer to concerted cultivation—propelled, possibly, by their wives, both of whom are teachers.) Yet when practiced by a white family in a relatively forgiving suburban environment, it may well be enough to ensure that his children maintain their class status.

Two of these men have only very young children, yet their circumstances are so different that without a significant amount of luck (good or ill), it seems likely that their outcomes will diverge as well. Chris's daughter, Hazel, is only three years old but has already begun her life with several strikes against her. Born addicted to drugs as a result of her parents' relapses, she was also several months premature. As Chris recounts: "She was tiny, smaller than my palm. . . . That was so hard to take, seeing this little tiny, totally innocent girl, hooked up to all these machines, all these wires going into her." Although he claims that "she's okay now," he has had little direct contact with her, due to restrictions placed by the state department of social services, as a condition for his girlfriend retaining custody. Perhaps the state intervention will be enough to help her avoid the fate of Boo-Boo's two young daughters, both of whom died, along with their parents, from AIDS.

Mokey's son, Rayford, is also three, but otherwise his young life stands in marked contrast to Hazel's. Although Mokey and his girlfriend, Karen, are not married, they otherwise seem to have followed the middle-class pattern of postponing children until their relationship and jobs were stable. Due to a car accident that has put her on disability, Karen, who has a college degree in special education, is able to stay home with Rayford. Mokey is an involved father, clearly in love with his son but concerned that he "watches too much TV"—traditionally a middle-class concern. These all bode well for Rayford's future, as long as Mokey is able to maintain his family's financial foothold in the middle class.

Thus, these men's experiences suggest that the cycle of intergenerational social reproduction can be disrupted if parents are able to gain and maintain a foothold in the middle class, thereby providing structural advantages for their children and potentially shielding them from many of the challenges their parents faced. For many, this includes (or, perhaps, is predicated upon) geographic as well as social mobility, a factor that has been associated with improved mobility prospects among disadvantaged youths in previous generations.[32] As Patillo-McCoy found in her study of the black middle class,[33] maintaining close ties with family and friends who remain mired in urban poverty can have negative repercussions; moving across the country can help weaken these ties. The mixed fates of Derek's two oldest children, both raised in the city where Derek grew up, illustrate this dilemma. But even among those who have cut the ties and moved away, lack of middle-class cultural capital can continue to be a handicap as their children move through the educational system. This is likely to be particularly severe for those who must negotiate race as well as class disadvantages, and may be particularly problematic for boys.

CONCLUSION

This chapter has provided a perspective on the Hallway Hangers and the Brothers that we believe is consistent with the one MacLeod elaborates in Parts One and Two of this book. In terms of where the Clarendon Heights peer groups have ended up, we argue that the Brothers and Hallway Hangers have largely realized the predictions of a social reproduction approach. This perspective does not predict that all who start at the bottom will remain there; simply that the odds of succeeding, when one starts with next to nothing, are far lower than the achievement ideology would suggest. It is, to repeat MacLeod's metaphor, a race in which competitors do not start at the same point. It's not that there "ain't no makin' it" at all, as the Hallway Hangers originally thought; it's that the odds of getting there are long, and heavily dependent on luck and structural circumstances. Though Slick and Mike have, in some sense, "made it," their positions are hardly secure. They are each an injury (Slick) or an economic downturn (Slick and Mike) away from a precarious economic situation. Although we certainly can (and should) laud the successes of Frankie and James, their positions in the middle of the income distribution hardly constitute a truly comfortable existence. Yet Frankie's union job offers him a degree of security the others lack. Indeed, it is quite possible that in another ten years, only Frankie will still be enjoying a stable job with benefits. For those without educational credentials, unions offer the only secure protection from labor-market fluctuations. The other Brothers and especially the Hallway Hangers are living only a bit above the poverty line at best and still must cope with the instability of an economically marginal existence. Even the tight labor market, an increase in the nominal minimum wage, and increases in economic productivity and growth of the late '90s did not significantly lift their boats (though they might have prevented a few from sinking).

Tracing the career trajectories of these men makes clear that at least one aspect of the achievement ideology is on target: Substance abuse and crime are, in the long run, straight routes to the bottom. Those who indulged most heavily and who were unable (or unwilling) to leave their habits behind, ended up on the street, in jail, or dead. Similarly, we see that the choices made by these individuals clearly matter, but the consequences of these choices are shaped by structural circumstance as well as "talent" and luck. In the unpredictable (certainly more than the achievement ideology would suggest) world of the formal economy, individuals can experience dramatic turnarounds when the personal and structural circumstances are right (Slick, Frankie), but also be constantly stymied when they are not (Juan, Mokey, Jinx). There is no single, well-marked path out of poverty and social marginality; one can make very different decisions along the way and still end up in the same location. But working entirely within the *informal* economy leads to instability, poverty, prison, or worse (Chris, Steve, Boo-Boo, Shorty). Hence, the life philosophies that several of the less successful Hallway Hangers have adopted: As Jinx put it, "Go with the punches, go with the flow. Like that, weeble, wobble, but we don't fall down."

It is also telling that the social service arm of the state has been of little or no help for these citizens who began life in a low-income housing project. Indeed, it seems as though those institutions and programs that were designed to protect others from them have been exemplary in their effectiveness, while those that might have helped them have been notable mainly by their absence. These men's contact with government agencies has been almost solely with penal institutions and their workers. Through the long arm of CHR, prison continues to have devastating effects on their careers even after they have served their time. The idea, then, of actually seeking services from the state could not have been further from these men's minds. Not only are the services not easily accessible but also one must be proactive to find out about their availability and persistent to actually receive them.* One wonders why Derek couldn't avail himself of the Family and Medical Leave Act when Faith was ill. One wonders why the child support debts accumulated while men were in prison. One wonders whether Chris will be able to kick his drug habit, now that substance abuse programs are being cut from prisons. One can further wonder, of course, about the possible impact of other social policies that have been shown to be consequential for the working poor but are unavailable in the United States: universal health care; parental leave; living-wage policies; better unemployment insurance; day care and early education programs; adult training and education programs; etc.** In other societies, the nature of these men's struggles would have been very different.

Bourdieu's framework, and in particular the concepts of capital and habitus, continues to provide a useful analytical frame for understanding these patterns, especially in grasping the complex interactions between structure and agency. Social structures not only set up the choices, but they also influence the choices

---

*Klinenberg discusses this issue in the context of the Chicago heat wave. He suggests that part of the problem is that the services are underfunded and only the most astute and determined consumers get what they need. There is also a problem insofar as the police—trained for paramilitary purposes—are often charged with providing social services. Eric Klinenberg, *Heat Wave: A Social Autopsy of Disaster in Chicago* (Chicago: University of Chicago Press, 2002), pp. 158–159, 232–233.

**Zuberi shows convincingly how specific social policies can be very consequential for the lives of the working poor. See Dan Zuberi, *Differences That Matter: Social Policy and the Working Poor in the United States and Canada* (Ithaca, N.Y.: ILR Press, 2006), pp. 151–165.

made through their influence on habitus. We can see that habitus is a dynamic entity—it changes to reflect current circumstance but continues to carry the past with it as well. It is a vehicle for both reproduction and for change—but more the former than the latter.

These interviews foreground another theme, one that has been evident from the start but has assumed far more importance as these men have aged: the search for respect. This is what originally led the Hallway Hangers away from the achievement ideology (similar to Bourgois's crack dealers), as noted by Frankie: "I was fucking mad. . . . The anger was just hopelessness, I guess. Always being looked at differently. Knowing. We were the kids who were never invited to your party, but we came anyways. . . . My perception is that people are looking at me as if I was less than. How do you overcome that? You impose your will upon 'em." Later: "I would have dreams of not being me. But I was who I was, and I had my boys back then. That was big to me. That was big. That was all I had."

But "the boys" did not last as a cohesive primary group, they did not "impose [their] will," and they could not sustain an alternate ideology. So over the years, the Hallway Hangers have slowly wandered back to the main path. Yet this has not been an easy route. We can see from these poignant interviews that, as Sennett and Cobb and Bourgois emphasize in different ways, the struggle for *respect* in the United States is deep and multilayered and has enormous consequences. Each of the interviewees reveals an inner search for pride in what he's doing and for respect from the outside world. Whether it's Slick's justification for some of his fights (you need to be able to "hold your head up high"), Jinx's desire to not be "a number" in a large company, Chris's refusal to "back down" to the guards while in prison, or Juan's pride in home ownership (evident as he speaks of being "involved with a house," almost as if it were a relationship), there's a tangible compulsion to vie for some degree of social honor, for some degree of distinction.[34] Unfortunately, the only time we see evidence of the Hallway Hangers or Brothers gaining a degree of respect, in any stable sense, is if: (a) they are self-employed (Slick and Mike); (b) they've done a good job working for someone who works with them (Jinx); or (c) they are committed to the people they are working with (Derek and Frankie).

More than thirty years ago, in *The Hidden Injuries of Class*, Sennett and Cobb argued that the American class structure and its supporting ideology produce a relentless pressure to prove one's worth:

> The idea of potential equality of power has been given a form peculiarly fitted to a competitive society where *in*equality of power is the rule and expectation. If all men start on some basis of equal potential ability, then the inequalities they experience in their lives . . . are the logical consequences of different personal drives to use those powers—in other words, social differences can now appear as questions of character, of moral resolve, will, competence.[35]

So where you end up is felt to be a deeply personal accomplishment. And there are strong incentives to feel a sense of accomplishment, no matter one's situation. Yet even if one properly "protects" oneself by setting a low bar, there is still a struggle to gain some measure of dignity and respect. Unfortunately,

> once respect is made the reward for human ability, no matter if the ability is seen potentially in all, the stage is set for all the dangers of individualism: loneliness for those who are called possessors, a feeling of individual guilt for those who do not come off as well.[36]

Indeed, in the interviews we find the loneliness of Mike and Slick at the top, as well as the social isolation of those at the bottom (Steve, Chris, Shorty)—and the lack of any collective political orientation (save for Frankie's trade union consciousness) in the others. Derek's decision to aim for the middle seems quite reasonable in this light.

The search for respect is deeply intertwined with the habitus of these men. Consider the decisions they made about how to deal with their substance-abuse problems. Despite his ongoing struggles with alcoholism, Juan describes himself as "too proud" to take part in any of the alcohol treatment programs offered to him; they "treat you like a loser." His hold on the main tenets of the achievement ideology makes it too difficult for him to accept that label—he is all too well aware that he *would* be seen as a "loser" from this standpoint, and to reinforce it in such a program is more than he can handle. Contrast this with Frankie, whose rejection of the achievement ideology early on gives him the self-confidence to accept that he's made mistakes and is thus able to embrace the "loser" label that is part of a process of recovery.* Thus, ironically, Juan, who played by the rules and still believes in them, struggles alone with his alcoholism, while Frankie, who early on rejected the accepted playbook, has been able to conquer his addictions and move forward.

These factors don't play out in the same way for everyone; habitus reflects a complex mixture of experience, aptitudes, and one's various stores of capital. And relationships: The lives of these men clearly show the importance of developing and maintaining stable social ties. Within such relationships, some modicum of respect can be found—even if it is in short supply in the outside world. In their youth, the Hallway Hangers had each other; but these ties could not be sustained into adulthood. Those who have done the best economically—Slick and Frankie— were able to forge meaningful relationships with others. Though more economically marginal, Stoney has also structured his life around a relationship—to his

---

*Note that peer-mediated programs like the twelve-step model fit relatively easily into Frankie's habitus. A professionally directed program, on the other hand, might not have worked as well for him, as suggested by Shorty's vehement rejection of the treatment programs he's participated in (though admittedly this was usually involuntarily).

wife and her family—and they provide him with an anchor and routine that, together with his music, give him a sense of satisfaction and accomplishment, as well as the strength and confidence to reach out and help others. He and his wife live with his struggling younger brother, on whom they exercise a positive influence. Shorty, as already noted, has pinned his hopes for redemption on his son, and strives now only to be worthy of him. And it seems as though Chris is groping for a similar anchor with his former girlfriend Colleen and his daughter, Hazel, though whether this will ever be more than a distant hope is unclear. (Even Chris realizes the long odds he faces in this struggle: "I've been on the inside [prison] so much.") Of the Brothers, only Super has not been able to develop and maintain a stable relationship outside of his family—and he is the least successful of the group.

Although we agree with and reaffirm MacLeod's political orientation (as stated on pp. 261–269), we close with the hope that some way can be found to accord respect to all human beings, independent of ability, independent of character. No matter what their past mistakes, no one should find themselves as Chris, Steve, and Shorty have—personally adrift, socially isolated, caught in a sea of lightly masked self-loathing with no clear sense of the way out. Chris, still in prison, is only the most desperate. Yet the human spirit is strong. Shorty clings to his son as his hope for salvation; Juan keeps plugging at Jim's Tow and funnels his search for respect into a house; Jinx finds some satisfaction transforming suburban lawns into works of art. And perhaps Chris will find solace in the Psalms. (It is doubly symbolic that MacLeod could gain physical access to Chris only in his role as a priest, and interpersonal access mainly on a spiritual level. Indeed, where has Chris found any peace in the secular world?) Though here we cannot outline a political means of severing the links among ability, inequality, and respect, we believe that the United States has the resources to ensure that no one is without adequate health care and that no one is below an adequate guaranteed minimum income. If the Brothers and Hallway Hangers can gain the modicum of respect that follows from such a safety net, their struggles in other domains will be that much less trying.

NOTES

1. Erik Olin Wright, *Class Counts: Comparative Studies in Class Analysis* (New York: Cambridge University Press, 1997); Robert Erikson and John H. Goldthorpe, *The Constant Flux: A Study of Class Mobility in Industrial Societies* (New York: Oxford University Press, 1992); Emily Beller and Michael Hout, "Intergenerational Social Mobility: The United States in Comparative Perspective," *The Future of Children* 16 (Fall 2006): 19–36.

2. Sennett's interesting ruminations were very helpful here. See Richard Sennett, *Respect in a World of Inequality* (New York and London: W. W. Norton, 2003), p. 3.

3. For similar findings, see Philippe Bourgois, *In Search of Respect: Selling Crack in El Barrio* (Cambridge, New York, and Melbourne: Cambridge University Press, 1996), and Elijah Anderson, *Streetwise: Race, Class, and Change in an Urban Community* (Chicago: University of Chicago Press, 1999).

4. Erving Goffman, *Presentation of Self in Everyday Life* (Garden City, N.Y.: Doubleday, 1959).

5. Loïc Wacquant, "The Rise of Advanced Marginality: Notes on Its Nature and Implications," *Acta Sociologica* 39, no. 2 (1996): 121–139.

6. Economic Policy Institute Issue Guide, www.epi.org/content.cfm/issueguides _minwage.

7. U.S. Department of Health and Human Services, http://aspe.hhs.gov/ poverty/05poverty.shtml.

8. Rose, *Social Stratification in the United States;* Jared Bernstein, Chauna Brocht, and Maggie Spade-Aguilar, *How Much Is Enough: Basic Family Budgets for Working Families* (Washington, D.C.: Economic Policy Institute, 2000); John E. Schwarz and Thomas J. Volgy, *The Forgotten Americans* (New York: W. W. Norton, 1992).

9. Bernstein, Brocht, and Spade-Aguilar, *How Much Is Enough.*

10. David S. Johnson, Timothy M. Smeeding, and Barbara Boyle Torrey, "Economic Inequality Through the Prisms of Income and Consumption," *Monthly Labor Review* 128 (April 2005): 11–24; Edward N. Wolff, *Top Heavy: The Increasing Inequality of Wealth in America and What Can Be Done about It* (New York: New Press, 1996); Rose, *Social Stratification in the United States.*

11. Lawrence Mishel, Jared Bernstein, and Sylvia Allegretto, *State of Working America 2006/2007* (Ithaca, N.Y.: ILR Press, 2006).

12. Ibid.

13. Ibid.

14. Ibid.

15. Katherine S. Newman, *Chutes and Ladders: Negotiating the Low-Wage Labor Market* (New York: Russell Sage Foundation; Cambridge: Harvard University Press, 2006).

16. Mark Granovetter, *Getting a Job: A Study of Contacts and Careers* (Chicago: University of Chicago Press, 1995).

17. William J. Wilson, *The Truly Disadvantaged: The Inner City, the Underclass, and Public Policy* (Chicago: University of Chicago Press, 1987).

18. Elijah Anderson, *Streetwise: Race, Class, and Change in an Urban Community* (Chicago: University of Chicago Press, 1990); Elijah Anderson, *Code of the Street: Decency, Violence, and the Moral Life of the Inner City* (New York: W. W. Norton, 1999); Mario Luis Small, *Villa Victoria: The Transformation of Social Capital in a Boston Barrio* (Chicago: University of Chicago Press, 2004).

19. Small, *Villa Victoria.*

20. Julia R. Henly, "Matching and Mismatch in the Low-Wage Labor Market: Job Search Perspective," in Urban Institute, *The Low-Wage Labor Market: Chal-*

lenges and Opportunities for Economic Self-Sufficiency (Washington, D.C.: U.S. Department of Health and Human Services, 2000).

21. Ernest Winsor, *The CORI Reader* (Boston: Massachusetts Law Reform Institute, 2003).

22. See, for example, Travis Hirschi and Michael Gottfredson, "Age and the Explanation of Crime," *American Journal of Sociology* 89 (November 1983): 552–584.

23. See Western, *Punishment and Inequality in America.*

24. Laub and Sampson, *Shared Beginnings, Divergent Lives: Delinquent Boys to Age 70.*

25. John U. Ogbu, "Variability in Minority School Performance: A Problem in Search of an Explanation," *Anthropology & Education Quarterly* 18 (December 1987): 312–334.

26. Richard Sennett and Jonathan Cobb, *The Hidden Injuries of Class* (New York: Vintage Books, 1972).

27. Loïc Wacquant, "Scrutinizing the Street: Poverty, Morality, and the Pitfalls of Urban Ethnography," *American Journal of Sociology* 107 (May 2002): 1499.

28. Ibid.

29. Samuel R. Lucas, *Tracking Inequality: Stratification and Mobility in American High Schools* (New York: Teachers College Press, 1999).

30. See Ann Arnett Ferguson, *Bad Boys: Public School in the Making of Black Masculinity* (Ann Arbor: University of Michigan Press, 2000).

31. Lareau, *Unequal Childhoods: Class, Race, and Family Life.*

32. See Laub and Sampson, *Shared Beginnings, Divergent Lives: Delinquent Boys to Age 70.*

33. Mary Patillo-McCoy, *Black Picket Fences: Privilege and Peril Among the Black Middle-class* (Chicago: University of Chicago Press, 1999).

34. See Pierre Bourdieu, *Distinction: A Social Critique of the Judgement of Taste*, Richard Nice, trans. (Cambridge, Mass.: Harvard University Press, 1984).

35. Sennett and Cobb, *The Hidden Injuries of Class*, p. 256.

36. Ibid.

AFTERWORD
Freddie's Final Say

This book began with the words of eleven-year-old Freddie Piniella: "I ain't goin' to college. Who wants to go to college? I'd just end up gettin' a shitty job anyway."

In fact, Freddie did go to college, and he and Isaac took the same sociology class. When the class was assigned to read the second edition of this book, Freddie borrowed a copy a few hours before the class discussion and skimmed it quickly. In class he raised his hand and said that he'd enjoyed the book and that it reminded him of his own neighborhood. Isaac laughed out loud and shouted, "Freddie, look who wrote it!"

I met up with Freddie for lunch near Clarendon Heights in April 2006. He's married with four children, completely bald, and has the same fire in his eyes that impressed and worried me twenty-five years earlier. He told me that he's doing well, working as a medical technician in a local hospital. "So have you 'made it'?" Silence, and then: "Hard to say. I'm proud of finishing high school and eventually making it through college. I'm supporting my family. But it ain't easy. I've just come off a shift working from five a.m. to one p.m. I'm not supposed to, but I'm heading out now to work a five-hour shift in a different hospital."

I asked Freddie what he liked about the book. He laughed. "I sure as shit didn't like all that theory at the beginning. What did I like? I'll tell ya. People look at me and they got no idea what I've done to get to where I am now. But it was all in the book. Growing up in Clarendon Heights we had to navigate around some sticky shit. You captured it pretty good."

APPENDIX 1

On the Making of *Ain't No Makin' It*

FIELDWORK: DOUBTS, DILEMMAS, AND DISCOVERIES

Few sociologists who employ qualitative research methods discuss the mechanics of fieldwork in their published writings. A frank account of the actual process by which research was carried out might disabuse people of the notion that sociological insight comes from logical analysis of a systematically gathered, static body of evidence. If my own experience is at all typical, insight comes from an immersion in the data, a sifting and resifting of the evidence until a pattern makes itself known. My research methods were not applied objectively in a manner devoid of human limitations and values. Of course, I had access to books that describe the various methods used in sociological field research. But many of these statements on research methods, as Whyte argues in the appendix of *Street Corner Society,* "fail to note that the researcher, like his informants, is a social animal. He has a role to play, and he has his own personality needs that must be met in some degree if he is to function successfully."[1] If, as I would argue, the best fieldwork emerges when the sociologist is completely immersed in the community under study, it means that his or her personal life will be inseparably bound up with the research. What follows, then, is a personal account of my relationship with the Clarendon Heights community and the way I came to understand the aspirations of its teenage members.

Walking through Clarendon Heights for the first time in the spring of 1981, I felt uneasy and vulnerable. Entering another world where the rules would all be different, I was naturally apprehensive. I might have been closer in class background to the people of Clarendon Heights than the great bulk of my university classmates were, but neither my lower-middle-class origins nor my attendance at a regional high school in rural New Hampshire made me particularly "at home" in the project. Most important, I was a university student, a status that could breed resentment, for it implied an upward social trajectory to which these people do not have ready access. To undertake research under such conditions would have been inconceivable. But that spring sociological research was far from my mind. I was at the project with two other university students to begin the Clarendon Heights youth enrichment program, with which I would be involved for the next four years. The youth program led to my interest in the aspirations of Clarendon Heights' young people and provided me with a role and an acceptance in the community without which the fieldwork would have been close to impossible.

Contrary to the expectations of the city's professional social workers, the youth program turned out to be a great success. We lived in the neighborhood during the summer months and established close relationships with the children in the program, their parents, and other project residents. Initial distance or coldness gradually gave way to trust and personal regard as the program's reputation and the rapport between counselors and community grew. Engaging nine boys ages eleven to thirteen in a varied mix of educational, cultural, and recreational activities, I gained more than acceptance by the project's residents—I also learned a great deal about their day-to-day problems and concerns. As my understanding of the community and sensitivity to the pulse of the neighborhood developed, so did my self-confidence and sense of belonging. Although class and racial differences could never be completely transcended, by September 1982 I counted among my closest friends many Clarendon Heights tenants.

It was during that second summer working in Clarendon Heights that my interest in the kids' aspirations really began to take shape. I was amazed that many of the twelve- and thirteen-year-old boys in my group did not even aspire to middle-class jobs (with the exception of professional athletics), but rather, when they verbalized aspirations at all, indicated a desire to work with sheet metal, in a machine tool factory, or in construction. The world of middle-class work was completely foreign to them, and as the significance of this fact impressed itself on me, I concerned myself more and more with their occupational aspirations. But at such a young age, these boys could not speak with much consistency or sophistication about their occupational hopes. To understand why aspirations were so low among Clarendon Heights youth, I would have to look to these boys' older brothers and sisters, to those in high school.

I say brothers and sisters because my study of aspirations should have included equal consideration of girls. That this study concentrates solely on boys puts it in the company of many other works in the male-dominated field of sociology that exclude half the population from research. But with class and racial barriers to overcome, I felt hard-pressed to understand the situation of the boys and would have been totally incapable of doing justice to the experience of girls because yet another barrier—gender—would have to be confronted. Already thus handicapped, I felt totally incapable of considering adolescent girls in Clarendon Heights, whose situation was so far beyond my own experience.

The boys presented enough problems. I'd had the least contact with Heights teenagers. I knew a few of the Hallway Hangers on a casual basis because Stoney, Steve, Slick, and Boo-Boo had younger siblings enrolled in the youth program. Still, no relationship extended much beyond the "Hey, how's it going?" stage, and although I was never hassled coming or going from doorway #13, I was still very much an outsider as far as the Hallway Hangers were concerned. My previous involvement in the community, however, had gained me a small degree of acceptance. They knew that I had been around for more than a year, that I worked hard, and that I got along well with many of the tenants, all of which ensured that I would be considered different from the typical university student. Had I been seen in such a light, I'm not sure I ever would have been accepted by the group, for college students were not welcome in doorway #13. My work with the Clarendon Heights youth program, however, allowed me to get my foot in the door and paved the way for future acceptance by the Hallway Hangers.

The Brothers were not so difficult. I played a lot of basketball with the kids in my youth group; we had a team of sorts and used to practice a few hours each week during the day. In the evenings, I invariably could be found at the park a block from Clarendon Heights playing a game of pickup basketball with the younger kids from the project. Many of the Brothers played, too, and I soon got to know them quite well. Some of them also had younger brothers and sisters in the youth program, so they were acquainted with me from the start. In addition, I had remained close to Mike, and my association with him helped me to befriend the others. For the Brothers my status as a college student was grounds for a measure of respect rather than suspicion. Nor did they seem to distance themselves from me because I was white. How they could endure the racist taunts of the Hallway Hangers and not come to resent whites in general is difficult to comprehend. It may be that I was insensitive to any covert racial strain between the Brothers and me, but I never felt its effects.

By November 1982 I had decided to write my undergraduate thesis on the aspirations of teenage boys in Clarendon Heights. I generally spent a few hours each week down at the project seeing the ten boys in my group anyway, but I began to increase my trips to Clarendon Heights in both duration and frequency. I also made more of an effort to speak to the older guys, particularly members of the Hallway Hangers. But I had an exceptionally heavy academic workload that semester; my real fieldwork did not begin until February 1983 when I enrolled in a course in sociological field methods.

The course introduced me to the mechanics of ethnographic fieldwork. From readings, discussion, and an experienced professor, I learned about the techniques of participant observation, oral history analysis, unstructured interviews, and unobtrusive measures. I realized that the real learning would take place through firsthand experience in the field, but discussion of methods and the examination of representative sociological work using qualitative methods served as a valuable introduction.

My initial research forays into Clarendon Heights were awkward and tentative. I wanted to determine the nature of the teenagers' aspirations and the factors that contribute to their formation. Sensing that there was a conflict between the achievement ideology promulgated in school and the experiences of the boys' families, I particularly was interested in how this tension was resolved. But although it was obvious that the Brothers and the Hallway Hangers experienced school in different ways, I had no idea of the extensive disparity in their outlooks. Most of my trips down to Clarendon Heights in February and March were spent as they always had been: in the company of the younger kids in the youth program, helping with homework, talking with parents, and generally maintaining contact with the families to which I had grown close. I also was spending some time with the Brothers, casually asking them about their aspirations, their high school programs, and their family backgrounds. This was possible because I had struck up friendships with Mike's closest friends: Super, Derek, and Craig. But with the Hallway Hangers my acceptance was progressing much more slowly. Those I knew would return my greeting on the street, but I still was subject to the intimidating glares with which those outside the group were greeted when walking past doorway #13. There was also an element of fear involved. I knew of the fights that took place in and around doorway #13, the heavy drinking, the drugs, and the crime. I also knew of the abuse the Brothers suffered at the hands of the Hallway Hangers and realized that, in their eyes, I was to some extent associated with the Brothers. I was fascinated by the activity in doorway #13, but I needed an "in" with the Hallway Hangers if they were to be included in the study.

Basketball provided the opportunity I was looking for. The city's Social Services Department opened up the gym in the grammar school located just across the street from the Heights for a couple of hours on two weekday evenings. The Brothers were the first to take advantage of this opportunity for pickup basketball, along with Hank White. Hank is a big, muscular fellow, slightly older than most of the Hallway Hangers, who commands the respect or fear of everybody in the neighborhood. After his sophomore year in high school, Hank spent eighteen months in a maximum-security prison for allegedly taking part in a rape behind the school building. With scars dotting his face, Hank conforms to the image of the stereotypical street "hood," and the manner with which he carries himself hardly dispels that impression. Nevertheless, he was the least racist of the Hallway Hangers, for in prison he had gotten to know and like a few blacks. He enjoyed playing basketball with the Brothers and was on good terms with all of them. We had seen each other around, but it wasn't until we were matched against each other on the basketball court one evening in early March that Hank took any real notice of me. Both of us are six feet tall, but Hank had the edge in strength and basketball ability. It was a good, hard game, and when it was over we walked back to the project together. It turned out he knew I was the student who ran the youth program. In parting, he grinned at me and told me to come back next week, "so I can kick your ass again."

Thus began my friendship with Hank. Only later would I discover that my new acquaintance was a convicted rapist, and by then I was prepared to believe the disavowals of his guilt. His apparent regard for me clearly influenced the light in which the other Hallway Hangers saw me and helped facilitate my acceptance by the group. If my team had won that evening, his friendliness may well have been enmity, and my status among his friends could have been of an entirely negative type. Still, basketball was turning out to be an important vehicle for gaining acceptance into the community.

The next week a number of the other Hallway Hangers turned up at the gym to play ball. Pickup basketball, around Clarendon Heights at least, only vaguely resembles the game played at the college and professional level. Defense is almost nonexistent, passing is kept to a minimum, and flashy moves are at a premium. We had access to only half the gym, so we played crosswise on a reduced court, a fortunate setup because none of us was in good shape. In fact, many of the Hallway Hangers would come in to play high or drunk or both. The games were nearly as verbal as they were physical. A constant chatter of good-natured kidding and self-congratulations could be heard from most players: "Gimme that fuckin' ball! I feel hot tonight. Bang! Get out of my face, Slick. I'll put those fucking fifteen-footers in all day." Matched up against Hank again, I responded to his joking insults with abuse of my own, being ever so careful not to go too far. The Hallway Hangers present noticed my familiarity with Hank and treated me accordingly. I was making progress, but it was slow and not without its problems. Every step I gained was accompanied by apprehension and doubt. That night on the basketball court a vicious fight broke out between two people on the fringes of the Hallway Hangers. Everybody else seemed to take it in stride, but I was shaken by the bloody spectacle. I was entering a new world, and I wasn't certain I could handle the situations in which I might find myself. It was an exciting time, but it also provided moments of anxiety and consternation.

The next week, while waiting outside the gym with the Brothers, I was asked to play on a team they were putting together. I readily assented. I sensed that they were confused by my developing association with the Hallway Hangers and in a sense felt betrayed. That I could enjoy their company as well as those who openly and maliciously antagonized them was incomprehensible in their eyes. So I was anxious to reestablish my allegiance to the Brothers and saw participation on their team as a good way of doing so. That same evening, however, after the usual pickup game, I was approached by Mark, one of Frankie's older brothers recently released from prison, who wanted me to play later that night for a Clarendon Heights team against another housing project across the city. I thought that there might be a league of some kind and, as I already was committed to a team, that I should forgo the opportunity. But this was simply a one-time game he had arranged, and after checking with the Brothers, I consented.

About nine of us piled into two cars and sped, screeching around corners, three miles to a grammar school gym adjacent to Lipton Park Housing Development. We lost the game, and I played horrendously, but in terms of my project significant advances were made. There is nothing like a common adversary to solidify tenuous associations and dissolve differences. That night I felt in some sense part of the Hallway Hangers and was treated, in turn, simply as a member of the group. Of course, there were still barriers, and I obviously was different from the rest, a fact that was lost on nobody when they dropped me off at the university on the way home. Nevertheless, even while they jokingly derided me for my poor performance as I climbed out of the noisy, run-down Impala, I felt a sense of belonging that hitherto had eluded me.

Only a week later, however, the status I had managed to achieve in both groups was threatened. The Brothers challenged the Hallway Hangers and their older friends to a game of basketball. Although considerably younger and smaller than the white youths, the Brothers were generally more skilled on the court and, with Craig playing, promised to give the Hallway Hangers a good game. Knowing nothing of the situation, I walked into the gym to find the younger kids cleared off their half of the court. Instead of playing floor hockey or kickball, they were seated in the bleachers, which had been pulled out of the wall for the occasion. At one end of the full-length court the Brothers were shooting at a basket; at the other end the Hallway Hangers were warming up. I heard Super blurt out, "Oh, yeah, here's Jay," but I also heard a voice from the other end bellow, "It's about fucking time, Jay; we thought we'd be playing without you." Both teams expected me to play for their side, and I had no idea what to do. To choose one team meant to alienate the other. My own inclination was to go with the Brothers. I remembered the contempt with which Juan had spoken of a white friend's neutrality when a fight had broken out at school between the Brothers and a gang of white kids. I had developed close friendships with Juan, Craig, Super, and Derek, and I didn't want to let them down. On the other hand, in terms of the dynamics of the fieldwork, I needed to move closer to the Hallway Hangers. Tying up my shoelaces, I frantically tried to think of a way out of the situation but came up short.

I walked out to the center of the court where a social service worker was waiting to referee the game. He seemed concerned about the possibility of the contest turning into a violent melee and looked none too happy about his own role. Trying to assume a noncommittal air, I sauntered over to the Brothers' side and took a few shots, then walked to the other end and did the same with the Hallway Hangers. The Hallway Hangers had Hank's older brother Robbie playing, a six-foot-four-inch hardened veteran of the army's special forces. I suggested that the Brothers could use me more, that with Robbie's playing for the Hallway Hangers the game might be a blowout anyway. The curt response was something to the effect that if I wanted to play with "the niggers," that was my prerogative. Before I could reply, the referee shouted for me to play with the Brothers to even up the sides, and, hoping this intervention would mitigate the damage done, I trotted over to play with the Brothers.

The game was close and very rough, with several near-fights and nasty verbal exchanges sparked off by elbows flying under the backboards. We were much smaller than the Hallway Hangers and somewhat intimidated, but with Craig playing we undoubtedly had the most skillful player on the court. I made one lucky play early on that probably did more to establish my credibility among teenagers in the neighborhood than any other single event. With Hank coasting in for an easy layup, I caught him from behind and somehow managed to block his shot, flinging the ball clear across the gym. The crowd, about fifty or sixty kids from the neighborhood, roared with surprise, for such ignominy seldom befell Hank. The Brothers whooped with glee, slapping me on the back, and Hank's own teammates bombarded him with wisecracks. I couldn't suppress a grin, and Hank, taking it well, just sheepishly grinned back. Fortunately, the referee had whistled for a foul, which enabled Hank to maintain some "face." We ended up losing the game by one point, not least because I missed a foul shot in the last minute, but although bitterly disappointed, the Brothers had shown a much bigger and older team that they would not back down to them. The significance of events in the gym extended well beyond its walls, which is why such games between the two groups were contested with intensity and vigor.

At game's end, I made a point of walking back to the Heights with the Hallway Hangers, despite the questions it must have raised in the Brothers' minds as to where my loyalties really lay. As far as both groups were concerned, there was no middle ground between them. Each wondered which side I was on; my attempt to sit on the fence, I began to realize, was going to be a difficult balancing job. There would be other instances, like the basketball game, where a choice would have to be made. It was an uncomfortable position, one that plagued me throughout the research, but I derived some comfort from the fact that at least it indicated I was getting on with the fieldwork.

The research, in fact, made some significant advances that night. I hung around with the Hallway Hangers outside doorway #13 while they smoked cigarettes and talked about the game. Frankie began to insult the Brothers in no uncertain terms, glancing at me to gauge my reaction. Sensing he was trying to find out where I stood, I let it all slide, neither agreeing with him nor defending the Brothers. Finally, apparently satisfied, he said that it was a good thing I had played for the Brothers, for it had evened up the teams. In fact, it hadn't made that much of a difference, but Frankie wanted to believe that it was the sole white player on the opposition who had made the game a close one. In any case, it became clear that although my playing for the Brothers had jeopardized my standing with the Hallway Hangers, I was to emerge relatively unscathed. Soon Frankie and the others were laughing about the confusion a white player on the other team had caused, about how they had nearly passed the ball to me several times, and about the look on Hank's face when I had blocked his shot.

When I boarded the bus heading for the university, I was surprised to find Frankie right by me. Heading to see a girlfriend, he took the seat next to me and struck up a conversation. When we passed Lincoln High School, he pointed to a window in the school and noted that inside was his classroom. "What subject?" I asked, in response to which Frankie launched into a fascinating description of the Adjustment Class and his teacher, Jimmy Sullivan. He told me he hoped to graduate in June, that he'd be the first of his mother's six sons to do so. After describing his brothers' experiences in prison, Frankie related in a candid and poignant tone the vulnerability he felt in his role at the Heights. "I gotta get away. I gotta do somethin'. If I don't, I'm gonna be fucked; I know it. I ain't ready for fucking prison, man." I had seen only Frankie's hard exterior, and this quite unexpected glimpse of his feelings took me by surprise. In time, I became used to some of the toughest individuals confiding in me things they rarely could reveal to their peers. This particular episode with Frankie created a small bond between the two of us that had crucial implications for my fieldwork. My friendship with Hank was important, but he spent relatively little time actually hanging in the neighborhood with the Hallway Hangers. Frankie, on the other hand, was a fixture in doorway #13 and the undisputed leader of the group. I knew from other ethnographies that good rapport with one key member is often sufficient to gain entrée to even the most closed group. William Foote Whyte's sponsorship by Doc allowed him access to the Norton Street gang,[2] and Elijah Anderson's relationship with Herman opened crucial doors to the social world of street-corner men.[3] With Frankie's friendship, my entrée into the Hallway Hangers' peer group was ensured.

I remember quite distinctly the first time I actually hung in doorway #13. Of course, I'd gone into that particular stairwell countless times, for one of the boys in my youth group lived in the entryway. Even then I felt uncomfortable making my way up the dark, littered stairway through the teenagers sitting sprawled on the steps and leaning against the walls laughing, drinking beer, and smoking marijuana. Walking in with Frankie, however, was entirely different. Everybody looked up when we came in, but when Frankie initiated a conversation with me, they all, as if on cue, continued on as if I weren't there. No one questioned my presence, and I found it not at all difficult to participate in the discussions. Frankie was collecting money to buy a half pound of marijuana, Chris was peddling cocaine, and at one point someone I'd never seen before came in wanting to buy some heroin but was turned away empty-handed. My presence seemed to have no effect; it was business as usual in doorway #13.

I knew then that I had crossed an important boundary. In the weeks that followed I was amazed at how quickly I came to feel accepted by the Hallway Hangers and comfortable hanging with them in Clarendon Heights. Despite the fact that my home was in rural New Hampshire and that I was a college student, neither of which I concealed from the Hallway Hangers, I was young (looking even less than my twenty-one years), and I was white. Those two characteristics and Frankie's friendship apparently were enough to satisfy the Hallway Hangers. Without consciously intending to do so, I began to fit in in other ways. My speech became rough and punctuated more often with obscenities; I began to carry myself with an air of cocky nonchalance and, I fear, machismo; and I found myself walking in a slow, shuffling gait that admitted a slight swagger. These were not, on the conscious level at least, mere affectations but were rather the unstudied products of my increasing involvement with the Hallway Hangers. To a large degree I was unaware of these changes; they were pointed out to me by fellow students involved in the youth program.

The world of Clarendon Heights and the world of the university were at odds with each other in almost every conceivable way. To stand with one foot in each often proved a difficult posture. It was only a ten-minute bus ride from the dark, squalid confines of doorway #13 to the richly decorated college dining hall with its high ceiling and ostentatious gold chandeliers. I remember turning up for dinner directly from the Heights and unthinkingly greeting one of my upper-class friends with, "Hey, Howard, what the fuck you been up to?" His startled look reminded me of where I was, and I hurriedly added, "I mean, how's your work going?" The dichotomy between the university and Clarendon Heights and the different standards of behavior expected of me in each were not sources of constant angst, but I found it somewhat difficult to adjust to the constant role changes. That I talked, walked, and acted differently on campus than I did in Clarendon Heights did not seem inconsistent, affected, or artificial to me at the time. I behaved in the way that seemed natural to me, but as Whyte points out in describing his fieldwork, what was natural at the project was bound to be different from what was natural on the college campus.[4]

In Clarendon Heights I found myself playing a number of roles, and the conflicts among these caused me the greatest consternation. In the first place, I was Jay MacLeod, human being with personal needs, including that of maintaining a certain level of self-respect. The Hallway Hangers' racism angered me a great deal, and the feeling was especially pronounced because of my proximity to the Brothers. The deep emotional scars left on the victims of racial prejudice were only too apparent. So naturally I often had the inclination to confront the racism of the Hallway Hangers, to tell them, in their terms, to "fuck off." But as a researcher I was striving to understand the boys, not change them. Challenging their racism also would be of no great help in facilitating my acceptance by the Hallway Hangers. Thus, I generally kept my mouth shut, neither questioning their racist views nor defending the Brothers against bigoted remarks, an exception being the conversation that is used to introduce the Brothers in Chapter 3.

If my roles as a person and as an ethnographer sometimes conflicted, then my role as director of the youth program complicated the picture further. What did the mothers of kids in the program think of me hanging in doorway #13 with Frankie and Hank and company? This was especially serious because by that time I was associated very closely with the youth program. I was seen not just as a counselor but as the major force behind its inception and continued existence. To invite disapproval was to invite condemnation of the program. I was particularly sensitive to this issue because the youth program was still my main priority in Clarendon Heights. I tried to minimize my visibility when associating with the Hallway Hangers, a feat not particularly difficult because they preferred to stay out of view of the police. Still, when lingering outside with the Hallway Hangers, especially if they were "partying," I stepped away from the group or otherwise tried to distance myself when a mother approached. Not surprisingly, this was not a very effective maneuver, and the problem was never resolved completely.

Late one Friday night, after a great deal of alcohol and drugs had been consumed and the noise level in the hallway reflected the decreased inhibitions of the group, a mother whom I knew quite well threw open her door and yelled at everyone "to shut the hell up." Noticing me, she shook her head uncomprehendingly and went back to bed more than a little bewildered. To ease the conflict between these two roles as much as possible, I simply kept up contact with the children's parents so they could see for themselves that I was undergoing no drastic character change. Although never confronted by any of the mothers about my association with the Hallway Hangers, I sensed that it was an issue for them and that it was discussed behind my back.

However, I was able to use this role conflict to my advantage in one respect. One of the stickiest issues with which I was confronted was whether to join in with the drinking and use of drugs in doorway #13. As the activity in the hallway revolved to a large degree around the consumption of beer, marijuana, and other intoxicants, I could fit in most easily by doing the same. Still, I was inclined to abstain for a number of reasons. First, both are illegal in the hallway because it is public property, and I had no desire to be arrested. I already had seen Stoney arrested in doorway #13 for possession of mescaline, and a number of older youths also had been apprehended for various drug offenses. Second, I needed to be alert and perceptive in order to observe, understand, and unobtrusively participate in the dynamics of the social relations. I had enough trouble participating in the discussions and writing up accurate field notes when I was completely sober. Third, drug and alcohol use would have hurt my credibility with the children in the youth program and with their parents. This last reservation was the only one I could express to the Hallway Hangers, but they understood and accepted it completely. Although I sometimes had a shot of peppermint schnapps or whiskey and smoked an occasional joint, I generally abstained from using intoxicants.

Other facets of the Hallway Hangers' subculture raised few problems. I learned to take and deal out playful verbal abuse; although my wit was never as sharp as Slick's or Frankie's, my capping ability certainly improved in time. I also became comfortable with the physical jostling and sparring sessions that took place in doorway #13, although I was more careful than the others to make sure they didn't erupt into serious bouts. My strongest asset was my athletic ability, but it probably was exaggerated by my sobriety, whereas the Hallway Hangers often were impaired in one way or another. In addition to basketball, we used to play football on the hardtop area between the project's buildings. The favorite sport of white youths in the Heights, however, was street hockey, and even individuals well into their twenties got involved in the neighborhood games. Once I rediscovered a long-abandoned affinity for goalie, I strapped on Jinx's old pads and attempted to turn away the shots Shorty, Chris, Stoney, and the others would blast at the homemade goal we set up against doorway #13.

Another element of the Hallway Hangers' subculture with which I had difficulty, however, was the blatant sexism. Involved tales of sexual conquest were relatively rare; the Hallway Hangers generally didn't discuss the intricacies of their sexual lives. Still, it was quite obvious that they saw the woman's role in their relationships as purely instrumental. Women were stripped of all identity except for that bound up with their sexuality, and even that was severely restricted; the Hallway Hangers always spoke about their own experience, never about their partners' experiences. Women were reduced to the level of commodities, and the discussions in doorway #13 sometimes consisted of consumers exchanging information. "Yeah, fuckin' right, Tracy'll go down on you, man. She's got that nice long tongue, too." Because of the discomfort these conversations caused me, I avoided or ignored them whenever possible. This was a serious mistake. An analysis of the gender relations of the Hallway Hangers could have been a valuable addition to the study, but with very few field notes on the subject, I was in no position to put forth any sort of argument. I managed to stomach the racial prejudice of the Hallway Hangers and in striving to understand their racism came to see its cultural, political, and theoretical significance. Put off by their sexism, I missed an opportunity to understand it.

My fieldwork with the Brothers did not pose nearly as many complications. Neither my status as a student nor my white skin seemed to be grounds for their distrust, and with the help of my long-standing relationship with Mike, I had little difficulty gaining acceptance by the group. But with his involvement in school athletics, Mike began to spend less and less time with the Brothers during the week, and I was often the sole white person in a group of eight or nine blacks, an anomalous position that was especially pronounced when we went into black neighborhoods to play basketball. I tried to fit in by subtly affecting some of the culturally distinctive language and behavior of black youths. It wasn't until I greeted a working-class black friend at the university with "Yo, Steve, what up?" and received a sharp, searching glance that I finally realized how unauthentic and artificial these mannerisms were. I dropped the pretensions and found that the Brothers were happy to accept me as I was. Although I naturally picked up some of their lingo, I felt more comfortable with the honest posture of an outsider to black culture. My ignorance of soul and funk music became something of a joke in the group, and they found my absolute inability to pick up even the most basic break-dancing moves greatly amusing.

The Brothers were interested in university life, both the educational and social sides; after a discussion of their attitudes toward Lincoln High School I invariably was called upon to relate my own college experiences. On a couple of occasions I invited them to productions sponsored by the university black students' association—plays and movies—and they seemed to enjoy and appreciate these outings. Personal friendships with each of the Brothers were much more easily and naturally established than with the Hallway Hangers and were less subject to the vicissitudes of status delineations within the group. Whereas the respect I was accorded by many of the Hallway

Hangers was based initially on my friendship with Frankie, with the Brothers I was able to establish a series of distinct one-on-one relationships. Spending time with the Brothers may have been less exciting than hanging in doorway #13, but it was certainly more relaxing and pleasurable. The only strain between me and the Brothers arose because of my continued association with the Hallway Hangers. Although I was never confronted directly on this issue by the Brothers (as I was by the Hallway Hangers), they began to recount with increased frequency stories of physical and verbal abuse at the hands of the Hallway Hangers. The implication of the stories and their searching glances was clear; although the Brothers never stated it directly, they wanted to know why I was spending so much time with the Hallway Hangers. Fortunately, it wasn't long before they were provided with an answer.

By April, having established a level of trust with both the Brothers and the Hallway Hangers, I felt ready to go beyond the unobtrusive research techniques I had thus far adopted. Hitherto I had been content to elicit as much information from the youths as I could under the guise of curiosity. I knew in which high school program each of the Brothers was enrolled and had an idea of the occupational aspirations of each boy. But for the Hallway Hangers, who were less tolerant of my questions, I had very sketchy data. I needed to explain to both groups the proposed study, my role as researcher, and their role as subjects. This I did in a casual way before initiating a conversation on their aspirations. I simply explained that to graduate from college, I must write a lengthy paper and that instead of doing a lot of research in a library, "I'm gonna write it on you guys down here and what kinds of jobs you want to go into after school and stuff like that." In general, they seemed happy to be the subjects of my research and patiently answered my questions, which became gradually more direct, pointed, and frequent.

Actually, I probably should have explained my project to them much earlier, but I wanted to be considered "okay" before springing on the youths my academic interest in them. I also was reluctant to be forthright about my research intentions because I was afraid some of the Brothers whom I'd befriended would see our relationship as based on academic necessity rather than personal affinity. This wasn't the case, although there was certainly an element of truth in it, which is doubtless why it bothered me. Neither the Brothers nor the Hallway Hangers, however, seemed as sensitive to this issue as I was. Although my researcher status added a new dimension to my relationship with each youth, all seemed willing to accept and distinguish between my academic agenda and my personal regard.

The revelation of my scholarly interest in the boys had one very important positive ramification. It gave me a special position in both groups, a niche that justified my continued presence but set me apart from the others. Whereas previously neither the Brothers nor the Hallway Hangers could understand my association with the other group, my involvement with both became much more explicable once I revealed in full my intentions. As Frankie explained to a fringe member of the Hallway Hangers who confronted me as I emerged from Super's apartment, "No, man, see, to do his shit right for his studies he's got to check out the fuckin' niggers, too." Likewise, the Brothers had more tolerance for the time I spent with the Hallway Hangers. Although simultaneous affiliation with both peer groups still caused problems for which there was no solution and with which I found myself constantly burdened, the situation improved significantly.

This position of being at once of and yet apart from the group had other positive implications, especially for my standing with the Hallway Hangers. There are many things that go along with membership in that subculture of which I wanted no part: the violence, the excessive consumption of alcohol and drugs, and the strident racism and sexism. Had I completely integrated myself into the group, I would have been expected to partake of all of the above. Fortunately, the unwritten rules that govern the behavior of the Hallway Hangers did not always apply to me. Had I been vociferously insulted by another member, for instance, I would not be confronted necessarily with the only two options normally open to an individual in that situation: fight or lose a great deal of social standing in the group. For this special status within the group I was thankful.

I was not, however, totally free of the group's status delineations. The fact that I spent a good deal of time with the Hallway Hangers talking, joking, exchanging insults, and playing sports meant that I could not stay entirely outside the group's pecking order, even if my position in it was very fluid. My friendships with Hank and, especially, Frankie must have troubled those who received less attention from them when I was present. I wanted to excel in some of the things that matter to the Hallway Hangers in order to gain their respect, but attempting to do so necessarily threatened the status of others in the group. It was the same situation I faced on the basketball court that first evening with Hank: I wanted to play well, but I didn't want to imperil his status on the court. Hanging in doorway #13, I learned to be acutely aware of status demarcations and the threat I posed to the standing of other individuals. I would try to placate those whose positions suffered at my expense by self-disparagement and by consciously drawing attention to their superiority over me. I'm certain that I was not as sensitive to these situations as I could have been, but I did come to realize the importance of minimizing the degree to which I could be regarded as a threat by other members of the group. The success of my project depended on good relations not just with Frankie and Slick, but with Shorty, Chris, Boo-Boo, Stoney, Steve, and Jinx as well.

Once I told the youths of my sociological interest in them, I set about gathering information more aggressively. I was intent on amassing material on their attitudes toward school and subsequent employment, but I was still very much at the reconnaissance stage; these unstructured interviews were a preliminary ground survey. Still, my conversations with boys from both groups often were quite lengthy and covered a great many topics. Taping the discussions or taking notes, obviously, was out of the question, so I was forced to rely on my memory. After a conversation with one of the boys, I'd hop on the bus and return to my dorm room immediately, preferably without speaking to anyone, and promptly write up the interview. At first, I made summary notes of the interview, remembering as much of what was said as I could and putting it in paragraph format. I was able to recall more, however, when I tried to reconstruct the interview word for word and wrote it up in script form with each question and answer. The more interviews I conducted and recorded, the better my concentration and memory became, until I could recall most of what was said in a thirty-minute discussion. Writing up the interview as soon as possible with no distractions was crucial. I remember having an excellent discussion with Super, Mokey, and Craig on the way to play basketball at the Salvation Army gym. But after playing two hours of ball, conversing on the way back to the Heights, and finally returning to my room to write up the interview, I had forgotten a great deal of it. Writing up interviews was extraordinarily tedious, especially because after conducting a good interview one wants to relax, but the importance of good field notes was impressed upon me by my professor and was indeed borne out by my own experience.

The requirements for my field methods course spurred me to conduct as many unstructured interviews as I could, for by mid-May I had to produce a paper on my project. By that time I had managed to conduct interviews with fourteen boys, eleven of whom would end up in the final study. I had information on all seven of the Brothers, but only on Chris, Boo-Boo, Stoney, and Frankie of the Hallway Hangers. Except in the cases of Mike and Frankie, the material was very thin, often including not much more than their high school programs, their attitudes toward school, and their expressed aspirations or expectations.

To gain a measure of understanding of the high school curriculum I obtained a detailed course catalog and conducted an interview with Karen Wallace, the school's career counselor. That I was compelled to examine and organize the data I had collected and search it for patterns and findings at that stage of the research was fortunate. Fieldwork is an organic process that should include a nearly continuous analysis and reorganization of the material into patterns and models that in turn guide the fieldwork in new directions. Writing the final paper for the class forced me to consolidate my research, and although a detailed picture of the social landscape did not emerge, I did gain a vantage point from which to formulate a strategy for exploring in greater depth the terrain staked out for study.

That strategy included fieldwork in the Lincoln School: observation in the classroom and semiformal interviews with teachers, guidance counselors, and administrators. I also planned to interview as many of the Hallway Hangers' and Brothers' parents to whom I could gain access as possible, a number I estimated at about one-half the total. Most important, I decided to conduct semiformal, in-depth interviews with all of the boys. My research demanded detailed data on each boy's family background and their experiences in and approaches to school and work, information I could elicit most effectively in private discussions relatively free of distraction. I was unable to construct with sufficient depth a portrait of each individual by piecing together the bits and pieces of data I collected on the street, no matter how much time I spent with each group; I needed to sit down and talk with each boy for an hour or so to gather simple data, such as family members' occupational histories, as well as to probe intricate issues like the degree to which each had internalized the achievement ideology. To this end, I drew up an interview guide, a list of issues that I wanted addressed in each discussion. I did not always stick to the guide, but having it before me in abbreviated form prevented me from missing crucial questions when the conversation got too intriguing. The guide also jogged my memory when I wrote up the discussion.

Unfortunately, the interview guide lay dormant for nearly two months, and much of the ethnographic strategy never saw the light of day at all. I simply was too busy with the youth program during the spring and summer to concentrate on the research. I failed to do any substantive fieldwork in the high school aside from conducting interviews with Bruce Davis and Jimmy Sullivan, and in Clarendon Heights I only managed to undertake interviews with Derek and Chris. But in September 1983 my work got a big boost.

Instead of returning to a university dormitory, I moved into a recently vacated, rent-controlled apartment in a large tenement building directly across the street from Clarendon Heights. It was a run-down, cockroach-infested dwelling, but it was large, cheap, and gave me a much-needed base where people could find me and I could conduct interviews. This move enhanced my research in vital ways. Spending time with the Brothers and the Hallway Hangers was no longer a commuting hassle but rather a break from studying, a way to relax and enjoy myself. Living so near Clarendon Heights, despite my continued status as a full-time student, also gave me a better feeling for the rhythm of the community and further reduced the degree to which I was an outsider, both in their eyes and in mine. Although my residence in the neighborhood was not free of complications, it marked a positive new development in my research and in my relationship with the entire community.

I began interviewing individuals in the apartment in October. Each interview would last approximately an hour, and I found that even if I made extensive notes it was difficult to recall with precision all that had been said. Finally, I decided that the formality of a tape recorder would be no worse than the formality of the interview guide. I tried it a few times, and although it certainly made people self-conscious at the beginning of the interview and probably deterred some of the Hallway Hangers from being as frank as they might have been about their criminal exploits, the benefits seemed to outweigh the disadvantages. Transcribing the tapes, however, was just as tedious as writing up the discussions from memory, for it generally took at least four or five hours and sometimes up to seven.

Both the Brothers and the Hallway Hangers regarded these interviews as a favor to me. The Brothers generally were more accommodating; I had little difficulty cajoling them up to my apartment for the required session. The Hallway Hangers were more elusive. Theirs is a world in which something is very seldom had for nothing, and they saw quite clearly that there was nothing in this project for them. I was the one meeting an academic requirement for a college degree, a principal attainment in my own pursuit of "success." In a year's time I would be studying on a scholarship in Oxford, England; most of the Hallway Hangers would be back in doorway #13, in the armed forces, or in prison. To be fair, I had contributed to the community through the youth program, as the Hallway Hangers were well aware. They didn't see me as "using" them. However, they did sense an imbalance in the relationship, and when I requested an hour of their time to level a barrage of personal questions at them, many of the Hallway Hangers vaguely expected something in return.

It soon became clear, however, that I had very little to give. I couldn't help the Hallway Hangers with their academic work as I did with the Brothers because those who were still in school very seldom did any. I did assist Slick briefly when he was looking into obtaining a GED, and some of the Hallway Hangers would approach me about legal or personal problems with the often mistaken hope that I could be of some help. More often, however, the requests were less innocent.

Like all the people age twenty or so who spent any time in doorway #13, I was asked to buy beer for the Hallway Hangers. These requests put me in a difficult position. I wanted to be of some use to the Hallway Hangers, but, well aware of the debilitating role of alcohol in their lives, I didn't want to buy them beer. Moreover, although the risk of police detection was not particularly high, other Clarendon Heights tenants easily might discover what I was doing. Nevertheless, I did make a couple of trips to the local package store for the Hallway Hangers. Those two trips attest, I think, to the unease I felt about the one-way nature of my involvement with the Hallway Hangers, to my desire to maintain my standing in the group, and, of course, to their powers of persuasion and manipulation. One of the biggest mistakes one can make in the company of the Hallway Hangers is to appear hesitant or uncertain; after I decided that buying beer for them was ethically dubious and pragmatically stupid, I answered their subsequent requests with an adamant "no" and was frank and honest in dealing with their appeals and protests.

Despite the fact that there continued to be much take and little give in my relationship with the Hallway Hangers, I did manage to get them all up to my apartment for a taped interview that autumn. In the end, sensing how important it was to me, the Hallway Hangers did the interviews as a personal favor. Some of them consented immediately, and we did the interview as soon as we had some common time free. Getting some of the others up to my apartment in front of the tape recorder was a significant achievement. Stoney, for example, is a very private person. Rather than undergo the weekly ordeal of having to talk about his "drug problem" with a counselor at the city's drug clinic, Stoney opted for a three-month stint in the county jail. In trying to gauge the influence his mother has on him, I asked in the actual interview if they had ever discussed his performance in school. "I didn't talk to her that much. I'm not the type of person who opens up and talks to people. That's why it took you so long to get me up here. I go to the drug clinic, and the lady just asks me questions. I hate it. I just ask her back why she wants to ask me this for. I'm not into it. I'm just doing this for a favor to you."

Once up in the apartment, many of the Hallway Hangers actually seemed to enjoy the interview. Boo-Boo and Frankie both stated that it was good to discuss and examine their feelings and thoughts. I was impressed by the honesty and thoughtfulness with which the Hallway Hangers answered my often probing questions. The Brothers were no less candid, but I had expected the Hallway Hangers to be less forthright and honest. Only Shorty refused to take the interview seriously and maintained a level of distance and invulnerability throughout the session.

Chris and Jinx came up to the apartment together. As Chris already had been interviewed, Jinx and I left him in the kitchen and went into the small room I used as a study where we talked for nearly ninety minutes. We emerged to find Chris sitting at the kitchen table smoking a joint. On the table was a mound of marijuana, probably a half pound, which Chris was rolling mechanically into thin joints at an amazing pace. Chris must have seen the look of surprise on my face because he immediately offered up a couple of joints to placate me. Jinx and I had a good laugh but were interrupted by the doorbell. My mirth faded quickly as I figured that with my luck the police were onto Chris and had picked this opportune moment to make the arrest. Fortunately, it was only Craig and Super inviting me to play ball in the park. I declined and quickly shut the door before they could catch a glimpse of Chris and Jinx or a whiff of the joint. I sat in the study and began to transcribe the tape while in the kitchen Chris rolled his joints and Jinx smoked.

I conducted a number of discussions with more than one individual, but one really stands out in importance for the amount of information it produced. On a cold afternoon in December I managed to assemble Frankie, Slick, Shorty, Chris, and Jinx in my apartment. The discussion, which lasted more than an hour and a half, began this way.

FRANKIE: Okay, man, ask us a fucking question, that's the deal.

JM: I wanna know what each of you wants to do, now and . . .

CHRIS: I wanna get laid right now. [*laughter*]

JM: Everyone tell me what they wanna be doing in twenty years.

SHORTY: Hey, you can't get no education around here unless if you're fucking rich, y'know? You can't get no education. Twenty years from now Chris'll prob'ly be in some fucking gay joint, whatever. [*laughter*] And we'll prob'ly be in prison or dead. [*laughter*] You can't get no education around here.

JM: How's that, though? Frankie, you were saying the other day that this city has one of the best school systems around. [*all laugh except Frankie*]

FRANKIE: Lincoln is the best fucking school system going, but we're all just fucking burnouts. We don't give a fuck.

SHORTY: I ain't a fucking burnout, man.

JINX: (sarcastically) You're all reformed and shit, right?

SHORTY: Shut up, potato head.

I had very little control of the interview and wasn't able to cover all of the ground that I'd hoped to, but the material that emerged as the conversation swept along from subject to subject was very rich and poignant. Disagreements and conflicts between individuals, some of which I actively probed, produced some fervid and well-argued viewpoints that never would have emerged from an individual interview. It took me an entire day to transcribe the discussion, and I never had time to conduct another one, but the yield from this group interview was very impressive. Although the ethnographer must weigh the impact of the dynamics of the discussion on its content, this added task should not deter researchers from cultivating this fertile area more thoroughly than I did.

By November, time constraints were cutting into more than my capacity to conduct group interviews. I had to scrap my plans to do any kind of extensive fieldwork in the school. Although I had interviewed only half the subjects in the study, I already had accumulated more than three hundred pages of field notes and interview transcriptions. I desperately wanted to interview as many of the youths' parents as I could, for I saw that as crucial to the study. In fact, I still see it as crucial to the study, but I simply did not have the time to conduct interviews with more than two mothers— Stoney's and Mokey's. Chapter 3, consequently, is incomplete, and I think the study as a whole suffers from the limitations on my research into each boy's family. Another important item on my fieldwork agenda that I never was able to carry out and that would have been quite enjoyable was hanging at Pop's, the little store where the Hallway Hangers and their friends congregated during the school day. These casualties of my research strategy were the unfortunate results of my full-time student status and of the community work with which I continued to be involved in Clarendon Heights.

After I moved into the apartment, I found myself entwined in the lives of many families to a degree I hadn't experienced before. Youngsters in the youth program would stop by to say hello or to ask for help with their schoolwork, as did the Brothers. During this period I became very close friends with Billy, the former member of the Hallway Hangers who had won a scholarship to college as a high school junior the previous spring. Billy was struggling with the academic workload of the Fundamental School, having recently switched from Occupational Education, so I ended up spending about ten hours a week assisting him with homework, advising him about college admissions, and generally just hacking around. I also became a regular tutor to an eighth-grader who had been in my youth group the previous three summers. He really was struggling in school, both academically and with respect to discipline, and at his mother's urging I met with his teachers, but to no particular avail. In none of these roles did I consider myself a social worker. I was simply a friend, and I probably got more out of these relationships in terms of personal satisfaction and fulfillment than they got from me. Sometimes the rewards were more tangible: A Haitian family to which I'd grown particularly close used to cook me a delicious West Indian meal about once a week, brought to my apartment wrapped in dish towels by nine-year-old Mark, fourteen-year-old Kerlain, or sixteen-year-old Rhodes.

Despite the fact that I never was viewed as a social worker, except perhaps as a very unorthodox and informal one, I was approached more and more often by people with serious problems. I stopped by to see Freddie Piniella, a tough little twelve-year-old kid whom I'd known for three years. He wasn't home, but his mother was. Mrs. Piniella always had maintained a cool distance from me, but suddenly she began to relate in a subdued, beaten tone her daughter Vicki's predicament. Vicki was a resilient fourteen-year-old girl whose violent temper, exceptionally loud voice, and strong frame made her at once an object of grudging admiration and resentment by her peers. Mrs. Piniella had found out that morning that Vicki was pregnant, well past her first trimester. She would need to have an abortion, but Mrs. Piniella had less than eighty dollars in the bank, and the cost of terminating such a late pregnancy was more than five hundred dollars. Mrs. Piniella, a part-time custodial worker at the university, was on welfare, but the state would under no circumstances, not even rape, fund abortions. I agreed to try finding a hospital or clinic that would carry out the operation at a reduced cost, but none of the places I contacted would do so for a pregnancy beyond the third month. Nor could Planned Parenthood or any other agency direct me to a hospital that would.

I returned the next day to report this news, only to hear from her very depressed mother that Vicki, it turned out, had gonorrhea as well. Eventually a social worker attached to the local health clinic located a hospital that would accept a reduced payment on a monthly basis, and Vicki had the abortion and was treated for venereal disease. I don't know how Vicki managed to cope with the strain of the whole experience, but I spoke with her the next week, and she seemed very composed. Her plight had quite an effect on me and pointed up the dichotomy between Clarendon Heights and the university more starkly than ever. It was an ironic contrast to learn of her predicament and then to hear the consternation my student friends were expressing about their upcoming midterm exams.

One morning in mid-December I was awakened by the door buzzer at four o'clock. It was a very cold Super, who had left home two days earlier after being beaten by his father. I found a blanket, and he slept on my couch. Later that morning we tried to decide what to do. Super was adamant in his refusal even to consider going home and trying to reach some sort of reconciliation with his parents. He had come that night from his uncle's apartment on the other side of the city, but reported that his uncle had a severe drinking problem and was prone to violent outbursts. With nowhere else to go, Super urged me to find a place for him in a home for runaways. So together we embarked on a very circuitous, time-consuming, and frustrating exploration of the social service bureaucracy. No shelter for teenagers would accept Super without a referral from a social worker, but the city's Social Services Department would not assign him one. Instead, they insisted on tracking down his family's social worker, a process that took four days. We finally got the woman's name and phoned her office repeatedly, but she must have been exceedingly busy because we never heard back from her. I called the high school, and Super finally managed to get one of the youth workers attached to the school to secure him a place in a teenage runaway home. By that time, however, all the beds were full, and he was put on a waiting list. Finally, after more than a week with me, Super moved into a youth home for ten days before returning to his family in Clarendon Heights. I always had assumed that the stories I'd heard from residents about the inefficiency and ineptitude of the social services bureaucracy were exaggerated. Now I was not so sure, although the problem clearly lay not with the social workers themselves; the problem was too little funding and too much work. It was, however, especially frustrating to be asked by those who could not deal effectively with Super's situation whether I was aware that it was against the law to harbor a runaway.

During the year I spent conducting research in Clarendon Heights I often was troubled by legal issues. By spending time with the Hallway Hangers in doorway #13 I quite clearly ran the risk of arrest, but this was not especially distressing. Had I been corralled in one of the periodic police raids of the hallway, the charges against me would have been minimal, if any were brought at all. Although being in the presence of those smoking marijuana was illegal, possession of narcotics, especially with intent to sell, is what the police were generally after. Still, I saw people arrested in Clarendon Heights for simply having a beer in their hand, so I had to contend with the possibility of arrest. Had that happened, I certainly would have had a lot of explaining to do: to kids in the youth program and their parents, to the Brothers, to university officials, and to my parents.

A greater cause for concern was my unprotected legal status as a researcher. Whereas lawyers, journalists, doctors, and clergy can withhold information to protect their clients, for academic researchers there is no clear-cut right of confidentiality. If any law enforcement official came to know about my study, my field notes could be used as evidence, and I could be put on the witness stand and questioned. In such a situation I would have two options: incriminate my friends or perjure myself. To avoid such a dilemma, my field methods professor urged me to explain to the youths that I preferred not to hear about their criminal exploits or at least not to record their accounts in my notes. But I found the criminal activity of the Hallway Hangers very interesting and quite relevant to the study. Besides, my legal position was no different from their own. The Hallway Hangers had all the information I did, undoubtedly more, and they had no legal coverage, nor were they particularly worried about it. I was a more likely source for the district attorney because as a university student I was presumably less concerned about indicting my friends than I would be about lying under oath. Not wanting to draw attention to this fact and risk losing the trust of the Hallway Hangers, I made no effort to remain ignorant of potentially incriminating information, although I destroyed or erased all the interview tapes and was exceptionally careful with my field notes.

In fact, one absolutely hallowed rule among the Hallway Hangers and a large proportion of the project's older residents was not to "rat" to the police. As an ethnographer I wasn't interested in passing an ethical judgment on this maxim. I was there to understand as much as I could, and selective noncooperation with the police seemed to make sense as a means of self-protection for a certain segment of the community. When I saw two young men who recently had been released from prison arrested while they sat quietly drinking bottles of beer on the steps of doorway #13 and realized that the "offense" would mean up to six months in prison for them as a violation of parole, I began to appreciate people's reluctance to cooperate with the police.

My own subscription to this maxim was put to a very serious test in mid-October. Paddy, a Green Berets veteran on the fringes of the Hallway Hangers, shot his girlfriend, Doreen, and I was the sole witness. Doreen, whom I knew well, wasn't critically wounded; the bullet pierced her arm and lodged in her breast, and after undergoing surgery she recovered rapidly and was out of the hospital in a few days. The details of the incident and subsequent events are too involved to relate here, so I'll concentrate on the issues I had to face as a citizen, as a researcher, and as a member of the Clarendon Heights community.

I was questioned by the police at the scene of the crime first as a suspect and then as a witness. I hadn't actually seen the shooting itself, but I had overheard the preceding altercation from within my apartment and knew what had happened. My first inclination was to relate everything, but I checked myself and repeatedly told the officers only what I'd seen after hearing the shot and running out into the street, thereby leaving out the key incriminating material I had heard. Doreen, it turned out, also refused to incriminate Paddy, but the police were nevertheless quite confident that he had committed the crime. He was arrested, but when Doreen refused to bring criminal charges, it looked as though the case might be dropped. Instead, the state decided to press charges, and I soon received a letter from an assistant district attorney asking me to phone him.

I was faced with a serious problem. Do I tell the whole truth, incriminate Paddy, and see justice done the American way? I had a number of doubts about this course, not all of them pragmatic, such as my physical well-being, my standing in the community, and the future of the study. Practically speaking, to "finger" Paddy would have had disastrous consequences, and I think most people under the circumstances would have balked at full cooperation with the authorities. I also happen to think that withholding information was not only expedient but also morally justifiable. Such an opinion may be pure self-delusion, as most people to whom I've related the incident seem to think, but from my position I couldn't help feeling that way.

As a member of the Clarendon Heights community and more particularly as a trusted associate of the Hallway Hangers, I felt in some ways that it was incumbent upon me to subscribe to their behavioral codes. There were obviously limits to this adherence; other duties or commitments (e.g., to justice) could override this allegiance to the group's rules of conduct, but I definitely felt in some sense drawn to respect the code of silence.

There were, of course, competing impulses. Paddy had shot and could easily have killed Doreen, and no community wants to tolerate that sort of behavior. Yet they were both very high and very drunk, and a violent argument had precipitated the incident. In addition, the shooting was not completely intentional (she was shot through a closed door), and Paddy immediately had repented of his action, rushing her amid hysterical tears to the hospital. Moreover, Doreen herself had lied in order to protect Paddy, and the two of them were back living together within a matter of days. But although I was conscious of these circumstances, they failed to diminish my conviction that Paddy should be punished.

Still, having spent the bulk of the previous summer researching prison life as part of a project undertaken by the kids in my youth group, and having tutored inmates at a state prison, I knew only too well what kind of impact a stint behind bars was likely to have on Paddy. In the end, this proved decisive. I was unwilling to jeopardize all that I had gained in Clarendon Heights in order to put Paddy in prison when he was likely to come out a much more dangerous person.

I decided to say nothing about the argument that preceded the shooting. When the trial finally took place in midwinter after a number of postponements, Paddy was found guilty despite my incomplete testimony, so all my speculation turned out to be academic. Convicted of illegal possession of a firearm, illegal discharge of a firearm, and assault with a deadly weapon, Paddy was sentenced to serve two years in a state prison. I didn't feel good about my role in the proceedings, especially refraining from providing information under oath, but neither did I lose sleep over the incident. Bourgeois morality has diminished relevance in a place like Clarendon Heights where the dictates of practical necessity often leave very little "moral" ground on which to stand.

During the fall of 1983 I felt myself drawn into the community as I had never been before, into its political and social life and into the web of personal, economic, and social problems that plague its residents. At the university, I had a full academic schedule, a work-study job, and a large extracurricular load. It was a very busy time, and I also found it emotionally draining, especially in trying to reconcile the two lives I led: the one on the university campus and the other on the streets of Clarendon Heights.

It was, of course, this study that bridged the two worlds. One of the most challenging (and rewarding) aspects of an ethnographic study is the synthesis the sociologist must create between a perceived intellectual tradition and the data daily emerging from the fieldwork. Without a theoretical framework to make some sense of the overwhelming quantity and variety of empirical material, the researcher would be swimming in a sea of field notes, each new interview tossing him or her in a different direction. By the same token, there is all too much theoretical abstraction with no experiential grounding whatsoever coming from scholars who are locked in their academic offices. This book began with a review of reproduction theory and, after the ethnographic material was laid out, moved on to a reconsideration of the theoretical perspective. That is the way this intellectual enterprise was actually carried out, although the progression was not nearly so linear. Since the beginning of the fieldwork in spring 1983 I had been studying the theoretical literature. The thinking of Bowles and Gintis, Bourdieu, Bernstein, and especially Willis (I didn't read Giroux until long afterward) informed my own thinking at every stage of the research. My empirical data and the theoretical perspective were held in a kind of dialectical tension, and I found myself moving back and forth between the two until my own ideas coalesced.

The emergence of my ideas was a slow, circuitous process; I had expected to have problems analyzing the data, but the earlier stage of simply organizing the empirical material proved more difficult than I had foreseen. By January 1984 I had in excess of five hundred pages of field notes. By March I had to turn this mass of data into a senior honors thesis. I knew the analytical and theoretical sections would prove intellectually taxing, but I didn't realize how difficult it would be to organize my notes into the basically descriptive chapters on the peer group, family, work, and school.

I failed to make theoretical notes throughout the months of research. I had plenty of notes depicting events and conversations, but kept no record of my more abstract sense of the observed phenomena. By November, the ideas that make up the backbone of Chapter 7 were beginning to emerge, albeit in a rough and rudimentary form. I was especially cognizant of these ideas in carrying out the remaining interviews and strove to collect information that would help determine the validity of my fresh theoretical discernments. The entire research period, in fact, involved a nearly constant appraisal and reappraisal of abstract ideas I thought could help me make sense of the data. But, ludicrously, I kept no written record of the development of these ideas. I would mentally cultivate and modify my views in line with the empirical material, but I should have noted after every interview how the new data had forced revisions in or had affirmed my previous thinking. Had I kept such notes, the stage between the end of my fieldwork and the beginning of the actual writing would have been considerably less hectic and would have filled me with much less dread.

I remember spending days reading through my field notes again and again, sifting through the material trying to come up with an organizational framework. I began keeping a record of all new insights, some of which would come to me at the most bizarre times and places, often touched off by a chance incident or a stray comment. In order to get some sort of grasp on the data, I developed a one-page index for each youth, on which I recorded information that struck me as particularly relevant or important. Perhaps the most useful organizing tool I employed was a huge chart that contained for each individual information on the following specifications: race, peer group, high school grade level, school program, expressed aspiration, acceptance of achievement ideology, faith in the efficacy of schooling, father in the household, employment of father, employment of mother, educational attainments of parents, duration of tenancy in public housing, duration of tenancy in Clarendon Heights, and whether the subject smokes cigarettes, drinks alcohol, smokes marijuana, or has been arrested. Once the data had been systematically laid out, patterns began to emerge.

Such patterns gave form and further meaning to the lives of these boys and helped me measure the relative significance of the various structural and cultural factors that shape aspirations. Ultimately, however, it was on the basketball court with the Brothers or in doorway #13 with the Hallway Hangers that I gained whatever understanding I eventually achieved.

SECOND HARVEST: NOTES ON THE 1991 FIELD EXPERIENCE

The fieldwork for the original study took place when I transformed a work site into a research venue in 1983. Having directed a youth program in Clarendon Heights, I was trusted by its teenage tenants, who agreed to help with my undergraduate thesis. When I returned seven years later to undertake research for the revised edition, Clarendon Heights had changed, and so had I. Moreover, the thesis had turned into a successful sociology textbook. I had maintained contact with some of the young men over the years, but many relationships had lapsed. Having taken up residence elsewhere, I no longer had a base in the community.

Thus I crossed the street to Clarendon Heights in July 1991 nearly as nervous as when I first arrived ten years earlier. I needn't have worried. "Hey, Jay," Steve rang out, "what the fuck brings you back to the Ponderosa?" I was coming back. My history in Clarendon Heights meant that its residents were even more affable, accommodating, and forthcoming this time than they had been in the 1980s. The anecdotal account that follows gives a brief sketch of my field experience in 1991.

Although the Brothers and the Hallway Hangers had scattered, tracking them down proved less troublesome than I expected. Several lived nearby and seemed glad to see me. They were excited about being the subjects of a book and pledged to help me with an updated edition. Mostly, they wanted to know how many millions of dollars I'd made on the book, why I'd spent four years in a Mississippi backwater as a community organizer, and why I was shortly returning to a place even more obscure—England. Informed of my intention to become an Anglican priest, a disclosure that instantly kills conversations in sociology circles, these guys were apt to ask about discounts for christenings, weddings, and funerals. The Brothers and the Hallway Hangers also pressed me for details about my wife.

In turn, I pressed each of them for an interview to discover how they had fared in the seven years since I'd done the original research. Most of the interviews were undertaken in the back of a neighborhood bar and restaurant that a friend of mine owns about a mile from Clarendon Heights. I spoke with others in their homes, at their work sites, and in my car. With their permission I recorded most of the interviews on microcassettes. Only Super was understandably dubious. I started slowly in that interview, and as his wariness eased he forgot about the recorder and spoke with surprising candor about his drug dealing.

Boo-Boo also spoke frankly about his criminal activities. This interview was done in my car because Boo-Boo was living several miles from Clarendon Heights. We decided to drive around while we talked, a dumb idea. Doing an interview while wheeling around a city will result in a bad interview, an accident, or both. I pulled into a suburban shopping center and parked the car as we talked on. After describing his night-deposit robberies, Boo-Boo told of being confronted by a pistol-waving partner over a crack sale gone sour. Suddenly, there came a knock on my car window. In the same instant several police cruisers converged on our car. I looked up into the grim face of a policeman who motioned with one hand for me to roll down the window, the other hand on his holster. I looked helplessly at Boo-Boo as I eased down my window. The other cops stayed in their cruisers. Bidden to get my license and registration and to get out of the car, I surreptitiously turned off the tape recorder and did as I was told. Shoppers stopped and stared. I was stunned. I figured that with all Boo-Boo's violent drug troubles in Raymond, there was bound to be a warrant out for his arrest. So I vowed neither to divulge Boo-Boo's identity nor to let on about the book. I showed the police officer my license. He asked me what we were doing.

JM: Just talking.

PO: Just talking, huh?

JM: Yessir.

PO: You come all the way up from Mississippi to have a little chat? Who's your partner?

JM: Actually, I'm shortly off to England, where I'll be training to be a priest.

PO: Uh-huh. Who's your partner?

JM: I'm not sure of his name.

This wasn't exactly convincing, so I explained that I studied at a nearby university years ago, ran a youth project in a poor neighborhood, and was close to Boo-Boo's sister Shelly. Because Boo-Boo is struggling with some traumatic personal problems, Shelly asked me to speak with him. As she is only his stepsister, I don't know his last name. It suddenly dawned on me that except for the last bit, this was quite true, and I stopped on a note of triumph. The officer showed rather less enthusiasm for the story. So I fumbled about in my wallet, hoping against all hope that I'd kept an old college ID, the only one with a decent photo. I found it, saved by my vanity. As the policeman turned the ID over in his hand, it seemed to dawn on him that my car trunk might not be full of heroin or assault weapons. Disappointed, he waved the other cruisers away but continued to question me closely. Pressed about Boo-Boo's identity and address, and about what we were doing, I ducked and drifted and parried weakly. I kept imagining the cop would reach into the front seat, pick up the tape recorder, and play back Boo-Boo's detailed disclosure of his criminal career.

Eventually the police officer called to his partner, who had been interrogating Boo-Boo, and they retired to their car. They seemed to spend ages on the radio, confirming our identities, checking my license and car registration, and comparing our stories. Then he returned to give me back my license and apologize for the half-hour inconvenience. He invited me to consider how suspicious we looked sitting outside a supermarket in a car with Mississippi plates. Instead of berating him for flouting police procedure and our civil liberties, I nodded meekly and he let us go. Evidently they didn't compare our stories too closely, for when I sank into the seat beside Boo-Boo and asked what he'd said, he replied, "Nuthin' really. Just our names, where I live, what we're doing, y'know, having an interview. He was real interested in your book."

As we drove away and resumed the interview (not such a dumb idea after all), Boo-Boo apologized for the incident as if it were his fault.

BOO-BOO: I'm sorry about that whole thing. You can't even sit in a car talking to me cuz I'm black. Shoot, these cops are so prejudiced around here.

Juan suggested I interview him as we drove to pick up his girlfriend. The drive took only fifteen minutes but he assured me she would be late. She was waiting at the curb when we drove up. Subsequently I struggled to set a time to speak with him. In the end, I went to Jim's Tow and caught him at work. I put in a tape, and Juan and I chatted as he painted a fender and then tinkered with an engine. When other employees began to pause as they passed by, I stuffed the small recorder into my pocket, thinking it would still pick up our conversation. That tape wasn't easy to transcribe. Juan's voice had been muffled even with the recorder perched on the car.

Slick's tape was also difficult to transcribe. I'd spent a few evenings hanging around his apartment, mostly playing with his baby son while he and Denise argued in an adjacent room. Without saying so, Slick seemed wary of doing an interview. The intervening seven years hadn't gone as he'd hoped. He was the proud father of two children. But he also had a difficult job, a girlfriend strung out on crack, and a run-down home. I stopped by one evening and the living room was full. Slick had just returned home from the construction site and was showering. Denise had three friends over, and there were three toddlers scrambling about on the floor. One child reached up and pulled a bottle of beer off a table. The women screamed, the babies shrieked, and Slick came in to suggest that we go out to do that interview. I knew that this was an escape from domestic duties and household chaos; I also knew that Denise was not pleased. But I jumped at the opportunity and lost little time in taking Slick to a cafeteria for dinner. "Turn the tape on," Slick commanded shortly after we sat down. "I don't give a fuck if people think I'm an FBI rat." We had an excellent talk over a good meal. Only later did I discover how easily voices are drowned out by background music and mealtime clatter.

The interviews done in prison were not tape-recorded. It shouldn't have been difficult to visit Stoney and Chris in prison, but it was. Stoney was in Carlisle State Prison twenty miles away. I called ahead to inquire about attire and was told not to wear jeans. I arrived fifteen minutes early, filled out the paperwork, placed the contents of my pockets along with my belt and wristwatch into a locker, and presented myself at the desk. "Sorry, you can't come in with that T-shirt on." I protested to no avail. Since it was a plain T-shirt, she explained, I could easily be confused with the prisoners. Shaking with anger, I extracted a promise that if I returned with a different shirt within half an hour, they would let me in. I ran back to the parking lot, jumped in my car, and raced into the surrounding countryside. Smack in the middle of a rural region, I sped along dusty lanes for fifteen frustrating minutes until I came upon a general store. They had one shirt, a massive T-shirt emblazoned with the cartoon character Roger Rabbit, protesting, "I was framed." I bought it.

Back at the visitors' desk, I was told this time that no T-shirts whatsoever could be worn into the prison complex. Fairly bursting with rage, I demanded to see the supervisor and was eventually let in because he found my story and my shirt so funny. I took off my shoes, strode through the metal detector, stopped to be frisked, and stepped into the steel trap. Finally I was ushered into the visitors' room, where I sat for thirty minutes. Eventually, a guard came up to tell me that Stoney had been moved that afternoon to Grassmoor Prison thirty miles away.

A few days later I turned up at Grassmoor and was told that Stoney was off the premises for a physical. I waited in the parking lot for an hour until a prison van drove up and Stoney and two other inmates climbed out, accompanied by two guards. Pleased to finally have Stoney in my sights, I waved like an idiot and received several searching stares. Then recognition broke over Stoney's face and he came to greet me. He had minimum-security status because of severe overcrowding in the state prison system, and so we went out in the yard and talked at a picnic table. He brought me up to date on his parents, brothers, girlfriend, ex-girlfriend, and children. He asked about Clarendon Heights, about each of the Hallway Hangers, and about me. I've always been close to Stoney's mother and brothers, but never had Stoney and I talked so easily. I felt less distance between us than ever before, and yet in an hour's time he would walk back to his cell and I would drive away in my car. And I wanted something first. I had come to interview Stoney, not just to visit him. Much as I hated to broach the issue directly, I knew better than to dance around it. I explained uneasily that the study had become a textbook and that I hoped to interview him for the revised edition. The subtext was plain: "Yes, Stoney, you're a friend, but first and foremost, you're an object of research. Otherwise, I wouldn't be here." Stoney was aware of the underlying message, I'm sure. But he graciously put me at ease and proceeded to pour his heart out for ninety minutes.

After the interview, Stoney led me around the prison and showed me a photo of his girlfriend. In the lounge area, we were surrounded by vending machines. He explained that prisoners had to pay for decent food, for clothes laundering, for most everything. Given only two dollars per day for his work in the prison kitchen, Stoney found this difficult. I offered him some money. He refused but then relented. Since it was against prison regulations and even a five-dollar bill would arouse suspicion, I tried to break up twenty dollars as best I could. It wasn't easy making various vending machines spew out quarters by the handful and then sneaking the booty into Stoney's socks!

I failed to learn my lesson when I visited Chris at Broadbottom State Prison. Broadbottom is part of a large farm complex, a crumbling Victorian structure where prisoners still slop out their cells. I arrived late and hurriedly dumped all my belongings into a basket at the desk, filled out a form, stepped through the metal detector, submitted to a search, and was herded with the other visitors into a small cafeteria. Every time a prisoner was brought into the room, I examined him closely. I hadn't seen Chris for several years and wasn't certain I would recognize him, or vice versa. When they did bring him in, I knew him straightaway, but he needed reminding who I was. He was surprised to see me. No one else had driven the two hours from Clarendon Heights to see him. Without his saying so, it was obvious that the first thing he wanted was some food. Everyone around us was shuttling back and forth to various vending machines, munching on candy bars, and downing cold drinks. Chris looked at them hungrily and I apologized profusely. Thinking the rules were the same as at Grassmoor, I had turned in my money with the rest of my things at the front desk. I had made lots of money on *Ain't No Makin' It,* and here I was without a couple of quarters to buy Chris a Coke.

In spite of this disastrous start, the interview went well from my point of view. Chris described in detached but vivid detail how his life had taken one disastrous turn after another. He'd alienated everyone, he told me. Having spent two hours with his mother the previous week, I knew this was no exaggeration. He had no money to buy deodorant or other essentials like socks and raised his foot above the table to prove the point. Before leaving, I promised to call his girlfriend, to visit his mother, to receive his collect call a week later, and to send him a twenty-dollar money order the next day. As we got up, Chris flashed me his old grin and said, "I know you're gettin' rich off me, Jay, with this book."

The issue of my financial gain bubbled up in several interviews, sometimes at my instigation, sometimes at theirs, and it was always there, simmering beneath the surface. Sometimes I felt like a manipulative, exploitative bastard. It's not just the money. It's also the power, privilege, and prestige this book has brought me. To the Brothers and the Hallway Hangers it has brought nothing outside of the satisfaction that their lives have had passing significance for several thousand college students. Most of them took pleasure in their anonymous notoriety. Some didn't. Mike didn't want to be part of the second edition. He had kept in touch with me in Mississippi. He had also called several times and talked of flying down with Craig. Once, on a trip up north, I showed him the book and gave him a copy. A few months later, I asked him what he thought. "Man, I just flipped through and looked at the stuff about me. I couldn't make any sense of that shit." When I returned to Clarendon Heights to research the revised edition, he said to leave him out of it. "I don't want everyone knowing my business, my personal stuff. I know you change the names and everything, but still." In the end, he relented only as a personal favor to me and because I eventually pushed the right button. Whereas with most of the young men the money I made from the book embarrassed me, this is what Mike respected. He was always railing at me for squandering a university degree to work for a pittance as a community worker. When I said that I needed his input for the revised edition to be a success, Mike came 'round to being included.

Having just spent four years in rural Mississippi, I was sensitive to the issue of "using" the young men for my own ends. In impoverished Holmes County, articles and books were there to be written, but I just could not generate the requisite analytical and social distance to turn my friends there into research subjects. Instead, I helped teenagers do their own fieldwork. Kids much like the Brothers ended up publishing two volumes of oral history interviews. They spent countless hours doing research, honing their questioning techniques, conducting interviews, transcribing tapes, editing their texts, preparing the manuscripts for publication, and promoting their book. Basically, they democratized the research process by converting it from a scholar's lone enterprise into an empowering learning process. Having masterminded this little revolution, I rode north and charged back into Clarendon Heights—as the lone researcher.

In 1983 I had been a youth worker in Clarendon Heights for several years. In 1991, however, I was just breezing through to satisfy my own research agenda. And yet writing this book is a way of giving something back to Clarendon Heights for all it has given to me. By striving to understand the young male world of Clarendon Heights on its own terms and then trying to translate and interpret that world for the wider culture, I like to think I have rendered a service to both. The outlook reflected in *Ain't No Makin' It* grew out of my work in the youth enrichment program. I saw many things on the streets that I could not fathom during those first summers in Clarendon Heights. When I looked closely and tried to suspend the biases, values, and assumptions I had imported from my own rural, white middle-class social world, I was driven to the fairly radical conclusions of this book. And so my political commitment, whether it is played out in Clarendon Heights, Holmes County, or Chesterfield, England, becomes another way of repaying the community for the privileged access it gave me.

Not much of this would wash with the Hallway Hangers. They know I owe them personally, and I was repeatedly asked for loans during the months of fieldwork in 1991. I gave Shorty ten dollars late one night. The money went straight into Super's pocket. "Thanks, Jay," Shorty said, grinning as he walked away to smoke the crack crystals. In 1983 I wouldn't even buy the Hallway Hangers booze. Now I was subsidizing a far deadlier addiction. I stood there feeling angry, guilty, and confused. That's fieldwork: It generates personal and intellectual satisfaction but also worry, ambiguity, and uncertainty.

I lent money to nearly all of the Hallway Hangers. At the time I knew these were gifts, and evidently they did too. Slick made out well. On the eve of my departure to England, I sold him my beloved '69 Chevrolet Impala with its beautifully rebuilt engine. Slick bought it for $1,300, so basically it was a gift. He paid me $500 in cash and signed a contract to send me the rest in monthly installments. I'm still waiting for the first one.

Many of the young men seemed to appreciate the opportunity to talk about their lives. At the end of a long interview during which the Jack Daniel's flowed freely, I asked Jinx if he had anything else to add.

JINX: I pretty much said what I gots to say. I hope it helps you out.

JM: I feel really privileged and lucky in a way that from way back people like yourself were willing to take me in, in a way. I mean, I'd worked down here for four years.

JINX: Uh-huh.

JM: So you knew I wasn't a narc and that I cared about the place, cuz you'd seen me with the kids, but I felt privileged then and even more so now comin' back, cuz I haven't seen people for a long time. And yet people are willing to sit down and talk about fairly personal things. Umm, so I appreciate that.

JINX: Hey, well, as I say, y'know, there are not too many people out there who you can sit down an' you can get stuff off your chest with. Y'know, a lot of times you don't want to talk to someone you're spendin' all the time in the world with. You'd rather talk to someone impartial, someone who you know it's gonna stay with. Y'know, cuz I keep a lot, I do, I keep a lot of shit in my system. An' then when the time comes, I let it out. Instead of letting it out when it comes, when it bothers me, I just absorb it all.

JM: When do you get a chance to talk about it?

JINX: A lot of times I don't. A lot of times I don't.

Frankie, Shorty, Boo-Boo, and Stoney were also grateful to slip out of their street front and to speak candidly about their lives.

I was depressed to discover how poorly many of the young men had fared in the seven years since my original research. The Brothers especially had been short-changed. Intellectually, this outcome confirmed the social reproduction thesis of the first edition. Emotionally, I was drained, disheartened, and disconcerted by their plight. As I listened to the men relate their experiences, my head was pulled in one direction and my heart in another. It was bizarre to feel simultaneously dispirited and vindicated by the poor employment prospects of the men, particularly the Brothers.

The interviews with the Brothers were more difficult for another reason. Whereas the Hallway Hangers had little stake in keeping up appearances, the Brothers' commitment to the American Dream meant that their relationship with me was more complex. The research relationship between a successful, white university graduate and a struggling, black high school graduate is inextricably bound up with the phenomena under analysis: class, race, education, opportunity, and marginality. In a sense, the subjects are inscribed in the object: The interview itself is a miniature realization of the broader topic under investigation. Friendship or not, there was a tendency for the Brothers to want to "look good" in my eyes and for the book. They may have been disposed, for example, to distance themselves from the twofold stigmata of race and poverty and to display their mastery of the dominant discourse of individual achievement. "No, we're not gonna use race and all the rest as an excuse." The crucial issue is whether their abiding belief in school and their dismissal of racism were trotted out for me as a white intruder, or whether the Brothers express these convictions among themselves.[5]

In 1983 I might have suspected that the Brothers' oft-stated belief in equality of opportunity was a symbolic gloss put on their experience for my benefit, had I not witnessed the practical outworkings of this belief in their everyday lives and conversations. Then I could corroborate their stories by firsthand observation; the new material relies on their word. Whereas an ethnography based on interviews and participant observation can compare a person's stated attitudes with his behavior, interviews alone have to be accepted at face value. Because every interview is partly an exercise in self-justification, then, my heavy reliance on interviews in Part Two is problematic. Lest this admission raise doubts about the data, let me say that I have complete faith in the candor and honesty of the interview material. When I suspected I was being fed less than the truth, I probed the issue and gently pushed the person to come clean. Invariably he did. If I was still unsure, I admitted as much in the text. In discussing Super's account of how the police planted drugs on him, for example, I allow that he "may be portraying his entry into the street economy in the best possible light." I am satisfied with the interview data, but the reader is required to trust my judgment.

To be sure, I was a participant observer as well as an interviewer in 1991. I spent countless hours hanging around with the Hallway Hangers and the Brothers, but often in their households and in neighborhood bars rather than on the streets. I stayed with Steve for a couple of weeks in Clarendon Heights. Given his hard exterior and often thoughtless behavior, I was surprised by his generosity as a host. It did me good to move back into Clarendon Heights, even for such a short time. It's so easy to forget the frustrations of project life: for example, the futility of keeping counters and cupboards clean when you're overrun by cockroaches anyway. One night I was awakened by a clamor in the living room. Steve was shouting, and I heard furniture shifting and things falling to the floor. I jumped out of bed and steeled myself for a fight as I peered through the doorway. There were Steve and his younger brother, hockey sticks in hand, chasing a rat around the room. Steve stunned the animal with a slapshot against the wall, picked it up by the tail, and flung it out the window to the street below. They collapsed in laughter. "Welcome to the Ritz," chortled Steve as I went back to bed. I moved out of Steve's place a few days later, the ever-present prerogative reserved for a researcher rather than a resident.

In late September 1991 I headed for Lincoln, England, to train for the Anglican priesthood. The contrast between Clarendon Heights and Lincoln Cathedral could not be sharper. In a moment of blind faith, I signed a contract with Westview Press to finish the revised edition by March 1992. I stole away from the library, lecture hall, and college chapel to transcribe the interviews and then to wrestle with eight hundred pages of transcripts and field notes that refused to be reduced to three new chapters. My wife, Sally Asher, and I devised all sorts of schemes to come to grips with the data. I highlighted the interviews using a complex color-coded scheme. Sally created a one-page index on each youth with crucial information. I developed intricate outlines, made reams of notes, created subject indexes, and distilled whole interviews down to a single sheet of paper. Reading the texts of the chapters now, I find it all seems so simple and straightforward. It wasn't.

Still struggling as 1993 loomed, I asked the bishop of Derby to postpone my ordination so that I could go home and finish the book that summer. I lived with my parents and commuted to Dartmouth College's library. Suddenly surrounded by more than theological tomes, I read far too widely and intensely. Important discoveries were the works of Philippe Bourgois and Loïc Wacquant. In addition, I gained access to census data for Clarendon Heights and the surrounding city. I agonized over how to present the new material, made several false starts, and went back to England to start my ministerial post in Chesterfield less than half-finished with the book.

The next year and a half were crazy. Immersed in a poor parish in a declining mining and industrial town, I met plenty of indigenous hallway hangers. I began working with disaffected teenagers in addition to my full regimen of visiting, counseling, praying, and performing funerals, baptisms, and Sunday services. But still I had the unfinished manuscript hanging over my head. I snatched bits of time in between my ministerial duties to work on it. My sermons began to sound like sociology essays and the book began to preach. Meanwhile, the patience of Dean Birkenkamp, my Westview editor, was wearing thin. I also wore out friends within and without the ranks of academia with drafts of chapters for their comments. Finally, with 1995 upon me, I printed this file for what I trusted was the last time.

I hope this book does justice to the young lives of the Brothers and the Hallway Hangers. I hope it provokes further study and sparks a critical attitude toward the American socioeconomic system. Most of all, I hope it spurs readers to struggle for a society that doesn't trample on the aspirations of its people.

CONFESSIONS: CLARENDON HEIGHTS REVISITED

I dialed the number and said, "Is Stoney there, please?" Long pause.

"Who's this?"

"Jay MacLeod. I used to—"

"No way! Jay! I don't believe this, dude! Holy shit! We were just talking about you the other day, no shit. Me and my brother. That's spooky. You callin' from England? Hey, how'd you get this number?" I explained that I was calling from my parents' home, that I hoped to interview him for a new edition of *Ain't No Makin' It,* and that the publisher had found his telephone number. Stoney suggested a time, told me how to find their place, and passed the phone to his younger brother Kyle. Kyle was one of the smartest kids in our summer youth program in the early 1980s, and I hadn't spoken to him for seventeen years. When I arrived at their place to interview Stoney, I spent the first hour catching up with Kyle around the kitchen table. I'd heard that Kyle had struggled as an adult but I was still shaken by his gaunt face and blackened teeth and by his matter-of-fact account of three brushes with death: beaten with a bar in a street fight; hit by a car in front of Clarendon Heights; and stabbed in the chest, resulting in a pierced lung and severe loss of blood. He has recovered fully from the traffic accident and the stabbing but still has intense, recurring head pain from the bar's permanent damage to his skull. Divorced and a father of two, Kyle has worked a series of construction jobs in siding, flooring, and framing—locally and in North Carolina. He currently works as a cook in a small pizza place. His childhood hopes in tatters, this was nevertheless the same Kyle, with his quick smile and quicker tongue. Back in the early 1980s I had lampooned his adolescent devotion to Ozzy Osbourne. Now Kyle delighted in pointing out that Ozzy is still a great performer as well as multimillionaire media entrepreneur and an exemplary father. Kyle related this as he showed me his bedroom jam-packed with amplifiers, speakers, and guitars (including one signed by all the original members of Black Sabbath, Osbourne's former band). Kyle asked me about my work and family and we reminisced about old times with the youth program. When Kyle left for work, I sat down with Stoney in the living room.

Back in 1983 Stoney found it difficult to talk about himself and actually opted for the county jail over weekly counseling sessions. I was expecting some of that diffidence when we sat down in his living room and I placed the small digital recorder and clip-on microphone on the table between us. I launched into a spiel about my gratitude to Stoney and the other men for the privileged access I've had to their experiences, thoughts, and feelings, and how through the book a generation of college students has been affected by the Hallway Hangers and Brothers. As I spoke, Stoney reached to the coffee table, picked up the tiny mike, clipped it to his black T-shirt, and said, "Let's do it." He smiled, and I realized Stoney was trying to put me at ease!

I first discovered the power of oral history from our youth program in Clarendon Heights. In the summer of 1982 the kids in my charge (Kyle among them) interviewed ex-convicts and published a magazine of their stories. The next summer they did the same with people who had been in the armed forces. Working as a community organizer in Mississippi, I helped teenagers publish two anthologies of oral history with their elders, many of whom were unsung veterans of the struggle for civil rights in the 1960s. In working-class British neighborhoods, oral history has proved an invaluable tool in parish ministry. Teenagers in Derbyshire and Lancashire have explored the social history of coal mining and cotton mills, respectively, and in my current parish adult learners have published four magazines that celebrate the stories of successive waves of Irish, Polish, Italian, Caribbean, South Asian, African, and East European immigrants. An oral history interview gives the interviewee a chance to order experiences and emotions, to set the past at rest, and to shore up a sense of self-cohesion. It can also be a painful experience of grudging self-exposure or of protective covering up. How would it be with the Hallway Hangers and the Brothers?

The crucial ingredient in an oral history interview is rapport. I was amazed by how graciously I was received by all the Brothers and Hallway Hangers and by how quickly rapport was reestablished. Our conversations were remarkably free from dissembling, and I was gratified by their willingness to speak honestly even when doing so portrayed them in a negative light. That's not to say that the interviews were devoid of posturing or self-justification, but fifteen years of parish ministry and pastoral visiting have helped me to discern when someone is being deceitful. There were certainly moments in the interviews when my credulity was strained, and this will have registered in my body language and sometimes in follow-up questions to probe the issue. The careful reader will note the contradiction in Shorty's interview, for example, between "I ain't been drinking at all" and his later assertion that he'd consumed three pints of liquor the previous day. The reader also understands that we have Shorty's rather unreliable perspective on his relationships, and that his girlfriend and son would see things in a rather different light. Reading between the lines is risky but natural and necessary, and oral history interviews are open to varied interpretation. Still, I was impressed by the honesty of the men. All in all (and I know how psychologically and sociologically naive this must sound), I believe that what is served up in these interviews is truth (if not quite *the* truth).

The interview with Stoney lasted just under two hours and ran to sixty-five pages of single-spaced transcript. Transcribing is immensely tedious, and it would have taken me up to twenty hours to transcribe Stoney's interview. I hated doing the transcribing for the first two editions of this book, as did friends and family who generously pitched in to help. So I was delighted to be able to hook up the digital recorder to my laptop, download Stoney's sound file, transfer it to a CD, and send it off to Westview Press for transcribing. The professionals did a good job. I don't know what the transcribers made of the content but Westview understands the importance of protecting the anonymity of the book's subjects and promised me that the interviews would be secure.

On March 15, 1984, I submitted my undergraduate thesis (Part One of this book, minus much of the theory) at the university's academic office. I was physically exhausted after several weeks of minimal sleep, but I was on an emotional high as I hurried down to Clarendon Heights with a copy of the bound manuscript. I dumped my backpack in my apartment and went in search of the Brothers to show them the thesis. I caught up with the Hallway Hangers later that evening in doorway #13. Both groups of guys were happy for me and expressed delight about seeing their words in print, and the Hallway Hangers took special pleasure in their unedited conversations. But when Frankie started to skim past the section on the Hallway Hangers to read about the Brothers, I made some hasty excuse and managed to get the manuscript from him. The next page contained quotes from the Brothers about how Frankie and his friends are lazy losers, and I knew that street violence might flow from a reading of the text. Even in 1995 when the expanded edition was published, I was afraid to give copies to the men because of how the Brothers and Hallway Hangers describe each other and the possibility of violent recriminations. But in 2006 I reckoned that risk was very remote, so after I finished the interview with Stoney I ran down to the car and fetched a copy for him. It was wonderful to hand it over, and Stoney's delight was obvious, but I also wondered what he'd make of it. It somehow felt right to give him the book after the interview, and I stuck to that pattern with the other men.

Stoney giggled when he came outside to wave me off and saw my car. I had borrowed my parent's car: a rusted-out, ocher-colored, 1991 sedan—surely the ugliest, most unwieldy vehicle Volvo has ever manufactured (and that's saying something). The car became something of a signature for my 2006–2007 fieldwork. My parents had bought a new car (new to them, that is) and the Volvo was mostly used for twice-weekly dump runs. The power steering is among the car's many casualties (as well as the radio), so driving for a half hour becomes a light workout. It occasioned much mirth among the men in the study, as well as Kyle and the other guys from the summer youth program.

Throughout this batch of research, I spent as much time with the men in the youth program as with the Brothers and Hallway Hangers. Like Derek, Mokey's younger brother Sammy followed Gary Santa to Utah many years ago. After interviewing Derek in May 2006 I drove upstate and found Sammy in a small public housing development. He's working construction and raising three children on his own. We had a wonderful couple of hours together. As I observed the family chemistry, I was quite simply in awe of Sammy: his energy, his patience, his relaxed mix of authority and affection. Back in the Clarendon Heights neighborhood, I met up for a meal with several of the guys in the youth program in spring 2006, and we planned a family barbecue for August—a twenty-fifth reunion of sorts. It was a wonderfully surreal gathering back on the Little League field near Clarendon Heights: fifteen men approaching middle age, wives and girlfriends, and about thirty kids.

Stoney came with Kyle and their younger brother, who had flown up from his military base in Florida for the event. Freddie Piniella ("I ain't goin' to college") and James's younger brother Junior helped to organize the gathering, and Mike also turned up. The city youth enrichment program continues to thrive after all these years, and some of the counselors joined us to discover that their current charges include sons and daughters of my old group. My sister works as a television reporter for a local cable news channel, and her station sent a reporter who did a piece on how city children and college students have changed each other's lives. We ate and drank and played softball. Then, much to everyone's amusement, including the passersby, my nine-year-old son and seven-year-old daughter got people playing cricket. At the end the mayor stopped by at the instigation of his friend and colleague Mark Thompson.

I stayed with Mark Thompson and his wife, Jo, while doing the new research for this third edition. I met Mark in 1981 when we were setting up the summer youth program. We modeled our program on one pioneered in 1970 in a large and notorious public housing development on the other side of the metropolitan area. Counselors there worked intensively with a small group of ten youngsters, engaging them in educational and recreational activities and taking them on field trips around the city and state. All the counselors lived on site, enabling them to forge relationships with parents and to be incorporated into community life. The counselors were young university students, black and white, many of them active in campus politics. But there was a joker in the pack: a local, working-class man who'd gone not to college but to Vietnam. This counselor was Mark Thompson. In 1981 he was an organizer for a small left-wing labor union and I was told to speak with him about the youth program. Thompson doesn't do small talk. I was prattling on about our hopes for the new summer program and he interrupted me in mid-sentence. "What do your parents do?" Taken aback, I replied, "My dad's a high school guidance counselor and my mom's a part-time PE teacher." Mark said, "Middle class, huh?" I began to nod but Mark shook his head and said, "You damn fool, you're working class. How the hell are you gonna teach these kids anything if you don't know your own self?" He scribbled on a scrap of paper and handed it to me: "Sennett and Cobb, *The Hidden Injuries of Class.*" "Read it." I did, and that book's wisdom still informs this study.

In 2006 Thompson was working for the mayor, an old friend and one of his fellow founders of the old summer program across the city. Down in Clarendon Heights two days later, I phoned Thompson. The surrounding area had been commercially revitalized and residentially gentrified, so there was no place to park my car without a permit. I was tired of feeding quarters into meters, moving the car, and getting plastered with parking tickets, and I was hoping the mayor's office could arrange for some kind of temporary residential permit. Gruff at the best of times, Thompson practically bit my head off over the phone. Who did I think I was? Everyone wanted a parking permit for around there. No chance. Thirty minutes later, he called back. "You know the Parkside [a bar half a mile down the road]? I called the owner. He says you can park there." Another half hour goes by and Mark calls again: "I've been thinking. Why don't you just use my car? It's got a residential permit on it."

The Thompsons' hospitality set the tone for the extraordinary generosity people showed me during the intermittent periods of research between April 2006 and

November 2007. Over and over again, the Hallway Hangers and the Brothers and their friends and families greeted me warmly. Having adapted to English etiquette, I was often taken aback by their effusive and demonstrative displays of affection. After interviewing street-scarred Steve, I shook hands with him and started to turn and open the car door. "Hey," he said, "give me a hug, guy. I love you, man." We embraced, and as I pulled off I could see Steve still waving in the rearview mirror. I was choked up. Here was a crack-smoking, girlfriend-beating, thrice-convicted felon teaching a Christian minister about the sanctity of human friendship.

In his interview, Derek speaks matter-of-factly (and all the more movingly because he doesn't make a big deal of it) about the personal and professional sacrifices he's made to safeguard the integrity of his relationships with people. I was aware then, as I am now, that as the author of this book I am using the men in just the instrumental manner that Derek resists. The Hallway Hangers and Brothers are partly a means to an end for me. I didn't seek them out until I needed them for this revised edition, and there is a huge imbalance of power and control in the relationship.

There is also the issue of my financial gain from the book. I discussed this with several of the men at the end of our interviews when I gave them one hundred dollars for taking the time out to talk to me. Many of them didn't want to take the cash, even after I explained about the royalty checks I've received since 1987. With the exception of Mike, I insisted they accept the money as compensation for doing the interview. I confided to some of the men that perhaps I should be giving them a lot more money, as there would be no book without the Hallway Hangers and Brothers. They invariably pointed out that I was doing all the work and graciously tried to ease my conscience. Slick was an exception. He rang me in May 2006 a week after our interview and on the eve of my flight back to England. He'd read *Ain't No Makin' It* and some reviews on the Internet, including some scholarly plaudits.

SLICK: It's a very insightful book. I liked it. I gotta tell ya, though, Jay, this hundred bucks you're giving each guy, it's a joke. Look at some of these guys. They're in the fuckin' gutter. Don't you think it would be good to help them out? See, we let you in because it was our way to help someone out. We had no hope but we could see you were on the way up. You've made a name for yourself with this book. You should be sharing more of the proceeds. Really, man, I'm dead serious. You've got a moral obligation to help them. You oughta be lookin' at givin' these guys a thousand dollars each, two thousand dollars each. A hundred bucks? That's spitting in their face.

JM: I hear what you're saying and it's something I've struggled with. You may be right. But if I gave Steve or Shorty or even Jinx a thousand dollars, where do you think the money would go?

SLICK: I see what you're saying, but the moral obligation is still there.

JM: It is still there. [*pause*] Listen, Slick, I've got other obligations too, and I think you'll understand this. I've got three kids. As a priest, I don't get a proper salary. I get what they call a stipend. It's barely enough for a family of five to live on. The thing is, I actually need the royalty money from the book, and it's not all that much. I'm not John Grisham or Dan Brown, writing best-selling novels.

SLICK: I'm holding your book in my hand right now. Know what it says on the front cover? "The best-selling classic"!

JM: [*laughing*] That's within sociology circles. It's like me saying, "Slick, the all-round best fisherman—in your household."

We laughed and talked amiably for another ten minutes. Slick thinks that the book should be made into a film and distributed widely so that more people understand the reality of neighborhoods like Clarendon Heights. "It's all about the environment. None of us chose that environment. Take any of those guys and put 'em in another environment? Guaranteed: They could do anything they want to in their life. I'm not that special." I know that Slick's concern about the money from the book may tie into his own feelings of guilt at having escaped Clarendon Heights. I also know that he may be right.

My status as a priest introduced a new dynamic into the research. I used it to gain access to Chris and wore my clerical collar to the jail. The impact on the tenor and content of our interview is obvious. But there were other times when I felt as much pastor as researcher, and sometimes it was difficult to generate the requisite social distance to ask the right questions from a sociological point of view. That's not to suggest I was constantly conflicted. In fact, a pastor learns early on to resist the natural temptation to jump in with solutions. People usually don't want or need you to fix their problems. More often, they just need you to get alongside and listen, and to ask the occasional question that prompts them to see themselves and their problems in a new light. To be sure, I had a research agenda and these were interviews rather than pastoral visits. But even way back in 1983 it was clear that some of the teenage Hallway Hangers and Brothers valued the chance to lay aside their street identities and to confide in me. Now entering middle age, some of the men seemed to use our interview to discern meaning in their lives and to reinforce their sense of self. For my part, I sometimes found it difficult to refrain from dispensing advice. This is obvious in the interview with Chris, but even in that first interview with Stoney, I was wanting him to deal with his huge child support arrears before he is arrested again for driving without a license.

Word spread quickly on the street that I'm a priest. But I had one evening of respite. Smitty's, the small bar adjacent to Clarendon Heights, is now a beauty parlor, so on my first evening in town I walked up a block to the Cape. Three-quarters of the Cape is a fine Portuguese restaurant but there is a separate neighborhood bar attached. The clientele at the bar used to be exclusively Portuguese, but I thought the old Clarendon Heights guard might have migrated up there. Everybody looked up for a long moment when I walked in and I scanned the faces. A few of the serious drinkers at the bar looked familiar, white guys who had frequented Smitty's twenty years ago. They had looked washed-up then; now they were barely hanging on. But there were also younger, healthier-looking men, some of them conversing in Portuguese, and two women. The two booths were empty, so I sat in the one that gave me a clear view of the bar and the doorway, hoping that Jinx, Steve, or Shorty would appear. I nursed a glass of Jack Daniel's and ordered some food. Soon I was enjoying a feast of the senses: a plate of *bacalhau* (barbecued codfish with baked red bliss potatoes, onion, garlic, and olive oil), Major League Baseball on one television and NBA playoffs on the other, and from the loudspeakers the sounds of Creedence Clearwater, Marvin Gaye, Warren Zevon, J. Geils, and Aretha Franklin. Denied such pleasures for so many years in England, I settled comfortably in my seat and wondered how I'd describe the rigors of fieldwork to my wife, Sally, back home with the children.

I didn't have much time to relax after that first night. The next day I loitered outside a coffee shop next to the Cape. Because customers can no longer smoke in bars, a steady trickle of people emerged from the Cape to light up before disappearing back inside. One of these was a middle-age man with several missing teeth and long, straggly hair. He looked familiar but I couldn't place him. "Didn't you use to work down here with the kids? You a priest now?" I had no idea how he'd heard. I'd been in town for only twenty-four hours and had divulged this information only to Mrs. Carlucci. I explained that I'm a priest in the Church of England rather than the Roman Catholic Church. He looked at me intently. "I guess you don't hear confessions?" In fact, I do hear confessions. The Church of England considers itself both Catholic and Reformed, and occasionally church members will ask to make a personal confession to a priest, receive some counsel, and be assured of God's forgiveness. The official title is the Ministry of Reconciliation, and I sometimes find it helpful myself. In the modern Anglican tradition, it's almost always done face-to-face rather than anonymously in a booth. This man was almost certainly Roman Catholic, so I said that I sometimes do hear confessions but that he'd be better off going to a proper Catholic priest. He looked at me long and hard. "I need a priest. Are you a priest or not?" So I ended up hearing his confession right there on the sidewalk. It was extraordinary, not just because of the setting and the seriousness of his sins, but because his penitence was so heartfelt. Hardened by twenty-five years in prison, he still broke down in tears several times. I was aware of people coming out of the Cape for a smoke and of pedestrians passing by, but he was oblivious. I gently probed some of the deeper wounds and we discussed how he might begin to make amends with some of those he has hurt. He began to regain his composure. Then, before I could pronounce any sort of absolution, a car horn blew, a man shouted at him to get in, and he was off! Perhaps most of the healing had happened already.

Ten minutes later, still loitering on the main street a block from Clarendon Heights and looking for any of the Hallway Hangers, I saw Steve approaching. I couldn't believe my luck. "Steve!" He recognized and placed me quickly. "Hey, Jay. Damn, how are you?" We shook hands warmly, and he said, "It's Curtis, by the way." No wonder he looked so good; this was Steve and Slick's younger brother—levelheaded, hardworking Curtis, briefly a participant in our youth program as a twelve-year-old. I explained about the book and he told me that Steve lives with their mother and gave me the phone number. Later that afternoon I caught up with Jinx at his son's Little League game. The next day I found Freddie and discovered that Juan's sister was still living in Clarendon Heights. Word was out that I was back in town, and people were starting to seek me out to renew lapsed friendships and to help me find the Brothers and Hallway Hangers. I was beginning to realize that this expanded edition of *Ain't No Makin' It* just might come to fruition.

Meanwhile, Mark Thompson was trying to arrange an informal meeting between me and members of the city school committee. He sent them copies of the book and invited them to a barbecue at his home in the hope that my insights could inform city policy. The not–particularly productive conversation showed how sociology can usefully illuminate a problem but struggles to suggest solutions. Indeed, sociology suggests that the sources of educational underachievement are often buried deep in the socioeconomic order and are resilient to policy tinkering. That's not a welcome message for any of us. I reiterated my argument about better schools (pages 263–267) and suggested that a way around the impasse is to turn students into sociologists themselves, that sociology should be seen as a survival skill as much as an academic discipline if young people like the Brothers and Hallway Hangers are to avoid the parallel pitfalls of blaming themselves or succumbing to pessimistic fatalism. Disadvantaged pupils can be helped to see both the structural constraints on opportunity and the spaces for agency and action. Not surprisingly, most of the committee were more concerned about teacher pay raises and whether to sack the superintendent.

At least one member of the school committee didn't need convincing. Isaac grew up in Emerson Heights, graduated from our youth program, and read *Ain't No Makin' It* in college. He has himself exploited those spaces for personal advancement while recognizing that in the end collective political action is required. Isaac and I had lunch, and part of the conversation is recounted in the introduction to Chapter 14 and in the afterword. We had a laugh about something else. When I was writing this thesis in 1983–1984, I didn't have the slightest clue that it would one day be published as a book. So when I was hurriedly thinking up pseudonyms to replace the men's real first names (which one does even for an undergraduate thesis to protect their anonymity), I borrowed nicknames from two kids in the youth program. I stole "Super" from James's brother and "Mokey" from Isaac. The real Mokey and the real Super have both now read the book. They are very different from the men in this book who assumed their names, but it did cause some confusion!

The reader remembers from the introduction to Chapter 14 that Isaac took me to task for failing to appreciate the power of continued structural constraints on the men's social mobility. One of the problems of oral history is that unseen structural forces tend to be forgotten and problems are seen in purely personal terms. As I was doing the interviews I began to question the whole sociological enterprise and wondered whether sense could be made of the interviews without flattening them. I was concerned to allow the men to emerge as individuals and to resist tying them too quickly to sociological theory.

In this I was influenced by what I happened to be reading at the time. Journeying by train and plane to interview James, Slick, and Derek, I was slowly making my way through William Faulkner's *Light in August*. Starkly realistic and cleverly symbolic, it's the story of complex characters who are trapped by childhood experiences and by racial and religious categories. The central character, already a victim of his past at the age of five, is tortured by self and others and as an adult becomes both crucifier and crucified.[6] Faulkner's imagination prompted me to wonder whether the richly textured lives of the Brothers and Hallway Hangers can profitably be ironed into sociological or even social-psychological categories. Certainly I was relieved that it would be up to Katherine McClelland and David Karen to make sociological sense of the men's lives.

In fact, Chapter 14 has restored my faith in sociology, as McClelland and Karen have found parallels and uncovered patterns that, far from flattening the lives of the men, help us to understand their complexity. Sociology helps us see how these men still swim against the current. Class and/or racial constraints on opportunity may become less strong as progress is made upstream in middle age. Or maybe the men have developed ways of coping with the current. In this period of economic boom, they may even have found placid little eddies relatively free from the undertow of structural constraint. But they (and we) are part of an unequal society in which the wealthy few are far freer than the many.

When I visited Chris in prison and he asked me about my faith, I suggested that spirituality can arrest our inertial drift into self-deception. My faith in a forgiving God allows me to face up to the truth about myself and to deal constructively with my sin. The United States is even more prone to self-deception than I am. We are in the grip of denial and resistance to the reality of our social sin, and sociology can help the world work through its ignorance of itself. Spirituality and sociology have parallel vocations. Spirituality reveals the truth about ourselves. Sociology reveals the truth about our society. Both spur us to struggle for justice, for in the end my redemption is linked to yours.

NOTES

1. William Foote Whyte, *Street Corner Society* (Chicago: University of Chicago Press, 1943), p. 279.

2. Ibid.

3. Elijah Anderson, *A Place on the Corner* (Chicago: University of Chicago Press, 1978).

4. Whyte, *Street Corner Society,* p. 304.

5. I am indebted to Loïc Wacquant for making these points in correspondence with me.

6. Edmond L. Volpe, *William Faulkner* (Syracuse, N.Y.: Syracuse University Press, 2003), pp. 151–174.

APPENDIX 2

Biographical Sketches of the Hallway Hangers and the Brothers in 2006

THE HALLWAY HANGERS

Frankie (pg. 278–291)

RACE/ETHNICITY: White/Irish
RESIDENCE: Living with his wife and son, one block from Clarendon Heights
EDUCATION: High school graduate (through Adjustment Class)
JOB HISTORY: Road crew with the state; union job, full benefits. Previous: City Housing Authority, twelve years; unemployed; restaurant/hotel jobs
DRUGS: Clean now (twenty-two months) through twelve-step program; most recently, addicted to prescription painkillers. Previous: alcohol and drugs
PRISON: Has a record, but no time served
WIFE/GIRLFRIEND: Carla
CHILDREN: Darren, twenty; college dropout
FAMILY*: In contact with mother, brothers, nephew
HEALTH: Heart attack in 2005

---

*of origin

Slick (pg. 335–349)

RACE/ETHNICITY: White/Irish
RESIDENCE: Living with his wife and children in a middle-class suburb in a southern state
EDUCATION: GED
JOB: Roofing contractor—self-employed since 1995. Previous: roofer, cocaine dealer, brief stint in the marines
DRUGS: Primarily alcohol; now sober
PRISON: Yes
WIFE/GIRLFRIEND: Denise
CHILDREN: Brad; Tyler, fourteen; two daughters, eight and nine
FAMILY: Younger brother is Steve (Hallway Hanger); telephone contact with mother and siblings; made peace with his father

---

Stoney (pg. 317–327)

RACE/ETHNICITY: White/Italian
RESIDENCE: Living with his wife in a run-down apartment in working-class town about twenty miles from Clarendon Heights
EDUCATION: High school dropout
JOB HISTORY: Part-time musician. Previous: Harley-Davidson store, welding, pizza shops
DRUGS: Beer and marijuana; has "cut back." Previous: Valium
PRISON: Yes, several stints, most recently for armed robbery
WIFE/GIRLFRIEND: Connie; met in between jail terms (in 1990), married in 1997
KIDS: Two sons: Buddy, twenty-one, and Jamie, eighteen, from a previous relationship
FAMILY: Younger brother lives in household; helps care for his mother-in-law
HEALTH: Suicide attempt in his twenties

Jinx (pg. 292–299)

RACE/ETHNICITY: White/Irish
RESIDENCE: Living with his girlfriend in a housing project near Clarendon Heights
EDUCATION: High school dropout
JOBS: Crew of landscape gardener, earning $12.50/hour. No benefits. Previous: chain automotive warehouse; family-owned "nuts and bolts" warehouse; computer quality control; hotel jobs
DRUGS: Marijuana, alcohol
PRISON: Arrested, but no convictions
WIFE/GIRLFRIEND: Currently living with his girlfriend, older sister of his previous girlfriend, Beth, with whom he stayed for eight years
CHILDREN: Two sons: Davey, twenty, and Jason, twelve
FAMILY: Very involved with brothers, sisters, and their children

---

Steve (pg. 311–316)

RACE/ETHNICITY: White/Irish
RESIDENCE: Living with his mother in working-class suburb near Clarendon Heights
EDUCATION: High school dropout; steam fireman's license (suspended)
JOBS: Unemployed; small-time marijuana dealer. Previous: painting, boilerman, roofing, construction, crack dealer
DRUGS: Alcohol, marijuana, various drugs. Previous: heroin
PRISON: Yes, several terms, including attempted murder; in prison most of the 1990s
WIFE/GIRLFRIEND: No
CHILDREN: Two daughters: Shelly, twenty, and Kerry, sixteen
FAMILY: Older brother is Slick (Hallway Hanger); younger brother Curtis tries to help him

Shorty (pg. 300–310)

RACE/ETHNICITY: White/Irish
RESIDENCE: Subsidized apartment near Clarendon Heights
EDUCATION: High school dropout
JOBS: On short-term disability. Previous: construction, carpentry, debt-collecting
DRUGS: Alcohol and prescription drugs
PRISON: Yes; also two terms in a state psychiatric facility
WIFE/GIRLFRIEND: Not currently. Previous: eleven years on/off with mother of his son
CHILDREN: One son, twelve
FAMILY: Parents deceased; contact with some siblings
HEALTH: Back problems since 1990s, from construction work, on partial disability for this

Chris (pg. 328–334)

RACE/ETHNICITY: Biracial (black/white)
RESIDENCE: Prison; previously homeless
EDUCATION: High school dropout
JOB: In prison almost constantly since 1991. When out: sold mobile phones at a local mall; dealt drugs
DRUGS: Yes, many, including heroin, cocaine, and crack
PRISON: Currently incarcerated, one of many terms; thirty offenses
WIFE/GIRLFRIEND: Girlfriend, Colleen, currently estranged
CHILDREN: Hazel, three
FAMILY: Close to sister Kerry, still in contact with mother and other sisters

Boo-Boo

RACE/ETHNICITY: Black
RESIDENCE: Many, including stints of homelessness
EDUCATION: High school dropout
JOB: Unemployed at time of death; previously drug trafficking, car wash, moving company
DRUGS: Yes, many
PRISON: Yes
WIFE/GIRLFRIEND: Wife, Ginger, deceased (AIDS)
CHILDREN: Two daughters, Natasha and Connie, also deceased (AIDS)
FAMILY: Half-brother of Derek (Brothers); grew up with mother and three siblings
OTHER: Died of AIDS in 1994, following the deaths of the rest of his family. Still mourned by brother Derek

THE BROTHERS

James (pg. 386–395)

RACE/ETHNICITY: Black
RESIDENCE: Living with his wife and children in a middle-class suburb in a nearby state
EDUCATION: GED; degree in computers from proprietary school
JOB: Computer help desk at a corporate headquarters, earning $52,000 annually. Previous: computer jobs of varying sorts with various corporations, and a temp agency prior to that
DRUGS: No
PRISON: No
WIFE/GIRLFRIEND: Wife (preschool teacher), married fourteen years
CHILDREN: Two sons, twelve and eight
FAMILY: Two-parent family growing up; father a strong influence but often absent

Mokey (pg. 351–359)

RACE/ETHNICITY: Black
RESIDENCE: Living with his girlfriend and son in Dover Plain (historically Irish quarter of the city)
EDUCATION: High school grad; dropped out of a liberal arts program at a community college
JOB: Night manager at Legal Documents. Previous: employee there, ski instructor out west, various jobs in the service industry
DRUGS: No; stopped drinking with work buddies after his son was born
PRISON: No
WIFE/GIRLFRIEND: Girlfriend, Karen, who is white; together for fourteen years, living together for nine

CHILDREN: Son, Rayford, three
FAMILY: Sees mother and younger sisters; younger brother has moved out west

---

Mike (pg. 370–375)

RACE/ETHNICITY: White; half Portuguese
RESIDENCE: Lives with his girlfriend and her daughters in suburban community twenty miles from Clarendon Heights
EDUCATION: High school graduate; less than one semester of college; real estate license
JOB: Real estate—self-employed. Previous: worked for the post office and a local fire department, and as a bank teller and a security guard
DRUGS: Occasionally drank "heavily" in the 1990s, then quit
PRISON: No
WIFE/GIRLFRIEND: Girlfriend, Rosa, who is Latina; together for fourteen years
CHILDREN: Rosa's two daughters, both teenagers
FAMILY: Employs his uncle

Derek (pg. 396–406)

RACE/ETHNICITY: Black
RESIDENCE: A western city, in a basement apartment in a small house
EDUCATION: High school graduate
JOB: Trainer for Internet firm, at $11.50/hour, with benefits. Previous: customer service and ramp work for several airlines; brief stint in the navy
DRUGS: No
PRISON: Military brig, after going AWOL from the navy
WIFE/GIRLFRIEND: Divorced from Faith in 1996; not currently in a relationship
CHILDREN: With Faith: Carlton, twenty-two, and Amy, nineteen (who has a three-year-old son); with girlfriend Winnie, sons Cole, five, and Corey, three
FAMILY: Hallway-Hanger Boo-Boo's half brother; grew up with mother and three other siblings

---

Juan (pg. 376–385)

RACE/ETHNICITY: African-Caribbean (Dominican)
RESIDENCE: Just bought a house with his fiancée in a working-class town thirty miles from Clarendon Heights
EDUCATION: High school graduate; some community college

JOB: Jim's Tow, on and off since 1984, as a driver and doing auto-body repair. Interspersed with stints at a fast food restaurant, as a stockboy, and a ramp worker at the airport
DRUGS: Alcohol; four DUI arrests
PRISON: Yes; one-year term in 2004, after his fourth DUI
WIFE/GIRLFRIEND: Fiancée, Brenda
CHILDREN: Five; oldest is seventeen. Juan lives with his fiancée's children now
FAMILY: Was close to his mother, who died in 1994. Still close to his sister

Super (pg. 360–369)

RACE/ETHNICITY: Black
RESIDENCE: Working-class neighborhood in the Clarendon Heights metropolitan area, with sister
EDUCATION: High school graduate; dropped out of community college
JOB: Casual work with a moving company; pay is $11/hour, no benefits. Previous: drug trafficking, occasional construction work (union), and several jobs in retail
DRUGS: Yes, many. Now clean
PRISON: Yes, at least three separate stints
WIFE/GIRLFRIEND: Married once, to the mother of his son; they are now divorced. Several girlfriends before and since, including the mother of his girls
CHILDREN: Three: a son, whom he hasn't seen in years, and two younger daughters
FAMILY: Several sisters, most of whom are doing well (one a college graduate). Lives with another sister, who is not. Remains in close contact with his mother, who is raising his daughters. Parents are still together; father has worked a union construction job for forty years

Craig

RACE/ETHNICITY: African-Caribbean
RESIDENCE: West Coast
EDUCATION: Bachelor's degree
JOB: Reportedly, fitness instructor. Previous: office work in a department store
DRUGS: None
PRISON: No
WIFE/GIRLFRIEND: Reportedly divorced
CHILDREN: No
FAMILY: Cut ties with his family in the 1990s when he moved
OTHER: Could not be located in 2007

BIBLIOGRAPHY

Anderson, Elijah. *A Place on the Corner.* Chicago: University of Chicago Press, 1978.
———. *Streetwise: Race, Class, and Change in an Urban Community.* Chicago: University of Chicago Press, 1990.
———. *Code of the Street: Decency, Violence, and the Moral Life of the Inner City.* New York: W. W. Norton, 1999.
Anderson, J., and F. Evans. "Family Socialization and Educational Achievement in Two Cultures: Mexican American and Anglo-American." *Sociometry* 39 (1976): 209–222.
Apple, Michael W. *Education and Power.* Boston: Routledge and Kegan Paul, 1982.
———. *Ideology and Curriculum.* Boston: Routledge and Kegan Paul, 1979.
Atkinson, Paul. *Language, Structure and Reproduction.* London: Methuen, 1985.
Bailey, Thomas, and Roger Waldinger. "The Changing Ethnic/Racial Division of Labor." In *Dual City: Restructuring New York.* Ed. John H. Mollenkopf and Manuel Castells. New York: Russell Sage Foundation, 1991.
Banfield, Edward C. *The Unheavenly City.* Boston: Little, Brown, 1970.
Banks, Olive. *The Sociology of Education.* London: B. T. Batsfield, 1976.
Beeghley, Leonard. "Individual and Structural Explanations of Poverty." *Population Research and Policy Review* 7 (1988): 207–219.
Beller, Andrea H. "Trends in Occupational Segregation by Sex and Race." In *Sex Segregation in the Workplace.* Ed. Barbara F. Reskin. Washington, D.C.: National Academy Press, 1984.
Bennett, T. *Popular Culture: History and Theory.* London: Open University Press, 1981.
Bernstein, Basil. "Social Class, Language, and Socialization." In *Power and Ideology in Education.* Ed. Jerome Karabel and A. H. Halsey. New York: Oxford University Press, 1977.
———. *Class, Codes and Control.* London: Routledge and Kegan Paul, 1975.

Bernstein, Jared, Chauna Brocht, and Maggie Spade-Aguilar. *How Much Is Enough: Basic Family Budgets for Working Families*. Washington, D.C.: Economic Policy Institute, 2000.

Bourdieu, Pierre. *The Logic of Practice*. Cambridge: Polity Press, 1990.

_____. *Homo Academicus*. Cambridge: Polity Press, 1988.

_____. *Distinction: A Social Critique of the Judgement of Taste*. Cambridge: Harvard University Press, 1984.

_____. "Cultural Reproduction and Social Reproduction." In *Power and Ideology in Education*. Ed. Jerome Karabel and A. H. Halsey. New York: Oxford University Press, 1977.

_____. *Outline of a Theory of Practice*. Cambridge: Cambridge University Press, 1977.

Bourdieu, Pierre, and Jean-Claude Passeron. *Reproduction in Education, Society, and Culture*. London: Sage, 1977.

Bourdieu, Pierre, and Loïc J. D. Wacquant. *An Invitation to Reflexive Sociology*. Chicago: University of Chicago Press, 1992.

Bourgois, Philippe. *Selling Crack in El Barrio*. Cambridge: Cambridge University Press, 1996.

_____. "From *Jíbaro* to Crack Dealer: Confronting the Restructuring of Capitalism in Spanish Harlem." In *Articulating Hidden Histories: Festschrift for Eric Wolf*. Ed. Jane Schneider and Rayna Rapp. Berkeley: University of California Press, 1994.

_____. "Growing Up." *The American Enterprise* 2 (May/June 1991): 28–33.

_____. "In Search of Respect: The New Service Economy and the Crack Alternative in Spanish Harlem." Russell Sage Foundation Working Paper No. 21. May 1991.

_____. "Shooting Gallery Notes." Russell Sage Foundation Working Paper No. 22. May 1991.

_____. "Crack in Spanish Harlem." *Anthropology Today* 5 (August 1989): 6–11.

_____. "In Search of Horatio Alger: Culture and Ideology in the Crack Economy." *Contemporary Drug Problems* (Winter 1989): 619–649.

_____. "Just Another Night on Crack Street." *New York Times Magazine,* November 12, 1989, pp. 52–94.

Bowles, Samuel, and Herbert Gintis. *Schooling in Capitalist America*. New York: Basic Books, 1976.

Bradbury, Katharine L., and Lynn E. Browne. "Black Men in the Labor Market." *New England Economic Review,* March/April 1986, pp. 32–42.

Bray, Rosemary L. "Growing Up on Welfare." *The Observer Magazine,* January 2, 1994, pp. 35–38.

Burris, Val. Rev. of *Learning to Labor,* by Paul Willis. *Harvard Educational Review* 50 (November 1980): 523–526.

Campbell, Anne. *The Girls in the Gang*. Oxford: Basil Blackwell, 1984.

Castro, J. "How's Your Pay?" *Time,* April 15, 1991, pp. 40–41.

Centre for Contemporary Cultural Studies. *The Empire Strikes Back*. London: Hutchinson, 1982.

Chinoy, Ely. *Automobile Workers and the American Dream*. Boston: Beacon Press, 1955.

Clark, Burton. "The 'Cooling-Out' Function in Higher Education." *American Journal of Sociology* 65 (1960): 576–596.

Corcoran, M., L. Datcher, and G. J. Duncan. "Most Workers Find Jobs Through Word of Mouth." *Monthly Labor Review* 103 (August 1980): 33–36.

"Corporate Executives Go to the Trough." *Dollars and Sense* 138 (1988): 10–11.

Corrigan, Paul. *Schooling for the Smash Street Kids*. London: Macmillan, 1979.

DeMott, Benjamin. *The Imperial Middle*. New York: William Morrow, 1990.

Dillon, David. "Does the School Have a Right to Its Own Language?" *The English Journal* 69 (April 1980): 13–17.

Dimaggio, Paul. "Cultural Capital and Social Success." *American Sociological Review* 47 (April 1982): 189–201.

Durkheim, Emile. *The Division of Labor in Society*. New York: Free Press, 1953.

Economic Policy Institute Issue Guide, www.epi.org/content.cfm/issueguides_minwage.

Edwards, Richard. *Contested Terrain*. New York: Basic Books, 1979.

Erikson, Erik H. *Gandhi's Truth*. New York: Norton, 1969.

Erikson, Kai T. *Everything in Its Path*. New York: Simon and Schuster, 1976.

Farley, Reynolds. "The Common Destiny of Blacks and Whites." In *Race in America*. Ed. Herbert Hill and James E. Jones Jr. Madison: University of Wisconsin Press, 1993.

Farrell, S., and J. Lorber, eds. *The Social Construction of Gender*. New York: Sage, 1991.

Featherman, David L., and Robert M. Hauser. *Opportunity and Change*. New York: Academic Press, 1978.

Ferguson, Ann Arnett. *Bad Boys: Public School in the Making of Black Masculinity*. Ann Arbor: University of Michigan Press, 2000.

Findley, Warren G., and Miriam M. Bryan. *Ability Grouping: A Review of the Literature*, part 3. Washington, D.C.: Office of Education, 1970.

Foley, Douglas E. *Learning Capitalist Culture*. Philadelphia: University of Pennsylvania Press, 1990.

Fordham, Signithia. "Racelessness as a Factor in Black Students' School Success: Pragmatic Strategy or Pyrrhic Victory?" *Harvard Educational Review* 53 (1988): 257–293.

Francis, David R. "Executive Pay in the U.S. Just Goes Up and Up." *Christian Science Monitor*, May 20, 1994, p. 9.

Freeman, Richard. *Black Elite: The New Market for Highly Educated Black Americans*. New York: McGraw-Hill, 1976.

———. "Employment and Earnings of Disadvantaged Young Men in a Labor Shortage Economy." National Bureau of Economic Research Working Paper No. 3444. September 1990.

Freire, Paulo. *Pedagogy of the Oppressed*. New York: Continuum, 1981.

Gambetta, Diego. *Were They Pushed or Did They Jump?* Cambridge: Cambridge University Press, 1987.

Gecas, Viktor. "Contexts of Socialization." In *Social Psychology: Sociological Perspectives*. Ed. Morris Rosenberg and Ralph H. Turner. New York: Basic Books, 1981.

Giroux, Henry A. "Theories of Reproduction and Resistance in the New Sociology of Education." *Harvard Educational Review* 53 (August 1983): 257–293.

———. *Theory & Resistance in Education*. London: Heinemann Educational Books, 1983.

Goffman, Erving. *Presentation of Self in Everyday Life.* Garden City, N.Y.: Doubleday, 1959.

Goldthorpe, John H. *Social Mobility and Class Structure in Modern Britain.* Oxford: Clarendon Press, 1980.

Gordon, Liz. "Paul Willis—Education, Cultural Production and Social Reproduction." *British Journal of Sociology of Education* 5 (1984): 105–115.

Gramsci, Antonio. *Selections from Prison Notebooks.* London: Lawrence and Wishart, 1971.

Granovetter, Mark. *Getting a Job: A Study of Contacts and Careers.* Chicago: University of Chicago Press, 1995.

_____. "The Strength of Weak Ties." *American Journal of Sociology* 78:6 (1973): 1360–1380.

Grubb, Norton. "The Economic Returns to Post-Secondary Education." Mimeo, School of Education, University of California at Berkeley, 1990.

Hagan, John. "Destiny and Drift." *American Sociological Review* 56 (October 1991): 567–582.

Haller, Archibald O., and Irwin Millers. *The Occupational Aspirations Scale.* Cambridge, Mass.: Schenkman, 1972.

Halsey, A. H., A. F. Heath, and J. M. Ridge. *Origins and Destinations.* Oxford: Clarendon Press, 1980.

Haraven, Tamara K., and Randolph Langenbach. *Amoskeag.* New York: Pantheon, 1978.

Hearn, J., and D. Morgan, eds. *Men, Masculinities and Social Theory.* London: Unwin Hyman, 1990.

Heath, Shirley Brice. *Ways with Words.* Cambridge: Cambridge University Press, 1983.

Henly, Julia R. "Matching and Mismatch in the Low-Wage Labor Market: Job Search Perspective," in Urban Institute, *The Low-Wage Labor Market: Challenges and Opportunities for Economic Self-Sufficiency.* Washington, D.C.: U.S. Department of Health and Human Services, 2000.

Hill, Herbert, and James E. Jones Jr., eds. *Race in America.* Madison: University of Wisconsin Press, 1993.

Hout, Michael. "Occupational Mobility of Black Men." *American Sociological Review* 49 (1984): 308–322.

Howell, Joseph T. *Hard Living on Clay Street.* New York: Anchor Books, 1973.

James, C. L. R. *Beyond a Boundary.* London: Yellow Jersey Press, 1963.

Jencks, Christopher. *Rethinking Social Policy: Race, Poverty and the Underclass.* Cambridge, Mass.: Harvard University Press, 1992.

Jencks, Christopher, and Paul E. Peterson, eds. *The Urban Underclass.* Washington, D.C.: Brookings Institution, 1991.

Jenkins, Richard. *Pierre Bourdieu.* London: Routledge, 1992.

Johnson, David S., Timothy M. Smeeding, and Barbara Boyle Torrey. "Economic Inequality Through the Prisms of Income and Consumption." *Monthly Labor Review* 128 (April 2005): 11–24.

Jones, Jacqueline. *The Dispossessed.* New York: Basic Books, 1992.

Jones, James E. Jr. "The Rise and Fall of Affirmative Action." In *Race in America.* Ed. Herbert Hill and James E. Jones Jr. Madison: University of Wisconsin Press, 1993.

Karabel, Jerome, and A. H. Halsey, eds. *Power and Ideology in Education.* New York: Oxford University Press, 1977.

Kasarda, John D. "Urban Industrial Transition and the Underclass." *Annals of the American Academy of the Political and Social Sciences* 501 (January 1989): 26–47.

Katz, Michael. *The Undeserving Poor.* New York: Pantheon, 1989.

Keddie, Nell. "Classroom Knowledge." In *Knowledge and Control.* Ed. Michael F. D. Young. London: Macmillan, 1972.

Kerkchoff, A. C. *Ambition and Attainment.* Washington, D.C.: American Sociological Association, 1974.

Kerkchoff, A. C., and R. T. Campbell. "Black-White Differences in the Educational Attainment Process." *Sociology of Education* 50 (January 1977): 15–27.

Kirschenmann, Joleen, and Kathryn M. Neckerman. "'We'd Love to Hire Them, But . . .': The Meaning of Race for Employers." In *The Urban Underclass.* Ed. Christopher Jencks and Paul E. Peterson. Washington, D.C.: Brookings Institution, 1991.

Kohn, Melvin L. *Class and Conformity: A Study in Values.* Chicago: University of Chicago Press, 1977.

Kornblum, William. *Blue Collar Community.* Chicago: University of Chicago Press, 1974.

Kornblum, William, and Terry Williams. *Growing Up Poor.* Lexington, Mass.: Lexington Books, 1985.

Lareau, Annette. *Unequal Childhoods: Class, Race, and Family Life.* Berkeley: University of California Press, 2003.

Laub, John H., and Robert J. Sampson. *Shared Beginnings, Divergent Lives: Delinquent Boys to Age 70.* Cambridge, Mass.: Harvard University Press, 2003.

Lemann, Nicholas. *The Promised Land: The Great Black Migration and How It Changed America.* New York: Alfred A. Knopf, 1991.

_____. "The Origins of the Underclass." *Atlantic Monthly,* June 1986, pp. 31–55, continued in *Atlantic Monthly,* July 1986, pp. 54–68.

Liebow, Elliot. *Tally's Corner.* Boston: Little, Brown, 1967.

London, Howard B. *The Culture of a Community College.* New York: Praeger, 1978.

Lucas, Samuel R. *Tracking Inequality: Stratification and Mobility in American High Schools.* New York: Teachers College Press, 1999.

Mann, Michael. "The Social Cohesion of Liberal Democracy." *American Sociological Review* 35 (June 1970): 423–439.

Mantsios, George. "Rewards and Opportunities: The Politics of Economics of Class in the U.S." In *Race, Class, and Gender in the United States: An Integrated Study.* Ed. Paula S. Rothenberg. New York: St. Martin's Press, 1992.

Marable, Manning. *Race, Reform, and Rebellion.* Jackson: University Press of Mississippi, 1991.

Marx, Karl. *Capital.* Harmondsworth: Penguin, 1976.

_____. *The Eighteenth Brumaire of Louis Napoleon.* In *Selected Works.* New York: International Publishers, 1968.

Marx, Karl, and Friedrich Engels. *The German Ideology.* New York: International Publishers, 1947.

Massey, Douglas S., and Nancy A. Denton. *American Apartheid: Segregation and the Making of the Underclass.* Cambridge, Mass.: Harvard University Press, 1993.

McNall, Scott G., Rhonda F. Levine, and Rick Fantasia. *Bringing Class Back In.* Boulder, Colo.: Westview Press, 1991.

Mehan, Hugh. "Understanding Inequality in Schools: The Contribution of Interpretive Studies." *Sociology of Education* 65 (January 1992): 1–20.

Merton, Robert K. *Social Theory and Social Structure.* New York: Free Press, 1968.

Michels, Robert. *First Lectures in Political Sociology.* New York: Harper and Row, 1965.

Miller, Charles, John A. McLaughlin, John Madden, and Norman M. Chansky. "Socioeconomic Class and Teacher Bias." *Psychological Reports* 23 (1968): 806–810.

Mishel, Lawrence, Jared Bernstein, and Sylvia Allegretto. *State of Working America 2006/2007.* Ithaca, N.Y.: ILR Press, 2006.

Mollenkopf, John H., and Manuel Castells, eds. *Dual City: Restructuring New York.* New York: Russell Sage Foundation, 1991.

Moynihan, Daniel Patrick, ed. *On Understanding Poverty.* New York: Basic Books, 1968.

Murray, Charles. *Losing Ground.* New York: Basic Books, 1984.

Neal, Donald. "A Theory of the Origin of Ethnic Stratification." *Social Problems* 16 (Fall 1968): 157–172.

Newman, Katherine S. *Chutes and Ladders: Negotiating the Low-Wage Labor Market.* New York: Russell Sage Foundation; Cambridge: Harvard University Press, 2006.

Ogbu, John U. "Variability in Minority School Performance: A Problem in Search of an Explanation." *Anthropology & Education Quarterly* 18 (December 1987): 312–334.

Omi, Michael, and Harold Winant. "Racial Formations." In *Race, Class, and Gender in the United States: An Integrated Study.* Ed. Paula S. Rothenberg. New York: St. Martin's Press, 1992.

Osterman, Paul. "Is There a Problem with the Youth Labor Market and If So How Should We Fix It?" Mimeo, Sloan School, MIT, February 1992.

_____. *Getting Started.* Cambridge, Mass.: MIT Press, 1980.

Patillo-McCoy, Mary. *Black Picket Fences: Privilege and Peril Among the Black Middleclass.* Chicago: University of Chicago Press, 1999.

Persell, Caroline Hodges. *Education and Inequality.* New York: Free Press, 1977.

Pomer, Marshall I. "Labor Market Structure, Intragenerational Mobility, and Discrimination: Black Male Advancement Out of Low-Paying Occupations." *American Sociological Review* 51 (1986): 650–659.

Portes, Alejandro. "Social Capital: Its Origins and Applications in Modern Sociology." *Annual Review of Sociology* 24 (1998): 1–24.

Powers, Brian. "Two Tracks to Nowhere." *Socialist Review* 19:2 (April–June 1989): 155–165.

Reich, Robert B. "As the World Turns." *New Republic,* May 1, 1989, pp. 23–28.

Rist, Ray C. "Student Social Class and Teacher Expectations: The Self-Fulfilling Prophecy in Ghetto Education." *Harvard Educational Review* 40 (August 1970): 411–451.

Rose, Stephen J. *Social Stratification in the United States: The American Profile Poster.* New York: New Press, 2007.

Rosegrant, Jane K. "Choosing Children." Thesis, Harvard College, 1985.

Rosenbaum, James E. *Making Inequality.* New York: Wylie and Sons, 1976.

Rosenberg, Morris. "The Self-Concept: Social Product and Social Force." In *Social Psychology: Sociological Perspectives.* Ed. Morris Rosenberg and Ralph H. Turner. New York: Basic Books, 1981.

_____. *Conceiving the Self.* New York: Basic Books, 1979.

Rosenberg, Morris, and Roberta G. Simmons. *Black and White Self-Esteem: The Urban School Child.* Washington, D.C.: American Sociological Association, 1971.

Rothenberg, Paula S., ed. *Race, Class, and Gender in the United States: An Integrated Study.* New York: St. Martin's Press, 1992.

Roy, David F. "The Role of the Researcher in the Study of Social Conflict." *Human Organization* 24 (Fall 1965): 262–271.

Rubin, Lillian. *Worlds of Pain.* New York: Basic Books, 1976.

Sassen, Saskia. "The Informal Economy." In *Dual City: Restructuring New York.* Ed. John H. Mollenkopf and Manuel Castells. New York: Russell Sage Foundation, 1991.

Schatzman, Leonard, and Anselm L. Strauss. *Field Research.* Englewood Cliffs, N.J.: Prentice-Hall, 1973.

Schultz, Charles B., and Roger H. Sherman. "Social Class, Development and Differences in Reinforcer Effectiveness." *Review of Education Research* 46 (1976): 25–59.

Schwarz, John E., and Thomas J. Volgy. *The Forgotten Americans.* New York: W. W. Norton, 1992.

Scully, Maureen Anne. "Coping with Meritocracy." Thesis, Harvard College, 1982.

Sennett, Richard. *Respect in a World of Inequality.* New York: W. W. Norton, 2003.

Sennett, Richard, and Jonathan Cobb. *The Hidden Injuries of Class.* New York: Vintage Books, 1972.

Shannon, Thomas R., Nancy Kleniewski, and William M. Cross, eds. *Urban Problems in Sociological Perspective.* Prospect Heights, Ill.: Waveland Press, 1991.

Sharff, Jagna Wojcicka. "The Underground Economy of a Poor Neighborhood." In *Cities of the United States: Studies in Urban Anthropology.* Ed. Leith Mullings. New York: Columbia University Press, 1987.

Shavelson, Richard J., Judith J. Hubner, and George C. Stanton. "Self-Concept: Validation of Construct Interpretations." *Review of Educational Research* 46 (Summer 1976): 407–411.

Small, Mario Luis. *Villa Victoria: The Transformation of Social Capital in a Boston Barrio.* Chicago: University of Chicago Press, 2004.

Son, Soo, Suzanne W. Model, and Gene A. Fisher. "Polarization and Progress in the Black Community." *Sociological Forum* 4:3 (1989): 309–327.

Spenner, Kenneth I., and David L. Featherman. "Achievement Ambitions." *Annual Review of Sociology* 4 (1978): 373–420.

Stinchcombe, Arthur L. *Rebellion in a High School.* Chicago: Quadrangle Books, 1964.

Sullivan, Mercer. "Absent Fathers in the Inner City." *Annals of the American Academy of the Political and Social Sciences* 501 (January 1989): 48–58.

_____. *Getting Paid.* Ithaca, N.Y.: Cornell University Press, 1989.

Sum, Andrew M. Personal interview, August 1991.

Sum, Andrew M., and Neal Fogg. "The Changing Economic Fortunes of Young Black Men in America." *The Black Scholar* 21 (January–March 1990): 47–55.

Sum, Andrew M., and Joseph Franz. "The Geographic Locations of Jobs Held by Employed High School Graduates." Unpublished paper, Center for Labor Market Studies, Northeastern University, May 1990.

Sum, Andrew M., and Joanna Heliotis. "Declining Real Wages of Youth." *Workforce,* Spring 1993, pp. 22–31.

Suttles, Gerald. *The Social Order of the Slum.* Chicago: University of Chicago Press, 1968.

Swartz, David. "Pierre Bourdieu: The Cultural Transmission of Social Inequality." *Harvard Educational Review* 47 (1977): 545–555.

Tawney, R. H. *Equality.* London: Allen and Unwin, 1938.

United States Bureau of the Census. Public Use Microdata Sample File, 1980 and 1990.

United States Department of Health and Human Services, http://aspe.hhs.gov/poverty/05poverty.shtml.

Volpe, Edmond L. *William Faulkner.* Syracuse: Syracuse University Press, 2003.

Wacquant, Loïc J. D. "Morning in America, Dusk in the Dark Ghetto: The New 'Civil War' in the American City." *Revue française d'études américaines* 60 (May 1994): 97–102.

––––––. "The State and Fate of the Ghetto: Redrawing the Urban Color Line in Postfordist America." In *Social Theory and the Politics of Identity.* Ed. Craig Calhoun. New York: Basil Blackwell, 1994.

––––––. "Bourdieu in America: Notes on the Transatlantic Importation of Social Theory." In *Bourdieu: Critical Perspectives.* Ed. Craig Calhoun, Edward LiPuma, and Moishe Postone. Cambridge: Polity Press, 1993.

––––––. "On the Tracks of Symbolic Power: Prefatory Notes to Bourdieu's 'State Nobility.'" *Theory, Culture, and Society* 10 (August 1993): 1–17.

––––––. "Urban Outcasts: Stigma and Division in the Black American Ghetto and the French Periphery." *International Journal of Urban and Regional Research* 17:3 (1993): 366–383.

––––––. "'The Zone': Le métier de 'hustler' dans le ghetto noir américain." *Actes de la recherche en science sociales* 93 (June 1992): 39–58.

––––––. "Making Class: The Middle Class(es) in Social Theory and Social Structure." In *Bringing Class Back In.* Ed. Scott G. McNall, Rhonda F. Levine, and Rick Fantasia. Boulder, Colo.: Westview Press, 1991.

––––––. "Sociology as Socioanalysis: Tales of *Homo Academicus.*" *Sociological Forum* 5 (1990): 677–689.

––––––. "The Ghetto, the State, and the New Capitalist Economy." *Dissent,* Fall 1989, pp. 508–520.

––––––. "The Puzzle of Race and Class in American Society and Social Sciences." *Benjamin E. Mays Monograph Series* 2 (Fall 1989): 7–20.

––––––. "The Rise of Advanced Marginality: Notes on Its Nature and Implications." *Acta Sociologica* 39, no. 2 (1996): 121–139.

––––––. "Scrutinizing the Street: Poverty, Morality, and the Pitfalls of Urban Ethnography." *American Journal of Sociology* 107 (May 2002): 1499.

Wacquant, Loïc J. D., and William Julius Wilson. "The Cost of Racial and Class Exclusion in the Inner City." *Annals of the American Academy of the Political and Social Sciences* 501 (January 1989): 8–25.

Waldinger, Roger. "Changing Ladders and Musical Chairs: Ethnicity and Opportunity in Post-Industrial New York." *Politics & Society* 15:4 (1986–1987): 369–401.

Waldinger, Roger, and Thomas Bailey. "The Continuing Significance of Race." *Politics & Society* 19:3 (1991): 291–323.

Weber, Max. *Economy and Society.* Berkeley: University of California Press, 1970.

Weis, Lois. *Working Class Without Work.* New York: Routledge, 1990.

Wellman, David T. *Portraits of White Racism.* Cambridge: Cambridge University Press, 1977.

West, Cornel. *Race Matters.* Boston: Beacon Press, 1993.

Western, Bruce. *Punishment and Inequality in America.* New York: Russell Sage Foundation, 2006.

Whyte, William Foote. *Street Corner Society.* Chicago: University of Chicago Press, 1943.

William, Terry. *The Cocaine Kids.* Reading, Mass.: Addison-Wesley, 1989.

Willis, Paul. "Youth Unemployment and the New Poverty: A Summary of a Local Authority Review and Framework for Policy Development on Youth and Youth Unemployment." Wolverhampton Information Centre, June 1985.

_____. "Youth Unemployment: Thinking the Unthinkable." Mimeo.

_____. "Cultural Production and Theories of Reproduction." In *Race, Class, and Education.* Ed. Len Barton and Stephen Walker. London: Croom Helm, 1983.

_____. "Cultural Production Is Different from Cultural Reproduction Is Different from Social Reproduction Is Different from Reproduction." *Interchange* 12 (1981): 48–67.

_____. *Learning to Labor.* Aldershot, U.K.: Gower, 1977.

Wilson, William Julius. *The Truly Disadvantaged: The Inner City, the Underclass, and Public Policy.* Chicago: University of Chicago Press, 1987.

_____. *The Declining Significance of Race.* Chicago: University of Chicago Press, 1978.

Winsor, Ernest. *The CORI Reader.* Boston: Massachusetts Law Reform Institute, 2003.

Wolff, Edward N. *Top Heavy: The Increasing Inequality of Wealth in America and What Can Be Done about It.* New York: New Press, 1996.

Yeakey, Carol Camp, and Clifford T. Bennett. "Race, Schooling, and Class in American Society." *Journal of Negro Education* 59 (Winter 1990): 3–18.

ABOUT THE BOOK

"I ain't goin' to college. Who wants to go to college? I'd just end up gettin' a shitty job anyway." So said Freddie Piniella, an eleven-year-old boy from Clarendon Heights low-income housing project, to Jay MacLeod, his counselor in a youth program. MacLeod was struck by the seeming self-defeatism of Freddie and his friends. How is it that in America, a nation of dreams and opportunities, a boy of eleven can feel trapped in a position of inherited poverty?

Author Jay MacLeod immerses himself in the teenage underworld of Clarendon Heights. The Hallway Hangers, who form one of the neighborhood cliques, appear as cynical, self-destructive hoodlums. The members of the other group, the Brothers, take the American Dream to heart and aspire to middle-class respectability. The twist is that the Hallway Hangers are mostly white; the Brothers are almost all black. Comparing the two groups, MacLeod provides a provocative account of how poverty is perpetuated from one generation to the next.

Part One tells the story of the boys' teenage aspirations. Part Two follows the Hallway Hangers and the Brothers into adulthood eight years later. MacLeod returns to Clarendon Heights to find the members of both groups struggling in the labor market or on the streets. Caught in the web of urban industrial decline, the Hallway Hangers—undereducated, unemployed, or imprisoned—have turned to the underground economy. But "crack capitalism" only fuels their desperation, and the Hallway Hangers seek solace in sexism and racism. The ambitious Brothers have fared little better. Their teenage dreams in tatters, the Brothers demonstrate that racism takes its toll on optimistic aspirations.

For this fully updated third edition, MacLeod returns to Clarendon Heights nearly twenty-five years after the first interviews. Part Three features thirteen

521

new interviews with the original Hallway Hangers and Brothers, now well into middle age and still negotiating precarious relationships with family, fatherhood, the job market, addiction, crime, and what it means to "make it." A new analysis chapter from Katherine McClelland and David Karen considers the latest dialogue and the implications for social reproduction theory today. This edition retains the vivid accounts of friendships, families, school, and work that made the first two editions so popular. The ethnography resonates with feeling and engrossing dialogue. But the book also addresses one of the most important issues in modern social theory and policy: how social inequality is reproduced from one generation to the next. MacLeod links individual lives with social theory to forge a powerful argument about how inequality is created, sustained, and accepted in the United States.

ABOUT THE AUTHORS

Jay MacLeod is a parish priest in England. Combining Christian ministry with community work, MacLeod still plays streetball, or tries to. His working-class parish is one of the most ethnically diverse square miles in Britain, and MacLeod works closely with members of the local mosques to engage disaffected teenagers and to foster friendships across the lines of race and religion. He and his wife, Sally Asher, have three children—Asher, Kate, and Toby.

Katherine McClelland and **David Karen** have been professors of sociology at Franklin and Marshall College and at Bryn Mawr College, respectively, since 1984. McClelland is currently engaged in a longitudinal study of race relations on college campuses; her other research and teaching interests include sociology of education, social stratification, and social psychology. Karen's research and teaching interests are in the areas of sociology of education, inequality, politics, social movements, and sociology of sport. He is also an elected school board member in Pennsylvania, where he and McClelland live with their children, Rachel and Joshua.

INDEX